Politics and Culture in the Developing World

The Impact of Globalization

THIRD EDITION

Richard J. Payne
Department of Politics and Government
Illinois State University

Jamal R. Nassar
College of Social and Behavioral Sciences
California State University, San Bernardino

PEARSON
Longman

New York • San Francisco • Boston
London • Toronto • Sydney • Tokyo • Singapore • Madrid
Mexico City • Munich • Paris • Cape Town • Hong Kong • Montreal

Vice President and Publisher: Priscilla McGeehon
Editor in Chief: Eric Stano
Acquisitions Editor: Vikram Mukhija
Executive Marketing Manager: Ann Stypuloski
Production Manager: Savoula Amanatidis
Project Coordination and Text Design: Elm Street Publishing Services, Inc.
Electronic Page Makeup: Integra Software Services, Pvt. Ltd.
Cover Design Manager: John Callahan
Cover Designer: Maria Ilardi
Cover Images: Courtesy of Getty Images
Photo Researcher: Christine A. Pullo
Senior Manufacturing Buyer: Alfred C. Dorsey
Printer and Binder: R. R. Donnelley and Sons Company—Crawfordsville
Cover Printer: R. R. Donnelley and Sons Company—Crawfordsville

Library of Congress Cataloging-in-Publication Data
Payne, Richard J., 1949–
    Politics and culture in the developing world : the impact of globalization / Richard J. Payne and Jamal
Nassar. — 3rd ed.
        p. cm.
    Includes bibliographical references and index.
    ISBN-13: 978-0-205-55057-9 (alk. paper)
    ISBN-10: 0-205-55057-6 (alk. paper)
1. Developing countries—Politics and government.   2. Globalization.   I. Nassar, Jamal R. (Jamal Raji)
II. Title.
    JF60.P44 2008
    320.9172′4—dc22

                                                                                    2007010980

Please visit us at **www.ablongman.com**

ISBN 13: 978-0-205-55057-9
ISBN 10: 0-205-55057-6

1 2 3 4 5 6 7 8 9 10—DOC—10 09 08 07

For Sami and Gina Nassar
and
Arlene and Don Winslow

BRIEF CONTENTS

DETAILED CONTENTS

Note: Each chapter ends with Summary and Review, Key Terms, Discussion Questions, Suggested Readings, Addresses and Websites, and Notes.

PREFACE

Our decision to write *Politics and Culture in the Developing World: The Impact of Globalization* grows out of our extensive professional and personal experiences. Our experiences in different parts of the developing world give us not only first-hand knowledge of those countries within it, but also a strong desire to share this knowledge with students. Although our connections to these areas remain strong, we have the additional advantage of being observers from a distance. The problems of developing countries are not abstract concerns for us. An important reason for writing this book is to improve our own understanding of the challenges that poor countries face and to think of possible solutions to some of them. As such, this third edition continues in the same spirit as the first and second editions. The nuclear crisis with North Korea, the war in Iraq, the Israeli-Palestinian conflict, the crisis over nuclear enrichment in Iran, and the constant threat of terrorism are all new reminders of the importance of studying the developing world.

For more than a quarter-century, we have been teaching courses on the global South, global issues, international relations, foreign policy, and American government. We have done extensive scholarly research and have published many articles and books on the developing countries. For more than a decade, we have shared with our colleagues a strong desire for a comprehensive textbook that is suitable for introductory courses on Africa, Asia, and Latin America. We wanted to write a book that dealt with issues that improve students' understanding of the developing world in an age of rapid globalization. Students are increasingly aware of the growing interdependence among countries and the fact that rich and poor countries are being drawn closer together. Rising rates of immigration from Latin America, Asia, and—to a lesser extent—Africa are contributing to profound demographic changes in the United States, Western Europe, Canada, and elsewhere in the industrialized world. These significant changes inspired us to write a text that treats developing countries as integral parts of an increasingly global society.

Globalization, a major theme of the book, makes it more difficult to separate the problems and concerns of rich countries from those of poor societies. Trade officials from the industrialized world are routinely pressured to negotiate agreements that include safeguards for environmental protection and the rights of workers in poor countries. Many of the world's largest corporations, such as Nike, negotiate with advocacy groups in the United States and Europe to develop new codes of conduct for global commerce in which many developing countries participate. Groups, which include many students, have effectively used the threat of protests and boycotts to persuade Starbucks Corporation to pay what they regard as a living wage to coffee bean growers in Central and South America. The anti-sweatshop movements on many American college campuses have influenced companies to make a greater effort to end child labor and oppressive working conditions in their factories in developing countries. Globalization has made these companies vulnerable to pressure from various groups that operate in both rich and poor countries.

We hope that our experiences in the developing world as well as in the classroom have enabled us to write a book that is relevant to our students' lives. We decided to make the text accessible without being simplistic. Based on feedback from our colleagues and students, we believe we have written a book that is intellectually engaging, interesting for students to read, and one that avoids a stereotypical treatment of developing countries. We have relied on carefully selected scholarly literature as well as real-life stories and current events to write this book. We have included pedagogical features that help students to understand the information, to develop critical thinking skills, and to think of ways to solve problems they will encounter beyond college, some of which will undoubtedly involve developing countries.

NEW TO THE THIRD EDITION

The success of the first two editions makes it necessary for us to continue to keep the book comprehensive and timely. This third edition incorporates recent developments and assesses their impact on relations with the United States. Unlike the previous two editions, this one incorporates more extensive coverage of the types of Islamic states and discusses how Islam and the West can co-exist. Another feature that expands this edition has to do with the role of women in developing societies. While we devote a whole chapter to this important issue, this third edition incorporates the subject into every chapter as well. Discussion of the theories of development has also been enhanced in this third edition. We now believe that our presentation of such theories is adequate for an introductory textbook such as this one.

TEXT PHILOSOPHY

Politics and Culture in the Developing World is based on an approach that consists of seven philosophical components that we believe students should get from a course on the developing world. Our emphasis on globalization as a major theme clearly indicates that our approach favors a comprehensive perspective. These seven philosophical themes are interwoven in the chapters throughout the book:

1. An understanding of basic concepts and theories and their strengths and weaknesses. Students should develop an ability to evaluate concepts and theories and to apply them to real-world problems.
2. An awareness of the powerful force of globalization. Students should realize how developing countries are linked to industrial countries (and to each other) by the increasing economic, cultural, political, and environmental globalization. This means that their lives are increasingly connected to the lives of people in Africa, Asia, and Latin America.
3. An appreciation of the complexities of developing societies as well as the similarities and differences among individuals throughout the world.

4. An understanding of how complex combinations of cultural, religious, political, environmental, and personal factors influence development and relations among countries.
5. A greater sense of the interdependence of different aspects of development and the various problems of many poor societies.
6. A recognition of the power of individuals, including students, to make a difference in the lives of people around them.
7. An ability to think critically, develop independent judgment, and sharpen their intellectual curiosity and imagination.

TEXT ORGANIZATION

We decided to organize the book around the general theme of how globalization is accelerating changes in the developing countries. Each chapter begins with a brief discussion of the impact of globalization on the particular issues covered in the chapter. This approach has the advantage of giving students a broader context in which to examine problems in the developing countries. Instead of seeing poor countries as being isolated from rich ones, we stress the growing interdependence of states. This organization underscores the point that students need to understand that many issues and developments in Asia, Africa, and Latin America cannot be neatly separated from issues and developments in Europe and the United States. To engage the student, the book first deals with the basic concepts and general issues that most students are familiar with.

Before discussing specific problems, we provide information on the cultural, religious, and political environments of Africa, Asia, and Latin America to give students a road map, as it were, to understand the more specific issues discussed in later chapters. The organization of the book is primarily thematic and, to a lesser extent, chronological. We focus on historical developments such as colonization, nationalism, and independence as a foundation for many of the contemporary issues we discuss later in the book.

Instead of presenting students with massive amounts of information, we made a deliberate and concerted effort to stress those issues of critical importance to developing countries as well as those that most students find interesting and controversial. We also decided to include a reasonable number of chapters. The book is composed of fourteen chapters to allow teachers to allocate a week to each chapter and still have enough time for review and exams. Our own experiences led us to the conclusion that it is better to cover a few topics well than to attempt to cover too many superficially. Organizing the book around fourteen chapters enables professors to have a greater degree of flexibility to include their own pedagogical approaches and supplementary reading.

We divided the book into four parts. Each part focuses on a general theme and provides a foundation for students to understand the next part. We take students from a general or macro-level analysis to more specific examinations of problems faced by developing countries. We remind students of these general concepts and analysis as we proceed with discussions of more complex issues.

Part One deals with the organization of people into political, cultural, and religious communities. It demonstrates that although nationalism continues to be a potent force, countries are also part of an increasingly interdependent and global society. Chapter 1 is the general introduction to the book. It contains a discussion of basic concepts that the students will encounter in later chapters. Chapter 2 shows how the forces of economic, cultural, political, and environmental globalization are creating closer and more complex connections among countries in the developed and developing world, and weakening the distinction between rich and poor countries. Chapter 3 looks at the cultural, religious, and political diversity of Africa, Asia, and Latin America and how culture and religion influence politics, development, leadership, and other aspects of life in countries in these areas. Chapter 4 looks at European colonization of Africa, Asia, and Latin America and the struggles of countries to gain their independence. Colonialism marks the beginnings of globalization and the division of the world into rich and poor societies. It helps explain the economic inequalities both among nations and within them, as discussed in Chapter 5.

Part Two focuses on issues that are generally regarded to be important by governments, interest groups, and international organizations. These include economic development, gender equality and the role of women in the development process, and the protection of individual freedoms and human rights. The four chapters in Part Two clearly demonstrate how changes are accompanied by both positive and negative consequences as well as the uneven and complicated nature of change. They give students insights about specific challenges that confront developing countries. To aid in that understanding, instead of writing a single chapter on development, we decided to write two chapters—one concentrating on efforts to achieve economic development and the benefits that accompany it in an increasingly global economy and another to stress the costs that usually result from development. This allows students to understand the process of development first and then evaluate its costs later. Thus, Chapter 6 is devoted to theories of development, specific efforts of various countries to develop, and some of the obstacles or impediments they encounter. Chapter 7 reminds students that congested urban areas, environmental degradation, and the loss of traditional cultures are some of the costs we pay as part of the bargain for economic improvement. Chapter 8 emphasizes that women are an integral and vital component of the development process, but that their participation is often limited by cultural and religious views of women and their roles. Chapter 9 shows that globalization has strongly influenced countries in the developing world to become more democratic and to be more respectful of human rights. But this chapter also points out that transitions to democracy and human rights are uneven and that success varies among countries in the developing world.

Part Three examines how political leaders set the agenda for change and how the bureaucracy is instrumental in transforming the dreams of leaders into reality. It brings into sharp focus the dynamic interaction of leaders, bureaucracy, and public policies that affect the lives of ordinary citizens. Chapter 10 addresses the roles leaders play in the development process, the different types of leaders, and how they operate within the framework of political and religious values and traditions. Chapter 11 discusses how the bureaucracy affects virtually everything a citizen does; problems of corruption; and the extent to which the bureaucracy can promote or impede economic, social, and political change.

Part Four concentrates on issues that are often considered to be primarily international concerns. It makes plain the fact that it is extremely difficult to separate many domestic problems from international relations. Unlike most textbooks on the developing world, our book includes a chapter on the foreign policies of countries in Africa, Asia, and Latin America. Chapter 12 deals with ethnic and religious conflicts that have escalated since the end of the Cold War. It looks at how ethnic conflicts are related to nationalism, and how they often undermine economic development as well as transitions to democracy. Ethnic conflicts force people to migrate, often involve neighboring states, and spill over into developed countries with large groups of immigrants from those countries engaged in ethnic strife. Chapter 13 specifically focuses on the problem of migration, including its causes and its consequences, for both the countries that migrants leave and those in which they settle. The United States, Canada, France, Germany, and Britain are examples of countries that are being transformed by migration. Chapter 14 examines how foreign policies of developing countries are influenced by both domestic and external factors, and how these policies are often linked to American domestic and foreign policies, such as free trade and the war on drugs. This last part of the book brings students back to the first part, which shows that countries are increasingly interdependent in an age of globalization.

PEDAGOGICAL FEATURES

We decided to adopt a writing style that makes the book accessible to students. We believe that a more conversational writing style engages the students, encourages them to relate what they read to the real world and their lives, and makes it easier for them to question what they read and sharpen their analytical skills. Our coverage of controversial issues helps students become active readers who interact with the material. Because students are also citizens who will play important roles in society, we have included pedagogical features that stimulate students to think critically about the consequences of problems in Africa, Asia, the Middle East, and Latin America for the people who live there as well as for themselves. Our emphasis on globalization and change as major themes of the book underscore the relevancy of many problems in distant places for the students' lives. The chapter on migration, for example, clearly demonstrates how the United States and other industrial societies are being transformed demographically, culturally, and politically by increasing numbers of immigrants from developing societies. Various pedagogical features underscore the complexities of developing countries as well as their differences and similarities. The book not only compares developing and developed nations, but also compares countries within the developing world to show students that those countries are not a monolithic bloc. We hope that our pedagogical features will make the book both informative and enjoyable for students.

"Globalization" Vignettes

We begin each chapter with a vignette on the impact of globalization on the topics covered in the chapter. These vignettes remind the students of the book's main theme. Issues in Africa, Asia, the Middle East, and Latin America are placed within a broader context that is familiar to most students.

Chapter Introductions

The vignettes on the impact of globalization are followed by an introduction to the chapter. The introduction provides a brief overview of the main points in the chapter, tells the students what is covered, and provides examples of controversial issues included in the chapter to stimulate the students' interest in the material.

Stories about Real People

Consistent with our decision to adopt an accessible writing style, we have included many stories throughout the book. These stories help students develop clearer images of the developing world. They also maintain the students' attention and interest in the material discussed in the chapter. We hope that our stories will encourage students to share their stories with their classmates and teachers.

"In the News" Boxes

These boxes provide brief accounts of interesting developments. Stories in these boxes highlight specific human experiences that are related to the main themes of the chapter. They illustrate major points, are interesting for students to read, help students understand how real lives are affected by issues, and motivate students to participate in class discussions. In addition to helping students remember the main points of the chapter, these boxes stimulate students' interest in reading major newspapers to obtain information on current events. They also help to underscore the main themes of globalization and change.

"Taking Action" Boxes

Many students wonder if they can have an impact on politics and society. These boxes demonstrate how an individual has helped to bring about significant changes and, in the process, helped to transform society. These boxes suggest to students that they can also be agents of change. A major goal of the boxes is to motivate students to make the connection between theories discussed in the book and ways to solve problems in the real world.

"You Decide" Boxes

These boxes ask students to be active participants. They discuss controversial issues and then ask students to make a judgment on them. Students are encouraged to engage in problem-solving activities and critically evaluate what they are reading.

We hope that by asking students what they think about specific issues and problems, these boxes will help students develop critical thinking skills and stimulate classroom discussions.

Maps and Photographs

Students usually want to know the location of countries being discussed. The maps will help put the issues in context and enable students to better grasp essential points discussed in the text. We have carefully selected photographs that portray specific developments and capture the students' attention and imagination. We have tried to select photographs that present an objective and realistic view of developing countries.

Tables

We have included many different tables in the book. Some tables show the differences between rich and poor countries. These tables contain data on the United States to enable students to see how the United States compares with other countries in terms of per capita income, health care, income distribution, and so on. Some tables summarize major points made in a section of the chapter, whereas others give a chronology of important events.

Key Terms and Definitions in Boldface Type

We have made a concerted effort to put definitions, key terms, and concepts in boldface type to draw the students' attention to them. Stressing their importance reinforces the point that they are building blocks of the chapter.

Marginal Notes

Marginal notes are designed to give students a quick reference to basic definitions and concepts. They provide a very brief review for the students.

Currency

Major developments in the news are integrated throughout the text. Many of the boxes concentrate on current issues to help explain general theories.

End-of-Chapter Summaries

These focus students' attention on the major points of the chapter and assist them in concentrating on the most important information as they review the chapter. We suggest that students also prepare their own chapter summaries as they read the chapter to improve their comprehension and retention of the information.

End-of-Chapter Key Terms and Discussion Questions

Most students believe that review questions at the end of each chapter are helpful. Our own students often tell us that review questions focus their attention on the most important information. These questions, concepts, and terms are designed to improve the retention of information, stimulate discussions, and help students prepare for exams. They may also assist teachers in the preparation of their own study guides.

End-of-Chapter Suggested Readings

We have included a list of suggested readings at the end of each chapter to familiarize students with the scholarly literature. This section helps students locate additional information on issues in which they are interested. We also provide the names, websites, addresses, and phone numbers of organizations that are involved in the issues discussed in each chapter to facilitate students' efforts to obtain more information.

Glossary

Most students use glossaries extensively. The glossary at the end of the text is a useful reference. It enables students to find major terms and definitions quickly.

Index

The index allows students to find key terms, concepts, and subjects discussed throughout the book. The index is especially helpful for reviewing for exams.

LEARNING BEYOND THE CLASSROOM

We believe that an important aspect of excellent teaching is interaction among students themselves and between students and teachers not only in the classroom but also in more informal settings. Feedback and questions from students are essential for learning and teaching. We encourage you to contact us by e-mail at **jnassar@ilstu.edu,** or write to us at the Department of Politics and Government, Illinois State University, Normal, Illinois 61790–4600.

ACKNOWLEDGMENTS

We are deeply indebted to numerous students and colleagues who made significant contributions to this interdisciplinary project. Because we wanted to make the book accessible to undergraduate students, we solicited feedback from many students over the years and encouraged several of them to assist us. Their questions, insights, suggestions, and research skills were invaluable. We are particularly indebted to Julie Edmunds, Richard Ehlers, Yu Bo, Sherri Replogle, Amentahru Wahlrab, Khalil Marrar, Doug Smith, Michelle Boyer, Aleksandra Malyszko, Sally Kwitkowski, Brennan Berg, and Jennifer Schlemmer. Anthony DiMaggio was extremely helpful in the second edition. Faculty here at Illinois State University and elsewhere were also very helpful, especially Rachitha Dayarante, Conrad Dyer, Marian Ide, Khalil Marrar, Jennifer Ngonga, and Ali Riaz. Dr. Riaz was especially helpful in his suggestions on the forms of government and the section on Islam. Dr. Nancy Lind was of great help as well. F. Tolu Aregbe did a superb job helping us revise the book to produce this outstanding third edition.

We are grateful to our colleagues, many of whom read parts of the manuscript and made helpful suggestions, based on their experiences teaching both large and small sections of courses on Africa, Asia, Latin America, and global issues. We would like to thank Denis Thornton, Bob Hunt, Carlos Parodi, Ron Pope, and Manfred Steger of the Department of Politics and Government at Illinois State University; Margaret Chapman of Illinois Wesleyan University; Roger Fisher of Harvard Law School; Maria Brisk of Boston University and Boston College; Elizabeth Davis of the Asia Pacific Center for Security Studies in Hawaii; Kelly Keogh, Normal Community High School; Dixie Mills, Dean of the College of Business at Illinois State University; Laura Berk of the Department of Psychology at Illinois State University; Valentine Moghadam, Director of Women's Studies at Illinois State University; Eleanor Zeff of Drake University; Kenneth Johnson of Eastern Kentucky University; William Crowther of the University of North Carolina–Greensboro; Julio F. Carron, University of Delaware; Earl Conreh-Morgan, University of South Florida; Michael Gold-Bliss, St. Cloud State University; Carl Lutrin, California Polytechnic State University; Steffen Schmidt, Iowa State University; Shawn Shieh, Marist College; Lionel Ingram, University of New Hampshire; Gardel Feurrado, The Citadel; and Lee Walker of the University of Kentucky.

We are especially indebted to Julie Edmunds and Sally Kwitkowski for their excellent research and word-processing skills, to Kay Stultz of Institutional Technology Service, and to Michele Ganschow of the Department of Politics and Government. We also need to thank Editor-in-Chief Eric Stano, Acquisitions Editor Vikram Mukhija, and Editorial Assistant Lucy Silberman, for their patience, hard work, and cooperation throughout the process. Above all, we would like to thank Elaine Graybill and Hanan Nassar for their insights, suggestions, and support.

RICHARD J. PAYNE
JAMAL R. NASSAR

CHAPTER ONE

Government, Politics, and Cultures in Africa, Asia, the Middle East, and Latin America

GOVERNMENT, POLITICS, AND CULTURES IN A GLOBAL WORLD

LET'S BEGIN WITH THE FIRST ESSENTIAL QUESTION: HOW DO WE INTERACT IN AN ORGANIZED SOCIAL SETTING? IT IS THROUGH POLITICS. OUR POLITICS ARE OFTEN BASED ON A COMMON CULTURE. BUT RECENTLY, POLITICS AND CULTURES HAVE BEEN GOING GLOBAL. WHAT HAPPENS IN ONE COUNTRY IS INCREASINGLY CONNECTED TO WHAT HAPPENS ELSEWHERE IN THE WORLD. FOR EXAMPLE, THE GOVERNMENT IN ONE COUNTRY MAY WISH TO HAVE A LOWER PRICE FOR OIL, BUT THAT IS BEYOND THE CONTROL OF ANY SINGLE GOVERNMENT. POLITICIANS IN ONE COUNTRY MAY WANT TO LIMIT THE TYPE OF INFORMATION THEIR CITIZENS RECEIVE. THAT, TOO, HAS PROVEN TO BE LARGELY BEYOND THEIR CONTROL.

IN OUR WORLD, GOVERNMENT, POLITICS, AND CULTURES ARE GOING THROUGH RAPID TRANSFORMATION AS A RESULT OF GLOBALIZATION. WE DO NOT EXACTLY KNOW THE SHAPE OF FUTURE POLITICS OR CULTURES. WE DO KNOW THAT OUR WORLD FACES NEW CIRCUMSTANCES WHOSE IMPLICATIONS ARE YET TO BE FULLY KNOWN. WHAT IS OBVIOUS IS THAT OUR INTERACTIONS IN ORGANIZED SOCIAL SETTINGS HAVE BECOME MORE COMPLEX.

INTRODUCTION

This book focuses on the politics and cultures of Africa, Asia, the Middle East, and Latin America in the era of globalization. These areas make up almost two-thirds of the earth's surface and are inhabited by approximately 80 percent of the world's population. Increasing globalization is creating closer and more complex relationships among the peoples of the developing countries in Africa, Asia, the Middle East, and Latin America and those of the developed countries such as the United States, Canada, Australia, Japan, and Europe. An understanding of the developing world is becoming more important as events in the developing world generally have an impact, directly and indirectly, on the lives of people in the developed world. September 11, 2001, was a reminder of such impact.

Before driving to a faraway place, most of us look at a map or the Internet to decide which interstate to take to reach our destination. Similarly, before learning about an area that is largely unfamiliar, we need to know the concepts or ideas that constitute the foundation of more complex issues. Concepts are like the interstate. They become the major link between students and their acquisition of a better understanding of the subject. Along the way, we hope that this book will spark a spirit of critical thinking. This chapter focuses on basic concepts, several of which may be familiar to many students. These concepts are used throughout the book. This chapter discusses concepts such as globalization, politics, government, culture, the state, sovereignty, the nation, and the developing world.

WHAT IS GLOBALIZATION?

globalization

The integration of markets, politics, values, and environmental concerns across borders.

This concept will be discussed in detail in Chapter 2. For now, you need to have a brief idea about the notion of globalization. In this book, we define **globalization** as the integration of markets, politics, values, and environmental concerns across borders. This process has been going on throughout history. During recent times, globalization has spread rapidly and its impact has become clear. Today, our global reality is one of interdependence and shared destiny. But globalization has serious consequences. The developing countries cannot live in isolation any longer. Events in other parts of the world affect them more seriously than developed and wealthier states. When the price of oil rises, it takes a greater toll on the poor than it does on the wealthy. When environmental controls are imposed, they have a greater impact on those who depend on the environment more directly. This book will review the impact of globalization in each of its chapters. By the end, you should have a good idea about how globalization affects the developing world.

WHAT IS POLITICS?

If you are a member of a fraternity, sorority, a student organization, or any other group, you know that the group has to have a way to manage its affairs. The group needs some system to decide on activities, to carry out such activities, or to settle disputes. Often, the system allows certain individuals to be in charge. Such individuals take, or are given, a certain amount of power over others in the group. It is this idea of power that is central to the concept of politics.

politics

The means by which a society organizes its affairs.

Politics may be defined as the means by which a society organizes its affairs. In old tribal societies, a chief took charge of organizing the affairs of the tribe. In modern societies, a government is usually formed for that purpose. So, when we study politics or political science, we generally study government. But that is not all, because in essence, what we study is the power relationships in societies. Although governments usually acquire the most power, other entities also have power. Public opinion, for example, is important. Certain groups acquire power on specific issues that relate to them. Labor unions could have a great deal of power when it comes to issues relating to labor. Farmers and farm bureaus are rather powerful on agricultural policies and

Every day since he arrived in Mexico City, Pedro Jasso Bravo, accompanied by his donkey, Shorty, has protested in the square across from the Metropolitan Cathedral and the National Palace. Protest is one of the many forms of political participation.

Source: Sergio Dorantes/Chicago Tribune Company

practices. The so-called gun lobby is powerful on issues of gun control. In the classroom, the teacher has certain powers that students do not. On the job, the manager or the boss has greater power than some of the other workers or employees. But whatever power an individual or group has, it is usually overshadowed by the greater power of government.

The **study of politics,** then, is the study of government and the use of power and its allocation in society. When we study national politics, we concentrate on the national government, its powers, and the powers of other groups that can influence the national government and its behavior. Courses on state and local politics look at state governments, county and city, or township governance. In public administration classes, you learn about governmental administration and the role of civil servants and their organization. The study of international relations, on the other hand, focuses on relations among nations and on international laws and organizations. In comparative politics, you would study other societies and their political forces, processes, institutions, and performances. In political science, you can also study political theory and methodology. Political theory courses try to understand theoretical and ethical notions underlying government and politics. Methodology refers to the methods employed by students, practitioners, and researchers to assess policies and their

study of politics

The study of government and power allocation in society.

TAKING ACTION

Individuals Can Make a Difference: Crossroads Global Handcrafts

In a time of free trade, fair trade principles are steadily gaining more attention. Fair trade is defined by a commitment to paying fair wages and providing equal opportunity, environmental sustainability, and safe working conditions for workers in the developing world. Charline Watts, head of the management team at Crossroads Global Handcrafts, located in Bloomington, Illinois, has played an instrumental role in this commitment to fair trade principles. Through her work at Crossroads, Charline and her co-workers have made an invaluable contribution to the fair trade movement. In affiliation with other groups committed to fair trade, Crossroads has successfully imported fairly traded products made in worker co-operatives throughout Asia, Africa, and Latin America. Worker co-operatives (co-ops) are defined as democratically empowering work environments existing throughout much of the world. In co-ops, workers are well paid for the products they make and, in turn, commit themselves to maintaining a work environment based on solidarity, environmental consciousness, and mutual respect for the rights of all workers—a commitment that has distinguished co-ops from low-paying, exploitive sweatshop environments. By dedicating their lives to paying a fair day's wage for a fair day's work, Charline and the management team at Crossroads, along with the artisans they work with, have sent a message that in an era of globalization, businesses do not have to rely on abusive, anti-worker policies, but can in fact do their part in improving the lives of workers and making this world a better place.

consequences. Whatever you study in political science, the subject will invariably touch on government.

WHAT IS GOVERNMENT?

Government is one of those concepts that we often use and know, but we have difficulty explaining. Like the concept of love, we all know what it is, but we can't easily define it. We can see government around us all the time. We see it in the police officer issuing a citation. We see government every time we see a fire engine zooming by, or whenever we pay sales tax on the purchases we make. Government seems to be with us all the time. It is in the air we breathe, as government regulates emissions from cars and factories. Government is in the food we eat and the water we drink, as government officials or employees draw guidelines on the permissible. Government builds roads and repairs potholes. It erects bridges and installs traffic lights. It maintains armed forces and police departments. It licenses teachers, doctors, real estate brokers, and car dealers. Government runs schools and universities. It is, somehow, everywhere. Government was there when we were born and it will be there when we die. In fact, we are not officially born until a government-certified individual signs a piece of paper called a birth certificate. Similarly, we do not legally die, and no one would dare bury us, until some government-approved individual signs a piece of paper called a death certificate.

So, what is this creature called government? Simply put, **government** is the institutions and processes that societies employ to organize their affairs and to protect them from internal or external threats. Often, that mechanism is a complex system of local, regional, and national organizations. Each set of organizations or institutions has particular tasks aiming at organizing and protecting society. Local government may include a mayor, a city council, a zoning board, a police commission, a health commission, a water authority, a fire commission, and a host of other authorities, each working in a specific sphere to organize and protect people inhabiting that particular community. Regional or state government is even more complex with a larger web of institutions. The national government is the largest entity and, often, the most complex. Our national government starts with the president, heading a very complex executive branch. Congress in the United States is bicameral (has two houses) and is the legislative branch. The Supreme Court is the highest authority in the judicial branch. Naturally, not all governments are organized in the same way. Some governments do not have such an extensive set of institutions with specialized powers. Some do not even have a president or a congress. Therefore, there are different forms of government. Let us take a look at those.

government

Institutions and processes employed by societies to organize their affairs.

FORMS OF GOVERNMENT

To simplify matters for our purposes, we can say that there are two basic forms of government: monarchy and republic. A *monarchy* is distinguished by having a monarch. A monarch may be called a king, queen, prince, emir, sultan, emperor, tzar, shah, or even pharaoh. Therefore, any government that is headed by somebody carrying such a title can be referred to as a monarchy. Similarly, a country that has no monarch can be called a *republic*. Therefore, the United Kingdom, having a queen, is a monarchy, whereas the United States, without a monarch, is a republic. This rather simple distinction, however, does not tell us enough. Saudi Arabia, for example, has a king and is, therefore, a monarchy. But the Saudi government is very different from the British government. Cuba does not have a king and is a republic, but we probably know that the Cuban and the U.S. governments are not alike. Therefore, there is a need for further distinctions among governments besides those of monarchy and republic. (See Figure 1.1.)

There are different types of monarchies and republics. These types can differentiate monarchies: limited, constitutional, and absolute. A **limited monarchy**

limited monarchy

A type of government where the monarch's powers are limited to ceremonial functions.

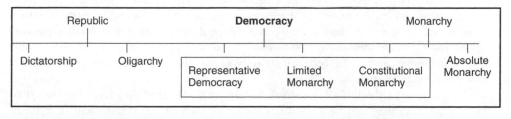

FIGURE 1.1 Forms of Government

constitutional monarchy

A type of monarchy where the monarch's powers are allocated in the constitution.

absolute monarchy

A type of monarchy where the monarch has absolute power.

dictatorship

A government in which a single person, who is not a monarch, has absolute power.

oligarchy

Rule of the few.

junta

A small group of military officers in charge of a country.

totalitarian system

All powers are concentrated at the center of government.

democracy

Any system where the majority rules is said to be a democracy.

centralized power

Decisions are made at the center of power.

decentralized power

Power is divided between a national government and smaller provincial or state governments.

is a monarchy where the monarch's powers are limited to ceremonial functions. The United Kingdom would be a good example of a limited monarchy. The British queen's functions are ceremonial. Real political power in Britain is in the hands of Parliament and its selected prime minister and cabinet. A **constitutional monarchy,** on the other hand, has a monarch whose powers are allocated in the constitution. In such a case, the monarch has real political power, but remains subject to the law. Other governmental institutions check the monarch's powers. Sweden's monarchy is a good example of a constitutional monarchy. Both limited and constitutional monarchies have democratic practices and people often call them democracies. For the purposes of this book, however, we will stay with the rigid distinctions among types of monarchies. A final type of monarchy is the **absolute monarchy,** where the monarch has absolute power. Here, the monarch is above the law and often makes the law. Prior to the Revolution of 1789, France had an absolute monarchy. Some may argue that a state like Saudi Arabia is an absolute monarchy. The Saudi king, however, is likely to disagree pointing to a system of consultation that exists in the country.

There are different types of republics as well. Some may be said to be dictatorships. A **dictatorship** has absolute power vested in a single person who is not a monarch. Many viewed Chile under Pinochet as a dictatorship. Another type of a republic can be grouped under the title of oligarchy. An **oligarchy** can be defined as rule by the few. The term *oligarchy* came from the old European feudal systems where the nobility ruled. It is now also applied to military regimes where a **junta,** or a small group of military officers, is in charge of a country. Military officers, as we shall see later, run many countries. Another example of minority rule was the apartheid system that existed in South Africa. Under apartheid, a 15 percent minority of whites ruled the country. It can also be argued that totalitarian governments constitute rule by the few, or an oligarchy. In **totalitarian systems,** all powers are concentrated at the center of government, which is often constitutionally held by the Communist party as exemplified by the former Soviet Union, China, Cuba, and North Korea. Naturally, rule by the few is not limited to republics. Sometimes a monarchy may have the nobility or a certain large family share power with the monarch. Similarly, limited or constitutional monarchies may have a democracy. Any republic where the majority rules is said to be a **democracy.** This is the third type of a republic. Most people like to think of their countries as being democratic, or ruled by the majority.

Another distinction among governments revolves around the distribution of power. Some countries have power **centralized** in the national government. This means that decisions are made at the center of power. Others have **decentralized** systems, meaning power is divided between a national government and smaller provincial or state governments. Often, governments that have a decentralized system also have a federal structure. In **federal structures,** smaller political units have certain major powers over their own affairs.

In summary, although all governments are similar in that they have the power to manage society, they can be very different from each other. What form or type of government a people have depends on many factors. Most important among those is the political culture that a group of people shares.

WHAT IS CULTURE AND POLITICAL CULTURE?

On Thanksgiving, many students head home for a family feast with turkey, dressing, and pumpkin pie. When families engage in such practices every Thanksgiving, this becomes part of a family's tradition. Tradition is a portion of culture. **Culture** is a set of traditions, beliefs, and behaviors that a people express and hold. The United Nations Educational, Scientific and Cultural Organization (UNESCO) defines culture as including "the whole complex of distinctive, spiritual, material, intellectual and emotional features that characterize a society or societal groups. It includes not only arts and letters, but also modes of life, the fundamental rights of the human being, value systems, traditions and beliefs."[1] When such traditions, beliefs, and behaviors relate to politics, they are called **political culture.** Many scholars who study political culture focus on attitudes toward politics and government.[2] Attitudes, of course, can also express themselves in beliefs and behaviors and are usually influenced by certain accepted traditions, but often a combination of these political attitudes translate themselves into laws and policies in society. It is the transformation of cultural norms into politics that makes an understanding of political cultures significant to our understanding of a society's politics. In general, every society tries to order its affairs in accordance with its own beliefs and attitudes. In some countries, the belief in the sanctity of human life contributed to banning the death penalty. In others, like the United States, a strong individualistic culture that emphasizes achievement makes it possible for government to enact laws that reward individual achievement.

The starting point of a culture is "its views on creation, the purpose of life and on an after life."[3] Therefore, a community's religious beliefs can be an indication of that community's culture. In theory, societies with religious diversity are likely to be more tolerant of the beliefs of others than a community without such diversity. Tolerance in religious beliefs often spills over to tolerance of other nonreligious beliefs. Naturally, different cultures see the world differently. But whatever cultures a people share, we all live in a rather small world and need to understand each other. Most people on earth live in what is called a *state*. Cultural diversity is becoming a common feature of modern states.

federal structures

Smaller political units that have certain major powers over their own affairs.

culture

A set of traditions, beliefs, and behaviors that a people express and hold.

political culture

Traditions, values, beliefs, and attitudes that relate to politics and government.

YOU DECIDE   **World Civilizations**

When you studied world civilization in high school, you learned a lot more about Europe than other parts of the world. In the process, significant civilizations were not presented. Consequently, some Americans may deal with those civilizations through stereotypes. Do you think that high school curricula should be revised to include more emphasis on civilizations outside of Europe? Or, is it best to leave such learning for college?

WHAT IS A STATE?

If you have ever traveled to Europe or to other countries, you know that you need a passport. To acquire a passport, you need a proof of citizenship. A birth certificate is usually sufficient to prove your citizenship. But if you were born in another country, a naturalization certificate may be required. Once abroad, your passport serves as your legal identification. Officials who request to see it will know that you are a citizen of your country. Citizenship in a country is equivalent to membership in a state. Today, states are the basic units of world society. Other units do exist, including labor unions, multinational corporations, nonprofit organizations, international and regional organizations, and a host of other professional and issue-oriented groups. Most people in the world live in states, or what many call countries. Legally and politically, a **state** is an internationally recognized, politically organized, populated, geographical area that possesses sovereignty.[4]

state

A legal and political unit that must be internationally recognized, politically organized, and have a populated geographic area that possesses sovereignty.

A state, then, is a legal and political unit that has five basic elements. Those include *recognition by other states*. Some scholars argue that recognition is not that important. But in international law, recognition by other states bestows legitimacy on a country or state. In northern Cyprus, for example, a Turkish invasion in 1974 led to the creation of a political unit that Turkey called the Turkish Federated State of Cyprus (TFSC). That "state" did not achieve recognition by the other states in the international community. As such, the TFSC was not admitted to the United Nations and was perceived by most other states as a mere extension of Turkey.

A second element of statehood is that of political organization. We have already seen that people organize their affairs politically by having a government. Therefore, *government is an indispensable element of statehood*. It would be hard to imagine a country, or state, without a government. In fact, such a thing does not legally exist. *A third element of statehood is population*. You cannot have a state without a people living there. Similarly, you cannot have a state without a geographic area or a territory. *Land, therefore, is the fourth element of statehood*. But having land, people, government, and

N IN THE NEWS

Olympic Torch Controversy

Organizers of the 2006 Winter Olympics, centered in Turin in northern Italy, faced the prospect of potentially embarrassing protests over the Games' sponsorship by the American soft drinks giant, Coca-Cola. There were doubts about the extent of Italian government funding for the Games, as well as heightened fears about possible terrorist attacks, and, later, threats by environmentalists to disrupt the games in protest at a new, high-speed rail link being built between Turin and the French city of Lyon. The Olympic torch itself was at the center of a row over Coca-Cola's sponsorship of the Games. Two municipal councils in Rome decided to ban it from passing through their streets in protest at what they said was the bad treatment of Coca-Cola workers in Colombia. The leaders of the campaign said more than 300 other councilors across Italy backed them. The president of the region, which includes Turin, urged the mayor of Rome to make the protesting councilors see sense.

Source: BBC News, 07 November 2005.

recognition are not sufficient by themselves. A state must also be sovereign. *Sovereignty is the fifth and final element of statehood.*

Hugo Grotius, a prominent scholar of international law, defined **sovereignty** as the power or authority "whose actions are not subject to the legal control of another, so that they cannot be rendered void by the operation of another human will."[5] What this means is that a state must be independent to be a state. This brings us to an interesting question: Are the fifty states of the United States really states? Given the earlier stipulation that a state must be sovereign or independent, the U.S. states are not considered states under international law. In most countries, such divisions within states are usually called provinces, not states. In the United States, because the thirteen original states were actually independent states, the founders saw fit to keep the title of "state" in the Constitution. In international law, however, California or Texas or any other state in the Union is called a *province*, not a state. A state is then really what people commonly call *country*. Most people today live in states. Most states today involve a territory or land that has a people who consider themselves to be a nation. Therefore, most states today are nation-states. By now, you have an idea about what a state is. Let us then take a look at the concept of nation.

sovereignty
The ability of a state to be independent and free from the control of another state.

WHAT IS A NATION?

Unlike the concept of state, which is concrete or tangible, the concept of nation is intangible. It is not grounded in something as clear as a passport or a birth certificate. A **nation** refers to a group of people who identify with each other as a political community because of common territorial, cultural, and other similar bonds. As such, the concept of nation is more dependent upon a feeling of identity rather than on legal qualifications, as in the case of the state.[6] As we have said before, membership in a state is defined by citizenship. Membership in a nation, on the other hand, is dependent on a feeling of belonging.

nation
A group of people who identify as a political community based upon common territory, culture, and other similar bonds.

Most states today are **nation-states.** This means that nations and states have acquired similar boundaries having people identifying with the nation and establishing a state for themselves. As such, we can say that most states are **homogeneous,** or have a single nation within their boundaries. Some states, however, are heterogeneous. **Heterogeneous,** or mixed, states have more than one nation inhabiting them. Until recently, the Soviet Union was a heterogeneous state. In the early 1990s, it split in a pattern that goes along with the various nationality groups that inhabited it. Similarly, former Yugoslavia transformed itself, in a bloody conflict, from a single heterogeneous state to a number of new nation-states.

nation-state
Nations and states have similar boundaries where the people identify with the nation and establish a state for themselves.

homogeneous state
A state with a single nation within its boundaries.

Some nations have developed a number of states as well. The Arabs, for example, have found themselves as citizens of many states, even though many of them see themselves as a single nation. The Koreans, the Chinese, the Vietnamese, and the Germans have or have had more than one state. But, in many cases, an eventual reunion between the state and the nation occurred. In most cases, people inhabiting a nation-state have developed over time a strong sense of belonging and pride in their national identity. That sense of belonging is called nationalism. In Chapter 3, we will discuss

heterogeneous state
A state that has more than one nation within its boundaries.

nationalism in more detail. For now, it is sufficient to say that nationalism is, perhaps, strongest in the developing world. But nationalism today is being challenged by the forces of globalization. We can define globalization as a process of integration of markets, politics, and environmental concerns across borders.

AFRICA, ASIA, LATIN AMERICA, AND THE MIDDLE EAST

The continents of Africa, Asia, and Latin America are often referred to as the *developing world*. The concept of the developing world is neither precise nor accurate. It includes very large areas of the earth and many peoples. It encompasses more than 160 countries in Latin America, Africa, the Middle East, and Asia. These countries account for three-fourths of the world's population. Even though the developing areas share some common features, they have many differences. Sometimes, the developing world is referred to by other names, including the underdeveloped countries, the Global South, the Third World, and the nonindustrialized countries. Essentially, what all such concepts refer to are the peoples and countries outside of Europe and North America with few exceptions.[7]

Societies outside of Europe and North America have many things in common. For the most part, Europeans ruled them for a long time. Also, their economies are largely agricultural based and their levels of industrialization, while varying widely, are relatively very low. In general, their peoples are poorer than those of Europe and

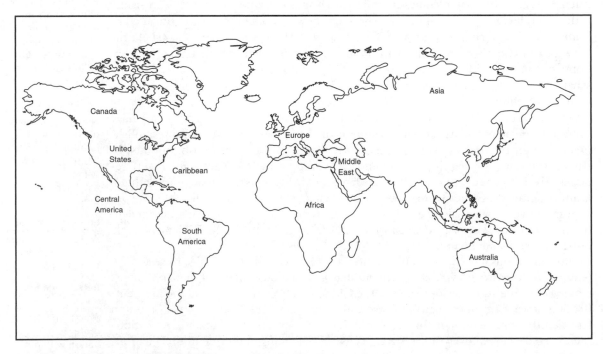

FIGURE 1.2 Africa, Asia, the Middle East, and Latin America

North America. They also have shorter life spans, lower literacy rates, and less urbanization. But even though they have many similarities, they also have differences. As such, generalizations about the developing world must be understood in that context, as generalizations. The many states of the developing world, while sharing some common features, have diverse cultures, political systems, economies, languages, religions, and aspirations. Let us now take a look at each of the continents as well as the region often called the Middle East, which crosses Asia and Africa.

Africa

Africa is rich in beauty, cultures, and minerals. Equally important is the reality that poverty and conflict also plague parts of Africa. Africa is second only to Asia as the world's largest and most populous continent, measuring 11,699,000 square miles and containing about 700 million people. Geographically, the Sahara Desert divides Africa into two areas known as North Africa and sub-Saharan Africa. For the most part, although the latter contains Africans identifying themselves as adherents of the continent's animist or local religions and Christianity, the former contains Africans identifying themselves as Muslims and sharing an affinity with Arab-speaking states of the Middle East. However, we must not assume that the predominance of one faith precludes another. For example, North African Egypt has a substantial population of Coptic Christians, whereas sub-Saharan African Senegal contains a Muslim majority. Moreover, many African nations—both north and south of the Sahara—speak more than one language. For example, the Moroccans speak Arabic, French, Berber, and Spanish. The Nigerians speak English, Hausa, Yoruba, Ibo, etc.[8]

Africa's diversity, with more than a thousand languages and hundreds of religious and ethnic groups, is unmatched by any other continent. Although 500,000 people or more speak fifty of Africa's languages, groups containing fewer than 500,000 people speak the rest of the

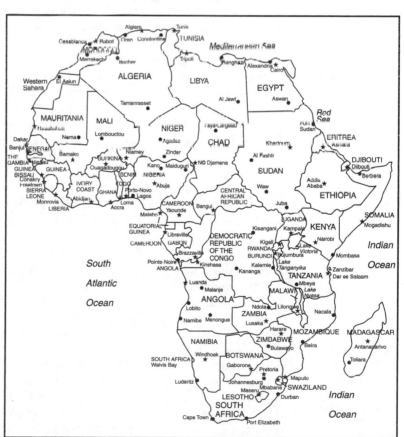

FIGURE 1.3 Africa

languages. Arabic, Swahili, and Hausa are among the most widely spoken languages in Africa. In many governmental and administrative affairs, however, many African states use the languages of the previous colonial empires (e.g., English, French, and Portuguese). This traversing of cultural entities—such as language—along different lines does not end with administration, but also exists among most ethnic groups, cultures, religions, and customs. Thus, for example, a female Nigerian Muslim woman may also ethnically be a Hausa, publicly speak English, pray in Arabic, and perform some rituals of an indigenous African religion. Indeed, many Africans may not identify with a certain group or custom, but rather may incorporate the practices of, and identify with, many different groups and religions. Thus, not only does there exist in Africa an abundance of horizontal diversity (i.e., many different cultures, practices, and customs), but there are many individuals who hold myriad beliefs, which we refer to as *vertical diversity*. This diversity is the result of Africa's rich and proud history, which most historians, archaeologists, and anthropologists argue is the oldest in the world. Africa holds the earliest human traces, which date back 5 million years. Moreover, traces of the closest ancestry of present-day humans also exist in Africa and date back 200,000 years. The first great civilization in Africa dates back 5,000 years. This civilization, dominated by the kingdom of Egypt, was located along the Nile valley and influenced global civilizations with many of its rich cultural, religious, political, and technological practices. Egypt's strategic Mediterranean location and its rich Afro-Asiatic heritage allowed it to influence the rest of the world in areas of human thought and activity. Ancient Egyptian sophistication led to the apex of ancient material development, of which the pyramids provide an example.

Africa's proud history and civilizations, although exemplified by ancient Egypt, do not stop in Egypt. The kingdom of Ghana is an example of the complex African trade and cultural traditions. Even after its decline by the eleventh century, Ghana passed on to its beneficiaries—North African Muslims and the South African kingdom of Mali—a rich structure of advancement. This intermixing created an amalgamation of many societies, symbiotically existing and influencing one another through trade routes, which encouraged not only the exchange of goods, but also the exchange of cultures and ideologies. This centuries-old process of regional cultural interaction and construction was not uninfluenced by other civilizations, however. During the late eighteenth century, new powers were to play a role in Afro-Asian affairs and forever change the African future.

European colonial posts existed in Africa well before the Berlin Conference of 1884–1885. However, it was at Berlin that the European states of Britain, France, Belgium, Portugal, Germany, and Italy officially carved up African territories and spheres of influence among themselves through the **General Act of Berlin.**[9] The European powers did not invite any Africans to the Berlin Conference and Africans were not in agreement with the provisions made at Berlin. Although resistance to European conquest was fiercest during the early years subsequent to the Berlin Conference, soon thereafter, the resistance was either co-opted by European guarantees of enrichment to a small elite of Africans or outright enslavement or murder of members of African resistance movements. After quelling the African resistance through the destruction of native state structures and turning Africans against one another, European exploitation of humans and

General Act of Berlin

A treaty that allowed certain European states different territories in Africa.

resources increased to levels unmatched in the history of the continent, even the world. This mode of exploitation continued and increased through World War I, when African raw materials such as rubber, grain, and human capital were needed to supply mass armies fighting on the European continent. Between the world wars, the demobilization of those armies, among many other developments in Europe, increased the level of exploitation in Africa to rebuild a shattered Europe.

The end of World War II, however, brought new hope for African resistance, which was now growing because of centuries of oppression. African soldiers returned to a lifestyle of misery under the same colonial states that they helped win the war. Exhausted after the horrors of World War II, European colonial powers found it less taxing to decolonize than to hold on to their restless possessions in Africa, in which peoples everywhere were yearning to live in freedom from oppression. The overthrow of European colonialism occurred first in North Africa and spread like a chain reaction throughout the continent. Mass parties emerged everywhere that not only called upon European powers to withdraw from their territories—sometimes through force and sometimes through diplomatic dialogue—but also promised their people a better life free from oppression, exploitation, and economic hardship.

Unfortunately, most of those nationalist visions for a better life did not materialize after the independence of African states. Instead, many of the same nationalist leaders who helped to overthrow the colonial regimes established their own systems of repression or were overthrown because of their failure to bring about an end to corruption, economic deficiency, oppression, etc. Nation building for many of the young African states proved to be the hardest task at hand. This was exacerbated by ethnic conflict, the result of the maintenance and solidification of nineteenth-century borders that often cut across ethnic lines, as well as famine, drought, and diseases such as AIDS.[10] Although most African countries possess the natural resources to overcome such problems, those natural resources are not worth much if they are untapped through technical expertise, adequate infrastructures, and general financial and human capital.

Asia

The largest of earth's continents, Asia covers an estimated 17,350,000 square miles and contains three-fifths of the world's population. Asia contains the Dead Sea, which is the lowest point on earth's surface, and Mount Everest, which is the highest. Asia's diversity lies not only in geography, but also in cultures, customs, beliefs, and civilizations. Asia is the center of most major world religions, including Buddhism, Christianity, Hinduism, Islam, and Judaism. It is also in Asia that we find both the Indian and the Chinese civilizations, which are among the oldest in human history. Asian civilizations were the first to create systems of governance to manage human affairs. Indeed, the dynamic civilizations that inhabit Asia are among the most diverse in the world.[11] To demonstrate the diversity of Asian peoples, we will turn our attention to comparing some of the present political and economic characteristics of two Asian nation-states, Japan and Bangladesh.

Since 1947, Japan has possessed a democratic, limited monarchy with a bicameral Diet (legislature) as the supreme organ of government. Members of the Diet designate a prime minister to conduct Japan's executive affairs. Although Japan has an emperor, he only has ceremonial powers. Japan's economy is one of the largest in the world, second only to that of the United States. In 2006, Japan's gross domestic product (GDP) totaled $4.167 trillion, which also makes Japan one of the largest producers of goods and services in the world. This economic prosperity stems from Japan's economic engagement in heavy industry—such as the manufacture of steel, motor vehicles, machinery, electronics, and chemicals—and an efficient, hardworking labor force. Because of this economic strength, Japanese citizens enjoy one of the highest standards of living in the world.

coup d'état

Military takeover of government.

In comparison to Japan, Bangladesh is one of the poorest nation-states on earth. Politically, Bangladesh has been plagued by a series of **coup d'états** (military takeover of government) since its conception in 1971. Presently, Bangladesh, like Japan, is a democracy headed by a prime minister. Bangladesh's economy is based on agricultural production. In 2005, the Bangladeshi GDP was estimated at $280 billion, which pales in comparison to Japan's GDP. Because of the poor economic conditions and the unstable political atmosphere in Bangladesh, many citizens suffer from a lack of basic necessities such as adequate nutrition, health care, and education. Although the comparison between Japan and Bangladesh may not be a fair one, it serves to demonstrate the diversity of the peoples inhabiting Asia.

Unfortunately, misconceptions about Asia's lack of diversity and major contributions still exist in many areas of our lives—even on our college campuses. Few Americans may not even be able to point to Asia on a map or if they are able to do that, they do not realize the significance of the timeless contributions that Asians have provided Europeans and Americans. We must not forget that the idea of the very pages that you are reading in this text emerged from Asiatic China. At a time when most people of the world used various inefficient and unrefined materials to write on, such as parchment and papyrus, the Chinese depended on the ingenuity and durability of

FIGURE 1.4 Asia

paper for centuries and introduced it to the rest of the world. Can you imagine where we would be without the luxury of paper? Asian contributions, however, do not stop at the material level. Asians have also provided us with most of our religious beliefs. Jesus, Abraham, Siddhartha, and Mohammad were all born and lived somewhere on the Asian continent. Those great figures of religion have influenced and continue to inspire billions of people. The ideas of those religious figures not only inspire people on a spiritual level, but also form the backbone of ethics responsible for the proper treatment of fellow human beings. Most of the religious beliefs in existence today have their origin somewhere in Asia. Thus, almost anywhere you look or anyone you speak to has certainly been influenced in some way by Asian contributions to global civilization. Asian contributions do not stop at religion; they also spill over into politics, which we turn to next.

The first forms of governments in existence developed in Asia. Because of their prehistoric origins, it is nearly impossible to know exactly when governed human settlements in Asia sprang up. Although, for example, written records did not appear in China until about 1700 B.C.E. under the **Shang Dynasty,** historians roughly place the earliest origins of Chinese civilization at about 3000 B.C.E. The early settlements, which formed the basis of Chinese civilization, were often—as in any other civilization—based on a feature that is of relative importance to human survival. Hence, the earliest traces of Chinese civilization are found along the Huang He or Yellow River, which is one of the most important rivers in China and second in size to the Yangtze. Along with the importance of human cooperation in organized settlements, which depended on fundamental elements to human sustenance such as fertile soil and water, governments were created to manage and ensure that cooperation.

> **Shang Dynasty**
> Chinese era when written records appeared.

Aside from the study of the origins of Asian civilizations in general and of governments in particular, the study of Asia is crucial to understanding the nature of who we are as a global community. Asia not only provided us with most of the things we identify with our existence such as religion and organized governance, but also is a model for human diversity, because it is the most diverse continent on earth in terms of geography, political structures, ethnicities, etc. This brief introduction to Asia is not designed to exhaustively inform the student of other global cultures. Instead, it is designed to shed some light on our human origins and what our present is shaped by. Aside from influences of politics, religion, and civilization, Asians have influenced us in many ways beyond the scope of this introduction.

Latin America

Although the term **Latin America** has raised many controversies in modern scholarship, for the purpose of this work, it will be used to refer to all territories south of the Rio Grande. South America is fourth in size to Asia, Africa, and North America, constituting 6,880,000 square miles, and politically containing thirteen countries, including Colombia, Venezuela, Guyana, Suriname, Guiana, Brazil, Uruguay, Paraguay, Argentina, Chile, Bolivia, Peru, and Ecuador. Also for the purpose of this work, Latin America will subsume the area between the Caribbean Sea and the Atlantic Ocean referred to as the "West Indies," an ambiguous and colonial term employed to describe the island

> **Latin America**
> Includes South America, countries of the Caribbean Sea, the Atlantic "West Indies," and Mexico.

territories of Cuba, Haiti, the Dominican Republic, Puerto Rico, and other smaller islands. Mexico is also considered a part of Latin America. Although Latin America may appear to be a region composed of homogeneous people, it is—like any other region—instead a very heterogeneous conglomerate of Euro-African and Native American cultures and languages. The **mestizos,** which are the descendants of Iberian and Native American ancestry, are an example of Latin American diversity. Moreover, Latin America contains another people of mixed Iberian and African ancestry, which, although less numerous than the *mestizos*, still compose a substantial ethno-national group. Throughout Latin America, Native Americans are most numerous in the highlands of the central Andean Mountains republics. Argentina and Uruguay hold the largest number of people of Spanish descent in Latin America. Meanwhile, Brazil is predominantly made up of Portuguese descendants, which are the prevailing Iberian element on the continent. In addition, Brazil holds a large number of African and racially mixed groups, while Guyana, Colombia, and Ecuador also contain a large number of people of African ancestry. Latin America also has significant settlements of people who descend from German, Japanese, Indian, Syrian, and Lebanese immigrants.

mestizos

Descendants of Iberian and Native American ancestry.

Between the 1960s and 1996, the Latin American population more than doubled, reaching 488 million. Even though this population increase is mostly attributed to natural phenomena, such as birthrate, some of it is attributed to migrations from, for example, post–World War II Europe. Ninety percent of Latin America's 310 million people are Catholic; however, we must emphasize that the continent also contains many other religious groups, including Protestants, Jews, Hindus, Muslims, Buddhists, and local religions. The reason for the Catholic majority in Latin America is grounded in the turbulent history of the continent. This turbulent history included conquest, colonization, and genocide by the European powers, initially, by Spain and Portugal, and later by France and Britain. Three of the four European powers—Spain,

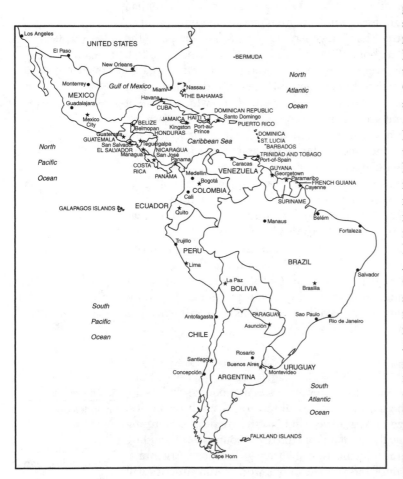

FIGURE 1.5 Latin America

Portugal, and France—contain a majority Catholic population, hence, the Catholic predominance in Latin America. To understand the Latin American past, we now turn to the continent's history.

Earlier, we described the island area between the Caribbean Sea and the Atlantic Ocean by the term *West Indies*. This term is the result of its author's confusion, that is, Christopher Columbus, who was commissioned by the Spanish and Portuguese government to find an alternative route to India in 1492. Upon reaching what he thought was India, Christopher Columbus wrongly referred to the area east of Latin America as the "Indies." Since that time, the term has gained permanent usage and was later simply qualified with the term *West*, which is how we end up with the term *West Indies*. Unfortunately, the historical errors of Europeans toward Latin America did not conclude with confusion of geography or terminology but continued into resource depletion, colonization, slavery, and ultimately, the genocide of millions of Native Americans and African slaves. After the Columbus landing in the Western Hemisphere, the floodgates opened for other numerous European "explorers," who were always sanctioned by one or more of the European powers to "discover" and ultimately claim, exploit, and colonize territories and peoples of Latin America. One of the best examples of European ruin wreaked upon the inhabitants of Latin America was Francisco Pizzaro, the Spanish conquistador whose curious explorations led to the subduing and destruction of an entire people, the Inca. In search for personal gains and riches for his native Spain, Pizzaro penetrated the gold-rich empire of the Inca in 1531. Within the brief period of five years—through the deadly use of European arms and pestilence—Pizzaro controlled the bulk of the Incan Empire, which included all of the gigantic areas of present-day Peru, Chile, and Bolivia.

The pattern of economic exploitation, colonization, and genocide continued as outlined—with increasing ferocity—for another 300 years. By the nineteenth century, a large part of the Native American population of Latin America was wiped out by disease and warfare. Meanwhile, millions of African slaves who were brought over by European colonization to work sugar and other agricultural fields perished as a result of exhaustion, disease, and maltreatment. Ironically, it is these conditions of oppression and murder that forced nineteenth-century Latin American colonies to be the first—in what is today referred to as the Third World—to undertake wars of national liberation against European domination. The Latin American struggle for independence—inspired not only by the French and American revolutions, but also by the Haitian revolution—occurred in two phases, the first from 1810 to 1816 and the second from 1816 to 1825. Although independence movements promised an improvement in the quality of life, those promises quickly diminished with increasing U.S. hegemony, stagnant economic conditions, the concentration of wealth in the hands of the church and a few wealthy families, and political turmoil.

During the twentieth century and up to the present, Latin American countries have undergone substantial change, which is part of a global phenomenon of modernization, industrialization, and rapid development.[12] Unfortunately, U.S. policy toward Latin American countries (i.e., Dollar Diplomacy and the Big Stick policy, which expanded the U.S. role in Latin America) further added to the economic and political difficulties of Latin American states. The early 1990s brought economic and political rejuvenation to Latin America with the improvement of Latin American markets and the end of the Cold War era, and U.S.-sponsored dictatorial regimes such as that of Augusto Pinochet in Chile. Despite the economic and political stabilization of most Latin American states during the 1990s, problems still remain, such as the growing gap between rich and poor, structural adjustment programs, factionalism of political parties, and ethnic-national and social tensions between groups competing for political and other resources. Such problems contribute to the rise in migration to the north. Many of the migrants cross the border without a visa or other documents.

The Middle East

Middle East

An ambiguous concept referring to countries of the eastern Mediterranean and parts of Africa.

The term **Middle East** presents scholars with a problem of ambiguity and confusion. Essentially, it is a European concept used to refer to those regions east of Europe. The Far East, the Middle East, and the Near East are all remnants of an old European colonial mindset, where Europe was viewed as the center of world civilization. Although the other two concepts are slowly disappearing from general usage, the Middle East remains very common. We will use this term in its broad context to refer to the area of modern-day Cyprus, Egypt, Iran, Iraq, Israel, the Palestinian Territories, Jordan, Kuwait, Lebanon, Saudi Arabia, Syria, Turkey, Yemen, and the states along the southern and eastern areas of the Arabian Peninsula, which include Bahrain, Oman, Qatar, and the United Arab Emirates. It was in the Middle East that the earliest civilizations emerged, namely in Mesopotamia (present-day Iraq), which is often called "the Cradle of Civilization" and in Persia (present-day Iran). Although there is no single defining cultural component of Middle Eastern peoples, a majority of people living in the Middle East identify themselves as Muslims. The reason for this prevalent Islamic identity dates back to events in the seventh century, which we turn to next.

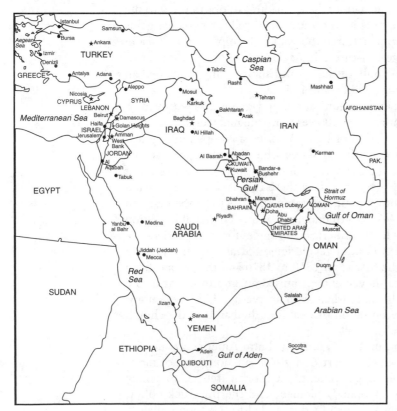

FIGURE 1.6 The Middle East

Upon receiving the revelations of an almighty God (Allah),

Mohammad, an Arab living in Mecca, in present-day Saudi Arabia, declared that he was given the ultimate form of revelation (Islam) to fellow Arabs. Because of Mohammad's revolutionary message, Meccans banished him to another town named Yathrib (Medina). This event became known as the Hijrah (622 A.D.) in Islamic history and became a focal point for all Muslims, and the beginning year of the Islamic calendar. While in Yathrib, Mohammed continued to spread his message and gained many followers identifying themselves as Muslims. In a short time, Mohammad returned to Mecca and succeeded in subduing his opposition and gaining political power over the town. By the end of Mohammad's life in 632, many of the old pagan adherents converted to Islam and identified Mohammad as the seal of all prophecy.[13]

Mohammad's sudden death fueled the determination of his followers to spread further his message, and hence that of God's, to all peoples surrounding Mecca. Within years, people throughout the Arabian Peninsula had converted to Islam and were as adamant as Mohammad's initial disciples to spread their beliefs. This became an organized mode of operation under Mohammad's successors (Khalifat al Nabi or Caliph), who not only headed the community of believers or Muslims, but also worked to export their religion. Taking note of the potential threat posed by Muslims, both the Sassanid Persian and Greek Byzantine empires attempted to eliminate that threat. Both ailing empires, however, were no match for the emerging Arab-Islamic power and were either swallowed in whole by the latter (as was Persia) or lost most of their territory (as did Byzantium).

The rapid Islamic expansion created an empire of universal beliefs rooted in the Judeo-Christian-Islamic tradition, the belief in one God, and stretched from present-day India, China, and Indonesia in Asia to France, Spain, and Portugal in Europe to Nigeria, Morocco, and Somalia in Africa. During the Golden Ages of the Islamic Empire (under the Arabs and later under the Turks), the world gained some of the greatest scientific and cultural contributions ever known, from translations and ultimate preservation of classical Greek works to innovations in mathematics, bureaucracy, and medicine. Indeed, the contributions to civilization made during the expansion of Islam have transformed the Middle East and the rest of the world forever. Thus, today we may read Plato's *Republic* because of its preservation by philosophers (Christians, Jews, and Muslims) living during the height of Islamic power or use the Arabic numerals in mathematics or understand the detrimental effects of germs on humans.

Despite the great advancements made by the Islamic civilization, changes in global affairs forced it to take a lesser place of importance. With the collapse of the Ottoman Empire in 1918, new nations emerged in the Middle East, but were still colonized by other powers, this time European. The British and French, both victors of World War I, carved up the Middle Eastern remains of the Ottoman Empire, through mandates, between themselves with the British colonizing the bulk of the Middle East from Iraq to Egypt and the French colonizing territories along the Mediterranean including Syria and Lebanon. One of the main reasons the British and French empires defeated the Ottoman Empire was the use of Arab nationalism against the latter. In return for fighting along with the British and French, Arabs were promised independence after the end of the war. Despite this promise, Arabs were forced to wait for another catastrophic war to gain independence from their colonizers.

Mohammad

Muslim prophet who was given the message of Islam to spread.

World War II not only caused the death of millions around the world, it also destroyed the empires that participated in it. Hence, by the middle 1950s and early 1960s, most of the Middle Eastern peoples were to gain their independence—except for the Palestinians, most of whose territory was turned into a Jewish State called Israel, and the Kurds, whose lands were carved up among the new states. As Middle Eastern states began to shape their own destinies, they found themselves caught in the middle of a Cold War between the Soviet Union and the United States on the one hand and a global economic system on the other. Because of their riches in natural resources and strategic global location, many territories of the Middle East remain coveted by regional powers, such as Saddam Hussein's Iraq, and by external powers, such as Russia and the United States. Although the endowments of location and resources may be perceived as a blessing by some, they have mostly brought suffering to the inhabitants of Middle Eastern countries through foreign-supported authoritarian regimes, corruption, arms races, and wars.

Palestinians and Kurds remain lacking in independence.

Presently, many Middle Eastern countries, like most developing countries, contend with problems of illiteracy, low life expectancy, high infant mortality, exploding populations, economic hardship, and political decay. Some Middle Eastern countries, however, enjoy a high socioeconomic standard of living such as the oil-producing states of the Gulf (with the exception of Iraq after its devastation in the Gulf War and years of economic sanctions). When compared with other countries in the developing world (e.g., Bangladesh, Afghanistan, Sierra Leone, Rwanda), Middle Eastern countries appear well off. Nevertheless, like other developing countries, Middle Eastern countries, with some exceptions, continue to fall behind. Even oil-rich countries—such as Kuwait—which possess an excess amount of wealth as a result of their petroleum-based economy, still suffer problems such as authoritarian rule, underdevelopment, and disproportionate gaps between rich and poor.

Summary and Review

A people are a group of individuals who make up a community. The way a people organizes its affairs is called politics. Essentially, the study of politics is the study of government and power allocation and use in society. Government is a mechanism that people employ to organize their affairs and to protect them from threats. In the United States, for example, people employ three branches of government—executive, legislative, and judicial—to enforce, pass, and interpret laws. Although people in the United States live in a republic, many people in other parts of the world live under monarchial forms of government, where a single monarch rules the state. There are different forms of monarchies. A limited monarchy is one in which the monarch's powers are limited to ceremonial functions, whereas a constitutional monarchy has a monarch whose powers are allocated in the constitution. In absolute monarchy, the monarch has absolute power. There are also different forms of republics, including dictatorship and oligarchy. A dictatorship has power vested in a single person who is not a monarch, whereas an oligarchy can be defined as rule by the few. Aside from politics, people also informally manage their affairs through culture. Culture is a set of traditions, beliefs, and behaviors that a people express and hold. Although culture and politics are often interdependent, they can be separated in order to study societies. Throughout the world, different cultural groupings often live under one state. A state is an internationally recognized, politically organized, populated, geographical area that possesses sovereignty. Aside from different cultures, states often possess many different nations, which are distinct from state and culture. A nation refers to a group of people who identify with each other as a political community because of common territorial, cultural, and other similar bonds.

Key Terms

politics 2	constitutional	federal structures 6	nonindustrialized
globalization 2	monarchy 6	culture 7	countries 10
government 5	dictatorship 6	elements of	underdeveloped
executive branch 5	oligarchy 6	statehood 8	countries 10
legislative branch 5	junta 6	state 8	the developing
judicial branch 5	apartheid 6	recognition 8	world 10
forms of govern	totalitarian	sovereignty 9	the South 10
ment 5	systems 6	nation 9	the Third World 10
limited monarchy 5	democracy 6	nation-state 9	
monarchy 5	centralized system 6	homogeneous state 9	
republic 5	decentralized	heterogeneous	
absolute monarchy 6	systems 6	state 9	

Discussion Questions

1. How do you define *government*? Explain how your government participates in the activities of your everyday life.
2. What are the different branches of government in the United States? Explain each branch by stating its highest authority.
3. Explain the basic forms of government. Give examples of each particular form of government by relating it to a country.
4. Explain the three different forms of monarchies. Give examples of each particular form of monarchy by relating it to a country.
5. What are the differences among dictatorships, oligarchy, and totalitarian forms of government? Give examples of countries that represent each case.
6. What does it mean when governments have centralized or decentralized forms of power?
7. What are the basic elements of statehood?
8. How significant is recognition to statehood? Explain the status of the "Turkish Federated State of Cyprus" today. Discuss other peoples or countries that may not be recognized by the world society.
9. Are the "states" in the United States of America real "states"? Explain.
10. Are nations limited to a particular area such as only within a state? Give examples of nations.
11. What are some of the basic features of the developing world?

Suggested Readings

Almond, Gabriel, and Sidney Verba. *The Civic Culture*. Princeton, NJ: Princeton University Press, 1963.

Alvarez, Sonia E., Evelina Dagnino, and Arturo Escobar, eds. *Cultures of Politics, Politics of Cultures: Re-Visioning Latin American Social Movements*. Boulder, CO: Westview Press, 1998.

Dierks, Rosa Gomez. *Introduction to Globalization: Political and Economic Perspectives for the New Century*. Lanham, MD: Roman and Littlefield, 2005.

Hechter, Michael. *Containing Nationalism*. Oxford, U.K.: Oxford University Press, 2000.

Jacobsen, Michael, and Ole Bruun, eds. *Human Rights and Asian Values: Contesting National Identities and Cultural Representations in Asia*. Richmond, VA: Curzon, 2000.

Jones, Anny Brooksbank, and Ronaldo Munck, eds. *Cultural Politics in Latin America*. New York: St. Martin's Press, 2000.

Mason, Colin. *A Short History of Asia: Stone Age to 2000 A.D.* New York: Palgrave, 2000.

Nassar, Jamal. *Globalization and Terrorism: The Migration of Dreams and Nightmares*. Lanham, MD: Roman and Littlefield, 2005.

Riaz, Ali. *Unfolding State: The Transformation of Bangladesh*. Whitby, ON, Canada: de Sitter Publications, 2005.

Thompson, Lloyd, Dapo Adelugba, and Egbe Ifie, eds. *Culture and Civilization*. Ibadan, Africa: Afrika-Link Books, 1991.

Weatherby, Joseph J., et al. *The Other World: Issues and Politics of the Developing World*. New York: Longman, 1997.

Addresses and Websites

APEC Secretariat
35 Heng Mui Keng Terrace
Singapore 119616
Tel: 65–6777–6012
Fax: 65–6775–6013
www.apec.org

Southern African Development Community
SADC Headquarters
Private Bag 0095, Gabarone, Botswana
Tel: (1267) 351863
Fax: (1267) 372848

African Union
Headquarters
P. O. Box 3243
Addis Ababa
Ethiopia
Tel: 1251 1 51–7700
Fax: 1251 1 51–7844
http://www.africa-union.org/

The African Union, formerly known as The Organization of African Unity, works toward the goal of Pan-African Unity among the vast nations within the African continent. The organization also aids African nations in economic development and cooperation while also allowing nations to maintain their sovereignty. This website provides an in-depth look at the organization and also gives various information about countries in Africa. This is an excellent place for beginners to find resources and information about Africa.

Cooperation Council for the Arab States of the Gulf (Gulf Cooperation Council (GCC))
Headquarters
P. O. Box 7153
Riyadh 11462
Saudi Arabia
Tel: [966] (1)482–7777
Fax: [966] (1)482–9089

League of Arab States
Al Tahrir Square
P. O. Box 11642
Cairo, Egypt
Tel: [20](2)575–0511
[20](2)575–2966
Fax: [20](2)574–0331
http://www.leagueofarabstates.org/

The League of Arab States is an organization consisting of many states in the Arab world. The organization, founded in 1945, was created to better the conditions of Arab countries and to help the states develop. It also works toward regional cooperation and the promotion of economic, cultural, and security plans. The website offers further information regarding the organization, including a list of member-states. A discussion on Arab civilization can also be found on the website.

Organization of American States
Headquarters
17th St. & Constitution Ave., NW
Washington, D.C. 20006
Tel: (202) 458–3000
http://www.oas.org/

The Organization of American States, founded in 1948, is a group that works toward unity and the promotion of regional cooperation among nations in North and South America. The website offers an in-depth look at the OAS, its charter and goals, along with contact information for the various missions or member-states. The site also offers various links pertaining to the organization, including different documents and information on cooperation and development.

http://www.asiasource.org/

This website provides a wonderful resource for information regarding the broader Asian society. From Iran to India to Indonesia to China, there is information on different cultural aspects, policies and government, economics and business, and societies and histories. Apart from being an archive for historical and cultural information, this website also offers information and news articles on current events in Asia.

http://www.channelafrica.org/

This website is a great reservoir of news from Africa. Using shortwave, satellite, and Internet radio, the site can connect browsers to current news and sports information, along with providing music from the continent. The website is available in many languages, including English, French, and Swahili. These languages and many more are also offered in the various links to Internet radio news and music.

http://www.lab.org.uk/

This is the website for the Latin American Bureau, which focuses on Latin American education. The organization also focuses on many aspects of Latin America, including developmental and human rights issues within the region and their relationship to the broader global society. The website is an excellent liaison for other websites that provide news regarding Latin America and house information on the region.

http://www.un.org/

This website takes you to the Internet home of the United Nations, the international governing structure in which many nations participate. The U.N. offers statistics and other useful information about various issues in countries. There are also numerous U.N. councils and programs, and information regarding them can be located on the site. This link is also an excellent source of information on international law and international affairs.

Notes

1. *Final Report of the World Conference on Cultural Policies* (Organized by UNESCO in Mexico City, 26 July–6 August, 1982), 41.
2. See, for example, Gabriel Almond and Sidney Verba, *The Civic Culture* (Princeton, NJ: Princeton University Press, 1963).
3. UNESCO, *Culture and Development* (Paris: UNESCO, 1994), 16.
4. H. B. Jacobini, *International Law: A Text* (Homewood, IL: The Dorsey Press, 1968), 49.
5. Hugo Grotius, *The Classics of International Law*, trans. F. W. Kelsey; vol. 2 (Oxford, U.K.: The Clarendon Press, 1925), 102.
6. For an argument against the idea of national belonging being an emotion, see Michael Hechter, *Containing Nationalism* (Oxford, U.K.: Oxford University Press, 2000).
7. There are many books on the topic. Among those are Howard Handelman, *The Challenge of Third World Development* (Upper Saddle River, NJ: Prentice Hall, 1996); and Joseph J. Weatherby et al., *The Other World: Issues and Politics of the Developing World* (New York: Longman, 1997).
8. See *African Make or Break: Action for Recovery* (London: Oxfam, 1993).
9. See Ali A. Mazrui, *The African: A Triple Heritage* (New York: Little, Brown, 1986).
10. See Kofi Annan, *The Causes of Conflict and the Promotion of Durable Peace and Sustainable Development in Africa* (New York: United Nations, 1998).
11. See Colin Mason, *A Short History of Asia: Stone Age to 2000 A.D.* (New York: Palgrave, 2000).
12. See Thomas E. Skidmore and Peter H. Smith, *Modern Latin America* (Oxford, U.K.: Oxford University Press, 2000).
13. Richard Bulliet, *Islam: The View from the Edge* (Irvington, NY: Columbia University Press, 1995).

CHAPTER TWO

Global Interdependence

GLOBALIZATION AND INTERDEPENDENCE

IN THE EARLY 1990s, PRESIDENT GEORGE H. W. BUSH, CELEBRATING THE DEMISE OF THE SOVIET UNION, DECLARED THE DAWN OF A NEW WORLD ORDER. SINCE THEN, THE FORCES OF GLOBALIZATION THAT CONTRIBUTED TO THE RISE OF THIS NEW ORDER HAVE BEEN ACCELERATING AT A DIZZYING PACE. THE NEW WORLD ORDER, HOWEVER, SHOULD NOT BE AN END IN ITSELF; RATHER, IT SHOULD BE A MEANS TO AN END. THE END OUGHT TO BE AN IMPROVEMENT IN THE HUMAN CONDITION GLOBALLY. HAVE WE ARRIVED THERE? SADLY, THE ANSWER IS NO. ALTHOUGH SOME PEOPLE IN THIS INTERDEPENDENT AND GLOBALIZED WORLD HAVE REAPED THE BENEFITS OF THIS NEW WORLD ORDER, OTHERS HAVE SUFFERED ITS NEGATIVE CONSEQUENCES. IT IS HOPED THAT, IN TIME, GLOBALIZATION WILL LEAD TO IMPROVED STANDARDS OF LIVING FOR EVERYONE. THE UNITED STATES LIKES TO VIEW ITSELF AS THE WORLD LEADER, THE CAPTAIN OF THE GLOBAL SHIP, SO TO SPEAK. BUT, ALTHOUGH THE CAPTAIN OF THE SHIP GETS THE LUXURY OF THE CAPTAIN'S CABIN, THE CAPTAIN ALSO GETS THE RESPONSIBILITY FOR THE WELL-BEING OF THE WHOLE SHIP. MANY AMERICANS, SOMEHOW, WANT THE LUXURY WITHOUT THE RESPONSIBILITY. THIS INTERDEPENDENT GLOBAL COMMUNITY OF OURS NEEDS CARING AND GLOBALLY MINDED LEADERSHIP, NOT A PAROCHIAL OR SELF-CENTERED ONE. SOME DAY, PERHAPS, THE MAJORITY OF AMERICANS WILL BE UP TO THE TASK OF PROVIDING THE WORLD WITH THE REQUIRED NEW WORLD LEADERSHIP.

INTRODUCTION

Imagine, for a moment, that as you leave the classroom and exit the building, you see strange creatures descending to earth and aiming their destructive beams upon structures and peoples all over the world. Clearly, these aliens are trying to conquer the earth. If that were to happen, it is feasible to expect soldiers everywhere to aim their guns and missiles toward the invading aliens and engage them in battle. American, Cuban, Iraqi, Bosnian, Serb, Arab, Israeli, North and South Korean, and soldiers of every state would suddenly forget their own state enemies and become instant allies in their struggle against the alien invaders. Should such a scenario ever occur, people everywhere would realize that we share one planet and a common destiny. You, as an educated college student, need not wait for such an invasion to reach this realization. Although our planet Earth is divided into independent states, it is also becoming increasingly interdependent. The growing interdependence of our global community is slowly changing the relationships of states and individuals. Simply put, local concerns have become global in implication. National problems are now global problems. Whether it is inflation, recession, environmental pollution, terrorism, monetary fluctuation, communicable diseases, drug trafficking, religious revivalism, or a host of other troubles, local or national solutions would not solve them. Global problems require global solutions. Our world of nation-states can offer mainly national solutions to global concerns. So far, the nation-state system has failed to solve many contemporary global problems.

THE GLOBAL REALITY

Scientists and space explorers have, so far, been unable to produce evidence that human life is viable anywhere in the universe outside of planet Earth. We have no options and no place to inhabit other than cohabiting this planet. There was a time on this planet when people lived independently of each other. Subsistence living, by definition, meant independent living where people produced a sufficient amount of food for their survival as an independent family unit. In time, people slowly became interdependent through the division of labor. Some food was produced, other food was traded, and service became a new trade item. Soon thereafter, society became so interdependent that individuals served only specialized functions—such as teaching, secretarial, construction, plumbing, etc.—whereas others produced their food or their other needs for survival. Today, our planet has become a web of global interdependence linked together in ways that our forebearers could not have imagined. Like individuals and families, peoples, nations, and states are all spinning this web while at the same time they are suspended in it. No state can any longer sustain its standard of living if it chooses to isolate itself from the rest of the world. Actions of one state have ramifications that go beyond its borders. Nor can states today escape the impact of developments outside their borders. In sum, the world we inhabit has become seamless and indivisible despite the borders that divide its many states.

Economically, the world is so interwoven that the livelihood of one depends upon the production of many others. When you go to visit a nearby mall, you are, in effect, entering a global marketplace rather than a mere local shopping center. Even in a single store, you are likely to encounter merchandise from many parts of the world. The shoes may come from Italy, the sweater may say "made in Malaysia," the jeans are likely to be made in the U.S.A., and the coffeemaker may come from Germany or Sweden. Even the single item that may say it was made in a specific country is likely to have many more sources outside of that country where it was produced. Take, for example, a dress that proclaims Singapore as the state where it was fabricated. The material for the dress is partly cotton and partly synthetic. The cotton, perhaps, came from Egypt or India. The petroleum for the synthetic may have originated in Iran or Saudi Arabia and been manufactured in England or South Korea. The lace on the dress may have come from Italy. The zipper made of a copper pull and plastic material might have started as copper ore in Chile and the plastic zipper in Mexico or Ecuador. Once cut and sewn in Singapore, the dress may have been hung on a Chinese-made hanger and placed in a Malaysian-made nylon bag. Once packaged, the dress could have been shipped on a Liberian-licensed cargo ship to Miami or Los Angeles for distribution to stores around the country. The increasing globalization of economic activity is most visible in the areas of production, trade, and finance. Electronic trading has opened the way for massive movements of funds. This weakened the effectiveness of governmental policy decisions in the areas of currency values and international trade. In the areas of production and trade, global interdependence is a visible fact of life. The production and trade of a dress, similar to the one mentioned earlier, can be an example of globalization in this area.

Interdependence is also evident in the area of minerals and other natural resources. Consumption of critical minerals has been on the rise and known reserves are concentrated in a few areas of the world. The reality is that no country is endowed with all the raw materials that it consumes. Some countries are rich in some minerals but lack others. Some lack most. Even a rich and large country like Germany can be poor in some resources vital to its economic activity. The United States, for example, is totally dependent upon others for its needs in chromium, manganese, and tin. All three materials are vital for the industrial economy of the country. The United States is also poor in its resources of many other minerals including aluminum, copper, iron, lead, nickel, potassium, tungsten, and zinc. In the area of energy, global interdependence manifests itself in the realm of politics. The Arab oil embargo of the early 1970s was a striking wake-up call to all nation-states. It highlighted the emergence of petroleum as a tool of foreign policy. The ramifications of the embargo were felt not only by the targeted states, but also by many other countries.

No country has all the raw materials it consumes.

NEWS IN THE

Dissent in the Digital Age

In Iran, a new form of dissent has taken root since 2001—known as *digital dissent*. Hanif Mazroui has gained attention as one of many dissidenters who are utilizing the Internet as a means of challenging the Iranian government's authority. Throughout Iran, web loggers, bloggers, and online journalists have been arrested and, according to some reports, tortured by the Iranian government in an effort to silence this new medium of protest. They are forced to publicly denounce their coercion and violence. The Iranian government has relied on force in order to quell challenges to its power and dominance over the Iranian public. Activists like Hanif, however, have identified the potential power of grassroots resistance in the face of extreme repression.

Source: The Los Angeles Times, 24 January 2005.

Interdependence is, perhaps, most evident in technology and communications. A technological or scientific breakthrough in the United States benefits not only Americans but also people everywhere. If, for example, a cure for cancer is found somewhere, cancer patients could benefit everywhere. As Lester Brown reported in 1972, "more and more, the new technology used in any given country originates outside that country."[1] His conclusion is even truer today. In communications, global interdependence is evident every time you turn on your television set or radio, log onto a computer network server, or read a newspaper. The combination of fax machines, universal telephone service (including cellular), and low-cost and high-speed computers enable us to communicate globally and instantly. Environmentally we inhabit a planet with a delicate ecological balance. In this planetary environment, there was a day when people could and did pursue their survival in isolation. We no longer can do so. Our numbers and our progress have made our fate as a species and as inhabitants of one ecological system interlocked and interdependent. An environmental disaster in one part of the planet is a disaster for the whole planet.

Food and agricultural interdependence is also evident every time you drink soda, order a hamburger, or have a cup of coffee. Some areas of the planet have an abundance of certain foods or agricultural products, whereas others have different ones. Even though the United States may be called the breadbasket of the world, it certainly is not the world's food basket. Although the United States exports a large amount of grain, it imports many other agricultural products, including beef, coffee, bananas, and other fruits and vegetables. Other areas of global interdependence include our own health when viruses and diseases travel beyond borders and infect people of all races and nationalities. Even our own neighbors may be the products of global interdependence. Migration now has become so common and easy with air transportation. No longer do we live in the same community of our birth. Today people are continuously on the move. Consequently, our modern societies are rapidly becoming multicultural and sometimes even multilingual. In sum, global interdependence has become a reality no state or individual can escape. No people can shut themselves off from "foreign" influences. When imperial China tried to do that some 500 years ago, it went quickly from "being the world's most advanced and powerful nation to becoming a poor backwater of the globe."[2] No nation can do that anymore. Perhaps, by now, some of you are thinking, "What do I care?" It is true that world affairs seem too far beyond your immediate interests. At this point in your life, you just want to finish college and get a decent job. You may have many other concerns. Some may be financial; others may relate to your circle of friends, your club, or your family. In sum, the world beyond seems too distant to worry about. This may be a good time to take a look at how events and developments that seem far may be very significant in determining the rest of your life.

GLOBAL INTERDEPENDENCE AND YOUR LIFE

We are going to tell you the story of a college student. Her name was Cindy. Cindy Marie Beaudoin was a first-year student at the University of Connecticut in September 1990. Just a month before Cindy went to college, Iraq had invaded Kuwait. As a soldier in the 142nd Medical Company of her state's National Guard, Cindy was called to active duty on November 17, 1990. Cindy had a month to go toward completing her first semester in college. In January 1991, Cindy and company were sent to Saudi Arabia. As the war began, Cindy and her unit moved into Iraq behind advancing combat units and later entered Kuwait. A few days later, the Iraqi army had been defeated and President Bush declared a cease-fire. But wars are not totally over with declarations. About 3:00 P.M. on February 28, Cindy's convoy was rocked by an explosion. Falling from her truck, she shouted: "They're firing at us." Moments later, she realized that she had been hit. We still do not know the cause of the explosion, but we do know that Cindy's abdomen was torn and her leg was gone. A medical helicopter picked her up but Cindy couldn't wait. She died during the flight. Cindy Marie Beaudoin was dead at the age of 19 without ever completing her first semester in college.[3]

Few months before her death in Kuwait, Cindy may have not known much or cared much about places like Kuwait, Saudi Arabia, or Iraq. Maybe Cindy didn't even know where these places were on a map. Yet, Cindy's life ended prematurely in Kuwait. You may now say that Cindy was in the National Guard, and because you are not, what happens in the world does not affect you. If so, you are wrong. When you turned eighteen, if you are a male, you were required to stop at a post office to register yourself in the Selective Service System. Should there be a major crisis, it is possible that you could be drafted into a branch of the military and, after a short boot camp experience, be sent to some faraway place to fight. If the draft is restored in an emergency, it is likely that it will also include females as well. In many other countries, military service is required of all those who are within a specific age group and are physically able to serve. Many recent college students found themselves in Afghanistan or Iraq and quite a few of them were killed or wounded.

TAKING ACTION

Cliff Kindy and the Christian Peacemaker Teams

Cliff Kindy's organization, the Christian Peacemaker Teams, remains a symbol of the strength of today's global antiwar movement. Christian Peacemaker Teams (CPT) organizes and sends activists throughout the world in an effort to lead by example in the effort to find nonviolent solutions to violent conflicts. Having recently spent time in Iraq protesting the U.S. war, as well as documenting human rights abuses throughout the country, Kindy is only one of many people dedicated to CPT who selflessly risk their lives to bring attention to grave human rights violations in conflicts ranging from the Israeli occupation of the Palestinian territories to the war in Iraq to the conflict between Colombian paramilitary forces and leftist guerillas. CPT's success in gaining global recognition in the battle to promote nonviolent solutions to global conflict is an excellent example of the extent to which global interdependence has allowed for human rights workers to operate across borders in order to find just and equitable solutions to increasingly global problems.

Source: The indy. Interview with Cliff Kindy of the Christian Peacemaker Teams. 8 October 2004, http://indy.pabn.org/news.php?id=426

Military service is not the only way in which global interdependence may touch your life. We all know about our military and political interdependence. Economically, environmentally, and even culturally we are all dependent upon each other on this planet of ours. Let us now take a detailed look at each of these areas.

ECONOMIC INTERDEPENDENCE

In the days of the old American west, many people went west and found a nice piece of land and settled on it. There, the family built its own log home and raised cows, pigs, and chickens. They planted and harvested their own vegetables and grains. The mother taught the children to read and write. In sum, in those days, the American family was independent or self-sufficient. Today, however, the average family in the United States or anywhere in the world has become interdependent. We now live in a world where specialization has replaced self-reliance. Our society today is similar to an assembly line where each person performs a specific function and countless others provide for the rest of that individual's needs. Just like people, states are no longer economically self-sufficient. All must engage in international trade in goods, services, and financial resources. Whether a state is rich or poor, whether it is capitalist or social-ist, every state is interlinked to the rest of the world. The United States is at the center of this global economic interdependence. Americans now own more than $2.5 trillion in shares and other assets located outside the United States. It is likely that some of the money paying for your college expenses comes from such assets. Foreigners also own plenty of shares and assets located in the United States. Today, more than $1.5 trillion in currency exchanges occur every single day. In more ways than we realize, our lives have become very dependent on a global economic system. This evening, you may order a pizza or eat egg rolls, tacos, or falafel. Even here, the food we eat reflects different cultures. The car you may buy may be a better example of interdependency. You may think that you are buying an American-made car when you purchase a General Motors product. The reality is that General Motors makes or assembles its cars in about thirty-four countries. The one you buy could be made in Finland, Kenya, or Brazil. Trade boomed in the twentieth century and the boom promises to continue in the twenty-first century.[4] The flow of goods and services has witnessed a tremendous jump in the last three decades. Table 2.1 shows the extent of growth in capital.

What could such rise in global trade mean to you? As a student, you are not a producer of goods; you are, however, a consumer. Purchasing is a major activity in your life. To a small child, milk does not come from cows, it comes from stores. Most small children have never seen a cow being milked, so in their world, milk comes from stores. What if there is to be a crisis of some sort that will prevent that child's parent or you from being able to purchase the barest of daily necessities such as milk, tooth-paste, cereal, bread, toilet paper, or soap? That would be a very unsettling experience. Such an event did happen. In 1974, for example, a national truck driver strike emptied store shelves within hours. Trade does not occur in the exchange of goods alone. It also involves services. Even though students generally are not producers of goods, many are producers of services that make a large part of trade. If you work at the

TABLE 2.1 PERCENTAGE OF WORLD TRADE IN GROSS DOMESTIC PRODUCTS AND EXPORTS FOR 2002

	Number of Countries	GDP (%) Advanced Economies	World	Exports of Goods and Services (%) Advanced Economies	World
Advanced Economies	29	100.0	55.7	100.0	74.8
United States		**37.9**	**21.1**	**16.5**	**12.4**
Euro Area	12	28.2	15.7	41.7	31.2
Germany		8.0	4.4	12.2	9.1
France		5.7	3.2	6.8	5.1
Italy		5.5	3.0	5.4	4.0
Japan		12.8	7.1	7.8	5.8
United Kingdom		5.6	3.1	6.8	5.1
Canada		3.6	2.0	5.1	3.8
Other Advanced Economies	22	20.9	11.6	39.4	29.5

		Developing Countries	World	Developing Countries	World
Developing Countries	125	100.0	38.1	100.0	20.3
Regional Groups					
Africa	51	8.5	3.2	9.2	1.9
Sub Sahara	48	6.5	2.5	6.8	1.4
Developing Asia	25	60.3	22.9	48.5	9.9
China		33.3	12.7	22.4	4.6
India		12.5	4.8	4.5	0.9
Other Asia	23	14.5	5.5	21.7	4.4
Middle East and Turkey	16	10.5	4.0	20.1	4.1

Source: IMF (2002), http://www.imf.org/external/pubs/ft/weo/2003/02/pdf/appendix.pdf

library, deliver pizza, or stock the shelves at a nearby grocery store, you are involved in a service activity. Today's trade activities involve services of architects, computer specialists, financial advisors, teachers, bankers, hotel managers, and a host of other services that people need. Almost half of U.S. exports are in services.

International investment is another form of international economic activity that is seeing rapid growth. Americans invest abroad often. Whenever an individual has stocks in some foreign company or when foreigners own stocks in U.S. companies, they are involved in international investment. Multinational corporations (MNCs) are at the forefront of the flow of international investments. They not only buy and sell stocks, but also have subsidiaries all over the world. Global monetary relations have also contributed to the growing global interdependence. Trade in money and currency exchange has reached a point where we can truly say that money has become a global commodity. The growth in economic activity may seem wonderful to many people. Governments and businesses usually encourage such activities and see them as

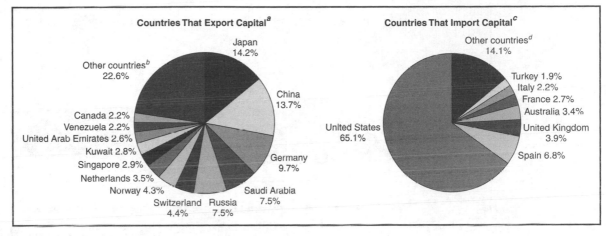

FIGURE 2.1 Major Net Exporters and Importers of Capital in 2005

[a]As measured by countries' current account surplus (assuming errors and omissions are part of the capital and financial accounts).
[b]Other countries include all countries with shares of total surplus less than 2.2 percent.
[c]As measured by countries' current account deficit (assuming errors and omissions are part of the capital and financial accounts).
[d]Other countries include all countries with shares of total deficit less than 1.9 percent.
Source: International Monetary Fund, *World Economic Outlook* database as of 27 March 2006.

signs of economic vitality as well as sources of profit, employment, and economic well-being. Of course, no growth occurs without some price to be paid for it. Economic growth has serious consequences to other areas of global interdependence. One of those is the well being of the environment. We simply cannot afford to keep the global economy on a collision course with our earth's ecosystem. Economic progress and environmental concerns are interlocked in a cycle of interdependence. The failure of one could spell failure for the other.

ENVIRONMENTAL INTERDEPENDENCE

Recently, developers in Houston drew up plans to build a new airport on a 200,000-acre wetland that is home to many species of birds. The Sierra Club attempted to block the new development. To do so, the Sierra Club joined forces with its nemesis, the National Rifle Association (NRA). The two strange bedfellows came together in 1995, when Marge Hanselman, a Sierra Club activist, set up a booth at a Houston gun show. After hearing ridicule from some visitors, she was asked by an NRA director why she was there. She made her case to the director, citing a long list of game birds that would be displaced if the airport were approved. The impressed director then introduced Hanselman to Sue King, a very active NRA member and a proud hunter of game birds. The two women soon became friends and put aside their differences for the common interest of protecting the wetland. The coalition of Sierra Club and NRA members proved too strong for the developers. Consequently, the city council recommended that the area be made a protected wetland.[5]

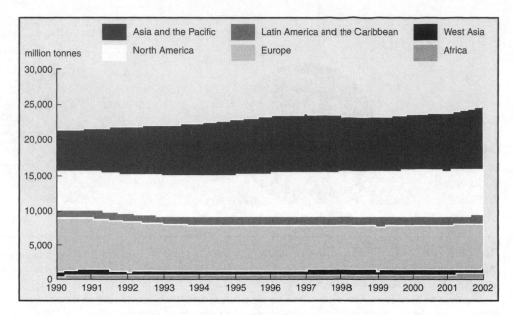

FIGURE 2.2 Carbon Dioxide Emissions by Region

Source: UNEP, *GEO Year Book 2006*, http://www.unep.org/geo/yearbook/yb2006/022.asp. GEO Data Portal based on United Nations 2005. The United Nations is the author of the original material.

Environmental issues may sound local in some instances. Their ramifications, however, are usually global.[6] Air pollution, global warming, nuclear waste, and acid rain have become a part of our common vocabulary. What they all denote is much more than preserving some species of game birds. The reality is that air currents travel without a visa and make no concern for state boundaries. Pollution of any sort in one place is invariably pollution in other places. The loss of the ozone layer affects not only people in the United States, but life on earth. Just like the NRA and the Sierra Club worked together to save game bird habitat in Houston, countries of the world must work together on a large scale to preserve our planet's health and well-being.

Economic growth that states seek in order to enhance the well-being of their people often leads to environmental degradation and loss of biodiversity that endanger all of us. A balance between economic growth and environmental protection is needed. To do so, countries must cooperate and plan together. The good news is that there has been progress made in this area. In 1972, the United Nations began the process of global discussions when it hosted the Conference on the Human Environment in Stockholm, Sweden. The result was the creation of a permanent program known as the United Nations Environmental Programme (UNEP). Since then, many international trade agreements incorporated environmental protection into their clauses. In 1987, the UNEP held a conference in Montreal, Canada, on the protection of the ozone layer. In time, countries committed themselves to reduce the emission of chlorofluorocarbons (CFCs). CFCs are used as a refrigerant but contribute to the depletion of the ozone layer.

In 1992, the **Earth Summit** in Rio de Janeiro, Brazil, addressed the issue of global warming and many countries signed on to reduce the emissions of gases that contribute to it.[7]

There has also been progress on a range of other environmental concerns including the dumping of hazardous wastes and toxic materials. But the progress so far falls far short of the needed drastic changes in the way we do things. Economic progress, sometimes seen as corporate interests, seems to outweigh global environmental well-being. This disparity was highlighted in 1999 when the World Trade Organization held its meeting in Seattle, Washington. That meeting drew 35,000 demonstrators and activists from environmental and labor groups concerned about the corporate role in the era of globalization. Action on environmental issues has gone global, in part, because of the dramatic revolution in global communication. This revolution in communication has contributed to greater cultural interaction at the global level.

Earth Summit

Addressed the issue of global warming.

CULTURAL INTERDEPENDENCE

Cultural globalization is, perhaps, the most familiar form of interdependence to most people. Almost everyone on earth knows the sports stars, the icons of popular culture, and the commercials for Coca-Cola. This was not the way it was fifty or so years ago. During the first part of the twentieth century, most people lived in remote villages that had never seen a television and were amazed at the sounds of the radio. Most were illiterate. Today, their grandchildren are on the move. They listen to music, watch television, and many participate in chat rooms and play games on the Internet.

McDonald's is a global corporation with outlets in many countries. This sign stands over one in Cairo, Egypt.

Source: Lauren Goodsmith/The Image Works

The world we live in today has become a web of global interdependence where the golden arches of McDonald's, Pepsi and Coca-Cola cans, Levi's jeans, Nike sneakers, and the idols who promote them are the same almost everywhere. Even the aspirations and dreams of children are becoming more alike as they become more exposed to the same television shows, news stories, and songs. Be it Kobe Bryant, Ricky Martin, Leonardo DiCaprio, or Britney Spears, children and teenagers the world over look up to them. You could walk on the streets of Accra or Jakarta and see images of such idols on clothing, in magazines, and on billboards. If you play Internet games, you may join a table with someone from Australia or Japan or South Africa. In sum, the world has become as interconnected in the area of cultural symbols and values as it has in other areas. The dominant culture is sweeping the world and sending messages that neither governments nor families abroad are able to control. American culture, with its emphasis on consumption, market economy, and individualism, has gone global. Of course, this dominance is not without opposition. Some intellectuals in Africa, Asia, and Latin America argue that their societies are now victims of "cultural colonialism." Some countries have tried to close their borders to outside cultural influences. Iran, for example, tried to do so in vain during the early years of its Islamic Revolution. Afghanistan, Saudi Arabia, and others have made similar attempts. In 1980, the majority of states at the United Nations meeting in Belgrade at the UNESCO General Conference even adopted a resolution that aimed at regulating the flow of information. Known as the New World Information and Communication Order, this resolution advocated respect for each people's cultural identity. Needless to say, resolutions do not necessarily translate into actions. This one did not.

The fact remains that information crosses borders without any regard to political divisions. Satellite transmissions and computer interactions need no visa. States seem helpless here. If they try to stop the spread of such technologies, they endanger their societies of falling farther behind. If they allow the spread, they risk unwanted consequences. Take, for example, a remote village in Yemen. People there still live in a traditional setting. Their homes are made of clay and they have no running water or electricity. The village has no school and most adults are illiterate. Imagine if one day the village elder comes back from the city with a battery-operated television set and a satellite dish to go with it. In the evening, when villagers usually sit around together to discuss their crops or livestock, the village elder now turns on the television. People watch the magic of seeing a new world unfold in front of their eyes as they view programs such as *Desperate Housewives*, *Two and a Half Men*, or some French or Italian movie. They see cars, streets, modern buildings, indoor plumbing, and a way of life they never imagined could exist. When the village elder clicks on the remote and removes the television set, everybody goes home to sleep on his or her dirt floors in their mud and clay homes. As they go to sleep, the villagers are likely to dream of having a car or installing an amazing faucet that brings water inside a home. We would like to call this process **migration of dreams** that follows the dissemination of information technologies. The wealthy and advanced countries are, in essence, encroaching on the dreams of the poor.

The migration of dreams is something that happens every day in every society. When you see a television program in a beautiful setting, you also may dream of going there someday. An old television show called *The Love Boat* contributed to tremendous

migration of dreams

The impact on the poor of television programs emanating from wealthier societies.

growth in the cruise industry. The idea of a commercial, in some way, is an attempt at intentional migration of dreams. Let us get back now to the village in Yemen. As the poor villagers begin to have greater dreams for themselves and their families, their level of expectation is sure to grow as well. Now, the villager may expect running water, roads, and even a car. The government of the country may be so poor that it cannot afford to provide running water or roads to every small village. That government may have greater priorities of providing for an infrastructure in the capital or in other cities. Or, perhaps, the government needs to put its limited resources into education or health care rather than bringing water or roads to such a remote place with very few people.

Social scientists tell us that the gap between expectations and achievement is a significant contributor to violence. They call this theory **relative deprivation.** Social scientists define relative deprivation as the gap between what a person gets and what that person thinks he or she should get. They tell us that the greater the gap between the two, the more likely an individual is to turn to violence.[8] If this popular theory is accurate, then it would be fair to conclude that the rising expectations of the poor in the Yemeni village or elsewhere could contribute to rising violence. That violence may be directed against a spouse, the children, the neighbors, or even the government. If some opposition group comes to the village to recruit fighters, arguing that the government is not doing its job well, more villagers are now likely to agree and, perhaps, join the opposition. Someone may argue that governments should do something to stop the migration of dreams. In fact, some governments, such as Saudi Arabia and China, have attempted to regulate the Internet. But the reality is that information technology has forged ahead of governmental abilities to control. Even in the United States, the government is scrambling to keep up with the speed by which information technology is developing. Moreover, governments in the poorer countries are being pushed to open up their markets to the world market. Most people refer to this as *globalization*, which is a subject deserving of more detailed discussion.

relative deprivation
The gap between what a person gets and what that person thinks he/she should get.

GLOBALIZATION

At the start of the twenty-first century, globalization has become a powerful concept in governmental, business, and even scholarly circles.[9] Governments often blame their failing economies on globalization. Corporations downsize or cut back on the number of workers, arguing that they need to be able to compete in the new global market. Scholars argue the merit of globalization and its direction. But globalization is not a totally new phenomenon. It has been around in some form or another for a long time. The whole process of interdependence is a process of globalization. What is new about globalization is its unchallenged spread during the past decade. Prior to the fall of the Berlin Wall, globalization was checked by a strong Soviet presence. After the demise of the Soviet Union, the challenge to globalization was left to some weak and barely organized nongovernmental organizations that are practically helpless to stop the momentum.

globalization

The integration of markets, politics, values, and environmental concerns across borders.

Globalization is the integration of markets, politics, values, and environmental concerns across borders. This process of integration is driven by both the desire for higher profits and hopes of greater world economic prosperity or a better future for the earth and its inhabitants. Those who oppose it fear greater economic disparities between rich and poor, loss of cultural distinctiveness, and environmental degradation. Multinational corporations see it as opening new markets to their products and services. Governments support it as the only available course to eliminate an inevitable isolation and economic disaster if they did not support it or as a means to enhance their economic positions. Labor unions fear it because it diverts jobs away to distant places where cheap labor and sweatshops could replace union work. Environmentalists fear the potentially unregulated production of goods for the sake of profit-producing environmental disasters. Investors in financial institutions and stock markets support it as a means for growth of their portfolios. In sum, globalization has become an extremely contentious issue. Scholars too have entered the debate on globalization. Benjamin Barber argues that globalization is leading to a homogenized **"McWorld"** in which American popular culture and consumerism are overtaking the globe. Rejecting such American and consumerist domination, other cultures are producing movements of resistance, which Barber refers to as "Jihad."[10] Whether it is Barber or some other scholar, the critics of globalization warn against unrestricted capitalism at the global level. One such scholar, Manfred Steger, refers to globalization as an ideology of market economy and calls it globalism.[11] It is also clear that globalization has highlighted concerns of human rights. Such concerns are discussed in more detail in Chapter 9.

McWorld

Term used to sum up Benjamin Barber's argument that American popular culture and consumerism is taking over the world.

Capitalism at the global level has, on occasion, had some serious ramifications. Take, for example, the case of a California billionaire who has paid $2 million to clone his dog, Missy. As CNN reported the story on March 22, 2000, some poor fellow in some remote African village may question this decision as unsustainable. A student or an executive corporate officer in New York or London, on the other hand, may see this as the billionaire's natural right to clone his dog. After all, he is using his own money to do so. To the average African, spending so much money on cloning a dog when people die from starvation on a daily basis would be seen as going too far. The CNN story may not have significant ramifications, other than engendering some resentment by the poor toward the rich.

How the rich sometimes make their money, though, could have serious consequences for the poor.[12] An example of such consequences would be the sweatshops that generate wealth for the rich and perpetuate poverty for the workers. Take, for example, the story of a young Pakistani boy named Iqbal Masih. Iqbal was one of the thousands of children in Pakistan who worked full time weaving "oriental" carpets. People around the world value such carpets. They fetch very high prices in countries like the United States. Pakistan is a major producer of "oriental" carpets, and the United States is its largest market. Pakistani carpets are often produced using child labor. Between 500,000 and 1,000,000 children between the ages of four and fourteen work fourteen hours a day, six days a week, making the

---

TAKING ACTION➤

The story of Iqbal Masih tells you that even a child can make a difference. What do you think you can do to make a difference? Perhaps you could join a Students Against Sweatshops chapter on your campus. If no such chapter exists, maybe you could start one. Students

Students Against Sweatshops

Against Sweatshops groups organize rallies and educational activities on campuses. They also pressure colleges and universities to divest any investments they have from companies that deal with countries that allow child labor.

---

beautiful carpets. Children as young as four are often chained to looms in carpet factories in Pakistan. These children are usually sent by their parents to work in the factories to help support the family. They are often thin and malnourished. Their size is small for their age, and their backs are curved from constant bending to the loom. Their hands are scarred, and they have difficulty breathing from the constant inhaling of cotton dust. In 1992, Pakistan adopted a law under international pressure outlawing the practice of making a payment to parents to bond children in labor. A Pakistani human rights group, the **Bonded Labor Liberation Front (BLLF),** began to visit factories to inform the children of the new law. Iqbal was one of those children freed from bonded labor by the BLLF. At age four, his parents had bonded him to a carpet manufacturer where he stayed until the age of ten in 1992.

BLLF

Bonded Labor Liberation Front.

Under the tutelage of the founder of the BLLF, Iqbal became an outspoken activist on behalf of other bonded children. He even traveled to Europe and the United States to expose the practice to potential buyers of Pakistani carpets. The energy, enthusiasm, and unique personality of Iqbal made him a very successful spokesperson for all bonded children of Pakistan. Between 1992 and 1994, Pakistan's carpet sales fell for the first time and the pressure on the country to enforce the law on bonded children mounted.

On April 16, 1995, a gunman shot Iqbal to death. The thirteen-year-old boy's death was blamed on what the founder of the BLLF called the "carpet Mafia." The practice of bonding children continues in Pakistan until this day. So does the pressure to end it. What this story tells us is that demand for "oriental" carpets in the rich countries contributes to production practices in other countries. Although the carpet manufacturers become wealthy, children suffer. Unless the buyers of the product are aware of such practices and are willing to boycott products produced by such means, exploitation of the underprivileged is likely to continue. The next chapter explores the gap between the rich and the poor. Now, let us take a brief look at the globalization of terrorism, which some see as a consequence of exploitation, poverty, and injustice.

TERRORISM AND GLOBALIZATION

On the morning of September 11, 2001, two passenger planes plunged into the World Trade Center leading to its collapse and the deaths of almost 3,000 innocent civilians. Another plane destroyed a section of the Pentagon, and a fourth plane went down into a field in Pennsylvania. For days, the world seemed to stand still. The shock of the terror was too grave for most people to take. Terrorism from abroad had reached the shores of the United States in a deadly fashion.

Those who engage in terrorism come from all colors and from all cultures. Terrorism is a symptom rather than a disease. It has many causes. Most definitions of the concept, however, seem to focus on the symptom and avoid any reference to its causes. What is clear after hundreds of years is that terrorism is a societal, rather than genetic, disease. Terrorist acts are not merely the acts of fanatics but are committed for clear purposes and by people with clear agendas. Terrorism may be traced back to two fundamental, underlying motivations: the struggle for power and domination and acts of desperation in response to this power struggle.

Terror has been global for a long time. The threats of nuclear, biological, and chemical attacks by terrorists are ominous. The "War on Terrorism" declared by President George W. Bush received a positive global reaction. The fight against terrorism must include not only military and intelligence global cooperation, but also rethinking of policies and activities. When the question of why terrorism is posed, issues of poverty, ignorance, injustice, and despair are often part of the answer. We address these issues in Chapter 6.

Summary and Review

The growing interdependence of our global community is slowly changing the relationships of states and individuals. Economically, the world is so interwoven that the livelihood of one depends on the production of many others. This relationship of interdependence transcends the economic sphere and includes environmental and political interests. In addition, the world has become smaller through efficient and low-cost traveling and the electronic media, such as the World Wide Web. Other areas of global interdependence include our own health when viruses and diseases travel beyond borders and infect people of all races and nationalities. AIDS, for example, does not discriminate on the bases of race, religion, nationality, sexual orientation, or any other human characteristic, immutable or otherwise. Indeed, global interdependence affects all of us, from the clothes we wear and the air we breathe to the food we eat and any forms of technology we use. Interdependence has yielded many positive as well as negative influences upon human life. Hence, for example, although jeans and baseball have become global cultural icons, many critics brand this trend as cultural colonialism, whereby American culture has spread to engulf a world where there exists no global minimum wage or labor laws to protect ordinary people from the exploitative tendencies of mass production.

Key Terms

subsistence living 25
global interdepen-dence 25
economic interdepen-dence 29

multinational corporations 30
global monetary relations 30
environmental interdepen-dence 31

cultural colonialism 34
New World Information and Communication Order 34
migration of dreams 34

relative deprivation 35
globalization 36
McWorld 36
Bonded Labor Liberation Front 37

Discussion Questions

1. What are the characteristics of subsistence living? Is subsistence living possible in today's world? Why or why not?
2. What are the attributes of globalization?
3. Describe the concept of McWorld. How can this concept pose potential harm to our world?
4. How does the saying "one person's mess is another person's catastrophe" apply to contemporary environmental conditions?
5. Is there any truth to the argument against cultural colonialism? Why or why not?
6. How have global monetary relations made the world a smaller place?
7. How do the Internet and other forms of rapid electronic communications affect the world we inhabit?
8. As state sovereignty decreases in favor of insurmountable pressures toward globalization, what negative impact can this trend have on people at risk from globalization pressures?
9. Can exploitative multinational corporations ever be rivaled by weak states, where the gross national product is less than the annual net profits of the MNCs?
10. Discuss how television and other media play a role in the migration of dreams and relative deprivation.

Suggested Readings

Anderson, Terry L., and Donald Leal. *Free Market Environmentalism Today.* New York: Palgrave, 2000.

Biel, Robert. *The New Imperialism: Crisis and Contradiction in North/South Relations.* London: Zed Books, 2000.

Cohn, Theodore H., Stephen McBride, and John Wiseman, eds. *Power in the Global Era: Grounding Globalization.* New York: St. Martin's Press, 2000.

Giddens, Anthony. *Runaway World: How Globalization Is Reshaping Our Lives.* New York: Routledge, 2000.

Jones, R. J. Barry. *The World Turned Upside Down? Globalization and the Future of the State.* New York: Palgrave, 2000.

Lutz, James M., and Brenda J. Lutz. *Global Terrorism.* New York: Routledge, 2004.

Nye Jr., Joseph S. *Power in the Global Information Age: From Realism to Globalization.* New York: Routledge, 2004.

Sjursen, Katrin, ed. *Globalization.* New York: H. W. Wilson, 2000.

Steger, Manfred. *Globalism: The New Market Ideology.* Lanham, MD: Rowman and Littlefield, 2001.

Lane, Jan-Erik, *Globalization and Politics: Promises and Dangers.* Burlington, VT: Ashgate, 2006.

Stott, Philip, and Sian Sullivan, eds. *Political Ecology: Science, Myth and Power.* Oxford, UK: Oxford University Press, 2000.

Addresses and Websites

Global Interdependence Center
Fels Center of Government
University of Pennsylvania
3814 Walnut Street
Philadelphia, PA 19104
Tel: (215) 898–9453
http://www.interdependence.org/

This web address is the site for the Global Interdependence Center of the University of Pennsylvania. It discusses the organization's intentions, which include looking at ways to develop new reasonable policies on critical economic issues. The organization also deals with finance and trade within free trade structures; however, they deal with other issues that relate to the broader theme of global interdependence, including the environment. Links to events and conferences sponsored by the organization are provided on the website.

North-South Centre/Centre Nord-Sud
Avenida da Liberdade 229–4°
1250–142 Lisboa—PORTUGAL
Tel: (351) 21 352 49 54

Fax: (351) 21 353 13 29
http://www.nscentre.org/

The North-South Centre considers itself a dialogical platform between Southern nations and Europe. It attempts to further public awareness regarding globalization and global interdependence. Although information about the organization can be found on the website, there are other areas of interest discussed as well. One of the major highlights of the website is the monthly close-up on particular issues pertaining to global interdependence.

http://www.un.org/

This website takes you to the Internet home of the United Nations, the international governing structure in which many nations participate. The U.N. offers statistics and other useful information about various issues in countries. There are also numerous U.N. councils and programs, and information regarding them can be located on the site. This link is also an excellent source of information on international law and international affairs.

Notes

1. Lester R. Brown, *World Without Borders* (New York: Vintage Books, 1972), 192.
2. Murray Weidenbaum, "No Way Out of Global Markets," *The Christian Science Monitor*, 19 (October 1995): 20.
3. John T. Rourke, *International Politics on the World Stage* (Sluice Dock, Guilford, CT: Dushkin/McGraw-Hill, 1999), 11.
4. See Jan Aart Scholte, *Globalization: A Critical Introduction* (New York: M. E. Sharpe, 2000).
5. "For the Birds," *Mother Jones* (February 2000): 22.
6. See Terry L. Anderson and Donald Leal, *Free Market Environmentalism Today* (New York: Palgrave, 2000).
7. For an excellent discussion of environmental politics, see Philip Stott and Sian Sullivan, eds., *Political Ecology:* *Science, Myth and Power* (Oxford, UK: Oxford University Press, 2000).
8. See, for example, Ted Robert Gurr, *Why Men Rebel* (Princeton, NJ: Princeton University Press, 1970).
9. See R. J. Barry Jones, *The World Turned Upside Down? Globalization and the Future of the State* (New York: Palgrave, 2000).
10. Benjamin Barber, *Jihad vs. McWorld* (New York: Times Books, 1995).
11. Manfred Steger, *Globalism: The New Market Ideology* (Lanham, MD: Rowman and Littlefield, 2001).
12. See Robert Biel, *The New Imperialism: Crisis and Contradiction in North/South Relations* (London: Zed Books, 2000).

CHAPTER THREE

Religion and Politics

GLOBALIZATION AND RELIGIOUS REVIVALISM

RELIGION HAS BEEN A GLOBALIZING FORCE THROUGHOUT HISTORY. IN SOME CASES, RELIGION HAS BEEN A SOURCE OF PEACE, NONVIOLENCE, AND HUMANITARIAN CONCERNS. IN OTHER CASES, RELIGION HAS BEEN USED TO INCITE TO VIOLENCE, WARS, AND HATRED. RELIGION HAS, IN SOME CASES, BEEN SUPPRESSED, WHEREAS IN OTHER CASES PROMOTED. IN ALL SITUATIONS, RELIGION CONTINUES TO PLAY A PIVOTAL ROLE IN THE VALUES SOCIETIES HOLD.

THE LAST QUARTER OF THE TWENTIETH CENTURY WITNESSED A REVIVAL OF RELIGIOUS FERVOR IN MANY PARTS OF THE WORLD. THIS REVIVAL OF RELIGION IS OFTEN CALLED FUNDAMENTALISM. FUNDAMENTALISTS USUALLY HOLD RATHER CONSERVATIVE VALUES THAT THEY WANT TO INCORPORATE INTO POLITICAL LIFE. BE IT ON ABORTION, GAY AND LESBIAN RIGHTS, GENDER ROLES, OR RELIGIOUS NATIONALISM, FUNDAMENTALISTS USUALLY HOLD STRONG VIEWS ROOTED IN SOME DIVINELY ORDAINED BELIEF SYSTEM. SUCH GROUPS OF FUNDAMENTALISTS NORMALLY CROSS THE BORDERS OF STATES AND ARE TRANSNATIONAL. WHETHER IT IS JEWISH, CHRISTIAN, ISLAMIC, HINDU, OR BUDDHIST FUNDAMENTALISM, THE PHENOMENON REMAINS SIMILAR IN THAT ITS ADHERENTS ARE TRUE BELIEVERS IN THE RIGHTEOUSNESS OF THEIR OWN BELIEFS. IN THIS GLOBAL ERA, RELIGION IS NOW A FORCE THAT CAN UNIFY OR DIVIDE PEOPLE ALL OVER THE WORLD. IT HAS THE POWER TO CREATE HARMONY AS WELL AS TENSIONS. AS OUR WORLD MOVES DEEPER INTO GLOBALIZATION, THE IMPACT OF RELIGION ALSO BECOMES MORE GLOBAL. IT IS INCREASINGLY IMPERATIVE THAT AN EDUCATED PERSON BE FAMILIAR WITH THE RELIGIOUS CULTURES OF OTHERS. NO MORE CAN WE SURVIVE ON STEREOTYPES. THE CONSEQUENCES COULD BE GRAVE.

INTRODUCTION

The countries in Africa, Asia, the Middle East, and Latin America are incredibly diverse in their cultures. Each region has a wealth of cultural diversity within its own. They defy easy generalizations. People in Africa, for example, not only have almost sixty countries, but also have a large variety of languages, customs, traditions, and religions. Very often, many people who live in the United States do not fully understand the cultures of others who live in distant places. Given the global nature of our existence, we all need to have a better understanding of each other. There are many reasons for that lack of understanding. One of them may have to do with an educational system that was originally designed to Americanize an immigrant population. More than 200 years later, the educational system still holds to the ideal of Americanizing a population that has become rather parochial. Another reason for lack of understanding may have to do with the media that depend too heavily on the sound bite. News of great events and peoples abroad is usually reduced to few seconds' or few lines' coverage where the adjective replaces real content. Therefore, major actors are often reduced to warlords, terrorists, fundamentalists, extremists, drug kingpins, or some other adjective leading to generalizations about other peoples and their cultures. There are many other reasons for the incomplete understanding of the cultures of others. The task here, however, is to introduce you to such cultures.

This book cannot provide you with the needed in-depth information about the many cultures of the world. What this chapter can do is try to introduce you to the major religious cultures of some of the peoples of the vast areas being covered. The interaction between religion and politics is rather obvious. This chapter discusses that interaction especially as it relates to the politics of development and change.

The last few decades have witnessed a religious revivalism in a variety of forms. This phenomenon is global. Religious revivalism is not limited to a specific region or religion. In the United States, for example, religious revivalism could be seen in the rise of the "Christian Coalition," or the demonstrations in front of abortion clinics, or even the killing of abortion clinic doctors and nurses. Similar revivalism can be found in the ranks of other religions including Judaism, Islam, Hinduism, and Buddhism. Four great religions dominate the regions under discussion. More than a billion people in Asia, the Middle East, and Africa are adherents of Islam. The majority of those who inhabit the Indian subcontinent are Hindu, whereas East Asia is mostly Buddhist. Most people in Latin America are Roman Catholic. Many others throughout adhere to some Christian denomination. Others are Jews, Sikhs, Baha'is, Zoroastrians, or even animists.

ISLAM

The brief introduction in Chapter 1 discussed the Middle East region and presented a historical overview of the region's Islamic culture. Islam, however, is practised in countries outside of the Middle East. In fact, one of the more common misperceptions is the one that equates Islam with Arabs. Contrary to this misperception, Arabs are a tiny minority among Muslims, or followers of Islam. Only one of every eight Muslims is an Arab. Moreover, many Arabs are Christian and some are Jewish. The most populous Islamic country is not even in the Middle East. That country is Indonesia, which is in Southeast Asia. Today, Islam is the fastest growing religion in the world. It is also the fastest growing religion in the United States. Yet the perception most Americans have of Islam is often colored by stereotypes such as the one on the Arabs. A rather common image of Islam

Arabs are a small minority among Muslims.

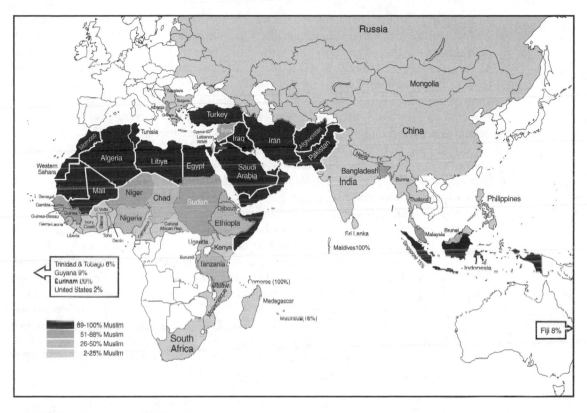

FIGURE 3.1 Muslims in the World

in the United States is that of a faith prone to fanaticism, extremism, and violence. As we already learned, all religions have some elements that are extremist, fanatic, and violent. Islam is not an exception. It is in the same boat as all other religions.

Islam is the product of the seventh-century Arabian Peninsula. The story of its origin is a success story. It produced an outstanding civilization that made major contributions to human development and progress. When the messenger of Islam, **Mohammad** (570–632 A.D.), was born, his native lands were in turmoil. For many decades Arabia had suffered an economic depression resulting from the decline of trade with Europe. Most people of the Arabian Peninsula were pagan and prayed to many gods. Mohammad preached to the people seeking to replace their paganism with loyalty to God, or Allah in Arabic. As other religious teachers before him, Mohammad lived simply and taught justice, love, and kindness.

When Mohammad was born, his father had already passed away. His mother died six years after his birth. He was raised and cared for by his grandfather and later his uncle. According to the Islamic holy book, the **Quran,** Mohammad grew up in poverty (Sura 93, v, 6f). He originally practiced the religious beliefs of his community. The community worshiped the gods of Hubal and al-Uzza, believed in spirits, a

Mohammad
Messenger of Islam.

Quran
Islamic holy book.

Satan, good and evil. Mohammad, however, was disturbed by the wars that tribes waged against each other. He reportedly was outraged at the practices of gambling, drinking, and the burial alive of unwanted infant daughters. As he matured, Mohammad learned about the Christian and Jewish monotheistic beliefs and seems to have been impressed by them. According to Islamic tradition, the angel Gabriel appeared to Mohammad in a cave at the base of Mount Hira, near Mecca, and revealed to him God's final revelation, The Quran. Shortly thereafter, Mohammad began to preach the message of God to the people of Mecca. The Quran recognizes the divine origin of the Old and New Testaments and that Mohammad received from God the final revelations as the last and greatest of the prophets. Many of the stories that appear in the Jewish Torah and the Christian Bible reappear in the Quran. The story of the creation and the stories of Noah, Abraham, Moses, and Jesus all are told in the Muslim Holy Book as well.

The doctrines and rites of Islam embodied not only features of the older revealed religions, but carried over and modified certain of their elements. It is such modifications that gave Islam a unique and, perhaps, an Arab character. One such modification had to do with the geographic center of the faith. Older monotheistic religions look toward Jerusalem in prayer. Even though Jerusalem remained important to Islam, Muslims look toward Mecca in prayer. Mecca, as you already know, was already an important center of Arab pagan worship. Islam also retained the idea of a holy day but changed the day to Friday. It was on a Friday that Mohammad brought on his first convert to Islam. Unlike Christianity and Judaism, Islam, however, did not make the entire day holy, but only that part of it spent in prayer.

The Teachings of Islam

The basic teachings of Islam could be found in the name itself.[1] *Islam* is a noun formed from the infinitive of a verb meaning to submit or to surrender. A *Muslim* is one who has submitted or surrendered to God. A good practicing Muslim, therefore, is one who surrenders his or her soul to God. A Muslim does that act of submission by living in accordance to the scriptures of Islam found in the Quran. Most important among those are five duties known as the **Pillars of Islam.** The five duties or pillars are:

Pillars of Islam

The five duties of a Muslim.

1. *Shahada or profession of faith:* A good Muslim must profess that there are no Gods but God and that Mohammad is God's messenger. Acceptance of this profession of faith and its faithful repetition constitute the first step in being a Muslim. These simple words are heard often among the Muslims. They are broadcast on loudspeakers from minarets throughout the Islamic world when the faithful are called to prayer.
2. *Salat or prayer:* A practicing Muslim must pray five times every day. The first is at sunrise, the second is at mid-day, and then mid-afternoon, sunset, and the fall of darkness. Muslims go through this ritual regularly. At prayer they recite praise of God and reaffirm their submission to His will. As mentioned earlier, Muslims look toward Mecca whenever they are praying.

3. *Zakat or almsgiving:* An important duty for Muslims is to give to those who are less fortunate. Almsgiving is a voluntary obligation for every Muslim to help those in need. Most Muslims either give direct gifts to the poor or make contributions to various charities.

4. *Sawm or fasting during Ramadan:* A practicing Muslim who is not sick, pregnant, or a child needs to fast during the holy month of Ramadan. A fasting Muslim does not eat, drink, smoke, or engage in sexual activity from sunrise to sunset. Ramadan is the month during which the Quran was revealed to Mohammad. Because Muslims use a lunar calendar, Ramadan varies on the Western calendars from year to year. As you probably know, Western calendars are solar ones with slightly longer years than those of the Muslim or Jewish calendars. The act of fasting gives Muslims the opportunity to feel the hunger of those who are hungry and the thirst of those who are thirsty. Whether you are a king or a factory worker, Ramadan allows you to become a more understanding human being as you feel the suffering of those who are less fortunate than you are.

5. *Hajj or pilgrimage:* Once in a lifetime, a Muslim is expected to make a pilgrimage to Mecca. It is also recommended that a Muslim complete the pilgrimage by visiting holy mosques in Medina and Jerusalem. The pilgrimage to Mecca is conditioned on its feasibility to a person. A person who is unable to do so because of financial ability, illness, or other similar reasons is excused from this duty.

Many Muslims around the world abide by these five duties. They are often committed to living a life of virtue and submission to what they believe to be the will of God. There are times, however, that interpretations of Islamic teachings clash with modern political and civic practices.

Islam and Politics

Strictly speaking, there is no independent political theory in Islam. Everything related to governance falls within the domain of the religion. Unlike Christianity, which proposed giving to "Caesar what is Caesar's and to God what is God's," Islam does not have a distinction between what is secular and what is religious. It may very well be this factor more than any other that has transferred the basis of loyalty in Islamic societies. The Muslim, who professes belief in God and the message of the Quran, is a member of the Muslim community, not on the basis of kinship, language, race, or nationality, but only on that of religion.

Politically, a strict Muslim community or state could be characterized by four main features:

1. The sole head of the community is God.
2. God's teachings as revealed in the Quran are the law and constitution of the Muslim community.
3. The function, form, and constitution of the community are eternal and cannot be changed regardless of time and place.
4. The purpose of the community or state is to uphold the faith.

shari'a

The totality of God's teachings in Islam.

It is clear from the characteristics listed here that the Quran and the totality of God's teachings known as the **shari'a** are to be the law for every Muslim. This makes Islam more than just a religion as known in modern Western society. Islam is rather an infallible doctrine of ethics prescribing the rules of conduct for an entire Muslim's life. This includes not only religious life but also a person's political, social, domestic, and private domains. Similar to the other great religions of our day, Islam is being rocked and battered by the revolutionary changes of today's world. Adherents of all major religions including Christianity, Judaism, Hinduism, Buddhism, and Islam are in the same boat. But the anguish and pain are in many ways greater for Muslims than they are for others. This is because Muslims, more than any of the others, are committed to the establishment of the Kingdom of God on earth. For them, there should be no separation between secular and religious, national and religious community, or civic and private duties. The advent of the modern nation-state and its incorporation of Western ideals have resulted in the dislocation of traditional Islamic political and cultural life. Islamic history did not prepare Muslims well for this fate. Their great history of success even during the life of the messenger of the religion made their current subservient role very hard to accept.

Four Turkish Women. Two are wearing traditional Islamic scarves and two are wearing Western clothing.

Source: Pete Souza/Chicago Tribune Company

As mentioned in Chapter 1, Islamic history is rather glorious and full of major contributions to world civilization. Students in the West study the Dark Ages and its practices of feudalism, serfdom, and witchcraft, and yet Islam of that same era had established a great empire that reached distant Spain on the west and central Asia to the east. As Muslims conquered the Byzantine Empire, they absorbed rather than destroyed. In the process they were able to transform old knowledge into a distinctive civilization. At the height of the Islamic Empire in the ninth and tenth centuries, Muslims contributed much to our knowledge. At the time Europe was practicing witchcraft in medicine, Muslims had hospitals and were practicing surgery. Many contributions in mathematics are still with us today as we use the decimal point, Arabic numerals, algebra, and the zero. When the Crusaders of Europe went to the Holy Land in the eleventh century, they found a civilization far more advanced than the Europe they left behind.

This glorious history clearly did not prepare Muslims for their current secondary role in global civilization. Consequently, some Muslim intellectuals began to ponder the fate of their people at various times in modern history. Some of those have argued that Islam should be adapted to fit modern technology. Others insisted that it is the people and not the religion that were the cause of their own downfall. Such intellectuals called for returning to Islamic scriptures and living by them. Yet others have proposed a separation between religion and modern political society. It is this last group that came to dominate most Islamic countries in the twentieth century. As a result, most Islamic states today have modern constitutions that are based on secular rather than religious principles. Some have developed well-managed, democratic structures. A few have even elected women to executive roles. Bangladesh, Pakistan, and Turkey have all elected women to the position of prime minister. Indonesia, the largest Islamic country, had a woman president. Other Islamic countries are still struggling to find an accommodation between religion and politics.

Essentially, there are three types of regimes in Islamic states: **Muslim states**, **Islamic states**, and **Islamist states**. Muslim states have Muslim majorities, but a secular system of government where religion is separated from government. Turkey would be an example of such a state. Islamic states have a Muslim majority that have a system of government that uses Islam for guidance in political affairs. Egypt and Indonesia are examples of such states. Islamist states, on the other hand, depend on Islamic law or Shari'a for governance. Saudi Arabia and Iran are such examples. Let us now look at one of those.

Types of Islamic States

Muslim, Islamic, and Islamist

Iran

Iran is the embodiment of a very old civilization. One of its early pioneers was Cyrus the Great, who created a major empire around 533 B.C.E. known as the Persian Empire, which spread its wings into many parts of the modern Middle East. With the rise of Islam, Iran became a major cornerstone of the Islamic Empire, and its people made major contributions to Islamic civilization. After the death of Mohammad, however, many in Iran disagreed with other Muslims over the issue of succession to leadership. That disagreement contributed to a split among the Muslims dividing them into Sunnites and Shi'ites. The Sunnites are today the large majority of Muslims, and they dominate among the Arab countries. Iran, on the other hand, which is not an Arab country, became the leader among the Shi'ites. In time, certain traditions and practices separated the two groups even further. Although Iran has a long and significant history, our concern in this chapter is with modern Iranian politics and its interaction with religion.

By the turn of the twentieth century, Persia, now known as Iran, was a monarchy ruled by a shah, or king. Historically, the country had an agricultural society in which few landlords owned most lands. As an urban class began to develop, resentment of the aristocracy grew. By 1906, the frustrated urban elements revolted and demanded a constitution giving them a share in power. In 1908, oil was discovered. The discovery of oil intensified a European rivalry over domination of Iran. With World War I breaking out in 1914, the British and Russian governments occupied the country. In 1917, the Russians withdrew after their revolution at home. The British, on the other hand, placed the country under their protection and attempted to maintain control over it.

The Shah of Iran naturally resented British meddling in his country's affairs. Consequently, his relationship with the British "protectors" deteriorated. In 1921, the British, working with elements in Iran's military, engineered a coup d'état, or military takeover, of the government. One of those collaborators with the British, Reza Khan, soon emerged as the next leader of Iran. He was crowned shah-n-shah, or king of kings, in 1925. His crowning marked the start of the Pahlavi Dynasty, which came to rule the country for a good part of the twentieth century. The new Shah proceeded to implement major domestic programs that aimed at modernizing the country. His flirting with Germany during World War II, however, brought on another occupation by British and Soviet forces in 1941. The British forced Shah Reza Khan to abdicate in favor of his young son, Muhammad Reza. The new Shah was too young to rule, and a Board of Regents was appointed to rule on his behalf. Feeling betrayed by his father, the British pressured the Board of Regents to allow more participation and create a system of government that would be more like that of Britain itself. They encouraged the

FIGURE 3.2 Iran

formation of political parties, elections, and greater empowerment of the prime minister. By 1951, the leader of the National Front, Dr. Muhammad Mossadeg, was elected prime minister on a platform that promised to nationalize Iran's oil.

United States Involvement The nationalization of Iran's oil that followed Mossadeg's election brought on the involvement of the United States. Fearing the spread of such policies of oil nationalization, the U.S. government initiated a very secretive operation to be implemented by the Central Intelligence Agency (CIA). In collaboration with the seven major oil companies, known as the **Seven Sisters**, that used to operate in Iran, a boycott of Iranian oil was declared. The aim of the boycott was to bring oil production in the country to a halt. Without the expertise of the oil companies, their shipping fleets, and pipelines, Iran could not drill, refine, or sell its oil. The consequence of such action was to drive Iran into an economic recession. The oil companies were hoping that the economic crises would weaken Mossadeg. Instead, they strengthened him. Nationalism gripped the Iranian public and turned their anger on foreign powers and corporations trying to undo the nationalization decision. Iranians took to the streets chanting anti-Western slogans and showing their support of Mossadeg. In time, some elements in Iran's parliament (the Majlis) began to question the prime minister's actions. In the summer of 1953, the prime minister dissolved the Parliament. In August 1953, the Shah fled the country under pressure from the prime minister's supporters.

> **Seven Sisters**
> Seven large oil companies that had monopolized the world's oil market.

Having failed to unseat the prime minister by the boycott, the CIA sent Kermit Roosevelt, director of its Near East operations, to the country with the objective of overthrowing Mossadeg's government. Within six days of the Shah's departure, military units took over the government and imprisoned Mossadeg and many of his allies. They called upon the Shah to return to his throne. The Shah returned to Iran triumphantly. It was not until twenty-five years later, in the summer of 1978, that the CIA declassified documents showing its central role in that operation.[2] By then, the Shah had smashed all opposition and created an autocratic regime dependent upon his wishes. With the help of his secret service agency, the **Savak**, the Shah consolidated his power and attempted to create a staunchly pro-Western regional force in Iran. His equating of Westernization with modernization, however, created new problems for the country. Severe poverty existed next to tremendous wealth, and corruption by the Shah and members of his family irritated many Iranians. In time, many people were ready to do the unthinkable—revolt.

> **Savak**
> The Shah's secret service agency.

The Iranian Revolution Shortly after the declassification of U.S. government documents about the CIA involvement in 1953, Iranian college students took to the streets to denounce the United States and the Shah's close relationship with it. The Shah ordered his troops to stop the demonstrators. In doing so, some students were shot and killed. Their funerals turned into larger demonstrations that included many other segments of the society. More troops were dispatched, leading to more deaths. Demonstrations spread to many parts of the country, and the cycle of deaths followed by more demonstrations continued until early 1979. This is not meant to say that the

Iranian Revolution was caused by the American announcement. Discontent with the Shah and his government had been mounting for many years. Social, economic, and political pressure had been building within the country for more than two decades. Opposition to the Shah came from very diverse groups that included religious elements, intellectuals, middle class, urban poor, and political parties, including the communist **Tudeh Party**.[3]

Tudeh Party

The communist party of Iran.

Although the Shah envisioned a strong Iran that would be a major regional power, his attempt at doing so backfired. Aside from irritating his neighbors, his spending on arms purchases diverted his attention from solving problems of poverty at home. Even though they knew that their country was rich in oil, the poor saw no oil money filtering down to their backward and impoverished villages. Consequently, Iran's poor resented his regime and joined the demonstrators. The Shah also managed to offend the religious elements in his society. Those people were upset with his Westernization of the culture and his 1961 land reform and the later exile of Ayatollah Khomeini. Although the revolution itself would later be called the Islamic Revolution, the fact remains that real revolutionary activities were not limited to the religious elements in the country. Instead, Iran's revolution started spontaneously and incorporated many segments of the society. The religious leaders, however, became more significant in time as they eventually managed to take over the revolution. The leftists of Iran were also significant participants in the revolution. Led by the Tudeh Party, this communist underground force was vehemently opposed to the Shah's close relationship to the United States, a country they viewed as imperialist. Communist party members were also determined to end the Shah's secret police, the Savak, and their torture chambers. After all, they were the target of the Savak. Other political parties in the country were also unhappy that they lost all power after the return of the Shah in 1953. The Iranian middle class, represented by the shopkeepers and others, were willing participants in the revolution. Corruption, mismanagement, and the feeling that they had no voice in government alienated them. Their children in colleges were the ones who started the cycle of demonstrations. This new educated youth had learned to question, and they demanded a better form of government for their society.

Together, these segments of Iran's society proved stronger than the Shah's armed forces. But they lacked common leadership. In time, many began to look to the **Ayatollah Khomeini**, who was exiled by the Shah more than a decade earlier, as the symbolic leader of their rebellion. The Ayatollah was now in his late seventies and had suffered one and a half decades of exile for his opposition to the Shah. Through the years, the Ayatollah continued to speak, advocating the overthrow of the monarchy in Iran. Audio recordings of his sermons were often smuggled into the country for his followers to hear. Soon after the Shah fled the country in January 1979, the Ayatollah came back to a hero's welcome. The Ayatollah's return gave the revolutionaries a common leader. However, many in the revolution were not thrilled about that leadership and argued for a modern secular political system. The transition that followed was characterized by a great deal of euphoria mixed with anxiety about the future. The Ayatollah's followers demanded the formation of an Islamic political system and the secularists expected an open and more democratic system.

Ayatollah Khomeini

Religious leader of Iran after the revolution of 1979.

The Constitutional Compromise A compromise was soon reached. A new constitution was adopted that seemed to bridge the gap between the secularist and religious elements. The constitution created a republic that incorporated separation of powers and Islamic ideals. It declared Ayatollah Khomeini as the country's "leader" and allowed for popular elections and representation. The leader became the supreme commander of the armed forces, appointed significant judicial figures, and approved the credentials of presidential candidates. The first presidential election was won by **Dr. Abulhassan Bani-Sadr**, a French-educated economist. Parliamentary elections brought a mixture of religious and nonreligious elements. To ensure that the **Majlis**, or parliament, would not enact laws that violate the teachings of Islam, the constitution set up a **Guardian Council** of twelve members. Their task is to scrutinize all legislation to ensure compliance with Islam. Thus the Islamic Republic of Iran was born.

Although the Iranian constitution remained the same, the collaboration between the religious elements and the secularists did not last long. In July 1981, President Bani-Sadr fled the country under pressure from the religious elements. Islamic Revolutionary Guards had executed some of his close associates and cabinet ministers, and his leadership had come into question as the country was losing battles in its recent war with Iraq. Bani-Sadr also became the target of ridicule by Islamic elements that held American diplomats hostage at the American Embassy compound in Tehran. Bani-Sadr clearly wanted to end the hostage crisis while his opponents wanted to drag it on.[4]

Soon after the United States admitted the deposed Shah into the country for cancer treatment, some Iranian students demonstrating in front of the American Embassy climbed the walls of the compound and took over the embassy. They feared that the Shah's entry to the United States was a part of a plot with the CIA aiming at bringing

Bani-Sadr

Iran's first elected president.

Majlis

Iran's parliament.

Guardian Council

Ensures that Iranian laws comply with the teachings of Islam.

N IN THE EWS

G8 Statement to Urge Iranian Response

The Group of Eight industrialized nations will call on Iran in a statement to respond soon to an offer by major powers over Tehran's nuclear programs. Iran's nuclear plans were the focus of discussion of ministers from the United States, Russia, Japan, France, Britain, Italy, Canada, and Germany who gathered at a city center mansion in Moscow to prepare for a summit of G8 leaders in mid-July. The statement would also indicate G8 disappointment that Iran has not, so far, formally responded to a six-power package of incentives offered to Tehran to get it to curb its nuclear development. The package was handed to Iran on June 6th by the five permanent, veto-wielding U.N. Security Council members—the United States, Britain, France, China and Russia—and Germany. The United States has accused Iran of having a secret program to build nuclear weapons. Tehran denies the charge, saying its nuclear program is solely for power generation.

Source: REUTERS/The New York Times, 29 June 2006.

the Shah back to Iran. They called the diplomats spies and the embassy the nest of spies. Such terms were in clear reference to the 1953 coup engineered by Kermit Roosevelt. Even after the Shah died of cancer, the American diplomats were not released. They remained there for a total of 444 days before their eventual release in January 1981. Relations between Iran and the United States remained strained into the early part of the twenty-first century. President George W. Bush even referred to Iran as an Axis of Evil state. The wars in Afghanistan to the east and Iraq to the west have placed U.S. troops on both sides of the country. Many Iranians feel that the United States plans to invade or attack their country in the near future, especially after Iran began to develop nuclear energy. Although Islam found its expression in Iran, it still has a long way to go before it can be the dominant political force in most other countries with Islamic majorities. Most of those have opted for systems that allow for some separation between religion and politics. Other religions have also found themselves in conflict with modern politics. Let us proceed to look at another one of those.

HINDUISM

Hinduism is a very old and diverse religion. Some of its doctrines date back to 3000 B.C.E. Hindus have a very wide selection of beliefs and practices. It is perhaps the most complicated of all religions in the world. Some have even argued that Hinduism is more than one religion. Today, Hinduism is the dominant religion in India and has more than 600 million followers. One of the reasons that Hinduism is complicated is that it has no founding figure like in most other religions. It developed over a long period and has incorporated many rituals and legends from many eras. To simplify a complex set of beliefs, we will emphasize those features common to Hindus regardless of the strain they may believe in. Most significant among those is the notion of Karma.[5] **Karma** refers to actions or deeds. Basically it is the belief or law that a person's thoughts, words, and deeds have an ethical consequence fixing his or her lot in future existences. You could simply view this Hindu law as essentially the same as the statement "as you have sown you shall reap."

Karma

The most significant belief in Hinduism that refers to actions or deeds.

Although the idea of retribution for our actions is not unique to monotheistic religions, Karma goes beyond the notion of souls going to heaven or hell. Hinduism firmly believes in the notion of **Samsara**, or rebirth. It is their belief that the soul of a person who dies does not (except in a single case) die, but rather it is reborn into another existence that will terminate in due time and necessitate yet another birth. Rebirth follows rebirth with a single exception, which will be explained later, in an endless chain. The successive births do not have to be on the same plane of being. It may occur in any of a series of heavens or hells. Or, it could occur on earth in any of the forms of life. Most Hindus believe that a person's soul could be reborn as a vegetable, animal, or human. What determines the nature of the rebirth is the law of Karma.

Samsara

The Hindu belief of rebirth.

Hindu teachings are directed to humans only. They emphasize the need to live a virtuous way of life similar to that taught by Christianity, Islam, and Judaism. But Hinduism does not insist on extreme virtue in one life. Because souls are reborn, salvation could be achieved over many existences. Therefore, Hinduism is, perhaps, more tolerant of deviations than the other religions as it does not insist on salvation in a single life. A person could live his or her entire life in a single existence seeking any of the following **Four Permissible Goals in Life**:

1. *Kama:* The desire for pleasure, especially through love, is an acceptable goal in life for a Hindu. It is seen as a sacred duty for a person to experience fulfillment in his or her own love life, as well as the fulfillment of that person's partner. Lust, pleasure, and love all represent acceptable behavior provided that the person remains within the bounds set by general social rules. It is understood, however, that this person will, in this life or in a future existence, come to the realization that pleasure alone is not enough. Eventually that individual would want and would pursue a more deeply satisfying goal in life.

2. *Artha:* Power and substance is the essence of Artha. It refers to material possessions or high social status. Seeking wealth and other forms of materialism or aspiring to positions of authority is a legitimate aspiration for a Hindu. But here again, it is understood that the person will eventually learn that a deeper satisfaction comes from following a greater path in life.

3. *Dharma:* Righteousness and discipline are more satisfying goals than either of the first two. Dharma is considered, in a strict sense, as a religious and moral law that sets the standard for a worthier and more deeply satisfying life. A person who chooses to follow Dharma is a disciplined individual who will renounce his or her personal desires and social success and seek the good of all. That person would do his or her duty toward others in the community, including family, caste, or the larger community. But again, the joy, however great, is not ultimate. There is one ultimate satisfaction that could be achieved by successfully following the fourth permissible goal in life.

4. *Moksha:* Liberation or salvation is the ultimate goal of a Hindu. It represents the final release of the soul from the cycle of rebirths. Moksha is the highest and only truly satisfying goal in life. To make Moksha your goal in life means living a life dedicated to work, knowledge, and devotion to Hindu teachings. Once liberated, the soul is forever satisfied. Although not all Hindus are in agreement on this, many later Hindus have come to accept the notion that when a soul achieves Moksha or liberation, it achieves Nirvana. Nirvana is mainly used in Buddhist teachings, but has been employed in Hindu texts. It refers to the ultimate state of liberation from rebirth. Hindu texts seem to have accepted the Buddhist definition of **Nirvana** as the fullness of being, which no human words can describe.

Even though Hinduism argues that a person's Karma determines his or her future rebirth into any of the forms of life, it also has a well-articulated division among humans. Rebirth as a human can occur at any of the castes or even at a lower level. That rebirth into a caste or out of it is determined by a person's Karma as well. It is not proper to define the Hindu castes as classes because classes represent economic divisions, whereas castes represent broader ones. Many authors, however, have made a linkage between the two because the caste system seems to also follow economic

Four Permissible Goals in Life

Goals in the Hindu faith that include Kama or the desire for pleasure, Artha or seeking wealth and positions of authority, Dharma or righteousness and discipline, and Moksha or liberation or salvation.

Nirvana

The fullness of being, which no human words can describe.

distinctions such as those between laborers, professionals, and aristocrats. The Hindu caste system has four castes of people grouped on the basis of their birth:

Brahmin
The highest caste in Hinduism, which includes the priesthood.

Ksatriya
The second caste in Hinduism, which includes the aristocratic nobility, warriors, or knights.

Vaisya
The third and largest caste that includes the peasants, merchants, and professionals.

Shudra
The fourth caste that includes all non-Aryans or those who are not of Indo-European origin.

outcastes or untouchables
Outsiders who are considered the dregs of society.

Brahmin: This is the highest of all castes and includes the priesthood. They are the people who are supposed to be devoted to the teaching of the religion.

Ksatriya: This caste includes the aristocratic nobility and the warriors or knights. In essence, the Ksatriya represent the ruling elite of society.

Vaisya: This caste is usually the largest and includes the peasants, the merchants, and the professionals. It could be referred to as the caste of the common people.

Shudra: This caste includes all non-Aryans or those who are not of Indo-European origin. Such people included blacks, Semites, slaves, servants, and even some prisoners of war. Further divisions came about over the centuries. But the most noted group is that of the **outcastes or the untouchables.** The outcastes are considered the dregs of society whose mere touch pollutes a caste. Such individuals have no hope of rising in the social scale. For centuries, the outcastes were stigmatized by Hindu society. Many were left to live in the misery of poverty and starvation.

For a long time the caste system was practiced as the norm in Hindu society. Even when the British dominated India for centuries, they left the practice intact. Just like there was a time when feudalism seemed inseparable from Christianity, the caste system also came to be seen as an integral part of Hinduism. When Indian independence became a reality in 1947, the new leaders of the independence movement did not hesitate to abolish it. But as we know from our experiences in the United States, ending slavery did not mean an end to prejudice and discrimination. The legal termination of the caste system in India did not fully terminate the long tradition of social prejudice. Its abolition, however, has signified that the caste system is not an essential feature of Hinduism.

Hinduism and Indian Politics

The new postindependence leaders of India found themselves clashing with religion over the caste system. Long before independence, however, the struggle they waged for independence found a way to accommodate itself to religion. India's struggle for independence benefited from the ideas of Mohandas Karamchand Gandhi, known as the Mahatma Gandhi. Gandhi was not a religious or spiritual leader as much as he was a political leader. However, he used the concept of *Satyagraha*, meaning holding fast to truth, and set out to entice his people to employ self-sacrifice in their struggle to liberate their homeland. Gandhi argued that his approach of "Satyagraha and its offshoots, non-cooperation and civil resistance, are nothing but new names for the law of suffering."[6] Gandhi was born in India, studied law in Britain, and worked briefly in South Africa. There, he resisted the discriminatory practices of the white South African government. In 1915, he went back to India and began a campaign to oust the British from his homeland. Drawing on Hindu principles of Dharma, the third permissible goal in life, Gandhi advocated the use of righteousness and virtue in a disciplined way to force the British colonists to leave India. In his own way, Gandhi was able to combine Hindu principles and nationalist ideals that, in time, came to symbolize India's struggle for independence.[7]

Although Gandhi accepted most Hindu traditions, including the principle of a caste system, he modified some of them. For example, Gandhi did not like the limitations imposed on the outcastes, or the untouchables. He called the untouchables the **Hajirans,** or the children of God. He attempted to integrate them into India's society and sought their participation in the struggle for independence. Working with India's Congress Party, Gandhi practiced nonviolent civil disobedience and was able to move hundreds of thousands of people into joining his cause. His many incarcerations and hunger strikes made him even more popular. Gandhi reasoned that the British continued to colonize India because they made a profit out of it. Therefore, he set out to take away that incentive. He urged his fellow Indians not to buy British-made clothing. Instead, he wanted them to make their own with the cotton they produced. Gandhi took on the loom as a symbol of his struggle and started weaving his own clothing. His famous Salt March marked a turning point in India's struggle and showed that suffering and self-sacrifice could achieve positive results.

Hajirans

The name Gandhi gave to the untouchables, meaning the children of God.

Even though Gandhi's approach of passive resistance did force the British to the negotiating table and out of India, India's partition into two states, India and Pakistan, resulted in mass murders and a massive refugee problem for both new states. Hindu extremists did not like his stance against their atrocities. On January 30, 1948, one such extremist assassinated the Mahatma Gandhi. Today, many Indians refer to Gandhi as the Father of India. His legacy, however, went beyond the borders of India. Dr. Martin Luther King, Jr., often referred to Gandhi's teachings in his struggle for civil rights in the United States. Other leaders struggling for justice from Burma to South Africa also were inspired by the work of Gandhi.

Recent Indian politics, however, have taken more religious tones as religious nationalists came to dominate recent elections. Consequently, tensions between the Hindu majority and the Muslim minority have, on occasion, escalated into bloody conflicts. The use of Hindu icons in politics is now a common feature of some political parties.

BUDDHISM

Buddhism arose in India as a direct challenge to the rigid caste system inherent in Hinduism. Its founder, Siddhartha Gautama (500 B.C.E.), known as the Buddha (the Enlightened One), was the son of an Indian king. He grew to adulthood under conditions of great comfort and splendor. Living on the palace grounds, the young Siddhartha had servants and slaves caring for his needs. At age 19, he was married to a beautiful princess, who bore him a son. It was at this time that Siddhartha began to take chariot rides into the city. Here, for the first time in his life, he came into contact with poverty, crippling diseases, old age, and death. One night, after a palace feast, Gautama left his sleeping wife and newborn son and ran away seeking enlightenment.

He wandered for many years, living the life of a beggar hoping to understand the meaning of life. He wandered from one village to another, one town to another, begging for food and seeking spiritual truth. He wandered for six years. One time, after forty-nine days of meditation, enlightenment came upon him. Siddhartha Gautama became a Buddha, or an enlightened one, and began preaching.

Early Buddhism was an outgrowth of Hinduism, and both religions have several significant beliefs in common. Among them is the idea that all living things are reborn into new lives (Samsara) and that all actions in this life will be compensated in the next (Karma). The main ideas of Buddhism are contained in the statements known as the

Four Noble Truths

These truths include life is suffering, suffering is caused by ignorance, sorrow ends when a person is enlightened, and enlightenment is achieved by a course of disciplined and moral conduct.

Four Noble Truths:

1. *Life is suffering:* Life, according to the Buddha, is full of suffering. It is a sorrowful state of existence. It should be the objective of every person to end the cycle of rebirth and the suffering that it brings.
2. *Suffering is caused by ignorance:* The most fundamental cause of the painful rebirth of every individual is ignorance. This ignorance leads to craving for life and its seeming pleasures. Our thirst to live and our desires to have a life based on pleasure and prosperity cause our rebirth, which continues the cycle of suffering.
3. *Sorrow ends when a person is enlightened:* Suffering ends when a person overcomes ignorance and becomes emancipated from "the will-to-live-and-have." Once a person is enlightened, that individual becomes exempt from the evil desire and their karma expires. Upon the end of that individual's current existence, he or she would achieve Nirvana. Nirvana is explained in Buddhist literature as "the fullness of being which no human words can describe."
4. *Enlightenment is achieved by a course of disciplined and moral conduct:* The life that concludes in the attainment of Nirvana requires a full understanding of the Four Noble Truths. The path to Nirvana is called the Noble Path of Buddhism **(Ariyamagga).** This path represents the essence of the Buddhist system of ethics. It presents eight specific means for achieving Nirvana. Those center on virtuous practice, mental composure, and wisdom.[8]

Ariyamagga

The Noble Path of Buddhism, which is the path to Nirvana.

Tripitaka

Buddhist holy books.

Buddhist writings are contained in the **Tripitaka,** or Three Baskets. In the Tripitaka, there is a great discussion of these concepts and an explanation of the Noble Path of Buddhism. Sometimes called the Noble Eightfold Path of Buddhism, it gives a clear picture of the ethical norms accepted in Buddhist literature.

The first norm of this Path is Right View, or Right Understanding. This involves an understanding of the power of the individual. Individuals have choices, and their future position is determined by their behavior and not predetermined by some supreme god or even by past action. Fate and determinism, therefore, are rejected in Buddhism.

Right Thought is the second norm of the Noble Path. This path bridges thought and action. It preaches the importance of having thoughts that are free from lustful relations or greed, free from hatred, and free from violent intentions. Thoughts, it is believed, lead to actions. Therefore, a good Buddhist must be free of improper thoughts.

The third step in the Buddhist Path is Right Speech. It involves avoiding false speech, slanderous speech, harsh speech, and frivolous talk. A Buddhist, therefore, must at all times seek to cultivate truthfulness and trustworthiness. He or she must also promote unity among those who are divided. A good Buddhist speaks in a pleasant and delightful manner. Finally, a Buddhist needs to cultivate meaningful, purposeful, and timely speech.

Right Conduct or Right Action is the fourth step in the Buddhist Path. It suggests avoidance of bodily harm to oneself or to others. Violence against all living things is warned against. Right Action means a life full of love, compassion, and abstention from wrongful gratification of your senses, especially in terms of sexual misbehavior.

Right Occupation or Livelihood is the fifth step and suggests a morally acceptable means of livelihood. Occupations that are materially rewarding but morally wrong must be avoided. Engaging in any occupation that could result in harming others is considered unacceptable in Buddhism. Such occupations include making or trading weapons, poisons, or animal flesh. A Buddhist monk has much more stringent conditions.

The sixth step in the Eightfold Path is Right Effort. The emphasis on effort is significant in Buddhism. Effort is the most important factor for the victory of morality over temptations within every individual. Individuals must be determined to prevent evil within themselves and to choose the moral alternative.

Right Mindfulness is the seventh step. This guides a person's mental, verbal, and bodily behavior toward a moral direction. Some may describe this path as the need to remain alert at all times in order to prevent any evil thoughts or actions.

The final step is Right Concentration or Meditation. This step requires clear and composed mental condition that helps in achieving wisdom and avoiding evil. Meditation is considered as a form of mental training for an ethical life of the Buddhist.

In his own way, Siddhartha Gautama introduced major ideas and suggested a way of life that is based on morality and ethics. Although Buddhism began in India, it did not last there for long. Soon it spread to other parts of Asia. Today, Buddhism and its variations is the dominant religion in Sri Lanka, Burma, Tibet, Thailand, Japan, North and South Korea, Mongolia, Cambodia, and even China. Buddhist universal ethics have influenced not only the cultures of such societies, but also their politics.

Buddhism and Politics

The image of Buddhism in Western society may be that of a religion of withdrawal. The reality of modern Buddhist societies is, however, very different. Buddhism in contemporary Asian society seems to stand for active engagement in social and political life. Two recent Nobel Peace prizes went to Buddhist activists. One was awarded to the Dalai Lama of Tibet and the other to San Suu Kyi of Myanmar or Burma. Buddhist monks throughout Asia advocate social change. Buddhists have also contributed a great deal to the conceptualization of nonviolent action for social justice in many corners of the world.[9] Although Buddhism is returning to China, it is still not accurate to call China a Buddhist country. After all, the People's Republic of China is a state run on the basis of communist ideology. Buddhist revival in China, however, is showing its impact on the country's politics as well. To have a better understanding of activist Buddhism, it may be better to look at some other state where Buddhist engagement in social and political reform is more obvious. One such place is Sri Lanka, where the majority of the people are Buddhist.

Sri Lanka

Sri Lanka, known as the Democratic Socialist Republic of Sri Lanka, is an island state in the Indian Ocean. The tsunami of December 2004 reminded people of Sri Lanka. Formerly called Ceylon, the country was colonized by the British and produced coffee, tea, and rubber on British-owned plantations. After a brief struggle by nationalist leaders, Ceylon was granted independence in 1948. More than 80 percent of the country's 18 million people are Sinhalese, who are generally Buddhist. About 18 percent are Tamil, who are generally Hindu. The rise of nationalism in the mid–1950s led to a government decree making Sinhala the only official language and providing state support for Buddhist institutions. This angered the Hindu Tamil minority, which led to the assassination of the country's leader by a Buddhist monk. The widow of the assassinated leader became the world's first female prime minister in 1960. In 1972, the country's name was changed to its original, precolonial name of Sri Lanka.

As discussed in Chapter 12, the Tamil minority resented the Sinhalese monopoly on political and economic power. In time, Tamils organized rebel groups that aimed at achieving a separate and independent Tamil state in the region populated by Tamils. Bloody violence erupted in 1983, and an agreement of limited Tamil autonomy in 1987 brought Indian troops to maintain the peace. The agreement failed and Indian troops were eventually withdrawn. So far, the conflict has claimed the lives of more than 64,000 people.[10] Although the conflict in Sri Lanka is significant and continues, Sri Lanka today has better social indicators than practically all developing countries with a similar level of income. It has, despite its civil war, set a new standard of development. Its approach to development has become a model to other states. This is, in part, due to the **Sarvodaya Shramadana Movement** and a vibrant society. The Sarvodaya Movement in Sri Lanka is one of the most successful self-help organizations in the world. Its concept of rural development links the Buddhist principles of loving kindness, compassion, the joy of living derived from making others happy, and steadiness of temper with concrete grassroots work that cares for the needs of ordinary people.

The founder of the Sarvodaya Movement, A. T. Ariyaratne, was a high school teacher in 1958 when he started to take his students from the city to do community work in poor villages. In 1966, he decided to carry out a village-awakening program in 100 villages in the country to celebrate Gandhi's 100th birthday. That was the start of a continuous development project that came to involve many people throughout Sri Lanka. It was at that time that the Buddhist school teacher expressed his philosophy in greater clarity. The explanation is

Sarvodaya Shramadana Movement

Self-help organization in Sri Lanka.

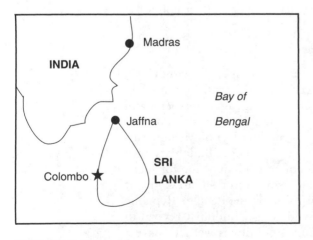

FIGURE 3.3 Sri Lanka

clearly rooted in Buddhist teachings. Sarvodaya's aim is to encourage every individual to work toward double liberation in the Buddhist sense: freeing the mind of its limitations and liberating the community in a nonviolent way from unjust socioeconomic conditions. After all, how could a person be liberated if his or her community is in chains? A person would work for community liberation by doing community work, by sharing, and by fully participating in the holistic development of the community.

In defining development goals, the Sarvodaya Movement identified a set of ten fundamental human needs in the villages of Sri Lanka:

1. A clean and beautiful environment
2. An adequate supply of clean water
3. Minimal supplies of clothing
4. An adequate supply of food
5. A modest home
6. Basic health care
7. Basic communication facilities
8. A minimal supply of energy
9. Holistic education
10. Spiritual and cultural needs

These fundamental needs were divided into further categories. People were asked to volunteer and to share. Volunteers built irrigation systems and wells. Farmland continues to be cleared, soil tilled, and roads built to access remote villages. Sanitary systems were developed and schools and village centers continue to be erected. In time, the Sarvodaya Movement was able to transform the Sri Lankan villages from their backwardness into models of progress and positive change.

Buddhist teachings are the basis of the Sarvodaya Movement's call to action. Such action, however, is based on the notion that all living creatures should enjoy good health and happiness, not just humans. Consequently, their model of development is biocentric and fosters protection of natural and environmental resources. It also fosters good human relations and encourages people to share and to perform constructive activities together. Eating and living together without considering class distinctions fosters the ideal of equality. The experiment waged by the Sarvodaya Movement has been hailed as a success story around the world. Today, this movement is active in more than 12,000 villages. Their call to action has transformed the lives of many people. The engagement of the Sarvodaya Movement not only helped villagers, but also helped the very volunteers. Their involvement often awakens compassion, kindness, and equanimity. Other movements around the world have also employed religion to achieve greater communal objectives. Either way, world history has proven the existence of a strong connection between politics and religion.

Today, Sri Lanka has a literacy rate of about 90 percent and a vibrant society that has continued to advance ahead of others in the region. Infant mortality is now 16 per 1,000. Life expectancy is seventy-one years for men and seventy-five for women. In sum, it is a country that continues to advance.

CHRISTIANITY IN AFRICA, ASIA, AND LATIN AMERICA

As you are well aware, Christianity began in the Middle East. Even though Christianity took root in Europe and the Americas, it also penetrated Africa and Asia. China, for example, has more than 10 million Christians, India has more than 2 million, and Japan has almost 1.5 million. A number of countries in Africa and Asia have Christian majorities. Ethiopia, Nigeria, the Central African Republic, the Philippines, and others are mostly Christian. Latin America is overwhelmingly Christian. Similar to other religions, Christianity in Africa, Asia, and Latin America has experienced religious revivalism. American and European missionaries and evangelical groups have established a foothold in many countries in Africa and Asia. They started schools where there were none and worked on projects designed to improve the physical well-being of the people there. Food and health projects are also among the many contributions of missionaries and evangelical activists. Regardless of motive, such projects tend to improve living standards of the poorest people in many parts of Africa, Asia, and Latin America. Christianity, therefore, is also used to achieve greater communal objectives. Local Christians even developed activist Christian doctrines to achieve justice for the less fortunate and the oppressed. Most prominent among those are the doctrines of liberation theology.

Liberation theology is rooted in the thoughts and actions of a number of Catholic priests and nuns working with the poor and oppressed. Although advocated only by a few, liberation theology has become an essential component of political life in many parts of Latin America. It has contributed to serious changes in Nicaragua, El Salvador, and Haiti. It even contributed to the rise of "people power" in the Philippines. Even though the Roman Catholic Church has historically taught conservative doctrines that advocated acceptance of authority, the experiences of Latin America in the last half of the twentieth century gave birth to new ideas of activism and rebellion. Some Latin American theologians attempted to make the Gospel of Jesus Christ relevant to the social, economic, and political situation in which many of the continent's poor found themselves. In a direct challenge to the established church doctrines, liberation theologians embarked on an interpretation of the scriptures that supported the poor and oppressed majority of Latin America.

Gustavo Gutierrez
Liberation ideology advocate.

One of the early advocates of liberation theology was a priest from Peru. **Gustavo Gutierrez** argued that poverty that dehumanizes people is an evil and an offence against God. Gutierrez lives and works among the poor in Lima, the capital of Peru. In 1971, he published a book that came to influence other theologians in Latin America.[11] In this book, Gutierrez argues that God takes the side of the poor and that poverty is the result of human failure to construct a world of justice. The Bible, then, has a promise of liberation not only from individual sin but also from oppressive systems that keep the majority of the people in Latin America in poverty. He insists that the practice of Christians should match their beliefs. Therefore, the church should be involved to correct injustices and to bring about a more equitable social, economic, and political system. In sum, liberation theologians like Gutierrez attempted to explain the relationship between the Christian faith and justice in the world.

The work of Gutierrez and others like him has emphasized the relationship between Christianity and justice. Latin American theology of liberation has influenced many people. Many Latin Americans found it justifiable to join revolutionary movements in countries such as El Salvador, Nicaragua, Colombia, and others. Even priests and nuns became active in revolutionary struggles. Government agents or troops murdered a number of them. Many of those were in El Salvador, where even the archbishop was murdered.

Archbishop Oscar Romero was gunned down in 1980 for his open criticism of injustices in his homeland. After the Sandinista Revolution in Nicaragua overthrew the repressive government, a number of liberation theologians who supported the revolutionaries took government posts in the new regime. In Haiti, the first democratically elected president was a former priest and liberation theologian, Jean-Bertrand Aristide. Latin American doctrines of liberation theology have influenced others beyond Latin America. African and Asian theologians developed similar arguments and organized for social justice. Even in the United States, black and feminist liberation thought developed along the lines of Latin American ideas of linking Christianity to a person's social experiences. Informal as well as formal contacts have developed among such theologians to the dislike of the Church's leadership in Rome. Let us now take a look at a case where a former priest who considered himself a liberation theologian actually took leadership of his country of Haiti.

Haiti

Christopher Columbus visited Haiti on his first trip to the West Indies. That visit was followed by disaster for the native **Tainos.** Spanish settlers brought them slavery, dispossession, and death. From an estimated population of 400,000 Tainos in 1492, Haiti, known then as Hispaniola, had only 60,000 left in 1508. In the seventeenth century, France invaded the area and made it into its colony, which it called Saint Dominique. Under the French, Haiti became the largest sugar producer in the West Indies. Imported enslaved Africans produced sugar on the plantations. In time, the slaves rebelled and took charge of the country. By the beginning of the twentieth

Tainos

Native people of Haiti.

century, the United States had become involved in Haiti's affairs. In 1915, the United States invaded Haiti in response to the overthrow of the government and the murder of its president. Anti-American sentiment grew when the United States occupied the country. An uprising in 1918 against U.S. occupation lasted for two years and left 2,000 Haitians dead. Opposition to the American occupation eventually grew within the United States. Today, Haiti remains the poorest state in our hemisphere.

In 1957, Francois Duvalier, nicknamed Papa Doc, took over the government and began an era of repressive government that continued after his death. His son, Jean-Claude Duvalier (Baby Doc), maintained the repression

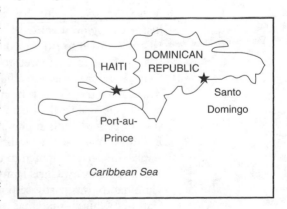

FIGURE 3.4 Haiti

until his departure in 1986. Tens of thousands of Haitians were murdered under the Duvalier dictatorship. Thousands more fled the country, many to the United States. An interim military government took charge of the country. Finally, the leading military general fled the country in 1990, and meaningful democratic elections became a possibility. The 1990 elections brought to power a charismatic liberation theologian. Father Jean-Bertrand Aristide won the presidency by a landslide. Orphaned in infancy, Aristide was raised by a Catholic order that dedicated itself to educating the children. Upon becoming a priest, he worked in the ghetto, where he ran an orphanage and a youth center. His popularity among the poor came from his services to them. His assignment as the priest in a ghetto parish made him an outspoken renegade clergyman who advocated social and political justice. His views and his activism in opposition to the Duvalier dictatorship led to his expulsion from his Salesian order in 1998.[12]

Aristide's presidency was interrupted by a military takeover in 1991. But with the support of the Haitian masses and U.N. resolutions backed by U.S. troops, Aristide was returned to power in 1995 to complete his term in office. Upon the end of his term of office later that year, Aristide transferred presidential power to his successor—which was the first time in the history of the country that one elected president gave up power to another elected president. During his short time in office, Aristide oversaw the least bloody and most democratic era in the country's history. He was able to tackle the drug problem, stop police brutality, end the practice of bribery in government, reduce the bureaucracy by 20 percent, raise the minimum wage, and end police extortion. These were major accomplishments for any leader. Given that Aristide was able to do so much in such a short time is a compliment to his record. Although his roots were in religion, Aristide's successes were in politics. In February 2001, Aristide ran for a second term of office and won. In 2004, however, he was driven out of the country by rebel groups. An election in 2006 brought Aristide's protégé, Rene Preval, back to office, and Aristide is set to return to the country.

Summary and Review

As we have seen in this chapter, religion has been used for good and for bad. Throughout history, religion was used for political purposes. Today, that trend continues. In Iran, Islam was used to rid the country of an oppressive absolute monarchy. Once in power, Islamic leaders attempted to use Islam to suppress opposition to their leadership. In India, Hinduism was also employed in the struggle for liberation. Gandhi's approach borrowed from the Hindu notion of self-sacrifice and Dharma in order to move a population to struggle against British colonialism. Soon after the British withdrew, the Hindu caste system caused India much suffering, and it is now used as a political tool by some. Buddhism was also used to bring about freedom from poverty. But as we have seen in Sri Lanka, it also contributed to the rise of extremist nationalism and a bloody conflict with a Hindu minority. Christianity has often been used to suppress others. In Latin America, Christianity was partly responsible for oppression against the native populations. The Catholic Church there has historically been identified with repressive regimes as well. But the Catholic Church also produced a brand of theology that contributed to the betterment of the region and its peoples. Religious revivalism is a phenomenon of our times. Some resent it; others praise it. In the areas we are looking at in this book, religion clearly had both effects. Although religion can be a tool for oppression, it also can be one for liberation. What matters here is that you have a better idea about the religious cultures of those regions and that you understand that all religions are in the same boat. They are all being rocked and battered by the revolutionary changes in today's world. As a result, religious leaders occasionally fight back. Some do so by rejecting modern practices; others do so by reinterpreting their scriptures to lead the process of change. That religion and politics relate is a simple fact. That religion is a globalizing force is also a simple fact, for better or for worse.

Key Terms

Arab 42	Savak 49	Satyagraha 54	Sarvodaya
Muslim 42	Karma 52	Four Noble	Shramadana
Five Pillars of	Samsara 52	Truths 56	Movement 58
Islam 44	Four Permissible	Tripitaka 56	liberation theology 60
Shari'a 46	Goals in Life 53	Dalai Lama 57	Tainos 61
Shah 48	Nirvana 53	Sinhalese 58	Jean-Bertrand
Seven Sisters 49	caste 54	Tamil 58	Aristide 62

Discussion Questions

1. What is the difference between an Arab and a Muslim?
2. What role, if any, did religious conviction play in the Islamic Revolution of 1979 in Iran?
3. Is the separation of religion and state possible under Islamic beliefs?
4. What is the Shari'a? How is the Shari'a affected by the Five Pillars of Islam?

5. How does the caste system affect Indian democracy?
6. What role do adherents of Buddhism play in politics?
7. What is liberation theology?
8. What was the impact of liberation theology in Latin America?
9. What is Satyagraha? Was it shaped by Gandhi alone, by Hinduism, or both? Explain.

Suggested Readings

Brown, L. Carl. *Religion and State: The Muslim Approach to Politics*. New York: Columbia University Press, 2000.

Esposito, John L. *Islam: The Straight Path*. New York: Oxford University Press, 1991.

Harris, Ian, ed. *Buddhism and Politics in Twentieth-Century Asia*. London, New York: Pinter, 1999.

Jain, Girilal. *The Hindu Phenomenon*. New Delhi, India: UBS Publishers' Distributors, 1994.

Kamitsuka, David G. *Theology and Contemporary Culture: Liberation, Postliberal, and Revisionary Perspectives.* New York: Cambridge University Press, 1999.

Krishna Iyer, V. R. *Religion and Politics.* Delhi, India: Konark Publishers, 1991.

Lane, Jan-Erik, and Hamadi Redissi. *Religion and Politics: Islam and Muslim Civilization.* Burlington: VT: Ashgate, 2004.

Larry Jay Diamond, Marc F. Plattner, and Daniel Brumberg, eds. *Islam and Democracy in the Middle East.* Baltimore, MD: Johns Hopkins University Press, 2003.

Primasiri, P. D. "Ethics of the Theravada Buddhist Tradition." In S. Cromwell Crawford, ed. *World Religions and Global Ethics.* New York: Paragon House, 1989.

Ratnapala, Nandasena. *Buddhist Democratic Political Theory and Practice.* Colombo, Sri Lanka: Sarvodaya Vishva Lekha Publishers, 1997.

Riaz, Ali. *God Willing: Islam in Bangladesh.* Lanham, MD: Rowman and Littlefield, 2004.

Addresses and Websites

OCRT—Ontario Consultants on Religious Tolerance
P. O. Box 514
Wellesley Island, NY
13640–0514
http://www.religioustolerance.org

Sponsored by the Ontario Consultants of Religious Tolerance, this website aims at promoting tolerance for various religions including Islam, Christianity, Buddhism, and Judaism. This site explores both positive and negative aspects of different faiths, while providing information about sociopolitical trends and perspectives of numerous religious beliefs. Agnosticism and atheism are also explained.

Buddhist Cultural Centre
125 Anderson Road
Nedimala
Dehiwala
Sri Lanka
Tel: 0094–1–734256
Fax: 0094–1–736737
http://www.lanka.net/bcc/

The Buddhist Cultural Centre website offers general information regarding Buddhism along with information and news of the events and activities of the Centre. Apart from general information on Buddhism, this website also shows how the faith can be applied to a person's life. The website also has information on meditation and hosts many articles pertaining to Buddhist philosophy and culture. Links to other Buddhist websites are provided.

Himalayan Academy
Kauai's Hindu Monastery
107 Kaholalele Road
Kapaa, HI 96746–9304
Fax: (1) 808–822–4351
http://www.himalayanacademy.com/

The Himalayan Academy is a not-for-profit institution that works to educate people about the Hindu faith. This website offers different information regarding Hinduism, including a discussion of the religious figures, the nine beliefs of the religion, karma, and reincarnation. There are many links to other Hindu websites located on this homepage, including a link to the monthly news magazine of Indian faith called "Hinduism Today."

The Sarvodaya Shramadana
Sarvodaya Central Office
No. 98 Rawatawatta Road
Moratuwa
Sri Lanka
Tel: 94 1 647159/647194/645255
Fax: 94 1 647084
http://www.sarvodaya.org/

As described in the chapter, the Sarvodaya Movement started as a development program for Sri Lanka. It aims to encourage every individual to work toward double liberation in the Buddhist sense: freeing your mind of its limitations and liberating the community in a nonviolent way from unjust socioeconomic conditions. This website is a reflection of these beliefs. It provides further information on the movement, including details of various projects in communities throughout Sri Lanka.

http://islam.org/

This website offers comprehensive information about Islam. It acts as a Muslim network for literature, ideas, shopping, travel, and various other resources. General information regarding Islam, the Hajj, and prayer, along with methods of practice, are also included. Also, the education link provides excellent information on the history of Islam and Muslim culture.

http://www.beliefnet.com

This website provides an excellent set of links to many of the world's religions.

Notes

1. For more detailed information on Islam, see John L. Esposito, *Islam: The Straight Path* (New York: Oxford University Press, 1991).
2. For more details on this CIA operation, see Kermit Roosevelt, *Countercoup: The Struggle for the Control of Iran* (New York: McGraw-Hill, 1979).
3. For details, see Eric Hoogland, *Reform and Revolution in Rural Iran* (Austin: Texas University Press, 1982).
4. See Gary Sick, *All Fall Down: America's Tragic Encounter with Iran* (New York: Random House, 1985).
5. For an excellent dictionary of Hindu concepts, see Karel Werner, *A Popular Dictionary of Hinduism* (Lincolnwood, IL: NTC/Contemporary Publishing Company, 1994).
6. Mohandas K. Gandhi, "Excerpts from *The Essential Writings of Mahatma Gandhi*," in Manfred B. Steger and Nancy S. Lind, eds., *Violence and Its Alternatives* (New York: St. Martin's Press, 1999), 294.
7. For an excellent discussion of Gandhi's discourse on nationalism, see Manfred B. Steger, *Gandhi's Dilemma: Non-Violent Principles and Nationalist Power* (New York: St. Martin's Press, 2000).
8. P. D. Primasiri, "Ethics of the Theravada Buddhist Tradition," in S. Cromwell Crawford, ed., *World Religions and Global Ethics* (New York: Paragon House, 1989), 40.
9. For a good survey of Buddhist engagement, see Christopher S. Queen and Sallie B. King, eds., *Engaged Buddhism: Buddhist Liberation Movements in Asia* (New York: SUNY Press, 1996).
10. For more information about Sri Lanka, see Lawrence J. Zweir, *Sri Lanka: War-Torn Island* (New York: Lerner, 1998).
11. Gustavo Gutierrez, *A Theology of Liberation*, ed. and trans. Sister Caridad Inda and John Eagleson (Maryknoll, NY: Orbis Books, 1988).
12. To read about Aristide's views, see Jean-Bertrand Aristide and Laura Flynn, *Eyes of the Heart: Seeking a Path for the Poor in the Age of Globalization* (Monroe, ME: Common Courage Press, 2000).

CHAPTER FOUR

Nationalism, Colonialism, and Independence

GLOBALIZATION AND THE NATION-STATE

EMPIRE WAS ALWAYS A GLOBALIZING FORCE. AN EARLIER PERIOD OF GLOBALIZATION LED TO THE EUROPEAN COLONIZATION OF AFRICA, ASIA, AND LATIN AMERICA. COLONIZATION, IN TURN, SOWED THE SEEDS FOR NATIONALISM AND INDEPENDENCE. TODAY, THE NEW WAVE OF GLOBALIZATION IS CREATING NEW CHALLENGES FOR NATION-STATES AND CONTRIBUTING TO AN EMERGENCE OF NEW FORMS OF NATIONALISM AND UNIVERSALISM.

TODAY, THERE ARE MORE THAN 27,000 NONGOVERNMENTAL ORGANIZATIONS (NGOS) THAT ADVOCATE GLOBAL REFORMS. WHETHER IT IS GREENPEACE THAT WANTS TO PROTECT THE ENVIRONMENT OR AMNESTY INTERNATIONAL THAT AIMS AT PROTECTING THE INDIVIDUAL, SUCH NGOS ARE SLOWLY CHANGING THE WAY GOVERNMENTS BEHAVE AND CREATING A WORLD SYSTEM MUCH MORE COMPLEX THAN ANY IN THE PAST.

INTRODUCTION

When we take a look at the world, we find that it is divided into countries. There are about 200 countries in the world today. In political science, countries are called states. Some states in the world are large and have large populations—such as the United States of America, China, or Russia. Others are small and have small populations—such as Kuwait or Singapore. Most states are nation-states. Because of that, many people have come to use the concepts of nation and state interchangeably. As discussed in Chapter 1, however, state and nation do not denote the same thing. *Nation* refers to a people who share common bonds. *State*, on the other hand, refers to a political unit commonly known as a country. As a result of colonialism, mass migrations, and natural disasters, among many other factors, many states throughout Africa, Asia, and Latin America do not possess one single nation. To understand both concepts of state and nation, let us begin by looking at nationalism.

WHAT IS NATIONALISM?

In his book, *In Retrospect: The Tragedy and Lessons of Vietnam*, former U.S. Secretary of Defense Robert S. McNamara argued that a major lesson to be learned from the Vietnam War is not to underestimate the power of nationalism. He went on to point out that his own Department of Defense, under both the Kennedy and Johnson administrations, did not understand the North Vietnamese and Viet Cong's ability to motivate people to fight and die for their beliefs and values. McNamara asserts that the United States continues to underestimate the power of nationalism in many parts of the world.[1] U.S. troubles in Iraq may be such a case.

What is this power that McNamara is blaming for America's defeat in the Vietnam War? **Nationalism,** then, is a state of mind or a feeling based on belonging to a nation. Sometimes the attachment may be to an ethnic group or even a religious one. The intensity of that feeling can, sometimes, be so strong as to drive a person to extremes. A person who may never be able to slaughter a chicken for food, may, under intense nationalism, not hesitate to shoot and kill another human being in the name of a nation. People tend to become this attached to a nation for many reasons. Among them is what has been called the **bonds of nationalism.** Scholars argue that these bonds give people a sense of identification and belonging. Although many scholars have discussed such bonds, their listing and order changes from one scholar to another. In this book, we will list only the most significant ones. They are:

nationalism

A state of mind or feeling based on belonging to a nation.

bonds of nationalism

Common territory; common language; common culture; common enemies.

1. *Common territory:* Let us say that this is time for spring break and you are now in Florida basking in the sun. You left cold New York behind for a week in the sun. Right next to you, a group of other college students spread their blanket on the beach while drinking cans of cold cola. As they sit down, one of them says to the others: "Isn't it great to be here in the sun rather than back in cold New York?" As soon as you hear New York mentioned, you are likely to raise your head and ask, "Are you from New York? I am from there too. Where in New York do you come from?" A conversation is likely to start and you may end up with new friends for the week. On the other hand, if that same person in the group had remarked that he or she was from Iowa, perhaps you would not have started a conversation. Being from the same area provided you with an instant bond with the group. Coming from the same territory makes both you and the group feel closer to each other than with someone from Iowa. Common territory, then, is a bond that gives people inhabiting that territory a sense of identification, belonging, and attachment to the territory and its inhabitants.

2. *Common language:* Say it is summer now. This summer you decide to tour Europe. While lost in Rome or touring the Vatican, you overhear a couple conversing in English. You are likely to approach them, asking where they are from and introducing yourself as an American or Canadian. "We are from Australia," one of the couple responds. Although Australia is much farther from North America than Italy is, you are likely to feel closer to this couple than you would to most Italians. You may complete the tour with them or you may even join them for lunch or on a tour the following day. Language, then, works to bond people or to give them a sense of mutual belonging.

3. *Common culture:* Students on your campus socialize in different ways with a variety of other students. If you pay attention to foreign students, you may discover that European students tend to socialize more with other European

students. They may even have a European Student Association. Muslim students are also likely to display similar processes of socialization. Even though Muslim students, or European students, speak different languages and come from different countries, they tend to feel closer to each other because of their common cultural bonds. Culture, then, whether in the form of religion, tradition, historical experiences, or general outlook, also works to bond people together.

4. *Common enemies:* Nationalism thrives on external crisis. It is strongest when the nation is perceived to be threatened. People tend to unite and work together more in crisis. When the common enemy is seen as evil, people join in their hatred of that enemy. In the United States, as elsewhere, the popularity of a leader soars in the presence of an "evil" common enemy. Such was the case in the aftermath of the September 11, 2001, attacks on the United States. People everywhere raised the flag and joined together in their hatred of the evil terrorists. When the Soviet Union existed, the perceived threat of "the imperialist West" was a major ingredient of its people's solidarity with their leaders. Similarly, the perceived communist threat played a unifying role in states like the United States. At times in the history of nations, nationalist fervor gets so strong as to see "the enemy" in less than human terms. Nazi nationalism, for example, reached the peak of bigotry and racism to the point where "the other" was perceived to be biologically inferior—a perception culminating in an attempt to exterminate the inferior other. Thus, during Nazi rule, German nationalism engaged in the ultimate expression of bigotry—genocide. Similarly, American frontier nationalism presumed a superior heritage of the white European over the native population and the African slaves.

To distinguish one nation from others, nations have created symbols that stand for its glory. The **symbols of nationalism** include:

symbols of nationalism

The flag, national anthem, slogans, legends, and historical sites.

1. *A flag:* Every nation has a flag and people are usually proud of the flag because it stands as a symbol of the nation. Many nations that have no states also have a flag. The Kurds or the Palestinians have flags but no states.

2. *A national anthem:* Just like a flag, every nation has a national anthem that glorifies the nation, its people, leaders, and lands. If you ever thought that the United States was the only "Land of the Free and Home of the Brave," you were wrong. Almost every national anthem praises its people as being free and brave.

3. *Popular slogans and legends:* You must have heard the statement so eloquently spoken by President Kennedy: "Ask not what your country can do for you, ask what you can do for your country." Statements like this or many others— such as "America: Love it or leave it," "The sun never sets on the British flag," or "My country, right or wrong"—are slogans that symbolize pride in your nation-state. They are symbols of nationalism that develop over time. Similarly notions symbolizing pride in the nation are stories and legends

about the nation's great leaders or founding elders. In the United States, the story of George Washington and the cherry tree is just one example of this symbol of nationalism. In China, the legend of Pan-Ku, the creator-god whose remains formed the five sacred mountains of China, was another example until the end of empire in that state.[2]

4. *Historical sites:* Nations also preserve certain buildings and erect monuments glorifying the nation, its leaders, or its beliefs. The home of George Washington is a well-preserved and visited site in the United States. Why would anyone want to preserve and visit a 200-year-old home if it was not for the fact that the country's first president and one of the founding fathers lived there? Other countries have similar sites that they maintain and visit.

Consequences of Nationalism

Nationalism is an important ingredient in the creation and maintenance of nation-states. It helps to maintain cohesion within nation-states. **Competition** among nations helps drive each to develop, grow, and excel; nationalism is a significant force. Nationalism could be credited for the competition that sparked the Industrial Revolution and the age of Renaissance in Europe. Nationalism is also credited for the rise of the new developing countries into **independence.** Among the landmarks of nationalism are the American and the French revolutions. The Declaration of Independence in what became the United States advocated a brand of nationalism that is based on equality, liberty, and secularism. French nationalism sparked revivals in many societies when its ideals were carried to faraway lands by Napoleon's invasions.

competition
Aids in the development and growth of nations.

independence
Occurs when a country is no longer subject to another country's rule

YOU DECIDE ✓   Can We Move Beyond Nationalism?

Nationalism can be a force that sparks innovation through competition. But it can also be a force for destruction, as evidenced by Nazi nationalism. It has contributed to a feeling of superiority based on nothing more than an accident of birth. Often, individuals who cannot slaughter a chicken for dinner are so moved by nationalist feelings that they become capable of killing another human being for the cause of the nation. Are we doomed to being nationalist? Is there a better way to organize ourselves? You may have seen the movie

Independence Day. The plot revolves around invading aliens trying to destroy and control our planet. In the battle against the aliens, many enemy nations join together to defeat the outside invaders.

Do we really need to wait for invading aliens to realize that nationalism tends to prevent us from seeing our common existence? Is there another way? Could you think of better ways to innovate without hate?

There were times when nationalism took on racist tones. Nazi German nationalism, American frontier nationalism, and white South African nationalism all presumed a superior biological heritage of one people over others. In Nazi nationalism, the nation was perceived to be more important than the individual. Consequently, racial purity became a Nazi obsession and those who didn't fit became targets of a genocide campaign. Nationalism is seldom as extreme and full of hate as in Nazi Germany, but the role of nationalism is rarely absent in modern nation-states. It is because of nationalism that each nation-state has become the center of its own universe. As a result, international morality has often become an extension of national morality. What is right for a nation is perceived by that nation to be right for all nations. Americans, for example, "take it for granted that democracy is a noble ideal."[3] It is hard for Americans to imagine that any people would choose communism over democracy. Should that happen, it would be assumed that coercion was used to force people into accepting communism. Little do Americans know that, even though the rights to vote or freedom of speech are noble ideals, they may be secondary luxuries to others in the world. The communist promise of right to shelter, food, and health care may legitimately be more appealing to those who are homeless, starving, or lacking health care provisions.

Early Western nationalism also contributed to the rise of colonialism. In their quest to be the best, most powerful, and greatest nation, European nation-states sought raw materials and new markets on other continents. In the process, Europeans came to rule peoples all over the world. In time, those ruled by the Europeans learned from their European masters many new ideas and practices. One of those was the idea of nationalism. Empowered with nationalist sentiments, the colonized peoples began to agitate for independence. **Wars of national liberation** ensued, and eventually the colonies began to emerge as new independent states. Many of those new states, however, did not have a homogeneous population. Ethnic strife developed in some states leading to internal conflicts and civil wars. Rwanda and Nigeria provide good

wars of national liberation

Battles of independence fought by colonized peoples.

N^{IN THE}**EWS**

Tuareg Rebels in Mali Peace Deal

Under the deal reached in Algeria, the Tuareg rebels have dropped demands for greater regional autonomy in exchange for poverty reduction. The government has promised to do more to develop Mali's northern desert regions, where the Tuaregs live. The attacks had raised fears of a return to civil war that ended in 1998.

Following the peace deal, many former Tuareg rebels were integrated into the army but some have

since deserted. Malian military officials say these deserters were behind the attacks on the towns of Kidal and Menaka. Malian officials say the deserters would be allowed to rejoin the army. There is a document, an agreement, that the Tuareg leadership is being expected to sign. Rebel spokesman Eglasse Ag Idar said that the deal "gives specifics on our region, on politics, development, and security. It is a good step for the development of our region."

Source: BBC News, 30 June 2006.

examples of ethnic divisions that contributed to domestic violence within the newly independent states. Nationalism also contributed to many **international wars.** World War I, for example, originated with ethnic nationalism in the Balkans.[4] World War II, was, in part, a consequence of the rise of Nazi German nationalism. Similarly, the recent conflict in the former Yugoslavia between Bosnians, Serbs, and Croats (or Albanians), is rooted in competing ethnic nationalism.

international wars
Wars in which numerous countries fight, such as the World Wars.

Nationalism, then, can be a force for good or bad. Recently, however, nationalism has been challenged by new developments in our world. Advances in military technology are making the nation-state more vulnerable. The rise of multinational corporations and international organizations is widely regarded as weakening national sovereignty. Transnational ideological and political movements are also challenging nationalism. In fact, global interdependence, the subject of Chapter 2, is a serious challenge not only to nationalism, but also to the life of every individual inhabiting the earth. In the past few centuries, however, nationalism was a defining phenomenon that shaped our modern world. As Europeans developed their own sense of nationalism and gained military superiority over the rest of the world, they went beyond Europe to colonize other parts of the globe.

COLONIALISM

Cecil Rhodes, one of Britain's most famous advocates of colonialism, once said that Britain "must find new lands from which we can easily obtain raw materials and at the same time exploit the cheap slave labor that is available from the natives of the colonies. The colonies also provide a dumping ground for the surplus goods produced in our factories."[5] With that objective, Europeans set out to colonize the rest of the world. Both nationalism and economic interests motivated colonialism. **Colonialism** has often been defined as a country's control of areas outside of its territory. By 1921, for example, Britain had controlled more than 25 percent of the land and population on earth. However, colonialism, in some form or another, had existed long before European dominance. Even Europeans were subject to non-European domination. The Huns, the Mongols, and the Turks had themselves dominated parts of Europe at various times in history. Therefore, the history of colonialism is not limited to the past 500 years when Europeans became dominant.

colonialism
A country's control of areas outside of its territory.

It will not be surprising if future historians look at the period from the sixteenth to the twentieth centuries as being the most significant time in human history. It was during that period that Europeans expanded beyond their continent to explore, dominate, and exploit peoples all over the globe. Now, as we move into the twenty-first century, colonialism in its traditional mode is over. Today, new forms of indirect domination and exploitation are common. Those are sometimes called imperialism or neocolonialism, which we will learn about in later chapters.

The legacy of colonialism is permanent. European conquest of the rest of the world transformed the colonized societies forever. Most of them were deprived of their major resources when Europeans exploited the silver, gold, diamonds, or other natural resources they came across. Many lost their own languages when Europeans

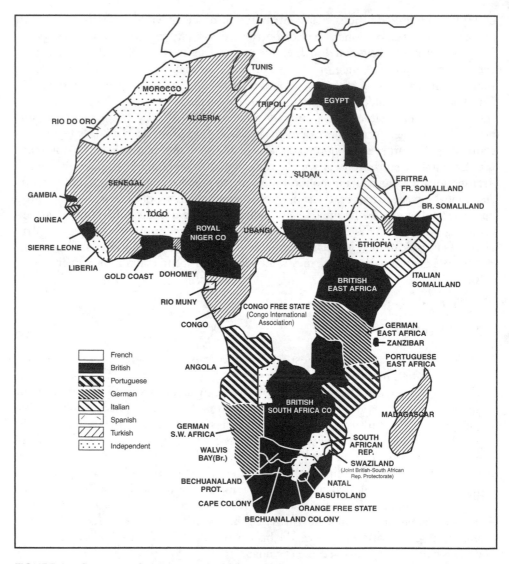

FIGURE 4.1 European Colonization in Africa, 1895

imposed their own language upon those under their control. It is no surprise that South Americans communicate in Spanish or Portuguese or North Americans in English. Similarly, the official languages of most of Africa are European ones. In some parts of South Asia, the official language is English. With the language went the culture, as European cultures came to be the dominant cultural norms for many of the elite of the colonized societies. Also lost were many of the historical artifacts and treasures of those ruled by Europeans. Egyptian artifacts and mummies, for example, are more abundant in European and American museums than they are in Egyptian ones.

In some cases, even many of the peoples who were ruled by Europeans were transferred to other parts of the world via the slave market. Some were exterminated. Also, very importantly, the economies of the colonized areas became permanently dependent upon those of Europe and North America. Their local precolonial economies were devastated and their new ones were tied to those of the powerful motherlands. The colonists did achieve prestige, acquisition of resources, control over sea routes, and global trade.

Colonialism also brought some advances. Education, health care, and transportation were improved with the advent of colonialism. Of course, the educational vision the Europeans had was a Euro-centered one that contributed to the devastation of local cultures. The enhancement of transportation was also essentially designed to facilitate European trade interests. For example, railway lines connected areas where mineral wealth was extracted to the ports from which it was transported to Europe and elsewhere. In time also, colonialism led to the rise of nationalism among the indigenous peoples who were colonized. The development of nationalism brought with it aspirations for independence. The European colonizers initially resisted the nationalist agendas of those it ruled. That resistance by the colonizers pushed many of the new nationalists into declaring wars of national liberation.

THE STRUGGLE FOR NATIONAL LIBERATION

Colonialism in time led to the rise of those colonized against the colonial rulers. As nationalism developed among the colonized, they began to agitate for independence. Often, the struggle for independence was long, cruel, and very costly in lives and material possessions. For some of the luckier states, that struggle was brief and less confrontational. Let us now take a look at some examples of the colonized states and their struggle for national liberation or independence.

India

When India became independent in 1947, it emerged as one of the "New States." It is ironic that a society as old as India's would be called a "New State." India is the home of great civilizations that spanned more than 5,000 years. That culture's contributions to human progress are significant. Yet, by the year 1600, Europeans were able to penetrate that great society and, in time, dominate it.

Trade in ancient times between Europe, India, and China had been carried on through the ports of Alexandria and Constantinople in the Middle East. But with the rise of Islam in the Middle East, Europeans started the Crusades against the Muslims. This created tensions that effectively blocked European access to the luxury goods and spices of Asia. The European explorations that followed were spurred on by the need to find new routes to Asia. You probably know that Christopher Columbus discovered the Americas while looking for a new route to India. In fact, when he landed on the shores of the New World, he thought that he was in India. Consequently, he called the inhabitants of the newly found lands "Indians."

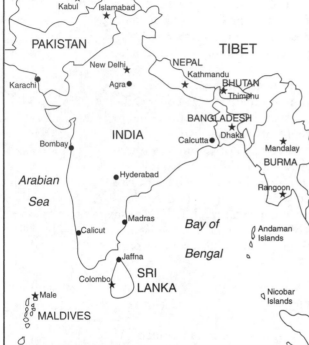

FIGURE 4.2 India

Among the earliest European adventurers were the Portuguese, who established settlements on the Indian subcontinent and used them as trading centers. The British first approached trade with India after Queen Elizabeth granted a charter to establish the East India Company in 1600. The East India Company set up its major trading centers in major cities. Later, the largest Portuguese settlement on the island of Bombay was given to the English monarch, Charles II, by the king of Portugal as part of a dowry. This made Bombay a British possession, which was used by the East India Company. The East India Company made its way toward political control of India by constructing large-scale forts to protect its employees from the counteractivities of the local rulers. The local rulers naturally saw the East India Company as a threat to their society and to their own authority. The forts, once established, required armed forces to maintain and defend. The East India Company brought into India its own armed forces that, by 1760, had military supremacy over the country. Thus, a British company came to rule a country many times larger than Britain. In 1773, the British Parliament passed a law placing the military arm of the company under government administration and in 1858 the British Crown totally abolished the East India Company and took direct control of India.

Prior to British control, India had had a thriving industry and a prosperous agriculture. By the time the British left India in 1947, the country was in economic ruin. The British were successful in making the country dependent upon the import of many European products for its basic necessities. Local industry was discouraged by the imposition of laws, and agriculture was turned into the production of raw materials for British industries. Those who watched the movie *Gandhi* may remember that Indians were deprived of the right to collect salt from the ocean and were required to purchase their salt and other needed supplies from British companies that had monopoly power over the Indian market. Discontent with the British was evident from the beginning. As the British began to dominate India, the local population's resistance became more organized and more persistent. In 1857, there was a major rebellion that the British refer to as the Mutiny of 1857. Later attempts at getting rid of British rule were crushed. In the twentieth century, nationalist groups had emerged with the objective of achieving independence. Most significant among those were the Congress Party and the Muslim League. Often, these two nationalist groups worked together to achieve their common objective of ridding the country of British domination.

As you already know, nationalism can be a very powerful force in society. British oppression contributed to the rise of Indian nationalism. A great nationalist Indian leader was a charismatic and spiritual man named **Mohandas Gandhi.** As discussed in Chapter 3, Gandhi returned to his native India in 1919 from South Africa. While there, Gandhi articulated a philosophy for nationalists resisting oppression. His philosophy of nonviolent resistance aimed at making colonialism expensive for Europeans to maintain. Soon after returning to India, Gandhi joined the Congress Party and began to preach and practice his philosophy known as **Satyagraha.** Satyagraha literally means holding fast to truth. Practically, it is a philosophy of nonviolent civil disobedience.

Mohandas K. Gandhi

Charismatic leader of the Indian struggle to gain independence from Britain.

Satyagraha

The philosophy of nonviolent civil disobedience.

Gandhi called for a boycott of British products and laws depriving Indians of their own resources. He argued that for Indians to fight the British while their clothes are made by them would be self-defeating. He took the loom and began to weave his own clothes. In time, millions of Indians followed suit, and the loom became a national symbol for India's struggle. Gandhi led Indians in the famous Salt March defying unjust British laws. When arrested, Gandhi never resisted and often went on long hunger strikes to mobilize the nation and the world behind the cause of justice to his people. In sum, Satyagraha was an active means of resistance that brought world attention to the injustice of colonialism. In the words of the Mahatma Gandhi "non-violence is infinitely superior to violence, forgiveness is more manly than punishment."[6]

Severely weakened by the devastation of World War II, the British were unable or unwilling to put up with the costs of controlling a defiant India. In August 1947, India gained its independence. A day before the country became free, Pakistan was declared independent. Pakistan was carved out of India in order to give India's Muslims a country of their own. The northeast and northwest regions of India, separated by a thousand miles, became a new country called Pakistan. These were areas where Muslims constituted a majority. In 1971, the eastern part of Pakistan split and declared itself an independent state called Bangladesh. Therefore, what used to be India under the British became three independent states: India, Pakistan, and Bangladesh.

When the British drew the borders between India and Pakistan, they left many Muslims in India and many Hindus in Pakistan. Fearing for their lives as minorities in new states, most left their homes

The Mahatma Gandhi used the ancient Hindu law of Satyagraha to guide a nonviolent struggle for the liberation of India.

Source: Hulton Archive/Getty Images

seeking refuge in their new "homelands." This created a massive refugee problem for both countries when more than 12 million people were on the move. Violence, starvation, and exhaustion killed about a million refugees. In one area between the two newly independent countries is the region of Kashmir. There, the population is mostly Muslim, but when the British were drawing the border in 1947, the governor was Hindu. Pakistan wanted Kashmir to be part of its country. The Hindu governor preferred to be with India. Since then, three major wars have taken place between India and Pakistan over the fate of Kashmir. In 1998, both countries tested nuclear weapons. Some people fear that the conflict over Kashmir may someday lead to a nuclear war between the two countries.

Algeria

In the early nineteenth century, Algeria was a rural society that found it possible to manage its own affairs. Algeria even exported grain and other products to the European market. It is said that it was this export of grain that eventually brought to Algeria the French colonizers. Historians tell the story of a French army purchase of wheat from two merchants in the capital city of Algiers in the 1790s. The French army, however, failed to pay for the purchase. The Algerian ruler, Husayn Dey (1818–1830), demanded payment to the two merchants. Instead of making payments, French merchants armed their factories in Algeria in violation of business agreements with the Algerian government. It is reported that at a meeting between the Algerian leader and the French Consul on April 29, 1827, the Algerian leader struck the French Consul with a flyswatter.[7] This insult, it is said, provoked a serious crisis that eventually led to the French occupation of Algeria.

The colonizers suppressed Algerian resistance to French occupation mercilessly. French settlers soon followed. The settlers had little respect for the Algerians and their culture. They desecrated Muslim mosques and treated the local population very harshly. They soon confiscated the best agricultural land and distributed it to settlers and French corporations. This, in time, brought more settlers from France. By the 1850s, more than 180,000 Europeans, mostly French, had settled in Algeria. The settlers concentrated on growing grapes and wheat for French consumption. French wines, after all, require plenty of good quality grapes. In time, the French declared the colony a district of France. Although Algerian resistance to French rule was continuous, it was not until 1954 that the Algerian War of Independence was declared. In that year, the **National Liberation Front (FLN)** was created with the stated objectives of achieving independence and establishing a democratic and socialist state. The FLN trained its fighters in the mountains and employed guerrilla tactics, attacking French interests and running to safety. The French response was to send 400,000 troops to Algeria to achieve total victory.

The French army's method of uprooting the Algerian fighters included torture, population resettlement, and major attacks on guerrilla bases. Many of the FLN's leaders were arrested and tortured. Those included Ahmed Ben Bella, who later became the country's first president. The French resolve to keep control of Algeria became solidified after the 1956 discovery of oil in the southern part of the country. With that

FLN

The National Liberation Front of Algeria.

resolve came greater atrocities. Stories of torture and ill treatment of the Algerian population gained the sympathy and support of many people in Africa, the Middle East, and even in Europe. The story of Jamila Buhrayd, for example, was later produced in an Egyptian film and published in French in a book. Jamila was a young educated woman who had joined the FLN. She was arrested by the French and subjected to brutal torture. Torture did not make Jamila confess about her comrades but, with the film and the book, it made the French authorities look bad and generated worldwide support for the struggle of the people of Algeria. In 1962, France concluded the Evian Agreement with the leaders of the FLN, which gave Algeria its independence. By then, more than 1 million Algerians had been killed (out of a population of 9 million), 800 villages were destroyed, and more than 3 million peasants were dislocated.

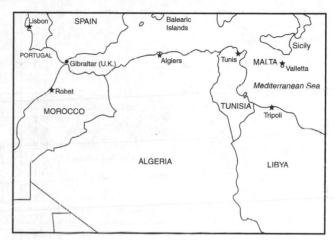

FIGURE 4.3 Algeria

Ghana

Ghana, on the west coast of Africa, is another state that experienced colonialism and a struggle to achieve its independence. Just like India and Algeria, Ghana represents an old civilization that had a thriving history. Archaeological remains indicate human inhabitance going back to the Bronze Age (4000 B.C.E.). In the ninth century, a famous Arab writer, Al Yaqubi, referred to Ghana as one of the three most organized states in Africa. While ancient Ghana was to the west of modern-day Ghana, the region had a glorious history. Its rulers were known for their wealth and skills. They were masters of trade and had lots of gold. In fact, Ghana was rich in gold and diamonds.[8]

Our image of precolonial Africa is rich in ignorance and stereotypes. Many in the United States and Europe still view Africa as "primitive," "tribal," and "backward." This is what one could call the "Hollywood Africa" or the "TV Land Africa." With movies like *Tarzan*, the image of the so-called Dark Continent is maintained. A similar phenomenon in Europe or the United States may be called a forest or a national park, but in Africa it is often referred to as a jungle. This condescending attitude toward Africa is being challenged. The term *tribe* is often applied to small villages as well as to large empires, and, in most cases, in conjunction with the adjective *primitive*. Are the Yorubas of Nigeria, with almost 40 million people, more of a tribe than the Swedes, Norwegians, or Irish? If not, then why not use the term to describe the less numerous European groups? If ethnic conflict in Africa is tribal, why not describe the conflict in Northern Ireland or Yugoslavia as tribal as well?

The dominant group of people in what came to make up Ghana is the **Ashanti.** Under a series of militant leaders, the Ashanti people expanded their rule and established a confederacy that became one of the most powerful kingdoms in the region.

Ashanti

The dominant group of Ghana.

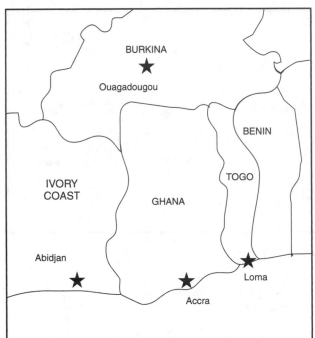

FIGURE 4.4 Ghana

Within their empire, the conquered territories were allowed to retain their own customs, and their leaders were given a seat on the Ashanti State Council. Each territory exercised a form of internal self-rule. Such a state of affairs existed when Europeans began their encroachment on Ghana. The first Europeans to arrive were the Portuguese. Prince Henry the Navigator arrived with his crew in 1471 and began to trade for gold, ivory, and pepper. He called this area the Gold Coast because of its abundance in that precious mineral. In 1482, the Portuguese built a trading post, the Elmina Castle, which still stands today. Today, however, the Elmina Castle stands as a reminder of European trade in African slaves. Within few decades, as gold and ivory resources began to dwindle, slave trade became the major export of the area.

The British made their way into the Gold Coast by creating the British African Company of Merchants in 1750. This company built and manned its installations, carried out trade, and defended its authority over areas under its jurisdiction. By 1875, the British became the dominant European power on the Gold Coast. In the 1880s, the British began to penetrate the northern areas of the region, and by 1902, the Northern Territories were declared a British protectorate—meaning, in practice, a colony. The Ghanaians resisted European encroachment all along. By the 1890s, they had formed an organized opposition with the establishment of the Aborigines' Rights Protection Society, which protested unfair land laws that violated traditional land tenure practices in the society. In 1920, a British West Africa Council was formed and demanded elected representation for all of the peoples of the region. Although such pressure seemed of little value at the time, it actually paid off in the years following World War II. The British were drained from that destructive war and soon thereafter their empire began to break away. The first sign of British acquiescence to Ghanaian demands came in 1946 when the British governor issued the Gold Coast Constitution. This constitution created a new legislative council that included elected members. Even though the council was only advisory to the British governor, it still was a bold move that gave Ghana a level of political participation not found anywhere else in colonial Africa.

With elections, political parties began to form. The first such group was formed in 1947 by a group of British-educated Ghanaians with the objective of achieving self-government. The United Gold Coast Convention (UGCC) wanted self-government "in the shortest possible time." Its leaders were arrested in March 1948 for political activism. Among those arrested was Kwame Nkrumah, who later broke with the UGCC to form his own party, the Convention People's Party (CPP) in 1949.[9]

The CPP demanded "self-government now" and identified itself with the working classes rather than the intellectual circles. Nkrumah's charisma and the slogans adopted by his party made the CPP very popular and worried the British administration. In 1950, the CPP started a campaign of "positive action" aiming at general strikes, boycotts, and other nonviolent resistance. But violence did occur. Consequently, the British arrested Nkrumah. His arrest, however, gave him more popularity among his people and made his party the undisputed winner of the colony's first national elections. The British governor had no choice but to release Nkrumah and offer him the job of "leader of government business," a position similar to that of prime minister. Using his political skills and popular support, Nkrumah was able to convince the British authorities to give him more power and, in time, to create a complete political system managed mostly by elected officials. Having effectively lost political power to Nkrumah's government, the British wanted to maintain some economic advantages. Therefore, at the request of the government of the Gold Coast, the British gave the country independence on March 6, 1956, so long as the new state remains a member of the British Commonwealth. The name adopted for the new country was Ghana, an old name used by the people of the area more than a century earlier.[10]

Brazil

It can be argued that Brazil does not belong in this section because it had no struggle for national liberation. Brazil is the largest state in South America and its only Portuguese-speaking nation. But unlike many other parts of Latin America, Brazil's independence was relatively peaceful. Even though South America experienced colonialism before Africa and Asia, it had similar struggles for independence.

Brazil is the largest state in South America.

Revolutionaries fought hard to achieve an end to mostly Spanish colonialism. Most prominent among the revolutionaries was Simon Bolivar, who led the struggle in many parts of the continent.

Brazil was colonized by Portugal in 1500. It was ruled by the Portuguese crown as a colony until 1808 when the royal family established its seat of power in Rio de Janeiro. The royal family did so when it escaped Napoleon's invasion of Portugal. Thus, the Portuguese government came to directly rule Brazil as a kingdom. When the Portuguese king returned home in 1821, his son declared himself emperor over an independent Brazil on September 7, 1822. The monarchy remained until 1889 when the marshal of the army took over the government and declared it a federal republic. Brazil remains a federal republic until this day.

Brazil covers nearly half of South America and is slightly smaller than the United States. With a population of more than 170 million, Brazil has few native inhabitants left (less than 1 percent of the population). The native inhabitants are mostly Tupi and Guarani Indians. Many Brazilians are of African or mixed origin. The majority of Brazil's population today are of white European origin. Most (more than 80 percent) are Roman Catholic. The United States imports coffee, cocoa, citrus, and beef from Brazil.

TAKING ACTION

Simon Bolivar

Simon Bolivar (1783–1830) was one of South America's most noted generals. His struggle against Spanish colonialism won independence for Bolivia (named after him), Panama, Colombia, Ecuador, Peru, and Venezuela. He was born on July 24, 1783, in Caracas, Venezuela. Bolivar joined a group of patriots at a young age and seized Caracas from Spain in 1810. His struggle with Spain continued through 1821 when his followers crushed the Spanish army in Venezuela. His army marched into other Spanish colonies liberating a half-dozen Latin American states.

FIGURE 4.5 Brazil

Summary and Review

As discussed in Chapter 1, nation and state do not denote the same thing. Nation refers to a people who share common bonds. State, on the other hand, refers to a political unit commonly known as a country. Even though most states today include a single nation, some do not. States that include a single nation are known as homogeneous states, whereas states that include many nations are known as heterogeneous states. All persons identifying with a nation exhibit some form of nationalism or a state of mind in which loyalty is given to the nation they belong to. Most nations possess common territory, language, culture, and enemies. Symbols of nationalism include a flag, national anthem, popular slogans and legends, and historical sites. Nationalism has many different consequences, some positive and others negative. Thus, although nationalism may promote competition among nations that produces growth and development, that competition may spawn wars and genocide. Nationalism may also lead to colonialism or the expansion of a nation beyond its territories. It was also nationalism that led to wars of national liberation, such as the American and the Indian revolutions from the British monarchy. Despite wars of national liberation, the legacy of colonialism on all countries that were either colonizers or colonized is permanent. Hence, Britain's riches extracted from overseas colonies remain a major source of wealth among Britons and

TABLE 4.1 FROM COLONIALISM TO INDEPENDENCE: SAMPLE STATES

Country	Colonizing Country	Year of Independence
Algeria	France	1962
Argentina	Spain	1854
Bahrain	Britain	1971
Brazil	Portugal	1822
Chile	Spain	1810
Djibouti	France	1977
Haiti	France	1801
India	Britain	1947
Indonesia	Netherlands	1945
Jordan	Britain	1945
Lebanon	France	1945
Nigeria	Britain	1961
Syria	France	1946
Tunisia	France	1956

in the British economy. Conversely, many territories possessed by Britain, such as Ghana, are still recovering from years of exploitation and enslavement, both of which directly resulted from British domination. Although the transfer of wealth under colonial enterprises has always been lopsided, the transfer of ideas has been more equal because Europeans and the people they colonized equally acquired many advances in civilization.

Key Terms

nation 66
state 66
nationalism 67
wars of national
   liberation 70
colonialism 71
East India
   Company 72

Congress Party 72
The Muslim
   League 74
Gandhi 75
Satyagraha 75
Kashmir 75
Pakistan 75
Bangladesh 75

Ben Bella 76
Jamila 77
Ashanti 77
Gold Coast 78
Elmina Castle 78
British African
   Company of
   Merchants 78

Nkrumah 78
UGCC 78
CPP 78
homogeneous 80
heterogeneous 80

Discussion Questions

1. Describe the differences among a nation, a state, and a nation-state.
2. What is the difference between homogeneous and heterogeneous states? Name a country that used to be heterogeneous.
3. How did nationalism affect the Vietnam War?
4. Name the bonds of nationalism and describe each.
5. Describe an extreme example of nationalism.

6. What are the symbols of nationalism, and how might they create a sense of nationalism?

7. Name some consequences of nationalism, and describe how they have affected the world.

8. Describe colonialism and the cultural, social, and economic impacts it had and still has on other civilizations.

Suggested Readings

Boahen, A. Adu. *African Perspectives on Colonialism.* Baltimore, MD: Johns Hopkins University Press, 1987.

Davidson, Basil, F. K. Buah, and Ade Ajayi. *The Growth of African Civilisation.* New York: Longman, 1965.

Martin, Meredith. *The Fate of Africa: The Hopes of Freedom to the Hearts of Despair.* Cambridge, MA: Perseus Books Group, 2005.

Nkrumah, Kwame. *Ghana: The Autobiography of Kwame Nkrumah.* New York: International Publishers, 1957.

Rodney, Walter. *How Europe Underdeveloped Africa.* Washington, D.C.: Howard University Press, 1981.

Zeigler, Harmon. *The Political Community: A Comparative Introduction to Political Systems and Society.* New York: Longman, 1990.

Addresses and Websites

ASEN—Association for the Study of Ethnicity and Nationalism
European Institute
London School of Economics
Houghton Street
London WC2A 2AE
Tel: 144 (0)20 7955 6801
Fax: 144 (0)20 7955 6218
http://www.lse.ac.uk/Depts/European/Asen/

This link is the homepage for the Association for the Study of Ethnicity and Nationalism. The organization aims to collect information and offer conferences, seminars, lectures, and workshops regarding the issues of nationalism and ethnicity. It also has a journal entitled *Nations and Nationalism.* This website provides further information about ASEN and its activities, along with brief information about nationalism.

UNITED for Intercultural Action
PB 413, NL-1000
AK Amsterdam
Tel: 131–20–6834778
Fax: 131–20–6834582
http://www.united.non-profit.nl/

This is the website for UNITED for Intercultural Action, a European network against nationalism, racism, and fascism and in support of migrants and refugees. It provides extensive information regarding the organization. This

website also provides information about hatred and inequalities that stem from nationalism, racism, and fascism. There are various links offered, including one that covers the organization's publications and leaflets.

World Citizen Foundation
211 East 43rd Street, Suite 908
New York, NY 10017
Tel: 11–212–973–9835
Fax: 11–212–973–9836
http:www.worldcitizen.org/

The aim of this organization is to unite people globally in the promotion of global democratic institutions. The website offers different articles pertaining to the mission of the organization, along with a brief list of international articles and laws. There is also a link for online polling regarding global events, as well as further information regarding the organization's view of democracy.

http://www.pbs.org/newshour/forum/ colonial2_1-3.html

This website offers some information regarding colonialism and its aftermath, particularly nations' statuses after the imposition of colonial rule. This link is a forum on economic independence following colonial rule, provided by the Public Broadcast Service (PBS). Forum questions are answered by Karen Parker, associate fellow for economic studies at the Council on Foreign Relations.

Notes

1. Robert S. McNamara, *In Retrospect: The Lessons of Vietnam* (New York: Times Books, 1995).
2. John B. Noss, *Man's Religions*, 4th ed. (London: Macmillan, 1969), 249.
3. Harmon Zeigler, *The Political Community: A Comparative Introduction to Political Systems and Society* (New York: Longman, 1990), 61.
4. See James Joll, *The Origins of the First World War* (Princeton, NJ: Princeton University Press, 1991).
5. Quoted in Edward Goldsmith, "Development as Colonialism," *The Ecologist* 27, no. 2 (March–April 1997): 70.
6. Mahatma Gandhi, "Excerpts from *The Essential Writings of Mahatma Gandhi*," in Manfred B. Steger and Nancy S. Lind, eds., *The Violence and Its Alternatives* (New York: St. Martin's Press, 1999), 293.
7. Lois A. Aroian and Richard P. Mitchell, *The Modern Middle East and North Africa* (New York: Macmillan, 1984), 133–34.
8. For more details on Ghana's civilization, see Basil Davidson, F. K. Buah, and Ade Ajayi, *The Growth of African Civilisation* (New York: Longman, 1965).
9. For a good book on Africa's view of colonialism, see A. Adu Boahen, *African Perspectives on Colonialism* (Baltimore, MD: Johns Hopkins University Press, 1987).
10. For more details on Ghana's struggle for independence, see Kwame Nkrumah, *Ghana: The Autobiography of Kwame Nkrumah* (New York: International Publishers, 1957).

CHAPTER FIVE

Global and Domestic Inequalities

GLOBALIZATION AND GLOBAL AND DOMESTIC INEQUALITIES

GLOBALIZATION, WHICH ENCOURAGES THE GROWTH OF FREE TRADE, OPEN MARKETS, AND COMPETITION IN THE WORLD ECONOMY, IS VIEWED AS CONTRIBUTING TO BOTH EQUALITY AND INEQUALITY AMONG AS WELL AS WITHIN COUNTRIES. GLOBALIZATION OFFERS OPPORTUNITIES TO STATES AND INDIVIDUALS WHO ARE ABLE TO TAKE ADVANTAGE OF THEM. BY MAKING NATIONAL BORDERS LESS SIGNIFICANT AND MORE POROUS, GLOBALIZATION CHALLENGES THE PREVAILING TENDENCY TO VIEW THE WORLD ALMOST EXCLUSIVELY IN TERMS OF RICH NATIONS VERSUS POOR NATIONS. ECONOMIC INEQUALITIES AMONG AND WITHIN COUNTRIES HAVE ALWAYS EXISTED AND CANNOT BE ATTRIBUTED PRIMARILY TO GLOBALIZATION. GLOBAL ECONOMIC INTERDEPENDENCE MEANS THAT MAJOR ECONOMIC PROBLEMS SPREAD FROM ONE COUNTRY TO ANOTHER, THEREBY HEIGHTENING THE SENSE OF ECONOMIC INSECURITY AS WELL AS WIDENING THE GAP BETWEEN RICH AND POOR. BUT GLOBALIZATION ALSO HOLDS THE PROMISE OF GREATER OPPORTUNITIES FOR THE POOR TO IMPROVE THEIR ECONOMIC POSITION BY GIVING THEM INCREASED ACCESS TO EDUCATION, TECHNOLOGY, JOBS, AND HOPE. COUNTRIES THAT ARE MORE INVOLVED IN THE GLOBAL ECONOMY TEND TO HAVE LESS POVERTY AND GREATER INCOME EQUALITY.

INTRODUCTION

Discussions about wealth and poverty are as old as humankind. Individuals, groups, and governments throughout the world have, at one time or another, wrestled with the issue of economic inequality and income distributions. Despite many efforts to narrow the gap between rich and poor individuals, groups, and countries, the adage that the rich get richer and the poor get children seems to be supported by continuing global and domestic inequalities. The fact that inequality exists is not in and of itself the major problem, especially if the standard of living for those on the bottom is improving. In a wealthy society, such as the United States, inequality is mitigated by access to social services, training, and education. Wide economic disparities are often narrowed in a growing economy and the possibility of upward mobility creates hope among the poor. Extreme and relatively permanent economic inequality within as well as among countries is widely viewed as detrimental to political stability and economic development. Extreme inequality, especially in societies with a weak middle class, often leads to the concentration of social and political power and the stifling of competition. As Chapter 9 shows, the existence and healthy functioning of democracy depends to a large extent on a significant degree of social and economic equality. Furthermore, extreme inequality generally negatively affects relations between the developing world and industrialized countries. Given the increasing levels of globalization, inequality among and within countries spills over into virtually all areas, from democratization and human rights to migration and ethnic conflicts. Following the attacks on the United States on September 11, 2001, poverty in the developing world was widely viewed as a major contributor to terrorism.

This chapter examines the widening economic gap between the rich countries of the industrialized North and the poor countries of the less-developed South, inequality within both rich and poor countries, the causes of unequal income distribution, and attempts to reduce poverty. It shows that the number of poor people continues to grow, partly because the population in the poorest societies steadily increases, making it more difficult for people to escape the cycle of poverty. Colonialism and its legacies are widely believed to also contribute to the growing gap between rich countries and poor countries. Most poor countries, just as they did during colonialism, continue to be exporters of primary products and importers of manufactured goods and technology from rich countries. However, globalization is changing this relationship, as companies in the industrial world locate manufacturing and production operations in many developing countries in an attempt to reduce costs and be competitive. Detrimental governmental policies, natural disasters, low literacy rates, widespread hunger and malnutrition, inadequate health care, and the rapid spread of AIDS and other infectious diseases in most parts of the developing world combine to reinforce inequality between the North and the South. This chapter points out that many developing states are the most unequal societies in the world. Some countries, such as India, have structured inequality based on rigid class systems. In both rich and poor countries, women are likely to be the poorest of the poor. Instead of just concentrating on the problems, this chapter also stresses that attempts to reduce poverty are as persistent as poverty itself.

GROWING INEQUALITY BETWEEN NORTH AND SOUTH

Although living standards have improved significantly in many countries over the past century, global inequalities have risen steadily. The vast majority, approximately 80 percent, of the world's population lives on about 20 percent of the world's income. The United States alone, which has 5 percent of the world's population, consumes 30 percent of the world's resources. Historic trends indicate that the richest countries will maintain their lead over the poorest countries for a long time. The gap between the richest country and the poorest country was 3 to

By the end of the twentieth century, the richest 20 percent of the world's population had 86 times as much income as the poorest 20 percent.

TABLE 5.1 INCOME GAPS BETWEEN RICH AND POOR COUNTRIES

	GDP Per Capita (US $) 2002
Rich Countries	
Luxembourg	47,354
Norway	41,914
Switzerland	36,687
United States	**36,006**
Denmark	32,179
Japan	31,407
Ireland	30,982
Iceland	29,749
Sweden	26,929
United Kingdom	26,444
Poor Countries	
Ethiopia	90
Burundi	102
Congo, Dem. Rep.	111
Guinea-Bissau	141
Sierra Leone	150
Malawi	177
Niger	190
Mozambique	195
Rwanda	212
Nepal	230
Low-Income Countries	**451**
Middle-Income Countries	**1,877**
High-Income Countries	**27,115**

Source: United Nations Development Program, *Human Development Report 2004* (New York: Oxford University Press, 2004), 184–87.

1 in 1820, 11 to 1 in 1913, 35 to 1 in 1950, 44 to 1 in 1973, and 72 to 1 in 1992. By the end of the twentieth century the richest 20 percent of the world's population had 86 times as much income as the poorest 20 percent.[1] To understand this income disparity between the rich countries and the poor countries, assume that Thomas Proctor lived in Britain in 1820 and Yusuf Kebede lives in Ethiopia today. Thomas's income in 1820 would be about six times that of Yusuf in 2005, 185 years later. Table 5.1 indicates such income gaps.

Economic development throughout Asia, Latin America, and, to a lesser extent, Africa has not significantly closed the gap between the North and South, despite rising incomes in the developing countries. In fact, the rich countries have experienced higher rates of economic growth than poor countries over the past twenty years. Per capita income actually declined in more than 100 poor countries, many of them in Africa. In other words, these societies have less income than they did twenty years ago. This economic polarization contradicts predictions by many economists, political scientists, development specialists, and others that developing countries as a whole would eventually catch up with industrialized nations. However, despite this gap, economic conditions for many individuals in the developing world have greatly improved. People are generally better off now than they were twenty years ago. Both China and India, the two most populous states in the world, illustrate the ever-widening income gap between the North and South. Between 1985 and 2006, both China and India experienced faster income growth than most rich countries. However, it is estimated that it would take approximately 100 years of constant growth at rates higher than those now experienced by industrialized states just to reach current American income levels.[2] Given the extremely high standard of living in the United States, both India and China would be relatively prosperous if they achieved half the income level of Americans. Table 5.2 shows the gross domestic product of ten of the richest countries and ten of the poorest countries. Singapore and Kuwait, two high income states, demonstrate that some formerly poor states have managed to achieve high rates of economic prosperity through the implementation of astute political, social, and economic policies (in the case of Singapore) and the possession of valuable natural resources such as petroleum (in the case of Kuwait).

Enduring Poverty in the South

Disparities in per capita income underscore significant economic differences between the North and the South. For more than two-thirds of humanity, poverty is an enduring reality, one that is only being slightly altered by the growing economies in the South. Although living standards are improving in the developing world and the middle class is growing, the number of poor people continues to grow, partly because the

TABLE 5.2 PERCENTAGE OF POPULATION LIVING ON $2 OR LESS A DAY

	Population Below $1 a day (%)	Population Below $2 a day (%)
Rich Countries		
United States	..	..
Canada	..	..
Japan	..	..
France	..	..
Sweden	..	..
Norway	..	..
United Kingdom	..	..
Australia	..	..
Germany	..	..
Netherlands	..	..
Poor Countries		
Zambia	63.7	87.4
Niger	61.4	85.3
Ethiopia	26.3	80.7
India	34.7	79.9
Rwanda	35.7	84.6
Nepal	37.7	82.5
Senegal	26.3	67.8
Kenya	23.0	58.6
Guatemala	16.0	37.4
Honduras	23.8	44.4

Source: United Nations Development Program, *Human Development Report 2004* (New York: Oxford University Press, 2004), 147–49.

population in the poorest societies steadily increases, thereby making the possibility of escaping poverty more difficult. For example, an estimated 204 million Latin Americans lived in poverty in 1997, compared with 200 million in 1990 and 136 million in 1980. Poor people, despite economic progress in Latin America, represented more than one-third of the region's population. In Haiti, where the per capita income is $415 and where 75 percent of the citizens do not have running water, four out of five Haitians live in absolute poverty, the lowest level of economic deprivation. The approximately

1.3 billion people live on less than $1 a day.

1.3 billion people who live on less than $1 a day share the hardships suffered by 80 percent of Haiti's population. The most extreme cases of poverty are Zambia, Guinea Bissau, Uganda, Niger, Ethiopia, and India.

In contrast to most inhabitants of poor countries, people who live in the highest income countries such as the United States, Canada, Japan, and Britain consume most of the world's resources. The top fifth of the citizens in the most affluent societies consume 58 percent of the world's energy, 65 percent of the world's electricity, and 46 percent of the global meat production; use 84 percent of the world's paper; drive 87 percent of the world's cars; and use 74 percent of all telephones. Whereas countries such as the United States, Sweden, and Switzerland have more than 600 telephone lines for every 1,000 people, poor countries average one line per 1,000 people.[3] For most of the people in Africa, Asia, and Latin America, life is a day-to-day struggle for survival. The harsh conditions that are the components of poverty reduce the average life expectancy for the world's poor, at a time when individuals in rich countries are living longer.

low literacy rates

Used as a measure of poverty because illiteracy and poverty are strongly connected.

Another measure of poverty in the South is the **low literacy rates,** especially among females. The connection between illiteracy and poverty is very strong. Industrialized societies are also very well-educated societies. Without high levels of education, these societies would not function effectively and would soon deteriorate economically. Just as education is essential to upward mobility for individuals, high literacy rates are an important part of any attempt to lessen poverty in developing countries in Africa, Asia, and Latin America. But poverty contains many vicious circles. Having few resources to allocate to literacy programs, poor countries often find themselves in a downward spiral of poverty. Those countries that

In India, less than half of all women are literate.

manage to increase literacy rates are likely to attract foreign investments, reduce population growth, improve health care and various public services, and, ultimately, create more wealth for the majority of their citizens. In Haiti, for example, almost half of all school-age children have never attended school. The same proportion of Haitians are illiterate. In India, where females have limited access to education, less than half of all women are literate. African countries not only are the poorest in the world, but also have the lowest literacy rates. This supports the conclusion that there is a direct relationship between wealth and high rates of literacy on the one hand and poverty and low literacy rates on the other.

malnutrition

An indicator of poverty that causes impaired vision, shorter life expectancies, and increased vulnerability to disease.

Hunger and **malnutrition** are generally regarded as even more obvious and important indicators of poverty than low literacy rates. Seriously malnourished children and adults are unable to function effectively. Chronic hunger and malnutrition are integral components of poverty and contribute to its perpetuation. Malnutrition causes impaired vision, an

Almost one-sixth of the world's population is malnourished.

inability to concentrate and to learn, greater vulnerability to disease and poor health, and a shorter life expectancy. It is estimated that almost one-sixth (840 million) of the world's population is malnourished. This number represents a decline from the 1969–1971 period, when almost 1 billion people were undernourished. Conditions have improved in China, Southeast Asia, Latin America, and the Caribbean. In Africa, however, malnutrition, especially among children, worsened.[4] But South Asia is the region with the highest rate of malnutrition and where more than half of all the malnourished children live, despite greater agricultural production.

Malnutrition leads to many health problems, including death. Two decades ago, every day 40,000 people died of malnutrition and related preventable disease. By 1990, the number declined to 35,000. Today, approximately 24,000 people die from hunger and hunger-related disease daily. The vast majority of the victims are children under five years of age. Where poverty is extreme, the youngest members of society tend to be the most vulnerable. Access to food is often determined by sex, control of resources, and social status. In some societies girls and women have lower status and generally receive less food. However, when women are the head of the household, they not only allocate more money to food, but also tend to favor a more equal distribution of food.[5]

In countries where ethnic conflicts are widespread and prolonged, famine usually results. **Famine** is generally defined as a situation in which food supplies are suddenly reduced, which causes a large number of deaths. Many people are severely malnourished, even when food is provided by international relief organizations and governments. This is partly due to the tendency of factions in civil wars to use food as a weapon.

TABLE 5.3 PREVALENCE OF CHILD MALNUTRITION

	% of Children under Age 5 (2001)
Rich Countries	
United States	..
Canada	..
Japan	..
Sweden	..
Norway	..
France	..
Germany	..
United Kingdom	..
Australia	..
Netherlands	..
Poor Countries	
Bangladesh	48
Cambodia	45
Nepal	48
Ethiopia	47
Niger	40
Mozambique	40
Vietnam	34
Philippines	32
Indonesia	25

Source: World Bank, *World Development Report 2004* (New York: Oxford University Press, 2003), 254–55.

They deliberately restrict the availability of food supplies in order to starve the population associated with a rival faction into submission. This strategy has been used in Ethiopia, Somalia, Angola, Sudan, and elsewhere. Conflicts also create hunger and starvation by diverting scarce resources away from food and other basic needs to weapons and general supplies for combatants. Furthermore, conflicts disrupt agriculture, livestock production, markets, transportation, and other activities related to growing and distributing food. In the southern part of the Sudan, famine and conflict, over a period of fifteen years, have claimed the lives of about 1.6 million people. Another 3 million Sudanese are starving.[6] Without the cooperation of warring factions or the government, attempts to diminish starvation are often only marginally successful.

Another indicator of the gap between the North and South, one that cannot be separated from poverty, is **inadequate health care** in less-developed countries. The vicious circles of poverty cannot be neatly isolated and analyzed. Malnourished children and adults are vulnerable to diseases, which, in turn, rob them of nutrients and their appetites. Chronic poor health drains individuals of energy needed to take care of themselves and their families, find and keep employment, and protect their environment. These problems are usually made worse by the government's inability

famine

A situation in which food supplies are suddenly reduced, which causes a large number of deaths.

inadequate health care

An indicator of the economic gap between the North and the South.

TABLE 5.4 POVERTY IN DEVELOPING COUNTRIES

Country	Population Without Access to Safe Water (%) 2000	Population Without Access to Sanitation (%) 2000
Chile	7	4
Costa Rica	5	7
Venezuela	17	32
Mexico	12	26
Thailand	16	4
Ecuador	15	14
Philippines	14	17
Brazil	13	24
Peru	20	29
Dominican Republic	14	33
China	25	60
Indonesia	22	45
Honduras	12	25
Guatemala	8	19
Nicaragua	23	70
Botswana	5	34
Lesotho	22	51
Zimbabwe	17	38
India	16	72
Kenya	43	13
Pakistan	10	38
Nepal	12	72
Nigeria	38	46
Madagascar	53	58
Bangladesh	3	52
Zambia	36	22
Senegal	22	30
Guinea Bissau	44	44

Source: United Nations Development Program, *Human Development Report 2004* (New York: Oxford University Press, 2004): 147–49.

or unwillingness to provide adequate sanitation and access to clean water and health care. Infectious diseases thrive in unsanitary conditions.

The AIDS epidemic clearly demonstrates inequality between the North and the South. With modern health care services and access to sophisticated drugs, Americans infected with HIV live with the disease for a relatively long time. Although families' resources are severely strained, it is unlikely that families will be reduced to poverty. In Africa, by contrast, where there are few safety nets, AIDS has devastating consequences for the society and for families. When a man or woman is sick, agricultural productivity declines, more resources are allocated to medicines and hospital expenses, and family members must take care of the sick person. In some cases, grandparents look after as many as twelve grandchildren whose parents died of AIDS.[7] Those countries most affected by AIDS are usually the poorest, and have many other diseases and a severe shortage of doctors, nurses, and other medical specialists.

Economic Inequalities Within Rich Countries

Economic prosperity in the industrialized countries often masks the reality of large income disparities among different groups of citizens. Although much of the focus is

The gap between rich and poor Americans is widening.

on the gap between rich and poor countries, it is increasingly obvious that economic inequality within societies, both North and South, demands greater emphasis. The globalization of the economy and the interdependence that characterizes the international system are challenging not only national boundaries but also how we perceive issues such as poverty and

Almost a Billion People Are Hungry

Despite many efforts to reduce starvation and hunger around the world, approximately 840 million people, more than 95 percent of them in Africa, Asia, and Latin America, suffer from hunger. The Food and Agricultural Organization, a special agency of the United Nations, found that from 1979 to 2005 the proportion of the population without enough to eat increased dramatically in Somalia, Afghanistan, Haiti, North Korea, Mongolia, Cuba, and Iraq. Causes of the rise in hunger include war, natural disasters, economic problems, the failure of agricultural programs, economic sanctions, and political mismanagement. The extent of the problem varies from one country to another. For example, hunger is more prevalent in Haiti than it is in Indonesia. More than 180 countries have pledged to decrease the number of hungry people by half in fifteen years. A few countries, such as Ghana and Nigeria, have made significant progress. However, the number of undernourished people is declining slowly, by only 8 million a year, worldwide. To reduce the number of hungry people by half by 2015, the global community will have to shrink the ranks of the undernourished by 20 million per year.

Sources: The Economist, 28 October 2000; and Somini Serigupta, "Hunger Worsens in Many Lands," *The New York Times,* 26 November 2003, A3.

YOU DECIDE ✓   Baby Formula and AIDS

It is estimated that between 1.1 million and 1.7 million infants are infected with the AIDS virus through breast-feeding. Companies that produce baby formula, such as Wyeth-Ayerst Laboratories and Nestlé, offered to donate tons of free formula to HIV-infected mothers to prevent the transmission of AIDS to babies. UNICEF, an agency of the United Nations that is responsible for protecting the interests of children, opposed accepting free formula, partly because it did not want to endorse the baby formula industry.

The conflict between UNICEF and the producers of baby formula began in the late 1970s, when Nestlé ran advertisements throughout the developing countries that featured healthy formula-fed babies. Nestlé distributed free samples of formula in maternity wards to influence women to purchase their product. By the time the free samples were used up, most women found that their own breast milk had dried up. Few women could afford to buy the formula. Many diluted the formula with contaminated water, starving their babies in the process. Activists organized an effective worldwide boycott of Nestlé's products. UNICEF also opposes Nestlé.

UNICEF argued that even if the formula protects a baby from AIDS, it could expose children to diarrhea and other deadly diseases in the developing world. Breast milk helps to protect children from these diseases. UNICEF officials believed that providing formula to HIV-infected women would undermine support for breast-feeding among healthy women, who are the vast majority of mothers.

How would you resolve this conflict between UNICEF and companies that produce baby formula?

Source: Alix Freedman and Steve Stecklow, "Bottled Up," *The Wall Street Journal,* 5 December 2000, A1.

income distribution. Within the United States, the gap between rich and poor Americans has widened since 1977. In 1999, the richest 2.7 million Americans, or 1 percent of the population, earned as much money as the poorest 100 million citizens, or 37 percent of all Americans. Although robust economic growth in the United States has benefited most income groups, the richest 1 percent of Americans received about 90 percent of the economic gains. In fact, since 1977, the gap has widened into a chasm. In 1977, the top 1 percent had as much as the bottom 20 percent or 49 million Americans.[8] In 1979, the top 1 percent received 7.5 percent of the national income, compared with 15.5 percent in 2000. During this period, the share received by the poorest 40 percent declined from 19.1 percent of the national income to 14.6 percent. In 2000, the top 1 percent earned an average of $862,000 each,

TABLE 5.5 HEALTH PROFILE

Country	HIV Prevalence (% ages 15–49) 2003	Tuberculosis Cases (per 100,000 people) 2002	Physicians (per 100,000 people) 2003
United States	0.2	4	279
Canada	0.3	5	187
Japan	0.1	44	202
United Kingdom	0.1	12	164
Chile	0.3	20	115
Kuwait	0.3	53	160
Costa Rica	0.6	19	160
Venezuela	0.7	54	200
Mexico	0.3	44	156
Cuba	0.1	14	596
Thailand	1.5	179	30
Philippines	0.1	540	115
Brazil	0.7	94	206
Turkey	0.1	50	123
China	0.1	272	164
South Africa	17.8	366	25
Indonesia	0.1	609	16
Egypt	0.1	38	218
Botswana	37.3	338	29
Zimbabwe	24.6	452	6
Swaziland	6.7	769	15
Kenya	1.3	579	14
India	5.4	344	51
Nigeria	16.5	565	27
Zambia	1.3	588	7
Haiti	5.6	392	25
Malawi	14.2	462	2
Ethiopia	8.5	508	3

Source: United Nations Development Program, *Human Development Report 2004* (New York: Oxford University Press, 2004), 156–59, 164–67.

compared with $21,350 each for the bottom 40 percent. In other words, the top 1 percent earned 40 times as much as the bottom 40 percent. By 2000, the top 10 percent of households in America had 44 percent of total household income.

The increase in income enjoyed by the wealthiest Americans is matched by losses among some groups, especially those with limited education. High school graduates have lost approximately 15 percent in wages between 1973 and 1993. As most students know, educational achievement determines income levels to a much greater extent now than previously. But a college education is more expensive and beyond the reach of an increasing number of Americans. Americans with higher family incomes have greater access to higher education, which, in turn, reinforces their economic advantage. The poor are generally at a disadvantage in a global economy.[9] By 2004, roughly 9.2 million working families, including 20 million children, were in the low-income category and struggled to survive financially. For the poorest Americans, life resembles that in many less-developed countries. For example, in Bayview, Virginia, on the Chesapeake Bay, many roads are unpaved, raw sewage runs through some streets during heavy rains, and rust-colored water is pumped by hand for bathing. Many homes have no running water or indoor toilets. Although shacks in this area of abject poverty rent for $45 to $50 a month, some of Bayview's 114 residents have difficulty paying it. In nearby Northampton, 28 percent of the population live in absolute poverty, 30 percent make less than $10,000 a year, and one-fifth have less than a ninth-grade education.[10] Due to grassroots efforts and an infusion of $3 million in economic development assistance, Bayview began to improve housing and living conditions for its residents in 2003.

Regional Inequalities

An emphasis on North-South economic disparities often obscures major differences among countries that are classified as part of the South. As we have seen, Africa, Asia, and Latin America differ in terms of their possession of natural resources. Whereas some parts of the Middle East have abundant petroleum supplies, many African and Latin American countries import petroleum. Africa's mineral resources are unmatched by most Asian states. However, countries in the same region and with approximately equal natural resources often experience different rates of economic growth and development, and countries with few natural resources may develop faster than countries with many resources.

Although Asia, Africa, and many countries in Latin America were in a similar economic position four decades ago, *there are now huge income gaps among them.* Countries in Asia, especially East Asia, occupy the top position in the developing world, with Latin America in the middle, and Africa on the bottom. Even though Asia and Latin America achieved significant industrialization and reduced their dependency on primary products such as oil, copper, bauxite, coffee, bananas, and cocoa, Africa's economic conditions essentially remained the same. In some cases they have deteriorated since 1960, when most countries became independent states. Most African countries are marginal players in international markets, and their per capita income remains extremely low. Almost 90 percent of Africa's export earnings come from primary commodities, compared with about 30 percent for East Asia.[11] Unlike Asia and Latin

America, where population growth has slowed and agricultural productivity has increased, Africa's population continues to grow faster than its food supply.

The Gulf Between Rich and Poor in the South

On June 9, 1998, a cyclone with winds of more than 100 miles per hour created a wall of water about eight feet high that inundated the vast, low-lying tidal mud flats of Kandla, on the west coast of India. These mud flats or salt pans produce sea salt that is harvested by some of India's poorest people. As many as 10,000 workers died when their shacks were swept away by the water. In a country with more than 1 billion people, the vast majority of whom live in poverty, such tragedies are common. What is also common is the general disregard for the poor. Kevin Sullivan argues that drivers who hit a cow on the streets of New Delhi face the very real threat of being attacked by a mob furious over the death of a sacred animal. But when thousands of people from society's bottom rung die, there is a collective shrug of resignation.[12] In most countries of Africa, Asia, and Latin America, there are two distinct worlds, one inhabited by the middle and upper classes and the other by the poor masses. Rich people in the developing world live like rich people in the North and are integrated in the world's economic and social system. The poor, by contrast, live in slums and marginal housing. They struggle to survive as agricultural workers, subsistence farmers, and manual laborers. Some regions are more prosperous than others. There are sharp disparities

---

TAKING ACTION

Yvonne de Mello and Brazil's Street Children

Yvonne de Mello was raised by a single parent, won a scholarship to study at the Sorbonne in Paris, and married a wealthy hotelier, with whom she has three children. For the past twenty years de Mello has been leaving her posh apartment with its idyllic view of Rio de Janeiro's famous Sugar Loaf Mountain to work with abandoned children in Rio's *favelas* (slums), where the stench of raw sewage is pervasive. It is estimated that thousands of children are homeless and abandoned in Rio. Brazil, one of the world's most unequal societies, has done little to help the children who roam the streets in search of food and work and who sleep on the streets at night. In some cases, the government has resorted to violence against them. Yvonne de Mello received international attention on the night of the horrific massacre of eight street children in July 1993. When off-duty police fired on street children, de Mello rushed to help the survivors. She stayed with them that night, singing songs and cradling them.

The massacre and de Mello's response motivated Bob Crites, an Oregon school counselor and former Peace Corps volunteer, to join de Mello in fighting poverty in Brazil. Crites formed Students Helping Street Kids International to provide scholarships for Brazilian children. The scholarship program, which is administered by de Mello, is funded primarily by American schoolchildren. They raise money for each child they sponsor. The goal of the program, which allows homeless children to attend private schools, is to transform lives and to groom future leaders to help Brazil's poor.

Source: Patrice M. Jones, "Brazil's Street Children Get Taste of Good Life," *Chicago Tribune,* 17 September 2000, Sect. 1, 3.

TABLE 5.6 DISTRIBUTION OF INCOME OR CONSUMPTION

Country	Year	Poorest 10%	Poorest 20%	Richest 20%	Richest 10%
Bangladesh	2000	3.9	9.0	41.3	26.7
Brazil	1998	0.5	2.0	64.4	46.7
Chile	2000	1.2	3.3	62.2	47.0
China	2001	1.8	4.7	50.0	33.1
Egypt	1999	3.7	8.6	43.6	29.5
Ghana	1999	2.1	5.6	46.6	30.0
India	2000	3.9	8.9	41.6	27.4
Indonesia	2002	3.6	8.4	43.3	28
Jamaica	2000	2.7	6.7	46.0	30.3
Kenya	1997	2.3	5.6	51.2	36.1
Mexico	2000	1.0	3.1	59.1	43.1
Nigeria	1997	1.6	4.4	55.7	40.8
Pakistan	1999	3.7	8.8	42.3	28.3
Panama	2000	0.7	2.4	60.3	43.3
Paraguay	1999	0.6	2.2	60.2	43.6
Philippines	2000	2.2	5.4	52.3	36.3
Sierra Leone	1989	0.5	1.1	63.4	43.6
South Africa	1995	0.7	2.0	66.5	46.9
Zimbabwe	1995	1.8	4.6	55.7	40.3
United States	**2000**	**1.9**	**5.4**	**45.8**	**29.9**

Source: United Nations Development Program, *Human Development Report 2004* (New York: Oxford University Press, 2004): 188–91.

between urban and rural areas, men and women, and among castes and ethnic groups. Brazil stands out as one of the most unequal societies in the world. The gap has been widening. In 1960, the poorest 50 percent of the population received 18 percent of the national income; their share fell to 11.6 percent by 1995. The income of the richest 20 percent rose from 54 percent of the national income in 1960 to 64 percent in 1995. In 1998, the richest 20 percent still received 64.4 percent of national income, compared with 2 percent for the poorest 20 percent. Regional inequalities in Brazil are also large. For example, in the North-East region, half of the children are enrolled in school, compared with 98 percent of the children in the Central-West region. Similarly, the Indian state of Bihar has an absolute poverty rate of 64 percent, compared to 25 percent for the states of Punjab and Haryana. In Swaziland in Southern Africa, King Mswati III, the last absolute monarch in sub-Saharan Africa, drives between his various palaces in a $500,000 Maybach 62 luxury sedan. Two-thirds of Swazis live below the U.N. poverty line, 20 percent receive international food aid, 40 percent are unemployed, and the elderly survive on $13 a month.[13]

Just as countries in the North are generally fearful of an invasion of poor migrants from the South, rich people within the South are fearful of the poor at home. Walls guarding the homes of the wealthy and gated communities are common throughout the developing world. Afraid of crime, especially kidnapping and car robberies, many of Brazil's elite are armoring their cars to protect themselves. The cost of armoring cars such as BMWs, Mercedes, Volvos, and Jeep Cherokees ranges from $20,000 to $35,000. This is in addition to the normal price of the car. But armoring cars is also another way of displaying status and the gulf between the rich and poor in Brazil. India is another country of great inequalities.

The Caste System: Structured Inequality Sometimes the gap between rich and poor within countries is rooted in cultural beliefs, attitudes, and values. Just as countries of the North are viewed as having unfair advantages by many leaders in the South, certain groups within developing societies are disadvantaged because of ethnicity or social class. When South Africa was governed by **apartheid laws,** the rigid social segregation of blacks, whites, Asians, and mixed-race groups was required. Apartheid also preserved a privileged position for whites only. But India's caste system is the most obvious and pervasive example of structural inequality. As we saw, the **caste system** is a rigid hierarchical system of social classes in Hinduism, which determines the status, rights, privileges, occupations, and social interaction of each person from birth. The lowest group in India is the **untouchables,** who are regarded as outcasts. This means that they do not belong to a caste or class. Brahmans (the priests and scholars) stand at the top, the Ksatriya (the military, law-makers, and rulers) are second, the Vaisyas (merchants, landowners, industrialists, and artisans) are third, and the Sudras (laborers and farm workers) are at the bottom of the caste system. Each caste is divided into numerous subcastes or **jatis.** The untouchables perform tasks deemed to be too polluted to be done by caste Hindus. These tasks include dealing with dead humans and animals and cleaning up human and animal waste. As seen in in Chapter 2, even though discrimination on the basis of caste was outlawed in India, old practices continue.

> *Although the caste system is outlawed, it is widely adhered to in Indian society.*

apartheid laws

South Africa's practice of rigid social segregation based on skin color.

caste system

A rigid hierarchical system of social classes in Hinduism.

untouchables

The people regarded as outcasts because they are the lowest group in India.

jatis

The subgroups of major castes.

Women: The Poorest of the Poor Women in most societies, in both the North and South, generally have fewer resources and opportunities than men. In many societies, the inequality of women is enshrined in both laws and customs, as we will see in Chapter 8. The inferior status of women plays a major role in their access to employment, the kind of work they perform, and their compensation. Equally important is the impact of how women are treated on their self-perception, their ability to provide for their children, their opportunity to obtain an education, and their attempts to help break the cycle of poverty. It is clear from discussions throughout this book that narrowing the gap between the North and South depends to a large extent on closing the gap between men and women.

The Causes of Inequality Between North and South

One of the issues debated most passionately by the international community is the cause for the persistent and growing economic disparity between rich and poor

Untouchable woman in India taking part in a small business to help change her socioeconomic status.

Source: Kim Barker/ *Chicago Tribune*

countries. There are many causes of inequality within countries and among them. These include (1) colonialism and its legacies, (2) the structure of the world economy that perpetuates the status of poor countries as exporters of primary products to and importers of manufactured goods and technology from rich countries, (3) increasing globalization of the economy, (4) overpopulation in the developing world, (5) ineffective and detrimental government policies or decisions, (6) political and economic instability, and (7) natural disasters. Although an examination of the causes of economic inequality among and within countries is necessary in order to find solutions, the discussion later in this chapter of ways to narrow the gaps indicates that it is much easier to identify the causes of inequality than to diminish inequality.

Colonization, it is generally argued, laid the foundation for the economic gap between rich and poor countries. Inequality breeds inequality because wealth tends to perpetuate wealth and poverty tends to perpetuate poverty. As we have seen, countries that were rich a hundred years ago, due partly to their colonization of the developing world, are generally still rich today. However, the ability of poor countries that were colonized to acquire wealth clearly demonstrates that these positions can change. Kuwait, Saudi Arabia, Singapore, and South Korea, now relatively rich, were considered poor until fairly recently. Nonetheless, it is widely argued that colonization has made it difficult for poor countries to close the North-South economic divide and to reduce the economic inequality within countries that began during colonization.

Structure of the World Economy Colonialism and historical experiences, as well as current practices, are seen as creating an unfair global economy that keeps poor nations poor and rich nations rich. The Scottish economist Adam Smith, who wrote *An Inquiry Into the Nature and Causes of the Wealth of Nations*, believed that governments should not interfere with the functioning of markets and that businesspersons would be led as by an invisible hand to do the best for society. However, many leaders of developing nations argue that governments and businesses in the rich countries work together to maintain an unfair world economy. They generally subscribe to what is called **dependency theory,** which holds that the South's reliance on exports of primary commodities, many of which were developed during colonization for the benefit of Europeans, puts it at an economic disadvantage. The prices obtained from their exports decline relative to the prices of manufactured imports. Many poor countries depend on one or two products for most of their income. Botswana depends on diamonds for almost 80 percent of its revenues, Nigeria receives 90 percent of its income from petroleum, and El Salvador relies on coffee exports for more than half of its money. When commodity prices decline, developing states' revenues plunge.

Although many developing countries still rely on exports of primary commodities, an increasing number of them are exporting manufactured goods to industrialized countries. Many of their citizens are experiencing greater prosperity as a result. The movement of assembly production out of the United States, Western Europe, and Japan to the developing world means that making clear distinctions between the economies of rich and poor countries are increasingly difficult. Developing countries effectively compete with technologically advanced countries as multinational corporations transfer machinery, skill-intensive technologies, management techniques, and capital to them and provide access to global markets for finished products. Many developing nations have an advantage due to the low wages workers get, despite their high rates of productivity. Another development that challenges dependency theory is the opening of new markets in other developing countries for goods and services produced by multinational corporations based in the South. Many developing countries cooperate with each other to produce manufactured products.[14]

Increasing Globalization **Economic globalization** is defined as free trade, open markets, and competition in the world economy and is viewed as causing both inequality and equality among and within nations. Globalization is a manifestation of the growing interdependence of states. It blurs distinctions between economic activities within countries and international economic activities. By making national borders less significant and more porous, *globalization* challenges the tendency to view the world exclusively in terms of rich countries versus poor countries. By heightening competition among as

dependency theory

The South's reliance on exports of primary commodities puts it at an economic disadvantage.

economic globalization

Free trade, open markets, and competition in the world economy.

well as within states, globalization helps to engender economic success or failure for groups in both rich and poor nations. Despite the gap between rich and poor countries, many citizens of developing countries are experiencing significant economic gains and enjoy a standard of living that is increasingly indistinguishable from that of middle-class Americans. Overall, globalization has produced many benefits for a large number of the inhabitants of the developing world. Most governments have implemented *free trade policies*, competition, and other aspects of globalization. But to compete effectively, governments are forced to adopt some policies that are seen as promoting greater inequality within their societies. For example, governments often reduce spending on social services, health care, subsidized food, and programs that benefit the poor, especially women and children, thereby increasing poverty for the most vulnerable citizens. To attract investment capital, it is argued that many governments further weaken the poor by engaging in what is seen as a race to the bottom in relation to wages. On the other hand, *foreign investment* contributes significantly to economic development, a process that is generally beneficial to the poor.

Skilled workers generally fare better than unskilled workers in both rich and poor countries. In India, for example, programmers and other computer experts, like their counterparts in rich countries, have enjoyed great financial success. Many are recruited to work for multinational companies such as IBM, Motorola, and Honeywell, which have branches in India. Global competition and free trade generally benefit most of the population by increasing job opportunities, weakening monopolies, and reducing consumer prices. Although wages in some industries also decline in rich countries and jobs are lost due to weakened labor unions, the relocation of industries from rich to poor countries, and corporate restructuring, cheaper imports from the developing world benefit American consumers and diminish inflation.[15] When General Motors or Eureka Company moves factories from the United States to Mexico, U.S. workers lose jobs but Mexicans gain jobs, improve their standard of living, and help narrow the gap between rich and poor within Mexico and between Mexicans and U.S. citizens. *Globalization contributes to both inequality and greater equality.*

Overpopulation is one of the most important causes of inequality. As we have seen, the economic chasm that separates rich countries from poor countries has widened over time. We have also seen that although population growth has decreased in the North, it has exploded in the South. Since 1950, the population in rich countries grew by about 50 percent, compared with 250 percent in poor countries. As will be discussed in Chapter 7, overpopulation results in part from deliberate personal choices. Poorer people generally have larger families. *Children are widely regarded as a source of social security* for aging parents and as contributors to the family income. Large families perpetuate poverty in most cases. Children are usually malnourished and unable to learn even if they have access to education because hunger destroys brain cells and retards development. Forced to work at menial jobs to help support the family, children fail to acquire skills essential to escape poverty. Their own children will probably face similar circumstances, thus ensuring the continuation of poverty. Lester C. Thurow contends that "people who are poor in poor countries with rapid rates of population growth are going to die in poor countries. Whatever one believes about the world's ability to provide enough food, huge income gaps will emerge not just with the first world but between those parts of the third world that have their populations under control and those that do not."[16]

Government policies play a key role in making global and domestic economic divisions. When Korea was divided into North Korea and South Korea in 1948, South Korea adopted capitalist policies that fostered economic success. North Korea, by contrast, decided to isolate itself from most of the world and to adopt a communist system of government based on norms of economic and social equality. When communism collapsed with the disintegration of the Soviet Union in the late 1980s, North Korea lost its external support and descended into famine, which took the lives of 2 to 3 million of that country's 24 million citizens. Government policies in North Korea produced and reinforced poverty. But decisions by governments that lead to prosperity can also spawn inequality, which demonstrates that inequality is a complex issue. People can actually be better off despite growing inequality. The People's Republic of China, for example, has gradually modified communist economic policies in favor of creating free-enterprise zones. China has experienced tremendous economic growth and prosperity, especially in coastal areas. As a result of China's economic policies, some Chinese are very prosperous—and yet the majority is less well off. In a sense, these policies created greater inequality. In many East Asian countries, governments pursued policies to ensure both rapid economic growth and equality in the distribution of income. Latin America, by contrast, has focused less on the poor and more on the rich and middle class. Instead of investing in the education of the poor, governments in Latin America allocate resources to disproportionately benefit the higher education of the wealthy. With limited education, the poor have remained trapped in the cycle of poverty.[17]

Civil wars, political and economic instability, and ethnic conflicts, which have plagued many parts of the developing world, directly contribute to economic disparities between the North and South. Even though stability is not always conducive to development, as was shown in the case of North Korea, those societies torn by civil war and ethnic conflict have little hope of getting out of poverty. In many cases, economic disadvantages suffered by ethnic groups cause conflicts that send poor countries into a downward spiral. For example, Sudan's Islamic government's unequal treatment of the country's Christians and **animists** (people who worship animals, stones, plants, and other objects) fuels a civil war that has made Sudan even poorer. As Chapter 12 shows, civil wars, ethnic conflicts, and political instability not only discourage foreign investment but also influence the best educated, most talented, and most financially successful citizens to flee or to invest their money outside the country. Instability reinforces the vicious cycle of poverty.

Natural disasters, such as drought, earthquakes, volcanic eruptions, and hurricanes, help perpetuate economic inequality among nations. These natural disasters destroy important economic sectors, create serious infrastructural problems, force the relocation of a large number of people, and lead to greater impoverishment. As population increases and land becomes scarce, unsafe areas are inhabited, making more people vulnerable to natural disasters. In many parts of Africa, both droughts and floods cause severe economic hardships and widespread starvation and famine, and help weaken governments and create political and economic instability. The cyclones that regularly plague many parts of Asia, especially Bangladesh, the Philippines, and India, help

animists

People who worship animals, stones, plants, and other objects.

perpetuate inequality by eliminating much of the progress achieved through economic development. Hurricanes frequently destroy major parts of the economies of the Caribbean that depend on tourism and the export of primary products such as bananas. In many ways, *geography contributes to North-South economic inequality.*

Narrowing the Gaps

Attempts to decrease the rich-poor divide are as persistent as the chasm between rich and poor is durable. As long as there are obvious economic disparities among people, it is likely that there will be efforts to bridge these gaps. Despite overwhelming evidence to support the adage that the rich get richer and the poor get poorer, there is also sufficient evidence to suggest that fortunes change and that many poor individuals are able to overcome poverty and become middle class, or even join the ranks of the rich. A poor person who lives in a rich country generally has a much greater chance of overcoming poverty than a poor person who lives in a poor country. But globalization and the interdependence of states hold the promise of more opportunities for the poor of the South to improve their economic position by giving them access to education, technology, and jobs. Governments and **nongovernmental organizations (NGOs)** (organizations that are not part of the government of a nation) can reduce poverty by investing in social and economic programs that uplift and empower the poor. In 2000, the United Nations issued the **Millennium Declaration,** which advocated the achievement of the Millennium Development Goals. These include cutting extreme poverty and hunger in half, reducing child mortality by two-thirds, providing universal primary education, and achieving equality for women by 2015. Ultimately, however, many solutions to the problem of global and domestic inequality must be found at the grassroots level by groups and individuals. Personal choices that reinforce poverty within families will eventually reinforce national poverty. As we have seen, there are many causes of inequality. This section offers some suggestions for narrowing the gap between rich and poor.

NGOs

Organizations that are not part of a government.

Millennium Declaration

Aim to dramatically reduce poverty, hunger, and infant mortality, and to secure greater equality for women.

Education and Family Planning One of the most effective ways to reduce inequality is through education and family planning. Education, especially for women, has a direct impact on the number of children a woman has and their level of education and quality of life. Educated women are more likely than uneducated women to use birth control, thereby reducing overpopulation, which is a major cause of inequality. Education for the society as a whole contributes directly to economic development, as we show in Chapter 6. Countries that make education and family planning priorities usually have smaller, healthier, more productive, and more economically and technologically competitive populations. These countries, such as Taiwan, Singapore, and South Korea, have effectively reduced domestic inequality as well as narrowed the gap between themselves and industrialized countries.

Democracy May Help Democratic governments, by definition, are generally responsive to the demands of voters and are less likely to engage in conflicts with other democracies. The poor, who are the majority in developing countries, can reward their political leaders for promoting their interests and the general welfare and punish leaders who ignore or damage their interests or are incompetent, corrupt, or irresponsible. Democracy reduces domestic conflict by providing greater access, representation, and institutionalized avenues of bargaining and compromise among competing ethnic groups. Democratic governments may be pressured to reduce economic inequalities by grassroots social movements, interest groups that represent the poor, and political parties that want the votes of the poor. For example, the untouchables of India have used their political power to influence their government to implement equal opportunity programs that reserve a percentage of all public service jobs for them.[18]

The Green Revolution Norman Borlaug and the Rockefeller Foundation worked together to increase food supplies by developing new varieties of wheat, rice, corn, and other grains. Through experimentation with different plant hybrids, Borlaug and his colleagues were able to develop a variety of wheat in Mexico that increased the average yield of eleven bushels per acre to thirty-nine bushels per acre. The new plants grew faster, produced more grain, and absorbed large quantities of fertilizer while remaining short and sturdy. This dramatic growth in food supplies is known as the **Green Revolution.** India was an early beneficiary of the development of high-yielding hybrids. Between 1965 and 1972, India's wheat production grew by 165 percent and its rice production grew by 35 percent. This revolution in farming enabled India to reduce widespread starvation by becoming self-sufficient in food grains.[19]

Green Revolution

Dramatic growth in food supplies due to agricultural advancements.

Even though the Green Revolution helped countries end their dependence on grain imports and become food exporters in some cases, it has been widely criticized for also creating inequalities within countries. The high-yielding varieties of grain require more fertilizer, irrigation, herbicides, pesticides, larger farms, and farm machinery. It is argued that smaller farmers lost their land as richer farmers expanded their farms. Furthermore, many small farmers could not obtain money to purchase expensive seed, machinery, fertilizers, etc. Many were unable to read and follow instructions to implement this agricultural breakthrough. Forced from their land, or staying on as agricultural workers for the new owners, these small farmers generally became poorer than they were before the Green Revolution. On the other hand, increased food supplies around the world contributed to lower food prices for many poor people. The Green Revolution also mitigates some of the major causes of inequality, such as overpopulation, natural disasters, and the unequal structure of the global economy. For example, the Green Revolution addresses the issue of overpopulation because it helps feed rapidly growing populations and lessens the need for more hands to provide labor to produce crops. The Green Revolution helps with the problem of natural disasters by providing crops that are more resilient to droughts and pests.

Diminishing Poverty Through Debt Reduction Debt reduction can be achieved through debt forgiveness and through restructuring and rescheduling debt. Debt reduction could stimulate economic growth and foster stability. It could also influence governments to abandon excuses for poor performance and implement social, political, and economic reforms. More money would be available to spend on programs to reduce infant mortality and malnutrition, improve educational opportunities for the poor, and build a modern infrastructure to facilitate economic development and enhance the quality of life.[20] Both the United States and Britain proposed writing off these debts entirely in 2004. In April 2006, Nigeria repaid the last of its $30 billion debt.

Government Policies and Free Trade Could Make a Difference Decisions made by governments in poor countries have been responsible for growing inequality both within and among states. Governments that make population control, access to education for males and females, health care, and free enterprise their priorities improve their societies' chances of reducing poverty. By implementing far-reaching economic reforms, China has attracted foreign investment, encouraged domestic entrepreneurship, and reduced population growth. As a result, China has a rapidly growing middle class and fewer poor people. By promoting free trade and foreign investments, Mexico has attracted many companies from the United States. These companies have significantly increased the number of middle-class Mexicans. However, economic prosperity for Mexicans is often seen as coming at the expense of American workers.

Development Assistance Economic aid can help to diminish poverty and enhance the quality of life in developing countries. To achieve these objectives, the cooperation of the government is essential. In many cases, aid never reaches the poor. Countries with free-market policies, institutions and values that discourage corruption and hold leaders accountable, and a commitment to social and economic equality are generally better able to use financial assistance to help the poor. Often, however, aid from rich countries goes to serve the national interest of the giving state rather than the needs of the poor. Remittances that go directly to individuals, as we discuss in Chapter 13, are far more effective than aid in diminishing inequality.

Summary and Review

Although living standards have improved significantly in many countries over the past century, global inequalities have risen steadily. The vast majority, approximately 80 percent, of the world's population lives on about 20 percent of the world's income. Historic trends indicate that the richest countries will maintain their lead over the poorest countries for a long time. The gap between the richest country and the poorest country was 3 to 1 in 1820, 11 to 1 in 1913, 35 to 1 in 1950, 44 to 1 in 1973, and 72 to 1 in 1992. By the end of the twentieth century the richest 20 percent of the world's population had 86 times as much income as the poorest 20 percent. Although the gulf between rich and poor varies along the North-South divide, on a country-by-country basis, the gap between rich and poor is greatest in Asia, Africa, and Latin America. Moreover, women in the South appear to be the poorest, least literate group. Along with great income gaps, malnutrition and famine are rampant. Today, approximately 24,000 people die from hunger and hunger-related disease daily. The vast majority of the victims are children under five years of age. Where poverty is extreme, the youngest members of society tend to be the most vulnerable. Access to food is often determined by sex, control of resources, and social status. In some societies girls and women have lower status and generally receive less food. The contemporary quandaries of inadequate health care, malnutrition, and poverty are attributable to natural disasters, personal decisions, colonialism and its legacy of inequality, wars, lack of equitable distribution, government decisions, and overpopulation. Ways to solve those problems include democracy, Green Revolution, debt reduction, free trade, development assistance, and nongovernmental organizations (NGOs).

Key Terms

literacy rates   88
malnutrition   88
hunger   88
famine   89
gap between rich
    and poor   90

caste system   96
apartheid laws
    96
dependency
    theory   98
globalization   98

overpopulation   99
animists   100
nongovernmental
    organizations   101
Green Revolution
    102

debt reduction   102
development
    assistance   103

Discussion Questions

1. Discuss reasons behind the gap between rich and poor. Why does it vary along lines of, for example, class and gender?
2. Does globalization contribute to the growing gap between rich and poor or does it diminish it? Why or why not?
3. What role do literacy rates play within the context of global inequalities?
4. What new and creative solutions can NGOs develop to alleviate suffering from hunger and malnutrition?
5. Discuss how dependency theories explain global inequalities. According to dependency theorists, what sort of future should most poor countries in Asia, Africa, and Latin America expect given the present condition of global systems? Will it be a future of prosperity and equality or one of failure and inequality?
6. Would government action be effective in inducing a trend toward equality? How or why not?
7. Is there a relationship between inequalities of health, nutrition, and wealth?
8. What forms should development assistance take? Should it only include South-South development assistance or strictly North-South?
9. How do caste systems contribute to inequality?
10. How could countries of the South rid themselves of neocolonial exploitation by countries in the North?

Suggested Readings

Birdsall, Nancy, et al. "How to Help Poor Countries." *Foreign Affairs* 84, No. 4 (July/August 2005): 136–152.

Cline, William R. *Trade Policy and Global Poverty*. Washington, D.C.: Institute for International Economics, 2004.

Elias, Juanita. *Fashioning Inequality*. Burlington, VT: Ashgate, 2004.

Elliott, Kimberly. *Delivering on Doha: Farm Trade and the Poor*. Washington D.C.: Institute for International Economics, 2006.

Isard, Peter. *The Macroeconomic Management of Foreign Aid.* Washington, D.C.: International Monetary Fund, 2006.

McBride, Stephen, and John Wiseman, eds. *Globalization and Its Discontents.* New York: St. Martin's Press, 2000.

Nkrumah, Kwame. *Neocolonialism: The Last Stage of Imperialism.* New York: International Publishers, 1966.

Rapley, John. *Globalization and Inequality.* Boulde, CO: Lynne Rienner, 2004.

Sachs, Jeffrey D. *The End of Poverty.* New York: Penguin, 2006.

Thurow, Lester C. *The Future of Capitalism.* New York: William Morrow, 1996.

Yusuf, Shahid, Weiping Wu, and Simon Evenett, eds. *Local Dynamics in an Era of Globalization: 21st Century Catalysts for Development.* New York: Oxford University Press, 2000.

Addresses and Websites

United Nations Economic Commission for Latin America and the Caribbean
Casilla de Correo 179-D
Santiago de Chile
Tel: (56–2) 210–2000–2085051
Fax: (56–2) 210–2000–2080252

http://eclac.org/default.asp?idioma = IN

This website is the home of the United Nations' Economic Commission for Latin America and the Caribbean. The commission works on the promotion of various issues in the region, particularly social and economic development, in order to lessen the inequalities surrounding these concerns. The website provides headline news regarding the region and the global community as it pertains to Latin America and the Caribbean. There are many links offered on this website, including analyses and research, U.N. publications, and statistical information pertaining to nations in the region.

Asian Development Bank
P. O. Box 789
0980 Manila, Philippines
Tel: (632) 632–4444
Fax: (632) 636–2444

http://www.adb.org/

This address is the home of the Asian Development Bank organization. The ADB, established in 1966, is a financial institution that aims to help eradicate poverty in Asia and thus works on a variety of development topics. The website offers information on Asia's general business and financial management, economics and statistics, and ways to aid in the development of Asia. Links to news and events, along with the organization's publications, can also be found on the website.

International Development Exchange
IDEX
827 Valencia Street Suite101
San Francisco, CA 94110–1736
Tel: (415) 824–8384

http://www.idex.org/

IDEX is an organization, based within the United States, that works toward economic justice in Asia, Africa, and Latin America. The group works with low-income nations in order to promote their goal of economic justice and to eradicate global inequalities as well. This website allows the browser to enter into the world of IDEX and its work. The organization currently assists eight nations, and the website offers brief information regarding economic conditions in these nations, along with information on their involvement with them.

Third World Conference Foundation
1525 E. 53rd Street, Suite 435
Chicago, IL 60615–4509
Tel: (773) 241–6688
Fax: (773) 241–7898

http://www.twcfinternational.org/

The Third World Conference Foundation works to discuss and tackle the challenges of development in the Third World. The organization brings people together from various backgrounds and professions in order to dialogue about development issues and global inequalities. This website offers further information regarding the organization and also describes their annual conference and other programs and activities.

Notes

1. U.N. Development Program, *Human Development Report 1999* (New York: Oxford University Press, 1999), 38.
2. Nancy Birdsall, "Life Is Unfair: Inequality in the World," *Foreign Policy* 111 (Summer 1998): 76; and Jeffrey D. Sachs, *The End of Poverty* (New York: Penguin, 2006).
3. U.N. Development Program, *Human Development Report 1998* (New York: Oxford University Press, 1998), 50.
4. Ibid.
5. American Dietetic Association, "Position Statement on World Hunger," *Journal of the American Dietetic Association* 95, no. 10 (October 1995): 1160–63.
6. Lydia Polgreen, "UN Agency Cuts Food Rations for Sudan Victims in Half," *The New York Times*, 29 April 2006, A3.
7. Michael Fleshman, "New Global Anti-AIDS Campaign Kicks Off," *African Renewal* (April 2006), 4; and Eileen Stillwagon, *AIDS and the Ecology of Poverty* (New York: Oxford University Press, 2005).
8. David Cay Johnston, "Gap Between Rich and Poor Found Substantially Wider," *The New York Times*, 5 September 1999, 14; and Laura D' Andrea Tyson, "How Bush Widened the Wealth Gap," *BusinessWeek*, 1 November 2004, 44.
9. Birdsall, "Life Is Unfair," 78; and Barbara Rose, "1 in 4 Working Families is Low Income," *Chicago Tribune*, 12 October 2004, Sect. 1, 1.
10. Sylvia Moreno, "Amidst Virginia's Plenty, the Third World Huddles," *The Washington Post National Weekly Edition*, 18 May 1998, 32; and Anne Raver, "Town of Worn Bootstraps Lifts Itself Up," *The New York Times*, 21 August 2003, D1.
11. Michael T. Rock, "Twenty-five Years of Economic Development," *World Development* 21, no. 11 (November 1993): 1790.
12. Kevin Sullivan, "That's the Way It Is, the Indians Say," *The Washington Post National Weekly Edition*, 13 July 1998, 16.
13. U.N. Development Program, *Human Development Report 2004* (New York: Oxford University Press, 2004), 189; World Bank, *India: Achievements and Challenges in Reducing Poverty* (Washington, D.C.: World Bank, 1997), 7; and Laurie Goering, "Rich in Tradition, Wretched in Life," *Chicago Tribune*, 16 April 2006, Sect. 1, 6.
14. Brian McDonald, *The World Trading System* (New York: St. Martin's Press, 1998), 12; A. S. Bhalla, *Globalization, Growth, and Marginalization* (New York: St. Martin's Press, 1998), 4; and Dale Neef, *A Little Knowledge Is a Dangerous Thing* (Boston: Butterworth, 1999), 56.
15. Norman S. Fieleke, "Is Global Competition Making the Poor Even Poorer?" *New England Economic Review* (November–December, 1994): 8; and Eddy Lee, "Globalization and Employment: Is Anxiety Justified?" *International Labor Review* 135, no. 4 (1996): 485–97.
16. Lester C. Thurow, *The Future of Capitalism* (New York: William Morrow, 1996), 91.
17. Kwan S. Kim, "Income Distribution and Poverty: An Interregional Comparison," *World Development* 25, no. 11 (1997): 1916; and Nancy Birdsall and Juan Luis Londono, "No Tradeoff: Efficient Growth Via More Equal Human Capital Accumulation," in Nancy Birdsall, Carol Graham, and Richard H. Sabot, eds., *Beyond Tradeoffs* (Washington, D.C.: Inter-American Development Bank, 1998), 1.
18. Celia W. Dugger, "The Lower Castes in India, Reaching for Power, Shake Up the System," *The New York Times*, 23 September 1999, A10.
19. Allen Kornmesser, "Changing Indian Agriculture," in C. Steven La Rue, ed., *The India Handbook* (Chicago: Fitzroy Dearborn Publishers, 1997), 123.
20. Lawrence H. Summers, "Debt Relief: A Fresh Start," *The Washington Post Weekly Edition*, 8 November 1999, 27; and "Debt Relief: Clean Slate," *The Economist*, 2 October 2004, 73.

CHAPTER SIX

Challenges of Development

GLOBALIZATION AND ECONOMIC DEVELOPMENT

GLOBALIZATION ACCENTUATES THE NEED FOR ECONOMIC DEVELOPMENT. BECAUSE HUMAN BEINGS SHARE A TENDENCY TO WANT TO IMPROVE THEIR STANDARD OF LIVING AND ACQUIRE MORE MATERIAL POSSESSIONS, GOVERNMENTS ARE PRESSURED TO EMBRACE ECONOMIC CHANGES AS PEOPLE IN POOR COUNTRIES BECOME MORE AWARE OF THE BENEFITS OF ECONOMIC DEVELOPMENT ENJOYED BY PEOPLE IN THE DEVELOPED WORLD. GLOBALIZATION DIRECTLY AFFECTS ECONOMIC DEVELOPMENT BECAUSE IT SPREADS TECHNOLOGY, MANAGERIAL SKILLS, AND INVESTMENT ESSENTIAL FOR ECONOMIC PROSPERITY. IT ALSO REQUIRES GOVERNMENTS TO PLAY A DIMINISHED ROLE IN THE ECONOMY AND TO REWARD PRIVATE ENTREPRENEURIAL ACTIVITIES. PRIVATIZATION OF PUBLIC ENTERPRISES BECOMES COMMONPLACE. FEWER SUBSIDIES, INCLUDING THOSE THAT BENEFIT THE POOR, ARE PROVIDED BY GOVERNMENTS THAT EMBRACE FREE MARKETS AS THE ROAD TO ECONOMIC DEVELOPMENT. THE GROWING TIES ACROSS GLOBAL MARKETS INCREASE THE LIKELIHOOD THAT ECONOMIC DIFFICULTIES WILL SPREAD FROM ONE COUNTRY TO ANOTHER. GLOBALIZATION MAKES IT MORE DIFFICULT FOR INDIVIDUAL GOVERNMENTS TO DETERMINE ECONOMIC DEVELOPMENT. HOWEVER, GOVERNMENTS STILL RETAIN CONSIDERABLE INFLUENCE ON THE PROCESS OF ECONOMIC CHANGE.

INTRODUCTION

Throughout history, human beings have attempted to have better lives. They advocated change and have resisted change. The idea of progress, which is generally accepted in the United States and Western Europe, is not always viewed positively by everyone in Western societies or in other parts of the world. Even when most citizens agree on the need for improvements, they may disagree about the pace of change, the degree of change, how to accomplish change, and how to deal with the positive and negative results of change. Who should benefit from change? Who should pay the cost of change? Because new ways of doing things and new ideas and values usually threaten those who benefit from the status quo, change is not only an economic issue but also a political issue. Both proponents of change and those who resist it often utilize politics to achieve their economic and social objectives. Consequently, the study of development, which is essentially about change to improve economic and social conditions, focuses on politics, economics, psychology, sociology, and other academic disciplines. Values, ideologies, institutions, resources, and technology play a crucial role in efforts to achieve and manage change. Countries throughout the world, regardless of their level of economic, social, and political achievement, are concerned with improving people's lives. Development is an ongoing process of change that is designed to meet new demands of different groups within societies to make life better. Development is also an uneven process. There are different levels of development not only among countries but also within countries. As we have seen in Chapter 5, the economic and social gaps between citizens within many developing societies are often wider than those between rich and poor countries. However, development is generally beneficial to most citizens. This is demonstrated in part by the **Millennium Development Goals** set by the global community. These include (1) eradicating hunger and poverty, (2) achieving universal primary education, (3) reducing child mortality, (4) improving maternal health, (5) combating infectious diseases, (6) ensuring environmental sustainability, (7) promoting gender equality and empowerment, and (8) developing a global partnership for development. This chapter discusses the nature of economic development, the role of governments in the process, and the factors that facilitate and impede development, such as cultural values, government policies, access to natural resources, and political instability. It concentrates primarily on the positive aspects of development.

Millennium Development Goals

Goals set by the global community to eradicate hunger and poverty, achieve universal primary education, and further human rights.

WHAT IS DEVELOPMENT?

The task of defining development is fraught with political as well as scientific difficulty. **Development** is usually defined as significant and measurable economic growth and the emergence of social, economic, and political institutions. The emphasis on economic growth leads some political scientists, economists, and others to equate development with industrialization. In response to the narrow focus on economic growth, others argue that a distinction should be made between growth and development.

For them, development is about the quality of life, environmental sustainability, and human development. **Growth** is seen as quantitative increases in economic activities, a larger economy, and more money. Development, on the other hand, is viewed as more equitable distribution of economic resources. Some governments in the developing world pursue egalitarian policies. Taiwan, Singapore, and South Korea are more egalitarian, whereas Brazil, Mexico, and South Africa have been less concerned with equality. But it is difficult to separate growth from development. A growing economy is more likely to produce greater benefits for more people than a stagnant or declining economy. A more useful definition of **economic development** encompasses growth, sustainability, equity, and human development.

development

Significant and measurable economic growth and the emergence of social, economic, and political institutions.

growth

Quantitative increases in economic activities, including a larger economy and more money.

economic development

Encompasses growth and equity or human development.

Growth is usually associated with the development of natural resources and the construction of an **infrastructure** to effectively utilize those resources. As countries mine copper, produce petroleum, manufacture steel, grow and process agricultural products, and make automobiles, they also build roads, bridges, ports, airports, railways, and lighthouses; develop communication networks; generate electricity; and provide reliable mail service, water, and medical services. The infrastructure—roads, bridges, etc.—is essential to development. Countries lacking a developed infrastructure attract little investment in manufacturing or

infrastructure

Items such as roads and bridges that aid in the effective use of resources.

services and generally suffer from low levels of economic growth and productivity. Computers are not very useful if countries do not have a reliable supply of electricity; factories cannot function efficiently without electricity and water; and products cannot be shipped on time without good roads, bridges, railways, reliable telecommunications systems, and ports.

Growth is also seen in terms of a country's **gross national product (GNP)** or its **gross domestic product (GDP)**. Most measures of economic development focus on either the total market value of all goods and services produced within a country (GDP) or the total market value of all goods and services produced by resources supplied by residents and businesses of a particular country, regardless of where the residents and businesses are located (GNP). Most countries prefer to use their GDP to measure economic performance. In an industrialized society, such as the United States, it is relatively easy to measure the market value of goods and services because of the availability of relevant information and resources to analyze the information. It is much more difficult to determine the GDP of most developing countries because of the poor quality of information and self-sufficiency. Many people in poor countries produce much of what they consume, and many economic transactions occur informally and are not recorded. Another problem with determining a country's GDP is deciding what to include. For example, the government of Colombia began to include money earned from the

Modern buildings in the developing world are indistinguishable from those in the United States and other developed countries.
Source: Chen Fei/China Features/Corbis Sygma

gross national product (GNP)

Total market value of all goods and services produced by citizens of a state regardless of where they are located.

gross domestic product (GDP)

Total market value of all goods and services produced within a country.

human development index

Measures the quality of life people experience.

gender-related development index

Index including the same measures as the human development index, but concentrating on inequality between women and men.

growth of illegal drugs within the country as part of the GDP. Although Colombian officials do not have precise measurements of drug production, they estimate that the illegal trade is worth $4 billion a year, or about one-third of the country's legal exports. Government economists argue that by including revenues from growing cocaine and other narcotics in the GDP, they are able to more accurately measure the total value of all economic activities in the country. However, they do not include money earned from the processing and trafficking of cocaine, marijuana, and heroin.[1] Such calculations do not take into consideration the equity and human development components of development.

The equity and human development aspect of development recognizes that economic growth is essential to achieve greater equality in society. Instead of measuring development in terms of GDP or GNP, the equity and human development component of development measures improvements in the quality of life for all citizens.[2] This means that basic needs should be satisfied. People should have access to adequate health care, housing, education, proper nutrition, a safe environment, an overall improved quality of life, and the enjoyment of freedoms associated with democratic governments. The United Nations Development Program (UNDP) developed a **human development index (HDI)** to measure the quality of life people experience in different countries. The HDI is based on a formula that takes into account life expectancy at birth, income, literacy, and access to education, measured by the average years of schooling. The **gender-related development index (GDI)** includes the same measures of the HDI but concentrates on inequalities between women and men.

Equity and human development focus on quality of life issues.

THE ROLE OF GOVERNMENT IN DEVELOPMENT

government institutions

Provide the essential framework within which development occurs.

As the discussion of theories and strategies for development indicates, governments may promote or impede development by implementing particular policies. There is a close relationship between economic development and political development. **Governmental institutions**—legislatures, judicial organizations, executive bodies, and bureaucracies—provide the essential framework within which development occurs. Institutions help structure social, economic, legal, and political behavior. They provide a great degree of certainty and stability. Institutions determine the rules of the game, protect property rights, and inspire investor confidence. Banks and other financial institutions can make investment capital available to entrepreneurs without fearing that they will be unable to secure repayment of the loans. Entrepreneurs can take financial risks without fearing the imposition of arbitrary government decisions that would deprive them of their property.

Many developing societies fail to make significant economic progress because they are unable to maintain order, collect revenues, enforce laws, and provide essential public services such as education and healthcare. Governments are primarily responsible for building the infrastructure to facilitate development. Many Asian countries, as will be discussed, developed the infrastructure and adopted policies to promote industrialization. The Mexican government initiated the **maquiladora program,** which encouraged U.S. manufacturing companies to locate their factories along the 2,000-mile border between the United States and Mexico to take advantage of lower wages in Mexico.[3] The Mexican government provided subsidies to encourage American companies to move to the border, passed laws to allow them to import machinery and raw materials without paying duties, and negotiated the **North American Free Trade Agreement (NAFTA)** to lower trade barriers among Mexico, the United States, and Canada. However, the forces of globalization contributed to a significant loss of jobs between 2001 and 2005 as companies moved from Mexico to China, El Salvador, and elsewhere in search of lower production costs, especially cheaper labor. Even though approaches to development vary, governments in all societies play a greater or lesser role in the process.

maquiladora program

A program initiated by Mexico that encouraged U.S. companies to locate on the Mexican-American border.

NAFTA

Designed to lower trade barriers among Mexico, Canada, and the United States.

The Classical Economic Model and Free-Market Capitalism

As discussed in Chapter 5, some scholars argued that individuals were primarily concerned with maximizing their economic interests. The price of goods and services are believed to be determined by **the law of supply and demand.** The classical economic model emphasizes competition among producers, the growth of production, the efficient allocation of resources, and relatively little governmental involvement in the market. Instead of government regulations and excessive taxation, the invisible hand of economic forces would regulate the market. The economic rationality of human beings would ultimately produce greater economic growth and enhanced living standards. Free-market capitalism or neoclassical economic theory is essentially an updated version of the classical economic theory. The neoclassical economists and free-market advocates favor low taxes, strong national currencies, the prohibition of monopolies in order to maximize economic competition, and minimum government regulations. The main economic role of government is to facilitate free-market competition.[4] Both domestic and international barriers to trade should be removed to build a global economic system. **Trade barriers** prevent the free exchange of goods and services and are therefore seen by some as an impediment to economic development.

law of supply and demand

Determines the price of goods and services.

trade barriers

Prevents the free exchange of goods and services.

YOU DECIDE ✓   ### Do the Costs of Privatization Outweigh the Benefits?

The emphasis on free trade, the removal of trade barriers, and the declining role of the government in the economy are generally accepted by most countries and international institutions that are involved in assisting countries with development. In many cases, free trade means that the government must allow private companies to take over some of its economic functions, many of which are viewed as beneficial to the poorest citizens.

Do you think that the costs of privatization outweigh the benefits?

privatization

The reduction of government involvement in economic activities and the increase in private influences on the economy.

Privatization increased rapidly in the developing world in the 1980s, especially after the fall of communism in the Soviet Union and Eastern Europe. The inefficiency and corruption often associated with government-controlled companies helped to strengthen the argument for privatization.[5] On the other side of the issue of privatization are those who benefit from government monopolies and subsidized services and products, especially food. In Nigeria, for example, trade union members view privatization as a direct threat to their job security. Who controls the new privatized economic activities also becomes a significant political issue in an ethnically divided country such as Nigeria. From the free-market perspective, the gains achieved by removing trade barriers and restricting governments' involvement in economic affairs clearly outweigh the costs for countries that want to develop.

State Capitalism

state capitalism

Gives the government a central role in economic development.

State capitalism stresses the importance of economic competition to secure growth. Private entrepreneurs, as in the case in free-market capitalism, are primarily responsible for promoting economic activities. Unlike free-market capitalism, state capitalism rejects the idea of the invisible hand as the regulator of the marketplace and gives the government a central role in economic development. Countries such as Japan, Singapore, Taiwan, South Korea, and China, which enjoyed rapid growth and equity, are leading proponents of state capitalism. State capitalists believe that individuals, driven by self-interest, cannot be relied on to do what is best for the society as a whole or to support national interests. Consequently, governments must decide national priorities and must assist industries that will help secure those national objectives. Furthermore, in addition to emphasizing the need for economic growth, state capitalism views equity as an equally important goal. In other words, they believe that both growth and equity are essential elements for development and that industrialization and urbanization should not result in the neglect of agriculture and rural communities.

Under state capitalism, the government makes resources and financial assistance available to selected industries and invests in education, especially technical education, health care, housing, infrastructure, and initially, in labor-intensive, low-skill manufacturing industries to produce shoes, apparel, and other consumer products for export. The abundance of cheap labor in these countries enabled these exports to effectively compete with goods produced in the United States and Western Europe prior to the implementation of global trade rules. As the Asian economies developed, the governments supported the building of larger and more technologically advanced industries. These included ship building, steel, automobile manufacturing, home appliances, and electronics.[6]

THEORIES OF DEVELOPMENT

Human beings develop theories as they deal with ordinary as well as not so ordinary problems and challenges in life. Parents and psychologists develop theories on how to raise children, and financial analysts develop theories about the stock market. The general purpose of a **theory** is to describe, explain, and predict how humans behave or how things work in the real world under specific circumstances. A theory is an orderly, logical, integrated set of ideas or statements regarding the natural environment, human behavior, and so on. All theories tend to simplify more complex realities. **Development theory** tries to explain how countries achieve specific economic and political improvements that are based on assumptions or things we take for granted. However, because different individuals and groups often make different assumptions, competing theories develop on how to achieve an objective.

Even though we try to find the one best theory, the complexity of reality demands the applications of several theories. Consequently, theories tend not only to compete, but also to overlap. Most scholars reject the view that there is a single theory of development. A theory often contains a strategy or strategies of how to make things work, and how to achieve the desired results. Economic development theory and practice vary from one period of history to another and from place to place. Medieval thinkers in Europe examined economic issues through the lens of Catholicism. Later, Protestants, especially Calvinists and Puritans, linked discipline, hard work, and high-quality work with honoring God. Economic theories, such as mercantilism, focused on economic development as an essential ingredient of national power. Theories change to take into account new developments; changing values and assumptions; and new social, economic, technological, and political realities. Societies borrow ideas about how to obtain higher standards of living and a better quality of life from other societies. Western Europeans borrowed ideas from the Chinese, the Arabs, the Turks, and the Egyptians to help Europe develop. European development later became a model for the rest of the world. Most theories of development are based on Western industrialization and modernization or in reaction to them. Marxism, dependency theory, Third World socialism, and other theories are, to some extent, influenced by Western models of development. Some scholars distinguish between individualist and structural theories. Individualism focuses on individuals as determinants of a country's economic performance, whereas structuralism views the structures of society and the global system as governing individual responses.[7]

Modernization Theory or Developmentalism

As many developing countries gained their independence after World War II, many advocates of economic development believed that the former colonies should emulate the capitalist, industrialized countries to achieve economic growth and build modern political institutions. A central belief was that all societies go through similar stages of development. Britain and France, for example, were once agrarian societies in which most of the inhabitants produced enough food for themselves. As technology improved, industrialization increased and more people found jobs making things for the rest of society. Improvements in agricultural methods resulted in greater agricultural productivity, which led to an increase in migration of people previously employed in farming from rural areas to the newly emerging urban

theory

Predicts how humans behave or how things work in the world under certain circumstances.

development theory

Explains how countries achieve economic improvements.

TABLE 6.1 MACROECONOMIC STRUCTURE

Country	GDP (US $ Billions) 2002	Primary Exports (% of Merchandise Exports) 2002	Manufactured Exports (% of Merchandise Exports) 2002	High-Technology Exports (% of Manufactured Exports) 2002
United States	**10,383.1**	**14**	**81**	**32**
Republic of Korea	467.7	8	92	32
Chile	64.2	80	18	3
Costa Rica	16.8	37	63	37
Mexico	637.2	16	84	21
Thailand	126.9	22	74	31
Philippines	78.0	8	50	65
Saudi Arabia	188.5	91	10	—
Brazil	452.4	44	54	19
Jamaica	7.9	27	64	—
Turkey	183.7	15	84	2
China	1,266.1	10	90	23
South Africa	104.2	37	63	5
Indonesia	172.9	44	54	16
Egypt	89.9	47	35	1
Zimbabwe	8.3	62	38	3
India	510.2	22	75	5
Ghana	6.2	85	16	3
Kenya	12.3	76	24	10
Pakistan	59.1	14	85	1
Nigeria	43.5	100	—	—
Bangladesh	47.6	8	92	—
Zambia	3.7	86	14	2
Haiti	3.4	—	—	—
Ethiopia	6.1	86	14	—

Source: United Nations Development Program, *Human Development Report 2004* (New York: Oxford University Press, 2004), 192–95.

centers where most manufacturing jobs were located. Ultimately, these societies became highly industrialized, technologically sophisticated, and predominately urban and service oriented. Subsistence agriculture gave way to mass production and consumerism.

Modernization theory, or developmentalism, embraces the classical economic model and free-market capitalism. It was strongly influenced by **naturalistic theories** in sociology and geography, which stressed the role of environmental factors in development, by Max Weber's emphasis on cultural aspects of development, and by structural functionalism, which combined naturalism with rationalism stressed by Weber. It argues that all countries go through stages of development, from traditional through transitional to modern. These stages are also identified as (1) underdevelopment, (2) take-off, and (3) modernity. The leading proponent of

naturalistic theories
Stress cultural and environmental influences on development.

the stages of development was **Walt W. Rostow.**[8] Traditional societies are characterized by ascription, fatalism, self-sufficiency, an emphasis on the present, loyalty to the family, strong kinship and ethnic groups, weak institutions, low levels of literacy and technology, and widespread superstition. These characteristics are believed to be barriers to development. Transitional societies contain both traditional and modern characteristics. They are far less focused on subsistence agriculture; literacy increases; village values are not as pervasive; and new social, economic, and political institutions emerge to challenge traditional norms and behavior. Modern societies are essentially Westernized. They are achievement oriented, increasingly urban, and literate, and they have a high quality of life and a great degree of personal and political freedom. The modernization theory holds that developing societies would have to change their values; adopt Western technology, economics, and political institutions; and create a climate that would attract foreign investment for industrialization.[9] Industrialization and modernization are largely perceived as synonymous. Modernization was the dominant theory for much of the 1950s and 1960s. Its emphasis on Western Europe and the United States as models of development for the rest of the world and on free-market capitalism was viewed as ethnocentric. It often ignored specific problems and conditions in developing countries and tended to treat African, Asian, and Latin American societies as a monolithic group, despite these areas' historical, cultural, economic, and political differences. Very little effort was made to understand or respect the values and cultures of the developing world.

Walt W. Rostow
The leading proponent of stages of development.

Marxist Theory

Karl Marx (1818–1883), a German economist, philosopher, and revolutionary, and Friedrich Engels (1820–1895), a German socialist and a successful industrialist in Manchester, England, articulated a philosophy of scientific socialism, which became known as Marxism. Marx and Engels developed their theory in numerous books, most notably, *The Communist Manifesto* and *Das Kapital*. **Marxism** is based on the philosophical method known as dialectical materialism, which emphasizes the dominance or primacy of economic determinants of history. The essence of dialectical materialism is that change occurs through the struggle of opposites. From the Marxist perspective, the history of society is essentially the history of class struggle, with those who control the means of production or the wealth occupying the dominant political and social positions. A specific class would rule as long as it represented the economically productive forces in society, but it would be challenged by another class and eventually replaced. Marx and Engels believed that dialectical materialism explained the movement of society away from agrarianism and feudalism to capitalism and ultimately to socialism and communism. All of these changes are determined by economics and are historically inevitable.

Marxism
Stresses the dominance of economic determinants of history and the inevitability of class conflicts.

Marxism holds that when human beings lived in agrarian societies, they were dominated by large landowners or feudalists. A class of artisans and merchants evolved to satisfy the demand of the feudalists for goods and services. When the artisans and merchants acquired wealth, they challenged the feudalists, a class struggle that gave rise to capitalism. Capitalism led to the expansion of the Industrial Revolution, which drew people from the countryside into the growing urban industrial centers. These industrial workers or proletarians were exploited by the owners of capital or the bourgeoisie. Capitalism, by its competitive nature, demanded more sacrifices from the workers to increase profits. From the Marxist view, capitalism led to unprecedented economic development on a global scale. However, it produced high levels of unemployment, subsistence wages, successively more serious economic crises, and other conditions that eventually influenced the workers to unite and overthrow the capitalist system. The workers would create a socialist society, in which the state would own and operate the economy. According to Marxist theory, economic development is determined and controlled by the government. Ultimately, after the economy is developed to the point where it can provide for everyone, the state will wither away because there will be no need for government.

Dependency Theory

Dependency theory, developed by Latin American intellectuals, students, and some religious leaders, is influenced by the Marxist emphasis on class conflict. It is closely related to **world systems theory,** articulated by Immanuel Wallerstein, which views the division of the world into economic groups as originating in the world capitalist economy developed in Western Europe in the sixteenth century. **Dependency theory** sees three classes of countries in the international system: (1) countries at the industrial core, (2) countries of the semiperiphery, and (3) countries at the periphery. The first group is composed of the industrial countries in Western Europe and North America and their multinational corporations. The second group consists of developing countries that have achieved significant levels of economic growth. The third class, the periphery, is the poorest developing countries. The relationship between the core and the periphery was established by colonialism for the benefit of industrial powers. Developing countries, formerly colonies, continue to be largely suppliers of raw materials to and importers of manufactured products from rich industrial countries. Instead of working to the benefit of all, capitalism reinforces dependency and economic inequalities among countries. Dependency theorists believe that economic development can occur primarily by restructuring the global economic and political system in a way that gives the poor a greater share of the world's resources. This view was at the heart of efforts in the United Nations and elsewhere by the **Group of 77** developing countries to create a **New International Economic Order (NIEO).** Dependency theory also advocates cooperation among poor countries in order to diminish their reliance on rich countries. One strategy suggested to accomplish this is the development of domestic industries for domestic consumption. This is also known as **import substitution.** Instead of importing finished products from industrialized countries, poor countries would make their own manufactured goods. From the dependency theory viewpoint, development is accomplished by a mixture of free-market capitalism and state capitalism.

world systems theory
Stresses the role of European capitalism in creating economic groups of countries.

dependency theory
Stresses the relationships among three classes of countries.

Group of 77
A group created by the developing nations that demanded that global wealth be redistributed.

New International Economic Order (NIEO)
An international platform for nations of the South to challenge the comparative strength of Northern countries to exploit weaker countries.

import substitution
The development of domestic industries for domestic consumption.

Third World and African Socialism

Many developing countries adopted variations of what is generally called Third World socialism to distinguish themselves from communist societies. Unlike state capitalism, in which private entrepreneurs are the main economic actors, **Third World socialism** called for less private enterprise and a greater role for government in determining economic priorities and in running industries. The most important features of Third World socialism include (1) industrialization through import substitution, (2) protectionism, (3) fixed exchange rates, (4) the development of state-owned companies, and (5) government control of agricultural prices.[10]

Import substitution was widely perceived as a strategy for stimulating economic growth through industrialization. Starting with the manufacture of textiles, shoes, and other basic consumer goods, governments later supported the manufacturing of construction materials, farm machinery, and the assembly of automobiles for the domestic market. Import substitution gave rise to protectionism because many of the new industries were inefficient, produced poor-quality products, and could not effectively compete with foreign companies. Governments, to protect their industries, violated almost all the rules of free-market capitalism. They imposed high tariffs, restricted how much of a particular product could be imported, and prevented the importation of other goods. Lacking competition, domestic firms had no incentive to become more efficient. Furthermore, even though they made imported goods, including raw materials and machinery needed for industry, cheaper, fixed exchange rates and overvalued currencies also made it more difficult for local producers of agricultural products to compete. In an effort to restrain imports, governments required importers to obtain special licenses and imposed high duties on imports.

A more specific variation of Third World socialism was **African socialism.** In 1967 the leader of Tanzania, Julius K. Nyerere, issued the Arusha Declaration, which called for greater self-reliance and egalitarianism. African socialism, based on the concept of **Ujamaa,** or familyhood, opposed both Marxism and capitalism. Instead, it drew upon African traditions of communalism and humanism. The government controlled many major economic activities.

Community and Grassroots Development

Community and grassroots development is essentially interchangeable. Other theories stress the role of government and multinational companies in development, whereas community and grassroots development assumes that the people most affected by poverty are able to improve their standard of living by using their own resources and adopting strategies that are consistent with their values and local conditions. This is a bottom-up approach to development. Traditional values, rather than being impediments to development, are utilized to promote economic growth and equity. Community development is based on the concept that people with common concerns can work together to deal with those concerns. It attempts to bring responsibility for development back to those who want to escape poverty.[11] An example of this strategy is the **Grameen Bank** in Bangladesh. The Grameen Bank is a small-scale credit program designed to help the poor,

Third World socialism
Calls for less private enterprise and a greater role for government in the economy.

African socialism
A theory that opposes Marxism and capitalism and draws upon African traditions of communalism and humanism.

Ujamaa
Traditional African concept of familyhood.

Grameen Bank
A small-scale credit program designed to help the poor, especially women, become micro-entrepreneurs.

especially women, become micro-entrepreneurs. Grameen's founder, Muhammad Yunus, won the Nobel Peace Prize in 2006. This is discussed in greater detail in Chapter 8.

Feminist Theory

Feminist theory emanates from the long struggle to achieve equal rights for women in Western Europe, the United States, New Zealand, Australia, and many parts of the developing world. Feminist theory, the essence of which is change, concentrates on inequality, poverty, and gender relations. It challenges traditional approaches to development, perceptions of women, and accepted views of women's roles in relation to economic development. Influenced by globalization, feminist theories broadened to include more of the concerns of women in the developing world. By the early 1980s, women were advocating the formulation and recognition of new theories of development that embraced feminism. Feminist theories focus on women's empowerment; active participation in economic development; and improved social, economic, and political conditions.

Sustainable Development

Believing that earth's resources were inexhaustible and viewing development as almost synonymous with the destruction of the natural environment, advocates of development, whether they applied the capitalist or socialist theory, were largely unconcerned with protecting the environment and preserving natural resources for future generations. In the 1960s and 1970s, students, environmental activists, and others challenged the idea of the inevitability of pollution and the destruction of the natural environment. The energy crisis of 1973–1974, which resulted from the oil embargo imposed on the Western industrial economies by the Organization of Arab Petroleum Exporting Countries (OAPEC), underscored the need to rethink the idea of inexhaustible and readily available energy supplies. The disappearance of some animals and plants drew attention to the need to preserve endangered species and to safeguard biodiversity. The destruction of the rain forests of the Amazon and the onset of global warming motivated individuals, groups, governments, and international organizations to treat environmental problems seriously. Out of this new awareness and shifting values came the theory of sustainable development. **Sustainable development** holds that growth is not inconsistent with using resources in such a way that future generations will have access to them and continue to experience both an adequate standard of living and equity. Sustainable development is essentially about recognizing the limits of natural resources and redefining development to reflect this reality.

sustainable development

Favors both growth and conserving natural resources.

FACTORS FACILITATING AND IMPEDING DEVELOPMENT

Nonetheless, major factors influencing development include (1) the values of both the leaders and citizens, (2) natural resources and natural disasters, (3) the international and regional economic environment, (4) population, (5) education and health care, (6) political instability, (7) corruption and economic development, and (8) debt and foreign aid.

Values of the Leaders and Citizens

At the heart of the various theories of development is culture. **Culture** is composed of beliefs, attitudes, values, moral codes, and institutions. Because culture is socially constructed, it is essentially subjective. Both positive and negative factors, which impinge on development, are found within any given culture. Values, which are widely shared assumptions about what is right and wrong, desirable or undesirable, good and bad, or just and unjust, influence how countries develop. The values of economic, social, and political leaders are usually viewed as the main determinants of development. If these leaders are committed to change, development is much more likely than when they want to perpetuate traditions that reject change.

culture

A social construct composed of beliefs, attitudes, values, moral codes, and institutions.

In Iran, for example, prior to the revolution of 1979, which created an Islamic Republic, the leaders embraced modernization. Iran experienced significant economic growth, as it did inequality. When Ayatollah Khomeini and other religious leaders seized power, Westernization was rejected and tradition was strictly enforced. The values of the new rulers, coupled with a war with Iraq, reversed the economic gains made prior to 1979. Asian values have been seen as the major reason for the economic success of Japan, Taiwan, South Korea, Singapore, and now China. These countries, it is argued, follow **Confucianism.** Confucian values spread from China to other parts of Asia. They include social harmony, adherence to a social hierarchy, obedience, loyalty, respect, strict morals, thrift, hard work, collective discipline, trust, and honesty. Japan, for example, stressed ethnic homogeneity and a powerful bureaucracy as important elements of Confucianism. However, these values are found in all societies to greater or lesser degrees. The United States is ethnically diverse and remains the world's leading economic power.

Confucianism

Belief in values that include social harmony, adherence to a social hierarchy, obedience, loyalty, respect, strict morals, trust, and honesty.

Natural Resources and Natural Disasters

Natural resources play a crucial role in the initial stages of development. The United States, with an abundance of natural resources, developed rapidly. Many countries in the developing world have also achieved rapid growth due to their ownership of gold, petroleum, copper, and other raw materials. South Africa's economy was built on gold, diamonds, and other valuable minerals. Saudi Arabia and many other countries in the Middle East used oil revenues to modernize their economies. Botswana also benefited from its diamonds and other resources. Access to resources alone does not determine development. Without effective leadership, entrepreneurship, an adequate infrastructure, access to international and regional markets, values that are conducive to development, and government policies that are designed to encourage economic growth, development is unlikely to occur even in countries with abundant resources. As will be discussed, poor management, corruption, political violence and instability, and weak institutions have combined to prevent resource-rich countries such as Nigeria, Zambia, and Zaire from achieving significant growth and greater equality. In fact, they have actually declined. Most developed countries achieved major breakthroughs in agriculture

Natural resources play a crucial role in the initial stages of development.

that enabled them to industrialize and focus on services. Africa's inability to launch an agricultural revolution is an important impediment to that continent's development. Even though countries such as South Africa and Zimbabwe are generally successful agricultural producers, most of Africa has not gone through the Green Revolution that resulted in large increases in agricultural output in Mexico, the Philippines, India, and elsewhere. Ghana, under the leadership of **Jerry Rawlings**, made agricultural development a national priority. His values and interests facilitated the beginnings of a Green Revolution in Ghana.[12]

Jerry Rawlings
Leader of Ghana.

Natural disasters can also impede or reverse development. Drought, desertification, and floods, caused in part by disregard for sustainable development, overpopulation, and urbanization, often have devastating consequences in the poorest parts of the world and the most economically vulnerable countries. The Red Cross International Federation found that in 1999 drought, flooding, deforestation, and soil problems forced more than 25 million people from their houses.[13] Indonesia experienced its worst drought in fifty years, which, together with forest fires caused by farmers and others, resulted in a sharp decline in agricultural productivity and an increase in food imports. This natural disaster also contributed to wider political and social problems, which escalated into food riots, political violence, and instability in Indonesia. In 1998, Hurricane Mitch caused extensive damage, an estimated $20 billion, to the fragile economies of Central America, a high-risk zone for earthquakes, hurricanes, floods, landslides, and volcanoes. In addition to destroying homes, businesses, and infrastructure, Hurricane Mitch destroyed much of the region's agriculture. Honduras lost much of its banana industry. Chiquita and Dole, two major producers of bananas, were forced to reduce their workforce by more than 70 percent, which further weakened an economy that is heavily dependent on banana exports. Just before the beginning of the tourist season in 1999, Hurricane Lenny destroyed many crops, businesses, hotels, and the infrastructure in much of the Caribbean. In 2004, Hurricanes Jeanne and Ivan caused extensive damage in the Caribbean. Flooding in Haiti caused 3,000 deaths. By far the most devastating natural disaster was the earthquake and tsunami that occurred in Asia on December 26, 2004. More than 165,000 lives were lost and the property damage was unprecedented. Asia continued to suffer from earthquakes and other natural disasters in 2006.

Natural disasters can impede or reverse development.

FIGURE 6.1 Central America

The International and Regional Economic Environment

An important component of the international and regional economic environment is **ideology** or a system of values, beliefs, and ideas. These values, beliefs, and ideas influence economic, social, and political activities.[14] During the period of colonialism, the prevailing ideology justified the economic arrangement between the colonies and the colonial powers. When the Cold War, an ideological struggle between the Soviet Union and the West, the United States in particular, began after World War II, the international environment was instrumental in both facilitating and stifling development. The United States and the Soviet Union assisted development efforts to demonstrate the superiority of their ideology. Countries such as Taiwan and South Korea benefited from this competition. However, many African countries suffered economically and politically as leaders focused on their own interests and used the East-West rivalry to advance their own interests. Development of a major country or group of counties in a region usually benefits other countries. The strong American economy contributes to the growth of Mexico's economy, and a prosperous South Africa benefits Botswana, Lesotho, and other countries in southern Africa. People from poorer neighboring states migrate to richer countries to find employment. The money sent home by migrant workers can help to stimulate development. **Regional economic development banks,** which provide loans for various economic projects and regional economic integration, often increase the development prospects of the member-states. Regional groupings, as well as individual countries, achieve greater economic growth and equity when the global economy is strong. Rich countries are more likely to grant poor countries greater access to their markets. On the other hand, a strong global economy may depend on the availability of inexpensive natural resources, thereby making exporters of these resources more vulnerable. Declining oil prices, for example, are widely viewed as positive development for oil-importing countries but are usually a disaster for members of OPEC.[15] This situation was reversed in 2006, as oil prices rose to more than $70 a barrel.

Although a strong international economy stimulates demand for some raw materials, it also reduces demand for others. For example, the strength of the U.S. currency and the American economy diminished the need of investors to protect their assets by buying and keeping gold. As the demand for gold decreased, prices also declined. The decision of Britain to sell gold further reduced prices. The implications of this international economic development are serious for South Africa, the world's largest producer of gold, and poor countries such as Mali, Tanzania, Uganda, and Ghana. Many of them had planned to expand gold production as an important component of their effort to further their development. Between 1997 and 1999, the price of gold fell from $325 an ounce to $255 an ounce. Approximately 103,000 gold-mining jobs were lost in South Africa. Mozambique and other neighboring countries that depend on gold mining in South Africa for employment were seriously affected by low gold prices.[16] However, by 2006, the price of gold had climbed to more than $660 an ounce.

Globalization profoundly affects development. Globalization has changed the way countries, as well as nonstate actors, interact. It has also diminished the ability of governments to exercise control over economic, political, and social developments within countries. Economic globalization also means that a crisis in one region usually affects

ideology

A system of values, beliefs, and ideas.

regional economic development banks

Banks that provide loans for various projects and regional economic integration.

other regions. For example, the Asian economic crisis of the late 1990s negatively affected Africa, Latin America, and other parts of the world. However, between 2002 and 2007, developing economies grew two and a half times as fast as developed economies.

Globalization profoundly affects development.

Globalization makes it easier for countries to develop if they have the essential technology and skills. Industries, or parts of industries, can be located virtually anywhere and, contrary to the view of dependency theorists, the hierarchy of core and periphery is becoming less meaningful. Companies from rich countries transfer assembly plants and information technology to developing countries that have the necessary infrastructure and skills. India, for example, is fast becoming an important center in the computer-dominated world. Location is largely irrelevant in the new global society. Companies reduce data-processing and other computer-related costs by moving their operations to India.[17]

Population

The size and growth rate of a country's population directly affects its development. A small population can impede development. Fewer consumers generally influence businesses to increase prices to cover basic operating costs. A small population is also likely to discourage most investments, partly because of the inability of fewer people to provide the infrastructure essential for industries to operate. Educational, health, recreational, and shopping facilities require a sufficient number of users to make them economical. In other words, small populations may prevent the realization of **economies of scale.** Economies of scale deal with the relationship between output and costs. Industries and organizations that are larger generally have a greater output and lower production costs. Most countries solve problems associated with small populations by pooling their resources and cooperating to achieve economies of scale. Relatively inexpensive transportation costs and the revolution in communications technology have enabled places with small populations to diminish some of their disadvantages.

economies of scale
Theory concerned with the relationship between output and costs.

Overpopulated countries are generally poor countries. Most of the societies with the largest populations and the highest growth rates are in the developing world. Roughly 97 percent of the growth of the world's population is occurring in Africa, Asia, and Latin America. Industrialized countries, such as Japan and countries in Western Europe, are experiencing declining growth rates and an aging population, which also have implications for development. An older population generally requires more expensive care than a younger population, but the strength of industrial economies and controlled immigration from the developing countries reduce the likelihood of serious economic problems arising in rich societies. The demographic differences between rich countries and poor countries are shown in Tables 6.2 and 6.3.

In India, where roughly 360 million people live in dire poverty and where 400 million people are illiterate, the population grows by about 33 persons a minute, 2,000 an hour, or 48,000 per day. By 2025, India will surpass China as the world's most populous country, with about 1.5 billion people, compared with China's 1.4 billion people. Asia alone, with the world's highest poverty rates, will account for more than half of the increase in the world's population in the next fifty years. China and India alone

TABLE 6.2 DEMOGRAPHIC TRENDS

Country	Total Population (Million)			Annual Population Growth Rate (%)		Population Aged 65 and Above (as % of Total)	
	1975	2002	2015	1975–2002	2002–2015	2002	2015
United States	**220.2**	**291**	**329.7**	**1.0**	**1.0**	**12.2**	**14.2**
Japan	111.5	127.5	127.2	0.5	—	18.2	26.0
Sweden	8.2	8.9	9.0	0.3	0.1	17.9	21.4
United Kingdom	55.4	59.1	61.3	0.2	0.3	15.9	17.8
France	52.7	59.8	62.8	0.5	0.4	16.2	18.5
Germany	78.7	82.4	82.5	0.2	—	17.1	20.8
Italy	55.4	57.5	55.5	0.1	20.3	18.7	22.3
Venezuela	12.7	25.2	31.2	2.5	1.6	4.6	6.6
Mexico	59.1	102	119.6	2.0	1.2	5.0	6.8
Thailand	41.4	62.2	69.6	1.5	0.9	5.8	8.1
Philippines	42.0	78.6	96.3	2.3	1.6	3.7	4.9
Saudi Arabia	7.3	23.5	32.7	4.4	2.5	2.7	3.4
Brazil	108.0	176.3	202.0	1.8	1.0	5.4	7.5
China	927.8	1294.9	1402.3	1.2	0.6	7.1	9.4
Indonesia	134.4	217.1	250.4	1.8	1.1	5.1	6.4
Egypt	39.3	70.5	90.0	2.2	1.9	4.6	5.4
India	620.7	1049.5	1246.4	1.9	1.3	6.3	5.4
Ghana	9.9	20.5	26.4	2.7	1.9	4.1	6.9
Pakistan	70.3	149.9	214.5	2.8	2.4	3.7	4.0
Nigeria	54.9	120.9	161.7	2.9	2.2	3.1	3.4
Bangladesh	75.2	143.8	181.4	2.4	1.8	3.8	6.2
Zambia	5.1	10.7	12.7	2.8	1.3	3.0	3.2
Ethiopia	3.1	69.0	93.3	2.7	2.4	2.9	3.2

Source: United Nations Development Program, *Human Development Report 2004* (New York: Oxford University Press, 2004), 152–55.

account for one out of every three children added to the global population. Africa is also growing rapidly, despite the devastating effects of AIDS. Comparing Europe and Africa illustrates the problem. Europe's population was three times larger than Africa's in 1900. By 2050, Africa will have more than three times the population of Europe.[18] Nigeria alone is projected to have 244 million people, Ethiopia 170 million, and Congo 160 million by 2050.

The rate of population change threatens the earth's carrying capacity. **Carrying capacity** refers to the maximum number of humans or animals a given area can support without creating irreversible destruction of the environment and, ultimately, of humans and animals themselves. Carrying capacity depends not just on the amount of available resources, but also on the values of the population. This means that overpopulation is a problem for rich countries as well as poor countries, depending on how they utilize their resources. Because rich countries consume more than poor countries, rich countries overtax the world's resources despite their smaller populations.

carrying capacity
The maximum number of humans and animals a given area can support without creating irreversible destruction.

TABLE 6.3 POPULATION

Country	Infant Mortality Rate per 1,000 Live Births		Contraceptive Prevalence Rate % of Women Aged 15–49	Total Fertility Rate Births per Woman	
	1980	2002	1995–2002	1970–1975	2000–2005
Angola	153	154	6	6.6	7.1
Bangladesh	132	51	54	6.2	3.5
Brazil	67	30	77	4.7	2.2
Chile	32	10	—	3.6	2.4
China	42	1	84	4.9	1.8
Egypt	120	35	56	5.7	3.3
Ethiopia	155	114	8	6.8	6.1
Ghana	100	57	22	6.9	4.1
Haiti	123	79	27	5.8	4.0
India	116	67	48	5.4	3.0
Jamaica	21	17	66	5.0	2.4
Kenya	72	78	39	8.1	4.0
Mexico	51	24	67	6.5	2.5
Mozambique	155	125	6	6.6	5.6
Nigeria	99	110	15	6.9	5.4
Pakistan	124	83	28	6.3	5.1
Philippines	52	29	47	6.0	3.2
Saudi Arabia	65	23	32	7.3	4.5
Singapore	12	3	62	2.6	1.4
South Africa	67	52	56	5.4	2.6
Zambia	90	108	34	7.8	5.6
Zimbabwe	82	76	4	7.6	3.9
Asia/Pacific	56	32	—	5.0	2.0
Latin America Caribbean	59	27	—	5.1	2.5
Middle East/N. Africa	96	48	—	6.7	3.8
South Asia	120	69	—	5.6	3.3
Sub-Saharan Africa	115	108	—	6.8	5.4
United States	**13**	**7**	**76**	**2.0**	**2.1**

Sources: World Bank, *World Development Report 1998* (New York: Oxford University Press, 1999), 202–3; and United Nations Development Program, *Human Development Report 2004* (New York: Oxford University Press, 2004), 152–59, 168–71.

For example, the average American consumes more than fourteen times as much as the average Bangladeshi consumes. However, most people do not want to live like people in Bangladesh. Because many desire to live like Americans, the world's carrying capacity will be reached with fewer people.

Education, especially for women, plays a crucial role in reducing fertility rates. It helps to determine other factors affecting population growth rates such as contraceptive usage, the age of marriage and childbearing, social status, employment opportunities outside the home, and residence. Educated women usually postpone childbearing, acquire information about their societies and cultures, become more aware of both employment opportunities and social options, are less constrained by traditional values, are more likely to use effective contraceptives, and exercise greater control over their economic and reproductive lives. Educated women have fewer children because

Educational achievement helps lower fertility rates.

they realize that in order to provide their offspring with a standard of living similar to or higher than their own, they will have to budget their resources carefully and concentrate them on a small family. Where women live also influences their fertility rates. Urban residents have fewer children, whereas women who work in agriculture in rural areas have larger families. Apart from the constraints of tradition, women in rural areas are likely to be less educated than women who live in cities.[19]

Government policies also promote population control in order to accelerate economic development. Many developing societies, especially those that embrace state capitalism, stress family planning and make contraceptives widely available. Although most countries rely on education to convince women in particular to have fewer children, India and China have adopted more aggressive approaches to control population

Exceptions to the one child policy are allowed.

growth. During the 1970s, Prime Minister Indira Gandhi of India implemented policies that allowed forced mass sterilization, an approach that Indians violently rejected. When Deng Xiao Ping decided to reform China's economy in 1979, he implemented the **one child policy.** China established a State Family Planning Bureau to formulate policies and procedures for enforcing the one child policy. Family planning committees at the local level are responsible for rewarding those who comply and punishing those who violate the One Child Pledge. However, although the one child policy is still officially in place, it has in practice been virtually abandoned because it is largely unenforceable in the cities and because about 100 million Chinese are constantly migrating. Under the one child policy, a couple can have only one child except in the following cases: (1) if the first child has a defect, (2) in the case of a remarriage in which one partner does not have a child, (3) if couples are involved in jobs such as mining, and (4) if both partners come from families with one child. The government strictly monitors women's contraceptive practices, although this is diminishing. Women are encouraged, and sometimes forced, to be sterilized, especially after the birth of a second child. Women are often pressured to have abortions. Failure to comply with the one child policy may result in the loss of benefits for the first child, fines, the loss of state employment, and seizure of property. Those who comply receive a monthly stipend until the child is fourteen years old; get preferential treatment when applying for housing, education, and health benefits for the child; and are granted a pension when they are old. In rural areas, where the one child policy is less rigidly enforced and often ignored, those who comply may receive a larger allocation of land, which is owned and controlled by the government.[20] By 2007, China was concerned about a shortage of girls and a rapidly aging population.

one child policy

Deng Xiao Ping's policy that limited couples to having one child.

Education and Health Care

As discussed in Chapter 5, rich societies are distinguished from poor societies not only by measures such as per capita income and GDP, but also by the number of physicians and nurses, access to clean water, sanitation, and literacy rates. Education is an essential foundation of development. Advances in agricultural productivity, the invention of industrial technologies and labor-saving devices, the growth of entrepreneurship, and the development of a productive labor force depend on access to information and training. Education challenges traditional values and social arrangements, empowers both women and men, and helps individuals actively participate in shaping their societies. Basic education allows farmers to read instructions for using modern agricultural techniques, enables them to develop effective marketing strategies, and improves their ability to obtain more resources from the government. American farmers are extremely successful partly because of their educational achievements, whereas African farmers are the least productive largely because of low literacy rates that range from 20 to 30 percent. Countries such as Taiwan, South Korea, and Singapore not only raised literacy rates, but also provided vocational, scientific, and engineering training to their citizens. In Taiwan, the government allocated 7.8 percent of its budget to education in 1952. By 1972, government spending on education had increased to 17.6 percent of the budget. Africa, which has experienced economic decline, spent only $15 per student in 1987, compared with $32 in 1980.[21]

Education is an essential foundation of development.

Many developing countries are caught in a vicious cycle of poor health and widespread poverty. Poor health reduces productivity, impedes access to education, limits mobility, diminishes employment opportunities, and places a severe economic and social burden on families and on the society as a whole. Countries in Asia that have experienced rapid industrialization heavily subsidized health care. They realized that an unhealthy population is detrimental to achieving economic development. Africa, the least developed continent, is plagued by diseases that have impeded both agricultural growth and industrialization. Africa's poverty reinforces its health problems. Few Africans can afford to buy drugs to treat diseases. Throughout the developing world, AIDS is severely undermining economic development efforts. India, Cambodia, China, Thailand, Brazil, Haiti, and most countries in Africa are seriously affected by the AIDS epidemic. Cultural values, inadequate medical resources, and low levels of education contribute to the rapid spread of AIDS in poor countries in general and in Africa in particular. Of the 34 million people with AIDS worldwide, 25 million of them are in Africa. More than 5,000 people with AIDS die each day in Africa. It is estimated that by 2007 more people in Africa had died from AIDS than from the bubonic plague, which killed 20 million people in Europe in the fourteenth century.[22]

AIDS is severely undermining economic development efforts.

AIDS is undoubtedly one of the most serious threats to Africa's development. It reduces valuable human resources, increases health and welfare costs, diverts resources away from productive investments, destroys communities, and further contributes to the economic and social marginalization of Africa. Asia, where AIDS is growing the fastest, will soon face many of the economic problems now confronting Africa. At Zambia's largest

TAKING ACTION

Brazil Fights AIDS

When AIDS became a major global health issue in the early 1980s, Brazil was one of the countries hardest hit by the deadly disease. Instead of denying that the problem existed as many governments in Africa, Asia, and other parts of Latin America and the Caribbean attempted to do, the Brazilian government adopted an aggressive strategy to prevent the spread of AIDS. Efforts were made to encourage Brazilians to talk about and use condoms, to talk about sex, and to talk publicly about people infected with AIDS. The government works with nonprofit organizations that provide support for AIDS victims. Brazil also manufactured its own generic AIDS drugs and distributed them free of charge to patients. As a result of these actions, less than 1 percent of Brazilians are infected with HIV.

cement company, absenteeism has increased dramatically since 1992. Uganda's railroad company loses 15 percent of its workforce each year. Barclay's Bank of Zambia has lost about 25 percent of its senior managers to AIDS. Forty percent of Uganda's military forces are infected with AIDS. Classrooms in Malawi are deserted because a third of the teachers have AIDS. Rural areas are also suffering. Many farmers are too sick to grow crops to feed their families, and many family members are too busy caring for those infected with AIDS to cultivate the land. Malnutrition is increasing, making more people vulnerable to contracting a variety of diseases. In 1998, for example, the production of corn by Zimbabwe's small farmers dropped by 61 percent because of illness and death from AIDS. Anti-AIDS campaigns have been launched throughout the developing world.[23]

AIDS is one of the most serious threats to Africa's development.

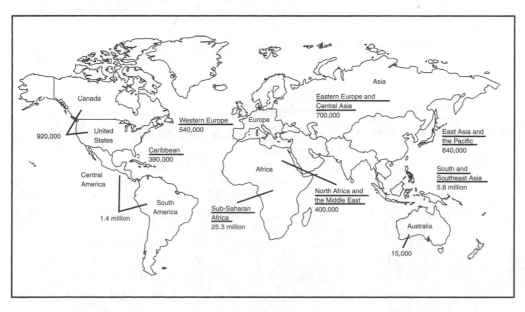

FIGURE 6.2 Number of People Infected with HIV/AIDS (36.1 million total)

Political Instability

Political instability and violence stifle development and, in many cases, have forced countries into economic decline. However, the process of development itself sometimes creates instability and violence, largely by destroying old institutions and values before new ones can be built to replace them and by bringing different groups into closer physical proximity. The challenge of development is to manage the forces of change that cause instability and violence while strengthening political, social, and economic institutions to achieve economic growth and social equity.

Political instability reinforces other impediments to development. Violence and instability have forced the best-educated and most talented citizens to leave, taking with them financial resources and skills essential for development. Civil wars increase risks for investors, destroy personal and state-owned property, seriously disrupt agricultural productivity and industrial activities, make normal trading arrangements difficult, disrupt communications by destroying the infrastructure, and consume valuable scarce natural resources. Nigeria, a country with abundant natural resources, experienced long periods of instability since its independence. In the late 1960s, it fought a civil war in which roughly 1.5 million people died. The Ibo, one of three main ethnic groups in the country, attempted to form a separate country, called **Biafra.** This part of the country, the eastern region, has large supplies of petroleum. Control over petroleum would have enabled Biafra to prosper as an independent country but would have harmed the rest of Nigeria. The government has deliberately kept the Niger Delta underdeveloped. The Delta produces about 2 million barrels of oil daily. Environmental degradation is widespread. Frustrated by their economic condition, residents of the Niger Delta have resorted to violence to change their situation. They routinely kidnap oil workers, damage oil pipelines, and take over oil stations. To safeguard the oil industry, Western oil companies that operate in the Delta provide electricity and water and build roads, bridges, schools, and hospitals—services for which governments are usually responsible.[24]

Political instability reinforces other impediments to development.

Biafra

The eastern region of Nigeria that has large supplies of petroleum.

Corruption and Economic Development

One of the most formidable obstacles to economic growth and social equity is widespread corruption. Corruption is endemic in Africa, Asia, and Latin America, with the poorest countries having the most serious problems. Indeed, many of these societies fail to achieve high levels of development precisely because corruption drains scarce resources away from vital public services and infrastructure projects. Much of the illegally obtained money is invested abroad to protect it—money that could be invested at home. Prime ministers, presidents, civil servants, politicians, and average citizens participate in bureaucratic corruption. **Bureaucratic corruption** is the illegal use of an official position or title for private gain.[25] This may include using your office to obtain bribes, stealing state property, embezzling public money, hiring your relatives for government jobs, and selectively enforcing the law or the delivery of public services.

bureaucratic corruption

The illegal use of an official position or title for personal gain.

Corruption makes everything in a society more expensive for most citizens. The average person has to pay public officials just to receive basic services. Citizens also have to pay higher prices for food, construction materials, automobiles, and other consumer goods because government officials cooperate with local businesspeople to overcharge the public or because government officials demand illegal payments from merchants. Customs officials usually must be bribed for individuals and companies to conduct legal and illegal trade. Bureaucratic corruption robs the state of money directly and indirectly. In some cases, corrupt officials simply take money from various government enterprises or pocket money that was allocated to build schools or bridges. In other cases, kickbacks and other illegal payments to officials drive up the cost of government contracts, equipment, and supplies. Roads may be poorly constructed, inferior materials may be used for building, and the state may be routinely overcharged for services. Official corruption spills over into the general population and becomes a way of life. Ultimately, costs escalate for almost everyone, cynicism grows, and political and social discourse that is essential for development is stifled because of repressive tactics that accompany corruption. Social, economic, and political institutions are weakened.

Corruption makes everything more expensive for most citizens.

There are several reasons for corruption in Africa, Asia, and Latin America. (1) Public officials are not held accountable for their actions by the people. Low levels of political participation, high levels of illiteracy, and other social and economic problems prevent the emergence of responsible governance or **good governance.** (2) Public servants believe that employment in government is more about private gain than public service. (3) Growing economic hardship is another reason for corruption. In many developing countries, public servants have to wait several months before they are paid because the governments do not have any money or because paying public servants is not a priority. Many public servants engage in corrupt activities to maintain their economic status or to survive. (4) Because politicians also engage in corruption, average persons find it easy to justify their own illegal behavior. (5) Values also contribute to corruption. What is usually seen as corruption in industrialized countries may be regarded as a legitimate social transaction. Loyalty to family, friends, and ethnic groups is still strong in most developing societies. (6) Finally, corruption is widespread because governments control much of the economy.[26]

There are six major reasons for corruption.

good governance
Responsible, responsive, and accountable government.

Nigeria has been consistently rated as one of the most corrupt countries in the world by **Transparency International,** a Belgian-based organization that monitors corruption. Nigerians generally regard corruption as a way of life, despite repeated promises by government officials and politicians to eliminate it. Despite its abundant natural resources, Nigeria has been declining economically, with its per capita income dropping from about $950 in 1985 to $328 in 2002. President **Olusegun Obasanjo,** Nigeria's first democratically elected leader in fifteen years, said that corruption was the greatest single cause of misery in society and had distorted and retrogressed society. He believed that unless corruption was fought decisively there could be no economic development in Nigeria.[27] Corruption has caused gasoline

Transparency International
A Belgian-based organization that monitors corruption.

Olusegun Obasanjo
Nigeria's first democratically elected president in fifteen years.

NEWS IN THE

Drugs and Corruption in Mexico

A court in Mexico upheld the seventy-one-year prison sentence on Jesús Gutierrez Rebollo, the former head of the National Institute to Combat Drugs.

Rebollo, the Mexican drug czar, was convicted on drugs and weapons charges. He received gifts, payments, and real estate from leaders of some of Mexico's most ruthless drug cartels.

shortages in a country that is a major oil producer and exporter. Because corrupt officials diverted more than $2 billion from state-owned refineries, refineries were unable to function and gas pipelines were never completed. As a result, Nigeria was forced to import refined fuels at higher costs and Nigerians waited in mile-long lines for gas.

In India, billions of dollars are stolen from the government's power stations. Customers bribe electrical company workers to slow down the meters, and bureaucrats and politicians sell jobs to supervising engineers. In Uttar Pradesh, India's most populous state and one of its poorest, more than 40 percent of the power generated is stolen. As in Nigeria, power failures are common, leaving factories idle and retarding economic growth.[28]

Debt, Foreign Aid, and Development

Weak economies often find themselves burdened with large external debt. Many countries borrowed heavily from commercial banks to finance development projects during the 1980s when interest rates were high. At the same time, prices for raw materials from the developing world declined, thereby preventing many countries from repaying their debts. Interest payments on the external debt deprived the countries of money that could have been used for development. The inability or unwillingness of governments to repay their debts further eroded their countries' access to additional credit from commercial banks. To prevent countries from defaulting on their loans, the **International Monetary Fund (IMF)** makes financing available. The IMF was created in 1944 to encourage world trade and international cooperation and to help countries with **balance of payments** problems.[29] A country's balance of payments is its record of economic transactions with other countries. If a country buys more from abroad than it sells abroad, it has a balance of payments problem and has to find ways to finance the difference. Poor countries often rely on the IMF to help them with balance of payments difficulties. However, the IMF's loans are given on the condition that governments adopt economic policies determined by the IMF. These include severely reducing government spending to balance the budget, eliminating trade barriers, cutting social subsidies, encouraging exports, devaluing currencies, and removing artificial barriers to foreign investment. Although these policies are intended to help

International Monetary Fund

An organization created to encourage world trade and international cooperation.

balance of payments

A country's record of economic transactions with other countries.

the poor countries, they have often resulted in increased income inequality, social strife, and poverty.

Overseas development assistance or foreign aid is usually designed to promote economic development. Organizations such as the United Nations and the U.S. Agency for International Development (AID) are actively supporting projects in agriculture, public health, housing, public administration, industry, trade, and many other areas. Foreign aid is a transfer of resources such as money, food, and technical assistance. These transfers are often gifts. Others, such as loans, are given on very favorable terms. Table 6.4 shows the major aid donors. Despite receiving substantial amounts of foreign aid, many countries have failed to achieve significant economic development. In many cases, governments abuse foreign aid. Governments have used food aid as a weapon against their adversaries. Much of the foreign aid has also been taken by corrupt officials for private gain. Aid is also seen as encouraging economic dependence and as detrimental to economic growth. For example, food aid may actually contribute to the decline of agriculture in a poor country by pushing local farmers off the market. In response to these problems, many donors have made aid conditional. To receive assistance, countries must eradicate corruption, implement economic reforms, and practice good government. Governments are also relying more on nongovernmental organizations (NGOs), groups that are not part of a government, to distribute aid in countries where corruption is a serious problem or where human rights and democratic practices are violated.[30]

TABLE 6.4 OFFICIAL DEVELOPMENT ASSISTANCE

| | Net ODA Disbursed | | | | |
| | Total (US $ Millions) | Gross National Income As % of GNI | | ODA per Capita of Donor Country | |
Country	2002	1990	2002	1990	2001 (US$)
United States	13,140	0.21	0.13	58	46
Norway	1,517	1.17	0.89	283	333
Japan	9,731	0.31	0.23	87	76
Sweden	1,848	0.91	0.83	170	207
Netherlands	3,068	0.92	0.81	164	190
United Kingdom	4,581	0.27	0.31	52	78
Canada	2,011	0.44	0.28	80	64
France	5,125	0.68	0.38	111	86
Switzerland	863	0.32	0.32	109	118
Germany	4,980	0.42	0.27	90	60
Denmark	1,540	0.94	0.96	213	286

Source: United Nations Development Program, *Human Development Report 2004* (New York: Oxford University Press, 2004), 196.

Summary and Review

Although change is a necessary part of life, some people often receive it negatively. Thus development, which encompasses change, is perceived differently by different people and different countries. However, with globalization and increasing interdependence among countries, countries throughout the world are concerned with issues of development. Numerous factors contribute to change, including a country's values, ideologies, institutions, resources, and technology. Many scholars believe that development is synonymous with industrialization and modernization. Developing an infrastructure is key to development. Even though development includes social and political aspects, the ultimate measure of development and growth of a country is through economic changes seen in the gross domestic product. Economic changes are also essential for social and equity changes that affect the quality of life. Governments are the major actors in development. Developing countries need social order, revenue, law enforcement, education, and health care to develop. These areas are largely in the hands of the government, although the global community has an increasing responsibility to help those countries struggling to develop.

Numerous theories have been created in order to advance development. These include (1) modernization theory or developmentalism, (2) Marxist theory, (3) dependency theory, (4) Third World and African socialism, (5) grassroots development, and (6) sustainable development. Modernization theory is based on the classical model and free-market capitalism. Competition, investment, and privatization are emphasized, as modernization theorists believe that all countries go through a series of stages on the way to development. Another theory of development is Marxist theory, which emphasizes dialectical materialism as the explanation of the movement of society away from agrarianism and feudalism to capitalism and ending in socialism and communism. Marxism relies heavily on the notion of class conflicts in each of the stages of development and views the elimination of these conflicts along with overcoming the dehumanizing effects of private property as the ultimate goal of development. The next theory is dependency theory, which states that the world economy is imbalanced and unfair and benefits industrialized nations. This inequity makes it extremely difficult for developing countries to get out of their current position. Third World socialism is another view that advocates the government taking a large role in the economy and favors less private enterprise involvement. African socialism is a specific type of Third World socialism that is based on the concept of familyhood and opposes both Marxism and capitalism. Some theorists also believe development must begin at the grassroots level through the community. Community successes and failures can be teaching examples of how to develop overall. In this type of development, traditional values are embraced. All contemporary theories of development are faced with a new argument about the limits of natural resources. Sustainable development argues that at current consumption rates, resources are running out, but development can be changed in order to not consume all resources to the detriment of future generations. Clearly, there are a variety of theories on development, originating from all parts of the world.

Development theories must also take into account factors that may impede or facilitate development when forming a plan of action. Some common factors impeding development are a lack of natural resources, hostile regional or international economic environment, high or low populations, poor health care, ethnic conflict, political instability, corruption, and a lack of foreign aid. The opposite of all the aforementioned can be facilitators of development as well. Natural disasters are major impediments to development. A lack of natural resources makes it extremely difficult for self-sufficiency. The AIDS epidemic in the developing world is also incapacitating their populations. Foreign aid, even when provided, can also cause problems for the developing world because of stipulations the developing world must follow in order to get aid.

Key Terms

development   108
growth   108
infrastructure   109
gross national
   product   109
gross domestic
   product   109
self-sufficiency   109
equity and human
   development   110

North American Free
   Trade Agreement
   111
free-market
   capitalism   111
state capitalism   112
modernization
   theory   113
dependency
   theory   116

Third World socialism
   117
African socialism   117
community
   development   117
sustainable
   development   118
ideology   121
economies of scale
   122

one child policy   125
AIDS   126
International
   Monetary Fund
   130
balance of payments
   130

Discussion Questions

1. How is growth commonly measured for countries? Are these valid measurements?
2. How are economic and political development linked?
3. Explain the importance of infrastructure to developing countries.
4. Discuss the stages of the modernization theory.
5. What is state capitalism and how is it different from free-market capitalism?
6. What are the features of Third World socialism? Is Third World socialism different from communism? Why or why not?

7. What do you think are the most important factors impeding development?
8. Can Africa ever gain an educated and healthy society?
9. Can development occur in a politically unstable country? Can development occur without creating political instability?
10. What role do foreign powers and their aid play in development?

Suggested Readings

Ben-David, Dan, Håkan Nordström, and L. Alan Winters. *Trade, Income Disparity and Poverty*. Geneva: WTO, 2000.

Goldin, Ian and Kenneth Reinert. *Globalization for Development*. London: Palgrave Macmillan, 2006.

Hansen, Keith. "A Plague's Bottom Line," *Foreign Policy* 137 (July/August 2003): 26–27.

Heineman, Ben, and Fritz Heinman, "The Long War Against Corruption," *Foreign Affairs* 85, no. 3 (May/June 2006): 75–86.

Kapstein, Ethan B. *Economic Justice in an Unfair World.* Princeton, NJ: Princeton University Press, 2006.

Lincoln, Edward J. *East Asian Economic Regionalism.* Washington, D.C.: Brookings Institution Press, 2004.

Schramm, Carl J. "Building Entrepreneurial Economies." *Foreign Affairs* 83, no. 4 (July/August 2004): 104–15.

Siegle, Joseph T., et al. "Why Democracies Excel." *Foreign Affairs* 83, no. 5 (Sept./Oct. 2004): 57–71.

Wiarda, Howard J. *Non-Western Theories of Development.* Fort Worth, TX: Harcourt Brace and Company, 1999, VII–VIII.

Addresses and Websites

International Labour Office—ILO
4, route des Morillons
CH-1211 Geneva 22
Switzerland
Tel: 41–22–799–6111
Fax: 41–22–798–8685
http://www.ilo.org/public/english/bureau/inst/bulletin/ictchlng.htm

The International Labour Office is an organization that revolves around various workers' rights. The ILO works on issues such as workers' rights, labor laws, equitable pay, child labor, and improvement of working conditions. The organization's membership consists of nations spanning the globe. Information on labor-related issues, including the ILO's own publications, can be found on the ILO homepage. This particular link on the ILO website provides information of development and the challenges that it faces.

International Centre for Trade and Sustainable Development—ICTSD
13 chemin des Anémones
1219 Châtelaine
Geneva, Switzerland
Tel: 41–22–917–8492
Fax: 41–22–917–8093
http://www.ictsd.org/

This website for the ICTSD offers information regarding the organization and sustainable development and trade. The organization works with policymakers and intergovernmental and nongovernmental entities on environmental and developmental issues by instigating a dialogue between the groups. Ultimately, this group looks to facilitate discussion on sustainable development.

The website can offer further information including links to their weekly and monthly publications.

Office of Public Information
The Carter Center
453 Freedom Parkway
Atlanta, GA 30307
Tel: (404) 331–3900
http://www.cartercenter.org/

The Carter Center is an organization that works toward human rights and the relief of human suffering. The organization seeks to promote democracy and freedom, while working on issues such as health and conflict resolution. Because peace and health-related issues are top priorities for the group, the website offers links to the various health and peace programs on which the Carter Center is currently working. Further information regarding the Carter Center and its projects can be found on the website.

International Development Exchange—IDEX
827 Valencia Street Suite 101
San Francisco, CA 94110–1736
Tel: (415) 824–8384
http://www.idex.org/

IDEX is an organization, based within the United States, that works toward economic justice in Asia, Africa, and Latin America. The group works with low-income nations in order to promote their goal of economic justice and to eradicate global inequalities, as well. This website allows the browser to enter into the world of IDEX and its work. The organization currently assists eight nations, and the website offers brief information regarding economic conditions in these nations, along with information on their involvement with them.

Notes

1. Larry Rohter, "Colombia Adjust Economic Figures to Include Crops," *The New York Times*, 22 June 1999, A3.
2. David Stoesz, Charles Guzzetta, and Mark Lusk, *International Development* (Boston: Allyn and Bacon, 1999), 117–18.
3. Altha J. Cravey, *Women and Work in Mexico's Maquiladores* (Lanham, MD: Rowman and Littlefield, 1998), 15.
4. Monte Palmer, *Political Development: Dilemmas and Challenges* (Itasca, IL: F. E. Peacock Publishers, 1997).
5. Ralph Van der Hoeven and Gyorgy Sziraczki, *Lessons from Privatization* (Geneva: International Labor Office, 1997), 4.
6. Howard Stein, "Policy Alternatives to Structural Adjustment in Africa," in Howard Stein, ed., *Asian Industrialization and Africa* (New York: St. Martin's Press, 1995), 18.
7. Howard J. Wiarda, *Non-Western Theories of Development* (Fort Worth, TX: Harcourt Brace and Company, 1999), VII–VIII; and S. Charusheela, Structuralism and Individualism in Economic Analysis (New York: Routledge, 2005), 8.
8. Walt W. Rostow, *The Process of Economic Growth* (New York: W. W. Norton, 1962), 307.
9. John Rapley, *Understanding Development* (Boulder, CO: Lynne Rienner, 1996), 17; and Wiarda, *Non-Western Theories of Development*, 6–7.
10. Michael F. Lofchie, "The New Political Economy of Africa," in David Apter and Carl G. Rosberg, eds. *Political Development and the New Realism in Sub-Saharan Africa* (Charlottesville, VA: University Press of Virginia, 1994), 147–50.
11. Stoesz, Guzzetta, and Lusk, *International Development*, 162.
12. Douglas Brinkley, "Bringing the Green Revolution to Africa," *World Policy Journal* 13, no. 1 (Spring 1996): 59.
13. Elizabeth Olson, "Increasing Disasters Threaten Poorer Countries," *The New York Times*, 24 June 1999, A11.
14. Richard J. Payne, *The Clash with Distant Cultures: Values, Interests, and Force in American Foreign Policy* (Albany, NY: State University of New York Press, 1995), 18.
15. Douglas Jehl, "Where Oil Is Plentiful But Cash Is Short," *The New York Times*, 16 January 1999, A6.
16. Donald G. McNeil, "As Britain Sells Some Gold, South Africa Howls," *The New York Times*, 7 July 1999, C1.
17. Robert Marquand, "Fast, Cheap, and in English, India Clerks for the World," *The Christian Science Monitor*, 30 April 1999, 7; and Mark Kobayashi-Hillary, *Outsourcing to India* (Berlin: Springer-Verlag, 2004).
18. David R. Francis, "Populations Growth Slows, and Elderly Ranks Rise," *The Christian Science Monitor*, 28 October 1998, 6; and Pamela Constable, "India's Clock Just Keeps on Ticking," *The Washington Post National Weekly Edition*, 30 August 1999, 16.
19. United Nations, *The World's Women 1995: Trends and Statistics* (New York: United Nations, 1995), 12–13.
20. Therese Hesketh and Wei Xing Zhu, "The One Child Family Policy," *British Medical Journal* (June 1997): 1685–87.
21. Stein, "Policy Alternatives."
22. Laurie Garrett, "The Lessons of HIV/AIDS," *Foreign Affairs* 84, no. 4 (July/August 2005), 63.
23. Ibid; and "AIDS in India," *The Economist*, 17 April 2004, 21–23.
24. Norimitsu Onishi, "Deep in the Republic of Cheveron," *The New York Times Magazine*, 4 July 1999, 27.
25. Kempe Ronald Hope, *Development in the Third World* (London: M. E. Sharpe, 1996), 130.
26. Ibid., 134; and Seth Mydans, "In Vietnam, Deep-Rooted Corruption Threatens Growth," *The New York Times*, 7 May 2006, A10.
27. Adio Waziri, "With Nigeria's Dictators Out, A Leader Grapples with Graft," *The Christian Science Monitor*, 4 June 1999, 7; and Celia W. Dugger, "Iraq, Susceptible to Corruption," *The New York Times*, 21 October 2004, A8.
28. Celia W. Dugger, "India Tries to Plug a Cash Drain: Its Power System," *The New York Times*, 6 February 2000, 4.
29. Graham Bird, *IMF Lending to Developing Countries* (London: Routledge, 1995), 7.
30. Sam Chege, "Donors Shift More Aid to NGOs," *Africa Recovery* (June 1999): 6.

CHAPTER SEVEN

The Costs of Development

GLOBALIZATION AND THE COSTS OF DEVELOPMENT

MANY OF THE COSTS AND BENEFITS ASSOCIATED WITH DEVELOPMENT ARE NOT CAUSED SOLELY BY GLOBALIZATION. HOWEVER, GLOBALIZATION CONTRIBUTES TO SOME OF THESE COSTS AS WELL AS TO FINDING WAYS TO DIMINISH THEIR IMPACT. RAPID URBANIZATION, HIGH CRIME RATES, TRAFFIC CONGESTION, HIGH LEVELS OF POLLUTION, DEFORESTATION, GROWING SOCIAL ALIENATION, THE DISAPPEARANCE OF MANY TRADITIONS, AND LOSS OF A UNIQUE CULTURAL IDENTITY ARE COSTS THAT OCCUR AS COUNTRIES MODERNIZE. BUT THE FREE-MARKET REFORMS THAT ARE PART OF GLOBALIZATION HAVE CONTRIBUTED TO HIGH LEVELS OF UNEMPLOYMENT AND RISING LEVELS OF POVERTY, GOVERNMENT DOWNSIZING, FAILING LOCAL BUSINESSES THAT ARE UNABLE TO COMPETE WITH MORE EFFICIENT GLOBAL COMPANIES, AND LOWER THAN EXPECTED FOREIGN INVESTMENTS. IT IS ARGUED THAT GLOBALIZATION LEADS TO AN INEVITABLE "RACE TO THE BOTTOM" IN LABOR AND ENVIRONMENTAL STANDARDS AS COUNTRIES COMPETE FOR FOREIGN INVESTMENTS BY LOWERING THEIR STANDARDS AND ALLOWING COMPANIES TO OPERATE FREELY. BUT THE COSTS OF DEVELOPMENT THAT ARE ATTRIBUTED TO GLOBALIZATION HAVE PROMPTED A GLOBAL EFFORT TO DIMINISH THEM. COMPANIES ARE PRESSURED BY ADVOCACY GROUPS AROUND THE WORLD TO PRACTICE NONDISCRIMINATION IN THE WORKPLACE, RECOGNIZE WORKERS' RIGHTS TO UNIONIZE, PROHIBIT FORCED LABOR AND EXPLOITATIVE CHILD LABOR, AND REDUCE ENVIRONMENTAL DAMAGE. IN SOME WAYS, GLOBALIZATION HELPS DRAW ATTENTION TO MANY COSTS OF DEVELOPMENT THAT WERE PREVIOUSLY OVERLOOKED.

INTRODUCTION

Economic development, which provides many benefits, is inevitably accompanied by various costs. However, not all of these costs are inevitable. Sometimes countries, and particular communities within them, pay a much higher cost for the positive aspects of economic growth than is necessary. Although development has greatly improved the lives of many people in the developing world, progress usually is achieved at a price. Students are all too familiar with the costs of obtaining a college education. Apart from allocating scarce resources to their education, they must also give up opportunities to do other things, due to limited time and money. But they pay the costs associated with getting a college education because of the many benefits that are usually derived from having a college degree. This trade-off is referred to as an **opportunity cost.** Some students, however, spend more time and money than they should on their education because of their own decisions or because of circumstances that are beyond their control. Policymakers, like students, must weigh the costs of development against the benefits of development. Equally important, they must determine if they can achieve the benefits of development at lower costs, or at no cost at all. In the final analysis, an evaluation of the costs of development is to some extent subjective and culturally influenced.

opportunity cost
Passing up an opportunity to achieve a greater benefit.

Developing and developed countries alike wrestle with costs that usually accompany the benefits of development. Given the growing interdependence of countries and increasing globalization, the costs of development often spread from one society to another. For example, pollution in China sometimes affects places as far away as the United States. Americans' demand for consumer items at low costs cannot be divorced from the growth of sweatshops in Asia and elsewhere. Many of the costs of development, however, are borne by people in the developing world. Taking into consideration the benefits of development, this chapter examines the many costs associated with economic progress, including (1) social and cultural costs, (2) economic and political costs, and (3) environmental costs.

SOCIAL AND CULTURAL COSTS OF DEVELOPMENT

Many small communities throughout the United States encourage companies to invest in them in order to improve their economics and the quality of life of the residents. As these communities grow, they become more aware of the loss of a sense of community; social alienation; the disintegration of families; a relentless pursuit of consumerism; a decline of their cultural identity; and an increase in drug abuse, alcoholism, and other problems that were largely confined to urban areas. Developing societies are confronted with many of these social and cultural costs. **Development,** by definition, involves some destruction of traditional values and cultures and the adoption of values and cultures similar to those found in industrialized societies, especially those in North America and Western Europe.

development
Involves the destruction of traditional values and cultures.

As societies develop economically, they become more socially and politically complex. The old sense of community is undermined by the demands of modernization. As more industries locate in these societies, people adjust to conform to their requirements. Personal appearance, dress, and a greater emphasis on punctuality are some of the most obvious changes. As more time is devoted to preparing for and getting to work, less time is available for interacting with families, neighbors, and friends. Increasingly, almost everyone is busy. The time that was invested in maintaining a sense of community is now allocated to individual endeavors. As greater emphasis is placed on the individual, less attention is given to the community. People become increasingly independent and isolated. As the infrastructure develops, there are more options for moving away from tightly knit communities. Members of the community, who once played essential roles, such as organizing the community to work on various projects or leading social and religious organizations, now live elsewhere, thereby depriving their old communities of valuable services. As more roads, bridges, and ports are constructed, the number of automobiles grows. Instead of walking or bicycling to work and other activities, people are more likely to drive. Even though the automobile gets them to their destination faster, it also isolates them from members of their communities. The social bonds that are nourished by walking are weakened by driving. People become more superficial in their relationships.

Social alienation, the pressure to make money, and the increased exposure to values of modern societies contribute to the rise of social problems. Many children, in search of meaningful connections, may engage in activities that are destructive to themselves and their communities. Even in relatively small and isolated societies, gangs begin to emerge and to tear the social fabric. Parents feel they can no longer control their children, despite their growing material wealth. Elders, who were once highly respected, are ignored as individualism replaces a sense of social and familial obligation. And parents themselves, along with children, adopt destructive lifestyles. Drug abuse, alcoholism, and prostitution become more widespread. For example, rapid economic growth in the United Arab Emirates has been accompanied by dramatic increases in alcohol and drug abuse. Despite earlier efforts to deny the problem, public campaigns against drug abuse and the establishment of rehabilitation centers were part of the Dubai society in 2006. These problems plague virtually all developing societies, especially those that are governed by secular laws. Prosperity often comes at a cost, but the benefits cannot be disregarded. Although traditional communities are weakened, new social organizations emerge. Many parents use newly acquired resources to enhance their children's education and social well-being. Prosperity, while bringing new social problems, also enables countries to solve old ones, such as overpopulation, poverty, and the low status of women.

Social alienation and the increased exposure to the values of modern societies contribute to the rise of social problems.

Instead of viewing development as a replacement for traditionalism, a more accurate view of development is that both modernization and traditionalism coexist in most societies, including those in the industrialized world. Most cultures are extremely durable, despite the adoption of new values. However, some cultures that are closely linked to location and the environment are threatened with extinction by the forces of change. Cultures of people in the Amazon rain forest, for example, are tied to the land. When the land is altered, these cultures are affected. Many are destroyed.

The challenge is to balance the costs of change against the costs of maintaining the status quo.

The cost of development for indigenous peoples in Latin America, Africa, and Asia is often extremely high. The challenge for many traditional cultures is to balance the costs of change against the costs of maintaining the status quo.[1] As will be discussed, development of the Amazon has generally ignored the desire of indigenous people to preserve their cultures. Greater efforts are being made to improve the economic and physical well-being of indigenous peoples without destroying their traditional cultures. It is doubtful, however, that this delicate balance can withstand the forces of change for very long.

One of the most important social costs of development is the escalation of criminal activities and a significant change in the nature of crimes committed. Modernization weakens many of the social bonds that helped reduce crime. As urbanization spreads; as communities are destroyed; and as individualism, alienation, and consumerism are strengthened, crime rates tend to rise. Although violence and other criminal activities occur in all societies, rising levels of prosperity, unequal distribution of benefits, the breakdown of traditional societies, and the failure of countries to establish modern institutions to replace traditional institutions make developing countries particularly vulnerable to widespread crime. The availability of things to steal due to the growing affluence that results from development is an important factor in the rising crime rate. As discussed in Chapter 5, development often widens the economic gap among various segments of the population. Those who have wealth often become the victims of those who do not.

Development is often accompanied by high crime rates.

Mexico City is often cited as a leading example of widespread and uncontrollable crime in the developing world. The vast majority of Mexico City residents are directly affected by crime. Muggings, burglaries, and car thefts are rampant. Many police officers are often victims of crime, partly because criminals want to demonstrate the ineffectiveness of the police. It is quite common for people to be mugged and beaten even when police officers are nearby. For example, a woman was mugged and beaten at the main entrance to the headquarters of the Mexico City police in late 1998, at a time when the new police chief, Alejandro Gertz Manero, vowed to reduce crime in Mexico City. In fact, more than 94 percent of all violent crimes reported to the police are never solved or prosecuted. In late 2004, people in Brazil and other Latin American cities protested against high crime rates and personal insecurity.[2] Part of the problem is that some police officers actually collaborate with criminals, largely due to economic reasons. Many police officers are paid approximately $200 a month, a salary that makes it difficult for most recruits to resist taking bribes from the public or payoffs from criminals involved in the drug trade and other illegal activities. In some cases, higher ranking police officers demand money from junior officers, who, in turn, prey on the public.[3] The escalation of crime in Mexico City diminishes the quality of life and imposes high economic costs on the country as a whole. Both the reality and widespread perception of insecurity undermine confidence in government institutions in general and law enforcement agencies in particular. Foreign companies are reluctant to invest in a crime-ridden society. If they do, they pass on the high costs of doing business in such a violent and uncertain environment to the consumers.

Development also facilitates crime by creating closer links among countries by enhancing transportation and communication among them, and by enabling individuals to acquire financial resources to engage in crime. The positive side of development is that it stimulates trade among countries that is both legal and beneficial to many people. The negative side of this, however, is that illegal activities also flourish.

As countries develop their infrastructure for legitimate trade, they also run the risk of having their ports, roads, airports, and telecommunications systems utilized for illegal trade. For example, the infrastructure for international trade makes it relatively easy for cars stolen in the United States to be transported to Mexico, Panama, Colombia, the Dominican Republic, China, and elsewhere in the developing world. A $70,000 Mercedes that was stolen in Miami was found a thousand miles from Florida. Its new owner was Mayra Sandoval, director of judicial affairs in Panama's Foreign Ministry. Ironically, Sandoval was responsible for negotiating an agreement between Panama and the United States to deal with the problem of stolen cars.[4] Americans who live in cities with ports or international borders are most likely to have their stolen cars shipped overseas. Miami, Jersey City, Memphis, New York, Tucson, Phoenix, and New Orleans are among the cities with the highest vehicle theft rates. The most frequently stolen vehicles include the Honda Accord, Toyota Camry, Oldsmobile Cutlass, Ford Mustang, Toyota Corolla, Nissan Maxima, and Jeep Grand Cherokee. In many cases, stolen cars are used to pay for drug shipments or to transport drugs or cash hidden in secret compartments, especially between Mexico and the United States.

Throughout the developing world, illegal drug cultivation, processing, and trafficking have emerged as one of the greatest social costs of development. Virtually all countries, large and small, are affected by illegal drugs. Development helps make economies and societies more interdependent, and it exposes developing countries to the problems generally associated with advanced industrialized societies such as the United States and Western Europe. Consumption of illegal drugs in rich countries influences poor countries with weak and corrupt governments to supply them. Suppliers usually become consumers, a development that has high social, economic, and political costs for poor countries. Even though a few individuals and groups benefit from drug trafficking, society as a whole suffers and development is often impeded. A few individuals become extremely wealthy from participating in illegal drug activities and are able to engage in conspicuous consumption, which influences others to get involved in drug trafficking to acquire wealth quickly and easily. The most obvious examples of countries involved in producing and selling illegal drugs are Colombia, Mexico, Afghanistan, and Thailand. But countries such as Jamaica, Nigeria, and South Africa also participate in the illegal drug trade as transit points and producers, and for facilitating financial transactions by international and domestic criminal organizations. Their modern communications networks, banking, and transportation systems facilitate not only drug trafficking but also hiding income derived from criminal activities. Eventually, banking, law enforcement, customs officials, and others in developing countries are pulled into a network of illegal activities based on the drug trade. Under these circumstances, violent crime flourishes.

> *Illegal drugs are one of the greatest social costs of development.*

Child Labor

Approximately 218 million children aged five to fourteen are working in developing countries. Roughly 317.4 million children work outside the home part-time. About half of them work full time, whereas the others combine work with school. Although the problem of child labor has always existed, to greater or lesser degrees, economic development and the increasing globalization of the economies of various countries have served as a catalyst for the growth of child labor. Developing countries must compete for foreign investment and must produce goods at low prices

Global competition is seen as fueling an increase in the use of child labor.

to gain access to global markets. As poor countries are pressured to compete with each other for investments and markets, they look for ways to reduce labor costs. As we discuss in Chapter 8, low-paid women replace higher-paid men in many of the footwear, plastics, toys, apparel, and electronics factories. Competition influences countries to find even cheaper ways to produce exports. This makes child labor, the cheapest labor of all, attractive to manufacturers. Most of the children do not work in industries that are connected to international companies or multinational corporations. The vast majority of them, about 70 percent, are employed in agriculture, forestry, and fishing. Another 8.3 percent work in wholesale and retail trade, restaurants, and hotels; 8.3 percent in manufacturing; and 6.5 percent in community, social, and personal services. Most child laborers are viewed as essential contributors to their families. Without their income, many families would not survive. Not surprisingly, the poorest countries are also those that exploit children the most. Countries of Asia, such as India, Pakistan, Bangladesh, Thailand, Indonesia, and the Philippines, employ approximately 153.5 million children. Africa, the poorest and least developed continent, has about 80 million children laborers, whereas Latin America and the Caribbean employ roughly 17 million children. But the developing countries are not the only societies with child labor problems. It is estimated that 300,000 to 1 million children are working illegally in the United States, primarily in agriculture.[5]

India, with roughly 100 million children working, has the largest number of child laborers in the world. Widespread poverty and an enduring **caste system** reinforce the practice of child labor. Both poverty and social attitudes make child labor acceptable to Indians, the majority of whom live in villages. Child labor on the farms and in the villages throughout India is considered part of the social and economic reality. Parents, many of whom are landless, illiterate, and hungry, worked when they were children and expect their own children to follow in their footsteps. For most parents, child labor is a way of life. With two children, ages eleven and sixteen, working with their father, a typical rural family in India may earn less than $1 a day. Overpopulation increases competition for even the lowest paid jobs in India and creates a vicious circle of poverty and dependence on child labor. Over time the positive aspects of development diminish the need for child labor.

caste system
A hierarchical system that is part of Hindu beliefs.

Children work in dangerous industries such as lead mining, metal manufacturing, fireworks, stone quarrying, brick kilns, brothels, and carpet weaving. Many of them as young as seven years old work long hours. They inhale dust and chemical fumes, and are exposed to other hazardous conditions. Many die before age forty, and those who live suffer from chronic pain and breathing problems caused by working conditions. Much of the attention has been focused on the carpet industry because it is a major source of income. Countries that import carpets from India and elsewhere find

A Child Laborer in India. Many children in the developing world are forced to work in difficult and often dangerous jobs to help support themselves and their families.

Source: Reuters/Corbis

themselves under pressure from various groups that oppose child labor. Responding to such pressure, the United States passed a law in 1997 to ban imports of goods made by child laborers. But India, which has numerous laws against child labor, does not regard children working at home for free as child laborers. In Uttar Pradesh and other parts of India, much of the carpet weaving is done in mud huts that are largely hidden from investigators from the outside world. Most Indian families are too poor to abandon the system of child labor. Educational opportunities are generally not available for the poorest children.[6]

Pakistan and Bangladesh also make extensive use of child labor. Until 1999, Pakistan relied primarily on child labor for its soccer ball industry. International pressure is forcing Pakistan to take steps to eventually eliminate the use of child workers and to employ women instead. Without the willingness of importers and consumers in the United States, Western Europe, and elsewhere to purchase soccer balls made by children, Pakistan realized that it had to change in order to maintain an important industry. Reebok, which purchased soccer balls from Pakistan, established a monitoring system at a new central production facility in Pakistan. It also affixed new "Made Without Child Labor" labels to its soccer balls. The company was clearly worried about the effect of negative publicity on its image and its sales. By 2006, the Pakistani soccer ball industry had largely abandoned child labor.

But the carpet industry in Pakistan has been the principal employer of children. Many poor families literally mortgage their children to carpet factories. Employers make it virtually impossible for child laborers to accumulate enough money to pay off the mortgages by overcharging them for food, housing, and even drugs. Many of these

NEWS | IN THE

American Teenage Workers

According to a 1999 study by the U.S. Bureau of Labor Statistics, approximately 25 percent of four-teen-year-olds and 38 percent of fifteen-year-olds have regular scheduled employment (as opposed to casual babysitting or yard work) during the school year. By the time they are seniors, 73 percent of young people work during at least part of the school year. The vast majority of them work for low wages as cooks, cashiers, waiters and waitresses, and office clerks. The average employed American high school student works seventeen hours a week during the academic year. Teens spent about $160 billion in 1999.

children die from disease and malnutrition. Although Pakistan is sensitive to international opposition against child labor, it has adopted policies that are similar to those of India. More of the carpets are made by families who rely on child labor.

Bangladesh, one of the poorest countries in the world and one that constantly suffers from natural disasters, employs around 7 million children. Most of them work between nine and fourteen hours a day and give their earnings to their parents. As is the case in India, many of the children work in agriculture for their families. But as modernization has reduced the amount of land available for small farmers, many rural residents are forced to migrate to urban areas in search of employment. Many children find jobs in the garment industry, which provides Bangladesh with about 70 percent of its export earnings. Women employed in these factories earn as little as $30 a month. Such low wages perpetuate the use of child labor to supplement the family's income. Furthermore, in order to obtain international funding for economic development, Bangladesh, which is highly dependent on foreign aid, adopted a **structural adjustment program.** This program required cuts in government spending on health care, education, nutrition, and other programs that benefit the poor.[7] Reduced government expenditures forced more families to rely on their children for income.

Latin America and the Caribbean are not as dependent on child labor as Asia and Africa. However, child labor is a serious problem in countries such as Haiti and Brazil. Under Haiti's **Restavec system,** impoverished parents who cannot afford to raise their children allow them to stay with wealthier families. The children are treated as slaves, psychologically abused, and beaten. They have no real freedom. They are not educated and are forced to do domestic work and menial jobs. The Restavec system is so widely practiced that many Haitians, who are the poorest people in the Western Hemisphere, regard it as an integral part of their society. Children are also laborers in Brazil's agricultural industry. For example, despite **Brazil's Labor Code,** which outlaws child labor, many children are employed to pick oranges and work in citrus-processing industries. Brazil is the world's largest exporter of orange juice and a supplier of major U.S. brands such as Minute Maid. But both domestic and international pressure, mainly from labor unions, are helping to end the use of child labor in the citrus industry.[8]

In response to widespread criticism of the use of child labor, several countries have enacted legislation banning child labor. Others have allowed industries to be inspected by outside investigators. Many countries, in cooperation with international organizations, produce products that carry labels indicating that they were not made with child labor. In India, for example, many carpet manufacturers use the **Kaleen** label and the **Rugmark** label to demonstrate their compliance with laws banning child labor. Inspectors carry out spot checks and fine violators. However, given the problems of poverty in India and persistent corruption, many manufacturers are able to circumvent the law and still obtain labels certifying that they do not use child labor. The **International Labor Organization,** a part of the United Nations that is based in Geneva, Switzerland, adopted an agreement in June 1999 to abolish the worst forms of child labor. These include slavery, debt bondage, trafficking in children, prostitution, child pornography, and the recruitment of children as soldiers by militias

structural adjustment program
Required cuts in government spending on programs that benefit the poor.

Restavec system
A system in Haiti that allows children of the poor to live with those who are wealthy.

Brazil's Labor Code
A Brazilian law that outlaws child labor.

Kaleen and Rugmark
Labels used by manufacturers to show compliance with child labor laws.

International Labor Organization
An organization of the United Nations that deals with labor-related issues, including child labor concerns.

and paramilitaries.[9] Yet poverty and the push for economic development are likely to make it difficult to enforce agreements banning child labor in the short run.

Sweatshops

Sweatshops are widely perceived as integral parts of developing economies. The connection between sweatshops and economic development is as old as the Industrial Revolution. Charles Dickens, the British novelist, wrote extensively about the horrific working conditions in industries throughout England from the middle of the eighteenth century to the middle of the nineteenth century. Many contemporary critics of factories in the developing world use the term *sweatshop* to portray the dangerous working conditions found in many of them. Characteristics of sweatshops include the dreariness of the work; the harshness of supervisors; difficult and hazardous jobs; frequent and serious accidents; long hours and low pay; few employee benefits and rights; and a generally toxic, polluted, and unsanitary working environment. Sweatshops are often portrayed as dismal places in which workers are exploited. Sweatshops also exist in the United States, especially in urban areas with large numbers of immigrants from the developing world. Like their counterparts in Asia and Latin America, most workers in American sweatshops are employed in the apparel industry.

Sweatshops are as old as the Industrial Revolution.

Sweatshops are characterized by dangerous conditions, long hours, and low wages.

For many inhabitants of the developing countries, sweatshops provide much-needed jobs. The existence of sweatshops in these societies reflects economic realities and their level of economic development. But they also underscore the need for multinational corporations from the developed as well as the developing countries to produce low-cost products for insatiable consumers throughout the world, especially in the United States. Sweatshops are part of the global economy. The poorest countries are most likely to have the worst working conditions and lowest wages, which make them attractive to many foreign as well as domestic investors. Many of these factories are actually small businesses that are owned by local entrepreneurs who make products for various companies. The pay ranges from less than 35 cents a day to more than $3 a day. Many workers earn less than $1 a day and labor twelve to fourteen hours each day six days a week. Work in the agricultural sector is often viewed as even more strenuous than a factory job and the pay is lower and infrequent. The poorest of the poor often must become garbage scavengers to survive. The economic crisis in Asia in the late 1990s resulted in high levels of unemployment and a greater willingness of the unemployed to do anything, including working in the sweatshops, to support themselves and their families.[10]

Sweatshops are part of the global economy.

The pay in sweatshops ranges from 35 cents to around $3 a day.

As more Western companies have moved parts of their operations to developing countries to take advantage of inexpensive labor and lower environmental standards and working conditions, they have encountered opposition from labor unions, environmentalists, humanitarians, and other activists. The global economy, increased and rapid communications, and the willingness of the media to expose exploitative labor practices by well-known personalities and corporations have made it easier for human rights activists and others to change the companies' practices. Companies such as Wal-Mart, The Gap, Reebok, Nike, Starbucks Coffee, Walt Disney, and Mattel have been criticized for taking advantage of sweatshop labor. One of the most dramatic developments occurred in 1996 when Kathie Lee Gifford, the famous television personality, was accused of promoting sweatshops by allowing her line of discount women's clothing to be manufactured in Honduras under sweatshop conditions. The Walt Disney Company was exposed for contracting with suppliers in Haiti who paid their workers less than the minimum wage of $2.40 a day. Similarly, workers in China making products worked up to sixteen hours a day, seven days a week, mostly without overtime pay. Wal-Mart was accused of using child labor in Bangladesh to make inexpensive clothing, and Mattel was exposed for its production of "Sweatshop Barbies." Starbucks Coffee was picketed by activists for buying its coffee beans from Guatemalan plantations that exploit their workers.[11]

> *Companies criticized for using sweatshop labor include Wal-Mart, The Gap, and Nike.*

Faced with global and domestic pressure, many of these companies have attempted to protect themselves by adopting various codes and labels. The **No Sweat** label is being used to verify that clothing, shoes, toys, and other products were not made in sweatshops or by children. Perhaps Nike has embraced the most far-reaching reforms after being faced with an effective boycott of its products in the mid-1990s. Nike developed a "Memorandum of Understanding" that is signed by factories that produce Nike shoes and other products. Nike's Memorandum of Understanding calls on companies to comply with the following: (1) government regulation of business; (2) safety and health regulations; (3) local laws providing health insurance, life insurance, and worker's compensation; (4) laws forbidding the use of forced labor; (5) environmental regulations; (6) laws promoting equal employment opportunities; and (7) efforts by external groups to certify that factories are complying with Nike's rules.[12]

No Sweat
A label used to verify that products were not made in sweatshops or by children.

> *Nike developed a Memorandum of Understanding.*

ECONOMIC AND POLITICAL COSTS OF DEVELOPMENT

Many economic costs of development are unavoidable because of the relatively weak bargaining position of poor countries. Some of these costs are not strictly economic but have significant economic implications. Overpopulation, for example, is caused by many noneconomic factors, as Chapter 6 points out. Advances in medical technology, improvements in transportation, and access to food contribute to population growth by reducing death rates. A growing population imposes a heavy economic burden on the developing world. Overpopulation threatens economic progress because of the enormous amounts of resources that are needed to sustain it. Schools, hospitals, roads, airports, harbors, electricity, water, sewage treatment plants, and other infrastructure projects must be provided. Governments must also deal with rising levels of unemployment as the population shifts from rural to urban areas.

To attract foreign investments, many governments provide incentives such as low taxes, free land for constructing factories, and the necessary infrastructure. These

To attract foreign investments, governments provide incentives such as low taxes.

costs are regarded as relatively insignificant when compared with the benefits a society can receive from foreign investments. But to attract foreign investments, many governments often alter their priorities, which results in one sector of the economy benefiting at the expense of others. This situation often leads to economic growth without economic equity. It also makes the whole economy extremely vulnerable to fluctuations in that particular economic sector. For example, countries that depend heavily on petroleum exports are vulnerable to changes in demand in importing countries. Another economic cost is the depletion of nonrenewable natural resources. In an effort to develop quickly, many countries allow their natural resources

The depletion of nonrenewable resources is a major cost of development.

to be exploited without paying much attention to sustainability. Careful management of resources, including recycling, can delay depletion of these resources and prolong economic benefits derived from them. Countries often go into debt to finance economic development. As we have seen, countries that are heavily in debt pay economic as well as social and political costs.

An economic cost associated with development is economic inequality. Inequality discourages investment on a wider scale and encourages the poor and their supporters to pressure governments to allocate resources to benefit those left behind by unequal

Economic inequality is a significant cost of development.

economic growth. High rates of inequality may encourage some members of society to be more productive and entrepreneurial. But such inequality usually leads to a concentration of political power and the stifling of economic competition. Poor people are deprived of opportunities to become productive and the powerful are inclined to be corrupt.[13] Ultimately, the poorest of the poor, who are usually women and children, pay the highest economic costs of growing inequality. They suffer most when the economy stagnates and when cuts are made in most government programs.

One of the main political costs of economic development is the decline of the government's ability to control what goes on inside the country or international developments that directly affect it. This relative loss

The relative loss of sovereignty is a part of the globalization process.

of *sovereignty*, or control over internal affairs, is part of the process of globalization and interdependence. This decline of sovereignty can also be viewed as a positive aspect of development. Few governments can influence the global economic competition, which is essentially determined by market forces. Communications technology and transportation have helped to weaken the ability of governments to control the activities of their citizens. As we have seen with child labor and sweatshops, organizations beyond a country's borders can have a significant impact on economic, social, and political decisions within countries. Reinforcing the role of globalization in undermining national sovereignty is the growing willingness of countries that provide economic assistance to attach certain conditions to that aid. Most governments regard these restrictions as important political costs.

Another short-term political cost of development is instability and the violation of human rights. As people from different ethnic, regional, and religious backgrounds are brought together by the forces of modernization, the likelihood of conflict increases. Instability is often caused by government economic policies, such as structural adjustment. Indonesia, for example, experienced political instability and violence when it agreed to demands of the International Monetary Fund to

Instability and human rights violations are short-term costs of development.

implement economic reforms that deprive the poor of various subsidies. Unstable political conditions, together with insecure governments and weak institutions, contribute to violations of human rights. Human rights abuses tend to occur most frequently in developing societies, when compared with traditional and modern societies. Many governments in the developing world also suffer from high levels of political corruption, which is a significant political cost that is closely linked to political instability. Political corruption is discussed in greater detail in Chapters 6 and 11.

Consumerism and Development

One of the most obvious changes brought about by economic development is a marked increase in consumerism and a dramatic change in what people consume, where they acquire consumer products, and how they relate to each other and the rest of the world. Societies throughout history have attempted to improve the quality of life for their people. A common measure of better life is usually greater access to more food, clothes, and better housing and the acquisition of various products that make life easier and more enjoyable. Many of the benefits are obvious. Yet these developments have negative consequences or costs. As discussed earlier, some of these costs are unavoidable and essential components of the overall positive nature of economic development. **Economic development,** by definition, implies growth and increased consumption of an ever-larger supply of products. Overconsumption, which is often a subjective evaluation, becomes more common as more products are made available at affordable prices to a large proportion of the population.

economic development
Implies growth and increased consumption.

Consumerism increases as countries develop, partly because many of the products are produced by them. As American, European, Japanese, and other local factories in developing societies produce electronics, appliances, automobiles, apparel, footwear, household furnishings, and other consumer items, people

Tourism alters consumer tastes and desires.

become more aware of these products, develop the need to acquire them, and, because of the jobs these industries create, are better able to purchase them. Industries such as tourism dramatically alter consumer tastes and desires. Tourists demand modern accommodations, restaurants, recreational facilities, and transportation. They also bring aspects of their own culture with them that influence people in the developing world to acquire a similar lifestyle. As tourism and other industries develop, more money flows into the society, which allows people from poor countries to travel to rich countries. Visiting or living in developed societies often profoundly changes consumption patterns. Most individuals are strongly influenced by the behavior and the habits of others around them. When travelers from developing countries return home, they not only take with them new ways of living, they also help to replicate consumption patterns of rich societies in their own countries. Development itself is therefore an engine that powers consumption. This consumerism is also positive because it contributes to further economic growth and increased economic opportunities.

Economic development brings countries and their cultures together to help create a global society. As we have seen, globalization is strengthened by revolutions in communications technology and transportation. People throughout the world are increasingly connected to each other by television, telephones, the Internet, and other forms of communications. Movies, videotapes, books, and magazines allow many people even in remote villages to see how people in rich countries live. They are also exposed to seductive advertisements that equate the acquisition of products with personal achievement and character. In other words, these advertisements attempt to convey the belief that you are what you consume. Traditional values are under pressure everywhere as global companies promote the homogenization of consumer tastes and cultural values.

Economic development helps create a global society.

Global companies undermine traditional values.

As more people in the developing world adopt the habits of people in developed countries, they also encounter the same problems. More people are involved in car accidents as roads become congested and speed is seen as being more important than safety. The consumption of fast foods and the sedentary lifestyles that characterize modern societies increase the number of overweight people, especially children, in poor countries. This rapid increase in the consumption of fast food is seen by the emphasis of McDonald's, for example, on building most of its new restaurants overseas. In the late 1990s, Hong Kong had the highest per capita consumption of McDonald's food in the world. Children throughout Asia and Latin America are suffering from obesity. In fact, there is a growing weight gap in the developing world, as the rich grow fat and the poor suffer from malnutrition and hunger. Overweight people outnumber underweight people everywhere except in South Asia, where 553 million are underweight, compared with 115 million people who are overweight. In North America, 153 million people are overweight, compared with 13 million who are underweight.

Obesity is a growing problem.

In Latin America, 152 million people are overweight and 32 million are underweight. Worldwide, there are as many overweight people, 1.1 billion, as underfed people. More than 230 million people worldwide suffer from diabetes, caused mainly by changes in lifestyle and diet.[14]

Consumption of fast food is only one of the costs of development. Other costs include poor diets in general, an increase in alcohol consumption, and smoking. Even though antismoking campaigns in the United States have reduced the number of smokers, just the opposite is happening in developing countries. Advertising and marketing of cigarettes have increased as tobacco companies have attempted to gain markets in poor countries to offset their lost markets in rich countries. As people in poor countries overeat, adopt sedentary lifestyles, abuse alcohol and drugs, and smoke, they begin to suffer from the same diseases that plague affluent societies. These include heart attacks, cancers, strokes, and diabetes. Longer life expectancies in the developing world, due to medical technology and improved diet, also increase the rate of chronic diseases in poor countries.

Urbanization and Development

Urbanization is an integral part of economic development. Cities grow as countries become more industrialized. Almost half of the people in the world live in urban areas. It is estimated that about 65 percent of them will live in cities by 2025. The urbanized population of the Middle East alone is predicted to reach 75 percent by 2010. Latin America and the Caribbean will have 80 percent of their populations living in cities by 2015.[15] It is important to point out that many governments, especially those in developing countries, do not know precisely how many people are living in urban areas. There is no effective way to count them. Many countries do not regard knowing the size of their cities as a pressing national priority, especially in light of all the pressing problems with which they are confronted. Furthermore, migration patterns, the tendency of people to reside in cities temporarily, and the reluctance of some people to be counted make it difficult for governments to collect accurate demographic data. Given continued population growth, it is clear that urbanization will only increase.

Patterns of urbanization are different in the developed countries than in the developing world. In most developed countries, there are many medium-sized and small cities and towns. By contrast, the developing countries have a few very large cities, often referred to as megalopolises. People from around the country come to these few cities, largely because of the economic, social, and political benefits they offer. These include hospitals, libraries, universities, modern shopping centers, transportation, social programs, employment opportunities, and various social, economic, and political organizations. Ten of the thirteen most populated cities in the world, with more than 13 million residents, are in developing countries. Five of these mega-cities are in Latin America, with Mexico City (24 million) and Sao Paulo in Brazil (22 million) taking the lead. Mega-cities in the poor countries include Jakarta in Indonesia, Seoul

The most populated cities are in the developing world.

TABLE 7.1 URBANIZATION

Country	Urban Population 2002	% of Total 2015
Angola	34.9	44.9
Bangladesh	23.9	29.6
Brazil	82.4	88.4
Chile	86.6	90.2
China	37.7	49.5
Costa Rica	60.1	66.8
Egypt	42.1	44.9
Ethiopia	15.4	19.8
Ghana	45	51.1
Haiti	36.9	45.5
India	28.1	32.2
Jamaica	52.1	54.2
Kenya	38.2	51.8
Mexico	75.2	78.8
Mozambique	34.5	48.5
Nigeria	45.9	55.5
Pakistan	33.7	39.5
Philippines	60.2	69.2
Saudi Arabia	87.2	91.1
Turkey	65.8	71.9
Zambia	35.4	40.8
East Asia/Pacific	40.2	51.0
Latin America/Caribbean	76.2	80.8
Middle East and North Africa	54.2	58.8
South Asia	29.6	34.3
Sub-Saharan Africa	35.0	42.4
United States	**79.8**	**83.6**

Source: United Nations Development Program, *Human Development Report 2004* (New York: Oxford University Press, 2004), 152–55.

in South Korea, Lagos in Nigeria, Bombay and Calcutta in India, Rio de Janeiro in Brazil, Buenos Aires in Argentina, Shanghai and Beijing in China, and Cairo in Egypt. The population density of cities in developing countries is usually higher than that in the developed world. For example, Mexico City, with a population as large as Australia's entire population, has twice the density of New York City, three times the density of Paris, and four times that of London. But Bombay and Calcutta, for example, have higher population densities than Mexico City.[16]

Large cities can have a number of positive effects. Urbanization in developing countries may help reduce pressures on the land imposed by rapid population growth. Urbanization makes more land available for agriculture and reduces activities, such as using wood for fuel, that contribute to deforestation and environmental damage. The efficient use of resources may also be enhanced in crowded areas. Mass transportation helps reduce the need for automobiles, and population density may produce economies of scale in industry as well as in the provision of public services, such as water, electricity, education, health care, and recreation. People in urban areas are likely to have a greater interest in and increased opportunities to recycle materials. They also become more aware of the need to use water, energy, and other resources efficiently.

Urbanization has many positive aspects.

Perhaps the most obvious benefit from urbanization, as discussed in Chapter 6, is the tendency of people in cities to have smaller families. Birthrates decline significantly because of the

Urban residents usually have smaller families.

restraints imposed on families by cities and the availability of contraception, educational opportunities, and exposure to modern technologies and ways of thinking.

A major problem is that urbanization tends to reduce responsibility and accountability. Very large cities encourage the fragmentation of environmental management. Although decentralization of authority to deal with urban problems is almost essential, decentralization can result in uncertainty about who deals with particular problems and who provides the necessary resources. Many local authorities in mega-cities are unable to raise revenues to build and maintain streets, collect garbage, and provide adequate sanitation services.[17] Another cost of urbanization is the increase of squalid shantytowns and uncontrollable urban sprawl. Most cities in the developing world lack access to adequate sanitation services. Raw sewage is routinely discharged into rivers, streams, lakes, and throughout the urban area. As more people move to the city, the demand for already scarce resources grows, making it difficult for governments to improve sanitation and diminish sprawl. When governments destroy shantytowns to promote urban development and public safety, residents of the squalid settlements recreate shantytowns elsewhere or become homeless. Urbanization also taxes scarce resources such as water. Many urban residents do not have adequate water supplies because the demand is too great, because much water is

Water shortage is a growing global problem.

wasted by industries and is not recycled, and because of the inability or unwillingness of governments to repair water pipelines and storage systems. Water shortage is a growing global problem.

Urban areas throughout the world, but especially in developing countries, have severe traffic and air pollution problems. These problems are so serious because of the rapid growth of urbanization and other changes brought about by economic development. Cairo, for example, has almost 2 million cars but only enough roads to handle a third of that number.

Traffic problems reflect the costs of development.

Mexico City is probably the most obvious example of traffic congestion and air pollution caused by automobiles. Efforts have been made to restrict automobile traffic by reducing the number of cars on the streets by almost half during some air pollution emergencies.[18]

Urbanization also contributes to the spread of disease. Unsanitary living conditions, limited access to clean water, extremely high levels of air pollution, exposure to

Urbanization contributes to the spread of diseases.

toxic and hazardous wastes, untreated sewage, and malnutrition create serious health problems for residents in developing countries. Mosquitoes, which transmit diseases such as yellow fever, malaria, and dengue fever, breed in the unsanitary conditions in urban areas. Discarded automobile tires, drainage ditches, irrigated urban gardens, water tanks, and garbage heaps provide ideal breeding places for mosquitoes. Increasing globalization also puts residents of developed countries at risk of contracting diseases that originate in poor societies. Shipping industries, airlines, and cruise ships facilitate the transportation of diseases from one country to another. For example, untreated sewage flowing into the

Globalization facilitates the spread of diseases, many of which originate in poor societies.

Bay of Bengal off Bangladesh was loaded into the bilge tanks of a freighter bound for South America. When the bilge tanks were emptied off the coast of Peru, a new strain of cholera, which was in the untreated sewage in Bangladesh, flourished in sewage from Lima, Peru. The cholera soon made its way into various cities as people ate contaminated shellfish from off the coast of Peru.[19]

The Decline of Agriculture and Economic Development

One of the main assumptions of modernization theory is that countries progress from being heavily dependent on agriculture to a greater reliance on industrialization. This has not occurred in most developing economies. Instead, agriculture has been neglected in many poor countries as they rushed to industrialize and as people migrated from rural areas to the cities. Asian countries, such as South Korea, Taiwan, and Thailand, have achieved high levels of industrialization as well as increased agricultural productivity. Latin America has also managed to balance agricultural development and industrialization. It is in Africa where agriculture has suffered most as a result of the pressures of economic development and government policies. In India, Mexico, Taiwan, South Korea, Brazil, China, and elsewhere in Asia and Latin America, the **Green Revolution** enabled farmers to produce more crops on the same amount of land by using hybrid seeds, chemical fertilizers, pesticides, herbicides, irrigation, and modern farm machinery. The Green Revolution largely bypassed Africa.

Green Revolution

Enabled farmers to produce more crops on the same amount of land via the use of technological advancements in the agricultural field.

urbanization

Takes valuable land away from agriculture.

Urbanization and the emphasis of many governments on rapid industrialization influenced many farmers to leave the rural areas in search of a better life in the cities. Fewer farmers, in the absence of improved agricultural productivity, meant that less food was being grown. **Urbanization** also helped take valuable land away from agricultural uses. As urban populations expanded, more land was lost to urban sprawl. Infrastructural projects essential to urbanization and industrialization require large amounts of land. Shopping malls, airports, roads and highways, tourist facilities, harbors, hospitals, schools, power plants, and so on reduce the amount of land available for agriculture. Deforestation, overgrazing, and some agricultural practices contribute to soil erosion and climate change. All of these contribute to the decline of agricultural productivity.

Environmental Costs of Development

One of the most obvious costs of economic development is environmental degradation. Urban areas throughout the developing world suffer from excessive rates of air and water pollution, toxic wastes, and the destruction of natural habitats for wildlife. Even small towns are plagued with environmental problems that result from development. Garbage

Cruise ships routinely pollute the oceans.

is recklessly disposed of in areas that were once pristine. Fragile beaches are destroyed as tourist facilities are constructed to fulfill the exotic fantasies of the rich and famous. Cruise ships routinely pollute once crystal clear waters in the Caribbean and elsewhere. Environmental destruction also results from the rapid and reckless exploitation of natural resources. Mining companies obtain contracts from developing countries that allow them to extract mineral resources without being responsible for protecting the environment. The need to develop puts countries in a weak bargaining position vis-à-vis multinational companies. In Indonesia, for example, mining companies have been largely exempt from complying with the relatively weak environmental laws. Consequently, mining activities have caused widespread destruction of surrounding forests and the pollution of rivers, lakes, and other water sources. The pollution of many rivers in the Philippines by wastes from copper mining has reduced fish yields by half. Oil companies have caused similar environmental damage in many oil-producing regions in Africa, Asia, and Latin America.

In Ecuador, for example, Texaco was the dominant oil company in the country until 1990. Its determination to maximize profits and its disregard for protecting the environment caused long-lasting environmental damage. Texaco poured low-grade crude oil on dirt roads it cleared to reduce dust, but the heavy rainfall in the Amazon soon carried the oil into

Texaco caused major pollution in Ecuador.

the fields and rivers, which contaminated crops and water supplies. In addition, millions of barrels of oil were accidentally spilled over a twenty-year period. Large pools of oil and other toxic wastes are everywhere in the oil-producing region of Ecuador. Trees and animals around them have died. In many places the soil is covered with a green and yellow liquid that releases a heavy odor of petroleum. The environmental costs were largely overlooked by a country that depends on oil and related products for 44 percent of its national budget. Revenues from the petroleum industry financed electrification of Ecuador and contributed to its industrial development.[20]

Water pollution is a major cost of economic development. The Green Revolution is also a significant cause of water contamination. Increased fertilizer and chemical usage improved agricultural productivity. However, heavy rains washed chemicals into rivers, lakes, and groundwater supplies. Farm chemicals in China are washed into the sea, creating massive

Water pollution is a major cost of economic development.

blooms of algae. In places such as Taiwan, many industrial plants are located in agricultural areas. Untreated industrial metals and wastewater contaminate some of the crops, especially rice, which requires a large amount of water to grow. Industrial development in Asia has resulted in heavily polluted rivers, lakes, and seas. For example, it is not uncommon to see many rivers and streams in China in which the water is so polluted that it is completely black and putrid.

Most of the water pollution in the developing world is caused by untreated human waste that is flushed into rivers, lakes, and the sea. India provides one of the best examples of how urbanization, water pollution, religious beliefs, and the contraction of dangerous diseases are intertwined. Almost half of India's 1 billion citizens live along the **Ganges River,** which stretches for 1,500 miles from the Himalayan Mountains to the Bay of Bengal. Most of the people do not have access to sewer and sanitation facilities, and the crowded cities dump millions of gallons of untreated human and industrial waste into the sluggish river. What makes the pollution of the Ganges River even more dangerous is the belief of many Hindus that bathing in the Ganges will wash away their sins. For them, the Ganges is India's holiest river. They believe that their bodies and souls are purified by drinking its water. Hindus also believe that if their bodies are cremated on the banks of the Ganges, their souls will escape from the material world's cycle of suffering.[21]

Air pollution is also a serious problem in the developing world. Economic development has helped to make many cities in Asia, Latin America, and Africa extremely dangerous to the health of their inhabitants. Beijing, Taipei (Taiwan), New Delhi (India), and Mexico City are among the most polluted cities in the world. Most of these cities are constantly covered with air that is so polluted that visibility is drastically diminished. Automobiles are a major source of the black haze that hangs over these cities. The number of cars has risen dramatically with economic development. Millions of cars now crowd the streets of New Delhi, Beijing, and Mexico City. Another major source of air pollution are the industries that are seen as essential to economic development. In China, for example, many of these industries use coal. Coal-powered plants spew harmful particles into the air and create the

Ganges River

A river in India along which almost half of the country's citizens live.

Major cities in the developing world are very polluted.

Developing countries are reluctant to favor the environment over economic growth.

Environmental Problems and Development

China's phenomenal economic growth has been accompanied by extraordinarily high levels of pollution. Poisons from mines contaminate land and water; new cars, air conditioners, and factories contribute to widespread air pollution. Farmland erosion and desertification are increasing, and industrial wastes are dumped untreated in rivers and landfills.

Can China continue to enjoy rapid economic growth and, simultaneously, clean up the environment?

haze that cannot be escaped in places such as Beijing. Adding to the problem caused by industry is the widespread use of coal by Chinese citizens to heat their homes and cook their food. Sixteen of the world's twenty most polluted cities are in China. The World Bank estimated that environmental problems and pollution cost China $170 billion a year. Toxic chemicals and climate-changing gases from the smokestacks of China's coal-burning power plants cross the Pacific to pollute California, Oregon, Washington, and other parts of the United States.[22] Few developing countries are willing to impose pollution restrictions on industries that fuel economic growth.

Pollution imposes significant economic and social costs on developing societies. Governments have to allocate more of their resources to efforts to reduce pollution levels and to pay for the health consequences of pollution. Taiwan, China, and Mexico are experiencing escalating rates of asthma and other respiratory diseases, lung and heart diseases, premature births and low birth weight, and premature deaths. In Beijing alone, more than 20,000 people died from pollution. The **World Health Organization (WHO),** an agency of the United Nations that attempts to improve the health of people around the world, studied the effects of contaminants in heavily polluted cities. It found that Mexico City's pollution is the most noxious for children. They are exposed to contaminants that are the equivalent of smoking two packs of cigarettes a day.[23] Children in Mexico City, especially those who live near city dumps, are never well. Many develop flulike symptoms, skin rashes, and almost constant throat infections. Although many urban residents realize the severity of pollution problems, they often feel unable to change their environment. Some governments have taken steps to deal with the problem. China, India, Mexico, and Brazil have increased gasoline prices by as much as 121 percent to reduce emissions of carbon dioxide. India is the world's largest producer of wind energy, and Bangladesh is relying increasingly on solar energy in rural areas. China is reducing its dependence on polluting coal and turning to cleaner sources of energy such as oil and natural gas. Despite these developments, poor countries, which are responsible for 30 to 40 percent of global pollution, believe that rich countries should bear most of the burden of emissions that cause the greenhouse gasses that are contributing to **global warming.** However, governments in developing countries are being pressured to change by environmental groups such as **Greenpeace** as well as by grassroots organizations that are concerned about the costs of environmental problems.

World Health Organization

An agency of the United Nations that attempts to improve the health of people around the world.

global warming

Caused mainly by emissions of carbon dioxide.

Greenpeace

A nongovernmental environmental group.

Deforestation

Deforestation is directly linked to the forces of modernization. Economic development, as Chapter 6 shows, involves building roads, airports, harbors, railroads, large reservoirs, dams, schools, hospitals, recreational facilities, storage facilities, and other projects. All of these require a large amount of land as well as forest resources.

Deforestation is linked to modernization.

Compared with productive agricultural land, forests are widely seen as less valuable. Destruction of the forests makes the land more valuable. Population pressures help speed up the process of deforestation in many ways. As population expands, the demand for fuel for cooking increases. Most of the trees that are cut down in developing countries are used for cooking and other domestic uses. About 90 percent of the African population depends on the forests for fuel. As urbanization and industrialization spread, more trees are destroyed. Land must be cleared to accommodate the growing number of urban residents. The pollution caused by industrialization and urbanization contributes to deforestation as more people use wood as fuel to boil contaminated water in an effort to purify it. Population pressures sometimes trigger ethnic conflicts. In an attempt to escape violence, many refugees live in the forests. They destroy many trees in order to obtain shelter and food. Population pressure also leads to deforestation by increasing the need for more agricultural land.

Most of the land that is cleared of forests is used for slash-and-burn agriculture. Many people in developing countries depend on traditional agricultural methods to produce enough food for themselves and their families. Commercial agriculture also contributes to deforestation. Millions of square miles of forests are cleared each year to grow coffee, tea, cocoa, rubber, palm oil, sugar cane, citrus, bananas, soybeans, and rice. Forests are also destroyed to create pasture to expand commercial cattle production. Cattle ranching has been a main cause of deforestation in Brazil and Central America. As commercial farming expands, the agricultural workers are usually replaced by machines. Unless new employment opportunities are created, many of the unemployed, landless workers see moving to the rain forest in search of land as their only option. In fact, many governments have aggressively supported deforestation in an effort to relocate people to less crowded areas. **Indonesia's Transmigration Program,** for example, attempted to relocate 140 million people and convert 2.5 million acres of rain forest to rice paddies. Similarly, Brazil constructed the **Trans-Amazon Highway** and encouraged millions of landless peasants to move to the Amazon and clear the land for cultivation. Both projects received funding from the World Bank.[24] Many of these agricultural projects fail because many rain forest soils are relatively poor in nutrients and are vulnerable to erosion caused by heavy rainfalls. Nevertheless, the Amazon continues to be destroyed by development.

Deforestation is also caused by commercial logging practices that do not focus on sustainable development of forest resources. The demand for tropical hardwoods such as mahogany is contributing to the destruction of forests in Southeast Asia, Central America, and elsewhere in the developing world. The demand for furniture and construction materials in developing countries themselves makes it difficult to practice

Indonesia's Transmigration Program

A program attempting to convert rain forest land to rice paddies.

Trans-Amazon Highway

Encouraged millions of landless peasants to move to the Amazon and clear the land for cultivation.

TAKING ACTION Protecting the Environment

In 1977, Dr. Wangari Muta Maathai of Kenya started the Greenbelt Movement to stop deforestation. In 2004, she became the first African woman to win the Nobel Peace Prize. Her movement planted more than 30 million trees across Africa.

sustainable development. In 2006, Indonesia signed an agreement with China that enables China to obtain wood from its forests for flooring, furniture, and construction. China promised to develop large palm oil plantations to replace trees destroyed in Indonesia. Many tropical woods are being harvested faster than they can be replaced. Development also creates a greater demand for paper products. This leads to more forests being exploited for pulp and paper production. The export of forest products is also viewed by many governments in the developing world as a relatively low cost and easily accessible source of revenue for funding domestic projects and to pay down their foreign debts. International pressures to repay loans used to fund various development programs hastened deforestation in many developing countries in the 1980s.

The export of forest products is seen as an easy way to obtain much-needed revenues.

One of the most common causes of deforestation is the deliberate setting of fires by small farmers, commercial farmers, ranchers, logging companies, and others. Satellite images of Brazil, Colombia, Indonesia, Tanzania, and elsewhere show that fires caused by people are destroying many tropical forests. Burning is widely practiced to clear brush and forest regrowth. However, many people set fires but do not have effective measures to contain them. Furthermore, burning forests is not generally perceived as a serious problem in most poor countries. In fact, burning is an integral part of agriculture and farming. Fire is used because it is cheap, fast, and effective—if it can be controlled. Another factor contributing to the increase in forest fires in the Amazon and Southeast Asia is selective logging. As forests are thinned out, humidity falls. Drier conditions facilitate the spread of human-made fires. The costs of these fires are high, in terms of human life, the destruction of property, and deforestation. Many people were killed in Indonesia in 1997. Smoke from forest fires impaired visibility to such an extent that an airliner crashed and two ships collided. Smog caused widespread illness and forced authorities to close schools and airports.

The costs of human-made fires are high.

Numerous problems are created by deforestation. Many plant and animal species are destroyed, thereby reducing the earth's biodiversity. The preservation of biodiversity is essential to many scientific advances in industry, agriculture, and medicine. Many of the human inhabitants of the forests also face the danger of extinction when their habitat is destroyed. Destruction of the rain forests is also seen as contributing to climate change. Areas become hotter and drier after forests are destroyed. Deforestation may actually change an area from being moist and humid to a desert. Because large rain forests, such as the Amazon, have an impact on the global climate, their destruction is seen as helping to create the problem of global warming and climate instability. Agricultural productivity declines as rainfall diminishes and as soil erosion becomes more extensive. In some

Deforestation threatens biodiversity.

Climate change is linked to deforestation.

areas, destructive floods become more prevalent even as groundwater reserves fall. Homes, farms, the infrastructure essential to development, and industrial plants are destroyed by extreme weather conditions. People who depend on forest products for their livelihoods must find other sources of income as deforestation expands. Forests provide a habitat for animals that help to pollinate plants and control agricultural pests.[25] Destruction of the forests ultimately threatens human survival.

Dam Construction

Economic development requires the availability of abundant and inexpensive energy to run industries, cities, and irrigation systems. Even though many developing countries have natural gas, coal, and petroleum, others have to import the energy. Alternative sources of energy, such as wind energy, solar energy, and hydroelectric power, are attractive to poor countries that want to reduce both costs and their vulnerability to unstable global energy markets. As with other aspects of development, the construction of dams carries costs as well as benefits. The choice between constructing a dam and preserving the environment was relatively easy for Egypt, a country in which almost the entire population is concentrated in less than 5 percent of the land area. Most of Egypt is a desert. The country has always depended on the water of the Nile River for its survival. Economic development and rapid population growth influenced the British, who ruled Egypt at the time, to build the Aswan Dam in 1902. A major objective was to store water to irrigate agricultural areas of the Nile Valley. In 1960, a hydroelectric power station was added to meet the rising demand for energy. When Gamal Abdul Nasser gained control of Egypt in 1954, he made the construction of another dam, the **Aswan High Dam,** the major component of Egypt's economic development program. The goal was to expand the amount of land for agriculture by providing relatively inexpensive water for irrigation. With the application of fertilizers and modern farming techniques, Egypt was able to plant two or three crops a year instead of just one. To build the dam, more than 90,000 people and many archaeological treasures had to be moved. Like most large infrastructure projects, construction of the Aswan High Dam generated much controversy.

One of the most controversial projects is the world's largest dam, the **Three Gorges Dam** on the Yangtze River in China. Like the Nile in Egypt, the Yangtze has played a central and often destructive role in China's history. The Yangtze flooded an area the size of New York state in 1931 and created about 14 million refugees. In 1954, the river flooded more than 6.9 million acres of land and killed more than 30,000 people. In 1998, the Yangtze flooded and nearly 14 million people were displaced and an undetermined number were killed. A principal reason for building the Three Gorges Dam is to prevent such disastrous floods, which not only take many lives, but also impede China's economic development. Other reasons for building the dam are to increase electrical power for **Pudong,** a major industrial development zone not far from Shanghai, and for relatively isolated inland areas that receive electricity infrequently. The dam's construction also made it easier for ships and barges to navigate the Yangtze further into the country's underdeveloped interior. But the costs of building the Three Gorges Dam are high. Apart from the $32 billion

Aswan High Dam

A dam built in Egypt to meet the rising demand for energy and to control flooding.

Three Gorges Dam

Located on the Yangtze River, it is the world's largest dam.

Pudong

A major industrial development zone in China.

allocated for construction, it is estimated that 1.2 million people have been removed from their homes. Hundreds of historical sites have been covered by water, and thousands of acres of fertile agricultural land have been lost. Many scenic areas that attracted tourists are now hidden. However, it is believed that the Three Gorges Dam itself will become a major tourist attraction.[26] It was completed in 2006.

Summary and Review

Economic development is inevitably accompanied by various costs. However, not all of these costs are inevitable. Sometimes countries, and particular communities within them, pay a much higher cost for economic growth than is necessary. Progress usually is achieved at a price. Developing and developed countries alike wrestle with costs of development. Many of the costs of development, however, are borne by people in the developing world. These include (1) urbanization; (2) pollution; (3) deforestation; (4) political instability and corruption; (5) the destruction of cultural artifacts and communities due to the construction of dams, airports, roads, and other infrastructure projects; (6) consumerism; and (7) the growing inequality within developing countries. These costs, even those that are obviously undesirable, are usually accompanied by many benefits. As modernization theorists argue, development, by definition, involves the destruction of traditional values and cultures and the adoption of values and cultures found in industrialized societies. One of the most important social costs of development is the escalation of criminal activities and a significant change in the nature of the crimes committed. Modernization weakens many of the social bonds that helped reduce crime. Two groups that most frequently bear the most severe negative consequences of development are women and children. Many argue that the destruction of the old social fabric, degradation of the ecosystem, and high levels of exploitation are hallmarks of development. Critics of such a "no pain, no gain" approach, on the contrary, argue that development can be achieved at sustainable levels and that the development of underdeveloped countries in Africa, Asia, and Latin America will not occur along the same destructive linear lines that they did in the developed countries of Europe.

Key Terms

Discussion Questions

1. Is sustainable development an achievable goal or a hopeless utopian dream?
2. What are the negative consequences of development?
3. How does increased globalization place pressures on societies of Asia, Africa, and Latin America to develop?
4. Is development possible without the destruction of the old social fabric?
5. What are the differences between "Westernization" and development?
6. Do you support development theorists in their claims that development occurs along a destructive linear path? Support your argument.
7. What are some ways of avoiding child labor?
8. Does Nike set a standard for other companies to avoid exploitation of developing societies, or is its Memorandum of Understanding a pathetic, normative attempt at disguising their exploitative guilt and co-opting public opinion?
9. Why should the world take an interest in multinational corporations paying a living wage to their employees in developing countries?
10. What kinds of conflict arise as a result of development?

Suggested Readings

Bass, Loretta E. *Child Labor in Sub-Saharan Africa.* Boulder, CO: Lynne Rienner, 2004.

Booth, Douglas E. *Hooked on Growth: Economic Addictions and the Environment.* Lanham, MD: Rowman and Littlefield, 2004.

Economy, Elizabeth C. *The River Runs Black: The Environmental Challenge to China's Future.* Ithaca, NY: Cornell University Press, 2004.

Esbenshade, Jill. *Monitoring Sweatshops.* Philadelphia, PA: Temple University Press, 2004.

Guimaraes, Roberto P. "The Environment, Population, and Urbanization." In Richard S. Hillman, ed. *Understanding Contemporary Latin America.* Boulder, CO: Lynne Rienner, 1997.

Isin, Engin F., ed. *Democracy, Citizenship, and the Global City.* New York: Routledge, 2000.

Linden, Eugene. "Seeing the Forest." *Foreign Affairs* 83, no. 4 (July/August 2004): 8–13.

Linden, Eugene. "The Exploding Cities of the Developing World." *Foreign Affairs* 75, no. 1 (January/February 1996): 52–65.

Yusuf, Shahid, Weiping Wu, and Simon Evenett, eds. *Local Dynamics in an Era of Globalization: 21st Century Catalysts for Development.* New York: Oxford University Press, 2000.

Van Schendel, Willem Abraham, and Itty Abraham. *Illicit Flows and Criminal Things.* Bloomington, IN: Indiana University Press, 2006.

Addresses and Websites

The Centre for Development and Population Activities
1400 16th Street NW, Suite 100
Washington, D.C. 20036
Tel: (202) 667–1142
Fax: (202) 332–4496
http://www.cedpa.org/

The Centre for Development and Population Activities specifically targets women with their efforts with development. The organization looks to provide women with reproductive health and family planning options, among other useful skills. This website offers information about women and development, including information on women and poverty. There are links to the organization's publications where further information can be obtained.

International Development Exchange—IDEX
827 Valencia Street Suite 101
San Francisco, CA 94110–1736
Tel: (415) 824–8384
http://www.idex.org/

IDEX is an organization, based within the United States, that works toward economic justice in Asia, Africa, and Latin America. The group works with low-income nations in order to promote their goal of economic justice and to eradicate global inequalities, as well. This website allows the browser to enter into the world of IDEX and its work. The organization currently assists eight nations, and the website offers brief information regarding economic conditions in these nations, along with information on their involvement with them.

Office of Public Information
The Carter Center
453 Freedom Parkway
Atlanta, GA 30307
Tel: (404) 331–3900
http://www.cartercenter.org/

The Carter Center is an organization that works toward human rights and the relief of human suffering.

The organization seeks to promote democracy and freedom, while working on issues such as health and conflict resolution. Because peace and health-related issues are top priorities for the group, the website offers links to the various health and peace programs on which the Carter Center is currently working. Further information regarding the Carter Center and its projects can be found on the website. This website also offers information on development, as well.

Society for International Development
Via Panisperna, 207
00184 Rome, Italy
Tel: +39–064872172
Fax: +39–064872170
http://www.sidint.org/

The Society for International Development is an organization that offers support regarding developmental issues and concerns at the local, national, and global levels. The organization sponsors a variety of programs, with issues ranging from health and globalization to women's concerns to knowledge, communications, and information technologies. There are numerous links provided on this website, including one for their development journal and other publications.

Notes

1. Alfonso Gonzalez, "Introduction," in Alfonso Gonzalez and Jim Norwine, eds., *The Third World* (Boulder, CO: Westview Press, 1998), 2.
2. Julia Preston, "In Defiance of Reforms, Crime Rises in Mexico City," *The New York Times*, 17 November 1998, A3; and "Crime and Policing in Latin America," *The Economist*, 2 October 2004, 35.
3. "Criminal Neglect: Mexico," *The Economist*, 1 November 1997, 36.
4. Chitra Ragavan and David Kaplan, "Why Auto Theft Is Going Global," *U.S. News and World Report*, 14 June 1999, 16; and Willem van Schendel and Itty Abraham, *Illicit Flows and Criminal Things* (Bloomington, IN: Indiana University Press, 2006).
5. Fiona Fleck, "Chipping Away at Child Labor," *The Christian Science Monitor*, 23 June 1999, 1; and Stephen Franklin, "Child Labor On Decline Globally," *Chicago Tribune*, 5 May 2006, Sect. 3, 1.
6. John Zubrzycki, "A Tough Buy: Child-Woven Carpets," *The Christian Science Monitor*, 30 October 1997, 1.
7. Jeremy Seabrook, "Reproach of Child Labor," *Financial Times*, 24 August 1999, 10.
8. Matt Moffett, "Citrus Squeeze," *The Wall Street Journal*, 9 September 1998, 1.
9. Elizabeth Olson, "World Panel Adopts Treaty to Restrict Child Labor," *The New York Times*, 18 June 1999, A12.
10. Nicholas D. Kristof, "Asia's Crisis Upsetting Effort to Reduce Sweatshop Blight," *The New York Times*, 15 June 1998, A1.
11. Debora L. Spar, "The Spotlight and the Bottom Line," *Foreign Affairs* 77, no. 2 (March/April 1999): 9.
12. "The Global Sweatshop," *Far Eastern Economic Review*, 19 September 1996, 5.
13. Nancy Birdsall, Carol Graham, and Richard Sabot, "Virtuous Circles in Latin America's Second Stage

Reforms," in Nancy Birdsall et al., eds., *Beyond Tradeoffs: Market Reforms and Equitable Growth in Latin America* (Washington, D.C.: Inter-American Development Bank, 1998), 2.

14. "World's Population Literally Bursting at the Seams," *The Pantagraph*, 5 March 2000, A1; and Marc Santora, "Concern Grows Over Worldwide Increase in Diabetes Cases," *The New York Times*, 11 June 2006, A12.

15. "Troublesome Trends: Population Growth, Distribution, Migration," *UN Chronicle* 31 (September 1994): 44; and UNDP, *Human Development Report 2004* (New York: Oxford University Press, 2004), 155.

16. Exequiel Ezcurra and Maria Mazari-Hiriart, "Are Mega Cities Viable," *Environment* (January–February 1996): 6.

17. The World Resources Institute, *World Resources 1996–1997* (New York: Oxford University Press, 1996), 27.

18. Roberto P. Guimaraes, "The Environment, Population, and Urbanization," in Richard S. Hillman, ed., *Understanding Contemporary Latin America* (Boulder, CO: Lynne Rienner, 1997), 193.

19. Eugene Linden, "The Exploring Cities of the Developing World," *Foreign Affairs* 75, no. 1 (January/February 1996), 57.

20. Diana Jean Schemo, "Ecuadoreans Want Texaco to Clear Toxic Residue," *The New York Times*, 1 February 1998, A10.

21. John Zubrzycki, "Pollution of Rivers in India Reaches a Crisis," *The Christian Science Monitor*, 29 October 1997, 5.

22. Elisabeth Rosenthal, "Beijing Officially Uncaps Filter on Its Staggering Pollution Data," *The New York Times*, 14 June 1998, A1; "China's Growing Pains," *The Economist*, 21 August 2004, 11–12; and Keith Bradsher, "Clouds from Chinese Coal Cast a long Shadow" *The New York Times*, 11 June 2006, A1.

23. Julia Preston, "A Fatal Case of Fatalism," *The New York Times*, 14 February 1999, A10.

24. Solon L. Barraclough and Krishna B. Ghimire, *Forests and Livelihoods* (New York: St. Martin's Press, 1995), 14; and Sander Thoenes, "In Asia's Big Haze, Man Battles Man-Made Disaster," *The Christian Science Monitor*, 28 October 1997, 1.

25. Janet Abramovitz, "Putting a Value on Nature's Free Services," *World Watch* 11, no. 1 (January–February 1998): 10–20.

26. Jean Ash, "Damming the Yangtze," *Forum for Applied Research and Public Policy* 13 (Fall 1998): 78–84; and Xiong Lei, "Going Against the Flow," *Science* (3 April 1998): 24–27.

CHAPTER EIGHT

Women in the Developing World

GLOBALIZATION AND WOMEN

MANY SIGNIFICANT CHANGES INITIATED BY WOMEN IN AFRICA, ASIA, AND LATIN AMERICA CANNOT BE ATTRIBUTED TO THE INFLUENCE OF GLOBALIZATION. HOWEVER, THE MAIN ENGINES OF GLOBALIZATION—COMMUNICATIONS TECHNOLOGY AND RAPID AND INEXPENSIVE COMMUNICATIONS—HAVE FACILITATED INTERACTIONS AMONG WOMEN AND THE FORMATION OF GLOBAL NETWORKS. MANY WOMEN FROM ELITE FAMILIES WHO WERE EDUCATED IN THE WEST MAINTAINED CONNECTIONS WITH INFLUENTIAL MEN AND WOMEN IN THE UNITED STATES AND WESTERN EUROPE. MANY WOMEN IN THE WEST PERCEIVE THE STRUGGLES OF WOMEN IN THE DEVELOPING WORLD AS LINKED TO THEIR OWN. CONSEQUENTLY, MANY OF THEM PRESSURE THEIR GOVERNMENTS AND INTERNATIONAL ORGANIZATIONS TO MAKE WOMEN'S ISSUES A PRIORITY IN THEIR RELATIONS WITH AFRICA, ASIA, AND LATIN AMERICA.

ONE OF THE MOST POTENT EFFECTS OF GLOBALIZATION IS ITS TENDENCY TO DIMINISH DIFFERENCES NOT ONLY AMONG CULTURES, BUT ALSO BETWEEN MEN AND WOMEN. GLOBALIZATION HAS HASTENED THE SPREAD OF THE MOVEMENT FOR GENDER EQUALITY BY MAKING WOMEN MORE AWARE OF THEIR STATUS AND THE NEED TO CHANGE IT. WOMEN, IN A GLOBAL SOCIETY, COMPARE THEMSELVES WITH THE MOST VISIBLE AND INFLUENTIAL WOMEN. FURTHERMORE, GLOBAL COMPANIES USUALLY PREFER TO EMPLOY WOMEN IN THE DEVELOPING WORLD, THEREBY GIVING THEM A MEASURE OF FINANCIAL INDEPENDENCE. WOMEN BECOME MORE EDUCATED AND ARE GENERALLY UNWILLING TO ACCEPT THE STATUS QUO. IN EFFECT, GLOBALIZATION HELPS WOMEN BECOME AGENTS OF CHANGE.

INTRODUCTION

Although it is common to discuss women in the developing world as a unified group, this oversimplification ignores the complexity that characterizes developing countries. Old values, challenged by new values, continue to influence relations between men and women and among women themselves. In some Islamic societies, some women insist on wearing a veil and yet others reject veiling. However, throughout the developing world women are the principal initiators of changes that will improve their lives. Modernization and globalization are eroding cultural boundaries and weakening the control that some men, the government, and some women exercise in an effort to maintain the status quo. Access to education and economic opportunities has enabled many women in Asia, Latin America, and Africa to develop a degree of social and financial independence that most women in the United States and other industrialized countries enjoy. The U.N. Development Program created the gender empowerment measure (GEM) to focus women's participation in economic and political activities. It also concentrates on gender disparities in government and economic opportunities.

Global changes have not affected all women in the same way. Development has, in some cases, helped widen economic and social gaps among women. Rural

Global changes have not affected all women in the same way.

women and urban women do not necessarily face the same problems or opportunities. Furthermore, each country has its own traditions and policies relating to women. These differences make it difficult to generalize about women in developing areas. Nonetheless, there is widespread agreement that women throughout the developing world are bringing about economic, social, and political change. This chapter discusses the roles and status of women, the practice of veiling, female genital mutilation, the sale of women, and "honor" killings in Africa, Asia, and Latin America. It also examines educational opportunities for women, the role of women in economic development, and women's political participation, including leadership roles.

THE ROLES OF WOMEN

socialization

The process in which values and perceptions help to determine our roles in society.

roles

Expectations regarding the duties, rights, and skills of individuals.

People in all societies have certain perceptions of themselves and others. How we see ourselves and those around us is shaped by values that we learn from parents, teachers, religious authorities, friends, and the media through the process of **socialization.** Values are widely shared beliefs and assumptions about what is right and wrong, proper and improper, just and unjust. These values, beliefs, and perceptions tell us how to relate to others and how they should relate to us. They tell us how to behave. In other words, values and perceptions help determine our roles in society. Many of these values and perceptions are reinforced by laws and policies made by governments. **Roles** can be defined as expectations regarding the skills, rights, and duties of individuals. Roles function as prescriptions for interpersonal behaviors that are associated with particular categories of persons.[1] But people constantly challenge prescribed roles, thereby changing societal perceptions of how men and women should behave and relate to each other.

In June 1998, the Southern Baptist Convention, America's largest Protestant denomination, issued a controversial statement that called on women to submit themselves graciously to their husbands' leadership.[2] When King Hussein of Jordan died in early 1999, his American wife, Queen Noor, did not attend the funeral. Because of

Muslim teachings that discourage the mixing of unrelated men and women, female relatives of King Hussein stayed at home to accept condolences from other women.[3] It may be argued that these two examples should not be equated. However, in both cases, religion and tradition support maintaining what many regard as different and distinct roles. These examples, although not equivalent, show that developed countries also have many stereotypes. At the same time, women are helping undermine those traditional roles. Many women in the United States disagreed strongly with the Southern Baptists. Several women in leadership roles, including Rima Khalaf, a member of the Jordanian senate, Queen Beatrix of the Netherlands, and President Mary McAleese of Ireland, attended King Hussein's funeral.

Most countries in Africa, Asia, and Latin America have traditions that make women primarily responsible for domestic work. Latin American societies generally view women as moral guardians of the family. Women teach values and morality by example. Susan Tiano maintains that according to the ideology of **marianismo,** the cult of Virgin Mary, the family is seen as being held together spiritually and emotionally through the mother's steadfast devotion. Marianismo supports the gender division of labor, which confines women to the house.[4] In some Islamic societies, religion assigns domestic roles to women. As will be discussed, the emphasis on women as guardians of the family virtue sometimes leads to extreme actions such as honor killings, when women violate social roles. In Bangladesh, India, and other Asian societies, women are responsible for taking care of their own families and their husbands' families.

Gender roles in poor countries are shaped to some extent by colonialism and the globalization of industry and trade. Plantation agriculture in Africa, for example, weakened the role of women as farmers. Colonial authorities imposed their own values on the Africans. They strengthened the role of men as heads of families, provided education for

Gender roles are shaped by colonialism and globalization.

men on a limited scale, hired men to work in agriculture, and emphasized training in domestic skills for women.[5] Many women, however, managed to continue as entrepreneurs. The decline of plantation agriculture contributed to the emergence of women as the primary producers of food. As countries industrialize, more women work in labor-intensive industries. Women, as will be discussed, are the majority of workers in the apparel, footwear, and electronics industries in Asia and Latin America. Increasingly, more women are gaining major positions in areas such as law, business, higher education, finance, medicine, and government, in addition to nursing, teaching, and other traditional fields. The roles of women are closely linked to their status.

THE STATUS OF WOMEN

Women generally have a lower status than men in most societies, including those in the industrialized world. **Status** refers to one's position in the social, economic, and political hierarchy. Men are generally regarded as occupying a higher place than

marianismo

An ideology in which the family is seen as being held together spiritually and emotionally through the mother's steadfast devotion.

status

One's position in the social, economic, and political hierarchy.

N **IN THE NEWS**

The Status of Women

A pregnant teenager was sentenced to receive 180 lashes with a cane by a Muslim (shari'a) court in northern Nigeria in September 2000. The seventeen-year-old girl was found guilty of having premarital sex and was to be flogged forty days after giving birth. The father of the child was apparently not charged with having premarital sex with the teenager.

social construct

Subjective standards used by societies.

dowries

Money given to a husband for marrying a particular woman.

Karma

Hindu belief that what happens to one in this life is determined by one's good or evil deeds in a previous life.

veiling

The covering of a woman's body with garments that preserve the notion of male dominance and female subservience.

women occupy in the social system. These positions are largely **socially constructed,** primarily by men. This means that societies use subjective standards to determine who will have a higher or lower status. These standards are subject to change as societies change. Tradition, religion, political and social beliefs, and economics determine status. Women in societies in which religion does not play a dominant role generally have a higher status than women in countries where social relations are based on religion. As societies become more industrialized and as women's economic position is strengthened, the gap in status between men and women narrows. The forces of modernization, economic necessity, and globalization are challenging notions of status based on tradition and religion.

Marriage illustrates the differences in status between men and women. Men in some Islamic societies are permitted by law and religion to have four wives and to divorce them. Women are allowed to have one husband and cannot easily obtain a divorce. A Muslim woman may not marry a non-Muslim man unless he becomes a Muslim. However, a Muslim man may marry a non-Muslim woman, but she too needs to convert to Islam. In Egypt, for example, the law allowed rapists to escape punishment if they married their victims. Parents and other relatives of rape victims have used the law to regain their family's honor. Parents of brides provide **dowries,** or property given at the time of marriage. Many women are killed in India, Pakistan, and Bangladesh because their husbands are not satisfied with the size of their dowries. Women in Bangladesh who have achieved a degree of financial success to enable them to refuse marriage proposals are often victimized by the rejected men. Some have had acid splashed in their faces and are blinded for life. Widows in India become dependent on their husbands' families, many of which perceive them as social and economic burdens. Eventually, many Hindu widows become social outcasts, a fate they believe happens to be their **Karma.** Karma is the Hindu belief that what happens to one in this life is determined by one's good or evil deeds in a previous life. The low status of women is further demonstrated by veiling, female genital mutilation, the selling of girls, and honor killing.

Veiling symbolizes gender segregation, the unequal relationship between men and women, and the complex nature of status in some Muslim countries. It also represents a broader cultural and political defense against Western cultural influences that appear to be irresistible even in very religious and traditional societies. But the main

YOU DECIDE ✔️   ## Veiling Women

Many women in the Islamic world wear the veil. As we have seen, the degree of veiling varies from one country to another and within societies. Many women and men in the United States and Western Europe regard veiling as an indication of male dominance over women. It is often argued that veiling is a matter of culture and should be seen in terms of cultural relativism.

Do you think that women and men from Islamic countries would have similar criticisms about the treatment of women in the West in relation to how they dress?

function of veiling is to preserve male dominance and female subservience and chastity. It is in countries where Islamic fundamentalism dominates that veiling is strictly enforced. Veiling varies from one Islamic society to another and covers a broad range of garments.[6] The veil in Morocco covers most of a woman's face and the rest of her body. In other countries, the veil leaves the face uncovered. Women in Afghanistan were covered from head to toe. In Turkey, Egypt, Tunisia, and other Muslim countries, the veil is used as a fashion statement and what it covers depends on the message wearers intend to communicate.

Afghanistan, Saudi Arabia, and Iran are examples of how veiling represents maintaining or returning to Islamic traditions. These countries are concerned with preserving their identity and their interpretation of Islamic heritage in the face of steady erosion of values and norms associated with a purer form of traditional Islam. All three countries have been exposed to Westernization and, in varying degrees, are resisting Western values. The Islamic **Taliban movement,** which ruled most of Afghanistan until 2002, was the most extreme of the Islamic fundamentalists. The religious police, in the General Department for the Preservation of Virtue and Prevention of Vice, came from villages in which contact between men and women who are not family members has always been forbidden. The Taliban strictly segregated men and women. Women were beaten if they allowed their faces, feet, or ankles to show beneath the mandatory head-to-toe shrouds. Women's bodies, including their ankles and feet, were seen as being sexually provocative. The veil in Afghanistan was equated with morality and female subservience. The defeat of the Taliban in 2002 by American and British forces ended many of the restrictions on women in Afghanistan. Saudi Arabia is a much more complex and less extreme society than Afghanistan. However, the moral police in Saudi Arabia also enforces strict dress codes. Women are not allowed to drive automobiles, wear short sleeves in public, or appear in public without covering their heads. Iran, which experienced significant social and economic changes before Ayatollah Khomeini took control of the country, struggles with both modernization and Islamic fundamentalism. Religious authorities in Iran enforce laws requiring women to wear the Islamic **chadore,** which covers their bodies completely. Women were forced to accept an inferior status by the Islamic state.

Taliban movement
Composed of extreme Islamic fundamentalists in Afghanistan.

chadore
A garment that women are required by law to wear in Iran and that covers the body completely.

Some women wear the veil for personal, political, and cultural reasons. Many women see Islamic dress as giving them both dignity and privacy in their societies. Modern women in urban areas may wear the veil in order to communicate their adherence to the Islamic moral and sexual code, while, at the same time, allowing them to interact with men. Women from traditional families and rural areas wear the veil in places such as Egypt to maintain a sense of identity. Coming from areas where men and women are segregated, women see the veil as providing security for women in sexually integrated settings. It also allows women to maintain outward signs of traditional behavior even as they participate in modern life. Some women also believe that wearing the veil is economical and protects them from male sexual harassment.[7]

Throughout the Islamic world, even in Afghanistan, Saudi Arabia, and Iran, women are challenging veiling and the values it represents. In fact, the renewed emphasis on veiling women reflects significant cultural change. Many Islamic fundamentalists adopt extreme measures precisely because they see their power eroding in the face of modernization and globalization. Practical economic concerns have always challenged the status quo. Many women in the United States, who once worked at home, now work outside the home because of economic as well as social reasons. As more women are educated, find employment, and live in urban areas, traditional forces are weakened. Veiling is at the heart of political conflict and social change. Men and women, primarily from less-privileged economic backgrounds, use religion and traditional values to assist the old order to maintain political and social control. Women who do not wear the veil are usually from the upper and middle class. These two groups clash because their interests and perceptions of women are fundamentally different.[8]

female genital mutilation

The practice of circumcising women for the benefit of men; it is often defended on the grounds of cultural relativism.

Female genital mutilation, also known as female circumcision, is an extreme form of social control. It is practiced in societies in which women are given a low social status. Even though both men and women are circumcised, female genital mutilation is largely done for the benefit of men. It enables them to control women by inflicting severe pain during sexual intercourse. There are varying degrees of female genital mutilation. It involves the removal of the clitoris in its less severe form, and all of the external female genitals in its most severe form. In extreme cases, vaginas are stitched shut, with only a small opening left through which urine and menstrual fluids can pass. These crude and painful operations are usually performed with knives and razors by traditional women practitioners. The main objective of female genital mutilation is to deprive women of any sexual feelings. By so doing, men are assured of women's chastity. Some women are severely injured and many bleed to death from the procedure. Chronic urinary tract infections are common, and childbirth is dangerous and extraordinarily painful. Egypt, Nigeria, Ethiopia, Somalia, Kenya, and the Sudan account for about 75 percent of the cases.[9] Like veiling, female genital mutilation is usually seen as a religious practice as well as a cultural issue by some Islamic conservatives. Muslims in Africa believe that the circumcision of girls is as much a religious requirement as the circumcision of boys. Parents and girls who are educated are increasingly opposed to the operation. Furthermore, some governments, despite opposition from religious and traditional leaders, have banned genital mutilation.

The **sale of females** remains an important indicator of the status of women in developing countries. Like other forms of human bondage, this trafficking of young girls and women is rooted in both traditional and economic considerations. People of lower social and economic status are generally vulnerable to extreme forms of exploitation and even death. In Asia and Africa, poor girls and women are often sold by their families as brides. In some parts of Kenya, for example, mothers encourage their daughters to remain chaste so that they may obtain a higher price for them. This preoccupation with virginity influences families and others to sell very young girls both as brides and as prostitutes. Unlike in India, where women pay dowries to men, tradition in Africa requires a man to pay a **bride price.** Girls who are educated are often sold for higher prices. Sometimes the bride's family will take her from her husband if he fails to make regular payments.[10] Modernization and generational change are challenging the custom of selling women.

Women throughout the world are forced or choose to go into prostitution primarily because of economic reasons. Young girls are especially vulnerable. India, Bangladesh, Thailand, Cambodia, and other Asian countries have long traditions of family-sanctioned prostitution. In Nepal, for example, as many as 40,000 girls and women have been sold and forced into prostitution, mostly in neighboring India. Many Nepalese girls from destitute families, especially those from low castes, often see leaving their homes as their only hope for a better life. This makes them easy victims for sex traffickers. Because of the low status of women and perceptions of prostitution as a business, not a moral issue, some families willingly sell their daughters. As in other Asian societies, Nepalese families tend to value sons more than daughters. Sons are viewed as assets, whereas daughters are viewed as liabilities. This facilitates selling daughters into prostitution. Similar practices are found in Africa and Latin America.[11]

Honor killings occur in societies in which women are basically regarded as bodies over which male relatives have absolute control, including the power to destroy them. Such murders are becoming infrequent and occur primarily in rural areas and traditional societies. Sex has always been a central reason for extreme forms of control exercised by men over women. Honor killing is the slaughter of women deemed to be unchaste by male relatives. An unchaste woman is regarded as a threat to the family's honor, or **sharaf.** Honor is defined in terms of the sexual purity of women. Female chastity is equivalent to honor and respect. An unchaste woman is often perceived as being worse than a murderer, even if she is raped, because she essentially destroys her family socially. Family members are usually ostracized. Only by killing unchaste women can the family's honor be cleansed and restored. Marrying or divorcing without the family's consent may also result in honor killings. Although honor killings are generally associated with Muslims in a few Arab countries, they also occur among Arab Christians in Egypt, Jordan, and Palestine, and in non-Arab countries such as India, Pakistan, and Turkey. In Brazil and other South American countries, men

In Jordan, more than a fourth of all murders each year are honor killings.

often kill women to protect their honor. Many Muslims who favor the practice use Islamic teachings to justify killing their unchaste female relatives. This perception is

---

sale of females

Practice of trafficking young girls and women into forced marriages and prostitution.

bride price

A tradition in Africa in which a man is required to pay for his bride.

honor killings

The slaughter of women who are deemed to be unchaste.

sharaf

A family's honor.

strengthened in Jordan, where one-fourth of all murders each year are honor killings. Jordan treats premarital sex as a criminal offense, equal to adultery. A pregnant, unmarried woman has no rights to her child, which is taken away at birth and raised in an orphanage.[12] It could be argued, however, that honor killing takes place in modern societies under the guise of "estranged husband" or some similar label.

WOMEN AND EDUCATION

Taliban

Islamic movement in Afghanistan that controlled the government until it was ousted by an international force led by the United States after the events of September 11, 2001.

Educating women is essential to economic and political development as well as to improving the status of women. Because educated women challenge traditional roles, men's control over their lives is weakened. Early marriages, an emphasis on childbearing, and religious beliefs have prevented women from achieving educational equality. In Afghanistan, for example, the **Taliban,** the Islamic movement that once controlled most of the country, outlawed education for women, closed educational institutions for women, and prevented women from teaching. The only schools that girls could attend were required to teach the Quran, the holy book for Muslims. Girls older than eight years could not legally attend school. Afghanistan represented extreme efforts to force women into inferior positions by depriving them of access to education. In the developing world, men have higher literacy rates than women, but this is changing as countries achieve greater economic growth. Literacy rates are essentially the same for women and men in rich countries. They are similar in the more industrialized societies in Asia and Latin America. Korea, Thailand, the Philippines, Mexico, Costa Rica, Brazil, and Chile have substantial gender equality in literacy. On the other hand, more traditional societies such as Saudi Arabia, India, Egypt, Pakistan, Bangladesh, and Ethiopia do not. In most poor societies neither women nor men enjoy much access to education.

Many governments have made deliberate efforts to educate women because they see them as the key to development. As part of its revolutionary approach, the new government in Egypt, which overthrew King Farouk in 1952, implemented equal educational opportunities for women. Education was made compulsory and free for all students between the ages of six and twelve. University education was opened to both men and women on a competitive basis, and the government not only made higher education free and accessible to those who qualified for admission, but also guaranteed them jobs after graduation. Women in urban and less traditional areas benefited most from these changes.[13] Egyptian society became more egalitarian and economically developed.

Improvements in education for women change women's perceptions of themselves and their status and roles in society. The empowerment of women through education has far-reaching implications for economic growth, gender equality, and social equity. The World Bank, the United Nations, and private organizations finance programs that allow women to attend literacy classes in private homes or small schools. They learn how

Girls in India between the ages of 1 and 5 are 43 percent more at risk of dying than boys, due to social values.

TABLE 8.1 WOMEN'S ACCESS TO EDUCATION

	Adult Literacy Rate (%) 2002		Combined 1st, 2nd, & 3rd Level Gross Enrollment Ratio (%) 2001–2002	
	Female	Male	Female	Male
United States	**99**	**99**	**97**	**91**
Canada	99	99	100	96
Japan	99	99	83	86
Sweden	99	99	100	95
United Kingdom	99	99	100	99
Korea, Rep. of	95.5	98.9	85	98
Chile	95.6	95.8	76	78
Kuwait	81.0	84.7	81	71
Costa Rica	95.9	95.7	70	69
Mexico	88.7	92.6	74	73
Thailand	90.5	94.9	59	58
Philippines	92.7	92.5	85	80
Saudi Arabia	69.5	84.1	57	58
Brazil	86.5	86.2	94	90
South Africa	85.3	86.7	77	78
Indonesia	83.4	92.5	61	68
Egypt	43.6	67.2	72	80
Zimbabwe	86.3	93.8	57	60
India	46.4	69.0	48	62
Ghana	65.9	81.9	43	50
Pakistan	28.5	53.4	31	43
Nigeria	59.4	74.4	41	49
Bangladesh	31.4	50.3	54	53
Zambia	73.8	86.3	43	47
Haiti	50	53.8	51	53
Ethiopia	33.8	49.2	28	41

Source: United Nations Development Program, *Human Development Report 2004* (New York: Oxford University Press, 2004), 217–20.

to write their names, read at a basic level, and do simple arithmetic. The programs are influencing Indian women to become more self-confident, to discard the veil, to be less dependent on their husbands, and to protect themselves and their children. Many women now challenge the customs of feeding girls less than boys and waiting longer to give girls medical attention. These customs result in high rates of malnutrition among girls and women. Girls in India between the ages of one and five are about 43 percent more at risk of dying than boys.[14] Women who are literate better understand how depriving girls of proper nutrition ultimately contributes to the birth of weaker sons. They also have fewer children and have higher expectations for themselves.

WOMEN IN DEVELOPMENT

Women's role in the development process is shaped to a large extent by how they are perceived in their societies. Although traditional societies limit women to specific occupations, in many parts of Asia and the Middle East, women are the backbone of the local economy. They gather fuel, get water, raise animals, manage local markets, and engage in business transactions in the barter economy. Several factors have caused women to become more active in all sectors of the economy. International development agencies such as the U.S. Agency for International Development (AID), the World Bank, and the United Nations have placed greater emphasis on the need to include more women in development programs. Economic necessity has also contributed to the participation of the growing number of women in the labor force. The most important reasons for the sharp rise in women's employment are globalization and the erosion of traditional values that rigidly defined women's roles. Global pressures have contributed to greater attention to gender responsive budgets that reflect governments' commitment to promoting gender equality through the allocation of public resources.

Many women in the developing world are solely responsible for their family's economic welfare. They engage in subsistence farming as more men migrate to cities.

Women are severely affected by structural adjustment policies.

Many reluctantly join the job market to help maintain living standards that have been undermined by economic crisis and structural adjustment policies imposed by the International Monetary Fund (IMF). Economic crises influence governments to reduce spending on social programs. As we have seen, the IMF will often require them to balance their budgets as a condition for receiving financial assistance. Latin America, with its huge debt burden, was forced to abandon cultural values that kept women at home when the region faced serious economic decline in the 1980s. This period of economic crisis is often called the **Lost Decade.** Even in

Lost Decade
The period of economic decline in Latin America in the 1980s.

TAKING ACTION

Dr. Nafis Sadik and Family Planning

Dr. Nafis Sadik, an obstetrician from Pakistan, became the executive director of the United Nations Population Fund in 1987. Working with independent family planning organizations, women's groups, and governments, she and other increasingly powerful women in the United Nations have transformed the debate over how to reduce population growth into a campaign for women's rights. Dr. Sadik helped put issues such as female genital mutilation, female reproductive rights, sexual violence, the sex trade, and AIDS on the agendas of governments and international organizations. Dr. Sadik tried to avoid emotional debates over cultural values by looking at these issues as public health concerns.

Source: Barbara Crossette, "Working for Women's Sexual Rights," *The New York Times,* 2 October 2000, A8.

Saudi Arabia, where women are strictly controlled, forbidden by law to drive, and segregated, more women are working outside the home. In 1996 the Saudi government made it legal for women to work in the private sector. The main impetus for change is economic decline. As the price of oil dropped from around $37 a barrel in 1979 and 1980 to about $10 a barrel in 1998, the Saudi per capita gross domestic product (GDP) plummeted from around $18,000 to $6,000. Similarly, the economic crisis in Asia in the late 1990s prompted more women to enter the labor markets.

Economic development in poor countries, increased educational opportunities and achievements for women, women's greater self-confidence and their growing sense of empowerment, declining fertility rates, and other forces of modernization contribute to the growth of the number of women in the workforce. Free trade and globalization changed not only how and where products are made, but also who makes them. Many jobs that were once performed mainly by women in the industrialized world are now done by women in developing countries for lower wages. Free trade intensifies global competition, which forces companies to produce high-quality goods at low prices. The growth of service industries further heightened the demand for low-cost, efficient labor. Globalization and the information technologies have led to what is called the **feminization of employment** in the newly created industries.[15]

feminization of employment

The increasing number of women working in the new global economy.

Women are leaving the home in increasing numbers to work in the industries of the new global economy. Although women are making significant gains in all areas of employment, most women are concentrated in the labor-intensive and low-wage industries such as clothing, textiles, shoes, electronics, and communications. Most of the jobs open to women require a willingness to take orders, manual dexterity, an ability to do monotonous tasks, and a willingness to work with the public. These jobs provide limited opportunities for upward mobility or decision-making authority and are closely linked to stereotypes of women's roles. Women in factories are still seen as nurturing, docile, subservient, and responsible. In the **maquiladora industry,** for example, single, childless women who have completed secondary school are the preferred workers. Occupational segregation by sex, a situation in which men get higher paying jobs than women, reinforces gender stereotypes.[16]

maquiladora industry

Prefers to hire single, childless women who graduated from high school.

WOMEN IN AGRICULTURE

Although more women are being employed in global factories, men are much more likely to be employed in the private sector than women. Men still receive most of the jobs in urban areas throughout the developing world. Many leave women behind in rural areas to engage in subsistence agriculture. Women are expected to grow enough food for

Women play a crucial role in agriculture.

their families and to produce cash crops to supplement their income. It is difficult to determine precisely how much of the agricultural production is done by women. The Food and Agriculture Organization (FAO) of the United Nations estimates that women's contribution to the production of food crops ranges from 30 percent in the Sudan to 80 percent in the Democratic Republic of the Congo.[17] Throughout the developing world, women play a crucial role in agriculture. However, many aid organizations often assume that men are the farmers and overlook or downplay women's contributions. Governments tend to give men more financial and technical assistance than women. Consequently, agricultural output remains low, especially in some African countries where up to 75 percent of the labor force is involved in agriculture.

Economic and cultural changes in developing countries are making it easier for women to become entrepreneurs. Advocates of community-based development and sustainable development tend to focus on women's economic contribution as essential to the overall development of a country. Although many efforts to include women in entrepreneurial activities occur at the grassroots level, much of the impetus for them comes from private voluntary organizations (PVOs), various nongovernmental organizations (NGOs), and individuals from outside the area. A key aspect of helping women to build their own businesses is helping them gain access to credit. Women's access to financial support assists the development process in several ways:

Women's access to financial support promotes economic development.

1. Women are able to contribute more to household expenditures and increase the value of their assets.
2. More money in the hands of women also means greater consumption, which stimulates more economic growth.
3. Women who work outside the home are likely to have lower fertility rates, greater access to health care, better nutrition, and increased self-empowerment.
4. As their financial status improves, many other aspects of their lives are likely to change.

They not only enhance their own educational opportunities and access to new cultural values and technologies, but also make sure that their children have similar advantages. Women must have access to credit to break the cycle of poverty by becoming entrepreneurs.

Women face several obstacles when they attempt to obtain credit. Major banks and other lending institutions attempt to minimize their risks by working with larger and more secure borrowers. Women are disadvantaged by their general lack of control over their financial resources and widespread cultural perceptions of women as minors who are dependent on men. Another problem faced by women is their role as homemakers. Throughout the world, women who work at home are not generally regarded in the same way as women who work outside the home. Women's reproductive lives are another disadvantage. Caring for large families makes

Women face several obstacles when they attempt to obtain credit.

it difficult to convince lenders that one can also manage a business simultaneously. Perhaps the most important barrier for women is **internal self-selection.** This refers to the tendency of individuals to decide not to apply for loans. In other words, they select themselves out of the process. Self-selection occurs for several reasons: (1) Some women believe that they do not need credit. (2) Others will not apply for loans because of their experiences with gender discrimination, which lead them to believe that they will be rejected. This creates a self-ful-filling prophecy. (3) Self-selection is often based on erroneous assumptions and information. Although women may correctly assume that their loan applications will be rejected because they lack sufficient income or collateral, they may also incorrectly assume they do not meet the criteria for financial support. Because of these reasons, many women in poor countries rely on the informal sector for their financial services.[18]

internal self-selection

The tendency of individuals to decide not to apply for loans.

Self-selection occurs for several reasons.

The **Grameen Bank** is the best example of an informal lending program that is targeted at rural women. More than 2.3 million people in Bangladesh have received microloans to start their own businesses. More than 94 percent of the borrowers are women. More than 150 organizations around the world, including some in the United States, have replicated the Grameen model to help women escape poverty and its negative consequences. The Grameen Bank was created in Bangladesh by **Muhammad Yunis.** He believed that banks and other financial institutions, by concentrating on individuals with collateral and reliable incomes, excluded the poor from the development process. Taking a grassroots approach to development, the Grameen Bank provides credit to members of the self-selected small groups, about five to seven women. These group members are responsible for each other, and their individual access to credit depends on the group's performance. To become a member of a group, women must be poor, cannot be related to others in the group, and must agree to help each other succeed in their entrepreneurial activities. This approach entails peer support as well as peer pressure. Women are required to learn the rules of the Grameen Bank and to memorize a social contract, known as the **Sixteen Decisions.** These include (1) a commitment to educating their children, (2) a refusal to take or give a dowry, (3) an emphasis on self-improvement and economic prosperity, and (4) a pledge to have small families. At the foundation of the Sixteen Decisions are **four principles:** discipline, unity, courage, and hard work. Women must pass an oral exam that tests their understanding of the bank's rules and its Sixteen Decisions. Once the group qualifies for participation in the program, only two members are allowed to apply for loans. These loans are small, ranging from $25 to $75. After the first two women make about five out of fifty payments, another two members qualify for microloans. The last member will receive a loan when the second two members make four payments. Members are eligible for larger loans after all of them have repaid the initial loans.[19] This program is widely viewed as being extremely successful in lifting women and their families out of poverty. In 2006, Yunis was awarded the Nobel Peace Prize for his work with the Grameen Bank.

Grameen Bank

An informal lending institution that targets rural women.

Muhammad Yunis

Created the Grameen Bank.

Sixteen Decisions

The social contract of the Grameen Bank.

four principles

Discipline, unity, courage, and hard work—the foundation of the Sixteen Decisions.

WOMEN'S POLITICAL PARTICIPATION

Women's participation in politics is influenced to a large extent by a particular society's perceptions of women, their roles, their status, and the country's level of economic and political development. As societies develop, women's political participation also rises. In most political systems, however, women experience varying degrees of political marginalization. Politics is still regarded as an activity for men. Barbara Nelson and Najma Chowdhury refer to this tendency as the **maleness of politics.** They argue that politics is closely connected to the traditional fatherly connotation of patriarchy, which excludes women from power, and to fraternalism. Politics has historically been the province of a brotherhood of men.[20] The American Revolution, the French Revolution, and others focused on the equality of men and fraternity. Nonetheless, women are experiencing unprecedented participation in politics. Women, as will be discussed, occupy important political offices and leadership positions in several developing countries.

Women's political rights have been gradually recognized, first by the right to vote and then by the removal of barriers to their access to public office. As women exercised their right to vote, political parties, interest groups, and other political organizations were pressured to include them in various political institutions. Furthermore, as the international system changes from a preoccupation with security issues to a greater concern with social and economic issues, women are better equipped to play a greater role in politics. Influenced by a sense of justice and strong opposition to gross violations of human rights, women mobilized to bring about change. The **Madres de la Plaza de Mayo,** Argentine mothers who marched daily in Argentina, drew attention to the "disappeared," their relatives who had been killed by the government. Women also led demonstrations in South Africa that eventually helped to end apartheid, or racial segregation and oppression.[21] Throughout the developing world, women's involvement in politics has reached unprecedented levels. Levels of participation among women vary from one part of the developing world to another.

Women in Africa and the Middle East are generally not as actively involved in politics as women in other developing areas. Most African countries are still dominated by cultural values that emphasize politics primarily as a male activity and stress the subordination of women. Women in the northern parts of Africa, where Islam is strong, must also contend with religious beliefs that allow men to control their lives. Husbands and fathers determine women's political participation. Another factor limiting African women's role in politics is education. Uneducated women are less likely than educated women to vote. Women who have access to financial resources—market women in West Africa, for example—are more engaged in political life. Finally, women must often work closely with men and concentrate on men's interests to succeed in a male-dominated political system. Politically active

maleness of politics
Politics regarded as an activity for men.

More educated women are less constrained by tradition and are more active politically.

Madres de la Plaza de Mayo
Mothers who marched in Argentina to draw attention to the "disappeared."

Women in Africa and the Middle East are generally not actively involved in politics.

women, usually better educated and wealthier than most women, often pursue class rather than gender issues.[22] Their interests and positions may be actually threatened by increased participation by women from lower social and economic backgrounds. All of these factors combine to diminish African women's political involvement.

Women in some parts of the Middle East, as we have seen, tend to be rigidly governed by religious and traditional beliefs that exclude them from politics. Furthermore, most countries in the Middle East are not democracies. However, women in countries such as Egypt and Iran vote. Despite restrictions imposed on women by Iran's Islamic government, women are making significant progress. In 2004, women held 12 of the 270 seats in Iran's parliament. Iran also had a woman vice president. It is important to point out that women in Iran had achieved a high level of education and many were indistinguishable from women in Europe and America before the Iranian Revolution of 1979 turned the country into an Islamic state. Since 1956, women in Egypt had the right to vote and to run for public office. Throughout the Middle East women are demanding more rights and governments, including in conservative Saudi Arabia. In October 2004, Crown Prince Abdullah received recommendations on reforms to improve women's rights.

Religion and tradition exclude women in many parts of the Middle East from politics.

Women in India, Pakistan, and Bangladesh have actively participated in politics and have become leaders in all three countries. India, known as the world's largest democracy due to its population, was ruled by Prime Minister Indira Gandhi from 1966 to 1977 and from 1980 to 1984. Although India is a democracy, traditional values, religion, widespread poverty, and the pervasive and deeply rooted caste system discourage women from fully participating in politics. However, economic progress in India is contributing to a growing number of women and men who are challenging the status quo. To bring more women into politics, India passed a constitutional amendment in 1993 that set aside a third of all **panchayat,** or village council seats, and village chief positions for women. It further allocated a percentage of those for women from the lowest rungs of the caste system, based on their percentage of the population.[23] This approach is consistent with India's policy of affirmative action for the low castes of society.

panchayat
Village council seats in India.

Pakistan, under Prime Minister Benazir Bhutto, attempted to bring more women and the poor into the political process. The **Pakistan People's Party (PPP)** ran on a platform that promised to eliminate barriers to women's political participation. Bhutto and the PPP wanted to (1) sign the U.N. Convention on the Elimination of All Forms of Discrimination Against Women, (2) improve working conditions and job opportunities for women, (3) introduce maternity leave, (4) repeal laws that discriminated against women, and (5) promote female literacy.[24] These promises were not implemented due to resistance from members of Bhutto's own party who held strong patriarchal views of women's status and roles in society. Furthermore, political problems that threatened the survival of Bhutto's government diverted attention away from women's issues. Political instability remains a major impediment to implementing reforms that empower women politically. Finally, Islamic fundamentalists in Pakistan have succeeded in reinforcing values that emphasize women's inferior status and exclusion from political life.

Pakistan People's Party
Promised to support women's equality.

Bangladesh, one of the poorest countries in the world, recognizes women's right to vote and hold elective office. Similar to women in India and Pakistan, women in Bangladesh encounter cultural and economic constraints to political participation, despite formal constitutional guarantees of political equality. Women who engage in political activities are often accused by religious leaders and others of violating the rule of **Purdah.** Purdah requires women to wear veils, restricts their mobility and social interaction, and limits access to employment. Many poor and illiterate women have formed village associations to challenge tradition and to secure their rights. They are demanding (1) an end to the illegal but common practice of **oral divorce,** which allows a husband to divorce his wife simply by telling her that he is divorcing her; (2) the abolition of dowries; and (3) ending the sexual harassment of women.

Latin American women are less constrained by tradition and are generally more highly educated than women in many parts of the developing world. The revolutionary tradition in parts of Latin America and the area's geographical and cultural proximity to the United States laid the foundation for women's involvement in political life. Influenced in part by the struggle of women in the United States for political equality, Brazilian women formed their own suffragist movement. Like the suffragist movement in the United States, the Brazilian movement was led by upper-class and professional women who strongly believed that women should have the right to vote. Some of the women had participated in women's international conferences, which heightened their awareness of gains made by women in other countries. By 1932, twelve years after American women won the right to vote, Brazilian women achieved their right to vote. Shortly thereafter, in 1933, **Carlota Pereira de Queiroz,** a physician from Sao Paulo and a member of a traditional and wealthy family, became the first woman to be elected to Parliament.[25] In 2006, Michelle Bachelet was elected as the president of Chile, and Portia Simpson-Miller was elected as the Prime Minister of Jamaica. As educational opportunities increased for women, more of them became politically active.

Women in Mexico have also made significant gains in politics. Women are well represented in Mexico's federal government workforce. Women held 22.6 percent of the seats in the 500-member Chamber of Deputies and 15.6 percent of the seats in the 128-member Senate in 2004. Women have held positions such as the comptroller general; the secretary of tourism; and the secretary of the environment, natural resources, and fisheries. In mid-1999, Amalia Garcia Medina was elected to head the Party of the Democratic Revolution (PRD), one of the three main political parties in Mexico. In 1995, Maria de los Angeles Moreno was appointed to lead the Institutional Revolutionary Party (PRI), the country's dominant political party. Women's political participation is rising as most countries in Latin America make a transition to democracy and embrace free trade.

Women in Turkey: A Case Study

Women in Turkey enjoy a unique position among women in the Muslim countries of the Middle East. Women's status and roles in Turkey are shaped by Turkey's historical experiences and the values and actions of **Mustafa Kemal Ataturk,** founder of the

---

Purdah

The rule that requires women to wear veils, restricts their mobility and social interaction, and limits access to employment.

oral divorce

Practice that allows a husband to divorce his wife solely by telling her.

Carlota de Queiroz

First woman in Brazil elected to Parliament in 1933.

Mustafa Kemal Ataturk

Founder of the modern Turkish state in 1923.

modern Turkish state in 1923. Ataturk's revolutionary changes must be seen in the context of Turkey's geographical position as the land bridge between Europe and Asia. Turkey emerged from the Ottoman Empire that had ruled the Balkans, the Middle East, and North Africa. Like previous empires, the Ottoman Empire gradually contracted and fragmented. The final blow came when it decided to ally itself with Germany in World War I. Countries such as Britain and France, which were allied against Germany, occupied parts of Turkey. Ataturk led a successful war of independence from 1919 to 1922. The Republic of Turkey, under Ataturk's leadership, was based on the model of parliamentary democracy. Ataturk deliberately and systematically dismantled much of the old social and political system in an effort to modernize the country. An essential part of this change was the abolition of theocratic or Islamic religious control and the imposition of some aspects of Western European culture and values. Many of the revolutionary changes directly affected the status of women and their participation in politics. Religious laws were replaced with secular laws. The system of religious education was abolished, religious courts were eliminated, and the constitutional provision accepting Islam as the state religion was repealed. Polygamy was outlawed, women gained equal rights to divorce and have custody of their children, and the government strongly supported legal and social equality between men and women. The veil was abandoned, due in part to Ataturk's campaign against wearing it. Both men and women were strongly encouraged to dress like Europeans.[26]

Although traditional values continue to influence contemporary politics and society in Turkey, a country in which 98 percent of the citizens are Muslim, the separation between church and state implemented by Ataturk endures. This distinction between religious and secular practices is clearer in large cities than in small towns and rural areas, where most Turks live. Women in urban areas continue to enjoy a legal status similar to that of European women. They can travel and work outside the home without having to obtain the permission of men, they have had a right to abortion since 1988, and they can marry whom they desire and get a divorce. Their participation in various professions is similar to that of European women. Numerous women are lawyers, engineers, doctors, diplomats, and educators. In 1993, **Tansu Ciller** became the first woman to lead Turkey. Women comprise between 43 and 50 percent of the workforce and generally receive equal pay for equal work.

Tansu Ciller

First woman to lead Turkey.

WOMEN LEADERS IN THE DEVELOPING WORLD

One of the most interesting paradoxes in the developing world is that countries that generally perceive women as inferior are often governed by women. These leaders share several characteristics: (1) They are from elite families, (2) they are usually highly educated, (3) they enter politics to continue the work of their husbands or fathers, and (4) they enter politics after their husbands or fathers have been assassinated while in political office or when they challenged the ruling elite. Women's ascent to power in countries that regard women as inferior demonstrates that gender is not the only consideration.

Women leaders share four key characteristics.

These are cases in which families are so powerful that gender becomes a secondary factor. Many of these families played a crucial role in their countries' independence struggles. Indira Gandhi of India, Aung San Suu Kyi of Burma, and Megawati Sukarnoputri of Indonesia came from such families.

Indira Gandhi

India's leader from 1966 to 1977 and from 1980 to 1984.

Indira Gandhi, leader of the world's second most populous country, is perhaps the best known of all the women who rose to leadership positions. She was the only child of Jawahar Lal Nehru, the head of the Indian National Congress Party, the country's dominant political party. Nehru, a leader in India's struggle for independence, became that country's first prime minister. Educated at Visva-Bharati University in India and Oxford University in Britain, Indira Gandhi served as her father's official hostess and unofficial advisor. She was elected to several leadership positions in the Congress Party before becoming prime minister in 1966, two years after her father died. Indira Gandhi ruled India for a total of fifteen years before she was assassinated by Sikh members of her security guard. Her government had implemented policy to forcefully suppress Sikh insurgents.

Benazir Bhutto

First woman to lead Pakistan.

Benazir Bhutto, a leader of Pakistan, was the first woman to lead a Muslim country. Pakistan, which was considered part of the British-ruled India, became a separate state when India gained its independence in 1947. As discussed in Chapter 3, Pakistan was formed for Muslims under the leadership of Ali Jinnah, a secular, charismatic lawyer. India, which is predominantly Hindu, has been involved in many conflicts with Muslim Pakistan. Although India remained a democracy, despite periods of political turbulence, Pakistan has suffered from political instability, military rule, and religious extremism. Benazir Bhutto, like Indira Gandhi, grew up in a political family. Her father, Zulfiqar Ali Bhutto, belonged to one of the most important landowning families in Pakistan. He became Pakistan's leader in 1971 following his country's defeat by India and the resignation of President Yahya Khan. In 1977 he was overthrown by General Zia ul-Haq and hanged in 1979. Benazir Bhutto, like Indira Gandhi, learned politics from her father. In the male-dominated society of Pakistan, her father favored her over his two sons and another daughter. A Muslim, Benazir Bhutto was educated by Catholic nuns before going to Harvard University for undergraduate studies and to Oxford, which her father attended, for graduate work. Bhutto returned to Pakistan in 1977 and protested her father's imprisonment and the military rule. She was jailed or placed under house arrest for much of the period between 1977 and 1984, when she was allowed to leave Pakistan to receive medical treatment in London. When General ul-Haq ended martial law and permitted political parties to function as a step in a transition to democracy in 1986, Benazir Bhutto returned to Pakistan. Largely due to her father's leadership of Pakistan and his murder by the military government, Benazir Bhutto enjoyed wide popular support. She became Pakistan's prime minister in 1988, shortly after General ul-Haq was killed in a plane crash.[27] She was ousted from power in 1996.

Violeta Chamorro

Leader of Nicaragua.

The rise to power of **Violeta Barrios de Chamorro** in Nicaragua in 1990 was similar to that of Corazon Aquino of the Philippines. Like Aquino, Chamorro came from a wealthy landowning family. Her education at Blackstone College in Virginia was interrupted by her father's death. Chamorro married a journalist, Pedro Joaquin Chamorro, from a wealthy landowning family that had been active

Ellen Johnson Sirleaf, a Harvard-educated banker who was imprisoned by Charles Taylor, was elected to be Liberia's president. She is Africa's first female head of state.

Source: Michael Kamber

in Nicaraguan politics. His opposition to the Somoza family that ruled Nicaragua began while he was a law student and continued when he became the editor of his family's newspaper, *La Prensa*. He supported the opposition to the Somoza regime, the **Sandinistas.** They were led by Daniel Ortega. Chamorro's support of the Sandinistas contributed to the Somoza regime's decision to assassinate him in 1978. His wife took over as *La Prensa*'s publisher. Her support of the Sandinistas, who eventually overthrew the Somoza regime in 1979, helped her gain a position in the new government. However, she soon became critical of the Sandinistas for their socialist policies and their close relationship with Cuba. When the Sandinistas allowed free elections to be held in 1990 Violeta Chamorro was elected to lead the country.

Sandinistas

A movement that overthrew the Somoza regime in Nicaragua.

EMPOWERING WOMEN

Between 1975 and 1995, the United Nations held four conferences on women. The first conference, held in Mexico City, focused on documenting gender gaps in education, employment, income, legal rights, and political participation. Subsequent conferences stressed the need to reduce poverty among women and to eliminate unequal treatment of men and women. The fourth conference on women, held in Beijing, was the most ambitious and widely publicized. Hillary Clinton attended the

TABLE 8.2 GENDER EMPOWERMENT INITIATIVE

Country	Seats in Parliament Held by Women (%)	Female Administrators and Managers (%)	Female Professional and Technical Workers (%)	Women's Share of Earned Income (%)
United States	**14**	**46**	**55**	**62**
Norway	36.4	28	49	74
Canada	23.6	34	54	63
Japan	9.9	10	46	46
Sweden	45.3	31	50	83
Netherlands	35.1	26	48	53
United Kingdom	17.3	31	44	60
Korea, Rep. of	5.9	5	34	46
Mexico	21.2	25	40	38
Thailand	9.6	27	55	61
Philippines	17.2	58	62	59
Brazil	9.1	17.3	62	42
Turkey	4.9	7	31	60
United Arab Emirates	0	8	25.1	–
Sri Lanka	4.4	4	49	57
Jordan	7.9	4.6	28.7	31
Iran	4.1	13	33	29
China	20.2	11.6	45.1	66
South Africa	28.4	17.4	46.7	45
Indonesia	8.0	6.6	40.8	69
Egypt	3.6	9	30	38
India	9.3	2.3	20.5	38
Pakistan	20.8	9	26	33
Bangladesh	2.0	8	25	56
Zambia	12.0	6.1	31.9	55

Sources: United Nations Development Program, *Human Development Report 1999* (New York: Oxford University Press, 1999), 142–45; United Nations Development Program, *Human Development Report 1998* (New York: Oxford University Press, 1998), 134–36; and United Nations Development Program, *Human Development Report 2004* (New York: Oxford University Press, 2004), 221–23.

Beijing Conference

A conference held by the United Nations where major concerns of women and their rights were emphasized.

conference and drew attention to the need for women's empowerment. The **Beijing Conference** outlined the major concerns that women have and emphasized respect for the rights of women. It stressed the following: (1) the right of women to decide all matters related to their sexuality and childbearing, (2) an end to the genital mutilation of girls and violence against women because their dowries are too small, (3) the right of women to have access to credit, and (4) the equal treatment of males and females. The Beijing conference reflected the growing communication among women about issues that affect them and an increase in grassroots efforts in developing countries to end discrimination against women. Despite continuing problems, women are making progress.

Summary and Review

Throughout the developing world, women are the principal initiators of changes that will improve their lives. Access to education and economic opportunities has enabled many women in Asia, Latin America, and Africa to develop a degree of social and financial independence that most women in the United States and other industrialized countries enjoy. The fact remains, however, that women throughout the world remain the largest marginalized group. In the developing countries of Africa, Asia, and Latin America, traditions make women primarily responsible for domestic work. Such gender roles in poor countries are shaped to some extent by colonialism and the globalization of industry and trade. Even though women's status continues to improve in many developing societies, most women suffer from an inferior status. Thus, throughout the world, including in the United States, women are seen by societies as inferior beings with many attempts at controlling them. Violating gender roles can often have serious ramifications. Gender often serves as a tool or justification for oppression. Just as in the United States, a sexual double standard exists, whereby promiscuous males are studs and promiscuous females are unchaste. Honor killings are often the result of such a gendered double standard. Throughout the developing world, women remain less educated and nourished on the bases of their sex and perceived gender roles. Women's achievements in the developing world, however, should not be overlooked. Hence, India, Pakistan, and Bangladesh have all seen women prime ministers and throughout the developing world women serve in leadership positions that run the gamut of public and private life.

Key Terms

gender roles 164
socialization 164
status 165
socially constructed views of women 166
dowries 166
Karma 166
veiling 166

female genital mutilation 168
bride price 169
honor killings 169
Lost Decade 172
feminization of employment 173
maquiladora industry 173

internal self-selection 175
Grameen Bank 175
maleness of politics 176
Madres de la Plaza de Mayo 176
panchayat 177

Pakistan People's Party (PPP) 177
Purdah 178
oral divorce 178
Beijing Conference 182

Discussion Questions

1. What role does socialization play in determining gender roles? Compare and contrast socialization trends in different parts of the developing world.
2. How do class and familial ties in Asia, Africa, and Latin America affect gender roles?

3. Discuss the reasons behind the Lost Decade.
4. How do politics often exclude women? What methods should be employed to equalize, among genders, access to political systems?
5. In what ways have women attempted to help themselves in developing countries?

6. What are some ways of punishing women for behaving inconsistently with their prescribed gender roles?
7. Discuss the achievements of the Beijing conference.
8. What are some characteristics of gender-based oppression?
9. Are females even more mistreated in the developing world than they are in the developed world? Why or why not?
10. How does the legacy of colonialism and globalization affect the roles of women?

Suggested Readings

Ahmed, Leila. *Women and Gender in Islam*. New Haven, CT: Yale University Press, 1992.

Coleman, Isobel. "The Payoff from Women's Rights." *Foreign Affairs* 83, no. 3 (May/June 2004): 80–95.

Coleman, Isobel. "Women, Islam, and the New Iraq," *Foreign Affairs* 85, no. 1 (January/February 2006): 24–38.

Counts, Alex. *Give Us Credit*. New York: Random House, 1996, XII.

Elias, Juanita. *Fashioning Inequality*. Burlington, VT: Ashgate, 2004.

Kwesiga, Joy C. *Central Yet Peripheral: The Rural Woman Farmer and Issues of African Development*. Ibadan, Nigeria: International Institute of Tropical Agriculture, 1999.

Lee-Smith, Diana, Florence Ebam Etta, et al., eds. *Women Managing Resources: African Research on Gender, Urbanisation and Environment*. Nairobi: Mazingira Institute, 1999.

Liswood, Laura A. *Women World Leaders*. London: Pandora, 1995.

Stromquist, Nelly P. "Roles and Statuses of Women." In Nelly P. Stromquist, ed. *Women in the Third World*. New York: Garland Publishing, 1998.

Addresses and Websites

Women's Environment & Development Organization (WEDO)
355 Lexington Avenue, 3rd Floor
New York, NY 10017–6603
Tel: (212) 973–0325
Fax: (212) 973–0335
http://www.wedo.org/

The Women's Environment & Development Organization is a group that works on environmental and development issues as they pertain to women. The organization asserts that they work to promote social and economic justice under the rubric of human rights. They break down their work into three program areas, economic justice, sustainable development, and gender and governance, all of which can be found on their website. This site also provides an excellent resource regarding various statistics and information pertaining to women, economics, and development. WEDO publications and links to news can also be located on the website.

International Center for Research on Women
1717 Massachusetts Avenue NW, Suite 302
Washington, D.C. 20036
Tel: (202) 797–0007
Fax: (202) 797–0020
http://www.icrw.org/

The International Center for Research on Women is an organization that targets many women's concerns, including issues of economic growth and poverty. The group looks to advancing women's human rights via the promotion of sustainable development. The website offers an in-depth description of the organization, its programs and advocacy. Media and publication links are provided, along with links on various topics pertaining to women. Other nongovernmental and governmental organizations can be linked from this site as well.

The Centre for Development and Population Activities
1400 16th Street NW, Suite 100
Washington, D.C. 20036
Tel: (202) 667–1142
Fax: (202) 332–4496
http://www.cedpa.org/

The Centre for Development and Population Activities specifically targets women with their efforts with development. The organization looks to provide women with reproductive health and family planning options, among other useful skills. This website offers information about women and development, including information on women and poverty. There are links to the organization's publications, where further information can be obtained.

The Association for Women's Rights in Development (AWID)
Toronto Secretariat:
96 Spadina Ave., Suite 401
Toronto, ON
Canada
M5V 2J6
Tel: (416) 594–3773
Fax: (416) 594–0330
http://www.awid.org/

The Association for Women's Rights in Development is an organization that seeks to promote women's human rights and equality and sustainable development for women. The organization aims at achieving improvements for women at the individual, state, and international level and offers various programs, which are elaborated upon on the website. The website also offers links to different publications and other websites of similar issues.

Society for International Development
Via Panisperna, 207
00184 Rome, Italy
Tel: 139–064872172
Fax: 139–064872170
http://www.sidint.org/

The Society for International Development is an organization that offers support regarding developmental issues and concerns at the local, national, and global levels. The organization sponsors a variety of programs, with issues ranging from health and globalization to women's concerns to knowledge, communications, and information technologies. There are numerous links provided on this website, including one for their development journal and other publications. Many of this organization's projects tend to focus on developmental issues as they relate to women.

Notes

1. Nelly P. Stromquist, "Roles and Statuses of Women," in Nelly P. Stromquist, ed., *Women in the Third World* (New York: Garland Publishing, 1998), 4.
2. Gustav Niebuhr, "Southern Baptists Declare Wife Should Submit to Her Husband," *The New York Times*, 10 June 1998, A1.
3. Douglas Jehl, "Following Tradition, An Affair for Men," *The New York Times*, 9 February 1999, A11.
4. Susan Tiano, "The Role of Women," in Richard S. Hillman, ed., *Understanding Contemporary Latin America* (Boulder, CO: Lynne Rienner, 1997), 239.
5. Paul Cammack, David Pool, and William Tordoff, *Third World Politics* (Baltimore, MD: Johns Hopkins Press, 1993), 212.
6. Leila Hessini, "Wearing the Hijab in Contemporary Morocco," in Fatma Muge Gocek and Shiva Balaghi, eds., *Reconstructing Gender in the Middle East* (New York: Columbia University Press, 1994), 41.
7. Leila Ahmed, *Women and Gender in Islam* (New Haven, CT: Yale University Press, 1992), 223.
8. Fatima Mernissi, *Beyond the Veil: Male-Female Dynamics in Modern Muslim Society* (Bloomington, IN: Indiana University Press, 1987), XI.
9. Barbara Crossett, "Senegal Bans Gutting of Genitals of Girls," *The New York Times*, 16 January 1999, A3.
10. Lara Santoro, "Kenya Brides That Can't Be Bought," *The Christian Science Monitor*, 13 October 1998, 6.
11. David Holmstrom, "Saving Nepal's Girls," *The Christian Science Monitor*, 14 April 1999, 11; and Somini Segupta, "Oldest Profession Is Still One of the Oldest Lures for Young Nigerian Women," *The New York Times*, 5 November 2004, A9.

12. Douglas Jehl, "Arab Honor's Price: A Woman's Blood," *The New York Times*, 20 June 1999, A1; and Christine Sbolar, "For Family's Honor, She Had to Die" *Chicago Tribune*, 17 November 2005, Sect. 1, 1.

13. Ahmed, *Women and Gender in Islam*, 210.

14. Uli Schmetzer, "Literacy Unchains Indian Women," *Chicago Tribune*, 13 February 2000, Sect. 1, 6.

15. Valentine M. Moghadam, *Women, Work, and Economic Reform in the Middle East and North Africa* (Boulder, CO: Lynne Rienner, 1998), 12; and Juanita Elias, *Fashioning Inequality* (Burlington, VT: Ashgate, 2004).

16. Richard Anker, *Gender and Jobs: Sex Segregation of Occupations in the World* (Geneva: International Labor Office, 1998), 411.

17. "Women Farmers: The Invisible Producers," *Africa Recovery* 11, no. 2 (October 1997): 11.

18. Mayada M. Baydas, Richard L. Meyer, and Nelson Aguilera-Alfred, "Discrimination Against Women in Formal Credit Markets," *World Development* 22, no. 7 (July 1994): 1075.

19. Alex Counts, *Give Us Credit* (New York: Random House, 1996), XII.

20. Najma Chowdhury and Barbara J. Nelson, "Redefining Politics: Patterns of Women's Political Engagement from a Global Perspective," in Barbara J. Nelson and Najma Chowdhury, eds., *Women and Politics Worldwide* (New Haven, CT: Yale University Press, 1994), 16.

21. Jane S. Jaquette, "Women in Power: From Tokenism to Critical Mass," *Foreign Policy*, no. 108 (Fall 1997): 27–28.

22. Margaret Jean Hay and Sharon Stichter, *African Women South of the Sahara* (New York: Longman, 1995), 203.

23. Celia W. Dugger, "Lower-Caste Women Turn Village Rule Upside Down," *The New York Times*, 3 May 1999, A1.

24. Anita Weiss, "The Slow Yet Steady Path to Women's Empowerment in Pakistan," in Yvonne Yazbeck Haddad and John L. Esposito, eds., *Islam, Gender, and Social Change* (New York: Oxford University Press, 1998), 134.

25. Fanny Tabak, "Women in the Struggle for Democracy and Equal Rights in Brazil," in *Women and Politics Worldwide*, 131.

26. Deniz Kandiyoti, "End of Empire: Islam, Nationalism, and Women in Turkey," in Deniz Kandiyoti, ed., *Women, Islam, and the State* (Philadelphia, PA: Temple University Press, 1991), 23; and Isobel Coleman, "Women, Islam, and the New Iraq" *Foreign Affairs* 85, no. 1 (January/February 2006), 24–38.

27. Laura A. Liswood, *Women World Leaders* (London: Pandora, 1995), 10.

CHAPTER NINE

Transitions to Democracy and Human Rights

GLOBALIZATION AND DEMOCRACY AND HUMAN RIGHTS

THE RAPID SPREAD OF COMMUNICATIONS TECHNOLOGY, THE GROWTH OF INTERNATIONAL TRAVEL, AND INCREASING CULTURAL GLOBALIZATION HELPED WEAKEN UNDEMOCRATIC GOVERNMENTS. THIS TREND WAS SIGNIFICANTLY STRENGTHENED BY THE FALL OF COMMUNISM IN THE SOVIET UNION AND EASTERN EUROPE AND THE SUBSEQUENT END OF THE COLD WAR IN THE LATE 1980s. BY CREATING GREATER INTERDEPENDENCE AMONG COUNTRIES, ESPECIALLY IN THE AREA OF COMMUNICATIONS, GLOBALIZATION IS INSTRUMENTAL IN ENCOURAGING TRANSITIONS TO DEMOCRACY AND PROTECTION OF HUMAN RIGHTS. GLOBALIZATION HAS CONTRIBUTED TO THE EROSION OF NATIONAL BOUNDARIES AND WEAKENED THE POWER OF GOVERNMENTS OVER THEIR CITIZENS. AN INTEGRAL COMPONENT OF GLOBALIZATION IS GREATER INDIVIDUAL AUTONOMY AND A RESPECT FOR FUNDAMENTAL FREEDOMS. JUST AS TRADE SPREADS FROM ONE COUNTRY TO ANOTHER IN A GLOBAL SOCIETY, CONCERNS ABOUT DEMOCRACY AND HUMAN RIGHTS ALSO TRANSCEND NATIONAL BORDERS. ECONOMIC GLOBALIZATION CREATES PRESSURES ON GOVERNMENTS TO END AUTHORITARIAN OR TOTALITARIAN RULE AND EMBRACE A MORE OPEN AND CIVIL SOCIETY. SOME GOVERNMENTS THAT FAIL TO CHANGE FACE ECONOMIC SANCTIONS AS WELL AS POLITICAL ISOLATION, ESPECIALLY IF THEY ESPOUSE ANTI-WESTERN POLICIES. GLOBALIZATION ALSO AIDS DEMOCRACY AND HUMAN RIGHTS BY MAKING AVAILABLE POLITICAL AND FINANCIAL RESOURCES TO MOVEMENTS CONCERNED WITH THESE ISSUES.

INTRODUCTION

Countries in Africa, Asia, and Latin America have struggled, in varying degrees, to achieve democracy and widespread respect for human rights. Their experiences with colonialism underscored the importance of instituting constitutional safeguards to protect citizens from arbitrary rule and violations of their fundamental freedoms. In some cases, such as in British India, colonization also brought Western democratic practices for a select few. To a large extent, struggles in the developing world for democracy and human rights were intertwined with movements for national independence. This was due in part to developments in Europe, especially the rise of Nazi

Germany and World War II, which made it obvious that greater attention had to be paid to protecting human rights and supporting democratic governments. Despite their initial enthusiasm for democracy and human rights during their struggle for independence, most governments in Africa, Asia, and Latin America became dictatorial and oppressive. The end of the Cold War and the fall of communism in Russia and Eastern Europe strengthened democratic movements in poor countries around the world. The majority of them, with help and encouragement from the United States and Western Europe, made a concerted effort to abandon dictatorships and to implement political systems that are committed to upholding democratic freedoms and human rights. In 2003, the United States invaded Iraq, partly to promote democracy in that country and in the broader Middle East. However, U.S. violations of human rights at Abu Ghraib prison in Iraq and at Guantanamo Bay in Cuba seriously undermined U.S. efforts to promote democracy.

This chapter discusses the difficult and uneven process of transition to democracy and protection of human rights. It focuses on the importance of institutions, such as constitutions, political parties, and independent judiciaries, in democratic societies. It examines the nature of democracy; the criteria for democracy; and the factors that contribute to the growth and stability of democracy, such as culture, the international and regional environment, historical experiences, and levels of economic development. This chapter shows that students and women have been instrumental in building democracy, especially in Latin America and Asia. International pressures and the forces of globalization also play critical roles in fostering the democratization of the developing world. Discussions of democratic transitions in Latin America, in particular, make it clear that many problems impede a full transition to and consolidation of democracy. Many ordinary citizens believe that democracy has failed to provide sustained economic growth or to end government corruption. Basic institutions, such as the courts, the legislatures, and political parties, are seen as ineffective. Africa and Asia face similar problems. Nevertheless, this chapter shows that significant progress is being made toward democratization. Discussions of democracy inevitably include human rights. This chapter looks at the evolution of human rights as a major international issue as well as conflicting perspectives on human rights.

demos

Greek word meaning people or populace.

kratia or kratis

Greek word meaning rule.

direct form of self-government

A system of governance where the people represent and vote for themselves.

DEMOCRACY

Democracy has been practiced by people throughout the world to varying degrees. However, the form of democracy found in most developed countries has its roots in ancient Greece. The word *democracy* is of Greek origin. It is derived from **demos,** meaning people or populace, and **kratia** or **kratis,** meaning rule. In other words, democracy is simply rule by the people. The people govern themselves. Democracy in ancient Greece was a **direct form of self-government.** This means that the people actually represented themselves and influenced decisions by voting for themselves. With the exception of small New England towns that hold town meetings, direct democracy is not practiced in modern societies. The United States and other democratic societies practice what is called representative democracy or indirect democracy.

Citizens elect representatives to vote for them and to safeguard and further their interests. **Democracy** is a system of government in which the majority of the people rule but the rights of the minority are protected. It is a system of government that is based not on the use of force to gain compliance but on the consent of the citizens. Democracies allow individuals and groups to freely compete for most positions of governmental power in an orderly manner. This means that free and fair elections must be held on a regular basis and that all adult citizens have a right to participate, with a few exceptions.

democracy

A system of government in which the majority rules but minority rights are protected.

Modern democratic societies have constitutions to protect the rights and freedoms of their citizens. A **constitution** may be defined as the fundamental legal framework or basic law of a country. A constitution assigns powers and duties to governmental institutions and agencies, indicates how decision makers are to be selected, defines the scope of governmental authority, establishes the nature of the relationship between the people and their government, and states how political leaders are to be held accountable. In essence, a constitution creates as well as limits power.

constitution

The legal framework or basic law of a society.

Constitutions may be written or unwritten. In either case, a constitution reflects the general agreement of a community about how it wishes to be governed. Although the American constitution is written, much of the fundamental law of the country is based on unwritten customs and traditions. The British Constitution, on the other hand, is unwritten. It is composed of traditions, customs, general understandings, legislative acts, and court decisions that are not compiled into a single document. The **British Constitution** is often referred to as a *received constitution*. The constitution of a country is generally regarded as the supreme law. All other laws, no matter how popular they are with the majority of citizens, must be consistent with the constitution. The courts of a country, and ultimately the supreme or highest court, must have the final authority to interpret the constitution. In other words, the supreme court or highest court makes the final decision on what is the law of a country. Because constitutions reflect political power and national values and priorities, they must be amended or updated through interpretation, new legislation, new customs, and formal changes in the document.

British Constitution

Composed largely of customs and traditions; it is not a single document.

Because constitutions reflect political power and national values and priorities, they must be amended.

Democratic societies emphasize the political equality of all citizens and guarantee that their fundamental rights and freedoms are not only protected but are viewed as sacred. People in a democracy have the right to freely express their ideas; to offer dissenting opinions; to be left alone; to form and join political, social, economic, and other organizations; to worship or not to worship as they see fit; and to live their lives without unreasonable governmental interference. These freedoms are not absolute. Governments must balance the rights of one individual or group against the rights of another individual or group. A fundamental aspect of democracy is the citizens' acceptance of responsibility for governing and for safeguarding the rights and freedoms of society as a whole. Democratic governments are supposed to respect the dignity of all individuals and protect the civil and human rights of all citizens, especially those of minorities that suffer from racial, ethnic, religious, and other forms of discrimination.

legitimacy

The power to govern based on the consent of the majority being governed.

presidential form of democracy

A government with clear separation of powers and a system of checks and balances.

parliamentary form of democracy

Governmental system where the legislative branch has greater powers over other branches.

There are many values and beliefs that are regarded as essential to the functioning of a stable and peaceful democratic society. One of the most important is the belief in the legitimacy of democracy. **Legitimacy** is the power to govern based on the consent of the majority of those who are governed. This is a fundamental principle of democracy, one that is closely related to the idea of a social contract articulated by John Locke and others. To a large extent, people's belief in the legitimacy of democracy depends on the performance of the government. The more successful the government has been in meeting the demands of the people, the more willing they will be to be ruled by it and to support it when it faces serious economic, social, or military challenges. Other beliefs that are important for maintaining democratic stability are (1) tolerance for different viewpoints, (2) willingness to compromise and cooperate with political opponents, (3) commitment to civility and pragmatism, and (4) willingness to get involved in the political process and to believe in one's ability to help achieve particular objectives.[1]

Modern democratic societies have either a presidential or a parliamentary form of democracy. The best example of a presidential democracy is the United States. In countries with a **presidential form of democracy,** there is a clear separation of powers and a system of checks and balances. The main branches of government—the executive, legislative, and judicial branches—are independent of each other and often in conflict with each other. The American system makes this conflict inevitable. The Framers of the Constitution, James Madison in particular, believed that the best way to protect democracy and individual freedoms was to implement a system in which separate branches of government would check each other's power. Members of Congress and the president are elected separately and independently of each other. This means that there can be divided government in the United States, with the Congress (or one house of Congress) controlled by Republicans and the executive branch led by a Democratic president. The president, who is both the leader of the government and the leader of the country, must work with Congress to get legislation passed. The judicial branch must determine the constitutionality of the actions of both Congress and the executive branch.

In the **parliamentary form of democracy,** there is no clear division between the executive and legislative branches of government. Instead of a president as the chief executive, parliamentary systems have prime ministers. The best example of a parliamentary democracy is Britain. There is relatively little conflict between the prime minister and the legislature or parliament because the prime minister is chosen

Saudis Hold First Elections

In August 2004, Saudi Arabia, working with United Nations experts, decided to hold elections for the first time to select half of the members of the 178 municipal councils, starting in November 2004.

Source: "Saudis Preparing for First Elections," *The New York Times,* 5 August 2004, A4.

TABLE 9.1 CRITERIA FOR DEMOCRACY

Inclusive citizenship: Citizenship must be open to all residents in the country.

The rule of law: The government operates under the law and individuals and minorities are protected against the "tyranny of the majority."

Freedom of expression: Freedom of religion, freedom of speech, and freedom of the press are vital components of a democratic society.

Free and fair elections: All citizens have the right to compete for elective office and government officials are chosen in frequent and fair elections.

Equality in voting: All votes are equal, with each person having one vote.

Citizen control of the agenda: Citizens ultimately decide the policies of the country.

Freedom of association: Citizens have the right to form and join organizations, including political parties and special interest groups.

Civilian control over the security forces: The armed forces, including the police, must be politically neutral and must be controlled by civilian authority.

Source: Adapted from Robert A. Dahl, *Dilemmas of Pluralist Democracy* (New Haven, CT; Yale University Press, 1982), 6; and Mary Kaldor and Ivan Vejvoda, *Democracy in Central and Eastern Europe* (London: Pinter, 1999), 4–5

---

by the majority in parliament. Unlike the American president, the British prime minister is elected as a member of the legislature first and is then chosen by members of the majority party to lead the government. In other words, the prime minister is both head of government and the leader of the majority party. The symbolic head of the country is Queen Elizabeth II.

Developing countries have varying views of democracy. They do not always see democracy in the same way as most people in the United States and Britain. It could be argued that, in reality, many developing societies have a partial democracy and are moving closer to the ideal democracy. Although Latin Americans declare their commitment to democracy, they are not generally enthusiastic about practicing it. Saudi Arabia provides another example of how some developing countries view democracy. Saudi Arabia is an Islamic country in which there is no separation of religious and secular authority. Most Islamic countries, including those that are

There is generally no clear separation of mosque and state in Islam.

democracies, view democratic rights and freedoms within the broader context of Islamic beliefs and customs. Unlike Western democracies, which believe that the people are sovereign, Islamic societies believe that God is sovereign and has ultimate authority and political power. Saudi Arabia's religious and historical background played a major role in shaping its contemporary political system. Muhammad ibn Saud, leader of a nomadic group, made an alliance with Abd al-Wahhab, an important religious scholar in the eighteenth century, for mutual protection. This combination of political and religious power is the foundation of the modern Saudi state.

A huge demonstra-
tion in Mexico City
to protest crime.
*The New York
Times*, 30 August
2004, A3.

Source: Hector
Guerrero/AFP/Getty
Images

Wahhabi tradition

A religious tradition
that is used as the
basis of Saudi law
and social behavior.

Saudi kings institutionalized the religious **Wahhabi tradition** as the basis of Saudi law and social behavior.[2] Although the Saudi leaders must consult with numerous princes and allow citizens to ask for favors from and express their opinions to the royal family, Saudi Arabia is not a democracy.

In sharp contrast to Saudi Arabia and Latin America, the English-speaking Caribbean countries are very democratic societies, despite occasional political problems. These islands hold free and fair elections regularly, allow the winning party to peacefully replace the governing party after elections, and protect the basic democratic freedoms of the people. Jorge I. Dominguez believes that this Caribbean achievement is far superior to that of Latin America and also to that of countries of Africa and Asia that acquired their formal independence from European powers after World War II.[3]

**political
participation**

Activities that
would include
voting, joining an
interest group,
and protesting or
running for a
position in
government.

Political Participation and Democratic Freedoms

Political participation and respect for civil liberties are basic to democracy. **Political participation** allows the people to communicate with elected officials and others in the government. Citizens must be able to express their viewpoints, make their concerns known, and demand certain actions or public policies from the government. In order to effectively communicate with and influence their representatives, people in democracies form political parties and interest groups, support freedom of the press and speech, and engage in informal activities.

Conventional political participation includes voting, supporting particular candidates for political office, running for a position in government, writing letters to the editor of a newspaper about a particular issue, and joining an interest group or an organization that tries to influence government policies or decisions. **Unconventional forms of participation** include mass demonstrations, civil disobedience, and sometimes even acts of violence. In many developing countries, political parties, interest groups, and the mass media are not very strong institutions. Political participation in many developing countries is done through **patron–client systems.** The patrons are intermediaries who have connections to both the modern and traditional parts of a society. They are often powerful landowners, religious authorities, bankers, and political figures. Their clients are usually poor people, agricultural workers and small farmers, small entrepreneurs, and laborers in urban areas. These patron–client systems contribute to political participation in several ways, including (1) providing a channel for the rural and urban poor to engage in politics, (2) influencing the making and implementation of public policies or decisions, and (3) serving as a communication link between their clients and the government.[4]

> **conventional participation**
> Includes voting, running for office, and joining interest groups.

> **unconventional participation**
> Includes mass demonstrations.

> **patron–client system**
> A system used in developing countries where patrons act as their clients' link to political participation and the government.

Freedom of the press and freedom of speech are essential aspects of democratic society. These freedoms allow people to express their opinions, to criticize government policies and behavior, to offer solutions to problems, and to engage in activities that may ultimately change the government and society. Freedom of the press and of speech means that there should be no prior restraint or censorship.

Freedom of speech and of the press are essential aspects of democracy.

This means that the government is not legally permitted to prevent people from writing or saying what they want. But these freedoms are not absolute. Governments may prevent speech that presents a clear and present danger to society; may outlaw fraudulent advertising, child pornography, and obscenity; and may punish those who engage in the defamation of the character of others.

Political parties play a crucial role in the democratic process. Political parties are defined as a coalition of interests whose goal is to gain control of the government by winning elections. To win, political parties must appeal to a wide range of interests. Ultimately, the goal is to win the majority of the votes cast by the people or the electorate. Some parties are organized to represent narrow interests and sometimes focus on a single issue. They realize that they are unlikely to win enough votes to enable them to control the government. In some societies, these minor parties may join with other larger parties to influence public policy. Political parties play the essential role of helping transfer power peacefully from the losers to the winners of regularly held elections. Political parties give the electorate choices by offering competing candidates for office and competing programs for society. Political parties help mobilize public opinion, offer alternative solutions to society's problems,

> **political party**
> A coalition of interests whose goal is to gain control of the government by winning elections.

Political parties help to peacefully transfer power.

The loyal opposition keeps the government accountable and responsible to the people.

and link the people to the institutions of government. Finally, political parties not only provide people to run the government, they also play the role of the opposition and help keep the government accountable and responsive to the people. The concept of loyal opposition means that the party out of power criticizes the ruling majority and suggests alternative policies and programs. The loyal opposition accepts the legitimacy of the ruling majority and does not adopt unconstitutional means to undermine it.

Political parties in developing societies are usually linked to the nationalist movements that were instrumental in achieving independence. Political parties are also formed in poor countries to deal with the challenges of economic development and to provide political stability. For example, the Republican People's Party in Turkey was an important part of the whole process of the modernization and Westernization of that country under the leadership of Mustafa Kemal Ataturk. The Indian National Congress Party, created in 1885, helped achieve India's independence from Britain in 1947 and built the foundation for India's democratic society. The Indian National Congress party served as an institution in which different viewpoints could be heard and compromises made on national objectives. The leaders of the party were strongly committed to democratic values such as a respect for the rule of law, tolerance of political opposition, and the reconciliation of conflicting interests.[5] Many developing societies have been dominated for a long period of time by one political party. The Institutional Revolutionary Party of Mexico (PRI) and the Indian National Congress Party are examples of dominant political parties. Both India and Mexico held elections regularly and allowed other parties to compete, although not always on a level playing field. Some developing countries instituted one-party systems. Gamal Abdel Nasser of Egypt, for example, created a one-party state and outlawed all opposition parties. Most developing countries have abandoned the idea of a single-party democracy. Many of them now face the problem of having too many political parties competing in elections. In Haiti, for example, there were about 2,930 candidates running for approximately 1,000 local and national political positions in the 2000 elections.[6]

Turkey provides an example of how a society that is committed to democracy and multiple political parties can justify excluding particular political parties. From an American point of view, banning a political party because of its religious beliefs is inconsistent with democratic principles. To understand Turkey's position we must put the issue of banning a religious party in the broader context of the creation of the modern Turkish state. Ataturk strongly committed his country to secularism and Westernization. He believed that the fall of the Ottoman Empire, from which Turkey emerged, was caused to a large extent by the leaders' misuse of Islam. When the Refah (Welfare) Party won 6 million votes, about 24 percent of all votes cast in the national election in 1997, a political crisis erupted in Turkey. The Refah Party is an Islamic party. Islamic parties in Algeria and Iran have contributed to the division in those societies. Many Turks viewed the Refah Party as a threat to Turkish society and secular values. In early 1998 the court banned it.[7]

Part of the reason for banning the Refah Party was the strong opposition of the military to what it regarded as the threat of Islamic filtration into Turkish society. Unlike in the United States, where the military is under civilian control, the military in Turkey,

Indonesia, and elsewhere in the developing world is an independent institution with a political role. By law, the military in Turkey has a right to intervene in politics if it believes that Turkey's secular society is threatened. The military's power in politics also stems from the fact that it is Turkey's most powerful and respected institution.[8]
Similarly, the military is the most powerful institution in Indonesia. As the country's stability was threatened due to the serious economic crisis in 1997, the military was widely perceived as the backbone of Indonesia. The Indonesian military has seventy-five reserved seats in the country's Parliament. Many government positions are held by military officers, including roughly half of the provincial governorships. Cabinet ministers, senior civil servants, ambassadors, and directors of state corporations are often soldiers. Military personnel are responsible for maintaining public order and monitoring political parties, nongovernmental organizations (NGOs), and religious and labor groups.[9]

Turkey's military has the legal right to intervene in politics.

Judicial systems are essential to maintaining democratic freedoms, including political participation. Democratic governments respect the **rule of law**. This means that no person is above the law and that all individuals are treated equally under the law. It also means that personal considerations are not allowed to determine how individuals are treated. The judiciary is critical to checking the power of the executive and legislative branches of government by making sure that their actions are constitutional or consistent with the constitution. A strong judiciary prevents political leaders from making arbitrary decisions and from depriving citizens of freedoms and basic human rights. It is the judiciary that determines the meaning of laws and holds political leaders accountable. The state bureaucracy or the administrative agencies also help to promote the rule of law and impartiality.

Many developing countries have weak and ineffective judicial systems. In some cases, the judicial systems do not safeguard the rights of all individuals or treat them equally. In some cases, the judicial systems are strongly influenced by religious beliefs and customs that are inconsistent with democratic ideals. In Saudi Arabia, for example, the legal system is based on **shari'a** or Islamic law. Shari'a courts have jurisdiction over criminal cases and civil suits dealing with marriage, divorce, child custody, and inheritance. In a shari'a court, the testimony of one man equals that of two women, and those who commit crimes against Muslims generally receive harsher penalties than those who commit crimes against non-Muslims.[10] In Jordan and Turkey, women are not treated equally. The law allows courts to treat men who have committed "crimes of honor" leniently.[11]

Interest groups, like political parties, are critical players in societies that are becoming or are already democratic. An interest group or pressure group is composed of individuals who share common concerns. They are generally not interested in gaining political power. They organize to influence the government to make decisions that are favorable to them. Unlike political parties, which try to build broad coalitions, interest groups usually focus on narrow issues. They are policy specialists in the sense that they concern themselves only with specific policies that

Access to the government is very important for groups trying to influence public policy.

judicial systems
Have the responsibility for ensuring that the laws are fair and that individuals' rights are protected.

rule of law
The rule that no person is above the law and that all individuals are treated equally under the law.

shari'a
Islamic law upon which the Saudi government is based.

interest groups
Groups composed of people who share common concerns and want to influence the government.

TABLE 9.2 CONSTITUTIONS IN LATIN AMERICA

Year of Independence	Country	Number of Constitutions	Year of Most Recent Constitution
1844	Dominican Republic	32	1966
1811	Venezuela	25	1961
1804	Haiti	24	1987
1822	Ecuador	19	1979
1825	Bolivia	15	1967
1821	El Salvador	14	1983
1821	Nicaragua	14	1987
1821	Honduras	14	1982
1821	Peru	13	1993
1810	Colombia	12	1991
1776	**United States**	**1**	**1789**

directly affect their group. Interest groups in both the developed and the developing world can only influence the government if they have access to it. Because most governmental institutions are located in urban areas, especially in developing countries, most interest groups are concentrated in cities.

Membership in interest groups reflects the level of development of a particular society. As economic development becomes more widespread, labor unions and agricultural groups begin to organize to protect their interests. Agricultural groups are often less powerful than labor movements because of their location in the countryside and the difficulties they face in getting members together and traveling to the urban areas to gain access to the government. Labor unions, on the other hand, are usually connected to industries that are vitally important to the country's economic prosperity as well as its political stability. Labor unions are most likely to be located in cities, close to the nerves of government. Their organization, importance in the economy, and ability to strike give them significant political power. College students are also strongly involved in politics in developing countries. They are some of the most articulate critics of government policies, have important organizational skills, and are much less bound by traditions and customs than most citizens. Students are usually located in areas that are close to government institutions. Because they usually belong to middle- and upper-class families, they have access to power as well as some protection against punitive actions by the government. But students must also eventually graduate and get jobs. This limits their ability to sustain their political activities.[12]

Students and labor unions are powerful groups in developing countries.

Factors Conducive to Democracy

A combination of factors provide a fertile environment for the growth and stability of democratic societies. Political scientists often refer to these factors as preconditions for democracy. Countries that are democratic share certain characteristics. One of the most important prerequisites for democracy is a **culture** or a set of values, beliefs, and attitudes that fosters toleration, bargaining, and compromise. Democracy requires a commitment to pragmatism and flexibility. Citizens must be willing to listen to different viewpoints with which they disagree and accept the policies voted for by the majority. The culture of a society also determines, to some extent, the degree of political participation that citizens enjoy. Another factor that is conducive to democracy are the social, political, and religious **beliefs** of the ruling groups. The **international or regional environment** also facilitates or impedes the development of democratic societies. For example, Spain and Portugal became democratic societies in the 1980s because of pressure from their European neighbors and their desire to be included in the wider European community. Closely related to the international and regional environment are historical experiences with democracy. India and the English-speaking Caribbean are examples of democracies that are rooted partly in their historical experiences with European colonialism. A final factor that is conducive to democracy is economic development.

Countries such as Botswana and Nigeria in Africa demonstrate that culture plays a major role in determining if a country will be democratic. Botswana, a country with about 1.5 million people, is a stable democracy. Among the reasons given for Botswana's democratic society are its political culture of political discussion, community consensus, and a tradition of nonviolence. Similarly, the political culture of Nigeria has helped make it difficult for many military regimes to gain legitimacy and institutionalize authoritarian rule. Nigerians' strong commitment to political and personal liberty has influenced military regimes to promise a transition to civilian rule and democratic government.[13] Although many of these promises were postponed by successive military regimes, Nigeria has periodically returned to democratic rule.

> *Culture plays a major role in determining if a country will be democratic.*

Cultural factors also help explain the existence of democratic governments in the Caribbean. The British brought many of their democratic institutions with them to their colonies in the Caribbean and implemented a process of decolonization that deliberately prepared the new countries for democratic government. The Westminster or British model of government had been in place, on a limited scale, from as early as 1639. The House of Assembly in Barbados, which began meeting in 1639, is the third oldest legislative body in the Western Hemisphere, preceded only by Bermuda's legislature and the Virginia House of Burgess.[14] British rule helped create a culture that emphasizes the rule of law; constitutional government; civilian supremacy; bureaucratic neutrality; and respect for social, economic, and political freedoms. Democratic competition was embraced and attempts were made to use government as an instrument for promoting social welfare and economic equality.[15]

Economic development also influences the adoption of democratic values. This does not mean that poor countries cannot be democracies or that all countries that have achieved a certain degree of economic progress are democratic. However, evidence shows that poor countries are less likely to be democratic than countries that are more prosperous. Poor countries generally do not have a relatively large middle

culture

A set of values, beliefs, and attitudes.

beliefs

A set of thoughts and values that encompass the social, political, and religious aspects of life.

international or regional environment

The surrounding societies that facilitate or impede the development of democratic values in other nations.

class; high rates of literacy; a vibrant and independent private sector; a well-developed infrastructure; or a large number of newspapers, radio stations, or televisions. Communication with the outside world is limited. All of these drawbacks make the growth of democracy unlikely. Africa provides a good example of how poverty stifles democracy.[16] Increased national wealth eventually expands the **middle class,** which many political scientists believe is essential to the acquisition and maintenance of democratic values. Many Asian and Latin American countries that have experienced rapid economic development, coupled with deliberate efforts by the government to reduce economic and social inequality, have adopted democratic values and practices.

middle class

The middle income group that is essential to the maintenance of democratic values.

Transitions to Democracy

Democratization is a process of changing from a previous authoritarian or totalitarian government to a democratic government that is widely regarded as legitimate and permanent. A democratic transition involves the negotiation and acceptance of democratic rules and procedures, the building or restructuring of political institutions, and the channeling of political competition along democratic lines.[17] An essential part of this process is deciding on a new constitution. Constitutions create power as well as limit power and help legitimize political power and unify the population. To achieve this, constitutions must be accepted by the people as a political creed. Compromises must be incorporated in constitutions for the documents to embody the values, beliefs, interests, and aspirations of the population.

Constitutions create as well as limit power.

Democratic transitions often begin with **liberalization** in what remains essentially a nondemocratic setting. Liberalization may include changes such as fewer restrictions on freedom of the press, the recognition of the right of workers to form trade unions, a movement away from arbitrarily arresting citizens, the release of political prisoners, and greater tolerance of political opposition. Democratization includes liberalization but is a much broader concept. Democratization involves the right of citizens to compete in elections to gain control of the government. But elections alone are not an indication of democratization. Many countries in Latin America—Guatemala, for example—have had many elections but have not completed the transition to democracy. Juan J. Linz and Alfred Stepan argue that a democratic transition is complete when there is widespread agreement on how to elect a government; when a government comes to power through a free and popular vote; when the government has the authority to make decisions for the country; and when there is a legal separation of executive, legislative, and judicial powers.[18] After a country achieves a democratic transition, it faces the challenge of consolidating democracy.

liberalization

Involves reducing restrictions on freedom.

Democratization involves the right of citizens to compete in elections and to control the government.

consolidation of democracy

Involves behavioral, attitudinal, and institutional changes.

The **consolidation of democracy** is a long-term process that continues after countries have made the transition to democracy. It involves behavioral, attitudinal, and institutional changes. Behaviorally, a democratic regime is consolidated when there is no significant effort to change the government by force. Attitudinally, a democratic regime is consolidated when a strong majority of the population believes that democratic institutions and procedures are most appropriate for their society. Institutionally, a democratic regime is consolidated when society as a whole, including the government, believes that there are certain laws, procedures, and institutions that must be used to govern society.[19] For democracy to be consolidated, **four conditions** are seen as essential:

1. The conditions must exist that make it relatively easy for a civil society to develop. Individuals must be able to form organizations that are autonomous from the government to protect their interests, inform the public, and challenge the government.
2. Specific arrangements must be made for groups and individuals to compete for political power. This usually means the development and functioning of core institutions such as political parties and interest groups.
3. Society must respect and uphold the rule of law, and an independent judicial system must exist to determine what the law is.
4. There must be an institutionalized economic society or significant degree of market autonomy and the right of individuals to own property.

The free market and private ownership of property are regarded as essential to the independence and liveliness of a civil society and, ultimately, the survival of democracy itself.[20]

Transitions to democracy do not occur in any specific order. What most countries that make the transition to democracy seem to have in common is a serious national crisis. The disruption of the status quo often creates rivalries within the nondemocratic government. Eventually, the government begins to disintegrate. Faced with unprecedented domestic

Transitions to democracy do not occur in any specific order.

and international pressures, most governments in these circumstances commit themselves to holding free elections and relaxing restrictions on fundamental freedoms. Elections usually change the old government and install new leaders. The **transitional phase of democracy** contains both democratic and nondemocratic elements. Several free and fair elections must be held and there must be a general societal consensus that there is no alternative to democracy before the transition to democracy is consolidated.[21] But democracies must also deliver. They must demonstrate that they can improve the economy, maintain order, and provide a better quality of life for the people to obtain legitimacy or acceptance by the people. A **full transition to democracy** is accomplished when basic democratic rights are an integral part of life and when people believe in the superiority of democracy over the alternatives.

Nondemocratic governments, especially those controlled by the military, attempt to manage transitions to democracy instead of making changes quickly. African governments provide many examples of **managed transitions.** They have essentially attempted to control the process of change in order to protect their own interests, to ensure stability, and to minimize concessions to the forces of change. In managed transitions, the military establishes a timetable for the return to democratic rule and determines the process for democratic elections.[22] These managed transitions occur in response to national unrest and economic crises. Some military leaders may initiate transitions to democracy because developments in the country, regionally and globally, indicate that military rule is no longer a viable option.

Whether they are managed or haphazard, transitions to democracy are influenced by pressures for change. The press, the business community, women, and students play a crucial role in bringing about political reforms. Nondemocratic countries that allow a measure of democratic freedom, such as limited freedom of the press and speech, are ultimately challenged by the press. In both Nigeria and South Africa, the press played a crucial role in creating the condition that eventually forced the government to implement democratic rule. Widespread access to information and ideas provided by a free press helps end the nondemocratic government's control of information and, eventually, its ability to control the population. Women in Latin America and Asia were instrumental in helping governments in those regions to become democratic. Women began to organize against worsening economic conditions and increased government brutality. The women's movement was led by upper- and middle-class professional women who not only were well educated but had lived in the United States and other democratic societies. They were joined by poor urban women who were struggling to take care of their families. Women were able to play a crucial role in transitions to democracy because (1) their activities were not viewed as threatening by the military rule; (2) the Catholic Church, an extremely powerful institution in these countries, urged women to participate in various nonpolitical activities; and (3) the military regimes were forced to commit themselves to political reforms in light of their serious economic failures.[23]

Transitions to democracy are influenced by pressures for change.

Women played a critical role in transition to democracy in Latin America.

International Pressure International pressure for democratic reform grew with the proliferation of human rights groups and nongovernmental organizations. As more citizens became actively involved in international issues, their governments became more responsive to their demands. The ideological conflict that characterized the **Cold War** had imposed restrictions on the ability of Americans to criticize American allies who violated their citizens' rights. This ideological barrier was no longer in place, and groups were now less restrained in their opposition to all governments that failed to practice democracy. When Indonesian forces attacked civilian demonstrators in 1998, the United States responded by pressuring the government to refrain from using excessive force. When violence erupted in East Timor, which voted for independence from Indonesia, the United States suspended military ties with and arms sales to Indonesia until the government stopped its soldiers and their allies from destroying the lives and property of the East Timorese.[24] Indonesia had to confront intense pressure not only from domestic groups but also from the United States, a longtime ally.

Cold War

The end of this ideological conflict contributed to democratization.

International pressure for transitions to democracy comes not only from governments and various human rights groups but also from the **Catholic Church.** In early 1998, Pope John Paul II visited Cuba, which is ruled by Fidel Castro and his communist government. Like other countries in Latin America, the majority of Cuba's population is Catholic. Unlike other Latin American countries, which have made a transition to democracy, Cuba continues to practice communism and to deny its citizens certain rights and freedoms found in other democratic societies. Pope John Paul II's historic visit to Cuba was designed to strengthen the role of the Catholic Church in bringing about democratic reforms in Cuba. As a result of the pope's visit, the Catholic Church in Cuba has gained greater freedom to advocate for social change.[25]

Catholic Church

A nonstate actor that influenced transitions to democracy.

Democratic Transitions in Latin America

Latin America has experienced more dynamic political changes than Africa and Asia. Between 1978 and 1993, fifteen countries made the transition from dictatorship and authoritarianism to democracy. Several factors contributed to the dramatic political changes in Latin America:

Six major factors contributed to change in Latin America.

1. Economic difficulties, symbolized by the debt crisis, destroyed the already low levels of legitimacy of many governments.
2. Military conflicts and military defeats weakened dictatorships in Nicaragua, El Salvador, Panama, and Argentina. The authoritarian government in Argentina, for example, was undermined not only by economic crisis, but also by its disastrous defeat in the Falklands (or Malvinas), a war it fought with Britain in an attempt to conquer the Falkland Islands (or the Malvinas).
3. Several authoritarian regimes were shaken by their inability to adequately respond to serious problems caused by natural disasters. These included an earthquake in Nicaragua and floods and droughts in already impoverished Bolivia.
4. Some governments were pressured by sanctions imposed primarily by the United States.
5. The demise of communism in the Soviet Union and Eastern Europe exposed the weaknesses of that ideology and made democracy a more attractive alternative.
6. The United States changed its approach to Latin America, beginning with the policies of President Jimmy Carter. America withdrew its support for dictatorships in Nicaragua, Argentina, Chile, Panama, Haiti, and the Dominican Republic.[26]

These changes reinforced pressures within the various countries for a transition to democracy. Despite their progress toward democracy, many Latin American countries face several problems that weaken the democratic process. Poverty continues to be the reality for many Latin Americans, despite growing economic prosperity in most countries. Corruption continues to erode the people's confidence in political, social, and economic institutions. Many ordinary citizens are not convinced that democracy can deliver. They do not believe that they are much better off under democratic governments than they were under authoritarian rule.[27]

Developments in Peru underscore the people's ambivalence toward democracy. Although Peru made the transition to democracy in the 1980s, the country has suffered from high levels of inflation, economic depression, and widespread violence. The most serious challenge came from the **Shining Path,** a rebel movement that was formed by university professors and students who subscribed to the philosophy of Mao Zedong (Mao Tse-tung), the first leader of China's Communist Party. The Shining Path used extreme violence against residents of impoverished villages, banned Indian and Christian holidays, and attempted to destroy the traditional family in an effort to create a new society. More than 30,000 people were killed and about 600,000 were displaced throughout Peru. The failure of the previous democratic government to end the violence and improve the economy led to the election of Alberto Fujimori as Peru's president in 1990. Fujimori not only ended much of the violence but also weakened the democratic process by dominating the legislature and the courts. Fujimori also exercised considerable control over the media and used undercover police agents to intimidate opposition leaders. By the end of 2000, Fujimori's government had collapsed. Fujimori went to Japan, where he claimed his rights to Japanese citizenship. Alejandro Toledo was elected as president of Peru in 2001.

Both Chile and Costa Rica have had relatively stable democracies for a long time. Chile's democracy was ended when **Salvador Allende,** the country's first elected Marxist president, was overthrown and killed by General Augusto Pinochet in 1973. Pinochet and the military ruled Chile until the restoration of democracy in 1990. Domestic and international pressure, as well as a growing middle class, influenced Pinochet to hold elections, which he lost. Chile returned to its democratic roots, despite retaining authoritarian tendencies and Pinochet's continuing role, as a senator-for-life, in the government. Political polarization diminished; there was greater national consensus of economic and social policies; and political parties, interest groups, and human rights activists were reinvigorated.[28] Ricardo Lagos from the Socialist Party won Chile's presidential election in 2000, and Michelle Bachelet (also from the Socialist Party) won the presidential election in 2006, thereby demonstrating the consolidation of democracy.

Costa Rica also stands out in Latin America as a country with a long history of democracy. Unlike most societies, Costa Rica does not have a military. It was abolished by the 1949 Constitution. The ministry of public security and the ministry of the presidency share responsibility for law enforcement and national security. The Constitution and various laws prohibit arbitrary arrest and detention, cruel and unusual punishment, and inhumane treatment of prisoners. The Constitution also protects the people's right to privacy and provides for freedom of religion. However, unlike the United States, which emphasizes the clear separation of church and state, the Constitution established Catholicism as the state religion. This is similar to England, where the Anglican faith is the state religion. However, people of all denominations freely practice their religion. The press operates freely. Newspapers, television stations, and radio stations are privately owned and operate independently of the government.[29]

Shining Path

A Peruvian rebel movement that was formed by university professors and students who subscribed to the philosophy of Mao Zedong.

Salvador Allende

Chile's first elected Marxist president; was killed by General Augusto Pinochet.

Mexico's democratic government has been dominated by the Institutional Revolutionary Party (PRI) since the 1920s. PRI has used its advantage of incumbency (its control over political offices) to consolidate its power. For example, PRI is often accused of systematically using state-financed aid programs to influence voters to support the party. Some voters are given groceries, scholarships, crop payments, and other benefits to encourage them to vote for PRI. Incumbents in most societies use their positions to enhance their chances of being reelected. They allocate the government's resources in a way that will influence the people to vote for them. This practice is referred to as **pork politics** in the United States. In Mexico, however, there are few checks to prevent politicians from abusing the power of incumbency. On the other hand, other political parties are beginning to successfully challenge PRI's dominance. In 1999, Vincente Fox of the National Action Party (PAN) became the president of Mexico, thereby ending seventy-one years of political dominance by the PRI.

pork politics
The name given to the activity of allocating the government's resources in a way to influence people to vote a particular way.

Mexico's judicial system is structured similarly to that of the United States. It has a system of local, state, and national courts, including a Supreme Court. Members of the Supreme Court do not serve for life. They are nominated by the president and must be approved by a two-thirds majority in the Senate. It is generally believed that the judiciary's independence is compromised to some extent by the fact that the Supreme Court judges can serve for no more than fifteen years.[30] The courts generally protect freedom of speech, freedom of the press, and other basic rights that are guaranteed by the Constitution. However, human rights abuses are a common problem in Mexico. There was an escalation in brutal murders connected to the illegal drug trade in 2006 and 2007. State authorities do not always prevent police officers and private militias from violating the rights of particular groups and individuals. Courts continue to admit as evidence confessions that have been obtained under torture, despite the Constitution's prohibition against the use of torture.

The judicial system in Mexico is undermined by official corruption. Because people lack confidence in the police, about 64 percent of crime victims in Mexico City do not even bother to report crimes to law enforcement authorities. In fact, many of the robberies are committed by the police. In some cases, especially in states along the U.S.–Mexican border, judges, police, and others posing as attorneys extort large sums of money, ranging from $3,000 to $10,000, from tourists to "fix" real or fabricated violations of the law.[31] The prison system reflects the corruption that is generally associated with the judicial system. Many detainees are able to bribe prison officials to have charges dropped before they were scheduled to appear before a judge. Many prisoners have to purchase their own food, medicine, and other necessities from prison guards. Prisoners also bribe guards to allow things they need to be brought in from relatives and friends. The poor conditions of the prisons, widespread poverty in Mexico, and the huge income gap between the rich and poor help to weaken the judicial system in particular and the democratic process in general. In 2006, results of the presidential election were contested for several months. The Federal Electoral Tribunal declared Felipe Calderón Hinojosa the winner on September 5, 2006. Nevertheless, Mexico remains committed to democracy.

Mexico's judicial system suffers from corruption.

Democratic Transitions in Africa

Most African countries briefly experienced democratic rule after achieving independence from Britain and France in the early 1960s. They inherited British and French institutions. However, many of these societies soon abandoned democracy. The governments in Tanzania, Ghana, and Guinea adopted socialist policies and stifled political opposition. In Nigeria, the military seized power, and ethnic and regional rivalries plunged the country into a devastating civil war in the late 1960s. Throughout much of their existence as independent states, African countries were directly or indirectly caught up in the Cold War. Many of the military conflicts that erupted during the Cold War were fought in Africa. In many ways, several African leaders used the rivalry between the United States and the Soviet Union to consolidate their authoritarian and military rule. Transitions to democracy were a low priority for African leaders as well as their external supporters. But many Africans remained hopeful that military dictatorships would end and worked to achieve that goal. Nigeria returned to civilian rule in 1979, but reverted to military rule four years later.

The end of the Cold War and an emphasis on global free trade by the United States and Western Europe pushed African societies closer to opening their societies and embracing democratic reforms. Military dictatorships came under increased domestic and international pressure to transfer power to freely elected governments. Because Russia itself was undergoing its own transition to democracy, Africans could no longer count on Russian support for their military regimes. Namibia, Mozambique, and Zimbabwe became more democratic, whereas Zaire (now the Democratic Republic of the Congo), America's staunchest African ally during the Cold War, resisted political reforms. Poverty and corruption became the hallmarks of Zaire under the leadership of Mobutu Sese Seko. In May 1997, Laurent Kabila overthrew Africa's longest dictatorship. The change was hailed as a major step toward democracy. But the bright promise soon faded as Kabila demonstrated his own preference for repression and dictatorship.[32] In January 2001, Kabila was assassinated and his son took over the country. Following a civil war in which more than 3 million people died, multiparty elections were held in July 2006. Congo remains unstable. However, the two most important transitions to democracy in Africa occurred in South Africa and Nigeria.

apartheid

Legal discrimination and racial separation.

South Africa implemented its system of racial separation, or **apartheid,** in 1948 under the leadership of the National Party. Under apartheid, the small white minority, descendants of Dutch, French, German, and English settlers, maintained a democratic system for themselves and oppressed the other South Africans. Apartheid established a racial hierarchy, with whites at the top and blacks at the bottom. But blacks and other nonwhite groups made up 85 percent of South Africa's population. Through extreme oppression and the implementation of divide-and-conquer strategies, the small white minority was able to rule South Africa. On the other hand, the democratic institutions that whites developed for themselves, in time, served as a foundation for the expansion of democracy for all South Africans.

African National Congress

Opposition to apartheid, led by Nelson Mandela.

Oppression by the white minority government influenced the formation of the **African National Congress (ANC),** led by Nelson Mandela. After Mandela and other leaders of the ANC were imprisoned for resisting apartheid laws, black South Africans believed that only a combination of armed struggle, trade union activity, mass demonstrations, various acts of resistance, and international pressure would force the white minority to abandon apartheid. As South Africa achieved higher levels of economic development, it became more dependent on black labor. Businesses eventually concluded that apartheid was outdated and costly. Many members of the business community advocated ending apartheid, especially in light of increased international economic sanctions against South Africa. Support from the Soviet Union enabled the ANC to launch military attacks against the apartheid regime. Churches around the world and within South Africa joined students and other groups to pressure the minority government to change. Faced with the reality that neither side could defeat the other, the National Party, under the leadership of **F. W. de Klerk,** and the ANC decided to negotiate an end to apartheid.[33] Nelson Mandela was released from prison, free elections were held in which all adults were eligible to vote, and whites were assured that their rights would be protected by a black majority government. South Africa, since 1994, adopted a new constitution, elected a new parliament, developed a new judicial system, and established a **Truth and Reconciliation Commission,** which tried to repair some of the damage caused by apartheid and to unite the various South African groups. Nelson Mandela was elected in 1994 to lead South Africa, and democratic rights have been observed.

Nigeria's transition to democracy is more uncertain than South Africa's. Nigeria's experience with democracy is limited. The rule of law has not been embedded in Nigerian society. Military rule in Nigeria impoverished the country and destroyed most of the democratic institutions. The courts were manipulated by military leaders, and the press, although relatively free, was frequently intimidated and disrupted by government officials. Human rights were routinely abused, excessive force and murder were used by the government to silence political opposition, and police officers often detained relatives and friends of suspects without charge to induce suspects to surrender. Prisoners such as **Ken Saro-Wiwa** and his eight co-defendants, who protested the government's oil policies and its oppression of the Ogoni people, were executed without receiving a fair trial by an impartial jury or judge.[34] Corruption was widely viewed as the norm, and government officials and their supporters used their positions to enrich themselves.

Nigeria's transition to democracy in early 1999 was influenced by many factors. Despite Nigeria's oil wealth, most Nigerians are desperately poor. Most of the revenues obtained from the country's petroleum were taken by political leaders. Widespread poverty, in such a potentially wealthy country, inspired Nigerians to try to end military rule. Another factor influencing the transition to democracy was the brutally oppressive actions of **General Sani Abacha.** General Abacha seized power after the results of Nigeria's presidential elections in 1993, which were designed to return the country to democratic rule, showed that Moshood Abiola would win. Abacha's ruthless dictatorship and unrestrained corruption resulted in Nigeria's isolation by the international community. This international pressure also contributed to political changes in Nigeria. After General Abacha's unexpected death in June 1998, his successor, General Abdulsalam Abubaker, implemented democratic reforms and promised to return Nigeria to civilian rule. Elections were held in February 1999. General Olusegun Obasanjo, a former Nigerian leader and the only general to give up power voluntarily to a civilian government (in 1979), won the presidential election.[35] However, Obasanjo and his supporters

F. W. de Klerk

Leader of the National Party; helped end apartheid.

Truth and Reconciliation Commission

An alternative to punishment by death or imprisonment for crimes against humanity.

Ken Saro-Wiwa

Executed for protesting Nigeria's oil policy.

General Sani Abacha

Military dictator whose oppressive rule led to Nigerian transition to democracy.

attempted to amend the Nigerian Constitution to enable him to seek another term in office. This effort was defeated in the Nigerian Senate in 2006. However, political struggles concerning elections continued in 2007 and corruption remained widespread.

Democratic Transitions in Asia

Rapid economic growth in Asia has served as a catalyst for democratic reforms. Countries such as Taiwan, South Korea, Thailand, Indonesia, and even China have been influenced to make transitions toward democracy. Although China remains a communist country, it has implemented far-reaching economic reforms and limited democratic freedoms. Taiwan and South Korea, for example, responded to pressure from prodemocracy movements and labor unions by ending authoritarian rule. Their economic prosperity and their integration in the global economy weakened the old system. Unlike Latin America, which suffers from high rates of economic inequality, many Asian countries attempted to reduce inequality and provide education, health care, housing, and employment for their citizens. A strong and growing middle class, as we have seen, plays a critical role in a country's transition to democracy. The middle class, especially students, moved the largest Islamic country, **Indonesia,** toward democracy during its economic crisis in the late 1990s.

Indonesia

The largest Islamic country; has transitioned toward democracy.

President Suharto of Indonesia, who came to power in 1965 after he led a military takeover of government, attempted to legitimize his authoritarian rule by building a strong economy. Suharto's government insisted that people minimize their differences and work together to develop the country. Indonesians agreed to accept fewer democratic rights in exchange for rapid economic development. But economic development strengthened the forces of change. Indonesia's economic success inevitably led to increased participation in society. When Indonesia's economy collapsed, the government had not built a large enough reservoir of political legitimacy to convince people to remain loyal and to keep their side of the bargain.

Students led the struggle against Suharto and his government. They called for Suharto's resignation, withdrawal of the military from politics, respect for the rule of law, immediate elections, a free press, competitive political parties, an independent and impartial judicial system that upholds basic freedoms, a strong legislative branch, and an end to corruption. Some Indonesians believed that such democratic reforms would endanger the country's stability and contribute to its disintegration. But the economic crisis had such a devastating effect on the majority of Indonesians that support for the status quo was seriously eroded. Middle-class people became more supportive of reform as they watched their wealth disappear when the stock market and the value of the country's currency, the **rupiah,** plunged. A major catalyst for change was the slaying of four students at Trisakti University by the security forces. Their deaths signaled to Indonesia's middle class that they were also vulnerable. The murder of the students, combined with the worsening economic crisis, triggered massive rioting that left more than 1,000 people dead. The security forces decided that only Suharto's resignation could prevent an escalation of the violence. But the end of Suharto's presidency only influenced students to demand

Students led the struggle against the Suharto government.

rupiah

The currency of Indonesia.

more political reforms. After two years of protests, the students saw Suharto's dictatorship collapse, the election of a new government, and a commitment by Indonesia's leaders to move forward with democratic reforms.[36]

China's transition to democracy is carefully controlled by the Communist Party. Although China is officially a communist society, generational change, rapid economic growth, the emergence of a strong middle class, and the government's embrace of capitalism and international trade are weakening the government's control over its citizens. In many ways, China is a paradox. The Communist Party is both the initiator of major changes as well as the guardian of conservatism and stability. China's huge markets and its growing economic power have entangled it with the global economic system. In order to be effective in global economic organizations, like the World Trade Organization (WTO), China has to reject many of its communist policies. It has to open up the society to outside forces of modernization. Economic development and globalization, especially the influence of revolutions in communications technologies, are gradually weakening the Communist Party and its ideology.

Changes in China's judicial system demonstrate the government's cautious approach to democratic reforms. In 1997, China revised its **Criminal Procedure Law** to give defendants the right to legal counsel, right to an active legal defense, and other rights of criminal defendants that are practiced in democratic countries. However, the judicial system, which is independent in theory, is strongly influenced by the Communist Party. The government places a higher priority on maintaining political and social stability and suppressing political opposition than on safeguarding individual rights. The government often dictates the sentences in politically sensitive cases. Arbitrary arrest and detention occur routinely. Officials often ignore procedures that are designed to give defendants a fair trial. In fact, prisoners are often forced to confess, and these confessions are admitted as evidence. The conviction rate is more than 90 percent.[37]

Criminal Procedure Law
China's revised law that granted defendants the right to legal counsel, among other rights.

The Communist Party restrains freedom of speech, press, and religion. However, it has also enacted reforms that facilitate the practice of these freedoms. Modern communications technologies connect China to the world. Many Chinese citizens in cities such as Beijing and Shanghai seem to constantly use cell phones. The Internet is used by an increasing number of Chinese, despite the government's efforts to control the content of materials available on the Internet. This is obviously a difficult undertaking. Many Chinese citizens have access to global television networks, especially in larger cities. Most Chinese enjoy personal freedoms that would have been unthinkable only a few years ago. However, political dissent is usually repressed by the government. Religious groups, including Protestants and Catholics, are required to register with and are monitored by the government. Although 15 to 20 million Christians are registered, approximately 30 million more worship privately in places that are not registered with the government. Religious groups that are perceived to be a challenge to the government are banned. The **Falun Gong,** or Buddhist law, for example, was banned in 1999 because of its religious and political activities. The Falun Gong is a popular spiritual movement that is based on Buddhism and Taoism. With more than 10 million members in China, it is the largest mass movement that is not controlled by the Communist Party.[38] Falun Gong received renewed attention in 2006 when one of its members interrupted President Hu Jintao's speech during his visit to the United States.

Falun Gong
Buddhist law and a banned religious group in China.

Grassroots democracy is being promoted across China. Influenced in part by Russia's difficulties with democratic and economic reforms, which were imposed by Russia's leaders, China has emphasized building democracy at the village level. About 900 million people, or about 75 percent of China's population, live in villages that practice limited democracy. As part of its managed transition to democracy, the Communist Party sent people to villages to train officials in the most basic principles of democracy and democratic procedures. The process started in 1989, shortly after hundreds of students and others protested in Tiananmen Square for democratic reforms and were killed by the Chinese military. Villages nominate and vote for committee candidates, without being controlled by the government.[39] Political participation at the village level, although not a serious threat to the Communist Party's control over China, is seen as an important first step toward a transition to democracy.

What Happens to Ex-Dictators?

Transitions to democracy have implications for the leaders of former nondemocratic societies. Most of these leaders usually escape punishment by the new democratic governments for the murders, torture, abductions, denial of political freedoms, and other abuses of human rights that occurred while they were in office. Many of these crimes were committed by the ex-dictators themselves. The fate of former dictators was highlighted at the end of the last century by attempts of Spain and other countries to extradite General Augusto Pinochet for gross human rights violations during his seventeen-year military rule in Chile. But many dictators avoid that much international media attention. Most new democratic governments are reluctant to prosecute ex-dictators for several reasons:

Six reasons given for not prosecuting ex-dictators.

1. The new democracies are too fragile to confront ex-dictators. The new leaders are more concerned about building democratic institutions and changing people's attitudes toward government.
2. Many ex-dictators play a critical role in transitions to democracy and are able to negotiate their exemption from prosecution when they leave office.
3. Ex-dictators usually continue to have strong support from the military, which is often the country's strongest and most legitimate institution. Putting former military leaders on trial could prompt armed forces to intervene in politics and end the democratic process.
4. The new civilian governments attempt to consolidate their power and put the past behind them by stressing the need for national reconciliation and forgiveness.
5. Some former despots escape punishment because of their ability to convince the new leaders that their brutality was justified by political circumstances or as part of an effort to develop the economy.
6. Some ex-dictators die before they can be tried for crimes committed under their leadership.

General Augusto Pinochet of Chile played a major role in the country's transition from his dictatorship to democracy. His treatment represents a movement away from the old practice of allowing dictators to escape prosecution. Pinochet overthrew the democratically elected leader of Chile, Salvador Allende, in 1973 and instituted a reign of terror that lasted until the country's transition to democracy began in 1990. At least 3,000 of Pinochet's political opponents were killed or "disappeared" during his seventeen-year rule. Pinochet also concentrated on Chile's economic development. Chile's record economic growth made it a success story in Latin America. As discussed earlier, economic development inspires political change. Pinochet eventually, under severe domestic and international pressure, permitted elections to be held, which he lost. Before stepping down, however, Pinochet's government wrote a constitution that gave him a lifelong Senate seat. Pinochet also retained his powerful position as the head of Chile's army until early 1998. However, countries such as Spain and France wanted to prosecute Pinochet for gross violations of human rights. As a member of Chile's Senate and leader of the conservatives in Congress, Pinochet was entitled to travel to Britain on a diplomatic passport, which theoretically protected him from prosecution. But Spain demanded his **extradition** from Britain so that he could be tried in Spain for crimes that were committed against Spanish citizens when he ruled Chile. Britain eventually ruled that Pinochet was too sick to stand trial. He was sent back to Chile in early 2000. His power was clearly diminished and his immunity from prosecution was immediately challenged. In August 2004, Chile's Supreme Court stripped Pinochet of immunity from prosecution.[40] Pinochet died in December 2006.

extradition
The process of making people go back to a country where they have been charged with a crime so that they can stand trial.

Human Rights in the Developing World

Respect for human rights and fundamental freedoms is, as we have seen, an essential component of democratic societies. However, there are conflicting perspectives on human rights and disagreements on how to deal with violations of human rights. **Human rights** are often equated with natural rights or God-given rights. These are rights that everyone has. People are born with these rights. These rights include the right to minimal subsistence, security against physical violence, the ownership of property, freedom of speech and religion, and the right to justice. Human rights are claimed by individuals, religious groups, political communities, women, ethnic minorities, and those not in positions of power. **John Locke** (1632–1704) and other proponents of human rights or natural rights argue that human beings are entitled to life, liberty, and property or, as Thomas Jefferson wrote in the American Declaration of Independence, the pursuit of happiness. The function of government, in their view, is to protect these fundamental rights. As this chapter has shown, many governments fail to respect human rights. In some cases, such as in Rwanda and Burundi, extreme violations of human rights—genocide and torture—have been prevalent. Many homeless children are killed in urban areas throughout Latin America by police death squads. Slavery still exists in parts of North Africa, especially in the Sudan.

Concerns about human rights can be found in all cultures, religions, and political systems, in varying degrees. Christianity, Judaism, Islam, Buddhism, Hinduism, Confucianism, and other religions have articulated rights and responsibilities of

human rights
Equated with natural or God-given rights.

John Locke
Leading proponent of natural rights who influenced Thomas Jefferson.

individuals and communities.[41] However, not all societies or religions have embraced the concept of individual freedom and the equality of all people. Although advocates of human rights embrace a universal or cosmopolitan view, others take a narrow and more limited view, generally referred to as relativism. **Universalists** or **cosmopolitans** believe that all people, no matter where they live, are entitled to basic rights simply because they are human beings. Greek and Roman philosophers, most notably **Cicero** (106–43 B.C.E.), believed in the idea of universal rights based on natural rights and natural law. Cicero articulated the view that governments as well as citizens anywhere in the world must obey the authority of the higher law of nature. All laws must be compatible with the law of nature, which can be discovered by right reasoning.

> **universalists or cosmopolitans**
>
> Those who believe that people everywhere are entitled to human rights.
>
> **Cicero**
>
> Roman philosopher and lawyer who believed in universal natural rights.

In sharp contrast to the universalists or cosmopolitans, proponents of relativism believe that rights enjoyed by individuals are determined by each society's specific culture and historical experiences. They view the government as the source of individual rights. One of the strongest proponents of relativism was Thomas Hobbes (1588–1679). An English philosopher, Hobbes believed that law was the command of the government or sovereign, and the only rights that individuals had came from government or the monarchy. Like Hobbes, Edmund Burke (1729–1797) argued that the rights of British people were derived not from abstract natural laws but from society's traditions, customs, and laws.

Proponents of relativism believe that rights are determined by each society's unique culture.

The rise of Nazi Germany and World War II dramatically focused the world's attention on human rights, including the rights of people living under colonialism to self-determination and independence. The debate on human rights after World War II took place within the broader context of the Cold War, symbolized by the rivalry between the United States and the Soviet Union. Countries focused on the different areas of human rights, depending on their ideology and level of economic development.

YOU DECIDE ✓   Are Human Rights Compatible with Islam?

The precepts of Islam, like those of Christianity, Hinduism, Judaism, and other major religions possessed of long and complex traditions, are susceptible to interpretations that often create conflicts between religious doctrines and human rights. Although governments may claim that their opposition to international human rights is justified by Islamic culture, the Muslims whom they govern may dismiss such claims as cynical appeals to religion, made with an interest to legitimize the vices of corrupt and undemocratic political systems.

Do you think that human rights are compatible with Islam? Make the argument for cultural relativism in relation to various practices in Saudi Arabia that are generally regarded as violations of human rights.

Source: Ann Elizabeth Mayer, *Islam and Human Rights* (Boulder, Co: Westview Press, 1999), xi–xiv.

The United States, Western Europe, and Canada believed that **negative rights** or the rights of individuals and groups against the government should be the priority. These rights, which include freedom of speech, freedom of religion, freedom of the press, and the right to a fair trial, are found in the International Covenant on Civil and Political Rights. The Soviet Union, China, and most developing countries focused primarily on **positive rights** or the rights of citizens to certain levels of economic well-being, health, education, and cultural amenities. Numerous human rights covenants have been passed by the United Nations. Some of them are the Universal Declaration of Human Rights; the International Convention on the Elimination of All Forms of Racial Discrimination; and the Convention Against Torture, and Other Cruel, Inhumane, or Degrading Treatment or Punishment.

The growing interdependence of countries and the decline of sovereignty have diminished the ability of governments to violate human rights without drawing international attention to the problems. Many governments and humanitarian organizations strongly support **humanitarian intervention,** or the use of military force against a country that engages in gross violations of human rights. As we have seen, even countries that are moving toward democratic governments continue to violate human rights. Democratic societies such as the United States and Britain are sometimes accused of violating human rights. The United States, for example, faced global condemnation in 2006 and 2007 for its human rights violation in Iraq, Afghanistan, and Guantanamo Bay (Cuba). Humanitarian intervention is used only in some of the most extreme cases. Generally speaking, those embracing cosmopolitan or universalist viewpoints are more likely to support humanitarian intervention than those who take a cultural relativist position.

Nongovernmental organizations, such as Amnesty International, Americas Watch, Asia Watch, Africa Watch, Medecins Sans Frontieres (Doctors Without Borders), and the Women's Environment and Development Organization, monitor human rights violations worldwide.[42] **Amnesty International** is one of the best known human rights groups. It was founded in London in 1961 by a group of writers and lawyers. It publicizes human rights abuses in different countries and encourages its members around the world to participate in letter-writing campaigns to seek the release of prisoners of conscience. These prisoners of conscience are individuals who are imprisoned because of their political, religious, social, and other beliefs. Many governments are sensitive to negative publicity, especially those that are integrated in the global economy. Human rights groups often pressure democratic

negative rights
Rights of individuals and groups to be protected from the government.

positive rights
Rights of individuals to economic well-being, health care, and education.

humanitarian intervention
The use of military force against a country that engages in gross violations of human rights.

Amnesty International
A leading human rights group.

TAKING ACTION

Amnesty International

There are many organizations on campus and in your community that are concerned with promoting democracy and protecting human rights. Amnesty International has chapters on many college campuses. You can attend a meeting of Amnesty International to learn more about human rights problems around the world.

governments to impose economic sanctions and other measures against countries that violate human rights.

Summary and Review

Most developing countries struggle to achieve both economic development and democracy. Some have achieved a remarkable degree of democratic freedom and respect for basic human rights, despite their relative poverty. Many, on the other hand, have experienced significant economic growth without making major progress toward democracy. Political development may be defined as the growth of modern and effective political institutions and practices such as those that are found in the United States, Canada, Britain, France, and other democratic societies. Judicial systems are essential to maintaining democratic freedoms, including political participation. Democratic governments respect the rule of law. Many developing countries, however, have weak and ineffective judicial systems. Interest groups, like political parties and judicial systems, are critical players in societies that are becoming or already are democratic. As economic development becomes more widespread, interest groups such as labor unions and agricultural groups begin to organize to protect their interests. Students are also strongly involved in politics in developing countries. Political scientists often refer to factors like judicial systems, interest groups, respect for the rule of law, opposition, and fair elections as preconditions for democracy. Economic development also influences the adoption of democratic values. Moreover, pressures for change influence transitions to democracy. Many of the pressures for change stem from women, international pressure, groups perceived to be marginalized in a political system, students, and many other less obvious variables. A major component of democratic societies is the respect for human rights and fundamental freedoms. Although transitions to democracy continue throughout Asia, Latin America, and Africa, they do not occur in any prioritized order.

Key Terms

democracy 189
legitimacy 190
presidential
    democracy 190
parliamentary
    democracy 190
separation
    of powers 190
checks and
    balances 190
Wahhabi
    tradition 192

political
    participation 192
patron-client
    systems 193
political party 193
Refah Party 194
rule of law 195
judicial system 195
shari'a 195
interest groups 195
managed transitions
    to democracy 199

Shining Path 202
apartheid 204
African National
    Congress 204
Truth and
    Reconciliation
    Commission 205
Falun Gong 207
grassroots
    democracy 208
Tiananmen
    Square 208

humanitarian
    intervention 211
Amnesty
    International 211

Discussion Questions

1. Is economic development a prerequisite for democratic transition? Why or why not?
2. Discuss important components of democracy.
3. Is it possible to achieve a quick transition to democracy? Can you think of some examples?
4. Discuss the belief outlined for democratic stability as outlined in this chapter.
5. What are the characteristics of a patron–client relation? Could a patron–client relationship be consistent with democratic values? Why or why not?
6. Why are the freedoms of press, assembly, opposition, and speech important for democratic societies?
7. Discuss the preconditions for democracy. Are there some preconditions that are more important than others? If so, which ones?
8. What is a managed transition to democracy?
9. How important are women to democratic transitions?
10. Do you believe that democracy occurs from the bottom up (grassroots to the social superstructures, i.e., statehood, religion, etc.) or from the top down (social superstructures to grassroots)?

Suggested Readings

Ambrose, Brendalyn P. *Democratization and the Protection of Human Rights in Africa: Problems and Prospects.* Westport, CT: Praeger, 1995.

Bell, Daniel A. *East Meets West: Human Rights and Democracy in East Asia.* Princeton, NJ: Princeton University Press, 2000.

Carothers, Thomas, and Marina Ottaway, eds. *Uncharted Journey.* Washington, D.C.: Carnegie Endowment for International Peace, 2005.

Finnemore, Barbara. *The Purpose of Intervention.* Ithaca, NY: Cornell University Press, 2003.

Goldman, Merle. *From Comrade to Citizen: The Struggle for Political Rights in China.* Cambridge, MA: Harvard University Press, 2006.

Hunter, Shireen T., and Huma Malik. *Modernization, Democracy, and Islam.* Westport, CT: Praeger, 2004.

Lex, Rieffel. "Indonesia's Quiet Revolution." *Foreign Affairs* 83, no. 5 (September/October 2004): 98–110.

Lindberg, Staffan. *Democracy and Elections in Africa.* Baltimore, MD: The Johns Hopkins University Press, 2006.

Liang-Fenton, Debra, ed. *Implementing U.S. Human Rights Policy.* Washington, D.C.: United States Institute of Peace, 2004.

Munoz, Heraldo, ed. *Democracy Rising.* Boulder, CO: Lynne Rienner, 2006.

Schell, Orville. "China's Hidden Democratic Legacy." *Foreign Affairs* 83, no. 4 (July/August 2004): 116–25.

Zakaria, Fareed. *The Future of Freedom.* New York: Norton, 2004.

Addresses and Websites

Citizen's Democracy Corps
1400 I Street, NW
Suite 1125
Washington, D.C. 20005
Tel: (800) 394 1945
Fax: (202) 872–0923
http://www.cdc.org/

The Citizen's Democracy Corps, founded in 1990, is a private organization that looks to help developing countries make a shift to a global, free-market economy. The organization provides foreign assistance and job opportunities for people and companies in regions that are making a democratic transition. It also helps these companies with both managerial and technical assistance to better working conditions and business results. This website offers further detail about the organization along with information about its various programs and countries in which the organization is operating.

Human Rights Watch
350 Fifth Avenue
34th Floor
New York, NY 10118–3299
Tel: (212) 290–4700
Fax: (212) 736–1300
http://www.hrw.org

The Human Rights Watch organization is a group that is dedicated to protecting human rights of all people across the globe. The organization works to uphold political freedom, bring offenders to justice, protect people from injustices and inhumanity during wartime, and prevent discrimination. This group does this by exposing human rights violations via in-depth investigations. This website is one of the most complete when it comes to global issues, economic justice, democracy, and human rights. It offers a vast amount of information regarding the organization and also has a wide range of information regarding human rights in various regions of the world. There is also a section on the homepage that provides information on various global issues.

Westminster Foundation for Democracy
2nd Floor
125 Pall Mall
London
SW1Y 5EA
United Kingdom
Tel: 144 (0) 207 930 0408
Fax: 144 (0) 207 930 0449
http://www.wfd.org/

The Westminster Foundation for Democracy, established in 1992, is an organization that looks to strengthen and build democratic institutions across the world. Although the organization works closely with the British government and Westminster political parties, its choices in projects and priorities are left up to the sole decision of the group. Some of the group's projects include promoting political parties, human rights, legal reform, democratic political institutions, and women's organizations. Its website offers further information about the organization, including extensive detail on their various projects that work to promote democracy. The website also offers other facts and provides program application and requirements for those who are eligible.

International Secretariat for Human Rights Without Frontiers
Avenue Winston Churchill 11/33
1180 Bruxelles
Tel: +132–2–345 61 45
Fax: +132–2–343 74 91
http://www.hrwf.net/English/english.html

The Human Rights Without Frontiers is an organization that promotes democracy and the rights of the individual. Under these goals, the group works on numerous projects including the promotion of freedom of religion and conscience, the eradication of trafficking of women, and the elimination of discrimination of minorities. This website offers more information regarding the organization and the issues on which it is currently working. Numerous resources can also be found on the website, including a link to other non-governmental and human rights organizations.

Notes

1. Larry Diamond et al., "Introduction: Comparing Experiences with Democracy," in Larry Diamond et al., eds., *Politics in Developing Countries* (Boulder, CO: Lynne Rienner, 1990), 16.
2. Thomas M. Magstadt, *Nations and Governments* (New York: St. Martin's Press, 1994), 289.
3. Jorge I. Dominguez, *Democratic Politics in Latin America and the Caribbean* (Baltimore, MD: The Johns Hopkins University Press, 1998), 14.
4. Gary K. Bertsch et al., *Power and Policy in Three Worlds* (New York: Macmillan, 1991), 580.
5. Jyotirindra Das Gupta, "India," in Larry Diamond et al., eds., *Politics in Developing Countries* (Boulder, CO: Lynne Reiner, 1990) 223.
6. "Despite UN Plea, Haiti Postpones Elections Indefinitely," *Chicago Tribune*, 5 March 2000, sect. 1, 9.
7. Scott Peterson, "Struck Down in Turkey, Islam Coils," *The Christian Science Monitor*, 20 January 1998, 6; and

Marina Ottaway and Thomas Carothers, "Middle East Democracy," *Foreign Policy* 145 (November/December 2004): 22–28.

8. Hugh Pope, "Turkey's Military Moves to Center Stage," *The Wall Street Journal*, 23 December 1997, A11.

9. Seth Mydans, "To Some Indonesians, Army Is Rock of Nation," *The New York Times*, 16 February 1998, A3.

10. U.S. Department of State, *Country Reports on Human Rights Practices for 1997* (Washington, D.C.: U.S. Government Printing Office, 1998), 1559.

11. Ibid., 1500.

12. Monte Palmer, *Political Development: Dilemmas and Challenges* (Itasca, IL: F. E. Peacock, 1997), 202.

13. Diamond et al., "Introduction," 18.

14. Richard J. Payne, *Opportunities and Dangers of Soviet-Cuban Expansion* (Albany: State University of New York Press, 1988), 125.

15. Dominguez, *Democratic Politics*, 26.

16. Michael Bratton and Nicolas van de Walle, *Democratic Experiments in Africa* (Cambridge, UK: Cambridge University Press, 1997), 239.

17. Geoffrey Pridham et al., "The International Dimension of Democratization," in Geoffrey Pridham et al., eds., *Building Democracy* (London: Leicester University Press, 1997), 2.

18. Juan J. Linz and Alfred Stepan, *Problems of Democratic Transitions and Consolidation* (Baltimore, MD: The Johns Hopkins University Press, 1996), 3.

19. Ibid., 6.

20. Ibid., 7–11.

21. Georg Sorensen, *Democracy and Democratization* (Boulder, CO: Westview Press, 1998), 39.

22. Bratton and van de Walle, *Democratic Experiments*, 171.

23. Sonia E. Alvarez, *Engendering Democracy in Brazil: Women's Movements in Transition Politics* (Princeton, NJ: Princeton University Press, 1990), 262.

24. Keith B. Richburg, "On Indonesia, It's Wait and See," *The Washington Post National Edition*, November 1999, 16.

25. Larry Rohter, "After the Visit: Mission Lies Now with Cuban Church," *The New York Times*, 27 January 1998, A3.

26. Robert K. Shaeffer, *Power to the People: Democratization Around the World* (Boulder, CO: Westview Press, 1997), 124.

27. Peter Hakim, "Is Latin America Doomed to Failure?" *Foreign Policy* 117 (Winter 1999–2000): 107; and "Democracy's Low-Level Equilibrium," *The Economist*, 14 August 2004, 35.

28. Felipe Aguero, "Conflicting Assessments of Democratization," in Felipe Aguero and Jeffrey Stark, eds., *Fault Lines of Democracy in Post-Transition Latin America* (Miami, FL: North-South Center Press, 1998), 3.

29. U.S. Department of State, *Country Reports*, 476.

30. Roderic Camp, *Politics in Mexico* (New York: Oxford University Press, 1996), 163.

31. U.S. Department of State, *Country Reports*, 574.

32. Howard W. French, "New Congo Leader's Star Steadily Loses Its Luster," *The New York Times*, 21 May 1998, A1.

33. Richard J. Payne, *The Nonsuperpowers and South Africa* (Bloomington: Indiana University Press, 1990), 245.

34. U.S. Department of State, *Country Reports*, 262–66.

35. Norimitsu Onishi, "Nigerians Vote, With High Hopes for Civilian Rule," *The New York Times*, 28 February 1999, A1.

36. Seth Mydans, "Indonesia's Students Pledge to Press Democratic Agenda," *The New York Times*, 9 November 1999, A8.

37. U.S. Department of State, *Country Reports*, 714–18.

38. John Pomfret and Michael Laris, "A Standoff Between Falun Gong and Government," *The Washington Post National Weekly Edition*, 8 November 1999, 15.

39. Matt Forney, "China's Democratic Experiment Hits Its Limits," *The Wall Street Journal*, 14 January 1999, A16; Orville Schell, "China's Hidden Democratic Legacy," *Foreign Affairs* 83, no. 4 (July/August 2004): 116; and Merle Goldman, From Comrade to Citizen: The Struggle for Political Rights in China (Cambridge, MA: Harvard University Press, 2006).

40. Clifford Krauss, "Pinochet, at Home in Chile: A Real Nowhere Man," *The New York Times*, 5 March 2000, A8; and "Chile's Top Court Strips Pinochet of Immunity," *The New York Times*, 27 August 2004, A3.

41. Seyom Brown, *Human Rights in World Politics* (New York: Addison Wesley Longman, 2000), 41–47.

42. Richard W. Mansbach, *Global Puzzle* (Boston: Houghton Mifflin Company, 1997), 558.

CHAPTER TEN

Political Leadership

GLOBALIZATION AND LEADERSHIP

IN THIS RAPIDLY CHANGING, TECHNOLOGY-DRIVEN WORLD, LEADERS NEED TO BE INNOVATORS. NO MORE CAN THE WORLD AFFORD OLD-STYLE LEADERS WHO WILL CONTINUE TO THINK IN NATIONALIST TERMS. THE WORLD WE LIVE IN IS A DIFFERENT WORLD, WHERE MOST OF OUR PROBLEMS ARE GLOBAL IN NATURE. NATIONAL SOLUTIONS CANNOT SOLVE GLOBAL PROBLEMS. TODAY, THE FORCES OF GLOBALIZATION ARE REDEFINING THE SOVEREIGN STATE. POLITICAL LEADERSHIP, HOWEVER, HAS NOT CAUGHT ON. NATIONALIST LEADERS STILL THRIVE. PATRIOTISM IS STILL A FORCE GREATER THAN HUMANISM. SOME WOULD ARGUE THAT NATIONALISM IS A FORM OF REACTION TO GLOBALIZATION. BUT RESISTANCE TO CHANGE CANNOT STOP THE CHANGE. IT ONLY SLOWS IT DOWN. IT ALSO COULD FORCE THOSE WHO DESIRE IT INTO A VIOLENT REACTION. AS PRESIDENT JOHN F. KENNEDY ONCE SAID: "THOSE WHO MAKE PEACEFUL CHANGE IMPOSSIBLE MAKE VIOLENT CHANGE INEVITABLE." THE ROLE OF LEADERS IS STILL SIGNIFICANT EVEN THOUGH THEY NO LONGER HAVE FULL CONTROL OF THE AGENDA.

INTRODUCTION

Although people are the foot soldiers of change, societies need leaders to direct the process of change. Some have argued that leaders are really no different from those who are led and that, although they occupy a special position, they are a mere reflection of their constituents. Others have argued that leaders are all important. They are the ones who shape society. Both positions are probably accurate to a degree. In situations of great change, such as the current process of globalization, leaders are, perhaps, more important. It is for this reason that we have decided to devote a chapter of this book to the role of political leadership. Africa, Asia, and Latin America are in the midst of a profound revolution. They are changing very rapidly. In times of change, when old structures are no longer respected and new ones are not yet fully developed, people often find it easy to attach their loyalty to an individual leader. This makes leaders in such societies more important. Political leaders play a critical role in developmental policies throughout the areas under study. We could classify leadership in Africa, Asia, and Latin America into a number of types. In many societies leadership is still patriarchal.

PATRIARCHAL LEADERSHIP

Patriarchy is at the core of all traditional systems where authority is closely related to family and kinship groups. The male head of the clan, tribe, or village acts in patriarchy as the head of a family and the group becomes the family. In some traditional societies, the nation becomes the family and the national leader becomes the patriarch or father of the whole nation. In such societies, who is the leader is more related to an accident of birth than it is to qualifications or an electoral process. A patriarchal leader leads because he is perceived to have a right to lead. His followers obey because they believe that it is their duty to do so. Patriarchal societies are often referred to as premodern. But if you visit such a country, you are likely to encounter modern appearances. You are likely to see high-rise buildings, modern dress, and up-to-date cars. This is where Professor Hisham Sharabi distinguishes between traditional patriarchy and what he terms as **neopatriarchy**.[1] Underneath that façade of modernity, the society remains patriarchal. Government remains rooted in the family unit as extended to include the whole nation. Prior to independence, most developing countries had patriarchal systems. After some years of independence, new types of leaders began to emerge. Initially, most came about as a result of **military interventions.** Some of the new military leaders wanted revolutionary change; others wanted incremental change; yet others took over the government so as to prevent impending change. In some cases, revolutions toppled patriarchal or military leaders and put forth the revolutionaries in power. More recently, some form of democratization has taken place and some countries have moved to yet a different type of democratically elected leadership.

patriarchal leadership

Leadership where authority is closely related to family and kinship groups, especially to the men in those groups.

neopatriarchy

A patriarchal system in a society that hides under the façade of modernity.

military intervention

A military takeover of government.

MILITARY LEADERSHIP

The phenomenon of intervention by military leaders in politics and their attempts to control governmental institutions is not limited to one region or area of the contemporary world. Such attempts have occurred on almost every continent. The majority of countries in Africa, Asia, and Latin America experienced one or more attempts of military intervention since independence. Even Europe and the United States did not completely escape this phenomenon of military intervention in politics in one form or another. There are examples of direct and successful interventions, as in Spain, Greece, and Portugal, as well as the unsuccessful, as in France in 1962. In the United States, indirect intervention is often indicated in the notion that the defense establishment enjoys excessive power, which is often used to influence governmental decisions and policies. Military intervention, especially in developing countries, has attracted the attention of social scientists because of its implications to stability and to international affairs. Yet, this area of study is still short of adequate theory or concepts to explain, let alone predict, such developments. Social scientists, and political scientists in particular, do not possess the proper information or the adequate analytical tools to deal confidently with events of military intervention in a certain society. Their generalizations are often not much more trustworthy than those of the journalists reporting the news according to their senses and personal preferences. Among the early scholars who investigated military intervention in the governments of the developing countries were Samuel P. Huntington and Morris Janowitz. Their work has had a major impact on later scholars in the field. Consequently, a brief look at their approaches is in order.

Huntington asserts that "military explanations do not explain military intervention"[2] because of the general politicization of all groups in the society. In an attempt to answer the question of why the military intervenes in politics, Huntington cites the "absence or weakness of effective political institutions in the society."[3] Morris Janowitz, on the other hand, attempts to relate military intervention to the organizational structure of the military establishment and the social background of the individual officers leading the intervention. In attempting to discover the causes of intervention, Janowitz points out the "characteristics of the military establishment" of the country and relates the capabilities of the leading officers to their "ethos of public service." He also discusses their skills "which combine managerial ability with heroic posture," their class origin from middle or lower-middle classes, and their internal cohesion.[4]

There is some evidence to support both arguments. Other theorists doing work on the subject either explained or employed one or both of these theoretical approaches. Others reminded us of some other factors contributing to the phenomenon of military intervention in politics. Regardless of theoretical reasons for intervention, the fact remains that many developing countries have had military intervention or are run by civilians dependent upon the military. When military officers carry out a successful intervention or coup d'état, new leadership suddenly emerges. Some are revolutionary, some are moderate, and others are conservative. Let us look at an example of each.

Revolutionary Military Leaders: Nasser of Egypt

Egypt represents an old civilization. Its history stretches back thousands of years. Modern Egypt, however, is a recent state. At the turn of the twentieth century, Egypt found itself under British protection. It had been declared a British Protectorate in 1882 after the British occupied the country. British interest in Egypt centered on the **Suez Canal,** a significant trade route that connects the Mediterranean Sea to the Red Sea.

Under British rule, the **capitulation system** allowed for many abuses in the country. The capitulation system exempted non-Egyptians from Egypt's laws. This exemption allowed British and other Western adventurers to rob the country of many artifacts. This is one reason so many Western museums have Egyptian mummies and other artifacts. In a way, we can be thankful that the Sphinx and the pyramids were too big and heavy to carry away; otherwise, they too would have ended up in some European or North American museum. Internally, Egypt had a feudal system. Under this system 2 percent of the people owned more than 70 percent of all the agricultural land. Most people lived and worked on the feudal estates. The small aristocratic elite lived in luxury while the Egyptian masses labored hard under Egypt's burning sun to produce for and serve the aristocratic families. Politically, Egypt had a monarchy with a king as head of state. Although there was a constitution, in practice, the king held

Suez Canal

A significant trade route that connects the Mediterranean Sea to the Red Sea.

capitulation system

System that exempted non-Egyptians from Egypt's laws.

absolute power in consultation with the British. By the end of World War II, King Farouk had been the monarch for almost a decade. His dependence on British advisors and his loyal aristocratic elite had grown. King Farouk by then was too involved in his own hobbies to worry much about government. In 1948, Egypt lost a war with the newly founded state of Israel.

It was at this juncture that Gamal Abdel Nasser and other military officers began to organize for the eventual coup d'état. Nasser, Anwar Sadat, and ten other young army officers began to meet to discuss ways to rid Egypt of corruption and place it on the right path to creating a more just society. Known as the Free Officers, the group eventually carried out a bloodless military takeover on July 23, 1952. King Farouk was forced to abdicate and leave the country. A year later, the monarchy was finally dropped

FIGURE 10.1 Egypt

in favor of a constitution that put power in the hands of the military officers. Nasser emerged as the sole and all-powerful leader of the country. His charismatic style made Nasser very popular among the Egyptian masses.

Now in power, Nasser began a series of activities designed to achieve his objectives for the country. As mentioned earlier, Nasser and his colleagues in the Free Officers group wanted to end feudalism, rid Egypt of British domination, and modernize the country. Feudalism was ended by decree. The **Agrarian Reform Act** limited land ownership and redistributed land among the peasants. The British role in Egypt, however, was a different story. It required a war. If you recall, British interest in Egypt revolved around the Suez Canal. The British, French, and the government of Egypt had collaborated to build the canal back in 1868. In return, the British and French were given rights to the canal for the next 100 years. Nasser did not have the patience to wait for the end of that term to rid his country of British troops in the Canal Zone. On July 26, 1956, Nasser decided to nationalize the Suez Canal Company and take sole control of the canal. In late October of the same year, Britain, France, and Israel invaded Egypt. The invasion of Egypt caused uproar throughout the Arab countries and the states of Africa, Asia, and Latin America. Other developing countries denounced the invasion as imperialist. In Britain itself, domestic opposition to the actions of the government threatened the ruling party's hold on power. The Soviet Union and the United States both opposed the invasion of Egypt and demanded the withdrawal of the invading forces. The pressure was too strong to resist. Consequently, the three countries withdrew from Egypt, leaving

Agrarian Reform Act

Limited land ownership and redistributed land among the peasants in Egypt.

Should the United States Have Helped Egypt?

Should the United States have helped Egypt construct the Aswan High Dam? Was it a mistake that the United States did not? Would Nasser have turned to the Soviet Union anyway if the United States had helped him? Remember Egypt and Israel were enemies and the United States was Israel's ally. Could you make an argument that if the United States helped Egypt with the dam, Arab-Israeli tension could have been eased?

Aswan High Dam

The largest dam in the world, brought about through Nasser's efforts in Egypt.

Nasser in a much stronger position. Although Nasser may have lost the battle, he clearly won the war. He emerged from the war as a great hero, not only to his own people, but also to other Arab, African, and Asian peoples. Finally, a Third World leader was able to stand up to the former colonial powers. Nasser became an instant celebrity and one of the most charismatic leaders of his day.

Another area of interest to the military leadership of Egypt was the modernization of the country. Aside from the usual modernization projects that include education, health care, and infrastructures, Nasser decided to build the largest dam in the world, the **Aswan High Dam** on the Nile River. As you may already know, the Nile is Egypt's mainstay. More than 90 percent of all Egyptians live around the river and depend on it for the production of their food. Every year, the Nile flooded, destroying crops in the process. By building a large dam on the river, Nasser hoped to control the floods, expand agricultural land into the desert, and generate hydroelectric power to help industrialize the country. The construction of the dam became highly publicized and internationally controversial. Loans and expertise were needed for the project. Nasser attempted to secure those from the United States, but when that failed, Nasser went to the Soviet Union for help. Doing so at the height of the Cold War turned out to be controversial. The Aswan Dam, however, did increase Egypt's cultivable land by about 2 million acres, and increased its power output tenfold. It also controlled the flooding that plagued the country's farmers. In additional, industrialization projects were created and Egypt seemed to be on the road toward modernization.

Population growth and the Arab-Israeli conflict, however, kept Egypt from joining the ranks of modern states. As the productivity grew so did the population, eating up any meaningful growth. The Arab-Israeli conflict also required that the country devote much-needed resources for military buildup and occasional wars. But Nasser's charisma and his personal integrity were never questioned by his followers. When he died of a heart attack in 1970, millions of Egyptians paid their respects, and he is still remembered as a great revolutionary leader by his countrymen.

Transitional Military Leaders: The Case of Nigeria

As we will discuss in Chapter 12, Nigeria is Africa's most populous state. With a population of more than 110 million, Nigeria is also potentially one of Africa's richest countries.

But ethnic problems, constant military interventions, and rampant corruption have kept the majority of Nigerians impoverished.[5] A former British colony, Nigeria achieved independence in 1960. Since then, for all but ten years, the country has been ruled by military regimes. One of the most notorious of those was the rule of General Sani Abacha from 1993 to 1998. During his reign, the country was dragged down by neglect, corruption, and mismanagement—despite its billions in oil revenues. Abacha ruled Nigeria with an iron fist that made it into an international pariah. Political opponents were imprisoned, exiled, or killed; the constitution was discarded; and violations of civil and human rights became commonplace.

On June 8, 1998, General Sani Abacha died after suffering a heart attack. He was mourned by very few. The commander of the country's armed forces and defense minister, General Abdulsalam Abubakar, took

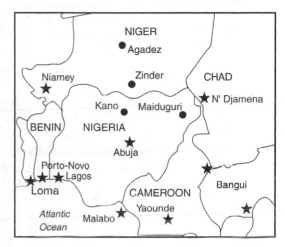

FIGURE 10.2 Nigeria

over as the new ruler. Under domestic and international pressure, Abubakar began a process to return the country to civilian rule. He invited all exiles to return home to help in rebuilding the country. He also released many political prisoners. On July 20, 1998, the new military leader of Nigeria released a plan to return power to civilian rule and to move the nation on a path of political and economic reform. May 29, 1998, was set as the date for swearing in a new civilian president.

A new constitution was adopted, political parties were chartered, and local elections were held. The presidential elections were held on February 27, 1999. With more than 60 percent of the votes, Olusegun Obasanjo was declared the winner. On May 29, 1999, the world watched as Obasanjo took over power from Abubakar. Nigeria had made its transition back to civilian rule. On the eve of the inauguration, Abubakar urged the new civilian rulers to seize the opportunity to change a nation wrecked by years of dictatorship.

Conservative Military Leaders: The Case of Chile

Chile is a beautiful coastal country with a rather long history of democracy. The people inhabiting the area tell a legend about their lands. It goes like this:

> *In the beginning of time, God created the world with all its wonders. Upon completion, God found that he had many pieces left. He had parts of rivers and valleys, of oceans and lakes, of glaciers and deserts, of mountains and forests, and of meadows and hills. Rather than let such wonders go to waste, God put them together and cast them onto the most remote corner of the earth. This is how Chile was born.*

Looking closely at Chile, we can understand the legend. Chile is a rather long and narrow country located in the extreme southwestern part of South America. It is geographically very diverse. In the north, Chile reaches the Andes Mountains and in the south the Antarctic zone. In between it has long beaches on the Pacific Ocean and behind the Andes lies the Atacama Desert. About 80 percent of Chile's population lives in urban areas. The country is rich in mining (mainly copper), agriculture, tourism, and fishing. Born out of Spanish colonization, Chile's constitution was, until 1973, one of the oldest in Latin America. The country had a republican form of government with elected presidents and a congress for 140 years.

In 1970, Salvador Allende, a medical doctor who led the Popular Unity Coalition, won the election for the presidency. With many Chileans suffering from malnutrition and the country facing shortages of food, housing, health care, and education, Allende pursued a socialist policy designed to redistribute the wealth of the nation. He began a land distribution program. He nationalized many industries and took over the foreign-owned copper mines and other natural resources. Such actions put him on a collision course with the United States, whose companies were severely affected. One major U.S. company that was affected was International Telephone & Telegraph (IT&T), which operated Chile's telephone system and owned copper mines there. In the 1972 U.S. presidential campaign, IT&T contributed $1 million to Richard Nixon's campaign. But the United States was moved more by Allende's perceived "Marxism" than by campaign donations. Allende's close relationship to Cuba and other communist countries further angered the U.S. government.

Aided by training and financing from the U.S. Central Intelligence Agency (CIA), a faction of the Chilean military, led by General Augusto Pinochet, carried out a coup d'état on September 11, 1973. Allende lost not only his job as president, but also his life. In the process, democracy in Chile came to an abrupt end, ironically with the help of the United States. A military regime was set up and the constitution was suspended.

Under Pinochet, Chile became an international outlaw state. To suppress the supporters of the previous government, Pinochet waged a campaign of terror that included raids, executions, disappearances, imprisonment, and torture of his opponents. In the four months following the coup, Amnesty International and the United Nations Human Rights Commission reported that 250,000 people were detained for political reasons. The government also halted the distribution of land and reversed many of Allende's policy decisions. Naturally, as in the case of all oppressive regimes, oppression did not end the opposition, it only strengthened it. Labor uprisings and nonviolent resistance by the Chilean masses continued, as did international pressure.

In 1980 Pinochet, under pressure, proposed a new constitution for the country. It provided that Pinochet would remain president until 1989 or possibly 1997. The proposed constitution allowed for the gradual return to some democratic forms of governance and restored a limited and appointed National Congress in 1990 and an elected president in 1997. But when the country went into an economic recession in the mid-1980s, opposition grew. Street protests, strikes, and symbolic resistance, such as people banging on pots, became commonplace. Consequently, Pinochet decided to hold a referendum on his presidency. The question voters were asked was whether Pinochet should remain president until 1997. The voters turned out in large numbers to defeat the proposition. Pinochet then made arrangements to step down as president but to remain head of the armed forces until 1998. After that time, he was to become senator-for-life.

N IN THE **EWS**

Pinochet Loses His Immunity

Augusto Pinochet, 90, was accused of stashing $27 million in bank accounts around the world and of crimes against humanity when he served as leader of Chile. Pinochet died in December 2006. His attorneys argued that he was too ill to stand trial. His daughter, however, is being charged with tax evasion. When she tried to enter the United States in 2006, Lucia Pinochet was arrested by the Department of Homeland Security and later sent back to the country she came from, Argentina.

Source: CNN News, 28 January 2006.

In 1990, the people of Chile voted for Patricio Aylwin to be president, and Chile was on its way back to democracy after seventeen years of oppressive military rule. Pinochet, of course, remained head of the military until 1998, when he became senator-for-life. Life did not go smoothly for the new senator, however. In October 1998, Pinochet was arrested in the United Kingdom when he was hospitalized for back surgery. His arrest was based on a Spanish request to extradite him to Spain for trial for the deaths of Spanish citizens killed in Chile under Pinochet's leadership. The Chilean government asked for his release, arguing that foreign courts have no jurisdiction for trying crimes committed on Chilean soil. The Spanish prosecutors argued that Pinochet's actions constituted crimes against humanity. Although the British eventually let Pinochet go back to his homeland, it took fifteen months of agonizing house arrest while British courts were looking into the matter.

Shortly after returning to his homeland, Pinochet learned that Chilean courts were stripping him of his congressional immunity as a senator-for-life, a privilege he granted himself in the constitution as a condition of his stepping down from the presidency. Pinochet's failing health prevented him from facing dozens of criminal cases involving the deaths and disappearances of many Chileans during his seventeen-year military rule over the country. His legacy of military dictatorship and reversal of change will remain for a long time.

Not all states in Africa, Asia, and Latin America have military regimes. Some are still monarchies, others have democratic systems, and a few have communist systems. Each has a different type of leadership and politics. Let us now take a look at some of those.

NONMILITARY LEADERSHIP

Many countries in Africa, Asia, and Latin America have civilian governments. In some cases, the civilian leadership is still dependent upon the military establishment to maintain its power. In other cases, the civilian leadership has the consent of the governed through a constitutional system that is supported by the people. In a few cases, the civilian leadership is accepted because of traditions and customs that the population seems to continue to tolerate. Saudi Arabia has such a system. In this part of the chapter, we will take a look at leadership in a monarchy, a communist system, and a democratic system.

The Monarch as Leader: Saudi Arabia

I will be father to the young, brother to the elderly,
I am but one of you; whatever troubles you, troubles me;
Whatever pleases you, pleases me.

THE LATE KING FAHD

The Kingdom of Saudi Arabia is the largest political unit in the Arabian Peninsula. A country that is almost entirely a desert, it has about one-fourth of the world's known oil reserves. The kingdom's founder was Abd al-Aziz Ibn Saud, who fought other tribal leaders to unite the country by 1927 under the name of the Kingdom of Hijaz and Najd and Its Dependencies. The country was renamed the Kingdom of Saudi Arabia in reference to Ibn Saud in 1932. Since that time, the country has been ruled by the descendents of Ibn Saud.

During the days of its founder, the person of the king combined executive, legislative, and administrative functions. Each tribal chief was responsible for the behavior of his people, and the Royal Army was ready to aid them if needed. In March 1958, legislative and executive powers were transferred to the crown prince, who also served as deputy prime minister. The king maintained veto powers. In May of the same year, a royal decree established a cabinet system with administrative powers. The cabinet, however, serves at the wishes of the king. Even today, Saudi Arabia has no constitution and maintains that the Islamic holy book, the Quran, is the guiding law of the land. The king still has absolute power and all government action is done by decree in the name of the king. No elections take place for any central government positions. Political parties are nonexistent.

Because no official census figures are available, the Saudi Arabian population is estimated. Latest estimates put that population at more than 21 million. That figure includes about one-fourth of the population who are nonnationals, or foreign. Until recently, nearly all Saudis were nomadic or seminomadic. Today, however, about 80 percent of the population is urban, the rest live in rural areas, and very few are still nomadic. Saudi cities look modern. High-rise buildings jot the landscape. Modern facilities shock first-time visitors.

The considerable influx of money from oil sales, especially in the 1960s and 1970s, generated many plans for development. Roads were built, universities were established, and industrialization was begun. Even agricultural projects were put in place, and this desert country became an exporter of wheat and other agricultural products. Industrialization targeted petrochemical products such as plastics, fertilizers, fiberglass, and other goods. Socially, the story is very different. Saudi Arabia is a rather conservative kingdom that attempts to maintain social cohesion through the application of Islamic principles. As such, even though the visitor may be impressed with modern buildings and amenities, they soon discover a society that is inward looking and very traditional. It was fitting then that, in 1992, when the country celebrated

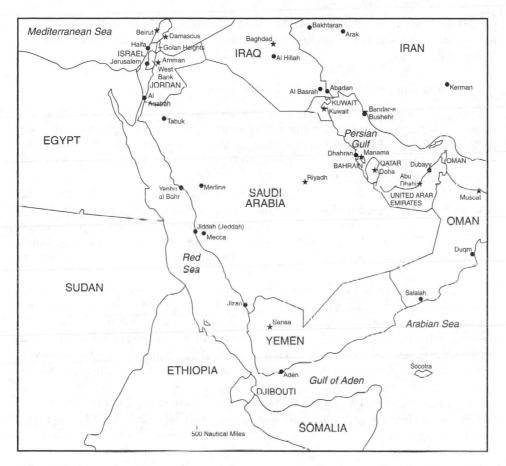

FIGURE 10.3 Saudi Arabia

its sixtieth anniversary, the Ministry of Information adopted the slogan of "Sixty years of progress without change."

Since its creation in 1932, Saudi Arabia had a total of five kings. The first was the country's founder, Ibn Saud. The rest were all his sons. An inner circle of his male descendants determines succession to power. When a king dies, the crown prince assumes the throne. King Fahd was the ruler until he died in 2005. The current monarch, King Abdallah, is the half-brother of the late King, and had acted on his behalf as crown prince due to King Fahd's health problems that had prevented him from carrying out the duties of ruling the country.

The person of the king combines legislative, executive, and administrative authority. Law is clearly guided by Islamic teachings as interpreted by the **ulema** or learned religious men. The king and the crown prince normally lead the Council of Ministers. The Council of Ministers is an appointed body that is vested with most

ulema

Islamic learned religious men.

powers with the king holding the right to veto their decisions. In sum, Saudi Arabia has a system of absolute monarchy supported by a patriarchal leader who acts as the father of the nation.

Communist Leaders: The Case of Cuba's Castro

Cuba is the Caribbean's largest island. It is also the only communist state in the Western Hemisphere. With 11 million inhabitants, Cuba has a long history that goes back to 3500 B.C.E. Europeans arrived only in the late fifteenth century. As in other parts of the Americas, the arrival of the Europeans brought with it slavery, wars, and misery to the inhabitants of the island.

Although Christopher Columbus sighted Cuba in 1492, he did not land there. It was Diego Velazquez de Cuellar who led an expedition to the island to claim it for the Spanish Crown in 1512. The Spanish slaughtered thousands of the native Taino-speaking **Arawaks.** Cuba was later used as the base from which expeditions to conquer Mexico were launched. As such, the island became Spain's gateway to South America.

Arawaks

Original inhabitants of Cuba.

The Spanish created large estates on the island where the local population was essentially enslaved under the pretext of teaching them Christianity. Exploitation, oppression, and European illnesses, to which the locals were not immune, led to the disappearance of the native population. Imported African slaves replaced the natives on the plantations. Tobacco was the major product of the island until sugar production became its major industry about a hundred years later. By 1820, Cuba became the world's largest sugar producer.

By 1825, Cuba and Puerto Rico were the only remaining Spanish colonies in the Western Hemisphere. As other Spanish colonies were freed, Cuba became a haven for Spanish loyalists escaping the victorious rebels. In October 1868, an attempt at independence from Spain took the lives of 200,000 people only to fail. In 1895, a similar attempt was made by a group of exiles led by a poet, Jose Marti. Marti was killed soon after he landed in Cuba, and his followers eventually were defeated.

In January 1898, an explosion destroyed a U.S. warship anchored at the Havana harbor. The U.S. government used this incident to achieve the eventual annexation of the Spanish colony. The United States declared war on Spain, and hostilities lasted for three months before the Spanish surrendered. By then Cuba had become a U.S.-occupied territory. An American governor was appointed, and a military base was created on Cuba's Guantanamo Bay. The U.S. naval base on Guantanamo Bay remains until today, reminding Cubans of the occupation of more than a hundred years ago. Cubans view the base as an insult to their nation.

Within two decades, U.S. companies came to dominate Cuba. American corporations gained ownership of two-thirds of the country's farmland, and tourism became a major industry run mostly by U.S. companies. Tourism was based on gambling and prostitution. In time, the country became known as the whorehouse of the United States. This was a time when the United States had a prohibition on alcohol.

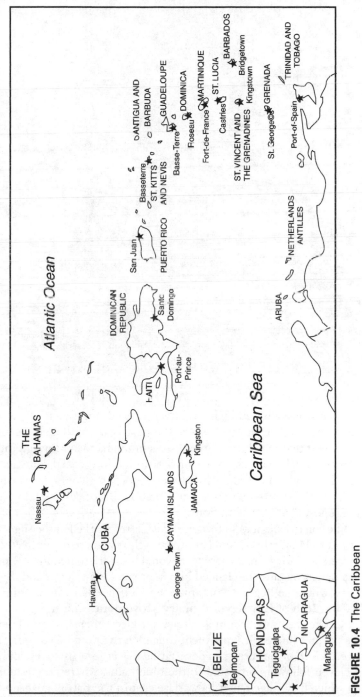

FIGURE 10.4 The Caribbean

February 11, 2005: President Fidel Castro speaks during a discussion at an international conference on economy and globalization in Havana, Cuba.

Source: Jorge Rey/AP/ World World Photos

A sergeant called Fulgencio Batista carried out a coup d'etat that overthrew the government in August 1933. Over the next two decades, Batista ran a very corrupt government that left the country's assets in the hands of foreign interests. The Batista dictatorship is known as an era of corruption and social injustice for many Cubans today. That sad era in Cuba's history ended when a young lawyer named Fidel Castro overthrew Batista after a three-year rebellion. Batista escaped the country, taking with him a reported U.S. $40 million.

The son of a plantation owner, Fidel Castro worked in the sugar cane fields as a boy. He went to Jesuit schools and later to law school, where he received a law degree. Castro practiced law in Havana, where he devoted his work to helping the poor. His opposition to the Batista dictatorship landed him in prison for a brief period. Eventually he went to Mexico where he began to organize the Cuban exiles into a fighting force, which he called the **26th of July Revolutionary Movement.** This movement of eighty-two men tried to overthrow Batista in an attack on December 2, 1956. They landed in eastern Cuba on the famous Granma yacht to launch their armed struggle. Most of the attackers were killed or captured in a devastating defeat for Castro. He did not give up. Castro and eleven followers retreated to the mountains, where they established a stronghold from which they waged guerrilla warfare against the Batista government.

The 26th of July Revolutionary Movement

Castro's group of 82 men who landed in Cuba in 1956.

Castro's movement grew after each attack. Numbering about 800, the movement scored many victories in small hit-and-run battles with government forces. Continuously growing, Castro's movement eventually became a serious threat to Batista. On January 1, 1959, Batista fled the country and Castro entered Havana as a liberating hero.

Soon after assuming power, Castro began to reform the economy. Decrees were passed cutting rents down, slashing electric rates, and nationalizing landholdings of more than 400 hectares. The United States was outraged at the nationalization of U.S. corporate interests. Telephone, electric, oil, and sugar companies were taken over by the government from U.S. corporate owners. Castro's offer of compensation did little to ease the tensions with the United States over Cuban actions. Castro simply wanted to take charge of his country's affairs to serve the poor and needy Cubans. Cuba's small elite, which included upper- and middle-class businesspeople and plantation owners, was similarly outraged. Most of them fled to Miami, where they have since orchestrated anti-Castro campaigns and influenced U.S. policy toward Cuba. The U.S. government imposed an **embargo** against trade with and travel to Cuba, which is still in place until this day.

The U.S. government also armed and trained a group of Cuban exiles to overthrow Castro's government. On April 17, 1961, this force of 1,300 exiles attempted an invasion of Cuba from the **Bay of Pigs** on the southern coast of the island. The invaders were defeated. But Cuban-U.S. relations worsened when Castro sought help and support from the Soviet Union in his confrontation with the United States. In a speech honoring the Cuban forces that defeated the invaders in April of that year, Castro said for the first time that the Cuban Revolution was socialist. Cuba's international behavior became more and more anti-American as Castro supported revolutionary forces in Central America and Africa. The Soviet Union also responded to Castro positively by giving Cuba massive amounts of aid.

The close Soviet-Cuban relations alarmed the U.S. government. In October 1962, a major crisis took place that brought the United States and the Soviet Union close to a nuclear holocaust. The United States discovered that the Soviet Union was setting up long-range ballistic missiles in Cuba. The U.S. president, John Kennedy, ordered a blockade of the island and demanded the removal of the missiles. Initially, the Soviet Union threatened to break the blockade, and a nuclear confrontation seemed imminent. That confrontation was averted when the Soviet Union decided to remove the missiles. If you have seen the movie *Thirteen Days*, you already have an idea about the crisis. For a long time after that U.S.-Cuban relations remained hostile. In the early 1990s, however, Cuba began to soften its anti-U.S. rhetoric and actually changed its constitution to drop any references to Marxism-Leninism. Relations with the United States remain cool, and the embargo against Cuba remains in place.

The Cuban society under the Castro regime has done relatively well. Through a state-supported agricultural system and ration program for basic nutrients, Cuba became the first underdeveloped economy to wipe out hunger and malnutrition. Cuba's public health system is so advanced that the World Health Organization recommended it as a

embargo

Legislation that restricts or bars some or all trade with certain countries.

Bay of Pigs

Failed invasion of Cuba by Miami exiles.

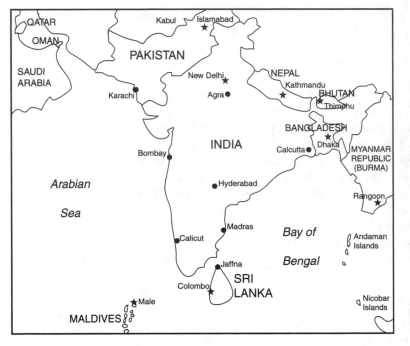

FIGURE 10.5 India

"model for the world." Cuba was successful in wiping out epidemics that infect most developing countries. Among Latin American countries, Cuba ranks best in life expectancy, infant mortality rate, literacy, and the number of doctors per thousand people. In sum, even though Castro's government had to deal with a harsh embargo, it was able to move Cuba in a direction that serves its people, especially the poor ones. Today, Castro is ill and has handed power to his brother, but his legacy still dominates the country.

Leaders in Democracies: The Case of India

Few countries in the world have such an ancient and diverse culture as India's. Stretching back 5,000 years, India's culture has been enriched by successive waves of migration that were absorbed into India's way of life. It is the physical, religious, linguistic, and racial variety that is the hallmark of India. As discussed in Chapter 3, India became independent in 1947 after centuries of British domination. The leaders who struggled for independence chose to remain within the British Commonwealth and retained many of the features of the British administration. India also adopted the British system of parliamentary democracy, making it the largest democracy on earth.

The Indian Constitution, adopted in 1950, safeguards all people from all forms of discrimination. Given the long history of the caste system in the country, this was a major break from tradition. It also caused severe hardships for the new government. The constitution also guaranteed freedom of speech, expression, and belief. The political system created a parliamentary democracy, where the House of Representatives decides on the prime minister who holds executive power. The Indian Parliament consists of two houses: the Rajya Sabha or the Council of States, and the Lok Sabha or the House of Representatives. The Council of States has 250 members, and the House of Representatives has 543 members. All legislation requires the approval of both houses. India has a ceremonial president elected by an electoral college drawn from both houses of parliament. The judiciary is independent and is headed by a Supreme Court. The country is set up as a federal state with twenty-five states and seven union territories represented in the federal system.

The achievement of independence in 1947 was just the first step for India's progress toward the creation of a modern state. The constitution set forth a number of goals for India's democracy. Economic growth, social justice, and self-reliance are most significant among them. To achieve such objectives, the country embarked on the promotion of five-year plans for development. Since then, India has come a long way in its progress toward development, but the process still has a long way to go. One thing is certain, however—India has created a democratic political system that could serve as a model for other countries in Africa, Asia, and Latin America. In Latin America, democracy has been on the rise. Sometimes, it has resulted in the rise of nationalist and revolutionary individuals to the top. Venezuela's Hugo Chavez and Evo Morales of Bolivia are such leaders.

Summary and Review

Africa, Asia, and Latin America are in the midst of a profound revolution. They are changing very rapidly. In times of change, when old structures are no longer respected and new ones are not yet fully developed, people often find it easy to attach their loyalty to an individual leader. This makes leaders in such societies more important. Political leaders play a critical role in developmental policies throughout the areas under study. We could classify leadership in Africa, Asia, and Latin America into a number of types. In many societies leadership is still patriarchal. Patriarchy is at the core of all traditional systems, where authority is closely related to family and kinship groups. Prior to independence, most developing countries had patriarchal systems. After some years of independence, new types of leaders began to emerge. Initially, most came about as a result of military interventions. The phenomenon of intervention by military leaders in politics and their attempts to control governmental institutions is not limited to one region or area of the contemporary world. Such attempts have occurred on almost every continent. This chapter focused on military interventions in the cases of Egypt, Nigeria, and Chile. In all of those countries, the military has served, for the most part, as a largely patriarchal authority that uses its powers to bring "order" to the society in which it operates. Countries in Africa, Asia, and Latin America—and all over the world—have varying degrees of patriarchal leadership. The latter, however, may stem from a communist background, as is the case in Cuba, or from democratic institutions, as is the case in India. Although not homogeneous in character or styles, leaders throughout Africa, Asia, and Latin America claim to represent their people's traditions, values, and political cultures.

Key Terms

patriarchy 217	free officers 219	Pinochet 222	ulema 225
military intervention 217	Agrarian Reform Act 219	International Telephone & Telegraph (IT&T) 222	Castro 228
capitulation system 218	Aswan High Dam 220		embargo 229
	Abacha 221		Bay of Pigs 229
Suez Canal 218	Allende 222	Ibn Saud 224	

Discussion Questions

1. What impact has rapid change had on governments and leaders in Africa, Asia, and Latin America?
2. Explain the lag between old systems of leadership and new ones.
3. Why are leaders important throughout the developing world? Is this importance similar to or different from the developed world?
4. What are some reasons behind the emergence of a new leadership?
5. Define patriarchy, and give examples as to how it plays a role in everyday life, political or otherwise.
6. Does military intervention only occur in the underdeveloped world, or is this a worldwide phenomenon? Provide examples.
7. Do authoritarian leaders, such as King Fahd of Saudi Arabia, respond to public opinion as do democratically elected leaders? How so? Give some examples.
8. How has the Bay of Pigs invasion solidified Castro's leadership?
9. What is meant by "progress without change"?
10. Compare the varying conceptions of order as they pertain to Cuba, Egypt, Saudi Arabia, and Chile.

Suggested Readings

Bakshi, S. R., S. R. Sharma, and S. Gajrani, eds. *Contemporary Political Leadership in India*. New Delhi, India: APH Publishing, 1998.

Boutros-Ghali, Boutros, et al. *Essays on Leadership*. Carnegie Commission on Preventing Deadly Conflict. Washington, D.C.: Carnegie Corporation of New York, 1998.

Bouvard, Marguerite Guzman. *Revolutionizing Motherhood: The Mothers of the Plaza De Mayo*. Lanham, MD: Rowman and Littlefield, 2004.

Dash, Anup Kumar. *The Political Elite in a Developing Society*. Delhi, India: Academic Foundation, 1994.

Kausar, Zeenath. *Women in Feminism and Politic[s]: New Directions Towards Islamization*. Selangor, Malaysia: Women's Affairs Secretariat (WAFA), IIUM, 1995.

Liswood, Laura A. *Women World Leaders: Fifteen Great Politicians Tell Their Stories*. London: Pandora, 1996.

Moens, Alexander. *The Foreign Policy of George W. Bush: Values, Strategy, and Loyalty*. Burlington, VT: Ashgate, 2004.

Javier Santiso, *Latin America's Political Economy of the Possible: Beyond Good Revolutionaries and Free Marketers*, Cambridge, MA: MIT Press, 2006.

Shevtsova, Lilia. *Putin's Russia*. Washington, D.C.: Brookings Institution Press, 2005.

Stern, Geoffrey. *Leaders and Leadership*. London: London School of Economics and Political Science, 1993.

Theakston, Kevin, ed. *Bureaucrats and Leadership*. New York: St. Martin's Press, 2000.

Westlake, Martin, ed. *Leaders of Transition*. New York: St. Martin's Press, 2000.

Addresses and Websites

Director, McConnell Center for Political Leadership
Ford Hall
University of Louisville
Louisville, KY 40292
Tel: (502) 852–3323

Fax: (502) 852–7923
http://www.mcconnellcenter.org/

The McConnell Center for Political Leadership was established in 1991 as a part of the University of Louisville in Kentucky. The main objective of the center is to make students more educated in political processes and stronger political leaders in the future. The center offers various programs, educational opportunities, and resources in order to promote strong political leadership among those who participate. Further information about the center and its political leadership aims can be found on the website.

International Secretariat for Human Rights Without Frontiers

Avenue Winston Churchill 11/33
1180 Bruxelles
Tel: + 32–2–345 61 45
Fax: + 32–2–343 74 91
http://www.hrwf.net/English/english.html

Human Rights Without Frontiers is an organization that promotes democracy and the rights of the individual. Under these goals, the group works on numerous projects including the promotion of freedom of religion and conscience, the eradication of trafficking of women, and the elimination of discrimination of minorities. This website offers more information regarding the organization and the issues on which it is currently working. Numerous resources can also be found on the website, including a link to other nongovernmental and human rights organizations. Because this organization offers many programs and educational opportunities, it is an excellent place to look for political leadership skills.

Global Interdependence Center

Fels Center of Government
University of Pennsylvania
3814 Walnut Street
Philadelphia, PA 19104
Tel: (215) 898-9453
http://www.interdependence.org/

This Web address is the site for the Global Interdependence Center of the University of Pennsylvania. It discusses the organization's intent, which includes looking at ways to develop new reasonable policies on critical economic issues. The organization also deals with finance and trade within free-trade structures; however, they deal with other issues that relate to the broader theme of global interdependence, including the environment. Links to events and conferences sponsored by the organization are provided on the website. This website is useful for those interested in global political leadership.

http://www.un.org/

This website takes you to the Internet home of the United Nations, the international governing structure in which many nations participate. The United Nations offers statistics and other useful information about various issues in countries. There are also numerous U.N. councils and programs, and information regarding them can be located on the site. This link is also an excellent source of information on international law and international affairs. Because the United Nations is the largest governing international body, it is a great source of information about political leadership at the global level.

Notes

1. Hisham Sharabi, *Neopatriarchy: A Theory of Distorted Change in Arab Society* (New York: Oxford University Press, 1988).
2. Samuel P. Huntington, *Political Order in Changing Societies* (New Haven, CT: Yale University Press, 1968), 194.
3. Ibid., 196.
4. Morris Janowitz, *The Military in the Political Development of New Nations* (Chicago: University of Chicago Press, 1964), 27–29.
5. For further reading on Nigeria, see Oladimeji Aborisade and Robert J. Mundt, *Politics in Nigeria* (New York: Longman, 1999).

CHAPTER ELEVEN

Bureaucracy

GLOBALIZATION AND THE BUREAUCRACY

THE BUREAUCRACY IS UNDER SERIOUS PRESSURE WITH GLOBALIZATION. NEW STANDARDS ARE COMING INTO BEING WITH DEREGULATION AND PRIVATIZATION. THE BUREAUCRACY OF THE OLD NATIONAL STATE HAD AUTHORITY AND CONTROL. TODAY, FORCES BEYOND THE CONTROL OF A SINGLE NATION-STATE ARE UNDERMINING THAT AUTHORITY. REGULATING TRADE, DRUG TRAFFIC, HEALTH, PORNOGRAPHY, AND MANY OTHER ACTIVITIES IS NOW HARDER THAN IN THE PAST. WITH THE GLOBAL NETWORKS THAT HAVE EASED THE FLOW OF INFORMATION, THE NATIONAL BUREAUCRACIES ARE SLOWLY LOSING THEIR GRIP IN THE AREA OF REGULATION.

THE NEW TECHNOLOGIES COULD ALSO MAKE THE WORK OF THE BUREAUCRACY MORE EFFICIENT. THE RAPID FLOW OF INFORMATION COULD ALLOW FOR THE SPREAD OF LESSONS FROM ONE BUREAUCRACY TO ANOTHER. FAILURE OF A PROGRAM SOMEWHERE MAY SAVE A SIMILAR PROGRAM ELSEWHERE AS INFORMATION BECOMES MORE READILY AVAILABLE. WITH CELLULAR TELEPHONES, BUREAUCRATS CANNOT HIDE AWAY FROM OFFICES. WITH THE INTERNET, MUCH NEW INFORMATION IS NOW WITHIN REACH.

INTRODUCTION

Let us say that the U.S. Congress passed a bill to construct a new interstate highway linking New York and California. The bill allocates $10 billion for the project. The president signs the bill and it becomes a national government decision. Who is going to plan, design, and oversee the actual construction of the interstate? Surely it will not be Congress or the president. It is likely to be the U.S. Department of Transportation. Who works there? It is civil servants or bureaucrats. They are the ones who administer government decisions.

The importance of administration is almost universally recognized. The **bureaucracy** is, in essence, the administrative arm of government. Political and economic development cannot be achieved without a competent bureaucracy. Policy decisions are not self-enforcing. The bureaucracy carries them out. Decisions by policymakers represent hope. It is the bureaucracy that must transform the hope or the dream into reality. Although bureaucrats are less visible than political leaders, their power usually is much greater in that it extends to every area of citizens' lives. If you need a driver's license, a passport, a birth certificate, a permit to add to a home, or a tax auditor, you will see a bureaucrat.

Bureaucrats also do much more than simply carry out orders by decision makers. They are the ones with information and expertise that is essential for policymakers. In essence, they are partners with the decision makers on issues of policy. In the countries of Africa, Asia, and Latin America, they not only administer laws, but, in the absence of parliamentary institutions, usually fashion them. They not only license, tax, and supervise, but often also organize and manage major financial, industrial, and agricultural enterprises. In order to modernize, the bureaucracy, therefore, ought to be the most permanent, the most expert, and the most efficient institution in the state.

As the core of the modern state, bureaucracy is very important in the process of modernization. The task of a modernizing bureaucracy involves not only running an ongoing system, but also developing new modes of operations, refining old norms, and building the new modern state. In all societies, the bureaucracy has the tasks of implementation and regulation. Let us take a look at such tasks.

bureaucracy

The administrative arm of government.

IMPLEMENTATION

Implementation is the stage in between the making of a policy decision and the consequences of the decision upon those people who are supposed to be affected by that decision. As already mentioned, policy decisions, such as the passage of a legislative act, are not self-executing. They need to be executed or carried out by someone else. As we saw earlier, a new interstate decision is likely to go to the U.S. Department of Transportation for implementation. Implementation involves the creation of a new agency or the assignment of responsibility to an existing one. It also takes the development of plans and guidelines for carrying out policy goals and the coordination of resources and personnel to achieve such goals.[1]

Implementation is not as simple as it may sound. It is a complicated process that involves the potential for policy failure. Planning, for example, does not always lead to success. The best-laid plans sometimes flunk the implementation test. Lack of clarity in the policy itself may contribute to differing interpretations and contrary results. Resources are not always readily available to carry out policies. Administrators may also be disposed to defeat a policy decision through inadequate implementation.

REGULATION

Government regulates all sorts of activities in society. Government regulates universities, hospitals, gambling casinos, businesses, environmental hazards, the sale of alcohol, and all types of activities. Regulation is often a controversial function of the bureaucracy. Policymakers usually give government agencies broad mandates to regulate industries, businesses, and a host of activities in society. Such regulations reach us on a continuous basis. When we discussed the role of government in Chapter 1, we saw that government is with us from the moment we are born to the moment we are buried or cremated. Any time we discuss government, we are, in essence, discussing the bureaucracy.

The idea that the U.S. economy is "free enterprise" is not entirely true. The reality is that government regulates our economy. Government regulates many sorts of activities. For example, if you want to buy or sell stocks, you will discover that the Securities and Exchange Commission has a hand there to protect you from potential fraud. If you work at a factory, a restaurant, or any other place, your relationship with your employer is regulated by the National Labor Relations Board. The Federal Trade Commission regulates advertising in order to protect consumers from deceptive practices. The Food and Drug Administration inspects the meat, the cereal, and most other foods we consume. The Consumer Product Safety Commission regulates even children's toys. In sum, government regulates so many activities in society that it is almost impossible to live outside the realm of regulation.

deregulation

The desire for less government regulation of the market.

Government regulates in order to protect us. But some people argue that too much regulation is not healthy for society. Such individuals want less regulation and less government in our lives. They advocate **deregulation.** The argument for deregulation is a popular one in many parts of the United States. The idea behind deregulation is that too much regulation raises prices, distorts market forces, and does not work. Consequently, the cry "get government off our backs" gets receptive audiences during national elections in many parts of the country. Popularity, however, does not necessarily equal accuracy. Regulation of society is very important to its own well-being. Some regulations have not worked and created problems; others have done a good service to society. It is because of regulations that we now breathe cleaner air, have lower lead content in our blood, and have children who are more likely to survive infancy.

THE BUREAUCRACY IN AFRICA, ASIA, AND LATIN AMERICA

As we have seen so far, bureaucracy is the core of the state. For the states of Africa, Asia, and Latin America, the bureaucracy is most important as they attempt to modernize their societies. Without a competent bureaucracy, modernization is destined to fail. In many of their states, the bureaucracy has gone a long way toward competency and efficiency; in others, it still has a long way to go. It is therefore difficult to make generalizations about the bureaucracy in so many countries. Instead, we will take a look at some common characteristics of modern bureaucracies in Africa, Asia, and Latin America.

Some of the common characteristics that may be typical of administration in Africa, Asia, and Latin America include structural uniformity, cultural variations, shortage of skilled staff, corruption, formalism, and operational autonomy. Let us now take a look at each.

Structural Uniformity

A basic pattern of the bureaucracy in Africa, Asia, and Latin America is imitative rather than indigenous. Modern bureaucracy in the states of Africa, Asia, and Latin America developed as they came in contact with the Europeans. That contact came in the form of colonial rule. The colonial powers established a new system of administration similar to those of the colonial motherland. The colonial administration was suited to the requirements of the colonial government rather than to the needs of the indigenous population. It was more elitist, more authoritarian, more aloof, and more paternalistic. The task of the colonial administration was to subvert the society to serve the needs of the dominant colonial power, not to serve the masses of people in the society. Remnants of these bureaucratic traits have inevitably carried over to the successor administration.

The transition from colonial administration to new independent state was not an easy one. The colonial structure remained almost intact. The function, however, changed. Once independence was achieved, the function was not to subvert the society to the needs of a ruling foreign government but to mobilize society for national development. With independence also came the loss of top executive officials. Those who ran the colonial bureaucracy were foreign officials who were nationals of the colonial motherland. With independence, those expert managers were reassigned back home or into some other colony. The new independent bureaucracy, therefore, had a colonial structure that was alien in origin, contradictory to native culture, and lacked the trained and experienced managers to run the system.

Cultural Variations

Few bureaucracies in the world have been in existence as long as those of Asia, the Middle East, or Africa. In fact, the bureaucracy was born somewhere there. Historians trace the earliest bureaucracy to Mesopotamia (today's Iraq). Others say it started in China, and some say it began in India. Europeans were left behind and developed their bureaucracies much later.

Although the inherited European system emphasized control and productivity, most African, Asian, and Latin American cultures put greater emphasis on values. In such cultures, being fair is more important than abiding by rigid bureaucratic rules. Often, rules are subverted to help an old person, someone in need, or a close friend or relative. There, bureaucracies tend to emphasize orientations that are not necessarily production-directed. Status based on ascription rather than achievement is common. In some countries, the cultural norms dominate, whereas in others, the legal-structural ones do. In Japan, for example, the bureaucracy benefited from the nation's strong sense of unity and ancient traditions of political centralization.[2] While employing European-based structures for its bureaucracy and improving them, Japan was able to make major strides toward the advancement of its people. In the process, Japan created an economy that is stronger than that of France, Italy, Spain, or many other European countries. Some countries in Africa, Asia, and Latin America, on the other hand, found their societies hindered by a burdensome bureaucratic structure that is essentially alien to their cultures.

Shortage of Skilled Staff

Bureaucracies in Africa, Asia, and Latin America have to deal with many problems when it comes to staffing. Often, they have a deficit in skilled staff necessary for carrying out the programs designed by their leaders. This shortage is not in the availability of employable individuals but rather in trained administrators with management capabilities, developmental skills, and technical competence. As the era of colonialism ended, the European powers withdrew their nationals to other assignments at home or in other colonies. Consequently, the newly independent states had to contend with training their own nationals to carry out the tasks of administration. As political instability occurred, so did instability in the bureaucracy. Top bureaucrats are replaced with new regimes, often by individuals who need time to develop the necessary experience to carry out their tasks. Technically competent bureaucrats often find opportunities to work in more technologically advanced and wealthier countries. When experience and know-how migrate, the bureaucracy suffers. This process of migration of technically competent individuals from poorer states to wealthier ones is called the **brain drain.**

brain drain

Migration of technically competent individuals from poorer states to wealthier ones.

Corruption

In Chapter 6, you read about corruption as a formidable obstacle to economic growth and social equity. You may remember that corruption is endemic in Africa, Asia, and Latin America, with the poorest states having the most serious problems. Corruption, of course, is not limited to the bureaucracy in any region or state on earth. It occurs in all states, including the wealthiest ones. The consequences of corruption, however, are greater in poorer societies lacking in resources. **Bureaucratic corruption** is the illegal use of an official position or title for private gain.[3] This could take place in many forms, including taking bribes, embezzlement, nepotism, patronage, or the selective enforcement of the law. Bribes are common in many societies. Often, bureaucrats are not paid a meaningful salary for survival. Bribes become a supplemental salary to allow public servants to make a living wage. This notion is generally accepted in some societies in which bribes are expected just like a tip for an airport or hotel baggage carrier. In the wealthier states, bribery takes place as well. But the consequences are often grave for the perpetrators.

bureaucratic corruption

The illegal use of an official position or title for private gain.

N IN THE NEWS

The Iraqi Oil for Food Scandal

In light of recent charges of corruption in the United Nation's Iraqi Oil for Food Program, two high-level U.N. officials have been suspended for suspected misconduct in relation to administering the program. Benon Sevan, responsible for heading the $64 billion program, and Joseph Stephanides, who currently heads the U.N. Security Council Affairs Division, have both been suspended without pay until they appear before U.N. disciplinary bodies set to resolve this dispute. Charged with having "tainted" the competitive bidding process used for companies to inspect goods shipped to Iraq under the program, the two bureaucrats allegedly conducted themselves in a way that was "ethically improper and seriously undermined the integrity of the United Nations," according to U.S. Federal Reserve Chairman Paul Volcker, who is leading the investigation into the Oil for Food Scandal.

Source: CBS News, 7, February 2005, http://www.cbsnews.com/stories/2005/01/18/world/printable667593.shtml

Some states in Africa, Asia, and Latin America are starting to take tough measures against corrupt officials. The People's Republic of China, for example, executed a senior parliament official on September 14, 2000, for taking bribes. Cheng Kejie was the highest Chinese official to be executed for bribery in more than fifty years of communist rule.[4]

Formalism

A prominent scholar on developing administration, Fred W. Riggs, used the concept of **formalism** to remind us of the widespread discrepancy between form and reality.[5] It is often the case in many countries that bureaucrats attempt to make things look as they ought to be rather than as they actually are. False reporting is, perhaps, the most common method of formalism. State Department official Roger Hilsman reported on such a practice during the Vietnam War. The United States was interested in developing statistical indicators to measure progress in that war. Once the request for such indicators reached a Vietnamese official, he responded: "Ah, les statistiques! Your Secretary of Defense loves statistics. We Vietnamese can give him all he wants. If you want them to go up, they will go up. If you want them to go down, they will go down."[6] Although very few bureaucrats will admit to that, it is nevertheless a common practice in some countries to fabricate statistics when necessary. Formalism could also take the shape of false reporting or by electing to disregard personnel regulations.

Cheng Kejie, former vice chairman of China's parliament, at his corruption trial before his execution.
Source: AFP/Getty Images

formalism

A concept used to remind people of the widespread discrepancy between form and reality, such as false reporting.

Operational Autonomy

Colonialism was essentially the rule of the bureaucrats with policy guidance from abroad. After independence, this pattern persisted in many societies, with bureaucrats having a monopoly over decision making with guidance from new masters at home. This pattern of operational autonomy is strengthened by the reality that the bureaucracy is usually the most permanent institution in the state. Government leaders

YOU DECIDE ✓ Can We Trust the Bureaucracy?

Working as a civil servant in a city's Department of Civil Engineering in Jordan, the city council once requested a report on housing units constructed in the previous two years and the numbers of adults and children inhabiting them. The request also asked for employment statistics of the dwellers of those units. Although I had information on the number of house construction permits issued,

I had no access to the remainder of the requested information. I promptly went to the chief engineer, who directed the unit to get advice on how I should proceed to gather the information. Pausing for a short while, the director then commanded: "Just make a report." Being the loyal employee I was, I did just that.

Source: Jamal R. Nassar on his own experience as a civil servant in the Ramallah Municipality in 1966.

usually make the major decisions, whereas bureaucrats determine the details and manage the day-to-day workings of the government.

The bureaucracy in the postcolonial states has many other problems. Some view these problems differently. For example, in writing about democracy and political development in India, Walter L. Weisberg asserts that "corruption helps the stability of society by allowing many individuals access to an otherwise impersonal bureaucratic machine. Greasing the wheels of the machine helps it work more quickly and smoothly."[7] Many experts have told us that cultural variations are wonderful and ought to be celebrated. Formalism could also help the poorer states receive low-interest loans and grants from wealthier countries or institutions. Operational autonomy could also be viewed as a form of participation and representation in authoritarian states. To be able to better understand the bureaucracy in so many countries is not a simple task. Generalizations just cannot do the job. A look at a few of those bureaucracies may allow us a better understanding of how the bureaucracy works in a few of those societies.

Bureaucracy in the People's Republic of China

As you already learned, China is a single-party state where the Communist Party is in command. When the communists took over in 1949, there were only 700,000 state employees in administrative and other posts. Within ten years, that number had jumped to more than 7 million.[8] Although administrative growth creates new problems, it also indicates the emphasis of the government on development. After all, it is the bureaucracy that transforms the dreams of political leaders into reality.

Control of policy at all levels in China rests with the Communist Party. The party makes policy and the bureaucracy carries it out. Although formally the State Council and the National People's Congress are the official bodies making policy, the reality is that the Communist Party dominates those and directs them. The way the whole Chinese system is organized revolves around the Chinese Communist Party (CCP). Significant government officials are CCP members. All levels of government have parallel party levels. Party committees watch over government decisions and operations all the way from the smallest community to the national government. The CCP also maintains control over every government organization through its members who are employed by such organizations.[9]

One interesting feature of China's bureaucracy is the periodic rotation that occurs. Top administrative officials are occasionally rotated down to the basic level where they have to handle matters that deal directly with the people. This serves as a reminder of the needs of the people the bureaucrats are supposed to serve. Although this approach is innovative and useful, China's bureaucracy is still plagued with occasional corruption, red tape, nepotism, and a host of other familiar problems of the bureaucracy.

Bureaucracy in Mexico

Mexico is a country that has been in the shadow of its neighbor to the north, the United States. Its economic problems have contributed to the constant migration, legal and illegal, to the United States. Even though Mexico is an oil-producing state, it is a country that has accumulated huge external debts. Its economy has improved with the country's entry into the North American Free Trade Agreement (NAFTA) in 1993.

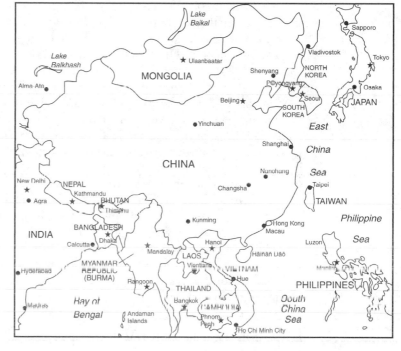

FIGURE 11.1 China

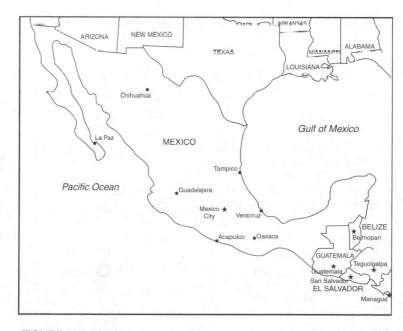

FIGURE 11.2 Mexico

From a colonial economy based largely on mining, especially silver, Mexico now has a diversified economy that includes strong agriculture, industry, and petroleum sectors. The Mexican bureaucracy is divided along federal lines into thirty-one states and a federal district. Historically, a single political party, the Institutional Revolutionary Party (PRI), dominated the bureaucracy, just like the federal government. The election of 2000, however, brought in a new party, the National Action Party (PAN), to power. On July 2, 2000, the PRI lost the presidency to Vicente Fox Queseda of the PAN, ending seventy-one years of PRI rule. The new president promised to improve the economy, reform taxes, overhaul the justice system, and give states more power. With Queseda in power, Mexico now has a government dominated by the PAN and an entrenched bureaucracy from the PRI. Many argue that the failure of the PAN government to improve the lives of its people is due to an entrenched bureaucracy.

Although the new government has promised more honest government, even prior to its assumption of powers, news broke out of less-than-honest dealings by the president-elect. On September 1, 2000, news reports surfaced about a scandal involving the president-elect using child labor to work on his ranch and freezing plant. The newly elected president conceded that he and his family had illegally used children as young as eleven years old and promptly fired those children after the story broke.

Bureaucracy in South Africa

You learned about South Africa earlier. You may remember that South Africa began as a colony. White settlers created the system of apartheid, which enforced racial segregation and kept the white minority in a dominant political and economic position.[10] The struggle led by the African National Congress (ANC) eventually brought about an end to apartheid.[11] Even though apartheid officially ended and black leaders like Nelson Mandela and Thabo Mbeki became presidents, the economic reality remains one of a small white dominant group and a large poverty-stricken black majority.

With so much frustration and a political and economic system dominated by a minority for so long, the new leaders had to find ways to reward their loyal supporters and party members. The easiest way to reward them is to hire them into the bureaucracy. This is called patronage. Common in many parts of the world,

FIGURE 11.3 South Africa

including in the United States, **patronage** is the use of political office to hire supporters. Patronage, however, can be harmful to the work of government. It often contributes to corruption. After all, it is a form of corruption in which the loyal supporters of leaders are hired rather than those best qualified to carry out the tasks of the bureaucracy. Patronage can also create a bloated bureaucracy with many unneeded civil servants on the payroll. Those civil servants on the payroll but without much to do contribute to lowering the morale of those actually needed to get the job done. Another way in which patronage can hurt is by creating a new class of civil servants who fear change. To them, change could mean that they lose their jobs. Therefore, a new class of civil servants would now do its best to block change.[12]

patronage

The use of political office to hire supporters.

Bureaucracy in Egypt

As you have already learned, most states in Africa, Asia, and Latin America have no provisions for unemployment insurance. Their socialist programs do not even include a welfare provision. Egypt is one of those states. Its leaders since the overthrow of the monarchy in 1952 have opted for a mild form of socialism that remains in place despite the many modifications over the years. To make up for the lack of unemployment insurance in their program, leaders have often resorted to using the bureaucracy as the dumping ground for the unemployed. During the days of Nasser, as many as one-third of all high school graduates ended up employed in the bureaucracy.

In 1950 about 2.2 percent of Egypt's population found work in the country's civil service.[13] This figure jumped from 350,000 in 1952 to 1.2 million by the time Nasser died in 1970. By 1986, 4.6 million Egyptians were employed in the bureaucracy, almost 10 percent of the entire population at the time. What impact do you think that large number of civil servants has on productivity or on politics? When the numbers go up, productivity normally goes down. This is due to the lower morale that results when you have a few who really work and many in the same office who do not even have tasks to do. They have their job instead of an unemployment check. The officials in charge

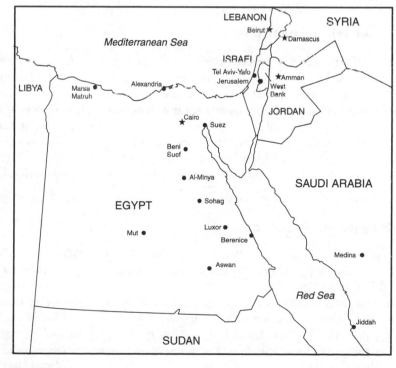

FIGURE 11.4 Egypt

also enhance their own power by granting the favor of a job to those desperate for one. The ones employed become loyal supporters of those who did them the favor.

Summary and Review

The entity that is responsible for administering governmental decisions is known as the bureaucracy. Although it is this governmental arm that transforms hope into reality, its powers extend far beyond administering public policy because the bureaucracy also holds valuable knowledge that other officials need in order to form policies and ultimately modernize the country. Thus, the bureaucracy is inextricably linked to a country's modernization process because it involves not only running an ongoing system, but also developing new modes of operations, refining old norms, and building the new modern state. Without the bureaucratic tasks of implementation and regulation, the country would most likely advance slowly, if it advanced at all.

Key Terms

bureaucracy 235
implementation 235

regulation 235
deregulation 236

structural
  uniformity 236

colonialism 237
cultural variations 237

Discussion Questions

1. What exactly is bureaucracy? Do all governments have some sort of a bureaucratic body?
2. Explain why it is that bureaucrats are often seen as having more power than the more visible public officials.
3. Discuss the tasks of implementation and regulation, both of which fall under the jurisdiction of the bureaucracy.

4. Why is it that governments are involved in the regulation of activities and institutions? Are governments too regulated?
5. Describe deregulation. Will less regulation help or harm citizens in the long run?
6. Discuss how colonialism has affected bureaucratic structures in Africa, Asia, and Latin America.

Suggested Readings

Almond, Gabriel, and James Coleman, eds. *The Politics of the Developing Areas.* Princeton, NJ: Princeton University Press, 1960.

Barlow, Max, ed. *New Challenges in Local and Regional Administration.* Burlington, VT: Ashgate, 2004.

Campos, Jose E., and Hilton L. Root. *The Key to the Asian Miracle.* Washington, D.C.: The Brookings Institute, 1996.

Dibua, Jeremiah I. *Modernization and the Crisis of Development in Africa: The Nigerian Experience.* Burlington, VT: Ashgate Press, 2006.

Dunleavy, Patrick. *Democracy, Bureaucracy and Public Choice.* New York: Harvester/Wheatsheaf, 1991.

Farazmand, Ali, ed. *Handbook of Comparative and Development Public Administration.* Switzerland: Marcel Dekker, 1991.

Heady, Ferrel. *Public Administration: A Comparative Perspective.* 3rd ed. New York: Marcel Dekker, 1984.

Ladeur, Karl-Heinz. *Public Governance in the Age of Globalization.* Burlington, VT: Ashgate, 2004.

Palmer, Monte, Ali Leila, and El Sayeed Yassin. *The Egyptian Bureaucracy.* New York: Syracuse University Press, 1988.

Riggs, Fred. *Administration in Developing Countries.* Boston: Houghton Mifflin, 1964.

Todaro, Michael. *Economic Development in the Third World.* 4th ed. New York: Longman, 1989.

Addresses and Websites

Transnational Crime and Corruption Center
221 Nebraska Hall American University
4400 Massachusetts Ave, NW
Washington, D.C. 20016
Tel: (202) 885-2657
Fax: (202) 885-1389
http://www.american.edu/transcrime/

The Transnational Crime and Corruption Center is a nonprofit organization designed to research organized crime and corruption. The organization offers information to other organizations, scholars, and governments, and it maintains six crime and corruption research centers internationally. The group has put on numerous conferences dealing with a wide variety of issues revolving around corruption and governments, corruption/crime and women, and corruption/crime threats to the global community. This website provides further details regarding this organization and crime and corruption throughout the world.

Global Coalition for Africa
1818 H Street Room H2-200
Washington, D.C. 20433
Tel (202) 458-4338
Fax (202) 522-3259
www.gcacma.org/Privatesector.htm

The private sector has been rightly recognized as the engine of growth. It is through activities of the private sector that new productive capacity and expansion of the existing capacity is usually achieved. The private sector also plays equally indispensable roles in providing services, and by engaging in both domestic and external trade. Providing income-earning employment opportunities to citizens is another well-known service of the private sector. Private sector development is thus a vital

requirement for the realization of country's development aspirations. In its work in this area, the GCA has considered what policies and institutional arrangements will facilitate the development of the private sector.

Nathanson Centre for the Study of Organized Crime and Corruption
Osgoode Hall Law School
York University
4700 Keele Street
Toronto, Ontario, Canada M3J 1P3
Tel: (416) 736-5907
Fax: (416) 650-4321
http://www.yorku.ca/nathanson/default.htm

This centre provides information regarding crime and corruption for Canada's government and the broader global community. It looks into the effects that corruption and crime can have on governments, people, and global interdependence. One of the organization's main efforts is education regarding corruption, crime, and the problems associated with the two. This website offers more information about the centre along with general information about crime and corruption. The website also offers links and publications on related issues.

http://www.cato.org/pubs/journal/cj16n1-6.html

This website is a useful link to an article on bureaucratic corruption in Africa. The article entitled "Bureaucratic Corruption in Africa: The Futility of Cleanups" by John Mukum Mbaku takes the reader into the bureaucracy in African nations and delves into the corruption that so often plagues bureaucracies across the globe. This is an interesting article for those who would like further information on bureaucratic corruption, particularly in the African region.

Notes

1. For an additional reading on the bureaucracy in the United States, see Michael E. Milakovich and George J. Gordon, *Public Administration in America*, 8th ed. (New York: St. Martin's Press, 2003).

2. See Rolf H. W. Theen and Frank L. Wilson, *Comparative Politics: An Introduction to Seven Countries*, 4th ed. (Upper Saddle River, NJ: Prentice Hall, 2001), 341–43.

3. For a good discussion of the bureaucracy in the developing countries, see Fred W. Riggs, "Bureaucrats and Political Development: A Paradoxical View," in Joseph La Palombara, ed., *Bureaucracy and Political Development* (Princeton, NJ: Princeton University Press, 1963).

4. CNN reported the execution after the Supreme People's Court issued the death sentence. The execution was carried out the next day with a single bullet to the back of the head.

5. See Fred Riggs, *Administration in Developing Countries* (Boston: Houghton Mifflin, 1964).

6. Roger Hilsman, *To Move a Nation* (Garden City, NY: Doubleday, 1967), 523.

7. Walter L. Weisberg, "Democracy and Development," in David E. Schmitt, ed., *Dynamics of the Third World: Political and Social Change* (Cambridge, MA: Winthrop Publishers, 1974), 57.

8. Victor C. Falkenheim, "The Politics of Revolution and Mobilization," in David E. Schmitt, ed., *Dynamics of the Third World: Political and Social Change* (Cambridge, MA: Winthrop Publishers, 1974), 288.

9. For a good introduction to China's political system, see William A. Joseph, "China," in Mark Kesselman, et al., *Introduction to Comparative Politics* (Boston: Houghton Mifflin, 2000), 485–544.

10. See Christopher Alden, *Apartheid's Last Stand: The Rise and Fall of the South African Security State* (New York: St. Martin's Press, 1996).

11. For a good study of how apartheid ended, see Patti Waldmeir, *Anatomy of a Miracle: The End of Apartheid and the Birth of the New South Africa* (New York: Norton, 1997).

12. For a good discussion of the impact of patronage in the United States, see Milakovich and Gordon, *Public Administration in America*.

13. Robert Springborg, *Mubarak's Egypt: Fragmentation of the Political Order* (Boulder, CO: Westview Press), 137.

CHAPTER TWELVE

Ethnicity, Ethnic Conflict, and Conflict Resolution

GLOBALIZATION AND ETHNIC CONFLICT

IN 1998, TURKEY CAPTURED ABDULLAH OCALAN, THE LEADER OF THE KURDISH GROUP AT WAR WITH TURKEY. KURDS IN GERMANY, BRITAIN, CANADA, AND ELSEWHERE VIOLENTLY PROTESTED HIS CAPTURE. INCREASED GLOBALIZATION, ESPECIALLY THE GROWTH OF TELECOMMUNICATIONS AND MIGRATION, HAS BROUGHT ETHNIC CONFLICTS IN DISTANT PLACES INTO AMERICAN CITIES. THE GROWING CONNECTEDNESS AND INTERDEPENDENCE THAT CHARACTERIZE GLOBALIZATION ALLOW PROBLEMS IN ONE AREA TO SPILL OVER INTO OTHER AREAS. GLOBAL TELEVISION NETWORKS AND THE INTERNET HAVE MADE IT ALMOST IMPOSSIBLE FOR MOST OF THE WORLD NOT TO KNOW ABOUT ETHNIC PROBLEMS AROUND THE GLOBE. INEXPENSIVE COMMUNICATIONS AND TRAVEL MAKE IT VERY EASY FOR ETHNIC GROUPS TO ORGANIZE ACROSS NATIONAL BOUNDARIES, IMPLEMENT THEIR PLANS, AND MAINTAIN STRONG ETHNIC IDENTITIES.

GLOBALIZATION ALSO WEAKENS ETHNIC IDENTITIES BY EXPOSING PEOPLE TO DIFFERENT IDEAS, BEHAVIOR, AND MATERIAL GOODS. BUT THE SPREAD OF CULTURAL GLOBALIZATION ACTUALLY INFLUENCES SOME GROUPS TO RESIST IT BECAUSE IT THREATENS THEIR IDENTITY AND SOLIDARITY. FURTHERMORE, ECONOMIC GLOBALIZATION SOMETIMES GIVES THOSE ETHNIC GROUPS WITH EDUCATION AND SKILLS AN ADVANTAGE OVER THOSE WHO MAINTAINED THEIR CULTURE. THOSE ETHNIC GROUPS THAT ARE DISADVANTAGED BY CHANGE OFTEN TURN AGAINST THE SUCCESSFUL MINORITY, AS IS THE CASE WITH THE TAMILS IN SRI LANKA. MILITARY GLOBALIZATION HAS CONTRIBUTED TO THE SPREAD OF LETHAL WEAPONS THAT ARE USED IN SOME ETHNIC CONFLICTS. THE GLOBAL DEMAND FOR DRUGS AND DIAMONDS FUEL ETHNIC CONFLICTS IN AFGHANISTAN, ANGOLA, SIERRA LEONE, AND ELSEWHERE BY PROVIDING ETHNIC GROUPS WITH THE RESOURCES TO FINANCE CONFLICTS. BUT THE NUMEROUS INTERNATIONAL ORGANIZATIONS THAT CHARACTERIZE POLITICAL GLOBALIZATION ALSO HELP PEOPLE COPE WITH CONFLICTS AND OFTEN CONTRIBUTE TO RESOLVING THEM.

INTRODUCTION

Ethnic issues and ethnic conflicts in the developing world have received increased attention since the end of the Cold War. Many of these conflicts developed independently of the East-West rivalry but were often held in check by the superpowers. Ongoing ethnic conflicts intensified without the restraint imposed by the United States and the Soviet Union on their allies. American involvement in ethnic conflicts in Somalia, Bosnia, and Kosovo reinforces concerns about the dangers of ethnic conflicts, not just for the societies directly involved, but also for neighboring countries, the United States, and Western Europe. Conflicts are extremely difficult to contain in one country in a world that is characterized by growing levels of interdependence and globalization. The proliferation of humanitarian groups has also helped make the world more aware of ethnic conflicts, especially those that result in widespread bloodshed. Americans are paying greater attention to ethnic conflicts because of major demographic changes in the United States that are altering its ethnic and racial balance.[1] Ethnic diversity within the developing world or in the rich countries does not automatically result in violence or conflict. Brazil, Mexico, Cuba, Trinidad and Tobago, Guyana, and Tanzania have not experienced many ethnic conflicts, despite their diversity.

This chapter discusses the nature of ethnicity and ethnic identity, the causes and costs of ethnic conflicts. In addition to direct casualties of ethnic wars, thousands of civilians are killed each year by landmines that are deliberately deployed to cause maximum physical damage and psychological terror. Many countries that experience severe food shortages and famine, such as the Sudan and Ethiopia, are also ravaged by ethnic wars. Conflict is clearly detrimental to both economic development and the consolidation of democracy. Sometimes the combination of widespread poverty and the economic success of some ethnic groups create the breeding ground for ethnic polarization and violence, as is the case with the Chinese in Indonesia and the Tamils in Sri Lanka. Although reference is made to several ethnic conflicts, this chapter focuses on recent and ongoing problems, including Rwanda, the Sudan, and Liberia in Africa; Sri Lanka, Indonesia, and the Kurds in Asia; and Chiapas in Latin America. This chapter also examines efforts to resolve these conflicts peacefully. As the case studies show, ethnic conflicts are often complex and are not always entirely about ethnicity. Indeed, ethnic identity has often changed quickly to fit changing circumstances.

ETHNICITY AND ETHNIC IDENTITY

tribalism

An outdated term used by Westerners to refer to groups of indigenous peoples in Africa, Asia, and Latin America.

Ethnicity, tribalism, and nationalism are often used interchangeably. **Tribalism** is usually regarded as an outdated term used by some Westerners to refer to small groups of indigenous people in Africa, Asia, and Latin America. Very large groups, some of them with millions of members, are also called tribes, both by some Westerners and by people in the developing world. Most scholars prefer to refer to these groups as ethnic groups. Sometimes ethnic groups are large and their members are spread across the boundaries of many different countries. These groups may aspire to have their own country. To achieve this, they develop a strong sense of **nationalism** and a nationalist movement. The Kurds are an ethnic group, some of whom have nationalistic aspirations. The Kurds live in Turkey, Iraq, Iran, Syria, and parts of the former Soviet Union. But most ethnic groups do not seek to form a separate nation. Some groups, such as the Tamils of Sri Lanka, want more autonomy within the established boundaries of their country.

nationalism

A state of mind in which loyalty is given to the nation to which an individual belongs.

An **ethnic group** is composed of individuals who generally share a sense of common identity based on a common set of historical experiences, national sentiments, religious beliefs, geographic location, a common language and culture, and, in countries such as the United States, arbitrary racial categories. Ethnicity is a subjective perception of who belongs to a particular group. Ethnic group members often have their own social organizations, support a particular political party, live in specific areas of the country, attend the same schools, develop business partnerships, and are associated with the same religious organizations. Ethnicity serves as a rallying point for mobilizing the members of an ethnic group to compete effectively for economic resources, positions in government and other social and economic institutions, government contracts and benefits, constitutional protections, and social and religious status.[2] Ethnic groups in America have a long history of economic, social, and political competition. Americans with African ancestry, for example, have used ethnicity to mobilize support for civil rights, economic opportunities, access to higher education, a share of government contracts, and greater political power.

ethnic group

A group composed of individuals who generally share a sense of common identity based on factors such as a common culture, geographic location, and religious beliefs.

Ethnicity is based on a subjective perception of group membership.

An essential component of ethnicity is a strong sense of identity or solidarity by individuals who perceive themselves as part of an ethnic group. **Identity** may be defined as a conception of the self, or a selection of physical, psychological, emotional, or social attributes of particular individuals.[3] The self is shaped by many different social, cultural, economic, and political factors. People may see their identity as defined by some moral or spiritual commitment, or they may characterize it in terms of nationality, ethnicity, or racial categories. Identity provides a framework within which people can determine their positions on various issues. This means that prejudice or prejudgment is an important part of identity. We make judgments about issues based not so much on objective criteria but on a belief about how we should react or what we should feel in a given situation. Our sense of identity influences our thought and behavior. As the case studies show, members of different ethnic groups are predisposed to think certain things about each other and to act on the basis of these views. Identity is about having a sense of belonging to a social group. To know your ethnic identity is often equated with knowing yourself, and ethnicity is thus believed to be a positive force.

identity

A conception of the self; a selection of physical, psychological, emotional, or social attributes of particular individuals.

Identity is about having a sense of belonging to a group.

Specific ethnic identities often emerge from shared experiences. The African American identity in the United States, for example, has been shaped by the unique experience of slavery, rigid racial segregation, and widespread discrimination. These experiences have contributed to the growth of a social identity that is characterized by feelings of community, similarity, and common purpose. Ethnic groups in the developing world may also share the same historical experiences, engage in struggles with outsiders, belong to the same religious groups, and speak a language that differentiates them from others around them. Individuals tend to believe that they belong to certain groups and that such membership has emotional and value significance. Personal identity, on the other hand, entails a sense of individual autonomy. It gives people a sense of place within a community or the larger society because of their own distinctive or unique characteristics.

Personal identity promotes greater individual autonomy.

ethnic pluralism

The presence of many different groups within a specific geographical boundary.

Ethnic pluralism, or the presence of many different groups within a specific geographical boundary, can be attributed to several factors. Ethnic diversity often results from conquest and annexation, when one distinct group of people is defeated by another and forced to live under the control of the conquerors. Another reason for ethnic pluralism was the decision by European colonial powers to put many different groups together in the same country. Some of these groups had been at war with each other and continued to be hostile toward each other in the countries created by the colonial rulers. Another factor contributing to the emergence of ethnic consciousness or ethnicity is the deliberate attempt by the European colonizers to divide people in order to control them. By emphasizing the differences among groups instead of their similarities, Europeans eventually convinced particular groups that they were indeed different. As the case study of Rwanda shows, this strategy continues to have devastating consequences for Africans today. Ethnic consciousness was created or reinforced by the British, who colonized Nigeria. The British allowed the northern Nigerians to maintain their traditions while encouraging the other Nigerians to adopt Western values, especially religion and education. Finally, population movement or migration, whether forced or voluntary, contributes to ethnic pluralism.[4]

Ethnic consciousness is often created by outsiders.

YOU DECIDE ✓ Is Ethnic Diversity a Threat to America?

The United States is one of the most ethnically diverse countries in the world. Many Americans perceive this diversity as a source of strength. They argue that Americans should not shy away from emphasizing their ethnic differences and that these differences should be respected.

Do you think this emphasis on ethnic diversity threatens American society? What developments in American society, in your view, help diminish the possibility of ethnic conflicts?

THE CAUSES OF ETHNIC CONFLICT

Although conflicts between ethnic groups are often seen as the result of "ancient hatreds," most ethnic conflicts are very complex and have very little to do with ancient animosities. Their causes are equally complex. Few ethnic conflicts are just about ethnicity. In many cases, ethnic divisions are com-plicated by the fact that they are inseparable from other divisions, such as skin color, religious affilia-tion, regional ties, and socioeconomic status.

> *The causes of ethnic conflict are complex.*

These divisions are increasingly difficult to maintain when economic development and globalization help to create a greater degree of interdependence among groups within countries as well as among countries. The causes of ethnic conflict include the following:

1. Geographic proximity
2. Group identity
3. Deliberate manipulation of negative perceptions by leaders
4. Competition for resources
5. Modernization
6. Weak political institutions
7. Transitions to democracy
8. Weapons proliferation

The most obvious cause of ethnic conflict is the geographic proximity of different groups. By bringing many different groups together to form countries, the European colonizers set the stage for ethnic conflict. But Africa's large number of ethnic groups found themselves in conflict with each other even without outside interference.

When a group's identity is based largely on adversarial relationships—on the basis of us versus them—conflict is almost inevitable. The adversarial approach influences mem-bers of different groups to expect only the worst from each other, put the worst interpre-tation on each other's words and behavior, and strongly distrust each other. The creation of an ethnic identity requires that group members be susceptible to viewing people not as individuals, but as stereotypes. The more one group focuses on how different it is from the other, the more likely it is not to see how much the groups have in common. This refusal or inability to

> *Conflicts strengthen boundaries between ethnic groups.*

see obvious similarities helps strengthen ethnic boundaries and the group's view of itself as pure and uncomplicated by outside influences. Ethnic conflict is often caused by delib-erate action by ethnic group leaders to preserve and reinforce group identity. Conflict helps strengthen the boundaries between the group and the outside world.

Another cause of ethnic conflict is the deliberate manipulation of negative per-ceptions by leaders to mobilize group support for their own political, economic, and social objectives. Leaders count on the emotional intensity and loyalty of the members of an ethnic group. They know that distrust can be used to fuel fears. Such fears usually override logical thinking. Consequently, despite misgivings individuals may have about engaging in or condoning violence against another group, their fears,

This young girl in Sierra Leone symbolizes the brutality and random violence generated by ethnic conflict. Innocent civilians suffer the most and continue to be victims long after the ethnic wars end.

Source: Malcolm Linton/Getty Images

sense of loyalty, and emotional commitment to their own group influence them to follow their leaders. The most obvious example of this is the violence in Rwanda that claimed as many as 800,000 lives in 1994. More than three-fourths of Rwanda's Tutsi population was killed because Hutu political leaders made a deliberate choice to incite fear and hatred among the Hutus to keep themselves in power.

Ethnic conflict is often used by leaders to promote their own objectives.

Competition among groups for scarce economic resources is a major cause of violent ethnic conflict. As discussed in Chapter 6, economic development often results in the unequal distribution of resources among individuals, groups, and regions within a country. Growing economic disparities may increase the fears of those ethnic groups that are disadvantaged. In Nigeria, for example, the Ibos fought to create a separate country because they did not

Competition for resources is a major cause of ethnic conflict.

want to share their wealth from the petroleum found in their region of the country. Modernization creates insecurity as well as increased confidence. Even groups that prosper from economic development sometimes feel insecure because the same forces of modernization that made their wealth possible also make them more vulnerable. Any significant change could alter their status. Economic decline in Asia, especially Indonesia, heightened competition among groups.

Modernization is another cause of ethnic conflict. Groups that participate in the development of the country acquire new values, have access to modern ways of life, and often have less tolerance for traditional cultures. Modernization tends to homogenize cultures, at least on the surface. The standardization of architecture, fast food, consumer items, automobiles, clothing, religion, education, and music threatens those groups that stress the uniqueness or purity of their own culture.[5] Modernization helps destroy the boundaries that are essential to ethnic solidarity and a sense of identity. Modernization creates new identities and rearranges the boundaries. These changes are threatening to many groups. Their leaders are usually unsure of their role in the new world created by industrialization and globalization. Ethnic conflict sometimes erupts from this sense of fear and uncertainty.

Modernization is a major cause of ethnic conflict.

Change creates uncertainty, which contributes to conflicts.

Closely related to modernization as a cause of ethnic conflict is the inability of political institutions in many developing countries to effectively manage differences that ultimately result in violence. Political leaders often respond to demands for political participation and economic opportunities by marginalized ethnic groups with excessive force, indifference, or ineffective policies. Afraid that strong ethnic identities could undermine national cohesion and stability, many leaders attempt to eliminate these differences, often with brute force. This approach often leads to ethnic conflict. The Kurds in Iran, Iraq, and Turkey, because of their sense of nationalism, have been suppressed by all three countries.

Weak political institutions often contribute to ethnic violence.

Transitions to democracy also contribute to ethnic conflicts. Change creates anxieties and threatens ethnic identities. Democratic transitions represent a major change in the status quo. Although equality is widely viewed as a positive democratic value, some groups lose their privileges and advantages in a system of government that is based on impartiality and the rule of law. Many ethnic group leaders are often unwilling to respect the emphasis on the individual, as opposed to the group, which is an essential part of a democratic society. Many ethnic groups are reluctant to compromise and respect different viewpoints, beliefs, and cultural practices. Some Muslims in Indonesia, for example, resist the right of Christians to freely practice their religion.

Transitions to democracy contribute to ethnic conflicts.

Democracy challenges ethnicity.

Finally, the proliferation of automatic weapons in developing countries is a significant cause of ethnic conflict. The availability of weapons increases the chances for conflicts among groups to escalate into violence. Conflicts in Sri Lanka, Turkey, Rwanda, and in many other developing countries are fueled by the willingness of countries as well as private groups to supply weapons to combatants. Many of these weapons were obtained from the Soviet Union, the United States, France, Britain, and other Western countries during the Cold War. When the Cold War ended, many ethnic conflicts intensified. Southern and Central Africa, for example, where many Cold War conflicts were waged, continued to be plagued by widespread warfare.

> *The proliferation of weapons is a cause of ethnic conflict.*

THE COSTS OF ETHNIC CONFLICT

Ethnic conflicts are extremely costly to developing countries. More often than not, the countries that can least afford to bear the costs of ethnic violence are those that suffer most. Their poverty and low levels of political development create situations that are conducive to ethnic conflict. The poor not only get poorer, but also are the most vulnerable to physical danger and psychological distress. Ethnic wars throughout the world have cost millions of lives. The exact number of lives lost will never be known because many poor countries have difficulty keeping an accurate count of the population. The conditions of war make it highly unlikely that the government, which is often preoccupied with its own survival, can keep an accurate count of the dead. Furthermore, many governments and their armed opponents use casualty figures for their own political purposes. However, estimates of the number of deaths from ethnic wars portray the devastating nature of these conflicts.[6]

> *Ethnic wars cost millions of lives.*

In addition to the direct casualties of ethnic wars, about 26,000 civilians are killed or wounded by land mines each year. The land mines are deliberately deployed to cause maximum physical damage and psychological terror. More than 100 million mines have been laid in about sixty-two countries, many of them in civilian and commercial areas. Land mines claim a new victim every twenty-two minutes. In Angola, for example, few families have escaped injury or death from land mines planted in agricultural areas, in forests, and around cities. It is increasingly common to see people who are handicapped as a result of accidentally walking on a land mine. Advances in technology have made land mines cheaper to produce but harder to find and remove. The cost of getting rid of a land mine ranges from $300 to $1,000. However, the cost of the mine itself is less than $25.[7] The economic costs associated with land mines are considerable. Not only are valuable resources allocated to planting and removing mines, these weapons cause such physical damage to individuals that many families suffer significant financial losses.

> *More than 26,000 civilians are killed or wounded by land mines each year.*

Economic costs of ethnic conflicts are especially severe for developing societies. These wars often destroy the country's best educated, best trained, and most valuable human resources. Individuals who are essential to the development process usually flee the conflict, leaving the country with decreased prospects of economic development. Instead of using scarce resources for economic development, governments are forced to spend money just to repair destroyed infrastructure projects. Industries are destroyed or cannot operate efficiently, and agricultural activities decline, as working in the fields becomes too dangerous. Foreign investments are lost and trade declines. Overall, the economy is devastated from civil strife and the insecurity that arises from it.

Transitions to democracy and the building of strong political institutions are difficult to accomplish in a violent environment. In fact, many of these ethnic

TABLE 12.1 ETHNIC CONFLICTS IN AFRICA, ASIA, AND LATIN AMERICA

Country	Estimated Deaths (years)	Description of the Conflict
Angola	600,000 (1975–2002)	Civil war between the MPLA government and UNITA rebels escalated after independence from Portugal in 1975.
Burundi	250,000 (1993–1999)	Tutsis and Hutus have been fighting since the Tutsis assassinated the first democratically elected president, a Hutu.
East Timor	307,000 (1975–2006)	Indonesian occupation of the former Portuguese colony resulted in 200,000 deaths in 1975. Indonesian militia groups killed about 7,000 East Timorese after East Timor voted for independence in 1999. Violence erupted in 2006.
Liberia	150,000 (1989–1997)	Rebellion to oust dictator and a subsequent struggle for control of the country.
Mexico	500 (1994–2000)	Indian communities, responding to poor living conditions (Chiapas) and threats to their economic well-being, attack the Mexican government.
Nigeria	1 million (1966–1970)	The Ibo region declared its independence, calling itself Biafra.
Peru	30,000 (1980–2000)	The Shining Path, an Indian rebel movement, subscribing to Chinese communist philosophy, attacked the government as well as Indian communities.
Rwanda	800,000 (1994)	Hutu troops slaughtered Tutsis and moderate Hutus.
Sierra Leone	15,000 (1992–2000)	Rebel and forces loyal to the previous government attempt to overthrow the new government.
Sri Lanka	62,000 (1983–2006)	Tamil rebels are fighting the Sinhalese government for a separate state.
Sudan	1.6 million (1983–2006)	Rebels from the Christian, animist South are fighting the Arab, Muslim government in the North.
Turkey	37,000 (1984–2006)	Kurdish groups are fighting for greater freedom and autonomy.

conflicts occur because of the lack of effective political institutions and democratic processes for resolving disputes peacefully. Democracy implies that citizens are willing to compromise on difficult issues and are willing to respect differences. The belief in fairness, tolerance, and trust enables democratic societies to avoid violence. Human rights, an important aspect of democracy, are clearly disregarded in ethnic conflicts. Most conflicts dehumanize individuals, which makes it easier to justify killing them and depriving them of the most basic human rights. Conflicts force millions of people to become refugees. Many of them remain in refugee camps long after the conflict has ended.

Neighboring countries as well as countries in which members of particular ethnic groups live are often negatively affected by ethnic conflicts in an age of globalization. Many countries throughout Africa have suffered as a result of the conflicts in Liberia, Rwanda, the Congo, Angola, and the Sudan. An entire region is affected as conflicts spill across borders or as ethnic groups, divided by national boundaries, become involved in the fighting to support members of their group. Because of global migration, ethnic conflicts in developing countries sometimes create violence in rich countries. When Abdullah Ocalan, leader of the Kurds, was captured in Kenya by Turkish agents in early 1999, Kurds living in Europe and Canada engaged in violent protests to demonstrate their outrage. Kurds occupied the Greek Embassy in London for three days. Three Kurdish demonstrators were shot and killed trying to occupy the Israeli consulate in Berlin. Violence erupted in Vancouver, Montreal, and Ottawa when Kurdish protestors demonstrated outside offices belonging to countries they believed had participated in the capture of Ocalan.

Neighboring countries often suffer from ethnic conflicts.

Ethnic conflicts often cause famine. Those regions of the world, which suffer most from malnutrition and starvation, are also very violent and politically unstable. Most countries in Africa, where most ethnic conflicts occur, have an abundance of rich agricultural land that has the potential to feed the continent's population. However, the worst famines and cases of malnutrition occur in Africa. A major cause of starvation is fighting between ethnic factions, and their tendency to use food as a weapon against each other and unarmed civilians. Conflict destroys agricultural productivity and other basic industries, such as oil and mineral production. The disruption of trade, as a result of war, makes it difficult for people to obtain food supplies. The Sudan is an example of a country in which ethnic conflict has caused widespread starvation. Roughly 2.6 million Sudanese face starvation. More than 2 million people have died from both fighting and famine. The government has used food as a weapon against its opponents. Most of the land, as much as 90 percent, is left uncultivated due to the ongoing conflict. The government encouraged militiamen on horseback, known as **murahaleen,** to not only kill civilians but also burn their crops and steal their cattle and other animals. Between 2003 and 2007, more than 2 million people fled Darfur to search for food and shelter elsewhere.[8] Many of them died in the process.

Ethnic conflicts are a major cause of famine.

murahaleen
Militiamen on horseback.

Environmental destruction is another major cost of ethnic conflict. Starving populations are unlikely to make environmental protection their priority. Large numbers of refugees take shelter in the forests and use the available resources to survive. Trees as well as animals are destroyed. Forests are cleared to plant crops and animals are killed for food. Ethnic conflicts in Rwanda and the Congo have destroyed much of the region's wildlife and the tourism industry that depended on it. More than 250 eastern lowland gorillas in Kahuzi-Biega National Park have been killed, and as many as 300 forest elephants have been slaughtered. The elephants are killed for meat and the ivory is shipped out of

Ethnic conflicts destroy the environment.

Africa to the Middle East and elsewhere. Gorillas are also slaughtered for meat. It is estimated that most of the 500 lowland gorillas in the Congo, as well as many in neighboring Rwanda, have been killed.[9]

Drug problems are often made worse by ethnic conflicts. Ethnic conflicts are costly, and a way must be found to finance them. In Angola and Sierra Leone, for example, diamonds are exported to obtain revenues to fund ethnic wars. In Peru and Colombia, drug cultivation and trafficking have been integral parts of guerrilla operations. The Shining Path rebels in Peru have relied on the Indian population to cultivate the coca plant, from which they produce cocaine for export. In Somalia's ethnic conflicts, drug use among armed young men esca-

Ethnic conflicts are often linked to drug problems.

lated. Drugs are often used to induce young men and boys to join groups involved in ethnic warfare. In fact, some of the worst atrocities in ethnic conflicts are carried out by boys who use drugs. The war in Afghanistan and ongoing violence among various ethnic groups in that country have directly contributed to the escalating drug problems in Iran, the neighboring countries, Western Europe, and the United States.

Iran, a very conservative Islamic country, accounts for as much as 85 percent of the worldwide seizures of opium. It has become the major area through which much of the world's supplies of opium, heroin, and hashish flow to markets in Iran itself and in the West. More than two decades of war have made Afghanistan a haven for drug smugglers, who are linked to various armed factions. The United Nations estimated that 3,500 tons of opium are produced each year in Afghanistan. Despite the U.S. invasion of Afghanistan, drug production increased in 2007. The Iranian government is ill-equipped to control the flow of drugs, largely because of the 1,200-mile border and the rugged terrain. But the drug smugglers are also well armed. Many of their weapons, including American-made Stinger antiaircraft missiles, were originally obtained by the Mujahedeen from Arab countries and the United States when Afghanistan was fighting the Soviet Union.

Drug smugglers use camels to transport drugs.

Vehicles are packed with opium and heroin and driven across the border areas at night. The drivers travel in darkness, using night-vision goggles to see their way. Drug smugglers also use camels to transport drugs. They separate a female camel from its newborn, leaving the offspring in Iran and taking the mother to Afghanistan. The smugglers use the mother as the lead camel for a camel caravan that is loaded with drugs because the mother will not stop until she reaches her young.[10] The caravan is watched by the drug traffickers from a safe distance. The cost to Iranian society is high: Roughly 1.2 million Iranians are addicts.

ETHNIC CONFLICTS IN AFRICA

No continent is more consumed by ethnic conflicts than Africa. From the South Atlantic to the Red Sea, African countries are at war. The conflict in Africa is so extensive that it has been called Africa's first world war. The Congo crisis, which began when Laurent Kabila's forces launched a successful war that overthrew Mobutu Sese Seko in 1997, has dragged in about eight countries and numerous ethnic groups. Many of the ethnic groups involved in the Congo war are supported by governments. Some governments seem to support one side or the other, based on the view that the enemy of an enemy is a friend. For example, the Ugandan government supports the Sudan People's Liberation Army (SPLA), which has been fighting the Sudanese government since 1983. Uganda supported the ethnic groups that fought against Kabila. In light of these alliances, the Sudanese government helped Kabila. Ethnic rivalries in Rwanda and Burundi spilled over into the Congo. Governments in Rwanda and Burundi are involved in the Congo crisis because the ethnic groups that threaten their stability operate from the Congo and are also participating in the Congo war.[11]

Nigeria

Nigeria is one of the most ethnically complex countries in the world, with more than 300 ethnic groups. With a population of more than 131 million, it is also Africa's most populous country. Once highly dependent on agriculture for its revenues, Nigeria's oil exports now account for 95 percent of its exports. This huge country, more than twice the size of California, is potentially one of Africa's richest states. But ethnic problems, together with years of military rule and "rampant" corruption, have kept the majority of Nigerians impoverished. Nigeria's ethnic problems are closely linked with other divisions in the country. The four main ethnic groups are the Hausa (21 percent), the Yoruba (21 percent), the Ibo (18 percent), and the Fulani (11 percent). These ethnic groups dominate different parts of the country, creating a regional divide as well as an ethnic divide. The Hausa and the Fulani are in the north, the Yoruba are concentrated in the west, and the Ibo live in the east. Each ethnic group has its own dominant language, although English is Nigeria's official language. Further complicating ethnicity in Nigeria is religion. The northern part of the country is dominated by Muslims and the southern and eastern regions are populated mainly by Christians. Economics has been at the heart of the country's ethnic struggles. The country's petroleum wealth is located in the Ibo region, the southeast. Finally, there is also the political and military divide. Northerners, primarily the Hausas, have ruled the country for most of its history. They have controlled the

Hausa, Yoruba, Ibo, and Fulani are the four main ethnic groups in Nigeria.

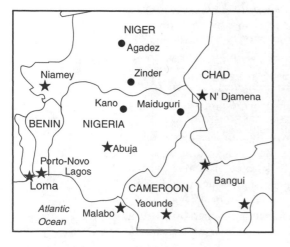

FIGURE 12.1 Nigeria

military regimes. The Yorubas, on the other hand, blame the northerners for the country's political and economic problems and have led the prodemocracy movements against military rule.

Nigeria's most serious ethnic conflict, the Biafran war, was rooted in the ethnic, religious, economic, regional, political, linguistic, and military divisions in the country. The northern part of Nigeria came under Muslim control as Islam expanded from North Africa into sub-Saharan Africa. The southern part of the country converted to Christianity under British colonial rule. The British implemented a policy of **indirect rule** in the north that allowed the Muslims to maintain their institutions, religion, language, culture, and economic and educational systems. The traditional rulers continued to control the areas they did before the arrival of the British. The British had some power over the traditional rulers and could influence them to implement certain policies. However, the northern part of Nigeria essentially remained traditional. The rest of the country came under greater British control or direct rule. The traditional institutions were challenged by Westernization, and many people adopted Western culture. British religious, educational, political, and social institutions competed with traditional ways. The different approaches used by Britain reinforced the regional differences.

Direct rule encouraged Westernization.

The discovery of petroleum in the Ibo region heightened competition among the regions. With their new wealth, the Ibo believed that the independence of their region would protect their interests. In 1966, the Ibo region declared its independence, calling itself **Biafra**. After four years of warfare, during which more than a million people died, Biafra was crushed by Nigeria. Nigeria imposed a food blockade that resulted in hundreds of thousands of deaths. The brutality of the Biafran war and the domination of the country's resources and politics by military regimes from the north continue to influence ethnic relations in Nigeria. In early 2000, ethnic violence erupted when Muslim leaders attempted to impose **shari'a,** or Islamic law, on Christians living in the northern part of the country. Between 2000 and 2007, more than 54,000 people were killed in conflicts between Muslims and Christians.

Liberia

Ethnic conflicts in Liberia are rooted, to some extent, in America's institution of slavery and its preoccupation with racial purity. Many leaders in the United States believed that the growing number of freed slaves threatened the institution of slavery and the practice of racial separation. Others believed that slavery was inhumane and incompatible with America's fundamental values and constitutional democracy. Both groups agreed that sending Americans with African ancestry to Africa was the solution to the problem. With the support of the **American Colonization Society,** the first group of freed American slaves landed in Liberia. They settled an area called Monrovia, named for President James Monroe, in 1822. The American settlers called themselves **Americo-Liberians.** They maintained their American values and discriminated against the Africans who lived in the area they colonized with the assistance of the American Colonization Society. In fact, as late as the 1930s, the

indirect rule
A governmental system, often implemented by colonists, that allows the people to maintain their institutions, language, culture, and economic systems.

Biafra
The Ibo region that declared its independence from Nigeria.

shari'a
Islamic law.

American Colonization Society
An American group that supported Africans' return to Africa.

Americo-Liberians
The name free slaves gave themselves once they landed in Liberia.

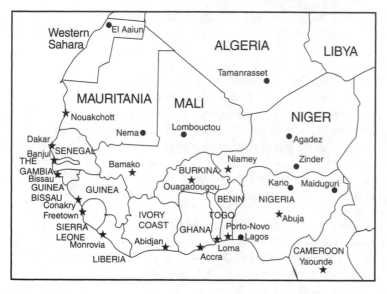

FIGURE 12.2 Sierra Leone and Liberia

Americo-Liberians enslaved some of the Africans from the interior of the country. Despite intermarriage between the Americo-Liberians and the Africans, the former remained a separate group. They spoke English, wore Western clothes, practiced Christianity, and adopted a lifestyle that was essentially American. They ruled the country until 1980.

Comprising about 5 percent of Liberia's population, the Americo-Liberians dominated the other groups. The major ethnic groups are the Kpelle (20 percent), the Bassa (14 percent), the Gio (9 percent), the Mano (7 percent), and the Krahn (5 percent). In the late 1970s, Liberia's economic problems heightened tensions between the privileged Americo-Liberians and the other ethnic groups. In 1980, **William Tolbert,** the Americo-Liberian president, was overthrown and murdered by a group of soldiers led by Samuel K. Doe, from the Krahn group. Once in power, Doe allowed the Krahn to dominate the country, just as the Americo-Liberians had done before he overthrew them. The Krahn were soon challenged by an alliance composed of the Gio and Mano groups. In late 1990, Doe was captured and tortured to death by Prince Johnson and members of the Gio group.[12] The war continued after Doe's death, as different factions struggled for power. Liberia, one of Africa's most prosperous countries and a close ally of the United States, descended into chaos and brutality. More than 150,000 people (out of a population of 3 million) were killed, 800,000 became refugees in neighboring countries and in Liberia itself, and starvation was widespread. Former Liberian President Charles Taylor, who was responsible for much of the brutality, was imprisoned in Sierra Leone in 2006, after attempting to flee Nigeria, where he was living. Taylor faced an international trial for war crimes.

William Tolbert

The Americo-Liberian president who was overthrown by Samuel K. Doe.

animism

The religious practice of worshiping animals, rocks, plants, and other similar objects.

trans-Sahara slave trade

A trade in which Arab countries enslaved Africans from south of the Sahara.

The Sudan

When Britain ruled the Sudan, it allowed the northern part of the country to maintain its Islamic religion and customs. The southern part of the Sudan was treated differently. Christian missionaries were allowed to convert the region's inhabitants. Many southern Sudanese continue to practice their traditional religion, or **animism.** Differences between the north and south are rooted in history. Just as there was a trans-Atlantic slave trade, there was a **trans-Sahara slave trade.** The Arab countries of the Middle East and North Africa enslaved as many as 10 million Africans from south of the Sahara. Although the Africans were ultimately integrated into the Arab societies, and are indistinguishable today as a separate group, Arabs and Africans remain distrustful of each other. Religious cleavages in the Sudan are reinforced by ethnic divisions. Many northern Sudanese, who are mainly Arab, are unwilling to treat southern Sudanese as equal citizens because of the legacy of slavery. In fact, some people in the northern part of the Sudan still refer to a person from the south as **abed,** or slave. This ethnic and religious conflict is complicated by the claims of both sides to territory that may contain huge oil reserves.

abed

A term meaning slave.

When Britain granted Sudan its independence in 1956, the stage was already set for ethnic conflict. The north and the south fought each other with varying levels of intensity from 1956 to 1972, when an uneasy truce was reached. In 1983, the Muslim government in the capital, Khartoum, declared that the entire country would be ruled by shari'a, or Islamic law. The Christians and animists in the southern part of the Sudan strongly resisted Islamic rule. They formed the **Sudan People's Liberation Army (SPLA)** to achieve a secular democratic Sudan. If that could not be done, their more radical goal was to make the south an independent country. The war has raged on. Many northern fighters use their religion to justify their own deaths. They believe that the highest aspiration of a Muslim is to die a martyr, or a **shaheed.** The government has prevented food supplies from reaching the starving people in the south and has bombed international relief centers. More than 2.6 million people have faced starvation, and more than 2 million people have died from famine and war. Both sides have committed gross violations of human rights. The north continues to enslave people from the south. The stakes in the conflict have increased with the export of petroleum. Both the north and south claim the oil fields.[13] Although the conflict continued in the Darfur region of Sudan, in January 2005 the Sudanese government and southern rebel leaders signed a peace agreement to end the civil war. The conflict in Darfur, seen as genocide, left 180,000 dead and created 2 million refugees by 2007. Despite the signing of a peace agreement between Sudan's government and the main rebel groups in 2007, fighting continued.

SPLA

Sudan People's Liberation Army; formed to achieve a secular democratic Sudan.

shaheed

An Arabic term for martyr.

Rwanda

When the Europeans made contact with the people who lived in what is now Rwanda, the area was ruled by a small group of cattle herders, who were predominantly **Tutsi.** The largest group was composed mainly of **Hutus.** There were many other smaller groups. They spoke the same language, shared the same culture, and practiced the same religion. Years of intermarriage made it difficult to neatly separate them into distinct ethnic groups. All groups supplied soldiers for their common ruler.[14] When the Germans colonized Rwanda (as well as Burundi) in 1899, they used indirect rule, relying primarily on the Tutsis to help them control the territory. The Tutsis made up 14 percent of the population, while Hutus formed the majority, 85 percent. The Germans brought with them **racial theories** that were common in Europe and the United States and believed that the Tutsis were superior to the Hutus. This racial thinking permeated Belgian policy in Rwanda when it took over both Rwanda and Burundi in 1916, following Germany's defeat in World War I.

Tutsis and Hutus

Two main ethnic groups in Rwanda.

racial theories

The theories that people are superior based upon their race or what skin color they have.

FIGURE 12.3 Rwanda and Burundi

Belgian authorities viewed the Tutsis and Hutus as distinct groups. Each group was seen as monolithic or homogeneous. They overlooked obvious similarities and common cultural practices and stressed the superiority of the Tutsis. The Tutsis were taller and were believed to be more regal and closer to Europeans in their physical appearance. But it was difficult to distinguish Hutus from Tutsis. The Belgians solved this problem by issuing mandatory identity cards to all Rwandans. This put each person into a fixed category, similar to the racial categories in the United States. The social mobility that was common among the groups ended. The Tutsis cooperated with the Belgians because of the privileges they received. Eventually, the Tutsis believed that they were indeed superior to the Hutus. To reinforce their belief in their superiority, the Belgians educated them while denying the Hutus equal access to education. The Belgians then blamed the low social standing of the Hutus on Hutu inferiority and passivity. The Belgians had created a superior and an inferior group. The Tutsis were allowed to exploit the Hutus. The Belgians reorganized the Rwandan society and deposed most of the Hutu chiefs. Most Hutus were placed under Tutsi control.[15]

Belgian missionaries, who believed in equality, democracy, and social progress, helped the disadvantaged Hutus obtain an education. Although educated Hutus were qualified to work in the colonial administration, they faced systematic discrimination that kept them out of the government. As their numbers grew, the educated Hutus began to challenge the system that gave the Tutsis significant advantages.

Belgium did not prepare Rwanda for independence.

They began to advocate for ethnic separation. In 1959, the Hutus rebelled and killed more than 20,000 Tutsi. When Rwanda became independent in 1962, a step for which Belgium did not prepare the country, Rwanda's Hutu majority gained control. The Tutsi in neighboring Burundi, also a minority, began to worry about developments in Rwanda. They feared that the Hutu majority would also gain control of Burundi. Their solution was to massacre every Hutu with an education, a government position, or financial resources. More than 250,000 Hutus were slaughtered in three months in 1972.

Ethnic rivalries in Rwanda escalated in 1990, when the power of the Hutus was challenged by the army of the Rwandan Patriotic Front. To restore a measure of peace and stability, moderate Hutus agreed to share power with the Tutsi minority in 1993. Hutu extremists began to kill both Tutsis and moderate Hutus. When a plane carrying Rwanda's President Juvenal Habyarimana, a Hutu, unexpectedly crashed on April 6, 1994, violence erupted with a force that stunned the world. The Hutus believed that the Tutsis were responsible for destroying the plane and its passengers.

The Hutus circulated lists of the names of people who favored a democratic transition and national reconciliation. They also set up roadblocks and demanded identity cards, which had been introduced by the Belgians to oppress the Hutus. Hutu militia leaders systematically searched each house and forced neighbors to turn against each other. Their goal was to eliminate every single Tutsi. Students were killed by their teachers, neighbors killed neighbors, and churches where Tutsis sought sanctuary became the scenes of some of the worst massacres. Several clergymen participated in the bloodshed. In some cases, husbands killed their wives, and then themselves, to save them from a more terrible death.[16] Almost 1 million people were slaughtered in thirteen weeks of fighting in Rwanda.

ETHNIC CONFLICTS IN ASIA

The fact that Asia is more economically developed and also has fewer ethnic groups and more logical national boundaries than Africa seems to limit the number and destructiveness of ethnic conflicts in that region of the world. Nonetheless, many parts of Asia suffer from ethnic violence. The conflicts in Sri Lanka and East Timor are two examples. Countries with large and ethnically and religiously diverse populations, such as India, Indonesia, and China, often experience periodic outbursts of ethnic violence. In the case of the Kurds, ethnic conflict stems in part from the desire of a people who share common political aspirations and culture to form a separate country or to be given a meaningful degree of autonomy. The countries in which they live—Turkey, Iran, Iraq, Syria, and parts of the former Soviet Union—are unwilling to change their boundaries or take any actions that would further promote ethnic separatism.

India

India, the world's largest democracy, is also one of the most complex countries on earth. Despite its diversity, India has managed to avoid prolonged and large-scale ethnic strife. Its strong commitment to democracy and secularism undoubtedly play an important role in reducing extremist tendencies in the society. Group competition can take place at the ballot box instead of through violence. India's political culture and its political system

TABLE 12.2 CASUALTIES FROM ETHNIC VIOLENCE IN PAKISTAN

Year	Number Killed	Number Injured
1989	18	102
1990	32	328
1991	47	263
1992	58	261
1993	39	247
1994	73	326
1995	59	189
1996	86	168
1997	193	219
1998	157	231
1999	86	189
2000	149	—
2001	261	495
2002	121	257
2003	102	103

Source: U.N. Development Program, *Human Development Report 2004* (New York: Oxford University Press, 2004), 75.

allow even the most disadvantaged groups to have equal voting power. This reality induces political leaders to compromise, moderate their positions on issues, and build coalitions in order to gain power. Although other democracies, such as Sri Lanka, experienced prolonged periods of ethnic violence, the Indian case shows that, generally speaking, democratic societies are more capable than nondemocratic societies of effectively managing differences and avoiding open warfare among rival groups.

India's strong commitment to democracy reduces ethnic strife.

India's worst ethnic violence occurred as British rule ended. Although India, under the leadership of **Jawahar Lal Nehru** and the Congress Party, strongly embraced secularism, many Muslims felt threatened by the Hindu majority. Led by **Ali Jinnah,** head of the Muslim League, the Muslims decided to form their own separate state in Pakistan. The creation of two countries out of what was British India was rooted in deep religious differences that erupted in horrific violence. When the Muslims living in India tried to get to Pakistan, where Muslims were the dominant majority, they encountered Hindus who had been living in Pakistan and were trying to get to India, where the Hindus were the dominant majority. Their encounter resulted in a slaughter that left more than 1 million people dead. More than 12 million became refugees. This horrifying violence shaped relations between India and Pakistan. Unlike 1947, when each side used crude weapons to butcher each other, both countries now have nuclear weapons.

Religious differences fuel the India-Pakistan conflict.

Conflicts among the various religious, ethnic, and social groups continue, but have not escalated into widespread fighting. The Sikhs and Jains have clashed with the government over religious issues. In fact, India's Prime Minister Indira Gandhi was assassinated in 1984 by her Sikh bodyguards in retaliation for the government's repression of the Sikhs in Punjab, for placing the Punjab under martial law, and for desecrating the **Sikhs' Golden Temple** in Amritsar. The Golden Temple, regarded as most sacred to Sikhs, became the center of controversy when Sikh rebels used it as a refuge from Indian security forces. Tamil separatists have also challenged the Indian government. In 1991, they assassinated Rajiv Gandhi, who became prime minister after his mother, Indira Gandhi, was killed. The rise of Hindu fundamentalism and nationalism has led to greater intolerance of other religious groups. Christians were the victims of many attacks by Hindu extremists, especially in 1998 and 1999. Nuns were raped, missionaries killed, and religious institutions were destroyed. Violence between Muslims and Hindus erupted again in March 2002, leaving more than 519 Muslims and 58 Hindus dead.

Jawahar Lal Nehru

Leader of the Congress Party in India.

Ali Jinnah

Leader of the Muslim League that founded Pakistan.

Sikhs' Golden Temple

The place most sacred to the Sikhs.

China

Although Han Chinese comprise about 93 percent of China's population, that country has many different ethnic minorities. These minorities live in regions of China that contain a large proportion of the country's natural resources, such as oil, coal, copper, gold, iron, lumber, and water. China recognizes its ethnic minorities and allocates significant resources to them. However, China has taken extreme measures to ensure that ethnic groups do not threaten the country's unity and stability. For example, China stationed almost 1 million troops in its western province of Xinjiang to suppress **Uighur separatists.** China brought the Uighurs and their territory under its control in 1949 and populated the area with Han Chinese, members of the majority group. Xinjiang, once known as East Turkestan, was regarded as geographically and culturally part of Turkic Central Asia. The Uighurs are Muslims and are perceived by China to be linked to foreign Islamic extremists. China is sensitive to the influence of Islamic fundamentalism not only in the Middle East, but also in parts of the former Soviet Union. Uighur separatists have attacked oil refineries, railroads, and bridges, and have planted bombs on buses, which killed several people. They also killed sixteen Chinese police officers in 1997 and have engaged in numerous hit-and-run raids on Chinese institutions. Apart from the Chinese policy of reserving the best jobs for Han Chinese, China has responded to the separatist movement with excessive force. More than 1,000 Uighurs have been executed and about 10,000 have been arrested.[17] The Uighurs' goal of independence is strongly resisted by China.

Uighur separatists

A minority group in China.

Sri Lanka

Sri Lanka, formerly known as Ceylon, gained its independence from Britain in 1948. Like other countries in southern Asia, Sri Lanka is ethnically complex. The most significant ethnic division is between the **Sinhalese,** who make up 74 percent of the population, and the **Tamils,** who comprise about 22 percent. The Tamils are equally divided between Ceylon Tamils, whose ancestors lived in Sri Lanka for many generations, and the Indian Tamils, whose ancestors arrived in Sri Lanka as agricultural workers in the late nineteenth century. Both the Sinhalese and the Tamils originally came from India, but the Tamils arrived more recently to the island and many still have connections with the Tamils of south India. The rest of the population is composed of Moors, Europeans, and the native people of Sri Lanka, known as **Veddah.** Similar to Nigeria, Sri Lanka is divided along religious, political, linguistic, regional, and economic lines as well. The Sinhalese are Buddhists and the Tamils are Hindu. About 8 percent of the population is Christian and 7 percent is Muslim. The Sinhalese speak Sinhala and the Tamils speak English and Tamil. The Tamils are concentrated in the northern part of the island country and the Sinhalese dominate the south. The Tamils were more exposed to Western influences than the Sinhalese majority. Missionary societies were allowed to function in Sri Lanka. These included the London Missionary Society, the Baptists, Wesleyan Methodists, and the American Missionary Society. All of them used English as the language of instruction. The American Missionary Society was extremely successful in educating a large number of Tamils. Education in English gave the Tamils an advantage in the British colonial government. Many migrated to the south, dominated by the Sinhalese, and successfully competed for jobs.[18]

Sinhalese and Tamils

Two main ethnic groups in Sri Lanka.

Veddah

The native people of Sri Lanka.

Competition between the Sinhalese and Tamils intensified as Sri Lanka moved closer to independence. The Sinhalese used their majority status to determine the design of the national flag (always an emotional issue) and to deprive all Indian Tamils of Sri Lankan citizenship, even though they were born in Sri Lanka or had lived there for many years.

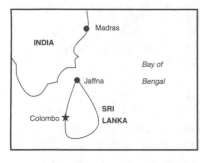

FIGURE 12.4 Sri Lanka

United National Party

United the Sinhalese and Tamils.

Sri Lanka Freedom Party

Stressed Sinhalese separatism.

Shortly after independence, the study of Sinhala was made a compulsory part of secondary education. Sinhalese nationalism grew when W. R. D. Bandaranaike left the **United National Party (UNP),** which united the Sinhalese and Tamils, to form the **Sri Lanka Freedom Party (SLFP),** which stressed Sinhalese separation and making Buddhism the national religion. Sinhalese nationalism was built to a large extent by leaders who mobilized feelings of resentment and fear against the Tamils. Although the Sinhalese were the majority, most of the important jobs were held by Ceylon Tamils. Furthermore, the Sinhalese perceived the Tamils in southern India, in the state of Tamil Nadu, as a threat because of their association with the Tamils of Sri Lanka. By 1958, riots broke out, in which Sinhalese nationalists killed hundreds of Tamils.[19]

The government, controlled by the Sinhalese majority, implemented a system of preferential university admissions for the Sinhalese students. Although only 22 percent of the population, the Tamils comprised 50 percent of the admissions to the engineering and medical schools. Their exposure to missionary education had given them a distinct advantage over the Sinhalese. Government policies led to a sharp reduction in the number of Tamil students in professional schools. By 1980, the number of Tamils with college degrees was one-fourth of the number of Tamils who had earned college degrees a decade earlier. The Sinhalese reinforced their attack on the Tamils by using their majority to implement constitutional reforms, which essentially reduced the status of Tamils to second-class citizenship. The government committed itself to protecting and fostering Buddhism as the dominant religion. Sinhalese Buddhist culture was supported, whereas Tamil culture was systematically undermined. The government banned the importation of literature and films from Tamil Nadu in India. Security forces attacked Tamil civilians who were attending the Fourth International Conference of Tamil Studies in 1974.[20] Violence escalated, leaving many people dead.

In 1978, Tamil separatists began to attack the Sri Lankan government. The government responded, like most governments, with increased violence, arbitrary arrests and detention, and a general disregard for fundamental democratic rights and protections. The underlying causes of the conflict were ignored. These actions helped sharpen distinctions between the Sinhalese and the Tamils and helped intensify adversarial feelings and behavior. In 1983, groups of Sinhalese, like the Hutus of Rwanda, obtained information about the location of Tamil homes, businesses, factories, and educational institutions. Armed with this information, they brutally attacked the Tamils. About 2,000 to 3,000 people were killed, thousands of homes were burned or damaged, and more than 100,000 Tamils were forced to leave their homes in Colombo, the country's capital. Approximately 175,000 refugees left Sri Lanka. The government did little to prevent the violence or to punish those involved. No gesture of empathy for the Tamils was given by government officials.[21] Under these circumstances, ethnic identities hardened, and moderates on both sides were either marginalized or killed. The Tamil rebels were led by Velupillai Prabhakaran.

Moderates on both sides are usually killed or marginalized in ethnic conflicts.

India, which had provided military assistance to the Tamil guerrillas, worried about the increasing number of Tamils who were taking refuge in India. Prime Minister Indira Gandhi decided to help the Tamils but also to seek a settlement with the Sri Lankan government that would protect Tamil interests in Sri Lanka. The **Indo-Sri Lankan Agreement to Establish Peace and Normality in Sri Lanka** was signed on July 27, 1987. It called for the introduction of Indian troops into Sri Lanka to enforce a negotiated end to the violence. The Indian Peace-Keeping Force would be stationed in the Tamil areas to establish order. Sri Lanka would be officially a multiethnic and multilingual country, meaning that the government would not promote one group or its culture over the others. Tamil, English, and Sinhalese would be the official languages. Finally, it called on the Tamil fighters to accept the cease-fire and to disarm. The Indian Peace-Keeping Force soon found itself at war with the Tamil guerrillas in northern Sri Lanka. Growing Indian casualties eventually forced India to withdraw from Sri Lanka in 1990.[22]

As the fighting escalated and the costs to the government climbed, Sri Lanka searched for a peaceful end to the ethnic strife. **Chandrika Bandaranaike Kumaratunga,** whose father had fanned the flames of ethnic violence shortly after the country gained its independence, promised to end the violence if elected as the country's president. She became Sri Lanka's president in 1994, a position held by her father and by her mother after her father was assassinated. Both her father and her husband had been killed as a

> *Tamil fighters made four demands.*

result of the ethnic conflict. She initiated talks with the Tamil Tigers, which resulted in a truce. The Tamil fighters made four demands that needed to be met for the truce to continue:

1. An immediate end to the embargo on food, gas, and other supplies to the areas under Tamil control.
2. Access to northern coastal waters for the Tamil fishing industry.
3. The removal of a government military camp from a strategic area in the Tamil territory.
4. Permission for the Tamil Tigers to carry their guns when in government-controlled territory.

The government rejected the last two demands. Fighting erupted after the government was unable or unwilling to allow food and other supplies to get to the Tamils. Although the embargo had been lifted, military distrust and hostility prevented making ending the embargo a reality.[23]

President Kumaratunga, realizing that the government could not defeat the Tamil guerrillas, unilaterally offered a peace agreement to the Tamils. She offered them regional autonomy in a federal system of government. The change from a **unitary system** of government, in which power is centralized, to a **federal system** of government, in which power is shared among different levels of government, required a constitutional amendment. The United National Party (UNP), which had been committed to reconciliation between the Sinhalese and the Tamils when Sri Lanka became independent,

Indo-Sri Lankan Agreement
An effort to end the conflict.

Chandrika Bandaranaike Kumaratunga
Sri Lanka's president.

unitary system
A system of government in which power is centralized.

federal system

A system of government in which power is shared among different levels of government.

opposed changing the constitution to create a federal system of government. President Kumaratunga's People's Alliance coalition had a slim majority in the Parliament and was unable to change the constitution without support from the UNP. Proposed constitutional changes in Sri Lanka require a two-thirds majority of the legislature to be passed. These changes must be ratified by a simple majority of the Sri Lankan electorate. Many Sinhalese believed that federalism would eventually lead to creating a separate country for Tamils on the island nation.[24] In February 2002 the government signed a cease-fire agreement with the Tamil rebel leader, Velupillai Prabhakaran. Although the Tamil Tigers withdrew from talks with the government in April 2003, the cease-fire remained in effect until 2006, when fighting escalated. The European Union responded by listing the Tamil Tigers as a terrorist organization. Conflict intensified in 2007.

Indonesia and East Timor

Between 1997 and 1999, ethnic violence spread across Indonesia, but it was concentrated in Jakarta, the Indonesia capital, and in East Timor. Indonesia is composed of more than 13,000 islands that stretch over a distance of about 3,000 miles. Although far from Saudi Arabia, where Islam originated, Indonesia is the world's largest Muslim country. Roughly 90 percent of the population is Muslim, 9 percent Christian, and Hindus and Buddhists account for the remaining 1 percent. Ethnic Chinese, who are a significant minority group in much of Southeast Asia, are the main targets of ethnic conflicts in Indonesia. Ethnic Chinese make up about 5 percent of Indonesia's population. However, they dominate the country's economy. Ethnic Chinese account for two-thirds of Indonesia's private, urban economy. They dominate the distribution network for food and other essentials. Ethnic Chinese were given preferential treatment by the Dutch who ruled Indonesia from 1610 to 1949. Indonesian leaders, bureaucrats, army officers, and entrepreneurs have collaborated with the powerful Chinese business community to enrich themselves.

Ethnic Chinese are a significant minority in much of Southeast Asia.

mosques

Places where Muslims worship.

As is the case in many other ethnic conflicts, economic success is usually at the foundation of the resentment that often leads to violence. Apart from being richer than the Indonesians around them, ethnic Chinese are mostly Christians. Their wealth has enabled them to build impressive churches not far from old **mosques,** places where Muslims worship. This combination of economic and religious success forms the breeding ground for ethnic polarization and discrimination. Indonesia has legalized discrimination against ethnic Chinese. Chinese-language schools are not permitted, Chinese-language reading materials and movies are banned, and it is illegal to celebrate the Chinese New Year.[25] Although many Indonesians believe that the Chinese are Indonesians who are entitled to equal treatment, a significant number of Indonesians have historically used violence against ethnic Chinese during economic crises.

The economic crisis that occurred between 1997 and 1999 sparked widespread violence against ethnic Chinese. As the economy declined, the cost of rice, cooking oil, kerosene, and other basic commodities increased dramatically. Because of the strong influence of the Chinese in Indonesia's economy, many Indonesians blamed them for the economic crisis. The homes, churches, and shops of ethnic Chinese were looted and burned. More than a thousand people were killed, many of them ethnic Chinese. Similar to ethnic conflicts in Bosnia and elsewhere, ethnic Chinese women were systematically raped. Human rights groups estimated that more than a hundred women were raped in Jakarta alone. Many rapes were not reported. Indonesian men used religious and ethnic differences to justify their violence against the Chinese.[26]

East Timor

The ethnic conflict in East Timor emanated from Portuguese colonization of the island. Unlike the British in Africa, Asia, and the Caribbean, the Portuguese did not prepare their colonies for independence. In fact, Portugal itself was ruled by civilian dictators until 1974, when a group of military officers overthrew the government in a bloodless coup. East Timor, ruled by Portugal from the sixteenth century until 1975, when the Portuguese withdrew, was invaded and annexed by Indonesia in 1975. The East Timorese, who are overwhelmingly Catholic, resisted occupation by Muslim Indonesia. An estimated 200,000 East Timorese, about 25 percent of the population, died as a result of Indonesian military action, starvation, and disease. Indonesia's occupation was never recognized as legal by the United Nations or any country. East Timorese continued to resist Indonesian rule, influenced the United Nations to call for East Timor's independence, and eventually gained the support of many countries and nongovernmental organizations.

Responding to growing international pressure, Indonesian President B. J. Habibie decided to allow the East Timorese to vote on the issue of independence for East Timor. This decision was made at a time when Indonesia was in political and economic turmoil. Militia groups in East Timor that favored maintaining the close ties with Indonesia began to acquire weapons, intimidated those who supported independence, and eventually killed dozens of their opponents. Despite the escalating violence, about 96 percent of the registered voters in East Timor participated in the referendum on independence. Eighty percent of them voted in favor of ending Indonesian rule over East Timor. Immediately after the referendum, violence erupted and East Timor became another killing field. Militia groups took control of

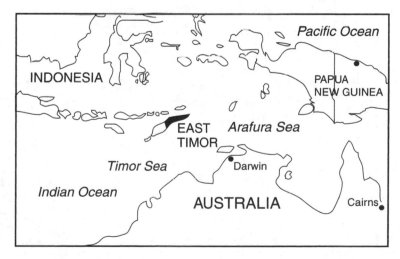

FIGURE 12.5 East Timor

the streets and indiscriminately killed thousands of East Timorese. Priests, nuns, and others associated with the Roman Catholic Church were systematically hunted down and killed. The head of **Caritas,** a Roman Catholic humanitarian agency, and about forty members of that organization were murdered. East Timorese who fled to churches in search of sanctuary were killed. More than 200,000 people, about one-fourth of the population, became refugees. The Indonesian military allowed the militias to slaughter the East Timorese. The international community was eventually "invited" by Indonesia to assist the Indonesians with peacekeeping in East Timor. By the time the Australians led the multinational peacekeeping force into East Timor, the damage had been done. East Timor became an independent country in May 2002. Violence erupted in 2006, forcing residents to seek refuge in churches, embassies, and nearby villages.

Caritas

Roman Catholic humanitarian agency.

The Kurds

The largest ethnic minority group in the Middle East, the Kurds established a separate identity as early as the fifth century B.C.E. As empires rose and fell in the Middle East, the Kurds came under the control of different powers. The rivalry between the Ottomans (Turkey) and the Persians (Iran) led to the division of Kurdistan (the Kurdish homeland) between Turkey and Iran. Like most groups in

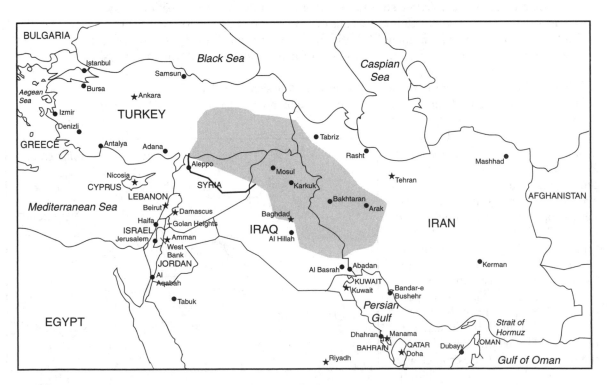

FIGURE 12.6 Kurdish Areas of Turkey, Iraq, Iran, and Syria

history, the Kurds were forced to change or modify their ethnic identity to survive. However, the Kurds have remained relatively cohesive culturally and politically. Although some have demanded a separate state, most of them have attempted to integrate into the various countries in which they live. For the last 500 years or more, the Kurdish population has been spread across Turkey, Iraq, Iran, Syria, and parts of the former Soviet Union. Turkey is home to the largest number of Kurds. It is estimated that as many as 15 million Kurds live in an area that covers 30 percent of Turkey, or 80,000 square miles. Iran has the second largest Kurdish population, followed by Iraq and Syria. The Kurds tend to live in the rural and mountainous regions of these countries. Although the Kurds are Muslims, they are Sunnis. In Iran, where the majority of Muslims are Shi'ite, Sunni Kurds are a religious minority.[27] As non-Arabs, the Kurds are an ethnic minority in predominately Arab Iraq.

The Kurds developed a separate ethnic identity many centuries ago.

Because the Kurds live in different countries, they have adopted different strategies to deal with their problems. A common cultural identity is weakened as more Kurds become part of the societies in which they live. Many Kurds, however, attempt to maintain their own culture. Some have struggled to gain greater political autonomy within the various countries, whereas others are committed to establishing an independent country. Iran, Iraq, and Turkey, for example, have violently suppressed them at one time or another. In some cases, Iran, Iraq, and Turkey have used the Kurds to achieve their own objectives. Iran supported Iraqi Kurds against Saddam Hussein's government, while treating its own Kurds harshly. Iraq also attempted to use Iranian Kurds against Iran. Iraqi Kurds were ruthlessly suppressed by Saddam Hussein. In 1988, during the Iran-Iraq War, Saddam Hussein's government used poisonous gas against the Kurds in **Halabja,** in northern Iraq, killing about 1,000 people. Following the Persian Gulf War in 1991, which forced Iraq out of Kuwait, Saddam Hussein launched a military attack against the Kurds and Shi'ites. As many as 30,000 Kurds and Shi'ites were killed. About half a million Kurds were forced from their homes and villages. Many died of cold and starvation in the hills along the Turkish border before the international community decided to give them humanitarian assistance and prevent further attacks by Iraq.[28] Following America's invasion of Iraq in 2003, the Kurds gained greater autonomy in northern Iraq.

Halabja
A Kurdish village against which Saddam Hussein used poisonous gas.

Turkey does not recognize the Kurds as a national, racial, or ethnic minority. There are no legal barriers against Kurdish participation in Turkish society and politics. Some Kurds have prominent positions in the society. Many members of Parliament and senior officials and professionals are ethnic Kurds. There has been a high rate of intermarriage between the Kurds and others in Turkey, and Kurds who live in the urban and industrial areas of the country have been generally assimilated into the Turkish society. But many Kurds want to maintain a separate identity. Others support the establishment of an independent state. The Kurdish movement for independence is led by the **Kurdish Workers Party,** known by its Turkish initials as the PKK. Turkey's 15 million Kurds are caught between the Turkish

Kurdish Workers Party
Movement for Kurdish independence.

government and the PKK, which has used violent methods to achieve an independent Kurdish state. Turkey responded forcefully to the actions of the PKK. Since 1984, when the guerrilla activities of the PKK intensified and grew more ruthless, Turkey has killed almost 37,000 Kurds. More than 3,000 Kurdish villages have been destroyed, and Turkey relocated at least 560,000 Kurds in order to depopulate rural villages that might harbor PKK supporters. Many Kurds fled the violence and poverty of the rural areas to live in urban areas in Turkey. Others migrated to Germany and other European countries. Turkey's war against Turkish Kurds was expanded to the Kurdish areas of Iraq, where PKK forces often hid. The growing autonomy of Kurdish areas inside Iraq, due to American and European protection of the Kurds, encouraged Turkish Kurds to seek refuge with Iraqi Kurds. Turkey had also imposed severe restrictions against the use of minority languages, including Kurdish, in the schools, the media, and by political parties. However, responding to pressure from the European Union, Turkey pledged to respect minority rights, allow limited Kurdish language broadcasts on state television, and released well-known Kurdish activists in 2004.[29] With the capture of **Abdullah Ocalan,** the leader of the PKK, in 1998, the Kurdish conflict with Turkey has been calmed. However, influenced partly by greater autonomy enjoyed by Kurds in Iraq, the PKK renewed the conflict in Turkey in 2006.

Abdullah Ocalan

Leader of the Kurdish Workers Party.

ETHNIC CONFLICTS IN LATIN AMERICA

Latin America has experienced relatively few ethnic conflicts, despite widespread violence in the region. Historical influences in Latin America have helped shape contemporary relations among ethnic groups. Brazil, Cuba, Mexico, Colombia, and other countries in Latin America were strongly influenced by their colonial rulers. Portugal, which colonized Brazil, and Spain, which ruled most of Latin America, maintained a system of slavery long after the rest of Western Europe had abolished the practice. Neither Spain nor Portugal emphasized racial or ethnic differences to justify human bondage. Jews, Moors, black Africans, and even Spaniards themselves were enslaved both in Spain and the New World. The institution of slavery was supervised by both the Catholic Church and the Crown. The general consensus was that the status of the slave was not permanent, and the distinction between slavery and freedom was perceived to be a result of misfortune. From the Catholic viewpoint, slaves were free and equal in God's sight, and their souls were as important as those of free people. The Catholic Church helped moderate ethnic relations in Brazil and established a foundation of tolerance. High rates of interracial and interethnic marriages have diminished the significance of both race and ethnicity in Latin America, especially when compared with the United States.

The Caribbean nations of Cuba, Trinidad and Tobago, and Guyana, despite their ethnic diversity, have not had serious violent ethnic conflicts. These countries, for various reasons, have not made ethnicity an overriding concern. People recognize their racial and ethnic mixture and stress the importance of their national identities and common cultures.[30] Latin American countries in which Native Americans are a significant proportion of the population, such as Peru, Guatemala, and Ecuador, have had conflicts erupt, but not strictly along ethnic lines. The **Shining Path** in Peru, as discussed in Chapter 9, represents the Indian population to some extent. However, Indians have also been its main targets.

Huge economic disparities between the relatively prosperous northern and central parts of Mexico and the poor southern areas of the country have contributed to ethnic

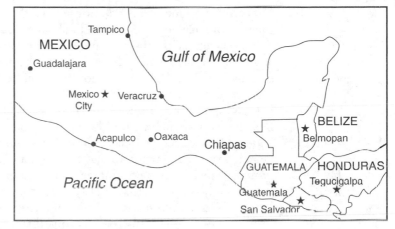

FIGURE 12.7 Chiapas

violence. The southern state of **Chiapas,** where entire Indian communities do not have electricity or running water, has been left in the preindustrial age. Although the northern and central parts of Mexico have benefited from the economic prosperity created by the North American Free Trade Agreement (NAFTA), the southern part of the country has not. In fact, many Indian communities in Chiapas and other parts of southern Mexico believed that NAFTA threatened their survival. The peasants and small farmers of the region felt that their corn and beans would be unable to compete with corn and beans produced on America's technologically advanced and highly productive farms. On January 1, 1994, the date after NAFTA went into effect, the Zapatista National Liberation Front (Zapatistas) launched attacks on the Mexican government in the state of Chiapas. The Zapatistas wanted the Mexican government to withdraw from NAFTA, ensure the fair treatment for Mexico's indigenous groups, and promote economic development of Chiapas. At least 500 people were killed between 1994 and 2000. The Mexican government negotiated with the Zapatistas and signed the **San Andres Accords,** which granted land and legal rights to the indigenous population.[31]

Shining Path

A Peruvian rebel movement that was formed by university professors and students who subscribed to the philosophy of Mao Zedong.

Chiapas

A southern state in Mexico.

San Andres Accords

An agreement that granted land and legal rights to the indigenous population of Mexico.

RESOLVING ETHNIC CONFLICTS

When ethnic groups disagree in democratic societies, they have the opportunity to compete for power and punish governments that mistreat them by participating in the electoral process. They have access to the courts. In the case of Chiapas in Mexico, the PRI government negotiated with the Zapatistas because it realized that rival political parties would take advantage of the government's inability to maintain stability. Democratic societies offer ethnic groups a chance to form coalitions with other groups with similar interests and problems.

As countries develop economically, most groups are able to meet their basic needs and are encouraged to work within the various institutions to achieve their goals. Governments also have more resources to allocate to ethnic groups with grievances.

However, if ethnic groups do not believe that the government is concerned about them, economic disparities brought about by economic growth may fuel ethnic conflict. Some ethnic conflicts can be resolved if the ethnic group is large and lives in separate parts of the country. In cases where the population is dominated by one group, such as in British India, a solution to ethnic conflict is to allow the ethnic group to form its own country. By drawing new boundaries, ethnic groups can become new nations, as was the case with India and Pakistan. India is predominantly Hindu and Pakistan is overwhelmingly Muslim. But many states are unwilling to redraw their national boundaries, especially if they have many different ethnic groups that want to be independent countries. In that case, military force is often used to crush the ethnic group, as the Nigerian government did when the Ibos formed Biafra.

In many cases, international organizations can help resolve ethnic conflicts. The United Nations plays a major role in encouraging groups to negotiate an end to hostilities. Increasingly, the United Nations intervenes militarily to end ethnic violence or to prevent it from escalating. Pressure from the United Nations and the willingness of Australia to lead an international peacekeeping force into East Timor helped end the bloodshed in East Timor and secured that country's independence from Indonesia. However, in 2006 violence again erupted in East Timor. Organizations such as the International Committee of the Red Cross, Amnesty International, and various human rights groups can help end ethnic conflicts by drawing international attention to them and by serving as mediators and neutral third parties. Regional military forces also help. As ethnic conflicts in Liberia and

International organizations play a key role in resolving ethnic conflicts.

ECOWAS is composed of sixteen West African states.

TAKING ACTION

Roger Fisher and Conflict Resolution

Roger Fisher, the Samuel Williston Professor of Law at Harvard University, strongly believes that scholarship must be applied to problems in the real world. Students should go beyond focusing on the causes of problems to find solutions to problems. In other words, students are ultimately practitioners. Raised in Illinois, Roger Fisher served in World War II with the U.S. Army Air Force, worked in Paris with the Marshall Plan, and served in Washington in the Department of Justice. He founded the Harvard Negotiation Project, which brings people from around the world, including individuals who are directly involved in trying to resolve conflicts, to learn how to be effective negotiators. He has advised numerous governments on conflict resolution and is always willing to share his insights with his students and colleagues. He has written many books on negotiations, including the international bestseller *Getting to Yes: Negotiating Agreement Without Giving In.* His wise and practical advice has helped to resolve many conflicts. Most importantly, he has demonstrated to students, by his commitment to applying his ideas to real problems, that they can also make a difference.

NEWS

Blood Diamonds in Sierra Leone

The United States, in January 2000, decided to support efforts to impose an arms embargo against Liberia and a ban on the export of diamonds, known as *blood diamonds*, in the U.N. Security Council. Liberia was widely believed to be instrumental in exporting diamonds from Sierra Leone and elsewhere in West Africa. Revenues from the gems were used to finance the brutal ethnic conflict in Sierra Leone.

Sierra Leone spilled across national boundaries and threatened the political and economic stability of the neighboring countries, the Economic Community of West African States (ECOWAS) decided to intervene militarily. Composed of Nigeria and fifteen other West African countries, ECOWAS is primarily concerned with regional economic integration. However, ECOWAS decided to create a military force, known as **Ecomog,** to restore order in Liberia and Sierra Leone.

A common solution to ethnic conflicts is to create **power-sharing arrangements.** Essentially, these arrangements divide political power among the different ethnic groups. However, unless periodic adjustments are made to reflect the changing demographics of the various groups, these arrangements tend to disintegrate and ethnic conflict erupts. In Lebanon, for example, government positions and political power were divided between the country's Maronite Christians and Sunni Muslims. But the power-sharing arrangement was not changed to reflect the rapid increase in the Muslim population. Failure to do so plunged Lebanon into a civil war that lasted from 1975 to 1990. The solution to this conflict included adjusting the division of power. **Federalism,** or the sharing of power between the central government and the states or provinces, also helps solve ethnic conflicts. Despite the continuing ethnic problems in Nigeria, India, and Mexico, the federal systems allow regions to have autonomy and flexibility to address ethnic conflicts.

Ecomog
The military force created by ECOWAS.

power-sharing arrangements
Arrangements that divide political power among different ethnic groups.

federalism
The sharing of power between the central government and the states or provinces.

Summary and Review

Ethnic issues and ethnic conflicts in the developing world have received increased attention since the end of the Cold War. Increased globalization, especially the growth of telecommunications, has brought ethnic conflicts in areas that were once thought of as being extremely remote into American homes. Despite the proliferation of media attention to ethnic conflict, ethnic diversity within the developing world or in the rich countries does not automatically result in conflict. Hence, even though Canada and the United States are two of the most ethnically diverse countries in the world, they are extremely stable politically and avoid serious racial and ethnic violence, despite past and present problems with race and ethnicity.

Ethnic group members often have their own social organizations, support a particular political party, live in specific areas of the country, attend the same schools, develop business partnerships, and are associated with the same religious organizations. Ethnic identity often functions to draw sharp distinctions among groups to promote group solidarity. Because of those distinctions, the most obvious cause of ethnic conflict is the geographic proximity of different groups. In addition, when a group's identity is based largely on adversarial relationships—on the basis of us versus them—conflict is almost inevitable. Other causes of ethnic conflict include the deliberate manipulation of negative perceptions by leaders, competition for scarce resources, modernization, governmental mismanagement, and proliferation of weapons along ethnic lines. Ethnic conflicts and warfare result in outrageous economic, political, and human costs to any society. Neighboring countries as well as countries in which members of particular ethnic groups live are often negatively affected by ethnic conflicts.

Key Terms

tribalism 248
ethnicity 249
identity 249
nationalism 249
ethnic pluralism 250
ethnic conflict 251
murahaleen 256
Biafran war 259
indirect rule 259
direct rule 259
American Colonization Society 259

Americo-Liberians 259
trans-Sahara slave trade 260
Sudan People's Liberation Army (SPLA) 261
shaheed 261
racial theories 261
Sikhs' Golden Temple 264
Muslim league 264
Congress Party 264
Han 264

Uighur separatists 265
United National Party (UNP) 266
Sri Lanka Freedom Party (SLFP) 266
federal system 267
unitary system 267
Kurds 270
Caritas 270
Kurdish Workers Party 271
Chiapas 273

Shining Path 273
North American Free Trade Agreement (NAFTA) 273
Zapatista National Liberation Front (Zapatistas) 273
San Andres Accords 273
power-sharing arrangements 275

Discussion Questions

1. Distinguish between ethnic conflicts and state conflicts. Why have ethnic conflicts been so prevalent since the end of the Cold War?
2. What are the bases of ethnicity?
3. Outline the causes of ethnic conflict.
4. What are the costs of ethnic conflicts?
5. Name the different ethnic groups in Nigeria. What were the reasons behind the Biafran war?
6. Explain how ethnic conflicts can involve several states.
7. How have European-imposed racial theories exacerbated ethnic conflicts in Africa?
8. What are some examples of ethnic conflict in the developed world?
9. How does the us-versus-them mentality affect ethnic conflict?
10. What can be done to resolve and prevent ethnic conflict?

Suggested Readings

Clement, Jean. *Postconflict Economics in Sub-Saharan Africa.* Washington, D.C.: International Monetary Fund, 2005.

Eller, Jack David. *From Culture to Ethnicity to Conflict: An Anthropological Perspective on International Ethnic Conflict.* Ann Arbor: University of Michigan Press, 1999.

Esman, Milton J. *Ethnic Politics.* Ithaca, NY: Cornell University Press, 1994.

Gberie, Lansana. *A Dirty War in West Africa.* Bloomington: Indiana University Press, 2006.

Jebb, Cindy R. *Bridging the Gap: Ethnicity, Legitimacy, and State Alignment in the International System.* Lanham, MD: Lexington Books, 2004.

Maundi, Mohammed O., et al. *Getting In: Mediator's Entry Into the Settlement of African Conflicts.* Washington, D.C.: U.S. Institute for Peace, 2005.

Payne, Richard J. *The Clash with Distant Cultures: Values, Interests, and Force in American Foreign Policy.* Albany: State University of New York Press, 1995.

Power, Samantha. *A Problem from Hell: America and the Age of Genocide.* New York: Basic Books, 2002.

Rothchild, Donald. *Managing Ethnic Conflict in Africa.* Washington, D.C.: Brookings Institution Press, 1997.

Szayna, Thomas S., ed. *Identifying Potential Ethnic Conflict: Application of a Process Model.* Santa Monica, CA: Rand, 2000.

Varshney, Ashutosh. *Ethnic Conflict and Civic Life.* New Haven, CT: Yale University Press, 2004.

Addresses and Websites

Association for the Study of Ethnicity and Nationalism—ASEN
European Institute
London School of Economics
Houghton Street
London WC2A 2AE
Tel: 144 (0)20 7955 6801
Fax: 144 (0)20 7955 6218
http://www.lse.ac.uk/Depts/European/Asen/

This link is the homepage for the Association for the Study of Ethnicity and Nationalism. The organization aims to collect information and offer conferences, seminars, lectures, and workshops regarding the issues of nationalism and ethnicity. It also has a journal entitled *Nations and Nationalism.* This website provides further information about ASEN and its activities, along with brief information about nationalism.

Conflict Resolution Center International—CRCII
204 37th Street
Suite 203
Pittsburgh, PA 15201–1829
Tel: (412) 687–6210
Fax: (412) 687–6232
http://www.conflictres.org/info.html

The Conflict Resolution Center International is an organization that strives to peacefully mediate conflicts at many levels. Its conflict resolution expertise ranges from issues pertaining to policy problems; environmental issues; or ethnic, racial, sexual, gender, or religious conflicts. Its website offers more information about the organization and the projects in which they are involved. There is also information regarding the center's six steps to conflict resolution and publications of the organization. This is an excellent website for those doing research on conflict resolution at the global levels.

Institute for International Mediation and Conflict Resolution
1424 K Street, N.W.
Suite 650
Washington, D.C. 20005
Tel: (202) 347–2042
Fax: (202) 347–2440
http://www.iimcr.org

The not-for-profit Institute for International Mediation and Conflict Resolution is an institution that offers various programs and services that promote peaceful conflict resolution methods. The aim of the institute is to provide future world leaders with these skills. This website provides information on the institute, its publications, symposia, and programs. There are also links to an online library on conflict resolution and world news published by the IIMCR.

Notes

1. Richard J. Payne, *Getting Beyond Race: The Changing American Culture* (Boulder, CO: Westview Press, 1998), 78.
2. Donald Rothchild, *Managing Ethnic Conflict in Africa* (Washington, D.C.: Brookings Institution Press, 1997), 4.
3. Virginia R. Dominguez, *White by Definition* (New Brunswick, NJ: Rutgers University Press, 1986), 266.
4. Milton J. Esman, *Ethnic Politics* (Ithaca, NY: Cornell University Press, 1994), 3.
5. Robin Wright, "Ethnic Conflict: An Overview," in Charles P. Cozic, ed., *National and Ethnic Conflict* (San Diego, CA: Greenhaven Press, 1994), 158.
6. "A World at War," *Chicago Tribune*, 14 November 1999, sect. 2, 1.
7. Boutros Boutros-Ghali, "The Land Mine Crisis," *Foreign Affairs* 73, no. 5 (September/October 1994): 8–11.
8. Ilene R. Prusher, "Inside an African Famine," *The Christian Science Monitor*, 9 October 1998, 7; and Jean Clement, *Postconflict Economics in Sub-Saharan Africa* (Washington, D.C.: International Monetary Fund, 2005).
9. Ian Fisher, "In Congo War's Wake, a Massacre of the Wildlife," *The New York Times*, 28 July 1999, A10; and Somini Sengupta, "In Sudan, No Clear Difference Between Arab and African," *The New York Times*, 3 October 2004, A3.
10. Colin Barraclough, "Iran Confronts a Long-Hidden Problem: Drugs," *The New York Times*, 29 August 1999, A10.
11. Ian Fisher, "Many Armies Ravage Rich Land in the First World War of Africa," *The New York Times*, 6 February 2000, A1.
12. Eghosa E. Osaghae, *Ethnicity, Class, and the Struggle for State Power in Liberia* (Dakar, Senegal: Codesia, 1996), 82; and Lansana Gberie, *A Dirty War in West Africa* (Bloomington: Indiana University Press, 2006).
13. Ian Fisher, "Oil Flowing in Sudan, Raising the Stakes in Its Civil War," *The New York Times*, 19 October 1999, A3; and Holli Chmela, "Rally Urges U.S. Role in Sudan," *Chicago Tribune*, 1 May 2006, sect. 1, 3.
14. Yahya Sadowski, "Ethnic Conflict," *Foreign Policy* 111 (Summer 1998): 13; and Richard F. Nyrop, *Rwanda: A Country Study* (Washington, D.C.: U.S. Government Printing Office, 1985), 1.
15. Alain Destexhe, *Rwanda and Genocide in the Twentieth Century* (New York: New York University Press, 1995), 40; Michael Ignatieff, *The Warrior's Honor: Ethnic War and the Modern Conscience* (New York: Metropolitan Books, 1997), 62; and Catherine Newbury, "Ethnicity

and the Politics of History in Rwanda," *Africa Today* 45, no. 1 (January–March 1998): 7–25.
16. Destexhe, *Rwanda and Genocide*, 31.
17. "China's Rebellious Province," *The Economist*, 23 August 1997, 29; and "The Hanification of Xingjiang Province," *The Economist*, 28 August 2004, 38.
18. Jack D. Eller, *From Culture to Ethnicity to Conflict* (Ann Arbor: The University of Michigan Press, 1999), 120.
19. Marshall R. Singer, "Sri Lanka's Ethnic Conflict," *Asian Survey* 36, no. 11 (November 1996): 1146; and "Monitor Says Sri Lanka Is at War," *The New York Times*, 14 May 2006, A4.
20. Eller, *From Culture to Ethnicity to Conflict*, 133.
21. Neelam Tiruchelvam, "Sri Lanka's Ethnic Conflict and Preventive Action," in Robert I. Rotberg, ed., *Vigilance and Vengeance* (Washington, D.C.: Brookings Institution Press, 1996), 150.
22. Eller, *From Culture to Ethnicity to Conflict*, 139.
23. Singer, "Sri Lanka's Ethnic Conflict," 1146.
24. Nilan Fernando, "Sri Lanka in 1997: Inching Toward a Durable Peace," *Asian Survey* 38, no. 2 (February 1998): 142–45.
25. Nicholas D. Kristof, "New Freedoms Feed Ethnic Frictions," *The New York Times*, 25 May 1998, A6.
26. Seth Mydans, "In Jakarta, Reports of Numerous Rapes of Chinese in Riots," *The New York Times*, 10 June 1998, A1.
27. Bill Bowring, "The Kurds in Turkey," in Kirsten E. Schulze et al., eds., *Nationalism, Minorities, and Diasporas* (London: I. B. Tauris, 1996), 25; and Eller, *From Culture to Ethnicity to Conflict*, 177.
28. Richard J. Payne, *The Clash with Distant Cultures: Values, Interests, and Force in American Foreign Policy* (Albany: State University of New York Press, 1995), 127; and Ted Robert Gurr, *Minorities at Risk: A Global View of Ethnopolitical Conflicts* (Washington, D.C.: U.S. Institute of Peace Press, 1993), 228.
29. U.S. Department of State, *Country Reports on Human Rights Practices* (Washington, D.C.: U.S. Government Printing Office, 1997), 1349; John Diamond, "U.S. Policy Toward Kurds Depends on Geography," *Chicago Tribune*, 21 November 1999, sect. 1, 6; and Susan Sachs, "Rebel Violence in Turkey Could Erode Kurds' Gains," *The New York Times*, 1 October 2004, A8.
30. Payne, *Getting Beyond Race*, 40–41.
31. Paul de la Garza, "Mexico Trying Again to Resolve Chiapas Muddle," *Chicago Tribune*, 12 September 1999, sect. 1, 6.

CHAPTER THIRTEEN

Migration

GLOBALIZATION AND MIGRATION

ONE OF THE OUTSTANDING FEATURES OF GLOBALIZATION IS THE INCREASED MOVEMENT OF PEOPLE WITHIN AND AMONG COUNTRIES. GLOBALIZATION STIMULATES MIGRATION IN MANY WAYS. BY INTENSIFYING ECONOMIC COMPETITION, GLOBALIZATION IS SEEN AS CREATING A "RACE TO THE BOTTOM," WHICH MEANS THAT COMPANIES LOOK AROUND THE WORLD FOR WAYS TO GAIN AN ADVANTAGE. THE POROUSNESS OF NATIONAL BORDERS, THE AVAILABILITY OF INFORMATION ABOUT ECONOMIC OPPORTUNITIES, EASY ACCESS TO RELATIVELY INEXPENSIVE TRANSPORTATION, AND EXISTING MIGRANT COMMUNITIES IN VARIOUS COUNTRIES MAKE MIGRATION A PART OF THE REALITY OF GLOBALIZATION. IMAGES OF ECONOMIC PROSPERITY AND FREEDOM IN WESTERN SOCIETIES OR IN URBAN AREAS OF DEVELOPING COUNTRIES ARE MADE READILY AVAILABLE THROUGH THE INSTRUMENTS OF CULTURAL GLOBALIZATION, SUCH AS TELEVISION, MOVIES, THE INTERNET, AND TOURISM. THE UNITED STATES, A LEADER OF GLOBALIZATION, IS HOME TO MIGRANTS FROM AROUND THE WORLD AND HAS MANY GLOBAL CITIES, SUCH AS NEW YORK, LOS ANGELES, CHICAGO, HOUSTON, AND MIAMI.

AN EARLIER PERIOD OF GLOBALIZATION IS A SIGNIFICANT CONTRIBUTOR TO MIGRATION. COLONIAL POWERS ENCOURAGED MASS MIGRATION TO RELIEVE POPULATION PRESSURES AND TO SETTLE LATIN AMERICA, NORTH AMERICA, AUSTRALIA, AND ELSEWHERE. THE CURRENT PERIOD OF GLOBALIZATION IS CREATING REVERSE MIGRATION, OR THE MOVEMENT OF PEOPLE FROM FORMER COLONIES TO FORMER COLONIAL POWERS. THE FORMER COLONIAL POWERS ARE VERY WEALTHY, THEIR CITIZENS ARE HAVING SMALLER FAMILIES AND ARE GETTING OLDER, AND THEY FACE A LABOR SHORTAGE. THIS INFLUENCES GREATER MIGRATION FROM OVERPOPULATED AND POORER DEVELOPING COUNTRIES. THE PROLIFERATION OF NONGOVERNMENTAL ORGANIZATIONS—A MANIFESTATION OF GLOBALIZATION—ALSO HELPS FOCUS ATTENTION ON MIGRATION, ESPECIALLY REFUGEE PROBLEMS, THEREBY MAKING MIGRATION AN IMPORTANT GLOBAL ISSUE.

INTRODUCTION

migration

The movement from one place to another.

Migration, the movement from one place to another, is an integral part of human behavior. People have always moved from one area to another for a variety of reasons. Our ancestors moved to find the best agricultural lands, better protection from potential enemies, and water and grass for their animals; to engage in religious conversions; to conquer land for new settlements; and in response to seasonal changes. The rich ethnic, religious, and cultural diversity of most countries, especially Canada and the United States, demonstrates the strong human tendency to leave one place and to go to another. Migration is strongly influenced by social, economic, military, and political developments. This chapter discusses the nature of migration in the twenty-first century and many of the factors that motivate people to leave their homes, such as political oppression, overpopulation, famine, environmental and natural disasters, employment opportunities, and family reunification. The poorest countries have the most problems with migration, primarily because they are, by definition, unable to provide economic opportunities for their citizens and are often politically unstable, abusive of human rights, and victims of natural disasters.

As we saw in Chapter 7, the dominant pattern of migration in the developing world is the movement from the countryside to urban areas. This chapter shows that the demand for labor in rich countries is a major cause of migration. In fact, the prosperity of the United States, for example, is dependent to some extent on the abundant and inexpensive labor provided by migrants. This is particularly true of the agricultural and building sectors of the economy. When the United States expanded westward and acquired territories from Mexico, the relationship between American farmers and agricultural workers from Mexico was established. France, Britain, Germany, and Japan also depend on migrants, to varying degrees. This chapter also examines the gains and losses, the advantages and disadvantages that result when large numbers of people cross national boundaries or move from one part of a country to another. It concludes with a discussion of the impact of migration on rich countries, including the United States, and how these countries are responding.

WHAT IS MIGRATION?

migrant

A person who moves from one country or area to another country or location.

refugee

A migrant who lives outside of his or her country but is unable or unwilling to return because of persecution.

The term *migration* is used in a general sense. It applies to both the movement of people within a country's geographical boundaries as well as movement across national boundaries. A **migrant** is a person who moves from one country or area to another country or location. Migrants may move from one part of a country to another location within that country or they may move to another country. Migrants can be refugees, displaced persons, or immigrants. **Refugees** are essentially migrants who live outside of their country but are unable or unwilling to return because of persecution or a well-founded fear of persecution. The previous chapter gave several examples of conflicts that created refugees. Refugees who attempt to get permanent residence in the country to which they fled, usually because of a well-founded fear of persecution, are referred to as asylum-seekers. The immigration laws of most countries make distinctions among asylum-seekers, refugees, and other types of immigrants.

A **displaced person** is someone who has been forced to leave his or her home because of violence, conflict, persecution, or natural disaster but has not crossed an international border. Displaced persons usually become refugees. Generally speaking, an **immigrant** is someone who goes to a foreign country to become a permanent resident. But many immigrants, both legal and illegal, tend to cross national boundaries frequently and do not view themselves as permanent residents in the foreign country.

Most migration occurs in a relatively limited geographical area, despite the increased **transcontinental migration,** or the movement of persons from one continent to another. People in search of physical security, economic opportunities, and education usually go to neighboring countries. Rwandan refugees go to Tanzania and Mexicans go across the border into the United States. Africa is the continent with the highest number of migrants (33 percent), followed by North America (21 percent), Europe (17 percent), Asia (15 percent), and Latin America (11 percent).

Men are more likely to migrate than women under ordinary circumstances. There are several reasons for this. Who migrates is determined to a large extent by the requirements imposed by countries, companies, or individuals who need labor. Many countries that recruit laborers often specify the need for male workers. Much of the work to be performed is culturally defined as work for men. Large numbers of men from Turkey, North Africa, and the Caribbean migrated to Germany, France, and Britain, respectively, after World War II to help rebuild these European countries that had been devastated by war. Men have also been recruited by companies involved in mining, construction, and industry. Cultural norms and sex roles within the sending countries

Men are more likely than women to migrate.

also help determine if men are more likely to migrate than women. Gender roles in North Africa and the Middle East, for example, restrict women's mobility. Gender roles also influence men to move in search of employment. Men are generally perceived as breadwinners in most countries, whereas women are seen as being responsible for raising the children and taking care of the home.[1] Economic development and greater access to education for women continue to change cultural views of what men and women are allowed to do and provide more employment opportunities for women.

Employment opportunities in neighboring countries often attract workers from other developing countries. Gold mining in South Africa, for example, attracted laborers from Lesotho, Mozambique, and Botswana. There is also **rural-to-rural migration.** Many people leave one rural area to live and work in another rural area. India, with most of its population living in small towns and villages, has a very high rate of rural-to-rural migration. Economic development creates many opportunities in urban areas. Many people move from rural areas to go to cities to search for employment and a better life. This **rural-to-urban migration** is the dominant pattern in the developing world. However, there is also **urban-to-rural migration.** In some countries, such as Brazil, China, Indonesia, and Tanzania, governments encourage (and sometimes force) people to leave the cities to settle new areas. Urban-to-rural migration is usually designed to encourage the economic development of the interior or the countryside and to redistribute people to relieve population pressures

displaced person

Someone who has been forced to leave his or her home because of violence, conflict, persecution, or natural disaster, but has not crossed an international border.

immigrant

Someone who goes to a foreign country to become a permanent resident.

transcontinental migration

The movement of persons from one continent to another.

rural-to-rural migration

The movement of people from one rural area to another.

rural-to-urban migration

The most dominant pattern of migration.

urban-to-rural migration

The movement of people from urban areas to rural areas.

seasonal migration

The movement of people from one area to another because of a seasonal demand for labor.

push factors

The factors that motivate people to leave their homes, such as human rights violations, violence, and political instability.

pull factors

The factors that motivate people to leave their homes, such as employment opportunities, higher wages, and educational opportunities.

on the major urban centers. Another type of migration is **seasonal migration.** People often move from one area to another because of seasonal demand for labor. Agricultural industries often demand more labor at certain times of the year than at others. Harvesting fruit, sugar cane, coffee, bananas, and other crops requires intensive labor for a short time. Seasonal migration is also driven by industries such as tourism. Tourism usually requires the employment of a large number of temporary workers during particular times of the year.[2] Workers in seasonal industries come from both rural and urban areas. Finally, migration may be voluntary or involuntary. Refugees, displaced persons, and enslaved persons are involuntary migrants. Most Americans with African ancestry were involuntary migrants. Voluntary migration, which involves mainly young men and women, occurs when people move to find better jobs, health care, educational opportunities, and an improved quality of life.

Migration may be voluntary or involuntary.

CAUSES OF MIGRATION

Migration is influenced by **push factors** as well as by **pull factors.**[3] Push factors are generally negative developments and circumstances that motivate people to leave their homes. These include human rights violations, political oppression, forced resettlement programs, violence and political instability, overpopulation, unemployment, poverty, natural and environmental disasters, and the lack of educational and cultural opportunities. An important push factor is the process of competitive exclusion. For example, many Mexicans migrate to the United States because they cannot compete with highly subsidized U.S. grain exports to Mexico under the North American Free Trade Agreement (NAFTA). Pull factors, which also attract people away from their homes, include employment opportunities, higher wages, political and social stability, a healthy environment, educational and cultural opportunities, and family reunification. These push and pull factors are affected by geographic proximity and individual initiative. They are also affected by new technologies; transportation; and social, political, and economic beliefs.

PUSH FACTORS

An important reason for migration is to escape human rights abuses. Religious and political oppression have pushed people from their

TABLE 13.1 TOP TEN COUNTRIES WITH MIGRANTS

Country	Migrants as Percentage of Total Population
United Arab Emirates	68%
Kuwait	49
Jordan	39
Israel	37
Singapore	34
Oman	26
Switzerland	25
Austria	25
Saudi Arabia	24
New Zealand	22

Source: United Nations Development Program, *Human Development Report 2004* (New York: Oxford University Press, 2004), 87.

home countries. The United States was settled by people who sought religious and political freedom. During the Cold War, many Europeans came to the United States to escape oppressive governments. The large influx of Cuban immigrants to Florida and other parts of America resulted from Cuba's system of communism under the leadership of Fidel Castro. Dictatorships in Africa, Asia, and Latin America pushed people away from those societies to democratic societies in North America, Western Europe, and parts of the developing world. Ethnic violence and civil wars, as we will discuss later, continue to create some of the most horrible violations of human rights and contribute to mass migration and refugee problems. Transitions to democracy, although reducing the flow of people seeking protection from human rights abuses, have contributed to an increase in migration for economic and social reasons. The fall of dictatorships and authoritarian governments removed many political obstacles to emigration. A common characteristic of authoritarian regimes is their tendency to control the movement of people, both within the country and internationally. The Castro regime in Cuba continues to regulate Cubans wanting to leave the country. Even though a transition to democracy in Cuba would influence some Cuban Americans to return to Cuba, it would also enable many Cubans to leave the island in search of better economic and social opportunities in the United States.

A major reason for migration is to escape human rights abuses.

Transitions to democracy contribute to migration.

   Overpopulation has been a major cause of migration. People move from overcrowded areas when economic opportunities decline to places that offer better opportunities. As population growth puts pressure on the land available for agriculture, people leave the countryside and move to urban areas in search of employment. Revolutions in communication and transportation have made it easier for people to migrate across national boundaries when their societies become too overcrowded. This trend is strengthened by the fact that even though the population of developing countries is increasing, rich countries in North America, Europe, and Asia are experiencing the aging and decline of their populations. In other words, overpopulation in poor countries is occurring at a time when rich countries are faced

Demographic factors influence migration.

overpopulation
Extreme population growth that threatens resources and causes overcrowding.

![N IN THE NEWS]

Economic Problems in Argentina

Argentina, Latin America's wealthiest country and one that is overwhelmingly populated by the descendants of European immigrants, was the world's seventh-richest nation at the beginning of the twentieth century. By 1998, the economy was so weak that tens of thousands of Argentines decided to seek the citizenship of their parents and grandparents in such nations as Spain, Italy, and Germany. By 2002, Argentina faced political instability, food riots, and serious economic problems. In 2004–2005, Argentina experienced rapid economic growth, enabling it to repay its $9.57 billion debt to the International Monetary Fund in January 2006 and to slow down migration.

underpopulation

Occurs when there is a strong decline in the population growth rate.

with **underpopulation.** Prosperity in rich countries influences women to stay in school longer, put more emphasis on work, marry later, and have fewer children, if any. As fertility drops, life expectancy increases. The net result is that industrialized societies are having fewer young people to support the larger numbers of elderly citizens. Italy, Germany, Greece, and Spain have more people over the age of 60 than there are people under the age of 20.[4]

Natural disasters, environmental problems, famines, and competitive exclusion push people away from their homelands or force them to relocate within their countries. Many of the world's displaced people are casualties of earthquakes, hurricanes, floods, volcanic eruption, environmental degradation, deforestation, soil erosion, and famine. Many of these disasters are caused by or made worse because of human activities, overpopulation, and a disregard for sustainable development. As we have seen, many of the world's worst famines are the result of deliberate policies of governments and warring ethnic groups. The famine in the Sudan, for example, was caused not just by poor agricultural production, but also by the government's policy of preventing food from getting to people in areas controlled by its military and political rivals. Famine in

Natural disasters, environmental problems, famines, and competitive competition are push factors.

places like North Korea is due to totalitarianism. Between 1995 and 1998, more than 3 million North Koreans died of starvation. Half a million people fled to China to escape the famine. Volcanic eruptions on the Caribbean island of Montserrat in the late 1990s caused the evacuation of most of the population and their migration to neighboring islands and Britain. The destruction left behind by Hurricane Mitch in Central America in late 1998 led to a huge increase in the number of people from Honduras, Nicaragua, El Salvador, and Guatemala who migrated to the United States. **Competitive exclusion** is a major cause of both rural-to-urban migration as well as international migration. This occurs when more land is taken by large agro-export companies, which increases land prices and decreases the land available to small subsistence farmers who are forced to migrate. As Chapter 7 showed, this process of competitive exclusion was a consequence of the Green Revolution. It is quite common in Latin America and Asia.

competitive exclusion

A major cause of migration; occurs when land is taken by large agro-export companies.

Several governments have both forced and encouraged people to migrate. China, for example, has sent millions of Han Chinese to settle areas in which ethnic groups challenge China's authority. This practice of subduing troubled regions through migration has been used by China's communist government and its imperial predecessors. When Chinese troops occupied Tibet in 1950, they began to change that

Cultural Revolution

A systematic effort to destroy everything that challenged communism in China.

Migration is often used to subdue troubled regions.

country's Buddhist culture. During China's **Cultural Revolution** (from 1966 to 1976), a systematic effort to destroy everything that challenged communist ideology, Mao Zedong's Red Guard stormtroopers detained Tibetan monks, destroyed temples, desecrated Buddhist sacred objects and scriptures, and punished those who practiced religion. China has an estimated 100 million people who are unemployed, and the government has encouraged many of them to move to Tibet. The migration of Chinese settlers has transformed virtually all aspects of Tibetan society, from music to architecture.

The low, humming chants of Tibetan monks now compete with loud Chinese disco music.[5]

Forced migration is also used to evict those who are hostile to the government or who disagree with fundamental or revolutionary social and political changes adopted by a new government. Large-scale emigration of certain segments or classes is viewed as an essential step to facilitate the economic, social, and political transformation of society. Forced migration is also used to achieve certain foreign policy objectives. Fidel Castro's leadership of Cuba influenced almost a million people to leave the country, especially those from the upper class. Castro's goal in evicting them or strongly encouraging them to leave was to more easily build a communist society. Castro has also used emigration as an instrument of his foreign policy toward the United States. Allowing a large number of Cubans to migrate to the United States is one way in which Castro can pressure the United States to take (or not to take) certain actions. Many other governments have forced people to leave for different reasons.[6]

China routinely uses forced migration to achieve economic and national security objectives. The Chinese government has forcibly removed people from urban to rural areas, from developed coastal areas to underdeveloped regions of the country's interior, and from its huge urban centers to remote border regions. However, as the coastal regions of China have achieved significant economic development, the government has tried to prevent people from moving to the coasts and abandoning the countryside. Various programs have been implemented to encourage economic development in other parts of the country. China's historical concerns about security have influenced it to settle people in border areas where Han Chinese are the minority or to areas that are sparsely populated and vulnerable to foreign invasion. However, the most ambitious forced removal program started in 1957 and intensified during the Cultural Revolution. An estimated 17 million young people from urban centers were sent to rural areas and border regions to reduce population pressures in the cities. The government also attempted to spread China's communist ideology and develop the remote areas of the country. These efforts were finally abandoned by the late 1970s.[7]

FIGURE 13.1 China and Tibet

forced migration
The act of evicting those who are hostile to the government.

China uses forced migration to achieve economic and national security objectives.

Violence and economic problems often combine to force people out of their country. Much of the violence results from conflicts between governments and rebel movements that challenge the governments' authority. As violence intensifies, governments are increasingly unable to protect the citizens. Colombia is an example of a country in which widespread domestic violence has created a serious refugee problem. Four decades of conflict between the government and various guerrilla groups and the proliferation of guns and drugs have made Colombia the most violent country in the world. Its murder rate is ten times that of the United States. It also has the highest number of kidnappings in the world. As the government escalated its war on cocaine producers, with American support, violence in civilian areas also increased, especially in Cali, home of many drug cartels. Between 1996 and 2000, more than 800,000 people, or 2 percent of Colombia's total population of 40 million, fled the country.[8] As is generally the case in countries plagued by violence, many of those leaving Colombia are young and highly educated.

Violence and economic problems force people to migrate.

Numerous ethnic conflicts and civil wars in Africa have left that continent with more than 4 million refugees. War in the Congo and surrounding countries has created many displaced persons. The conflict in East Timor resulted in more than 200,000 refugees, many of whom have since returned home. Violence against the Kurds has not only led to the growth of Kurdish refugees in the Middle East, but also influenced many Kurds to seek refuge in Europe and North America. There are more than 500,000 Kurds in Western Europe. Germany and France are home to most of them (Germany has about 400,000 and France has 60,000). The Vietnam War and economic problems produced a mass exodus of Vietnamese. More than 132,000 people left Vietnam shortly after the communists defeated the South Vietnamese army, which was supported by the United States. Most of the Vietnamese refugees came to America. As economic conditions worsened and as the communist government consolidated its power in the country, many Vietnamese sought refuge in neighboring countries. More than 200,000 ethnic Chinese from Vietnam fled to China when conflict between China and Vietnam erupted in 1978 and 1979. Most of the Chinese in Vietnam lived in South Vietnam. Another 70,000 Vietnamese arrived in Hong Kong in small boats or were rescued from small boats by ocean-going ships on their way to Hong Kong.[9] By 2007, there were more than 1 million Iraqi refugees living in Syria, Jordan, and elsewhere. There were roughly 1 million internally displaced Iraqis as a result of America's invasion and occupation of the country.

The Vietnam War caused a mass exodus of Vietnamese.

Women and children make up the majority of the world's refugees. They are the most vulnerable to violence. Although women leave for the same reasons as men, women are often victims of human rights abuses and violence directed primarily at women. In most wars and ethnic conflicts around the world, women are victims of rape. In some cases, such as in Bosnia and Kosovo, rape was used to intimidate people and force them to leave their homes. Women also flee because of their fear of persecution in countries that practice honor killings or abuse women who violate traditions and religious beliefs. An increasing number of women from Africa and the Middle East have fled their societies to avoid practices such as female genital mutilation. However, women refugees often experience sexual violence when they try to escape from war and ethnic conflicts. They are also victimized in many refugee camps by male refugees, by those in charge of

Women and children are the majority of refugees.

refugee camps, and by men from surrounding areas. A large number of Vietnamese boat women were abducted and raped by pirates while at sea in the 1980s. Somali women who fled interclan fighting, famine, and disease were raped in refugee camps in Kenya. Many women who are raped are shunned by their families and are punished socially and economically by their communities.[10]

Palestinian Refugees

The creation of the state of Israel in 1948 and wars between the Israelis and the Arabs led to a serious Palestinian refugee problem. Between 1947 and 1948, approximately 800,000 Palestinians became refugees from areas of Palestine that were occupied by Israel. Even though many Israelis claim the Palestinians left more or less voluntarily, most Palestinians regard this exodus as the result of Israel's strategy to force the Palestinians out of Palestine. There are roughly 3.5 million Palestinian refugees. More than a million of them live in refugee camps throughout the Arab world. Many of the refugees have lived in these camps for more than half a century. Their children and grandchildren were born and raised in refugee camps. The 1967 War, during which all of historic Palestine came under Israeli control, led to a second wave of Palestinian refugees. About 400,000 Palestinians, out of a population of 2.5 million, left Palestine for Jordan, Lebanon, and other Arab countries. The civil war in Lebanon and Israel's invasion of Lebanon in

There are roughly 3.5 million Palestinian refugees.

1982 forced more Palestinians to become refugees again. Some of them left for Europe and the United States. There are more than 200,000 Palestinians living in the United States and Canada, and about 200,000 are living in Europe.[11] Many Palestinian refugees migrated to oil-producing Arab countries that needed both skilled and unskilled labor. However, when Iraq invaded Kuwait, many Palestinians were perceived as being sympathetic to Iraq. The politics of the Gulf War in 1991 contributed to the expulsion of about 350,000 Palestinians from Kuwait alone. Palestinians also left Iraq and Saudi Arabia. Most of the Palestinians who were expelled from Kuwait became refugees in Jordan. Although many Palestinian refugees hope to return to Palestine, the Palestinian refugee problem is likely to remain unresolved for a long time.

Widespread refugee problems in Europe during and after World War II influenced the United States, Western Europe, the Soviet Union, China, and Japan to develop institutions to deal with refugees. The office of the United Nations High Commissioner for Refugees (UNHCR) was established in 1950 to help refugees. Most of the funding for UNHCR activities comes from governments, private organizations, and individuals. The proliferation of ethnic conflicts and natural disasters has put a tremendous strain on UNHCR's resources. Other U.N.

The United Nations High Commissioner for Refugees was established in 1950.

agencies, the International Committee of the Red Cross, and various nongovernmental organizations are also involved in helping refugees. Their task is often made more difficult by inability or unwillingness of some countries to separate fighters from innocent civilians in refugee camps, despite the existence of international legal

humanitarian intervention

The military invasion of a country to prevent or limit human rights abuses.

guidelines for doing so. Failure to separate them often results in refugees and aid workers becoming targets in ethnic conflicts. Increasingly, the United Nations is being pressured to prevent the escalation of ethnic conflicts that are a major cause of the refugee problem. More countries, including the United States, favor selective **humanitarian intervention,** or the military invasion of a country to prevent or limit human rights abuses that influence people to leave their homes.

PULL FACTORS

The availability of economic opportunities, especially the demand for labor, have influenced people to migrate. People leave rural areas to work in the growing manufacturing and service industries in urban areas; to improve their education; and to gain greater access to health care, consumer services, and a modern way of life. This rural-to-urban migration, the movement of people away from agricultural activities and into industries, is an integral part of modernization. However, as cities become overcrowded, many governments implement policies that encourage the development of rural areas. Brazil and China, for example, have attempted to reduce urban population pressures by promoting the urbanization of the countryside. In 1985, the Chinese govern-

Spark Plan

An effort to modernize rural Chinese industries through technological innovations.

Economic development encourages migration.

ment implemented a **Spark Plan,** which was designed to modernize rural industries through technological innovations. It adopted an export-oriented development strategy in 1987 that facilitated the export of products made in rural areas.[12] These policies stimulated economic development and job growth. People migrated from rural areas to the small towns that were built around these new industries. Infrastructure projects that are seen as essential to economic development often cause people to migrate. The construction of large dams in China and elsewhere in the developing world has forced many people to leave their homes. The building of industrial factories, airports, highways, power stations, and various public works projects uproot an estimated 10 million people in the developing world every year.[13]

The need for inexpensive and reliable labor to work in the gold and diamond mines in South Africa led to the systematic recruitment of workers from Mozambique, Lesotho, Botswana, and Swaziland. Many petroleum producers in the Middle East and the Persian Gulf have depended on hundreds of thousands of workers from the region and from other countries to meet the demand for labor in the oil and natural gas industries. Singapore and Malaysia have relied on China, Indonesia, India, and other countries for inexpensive migrant labor to fuel their economic boom.[14]

Globalization is increasingly one of the most significant pull factors in relation to migration. Globalization erodes national borders and strengthens the interdependence of countries, nonstate actors, and individuals. When people travel to distant places, they take with them important aspects of their culture. Westerners who go to developing countries

Globalization is a major cause of migration.

project an image of prosperity that poor people in those countries tend to associate with all Westerners. The images obtained through interaction with Western tourists are reinforced by images on television. Furthermore, the global system of communication provides individuals with information about economic and social opportunities in rich countries and how to get there. Low-cost transportation and the increasing flow of people across national boundaries facilitate movement from one part of the world to another. Distances are no longer an insurmountable barrier to migration.[15] **Global cities** like Los Angeles,

Globalization strengthens the interdependence of countries.

New York, Miami, Chicago, Houston, London, Paris, Shanghai, and Hong Kong enable immigrants to blend in and become low-wage workers in hotels, restaurants, sweatshops, and the homes of American families. This demand for labor and the strong desire of people from the developing world to escape poverty have enabled labor recruiters to serve as a link between employers in rich countries and migrant workers.

global cities
Cities such as New York and Chicago that enable immigrants to blend in and become low-wage workers.

An important cause of increased migration is the proliferation of groups that recruit laborers from poor countries and often smuggle them into the United States, Canada, and Western Europe. Labor recruiters and smugglers charge substantial sums of money to transport migrants to labor markets and to secure employment for them. Labor recruiters and smugglers are well organized and take advantage of global communication and transportation to engage in trafficking in human beings. Leaders of smuggling operations employ

Labor recruiters and smugglers facilitate migration.

several subcontractors—people who find migrants as well as those who transport them or arrange their transportation to countries that provide employment opportunities. Many smuggling operations are linked to various illegal activities, including drug trafficking and prostitution. Weak governments, widespread corruption, and poverty create an environment that is conducive to human trafficking.

Asia, with its serious overpopulation problems and poverty, is the area of the developing world that has the most organized and sophisticated network involved in recruiting and smuggling laborers. Overseas Chinese organizations cooperate with mainland Chinese organizations. Many illegal Chinese immigrants come to the United States by plane, ship, and automobile to work for sweatshops, slumlords, and gang bosses. Smugglers in Indonesia and other parts of Asia work with corrupt government officials to obtain the necessary permits and

TABLE 13.2 TOP TEN CITIES WITH FOREIGN-BORN POPULATIONS

City	Percentage of City's Population Foreign-Born
Miami	59%
Toronto	44
Los Angeles	41
Vancouver	37
New York City	36
Singapore	33
Sydney	31
Abidjan	30
London	28
Paris	23

Source: United Nations Development Program, *Human Development Report 2004* (New York: Oxford University Press, 2004), 99.

documentation to enable them to send large numbers of young women to work as domestic servants in Saudi Arabia and the Gulf states.[16] Smugglers in Italy, for example, engage in a lucrative business of transporting illegal immigrants from Turkey into Europe. Because Italy is part of a group of the European Union, which has eliminated border checks, illegal immigrants, once they have entered Italy, often go to Germany and France, countries that already have large immigrant populations. It is estimated that labor recruiters and smugglers along the U.S.-Mexican border make $900 million a year, roughly the same amount spent by the U.S. Border Control nationwide to prevent illegal immigration. Migrants are recruited in Mexico; guided across the border by "fence jumpers;" and driven to safe houses in border towns in Arizona, Texas, New Mexico, and California, where they are held until smugglers are paid. Once in the United States, migrants take advantage of the country's openness and transportation systems to locate in cities and towns throughout America.[17] The construction of a combination of walls and fences along the U.S.-Mexican border by the United States in 2007 is designed to reduce the flow of illegal immigrants.

Case Studies

The United States The demand for labor in the United States, together with poverty, conflict, and oppression in Europe, led to the migration of large numbers of Europeans to America. The first and most significant groups of workers to come to the United States from what is now called the developing world were enslaved Africans. Chinese immigrants came to California in the 1850s to work in the gold mines, on the railroads, and in the agricultural industry. Japanese laborers also immigrated to Hawaii and California to work in agriculture. Many Mexicans were already living in territories that became part of the United States following the **Mexican-American War,** which lasted from 1846 to 1848. More than 100,000 Mexicans decided to remain in Texas, California, Arizona, New Mexico, Utah, Nevada, and Colorado—parts of Mexico that were conquered by the United States. The need for inexpensive and reliable labor continues to draw migrants from Latin America, Asia, and Africa to the United States, a fact underscored by the immigration protests and debates in the United States in 2006.

From Oregon to Massachusetts, from California to Florida, farmers depend on migrant workers to harvest apples, pumpkins, cherries, lettuce, strawberries, oranges, and most agricultural produce. Although many of the laborers on the East Coast come from Jamaica and other parts of the Caribbean, farmers on the West Coast and in the Southwest depend on workers from Mexico and other Latin American countries to harvest the crops. Immigrants from the developing world are an important part of the labor force throughout the United States. Most taxi drivers in cities such as Washington, D.C., New York, Chicago, Boston, Miami, Houston, and Los Angeles are immigrants from Asia, Africa, and Latin America. Restaurants, hotels, hospitals, universities, and various industries rely on immigrants from developing countries. Most of the discussion on immigration in America focuses on the large and growing number of Mexican workers in the country.

Mexican migration to the United States has been largely influenced by economic opportunities in America and difficult economic circumstances in Mexico. The annexation of Mexican territory by the United States did not significantly alter migration

Mexican-American War

Lasted from 1846 to 1848.

U.S. Dependence on Illegal Migrants

Farmers, builders, manufacturers, homeowners, and virtually every sector of the American economy depend on migrant workers. Illegal immigrants are an integral component of American life. What do you think should be done about illegal migrants?

across the newly established borders. The Mexican Revolution of 1910 forced many Mexicans out of Mexico and into the United States. The economic and political problems in Mexico at the time served as push factors, and the need for labor in agriculture and on the railroads in the western United States functioned as pull factors. Demand for labor in the United States during World War I drew more Mexicans to the country.[18] This demand lasted until 1923, when European immigrants began to replace Mexican immigrants. Although many employers began to see European immigrants as troublemakers and preferred the more cooperative Mexican workers, the economic devastation of the **Great Depression** of the 1930s led to the deportation of thousands of Mexican workers and their families. But the demand for labor in the United States during World War II brought Mexicans back under the **Bracero Program.** The Bracero Program was a set of agreements between the United States and Mexico that facilitated the migration of Mexican workers, on a temporary basis, to work primarily in agriculture in the United States. The increase in legal migration under the Bracero Program was accompanied by the growth of illegal immigration. From 1942 to 1952, roughly 900,000 Mexican workers entered the United States under the Bracero Program, compared with more than 2 million illegal workers over the same period. In response to economic competition and fears about communists entering the country through Mexico, the United States launched **Operation Wetback,** in which hundreds of thousands of Mexicans were rounded up and deported. However, by the time the Bracero Program ended in 1964, the relationship between Mexican workers and American employers was so well established that controlling the flow of migrants across the U.S.-Mexican border was extremely difficult.[19] Immigration from Mexico, both legal and illegal, became a reality of American life. In 2006 and 2007, immigrants and their supporters demonstrated throughout the United States to show their importance to the U.S. economy and to obtain more immigration rights.

> *The Mexican Revolution forced many Mexicans out of Mexico and into the United States.*

Great Depression
Led to the deportation of Mexican workers.

Bracero Program
Allowed Mexican workers to temporarily migrate to the United States.

Operation Wetback
An American initiative that rounded up and deported Mexican workers.

Immigrant laborers in Houston, Los Angeles, and other cities in the West and Southwest wait each morning to be offered employment. Employers and their agents hire them to paint houses, repair roofs, dig ditches, hang drywall, build houses, cook, do gardening and yard work, work in the fields, clean houses, and perform many other jobs that most Americans may not want to do themselves. Immigrants

Immigrants demonstrated throughout the United States in 2006 to show their importance to the economy and for immigration rights.

Source: E. Jason Wambsgans/*Chicago Tribune*

provide most of the labor in dangerous meatpacking plants. In Storm Lake, Iowa, meatpacking plants attract so many immigrants from Mexico that the town has been transformed. Although most Americans regard jobs in meatpacking plants as dangerous, most immigrants often disregard the danger in order to make $7 to $10 an hour. Although the pay is low by American standards, it is very high compared with the $4 a day many unskilled laborers earn in Mexico. Because of the economic benefits of cheap labor, employers hire recruiters to find workers for them in Mexico. They also pay workers bonuses of up to $150 for finding immigrants who become employees in the meatpacking plants.[20] American society is very dependent on cheap immigrant labor.

France The influx of large numbers of immigrants from the developing countries into France must be seen in the broader context of French colonialism and the demand for labor in France. France's tradition of respecting the civil and human rights of foreigners also facilitated immigration from poor countries. France adopted a **policy of assimilation** toward its colonies in Africa, Asia, the Caribbean, and the Pacific. Under this policy, many residents of French colonies gained French citizenship and were free to migrate to France. Many Africans and Asians found employment in France, especially after World War I, which had such a devastating impact on the French population that the country had to import labor for its industries. Even after Algeria,

policy of assimilation

A French policy that allowed residents of French colonies to gain citizenship and migrate freely to France.

Tunisia, Morocco, and other French colonies gained their independence in the 1950s and early 1960s, the status of these former "citizens" was not changed. Many of them continued to arrive in France. The largest number of immigrants came from North Africa until the 1980s. After that time, immigration from Senegal, the Ivory Coast, and other West African countries increased.[21] Despite significant opposition to immigrants from the developing world from politicians such as **Jean-Marie Le Pen,** France continues to attract migrants from poor countries. Even Le Pen moderated his anti-immigration position in the 2007 French elections.

Jean-Marie Le Pen

French politician who strongly opposes immigration from the developing world to France.

Germany   Prior to the 1950s, Germany encouraged its citizens to emigrate to North America, Eastern Europe, Latin America, and elsewhere. Between 1920 and 1950, almost 7 million German immigrants settled in the United States. Germany's need for labor from the developing world was due to the destruction Germany experienced in World War II. When West Germany began to rebuild its industries, the demand for manual labor could not be met by the domestic labor force, especially after the flow of migrants from East Germany ended with the construction of the **Berlin Wall** (by the Soviet Union) between the two countries. The growing domestic and international market for West Germany's cars, machine tools, appliances, and other manufactured products influenced the government to recruit foreign workers, mostly from Spain, Greece, Turkey, and Portugal. The government and the unions agreed that Germans and foreigners would receive equal wages. Under the **Gastarbeiter rotation system,** foreign workers or guest workers would stay in Germany for one to three years and then return to their home countries.[22] But many guest workers did not go home. Instead, many made Germany their home and brought their families to join them. Employers wanted these temporary workers to stay because of the economic benefits they derived from them. By 2000, Germany was home to about 2 million Turks, some of the poorest and most visible migrants in the country. Outbreaks of violence against them occur frequently.

Berlin Wall

A wall that formerly separated East Germany from West Germany.

Gastarbeiter rotation system

A German system that allowed foreign workers or guest workers to stay in Germany for one to three years and then return to their home countries.

Japan   Although Japan emphasizes ethnic and cultural homogeneity as a positive value, immigrants from Asia, Latin America, and, to a lesser extent, Africa are gradually transforming the ethnic composition of Japan. Despite Japan's reluctance to encourage immigration, the country's need for labor has forced it to modify its position. During World War I, labor shortages in Japan prompted manufacturers and mine owners to import Korean workers. More than 2 million Koreans were brought to Japan during World War II to help meet the demand for labor. Most of them were sent back to Korea when the war ended. Labor shortages plagued Japan in the late

Korean workers were brought to Japan during World War I and World War II.

1980s because the economy had expanded rapidly and the country's population was not only declining but also aging rapidly. Japan's industrial growth after World War II was fueled largely by labor from rural areas of the country. As Japanese citizens became prosperous, they discouraged their children from doing manual labor and encouraged them to get a university education. Younger Japanese began to avoid jobs that were considered to be dangerous, dirty, and physically demanding. Although Japan's economic growth had slowed considerably by the end of the last century, the country still depends on immigrants to do many of the jobs that Japanese citizens avoid. Japan's high standard of living has attracted workers from Thailand, the Philippines, Malaysia, South Korea, Vietnam, China, Indonesia, Iran, Bangladesh, and parts of Africa. Crime syndicates based in Japan, Hong Kong, Taiwan, Thailand, and the Philippines facilitate the flow of illegal immigrants into Japan. Japan also relies on immigrants from Latin America to meet its demand for labor. Since 1989, Japan has allowed Latin Americans of Japanese ancestry (or **Nikkeijin**) to gain virtually unrestricted access to employment in the country. Immigrants of Japanese ancestry come mainly from Brazil, Peru, Argentina, Bolivia, and Paraguay. From Japan's viewpoint, these immigrants do not change the country's ethnic homogeneity.[23]

Nikkeijin

Latin Americans of Japanese ancestry.

THE IMPACT OF MIGRATION ON POOR COUNTRIES

Increasing globalization, the removal of political obstacles to freedom of movement, overpopulation pressures, national disasters, wars, ethnic conflicts, and the search for economic opportunities influence many people to leave developing countries. Migration, by its very nature, usually deprives a region or a country of some of its valuable human resources. However, staying in a poor country often stifles the development of human capital and only helps perpetuate poverty and other problems. In other words, the impact of migration on poor countries is not always straightforward and uncomplicated. There are both gains and losses, advantages and disadvantages, that result when large numbers of individuals cross national borders or move from one part of the country to another to improve their lives.

brain drain

The migration of highly educated and trained people from poor countries to rich countries.

Brain drain, or the migration of highly educated and trained people, is viewed as a serious problem in many parts of the developing world. Many European countries, especially after World War II, worried about the loss of talented individuals who were attracted to better opportunities in the United States. However, most European countries had the ability to train others to lessen the problems caused by brain drain. Most of the concern about the loss of expertise has been focused on Asia, Africa, and Latin America, especially after many countries in these areas gained their independence in the 1960s. Many developing countries had relatively few educated individuals at the time of independence. As political instability and economic problems increased, doctors, lawyers, engineers, scientists, and people with valuable technological skills emigrated to the United States, Canada, France, and other developed countries. Many students from poor countries who were educated in rich countries did not return, thereby contributing to the brain drain. The lack of political stability, a general disinterest in or poor understanding of what educated persons did, and the unavailability of proper equipment, research facilities, and a supportive environment influenced many of them to remain where they received advanced education and technical training.[24] Economic opportunities were also a powerful inducement to stay in rich countries. Although the loss of expertise due to migration remains an important concern, most developing countries are better equipped to train a large number of people to contribute to economic, social, and political development. The brain drain issue is now more complicated.

It is estimated that half of the recent graduates from the prestigious Indian Institute of Technology leave for the United States. They are driven out of India by overregulation, high taxes, stagnant career paths, and numerous entrepreneurial impediments. Many are attracted to the United States by greater economic opportunities and an environment that is conducive to economic success and personal growth.[25] But this migration of talented individuals is seen as detrimental to India. India is deprived of innovative individuals, the economic benefits that they could provide, and role models for younger Indians. Brain drain also costs poor countries. The money they invested in these individuals' education, training, and general development is essentially lost. Countries that attract migrants benefit from the investments made by poor countries.

On the other hand, many poor countries are unable to absorb the available skilled labor. What is usually perceived as brain drain is often **brain overflow.** Poor countries, such as the Philippines and Egypt, become exporters of highly trained individuals because of their inability to use them. Many skilled migrants, in an increasingly global society, maintain contacts with their home countries and often return to them. In effect, they take back much-needed capital for investment and advanced technologies and technical knowledge they acquired in rich countries. The computer chip industry in Taiwan is an example of how migrants eventually transfer technology from rich countries to their homeland. China, India, and other developing societies systematically encourage migrants to invest in and transfer technology to their country of origin.[26] Migrants also make valuable contacts in rich countries that enable them to raise money for investments back home. They often manage to encourage experts from rich countries to help with development projects in poor countries. Many migrants become valuable assets to their homelands. Sammy Sosa, for example, was extremely valuable to the Dominican Republic as a promoter of tourism to that country because he migrated to the United States to play baseball.

Remittances from migrants play a crucial role in the economic development of many poor countries. Migrants throughout the world tend to send money to their families. In some cases, poor countries make arrangements with rich countries to recruit migrants for temporary work. Part of the migrant's pay is sent directly to the governments of poor countries. Money sent to families is used to buy food and clothes, build houses, purchase agricultural land, and help educate family members. Many migrants send money to their relatives to save, invest in small businesses, or help develop community services. Remittances from emigration, to governments and to families, are extremely important to the economic well-being of many countries. Mexico, the Philippines, Egypt, Turkey, Algeria, India, and many other countries depend on remittances as a main source of foreign exchange.

Many of the estimated 6 million Mexicans who live in the United States send money to Mexico. Remittances from migrants have transformed many parts of Mexico. Communities in Mexico receive money not only to purchase food, clothes, shoes, education, and other essentials, but also for investment purposes. For example, Mexicans who left the state of Guanajuato in search of jobs in Chicago, Atlanta, Houston, Dallas, Los Angeles, Phoenix, and other U.S. cities invest their money in Guanajuato to create jobs. Many, with the help of the Mexican government, invest in

brain overflow
Inability of poor countries to use highly trained individuals.

remittance
Money that migrant workers send back to their families or countries.

TAKING ACTION

Immigrants' Strategies for Economic Success

Immigrants from many developing countries have relied on informal lending systems to secure funds to start businesses, finance college education, and purchase homes. Instead of relying on American lending institutions for loans and then paying them interest, they tap into a homegrown cash flow system. An example of this system is found in many Caribbean communities in the United States. The system, called "susu" or "partner," is an informal rotating-credit arrangement with roots in Caribbean culture. A group gets together to pool its savings, and members can withdraw funds from the pool when they need money. In a typical susu, about twenty close family members and friends make a weekly contribution of a certain fixed amount to the fund. If each member is contributing $100 a week over a period of twenty weeks, each member is entitled to draw $2,000 during the twenty-week period. The money changes hands across kitchen tables and in living rooms, with mostly women negotiating the transactions and serving as bankers. Those who receive their share early get, in effect, the equivalent of a cash advance against future deposits, but without having to pay interest. Those who draw their funds at the end use the system as a savings program to help friends and family members. This system is increasingly used in combination with bank loans or other funding.

Source: Meera Louis, "Caribbean-Type Saving Helps Build Businesses," *The Wall Street Journal,* 17 October 2000, B1.

maquiladoras

Export factories in which the Mexican government invests.

maquiladoras, or export factories, to enable other Mexicans to find employment in their communities. More than 1,000 jobs were created by 1998, just one year after the program started.[27] Many migrants invest their money in building homes. In fact, constructing a house is a major incentive for emigration. Even though many migrants build large homes to display the relative economic success they achieved in the United States, most of them add rooms to their parents' homes or build modest modern homes for themselves. These investments generate employment for Mexicans who remain in their communities and provide revenues for the Mexican government. Remittances are now seen as an important component of many countries' economies. For example, Mexico's central bank estimated that Mexicans transferred more than $6 billion from the United States to Mexico in 1998. By 2007, this figure had increased to more than $12 billion. These remittances were the third largest source of foreign revenue for Mexico. Only revenues from oil and tourism were larger.[28]

Because many countries are so dependent on remittances from migrants, economic problems in countries that employ them have a direct negative impact on sending countries. The economic crisis in Asia at the end of the last century forced governments to devalue their currencies, abandon ambitious development projects, and expel immigrants who provided the cheap labor that fueled the economic boom. The expulsion of domestic, construction, and plantation workers had a devastating effect on countries such as the Philippines, Indonesia, and Bangladesh. Migrant workers from the Philippines, for example, are the country's primary source of foreign revenue. Tens of millions of people in the Philippines depend on remittances from relatives working abroad. Migrants in southern Africa have also been severely affected by low prices for gold and unemployment in the mining industry. Lesotho, for example, depended on remittances from miners in South Africa for a quarter of its gross domestic product (GDP). The unemployment rate in Lesotho is around 50 percent. The United Nations has consistently ranked Lesotho as one of the world's poorest countries. The decline in remittances from migrant workers only worsened Lesotho's economic situation.

THE IMPACT OF MIGRATION ON RICH COUNTRIES

Migration's economic impact on rich countries is difficult to measure precisely. But as this chapter shows, migrants provide inexpensive labor that contributes to economic growth and prosperity in rich countries. As the populations of developed countries grow older and decline, migrants from poor countries are increasingly supporting an aging population. Migrants also help keep inflation low by keeping wages from rising rapidly. Most rich countries are concerned about the social and political impact of immigration. France, which is predominately Catholic, worries about the large number of Muslims from North Africa who, unlike earlier generations of migrants that adopted French culture, are maintaining their own distinct ethnic identities. Many children of migrants, who were born in France, reject much of French culture, view Islam as being incompatible with French morality, and separate themselves from the larger French society. France, which has stressed the separation of church and state and the importance of a secular society, has reacted strongly to symbols of Islam, such as the scarf, in public schools. Germany is also facing cultural problems due to the large number of Turkish guest workers in the country. Although Turks make up one-fourth of Germany's immigrants, their relative poverty, lack of education, and practice of Islam make them the focal point of Germany's concern about migration. Germany regarded the Turks as temporary residents. Even though many of them were raised in Germany, they were not given German citizenship. Germany's refusal to see itself as a country of immigration has contributed to the Turks' reluctance to fully integrate into German society. Christian churches and labor unions have consistently urged the government to treat guest workers the same as German citizens. In 1996, Germany changed its policy on citizenship for the Turks, and made 46,300 Turks German citizens. Despite progress in this area, frictions between Turkish migrants and Germans often erupt in violence. Germany is also concerned about the impact of a large influx of Turks on German culture and society.

Migration is rapidly changing the American society. Although immigrants came from Germany, Canada, Poland, the Soviet Union, and other European countries prior to 1965, most immigrants now come from Mexico, the Philippines, China, Cuba, India, Vietnam, and other developing countries. The large number of Latinos or Hispanics in the United States, estimated at 34 million in 2007, is profoundly altering American political and social institutions. Politicians are aware of the growing political power of Latinos and have begun focusing on their interests and concerns. Latinos have great

Migration is rapidly changing the American society.

electoral votes

The votes that actually elect the president of the United States.

potential political power because they are concentrated in states with the most **electoral votes,** the votes needed to elect the president of the United States. These states include California, Texas, Florida, New York, and Illinois. Spanish is widely perceived to be America's second language, and the border town of El Cenizo in Texas adopted Spanish as its official language in 1999. It also declared the community to be a safe haven for illegal immigrants. The growing power of Latinos and other immigrants from the developing world is often viewed by some U.S. citizens as a threat to American culture.[29] Several groups in the United States advocate limiting immigration and making English the country's official language. Following massive demonstrations by immigrants and their supporters in 2006, the U.S. Congress passed resolutions supporting English as the official language. President George W. Bush increased the number of National Guard units along the border. Building additional walls and fences to keep Mexican migrants out of the United States was also approved by Congress.

The globalization of the economy; the ease with which people can cross national borders; and the extensive family, cultural, educational, and business links that are already established among countries make immigration a permanent feature of the global society. Although many countries want to stop the flow of migrants for both economic and cultural reasons, economic and social realities in an increasingly borderless world make this difficult to achieve. Few consumers are willing to do anything that would threaten the bountiful supply of cheap food, despite their opposition to immigration in the abstract. Many parts of the American economy, especially agriculture, construction, and the service industry, are very dependent on immigrants.

Summary and Review

Migration, the movement from one place to another, is an integral part of human behavior. People have always moved from one area to another for a variety of reasons. Our ancestors moved to find the best agricultural lands, better protection from potential enemies, and water and grass for their animals; to engage in religious conversions; to conquer land for new settlements; and in response to seasonal changes. The rich ethnic, religious, and cultural diversity of most countries, especially Canada and the United States, demonstrates the strong human tendency to leave one place and to go to another. There are many different types of migration and migrants. The latter can include internally displaced people, refugees, and migrants, and the former includes transcontinental migration, rural-to-rural migration, urban-to-rural migration, and seasonal migration. Two broad reasons behind migration are known as push and pull factors. Push factors motivate people to leave their homes and include human rights violations, political oppression, forced resettlement programs, violence and political instability, overpopulation, unemployment, poverty, natural and environmental disasters, and the lack of educational and cultural opportunities. Pull factors include employment opportunities, higher wages, political and social stability, a healthy environment, educational and cultural opportunities, and family reunification. Most of the refugees and internally displaced people throughout the world can be found in Africa and Asia. Since 1948, the United Nations High Commissioner for Refugees (UNHCR) has been actively working with nongovernmental organizations and states to help aid refugees and resolve problems creating the displacement of people throughout the world. Migration is rapidly changing the underdeveloped as well as the developed worlds.

Key Terms

migration 280
migrant 280
refugee 280
displaced
    person 281
immigrant 281
transcontinental
    migration 281
rural-to-rural
    migration 281

urban-to-rural
    migration 281
rural-to-urban
    migration 281
seasonal
    migration 282
push factors 282
pull factors 282
Cultural
    Revolution 284

forced migration 285
Palestinians 287
United Nations
    High
    Commissioner
    for Refugees
    (UNHCR) 287
Spark Plan 288
humanitarian
    intervention 288

globalization 288
global cities 289
Operation
    Wetback 291
assimilation 292
guest workers 293
Nikkeijin 294
brain drain 294
brain overflow 295
maquiladoras 296

Discussion Questions

1. Describe the reasons behind migration.
2. What are the effects of migration on the developed and the underdeveloped worlds?
3. Distinguish between push and pull factors.
4. What are the differences between a refugee and a displaced person?
5. How has globalization contributed to migration?
6. How can the UNHCR work more effectively at repatriating refugees?

7. What are the reasons behind China's forced migration policies?
8. How healthy are national policies of assimilation?
9. Is it possible to have a world without migration?
10. What factors underlie xenophobic tendencies of countries that host large migrant communities?

Suggested Readings

Castles, Stephen, and Alastair Davidson. *Citizenship and Migration: Globalization and the Politics of Belonging.* New York: Routledge, 2000.

D'Arcy, Michael, et al. *Protecting the Homeland 2006/2007.* Washington, D.C.: Brookings, 2006.

Ghosh, Bimal, ed. *Managing Migration: Time for a New International Regime?* New York: Oxford University Press, 2000.

Huntington, Samuel P. "The Hispanic Challenge." *Foreign Policy* 141 (March/April 2004): 30–45.

Kapur, Davesh, and John McHale. "Migration's New Payoff." *Foreign Policy* 139 (November/December 2003): 48–57.

Martin, Phillip, et al. *Managing Labor Migration in the Twenty-first Century.* New Haven, CT: Yale University Press, 2006.

Martin, Susan Forbes. *Refugee Women*. Lanham, MD: Lexington Books, 2004.

Organisation for Economic Co-operation and Development. *Globalisation, Migration, and Development*. Paris: OECD, 2000.

Picciotto, Robert, Warren van Wicklin, and Edward Rice, eds. *Involuntary Resettlement: Comparative Perspectives*. New Brunswick, NJ: Transaction Publishers, 2001.

Schiff, Maurice, and Caglar Ogden, eds. *International Migration, Remittances, and the Brain Drain*. London: Palgrave Macmillian, 2005.

Toro-Morn, Maura I., and Marixsa Alicea, eds. *Migration and Immigration*. Westport, CT: Greenwood Press, 2004.

Addresses and Websites

Center for Migration Studies of New York, Inc.
209 Flagg Place
Staten Island, New York 10204–1199
Tel: (718) 351–8800
Fax: (718) 667–4598
http://www.cmsny.org/

The Center for Migration Studies of New York, founded in 1964, is one of the foremost institutes for migration research. The group covers a wide range of information regarding migration and tracking refugee movement throughout the world. One of the organization's main efforts is to educate people on migration and refugee issues and concerns. This website offers an in-depth look at the Center for Migration Studies and general information regarding migration. The website also offers information on the Center's current projects, publications, and a library archive of refugee and migration resources.

United Nations High Commission for Refugees— UNHCR
Public Information Section
CP 2500
1211 Genève 2 Dépôt
Switzerland
http://www.unhcr.ch/cgi-bin/texis/vtx/home

This is the home of the United Nations High Commission for Refugees (UNHCR). This arm of the United Nations was founded in 1950 by the U.N. General Assembly in an effort to aid in the increasing refugee problem in the world. The UNHCR works toward helping refugees with their needs, including providing them with food, medicine, and water. The UNHCR looks toward finding long-term solutions to end crises of refugees and displaced peoples. This website provides extensive information about the UNHCR and refugees across the globe. This is one of the most comprehensive refugee websites available.

Immigration and Refugee Services of America— IRSA
1717 Massachusetts Ave., NW
Suite 200
Washington, D.C. 20036
Tel: (202) 797-2105
Fax: (202) 347-2460
http://www.irsa-uscr.org/

The Immigration and Refugee Services of America is an organization that aims to find viable solutions to refugee concerns and problems associated with refugees. The group provides many assistance and educational programs to help refugees and promote and defend human rights. Their website offers links to the numerous refugee projects on which the organization has been working. There is also information on special needs of refugees including disease epidemics including hepatitis and HIV. This website provides ample information about refugees and even has a news and updates section to keep the website up to date.

Migration and Refugee Services
1900 South Acadian Thruway
P.O. Box 4213
Baton Rouge, LA 70821–0220
Tel: (225) 346-0660
Fax: (225) 346-0220
http://www.brmrs.org/

The Migration and Refugee Services is an organization that works with refugees within the United States. This Catholic-sponsored organization aids immigrants and refugees via counseling, educational efforts, and promotion of economic self-sufficiency. The website has further information regarding the organization and also provides links to career-counseling services and a governmental workforce website. A more in-depth list of the group's services can also be found on the website.

Notes

1. Sylvia Chant and Sarah A. Radcliffe, "Migration and Development: The Importance of Gender," in Sylvia Chant, ed., *Gender and Migration in Developing Countries* (London: Belhaven Press, 1992), 16.
2. Sylvia Chant, ed., *Gender and Migration in Developing Countries* (London: Belhaven Press, 1992), 11.
3. Kimberly A. Hamilton and Kate Holder, "International Migration and Foreign Policy," *The Washington Quarterly* (Spring 1991): 196.
4. Michael Specter, "Population Implosion Worries a Graying Europe," *The New York Times*, 10 July 1998, A1; and Philip Martin, et al., *Managing Labor Migration in the Twenty-first Century* (New Haven, CT: Yale University Press, 2006), 7.
5. Kevin Platt, "Chinese Migrants Change Face of Tibet," *The Christian Science Monitor*, 10 September 1998, 8; and Hal Kane, "Leaving Home," in Lester R. Brown, ed., *State of the World 1995* (New York: W. W. Norton, 1995), 137.
6. Myron Weiner, *The Global Migration Crisis* (New York: HarperCollins, 1995), 30.
7. Lin You Su, "Migration and Urbanization in China," in Gavin W. Jones and Pravin Visaria, eds., *Urbanization in Large Developing Countries* (Oxford UK: Clarendon Press, 1997), 71.
8. Larry Rohter, "Driven by Fear, Colombians Leave in Droves," *The New York Times*, 5 March 2000, A8.
9. Ronald Skeldon, "Hong Kong's Response to the Indochinese Influx, 1975–1993," *Annals of the American Academy of Political and Social Science* 534 (July 1994): 92.
10. Amnesty International, *Amnesty International Report 1997* (London: Amnesty International, 1997), 2.
11. Samih K. Farsoun and Christina E. Zacharia, *Palestine and the Palestinians* (Boulder, CO: Westview Press, 1997), 138–39; and Michael Fischbach, *The Peace Process and Palestinian Refugee Claims* (Washington, D.C.: U.S. Institute of Peace Press, 2006).
12. Gabe T. Wang and Xiaobo Hu, "Small Town Development and Rural Urbanization in China," *Journal of Contemporary Asia* 29, no. 1 (1999): 80.
13. Kane, "Leaving Home," 137.
14. Ben Dolven, "The China Factor," *Far Eastern Economic Review* 18 March 1999, 54.
15. Weiner, *The Global Migration Crisis*, 25; and Lester C. Thurow, *The Future of Capitalism* (New York: William Morrow, 1996), 93.
16. Ozay Mehmet, et al. *Towards a Fair Global Labor Market* (London: Routledge, 1999), 27–28.
17. Alan Zarembo, "People Smugglers Inc.," *Newsweek*, 13 September 1999, 36; and Jennifer Lee, "Human Smuggling, for a Hefty Fee," *The New York Times*, 28 May 2006, sect. 3, 2.
18. David M. Reimers, *Still the Golden Door: The Third World Comes to America* (New York: Colombia University Press, 1992), 2.
19. Kitty Calavita, "U.S. Immigration and Policy Responses," in Wayne A. Cornelius et al., eds., *Controlling Immigration. A Global Perspective* (Stanford, CA: Stanford University Press, 1994), 59.
20. Stephen J. Hedges and Dana Hawkins, "The New Jungle," *U.S. News and World Report*, 23 September 1996.
21. James F. Hollifield, "Immigration and Republicanism in France," in Cornelius et al., eds., *Controlling Immigration*, 153.
22. Philip L. Martin, "Germany: Reluctant Land of Immigration," in Cornelius et al., eds., *Controlling Immigration*, 199; and Hermann Kurthen, "Germany at the Crossroads," *International Migration Review* 29, no. 4 (Winter 1995): 922.
23. Wayne A. Cornelius, "Japan: The Illusion of Immigration Control," in Cornelius et al., eds., *Controlling Immigration*, 396.
24. D. Chongo Mundende, "The Brain Drain and Developing Countries," in Reginald Appleyard, ed., *The Impact of International Migration on Developing Countries* (Paris: OECD, 1989), 184; and Laurie Goering, "WHO: 57 Nations Short of Skilled Health Workers," *Chicago Tribune*, 8 April 2006, sect. 1, 6.
25. Stephan-Gotz Richter, "The Immigration Safety Valve," *Foreign Affairs* 79, no. 2 (March–April 2000): 15.
26. Weiner, *The Global Migration Crisis*, 39.
27. Paul de la Garza, "Emigrants Help Out Back Home," *Chicago Tribune*, 23 March 1998, sect. 1, 1.
28. Devesh Kapur and John McHale, "Migration's New Payoff," *Foreign Policy* 139 (November/December 2003), 50.
29. "Texas Town Approves Spanish As Its Language," *Chicago Tribune*, 15 August 1999, sect. 1, 7; Samuel P. Huntington, "The Hispanic Challenge," *Foreign Policy* 141 (March/April 2004): 30–45; and Dahleen Glanton, "Migrants Brace for State Laws," *Chicago Tribune*, 10 April 2006, sect. 1, 1.

CHAPTER FOURTEEN

Foreign Relations of the Developing Countries

GLOBALIZATION AND FOREIGN RELATIONS

AS GLOBALIZATION INCREASES, THE FATE OF RICH COUNTRIES IS INCREASINGLY LINKED TO THAT OF POOR COUNTRIES, TO VARYING DEGREES. TERRORIST GROUPS, BASED IN AFGHANISTAN, USED THE INSTRUMENTS OF GLOBALIZATION TO INFLICT A DEVASTATING BLOW ON THE UNITED STATES ON SEPTEMBER 11, 2001. THE UNITED STATES FOUND ITSELF FIGHTING THE FIRST WAR OF THE TWENTY-FIRST CENTURY IN AFGHANISTAN, ONE OF THE POOREST COUNTRIES IN THE WORLD. IN 2003, THE UNITED STATES INVADED IRAQ, OVERTHREW THE GOVERNMENT, ARRESTED ITS LEADERS, AND OCCUPIED THE COUNTRY, THEREBY BECOMING DEEPLY INVOLVED MILITARILY IN THE HEART OF THE ARAB WORLD. ALTHOUGH MUCH OF THE DISCUSSION OF FOREIGN POLICY AND INTERNATIONAL RELATIONS IS FOCUSED ON DEVELOPED COUNTRIES, ESPECIALLY THE UNITED STATES AND MEMBERS OF THE EUROPEAN UNION, FOREIGN RELATIONS ARE ALSO EXTREMELY IMPORTANT TO MANY DEVELOPING COUNTRIES, DESPITE THEIR BUREAUCRATIC, ECONOMIC, AND DIPLOMATIC WEAKNESSES. THE POVERTY OF DEVELOPING COUNTRIES HEIGHTENS THEIR VULNERABILITY TO EVENTS BEYOND THEIR BORDERS, EVENTS OVER WHICH THEY HAVE RELATIVELY LITTLE CONTROL. ETHNIC CONFLICTS IN RWANDA, INDONESIA, AND ELSEWHERE IN THE DEVELOPING WORLD ATTRACT THE ATTENTION OF HUMAN RIGHTS ACTIVISTS IN EUROPE AND AMERICA. THESE ACTIVISTS PRESSURE THEIR GOVERNMENTS AND INTERNATIONAL ORGANIZATIONS TO TAKE ACTIONS TO END THE CONFLICTS. ORGANIZATIONS SUCH AS THE INTERNATIONAL MONETARY FUND AND THE WORLD BANK ARE ROUTINELY CRITICIZED FOR DAMAGING THE ECONOMIES AND THE ENVIRONMENT OF DEVELOPING COUNTRIES. SOME POOR COUNTRIES POSE DIRECT THREATS TO RICH COUNTRIES. SOME HAVE IMPOSED OIL EMBARGOS, WHEREAS OTHERS HAVE SUPPORTED VIOLENCE AGAINST THE UNITED STATES AND COUNTRIES IN WESTERN EUROPE. OTHER POOR COUNTRIES ALLIED THEMSELVES WITH THE SOVIET UNION DURING THE COLD WAR, THEREBY INCREASING AMERICAN SECURITY CONCERNS. CUBA, FOR EXAMPLE, WHICH BECAME A STAUNCH SOVIET ALLY, CONTINUES TO INFLUENCE AMERICA'S DOMESTIC AFFAIRS AS WELL AS ITS FOREIGN POLICY.

INTRODUCTION

The **study of international relations** is primarily about the interactions of countries or states. Just as individuals have relations with other individuals, states have to deal with each other. Their relationships are characterized by cooperation as well as conflict. Just as individuals attempt to achieve their goals by working with others, states reach agreements with each other to achieve their objectives. However, just like when conflict is an integral part of human relationships, states often disagree and sometimes engage in violent conflict to settle their disputes. Like rich countries, poor countries rely on both diplomacy and military might to safeguard their interests.

An important characteristic of all states is **sovereignty,** or control over their internal affairs and external relations. But the degree of control a state has depends on many factors, including its level of economic development; its geographic location; and the quality of its leadership and political institutions, including the bureaucracy. Powerful countries generally have a greater degree of independence than weak countries. The concept of sovereignty emerged with the rise of the modern state at the end of the Thirty Years' War, which concluded with the **Peace of Westphalia** in 1648.

In addition to sovereignty, which includes independence, states generally have defined boundaries, people who have separate national identities, and governments. In many cases, boundaries are not well defined and people identify with others in a different state, which complicate relations among countries. Furthermore, the rise of nonstate actors and transnational organizations changed how states interact with each other. Revolutions in technology and transportation have contributed to the creation of what is becoming a borderless world. Developing countries conduct their foreign relations in an increasingly interdependent world. Given their level of economic development, poor countries are as concerned with the activities of multinational corporations, humanitarian organizations, and nongovernmental organizations as they are with other countries. This chapter discusses the process of foreign policy making in developing societies, factors shaping these policies, the relationship between the developing world and the United States, and conflict as well as cooperation among developing countries. The chapter focuses on the foreign relations of specific countries, such as China, India, Egypt, Mexico, and Cuba. Special emphasis is placed on their relations with the United States.

MAKING FOREIGN POLICY IN DEVELOPING COUNTRIES

In a general sense, foreign policy deals with efforts on the part of one country to influence the behavior and attitudes of other countries, nongovernmental organizations (NGOs), transnational actors, and international institutions. The foreign policies of developing countries are expressions of what governments, groups, and individuals determine to be national interests. **National interests** may be defined as a set of goals that are essential or beneficial to a country's survival, its economic prosperity, the psychological well-being of its population, and its status and prestige in the region and in the larger international community.[1] This definition implies that foreign policy issues are often difficult to distinguish from domestic concerns. In fact, most foreign policies

study of international relations

The study of the interactions among countries or states.

sovereignty

A country's control over its internal affairs and external relations.

Peace of Westphalia

Ended the Thirty Years' War in 1648.

national interests

A set of goals that are essential or beneficial to a country's survival, status, and economic prosperity.

are designed to achieve domestic policies through interaction with other states as well as nonstate actors. Efficient foreign policies are usually based on an objective analysis of a hierarchy of interests or national priorities. In order of importance, these priorities are as follows:

1. Survival interests, where a state's existence is at stake.
2. Vital interests, where serious harm to a country would occur if strong actions were not taken relatively soon.
3. Major interests, where a country could suffer if nothing is done to counteract a threat.
4. Peripheral or minor interests, where little damage would result if a wait-and-see policy were adopted.[2]

foreign policies

Decisions influenced by a combination of factors.

The **foreign policies** of developing countries are influenced by many factors, including (1) the country's geographical location, (2) the level of economic development of the country, (3) the nature of the country's political system and the quality of its leadership, (4) the military capabilities of the country, (5) the nature of international public opinion and the priorities of major countries and nonstate actors, and (6) cultural ties with other countries. Geographic location and physical terrain have always determined, to a great extent, countries' international relations. Poland's low terrain made it relatively easy to be conquered by its neighbors. England's separation from the European continent protected it from foreign invasions. Mexico's proximity to the United States limits the kinds of policies Mexico can pursue. A country's level of economic development influences its selection of foreign policy goals and how it tries to accomplish them. Richer countries tend to have more interests and the resources necessary to pursue and protect them. Poorer countries are usually more dependent and subservient in their relations with rich countries. The cost of developing independent foreign policies is often too high for poor states. However, some states resist efforts by stronger countries to control their international behavior.[3] Many of these countries are ruled by authoritarian regimes. Their leaders often use confrontation with powerful states to consolidate their power over their societies. Fidel Castro, for example, has maintained his control over Cuba by defiantly resisting efforts of the United States to influence Cuba's foreign policies and its internal affairs.

Economic factors influence foreign policy.

Foreign policies are shaped by the nature of a country's political system and the quality of its leadership. Most developing countries, despite their transitions toward democracy, are ruled by a small group of individuals. In countries where one individual dominates, foreign policy is often determined by the personal preferences and interests of that individual and his or her supporters. In Indonesia, for example, foreign policy reflected the interests of the country's elite. Many African countries are still ruled by personalized authoritarian regimes. Leaders have significant influence on the making of foreign policy. Unlike in democratic societies, where leaders are held responsible for their behavior, rulers in

Foreign policies often reflect the interests of the country's elite.

many parts of the developing world are not strongly influenced by public opinion and are not generally held accountable for their actions. This does not mean that leaders are not restrained by domestic and international considerations. The weak political institutions and widespread corruption and bureaucratic inefficiency that characterize most developing countries directly influence the quality and nature of the foreign relations of these states.

The military capabilities of a country shape its foreign policy objectives and how it attempts to accomplish them. Both South Africa and Nigeria have used their military superiority in their respective regions to try to end ethnic conflicts and restore order. Egypt's military might allowed it to play a leading role in the Arab-Israeli conflict. Egypt's participation in the Gulf War was also extremely important. The stronger a country's military capabilities, the more likely it is to have broader national security interests. Without Egypt's willingness to fight Israel, the Arab countries were unable to confront Israel militarily. Iraq's dominant military position in the Gulf was a factor in its decision to invade and occupy Kuwait. But these countries' military capabilities are often constrained by the interests of major powers, international public opinion, and their relationships with the major countries.

Military capabilities shape a country's foreign policy.

In many cases, the foreign policies of developing countries are strongly influenced by the priorities of major countries and nonstate actors. Colombia, Mexico, and Jamaica, for example, have made fighting drug trafficking a major foreign policy objective, largely because the war on drugs is a primary interest of the United States. Human rights have become a major concern of many poor countries because of the influence of other countries and organizations such as Amnesty International. International groups and international public opinion often prevent countries from pursuing certain policies toward neighboring states. Due in part to international public opinion, Indonesia eventually granted East Timor its independence. South Africa not only abolished its system of apartheid, it also ended its policy of using military force to destabilize neighboring countries, partly because of international public opinion and the activities of various international

The priorities of other countries and nonstate actors shape foreign policies.

YOU DECIDE ✓ The War on Terrorism

The war on terrorism demonstrates that foreign policies of developing countries profoundly affect the security interests of the United States. The foreign relations of Pakistan, Afghanistan, Iran, Syria, Iraq, and various Persian Gulf countries became closely linked to America's concerns with global terrorism.

In your view, what can the United States do to ensure that developing countries' foreign policies contribute to its fight against terrorism?

organizations. The foreign policies of Afghanistan, for example, were widely perceived as being strongly influenced by Al Qaeda, a terrorist group based in Afghanistan and headed by Osama bin Laden.

cultural ties

Common values, family ties, and historical experiences shape foreign policy.

Cultural ties with other countries often help shape a country's foreign policy. Countries that share common values, beliefs, attitudes, and historical experiences tend to develop close relationships. These relationships are often cemented by family ties, cultural activities, and frequent interaction between people from the various countries. Mexico's relations with the United States, for example, are influenced by its cultural and family ties to America. These connections are strengthened as more Mexicans migrate to the United States. In the case of Cuba, the large Cuban American community in the United States not only helps determine American relations with Cuba but also influences Cuba's relationship with the United States. Strong cultural links between the Palestinians and the Arab countries play a role in those states' policies toward Israel and the United States. Cultural ties also influence how countries deal with problems that arise among them. The closer the countries are linked together by culture, the more likely they are to try to resolve their conflicts peacefully and to work together to achieve their foreign policy objectives. The greater the cultural differences among states, the more likely they are to resort to violence to settle disputes.[4]

When developing countries focus primarily on foreign affairs, they concentrate mostly on regional issues or broad international concerns, such as creating a New International Economic Order (NIEO) and international human rights. Within each region, there is usually a leading developing country that plays a dominant role. For example, Brazil and, to a lesser extent, Argentina are able to exercise considerable influence in relation to the other South American countries. Mexico's leadership in Central America remains strong. India's power in South Asia, although challenged by Pakistan, is recognized by states in the region. Nigeria, the most powerful country in West Africa, has used its military strength to end ethnic conflicts in Sierra Leone and Liberia. South Africa has long played the role of southern Africa's superpower, often with disastrous consequences for countries in the region. China, a leader in East Asia, is also a major power in the international community. Its large population, considerable resources, and economic growth are likely to enable it to eventually challenge the United States for global leadership. Finally, Egypt is the leading country in the Arab world. Its policies, especially in relation to the Palestinian-Israeli conflict, have had profound implications for broader Arab-Israeli relations.

As several chapters in this book have shown, developing countries are primarily concerned with economic issues. These concerns are reflected in their foreign policies.

Foreign policies of developing countries focus on economic issues.

Developing countries' foreign policies attempt to promote economic development by attracting foreign investments and international assistance. They also try to pursue policies that are designed to narrow the economic and technological gap between themselves and the developed countries. An important part of this effort is to gain access to the markets of rich countries for their primary and manufactured products. Many poor countries make sustainable development and protection of the environment foreign policy priorities. Costa Rica is an example of a country whose foreign policy is directly linked to conservation efforts. Developing countries' foreign policies also deal with debt relief and gaining access to and sharing water supplies. Many landlocked countries develop relations with their neighbors to gain access to the oceans. For much of the 1970s and 1980s, developing countries focused their foreign policy efforts on gaining control over fish, oil, and other resources in an exclusive economic zone that extended 200 miles from their coasts. They also attempted to control exploitation of resources beyond this area by using their numerical majority in the United Nations to declare the resources outside the economic zones "the common heritage of mankind." Finally, as we have seen, foreign policy in developing countries often involves dealing with ethnic conflicts, refugees, migration issues, famine, and humanitarian intervention.

Developing countries use several **foreign policy instruments** to influence others. The instruments of foreign policy that are available to any country depend on a particular country's capabilities. Rich counties have more resources to use to accomplish their foreign policies. Many developing countries often rely on military force and diplomacy to achieve their objectives. However, their military power is limited and can easily be neutralized by rich countries such as the United States and Britain. For example, Argentina's invasion of the Falkland Islands or Malvinas was ended by superior British forces. The relative military weakness of developing countries induces them to rely less on military power and more on diplomacy when dealing with other countries. During the Cold War, several developing countries allied themselves with either the Soviet Union or the United States. However, most poor countries opted for a **policy of nonalignment.** This meant that they were not formally allied with either the Soviet Union or the United States. Theoretically, they were independent of both superpowers. Under the leadership of Yugoslavia, India, Egypt, Ghana, and other developing countries, they formed the Nonaligned Movement. Another instrument of foreign policy used by developing countries is regional, political, and economic integration. Regional organizations and military alliances have also been formed by several countries to deal with external as well as domestic threats.

foreign policy instruments

A combination of military power, diplomacy, and economic might.

policy of nonalignment

Policy of not being formally allied with the United States or the Soviet Union during the Cold War.

THE DEVELOPING WORLD AND THE UNITED STATES

Relations between developing countries and the United States demonstrate the growth of global interdependence in world politics and economics. As the case study of Afghanistan shows, some developing countries' actions have significant implications for the United States. America's behavior is often even more consequential for poor countries. The United States' position as the world's leading economic, military, and political power draws it into the major foreign policies of developing countries. Increasing migration of people from the developing world to the United States reinforces U.S. concerns about poor societies. Poor countries as well as developed societies expect the United States to get involved in the affairs of other

America's position in the world draws it into the foreign policies of developing countries.

countries, especially when these countries' actions threaten global peace and stability or constitute gross violations of human rights. As the discussion of specific countries' foreign policies shows, the United States is often directly or indirectly involved in most regional conflicts. In many cases, the United States has intervened militarily to bring an end to conflicts or promote a specific national interest. Often, instead of using its own forces to restore stability to an area, the United States supplies countries with military and economic aid to enable them to protect themselves and maintain peace in the region.

Afghanistan: A Case Study

Al Qaeda

Terrorist group
headed by Osama
bin Laden.

On September 11, 2001, terrorists from the **Al Qaeda** organization, based in Afghanistan and headed by the Saudi Arabian exile Osama bin Laden, hijacked four American passenger jets loaded with fuel and used them as missiles to bomb the World Trade Center in New York and the Pentagon in Arlington, Virginia, just outside of Washington, D.C. The terrorists took flying lessons in the United States; relied on the Internet, telephones, and fax machines to communicate with each other; and, armed with box cutters, seized control of American planes to inflict the greatest damage the United States has experienced on its territory. Almost 3,000 people were killed; the World Trade Center and many other buildings were completely destroyed; the Pentagon was badly damaged; and the economy, already weak, was pushed into a recession. This attack on the United States demonstrated America's vulnerability to problems and violence in other parts of the world in an age of globalization. Conflicts in the developing world in which the United States is or has been involved, such as those in Iraq, Afghanistan, and the Middle East, are widely perceived in the developing world as factors contributing to terrorism against America. This attack and America's response to it also showed that the United States needs the cooperation of developed countries to achieve some of its foreign policy and national security objectives.

Afghanistan is one of the least developed countries in the world. One in every four children dies before the age of five; life expectancy is about forty-three years; only 12 percent of the population has access to clean drinking water; barely 30 percent of the men and 15 percent of the women are literate. Afghanistan's infrastructure has been almost completely destroyed by more than two decades of war, first against the occupation by the Soviet Union and then conflicts among various ethnic groups within the country. Afghanistan's population, estimated at 25 million, is made up of a

FIGURE 14.1 Afghanistan

large number of ethnic groups. These include the Pashtun (38 percent), Tajik (25 percent), Hazaral (19 percent), and Uzbek (6 percent). This ethnic diversity is reinforced by significant language barriers. Most of the population speaks Dari, an Afghan form of Persian. Others speak Pashto, or one of more than thirty different minor languages.

U.S. involvement in Afghanistan is an outgrowth of its interest in maintaining access to Persian Gulf oil and its commitment to containing communism in South Asia as well as the Middle East following World War II. Although America's main concern was its relationship with Pakistan, it provided financial assistance to Pakistan's neighbor, Afghanistan, to promote political stability and minimize the ability of the former Soviet Union to dominate Afghanistan or use it as a base from which it could spread communism to South Asia. When the Soviet Union invaded Afghanistan in 1979, the United States increased its support of Pakistan and implemented largely ineffective sanctions against the Soviet Union. The United States also gave military aid to Afghan resistance movements, known as the **Mujahedeen** (holy warriors), to strengthen resistance to Soviet occupation. America's Central Intelligence Agency (CIA) trained Islamic freedom fighters to resist the Soviets. Many of the leaders of the Taliban emerged from the Islamic freedom fighters. Muslims from other countries, including Osama bin Laden, went to Afghanistan to join the Mujahedeen. When the Soviet Union withdrew its troops in 1989, Afghanistan disintegrated into a civil war.

Mujahedeen
Holy warriors.

Pakistan, under Prime Minister Benazir Bhutto, supported the Taliban, enabling it to gain control of roughly 90 percent of Afghanistan. Osama bin Laden, the son of a Saudi Arabian construction magnate, opposed America's stationing of its troops in Saudi Arabia as well as the U.S.-led coalition that went to war in 1991 against Iraq to force it to end its military invasion of neighboring Kuwait. Due to opposition to the Saudi government, bin Laden was stripped of his Saudi citizenship and forced to go into exile, first in the Sudan and later (1996) in Afghanistan. In return for the safe haven provided by Afghanistan, bin Laden provided the Taliban with thousands of fighters and millions of dollars. Bin Laden eventually gained enough influence over the Taliban to allow him to transform Afghanistan into his own personal training center for global terrorists. America's war against terrorism began with the bombing of Afghanistan in October 2001. The U.S. invasion and occupation of Iraq were also linked to fighting terrorism. America found itself deeply engaged in the developing world. The United States' "global war on terrorism" made Iraq the focus of American foreign policy by 2006. The failure of U.S. policy in Iraq, Iran's growing power and its nuclear program, and growing violence in Palestine and Lebanon made the Middle East the focus of U.S. foriegn policy in 2007.

ECONOMIC GLOBALIZATION AND FOREIGN POLICIES

The Asian economic crisis, which began in late 1997, shows how developments in poor countries ultimately affect America's economy and its foreign policy. The United States decided to play the leading role in preventing the financial turmoil in Asia from spreading and creating serious political problems. Several parts of the U.S. economy were affected by the Asian crisis. American agricultural exports declined because Asian countries could not afford to purchase American beef, corn, pork, and other products.

devaluation of currency

Devaluation occurs when a country's currency loses monetary value and its people have to spend more money to purchase the same amounts of products.

Devaluation of the currencies of Thailand, the Philippines, South Korea, Malaysia, and Indonesia meant that U.S. farm products became too expensive to purchase. These countries had to spend more of their money to purchase the same amount of corn, beef, and pork. Livestock and poultry producers in Asia that imported feed grain from the United States were faced with higher costs as the exchange rates plummeted. Severe economic problems in these societies prevented producers from passing on increased costs to consumers, many of whom were unemployed. U.S. airlines were forced to cancel flights, reduce operations, lay off employees, cancel aircraft orders, and delay aircraft deliveries. The Asian crisis severely reduced the number of Asian tourists who visited the United States. As the U.S. dollar increased in value in relation to South Korea's won, Indonesia's rupiah, Thailand's baht, and the Philippine peso, it became more expensive for travelers from those countries to come to the United States. Hawaii, with an economy that is dependent on tourism, lost substantial revenues.[5]

The economic decisions of developing countries and the U.S. use of economic sanctions as an instrument of foreign policy have important consequences for American consumers. For example, when OPEC reduced oil production in early 2000, oil prices climbed from $10 to $30 a barrel. The war in Iraq, growing instability in the Middle East, and Hurricane Katrina helped to push the price of a barrel of oil above $70 in 2006. Soaring oil prices affected many areas of the U.S. economy and demonstrated the country's vulnerability to foreign policies of oil-exporting countries. Rising gasoline prices, which are the most visible prices in a society that depends on automobiles, became both an economic concern as well as a political issue.[6] Political leaders attempted to persuade the oil exporters to increase production in order to lower gasoline and heating oil prices. On the other hand, when Brazil exported low-priced steel to the United States, the Clinton administration imposed restrictions on steel imports. The lower steel prices, although beneficial to the consumer, were opposed by labor unions whose members' employment was threatened by cheaper steel imports from Brazil, South Korea, Japan, and Russia. The United States negotiated an agreement with Brazil that enabled Brazil to avoid tariffs of about 50 percent on its steel by "voluntarily" reducing steel exports to the United States. In 2007, the United States filed two complaints against China's trading policies with the World Trade Organization.

To achieve specific foreign policy objectives, the United States often imposes economic sanctions against other countries. For example, following the destruction of Pan Am Flight 103 over Lockerbie, Scotland, in 1988, the United States imposed sanctions against Libya for its alleged role in the bombing. Libya's leader, Muammar Qaddafi, was believed to be involved in a number of attacks against the United States and its allies. Although the sanctions hurt Libya, they were also costly for the United States. American policy toward Libya deprived American companies access to Libya. U.S. farmers, who were suffering from low grain prices, could not export grain to Libya. Boeing, based in Seattle, could not compete with **Airbus,** the European consortium, to sell Libya passenger jets.[7] These examples show how U.S. relations with developing countries affect American consumers and workers. In 2004, the United States lifted sanctions against Libya following Qaddafi's decision to abandon developing weapons of mass destruction and offer compensation to families of the Lockerbie tragedy. In 2006, America restored diplomatic relations with Libya.

Airbus

A European consortium that sold passenger jets to Libya.

CONFLICT AND COOPERATION AMONG DEVELOPING COUNTRIES

Relations among developing countries are characterized by both conflict and cooperation. Despite their many similarities, poor countries have many different interests and different approaches to achieving their foreign policy goals. Some developing states have closer relationships with European nations. Others are closer to the United States. Their geographic location, level of development, and degree of economic interdependence ultimately influence the extent to which they work together. Although poor countries emphasize international cooperation, they are far from being a unified group. There are many examples of conflict between poor countries. India and Pakistan, as we discuss later, have had hostile relations since they gained their independence from Britain in 1947. China and India have clashed over boundary disputes and ideological differences. In fact, China has supported Pakistan and Russia has sided with India. China fought Vietnam, after supporting North Vietnam during its war with the United States. Vietnam invaded Cambodia. Many poor countries in Asia are faced with direct or indirect threats from each other. Peru has a history of strained relations with Chile and a border dispute with Ecuador, which erupted into hostilities in early 1981. Guyana and Venezuela have clashed over a territorial dispute, despite efforts to settle the conflict peacefully. Chile has had a lengthy dispute with Argentina over the ownership of three islands in the Beagle Channel.

Territorial claims led to war between Ethiopia and Somalia in 1977. Both Ethiopia and Somalia claimed the Ogaden region, where many Somalis live. Although the boundaries drawn by Britain and Italy, the colonial powers in the region known as the Horn of Africa, were accepted by Ethiopia, Somalia persisted in claiming territory within the boundaries of Ethiopia. Boundary problems also caused military conflicts between Ethiopia and Eritrea. After losing a war that was designed to conquer Ethiopia, the defeated Italians managed to carve out a colony along the Red Sea, called it Eritrea, and governed it as a separate entity from 1890 until World War II. After Italy was defeated in World War II, **Haile Selassie,** Ethiopia's leader, attempted to annex Eritrea in order for Ethiopia to have access to the Red Sea and avoid being landlocked. By 1962, Ethiopia had succeeded in annexing Eritrea. This marked the beginning of the Ethiopian-Eritrean conflict.[8] After Eritrea gained its independence from Ethiopia in 1993, the two countries became allies. However, unresolved territorial disputes led to renewed conflict in 1998. In early 2000, Ethiopia faced massive starvation, but continued fighting with Eritrea. In 2007, Ethiopian forces invaded Somalia to support their allies in that country's civil war.

Haile Selassie
Ethiopia's leader.

Developing countries in the Middle East have also fought each other. Despite their many similarities, these countries have serious disagreements about territorial boundaries. There are also religious and ethnic differences between them. For example, although Iran and Iraq are both predominantly Islamic countries, they represent two different branches of Islam. Iran's population is largely Shi'ite, whereas Iraqis are Sunnites. Iraq is much more secular than Iran. Iraq's population is Arab and Iran's is Persian. Conflicting territorial claims along their 750-mile border led to war in 1980, when Saddam Hussein, Iraq's leader, invaded Iran. More than any other issue, Iraq's determination to maintain control over the Shatt al Arab waterway generated serious confrontation with Iran. Territorial disputes as well as Iraq's claim to all of Kuwait led to Iraq's invasion of Kuwait in 1990 and the Gulf War. The United States and West European states have been involved in most of the conflicts between developing countries.[9]

Conflicts among developing countries are generally overshadowed by the level of cooperation among them. Many poor countries attempted to maintain their newly won independence during the early days of the Cold War by joining the Nonaligned Movement, as discussed earlier. Because economic development is of paramount importance to developing countries, cooperation among them has focused on common needs such as access to export markets, higher prices for their products, and greater access to foreign investment and technology. Economic cooperation among poor countries, also known as South-South cooperation, grows out of the realization that they can enhance their chances to develop by pooling their limited resources and building political coalitions. As early as 1967 developing countries formed the **Group of 77** at the United Nations, which is now composed of about 133 countries, to promote South-South cooperation and to strengthen the bargaining position of poor countries in their negotiations with rich societies. Increased economic competition and globalization underscore the need for South-South cooperation. In early 2000, the leaders of the Group of 77 met in Havana, Cuba, to attend the South Summit. They discussed the implications of the globalization of the world economy, technology in developing countries, ways to increase cooperation among poor countries, and improving relations between the rich and poor societies. One of the most important efforts by developing countries to enhance their economic position vis-à-vis the industrialized world was their call in 1974 for a New International Economic Order (NIEO). The NIEO included demands for the following:

Group of 77
A political and economic coalition formed by developing countries.

The New International Economic Order was designed to enhance the economic position of poor countries.

1. A transfer of technology from rich countries to poor countries.
2. Greater access to rich countries' markets for manufactured products from the developing world.
3. Increased economic assistance for poor countries.
4. Higher and more stable prices for raw materials from developing countries.
5. A code of conduct for multinational corporations.
6. Greater voting power for poor countries in the International Monetary Fund (IMF), the World Bank, and other international institutions.

REGIONAL ECONOMIC AND POLITICAL INTEGRATION

Widespread destruction caused by World War II prompted European leaders to consider economic and political integration as part of their larger effort to create a lasting peace on the continent. The formation of the European Economic Community, established by the Treaty of Rome in 1957, brought European countries into an economic alliance that has also strengthened their political ties. As the Europeans moved closer to unification, other countries were also promoting economic and political integration as an essential component of economic development. NAFTA was created partly to enable the United States to counterbalance the growing economic power of the European Union (EU). Many poor countries were influenced to form regional economic groups by their close relationship with several European states during colonialism. The fall of communism and the spread of free markets

The Treaty of Rome fostered European economic and political integration.

as a path to economic development facilitate the growth of regional integration in the developing world. In this sense, regional integration is, in part, a product of globalization. Globalization influences poor countries to form trading blocs to avoid economic marginalization. A major goal of economic integration in the developing world is to achieve economies of scale. By combining their resources to build industries that serve a large number of people, poor countries not only lower prices for

Economies of scale deal with the relationship between output and costs.

their consumers, but also conserve more of their scarce resources. Economic integration is also perceived as a way of helping poor countries improve their bargaining power with respect to industrialized societies and to compete more effectively.[10]

An important component of economic integration in the developing world is the creation of **regional economic development banks,** which are modeled after the World Bank. Each region has its own bank. There is an African Development Bank, an Asian Development Bank, the Inter-American Development Bank, and a Caribbean Development Bank. They all share similar objectives, including providing capital to governments to stimulate economic development, promoting regional economic integration, and providing policy and technical assistance. Membership in these banks is not limited to developing countries. For example, the United States is a founding member of the Washington-based Inter-American Development Bank. Britain and Canada are members of the Caribbean Development Bank. These banks give poor countries access to vital financial resources. Like the World Bank, regional development banks raise money through the contributions of their members and by borrowing from international financial institutions.[11]

regional economic development banks
Regional banks and loan institutions that are modeled after the World Bank.

Regional economic and political integration is inseparable from international relations. OPEC is perhaps the best example of how developing countries have employed economic collaboration to achieve both economic development and greater political power in the international system. The Southern Cone Common Market (Mercosur), the Organization of American States (OAS), the African Union, the Association of South East Asian Nations (ASEAN), the League of Arab States, the Economic Community of West African States (ECOWAS), and the South Asian Association for Regional Cooperation (SAARC) share the common goals of economic development, political, cultural, and technological cooperation, and enhanced bargaining power in their relations with the industrial world.

The Organization of Petroleum Exporting Countries (OPEC) was created in response to the power of large oil companies in relation to oil-producing states. Until the mid-1950s, most of the world's petroleum was controlled by seven large

---

TAKING ACTION ➡ ## Energy Independence

The International Energy Agency estimated that there is sufficient petroleum to meet global demands for thirty years. Global economic development in general and China's rapid growth in particular contributed to the increased demand for petroleum. In 2004, oil prices rose to $55 a barrel, an increase of 70 percent.

What can be done to reduce America's dependence on oil?

Seven Sisters

The name given to seven large oil companies that controlled most of the world's oil until the mid-1950s.

OPEC

Formed in 1960 to counteract the power of the oil companies.

oil companies, known as the **Seven Sisters.** Five of them—Esso, Mobil, Standard of California, Gulf, and Texaco—were American companies, one (British Petroleum) was British, and one (Shell) was jointly owned by the British and the Dutch. The major oil-producing countries were extremely poor, despite the abundant supply of petroleum under their land. Few of them had the technical expertise to develop an oil industry on their own or to transport the oil to markets in societies that needed petroleum. Developing countries were completely dependent on the oil companies for the extraction, transportation, refining, marketing, and pricing of petroleum. Under agreements worked out between poor countries and oil companies, the oil companies owned the petroleum they found in the countries. The power of the Seven Sisters was reinforced by their practice of making decisions about petroleum together. In other words, the oil companies exercised monopoly power. Their behavior was inconsistent with the free market and economic competition. Oil-producing countries were clearly at a severe disadvantage under these circumstances.

Significant change in the relationship between the Seven Sisters and petroleum-producing states began to occur as these countries became more economically developed and as an educated elite began to grow. As part of their agreement with oil producers, the Seven Sisters provided technical training and education for a small number of citizens from oil states. Eventually, these educated citizens helped improve the bargaining power of their countries. Economic and educational progress gave these countries greater confidence to challenge the oil companies' dominance. The step toward the formation of OPEC took place when Iran and Venezuela participated in the first Arab Oil Congress in Cairo in early 1959. These two non-Arab countries strengthened the oil producer's opposition to price reductions (determined by the oil companies). They also initiated discussion about the possibility of creating an organization that would be composed of all oil-producing countries, not just the Arab states.[12] **OPEC** was formed in Baghdad, Iraq, in September 1960 by Iran, Iraq, Kuwait, Saudi Arabia, and Venezuela. Algeria, Indonesia, Libya, Nigeria, Qatar, and the United Arab Emirates joined OPEC in the late 1960s. Oil-producing countries such as Mexico and Norway, although not members of OPEC, work closely with the organization to prevent oil prices from falling too low.

The **Southern Cone Common Market** or the **South American Free Trade Area,** known as **Mercosur,** was formed by the Treaty of Asuncion in 1991. Composed of Brazil, Argentina, Uruguay, and Paraguay, Mercosur is the world's third largest trading bloc (Chile and Bolivia are associate members of Mercosur). The main objective of Mercosur is to reduce trade barriers among its members. Brazil and Argentina are by far the largest countries in Mercosur and also the most antagonistic toward each other. Brazil and Argentina fought a war against each other (1827), and as late as the 1980s Brazil was still constructing its railroads with wider tracks than Argentina's, to impede potential invaders. But just as Germany and France were able to overcome their historical antagonism to play a leading role in promoting European economic integration, Brazil and Argentina are downplaying their historic rivalry to further their economic development. Mercosur is cooperating with the European Union to build a counterweight to the U.S. global economic power. Historical ties between South America and Europe, especially Portugal, Spain, Britain, and Germany, are facilitating greater economic cooperation between the two regions.[13]

Mercosur

Economic bloc in South America.

The **Association of Southeast Asian Nations (ASEAN)** was founded in 1967 by Thailand, Indonesia, the Philippines, Malaysia, and Singapore. It now includes Brunei, Burma, Vietnam, and Laos. The major purpose of ASEAN is the promotion of economic, social, and cultural progress through international cooperation. Most of the members of ASEAN have achieved significant economic growth, especially when compared with countries in Latin America and Africa. Rapid economic development in Asia has influenced the growth of democratic movements. These forces of democracy believe that ASEAN members should move beyond their focus on economic development and concentrate on creating democratic societies. ASEAN has avoided dealing with political issues because its members believed in a policy of noninterference in each other's internal affairs. ASEAN was created during the Vietnam War, and the member countries were not only concerned about the spread of communism but also preoccupied with insurgencies and ethnic conflicts at home. Their emphasis on economic growth would have been undermined if they had attempted to address broader political issues. China, India, and Japan are determined to increase their involvement in ASEAN. Japan is generally admired by ASEAN for its economic success, its management strategies, and its advances in technology. However, ASEAN is also concerned about the likelihood of Japan becoming the dominant military power in the region, largely because of Japan's brutal treatment of many Asian countries during World War II.[14]

ASEAN

Founded in 1967 to promote economic and cultural cooperation in southeast Asia.

The **Organization of American States (OAS)** was established on April 30, 1948, in Bogota, Colombia. Composed of the Latin American countries, the Caribbean, the United States, and Canada, the OAS attempts to (1) promote solidarity among the member countries; (2) strengthen their collaboration and defend their independence and territorial integrity; (3) promote the economic, social, and cultural development of member states; and (4) work toward regional economic integration. The OAS, supported by funding from international organizations, deals with a wide range of issues. These include river basin management, biodiversity, conservation, planning for natural disasters, the removal of land mines, the prevention of drug trafficking, and addressing threats from international terrorism. The management of

OAS

Created in 1948 and composed of Latin American and Caribbean countries, the United States, and Canada.

natural resources and sustainable development are major concerns of the OAS. Because of the power of the United States, the OAS has focused on issues in which the United States is involved. The United States' relationship with Cuba, for example, has created division and tension within the OAS. The conflicts in Central America in the late 1970s and most of the 1980s, and the United States' handling of them, resulted in serious disagreements within the OAS. During the Falkland or Malvinas Islands crisis, the United States was perceived to have supported Britain against Argentina, a member of the OAS. Despite these tensions, the OAS has strengthened relations among the Latin American countries.

African countries relied primarily on the **Organization of African Unity (OAU)** to achieve many of their foreign policy objectives. Founded in Addis Ababa, Ethiopia, on May 25, 1963, the OAU committed itself to (1) promoting the unity and solidarity of the newly independent African countries, (2) coordinating the efforts of member states to improve the standard of living for Africans, (3) defending the independence and territorial integrity of African states, and (4) ending colonial rule and white minority rule in Africa. From its inception, the OAU formulated a general strategy for undermining white minority rule in southern Africa. This strategy contained three interrelated components. The first involved isolating South Africa and other countries ruled by a white minority on the African continent. The second part of the strategy called for mobilizing international support to isolate minority-ruled countries economically, politically, culturally, and militarily. The final component focused on assisting the armed struggle against minority rule in Africa by providing support for various groups or liberation movements that were resisting minority governments.[15] In 2002, the OAU was replaced with the **African Union,** which includes an emphasis on integrating Africa into the global economy. The African Union was primarily responsible for trying to prevent the spread of violence in Darfur in the Sudan in 2007.

> **OAU**
> Founded in 1963 to promote African solidarity and independence.

> **African Union**
> Replaced the OAU in 2002.

FOREIGN RELATIONS OF DEVELOPING COUNTRIES

A brief discussion of the foreign policies of specific developing countries shows that each region has at least one major country that attempts to influence developments in the area. Because the United States is a global power with global interests, major developing countries often find that their pursuit of their foreign policy objectives in their regions collides with the interests of the United States. Sometimes developing countries have the same interests as those of the United States and find it advantageous to cooperate with it. The policies of all the countries discussed—China, India, Egypt, Mexico, and Cuba—have implications for American foreign policy. Some countries, such as China and Mexico, are more important than others, such as Cuba and South Africa. However, the emotional intensity among Cuban Americans in relation to Fidel Castro helps exaggerate Cuba's significance in U.S. foreign policy.

China

The world's most populous country, China also has one of the world's oldest and greatest civilizations. China was the world's leading military and economic power many years ago, more than a century before Western Europe conquered much of Asia, Africa, and Latin America. China was severely weakened by internal divisions and foreign military interventions for much of its history. As a major economic power with nuclear weapons, and one of the five permanent members of the U.N. Security Council, China sees itself as a leading world power. With a population of 1.3 billion, China has attracted investments from around the world. China believes that it is entitled to the international respect and recognition that many major countries enjoy. This quest for international prominence and its growing demand for natural resources motivate China to establish relations with other developing countries and establish itself as a champion of world peace and justice.[16] By 2007, there were significant Chinese investments in Africa, the Middle East, Latin America, and Asia.

An overriding objective of China's foreign and domestic policies is the restoration of its dynastic borders. Unlike the European powers, which colonized much of Asia, Africa, and Latin America, China did not acquire overseas colonies. This historical fact strengthens China's determination not to give up any of its territory. In 1997, China regained control of Hong Kong, part of China that had been ruled by the British since 1842. Britain had occupied Hong Kong during the **Opium Wars** of 1839 to 1842, in which Britain fought China to maintain the lucrative British trade in opium. Preventing Taiwan's independence is one of the most important goals of China's foreign policy. China has systematically and vigorously opposed Taiwan's efforts to become an independent country. China warned the Taiwanese in early 2000 that if they elected Chen Shui-bian, who had advocated Taiwan's independence, such a development could provoke a war between Taiwan and China. Chen Shui-bian was elected. However,

Opium Wars
Britain fought China to maintain the lucrative British trade in opium (1839–1842).

Preventing Taiwan from gaining independence is a major goal of China's foreign policy.

he backed down on calls for Taiwan's independence and China backed away from its threat to invade Taiwan.[17] The possibility of war worried Asia as well as the United States. China also has territorial disputes with several countries over Mischief Reef, the Spratly Islands, and the Paracel Islands in the South China Sea. These islands are also claimed by the Philippines, Taiwan, Malaysia, Vietnam, and Brunei. Although China emphasizes economic cooperation with these countries, which are members of ASEAN, Chinese leaders are unwilling to compromise on the issue of sovereignty over areas believed to be part of China. Chinese ownership of these islands gives it access to valuable fishing grounds and oil and gas deposits. Conflict between China and other countries that claim the islands would undermine regional stability.[18] China is becoming increasingly assertive as it becomes stronger militarily and economically.

China's leaders view Chinese nationalism as an organizing principle of the country's domestic and foreign policies. China's nationalism is utilized to strengthen the increasingly uncertain legitimacy of the **Chinese Communist Party (CCP),** which controls the country. China's rapid economic growth and growing exposure to Western ideas and international developments have weakened communism. Nationalism is being used as an alternative to communism to unify the Chinese people. Conflict with Taiwan and Tibet is often used by the CCP to promote Chinese solidarity and a national sense of common purpose. Many Chinese perceive an independent Taiwan as posing a threat to their country's security.[19]

Chinese Communist Party
Controls China.

Mao Zedong

Founder of Chinese communism and leader of China.

China's relations with the United States are shaped, to a large extent, by China's adoption of communism under the leadership of **Mao Zedong** in 1949. China was allied with the United States against Japan and Germany during World War II. When the Communist forces defeated the Nationalists, led by Chiang Kai-Shek, the United States recognized the Nationalists, who retreated to Taiwan, as China's legitimate government. America's support of Taiwan was reinforced during the Korean conflict (1951–1953), the first major conflict of the Cold War. Communist North Korean troops invaded South Korea, which brought China and the United States into direct conflict in Asia. Although the United States insisted that Taiwan,

TABLE 14.1 CHRONOLOGY OF CHINA'S RELATIONS WITH THE UNITED STATES

Year	Major Developments
1949	Mao Zedong's Communist forces defeat Chiang Kai-Shek's Nationalists, who retreat to Taiwan. The United States recognizes the Nationalists as China's legitimate government.
1951–1953	The Korean War leads to conflicts between Chinese and American troops.
1954	The United States and Taiwan sign a mutual defense agreement.
1955–1970	American and Chinese ambassadors meet occasionally in Geneva, Switzerland, and in Warsaw, Poland.
1971	China's Prime Minister Zhou Enlai invites an American table tennis team to China. U.S. National Security Adviser Henry Kissinger makes a secret trip to China.
1971	China takes over Taiwan's U.N. seat, thereby reinforcing its view that it represented the Chinese nation.
1972	President Richard M. Nixon visits China. He signs the Shanghai Joint Communiqué, which declared that there is only one China and that Taiwan is part of China.
1979	China and the United States establish diplomatic relations. China's leader, Deng Xiaoping, visits the United States. Congress passes the Taiwan Relations Act, which reaffirmed America's commitment to Taiwan and its willingness to continue selling military weapons to Taiwan, despite opposition from China.
1982	The United States pledges not to increase arms sales to Taiwan.
1989	President George Bush visits China. Chinese troops fire on prodemocracy demonstration in Tiananmen Square. The United States imposes sanctions against China.
1992	President Bush approves the sale of F-16 fighter jets to Taiwan.
1993	President Bill Clinton links trading with China to human rights.
1994	President Clinton drops policy linking trade to human rights.
1997	China's President Jiang Zemin visits the United States.
1999	President Clinton visits China.
2000	The United States agrees to China's full membership in the World Trade Organization.
2001	U.S. spy plane is damaged by Chinese fighter jet and forced to land in China.
2001	President George W. Bush attends the APEC Summit in Shanghai.
2002	President George W. Bush discusses terrorism and trade in Beijing.
2004	Chinese Premier Wen Jiabo visits the United States. U.S. Secretary of State Colin Powell makes several trips to China to try to resolve the nuclear weapons dispute with North Korea.
2005	President George W. Bush visits China.
2006	Chinese President Hu Jintao visits the United States.

with less than 20 million people, represented China, it could not ignore the 1.2 billion people on mainland China.

President Richard M. Nixon and Henry Kissinger, the national security adviser, saw improved U.S. relations with China as a way of diminishing the power of the Soviet Union. They also wanted to pave the way for American companies to compete with the Japanese and the Europeans for markets in China. China's Prime Minister Zhou Enlai invited an American table tennis team to China in 1971, a development that was called **ping-pong diplomacy.** This was followed by a secret visit to China by Kissinger. With the support of the developing countries, the Soviet Union, and many European nations, China took over Taiwan's seat in the United Nations, thereby strengthening its claim as the legitimate representative of the Chinese people. President Nixon visited China in 1972 and signed the **Shanghai Joint Communiqué** with China, which declared that there is one China and that Taiwan is part of China. This was a major victory for China. This development paved the way for the establishment of diplomatic relations between China and the United States in 1979. But the passage of the **Taiwan Relations Act** by Congress in 1979 reaffirmed the U.S. commitment to Taiwan's security.

America's relations with Taiwan, and China's determination not to allow Taiwan to become independent, often lead to tensions between the United States and China. China's violations of human rights and its decision to use troops to crush prodemocracy demonstrations in Tiananmen Square in Beijing in 1989 further strained relations between the United States and China. In an effort to gain China's support for the U.S.-led coalition against terrorism following the attack on New York and Washington on September 11, 2001, America tried to improve its relations with China, and President George W. Bush went to China.

China's rapid economic development has generated an unprecedented demand for natural resources and access to overseas markets for its growing manufactured products. Given the expansion of China's middle class, urbanization, and greater reliance on automobiles, China's foreign policy is strongly influenced by its need for petroleum. In April 2006, President Hu Jintao stopped in Saudi Arabia, following his visit to the United States. Partly due to growing disenchantment with America, many Middle Eastern oil producers view China as an alternative to their reliance on the United States and have signed various agreements that strengthen cooperation with China in areas such as energy exploration, trade, and security. China has significant economic ties with several African countries, including the oil-producing states, such as Nigeria, Sudan, and Angola. China's foreign policy toward Asian countries is also changing. Instead of focusing on territorial claims, China stresses diplomacy, economic assistance, and trade to gain greater access to the region's resources. Of increasing concern to the United States is China's active growing involvement in Latin America. Latin America is now a significant source of raw materials. Furthermore, many Latin Americans perceive China as potential check on U.S. power in the region. China's rapid economic growth and its expanding economic ties with developing countries are widely seen as a direct challenge to American interests and global leadership.[20]

ping-pong diplomacy
A diplomatic initiative that sent an American ping-pong team to China in 1971.

Shanghai Joint Communiqué
A 1972 declaration of a single China.

Taiwan Relations Act
An act passed by Congress that reaffirmed the U.S. commitment to Taiwan's security.

India

The world's largest democracy and the second most populous country, India's foreign policies reflect its concerns with its positions as the leading country in South Asia and in the Nonaligned Movement. As one of the earliest countries in Asia and Africa to gain its independence after World War II, India perceived itself as a model for other developing countries that also experienced colonialism. India's early leaders believed that their country should play a prominent role in world politics, especially in relation to the developing nations and international organizations. India's geographical proximity to China and the Soviet Union, plus its strong commitment to democracy, complicated its foreign policy. On the one hand, India adopted many socialist economic policies and established close relations with the Soviet Union, partly to protect itself from China. On the other hand, despite its many economic and social problems, India remained a secular and democratic society. India's socialist policies and its ties to the Soviet Union created tensions in its relations with the United States. However, India and the United States shared a commitment to values that brought them together at a time when there were few democratic societies in the developing world.

Like other regional powers in the developing world, India has traditionally focused on the security of its area of the world, the South Asian subcontinent. In addition to strengthening its military power, which now includes nuclear weapons, India has attempted to consolidate its position in the region through cooperation with the neighboring states. India also realizes that only through cooperation with other countries can it reduce widespread poverty at home and in the region. The economic success of ASEAN is also a motivating factor in India's decision to promote regional

Leaders of India and Pakistan meeting to ease the tensions between the two nuclear powers.

Source: Chip East/Reuters/Corbis

cooperation. However, ongoing tensions between Pakistan and India, which have existed since the Indian subcontinent was partitioned to form India and Pakistan in 1947, makes cooperation difficult. Despite these problems, the **South Asian Association for Regional Cooperation (SAARC)** was formed in 1985. Composed of India, Pakistan, Sri Lanka, Bangladesh, Bhutan, Nepal, and the Maldives, the organization focuses on trade, development, and stability in order to overcome regional challenges of poverty, underdevelopment, low production levels, and over-population. Although the countries have moved closer toward regional economic integration, India's economic dominance has heightened Pakistan's fear that it will be at a competitive disadvantage. India views economic and political development as essential prerequisites for projecting its power beyond South Asia and for an enhanced international role.[21]

SAARC

Formed in 1985 to promote regional economic development in South Asia.

One of India's most important foreign policy achievements was its role in ending apartheid, or racial separation, in South Africa. India's interest in South Africa predates its own independence. In fact, the quest for racial equality in South Africa was connected to India's struggle for independence through the activities of **Mahatma Gandhi** in both countries. For more than twenty years Gandhi had attempted to influence the white minority government in South Africa to end discrimination against nonwhite South Africans, particularly those of Indian descent. Gandhi's strategy of nonviolence, which he used to achieve change in South Africa, was also used in India during his efforts to gain India's independence from Britain. Gandhi's pivotal role in India's fight for independence and the fact that Indians in South Africa were victims of discrimination influenced the Indian government to

Mahatma Gandhi

Used nonviolent strategies in both South Africa and India to effectuate change.

India played a leading role in ending apartheid.

initiate an international campaign to end apartheid. When the U.N. General Assembly met for the first time in October 1946, India, a self-governing territory within the British Empire, introduced the issue of the unjust treatment of Indians in South Africa. India's actions put the white minority government's racial practices on the international agenda. India continued to support efforts to end apartheid until 1994, when South Africans voted to end white minority rule. By championing a cause supported throughout the developing world, India strengthened its position in international relations and among the developing countries.[22]

More than any other issue, India's relations with Pakistan have dominated its foreign policy. The process by which India and Pakistan were created has shaped how the two countries deal with each other and the problems that keep them in a state of conflict. The violence that erupted between mostly Hindu India and Muslim Pakistan when both countries became independent had a profound impact on how they relate to each other. Central to the conflict between them is the issue of Kashmir. As Barry Bearak put it, "for a half century, India and Pakistan have fought over this land (Kashmir), sustaining a hatred so venomous as to rival any in the world. For each, possessing Kashmir is a matter of life and death, with both persistently willing to forsake the former for the latter."[23] However, by 2007 tensions had deescalated and several effects had been made to improve relations between India and Pakistan.

The Kashmir problem grows out of the partitioning of British India. Like India and Pakistan, Kashmir (also known as the princely state of Jammu and Kashmir) wanted to

Instrument of Accession

An agreement between India and the leader of Kashmir that gave India jurisdiction over Kashmir's external affairs, defense, and communications.

become a separate, independent country. However, the Hindu leader of Kashmir made an agreement with India in 1948 to protect Kashmir from invaders from Pakistan. The agreement, known as the **Instrument of Accession,** gave India jurisdiction over Kashmir's external affairs, defense, and communications. This agreement was to be voted on by the people of Kashmir, but Kashmir's ethnic and religious diversity created a problem. Muslims, Hindus, Sikhs, and Buddhists dominate different parts of Kashmir. India's first prime minister, Jawahar Lal Nehru, believed that Kashmir's future should be determined by the majority. However, Pakistan invaded Kashmir before the Kashmiris were allowed to vote on the future of their territory. This invasion led to the first war between India and Pakistan. The U.N. Security Council called for the withdrawal of Pakistan's troops, to be followed by an election that would allow Kashmiris to decide their future. India and Pakistan refused to give up the territory they controlled. Roughly two-thirds of Kashmir is controlled by India, one-third by Pakistan, and a small area (known as Aksia Chin) is claimed by China. Both India and Pakistan have stationed troops along the "line of control," which divides Kashmir into Pakistani and Indian sections. Tensions along the line of control remain high. India and Pakistan have fought three wars over Kashmir. Both countries view Kashmir as part of their own territory. China continues to maintain control over its part of Kashmir.[24]

Conflict over Kashmir has heightened the insecurity of both Pakistan and India. Their fears motivated both countries to acquire nuclear weapons in 1998. Pakistan, with about 140 million people, faces India, which has more than a billion people. India

Both India and Pakistan have nuclear weapons.

has always had the stronger military. In fact, in 1971, India supported a nationalist, separatist movement that eventually severed East Pakistan from West Pakistan to create the independent country of Bangladesh.

Given the unwillingness of India and Pakistan to engage in sustained negotiations over problems that have lasted more than fifty years, a nuclear arms race between them is extremely dangerous. The United States imposed economic sanctions against India and Pakistan in 1998 to persuade them not to engage in nuclear proliferation. These sanctions were lifted in 2001 as a part of America's effort to build a global coalition against terrorism. India accused the United States, the leading nuclear power, of hypocrisy. India believes that its security can only be protected either by global nuclear disarmament or by the exercise of the principle of equal and legitimate security for all countries.[25] America's concerns about nuclear proliferation on the Indian subcontinent may have influenced President Bill Clinton to visit India, Pakistan, and Bangladesh in March 2000. Clinton urged closer economic and technological cooperation between India and the United States, focusing on finding ways to encourage Indian Americans, who had more than 750 companies in the Silicon Valley, to help develop India's growing software industry.

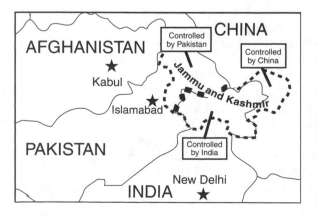

FIGURE 14.2 Kashmir

Technological development and global trade are seen as essential components of efforts to deal with hunger, disease, pollution, and other problems in India. In 2006, President George W. Bush also attempted to consolidate relations between India and the United States. During his visit to India, President Bush signed an agreement that gave India greater access to U.S. nuclear technology. This agreement was opposed by Pakistan as well as by countries and groups concerned about nuclear proliferation. In 2007, India successfully fired its first Agni III missile, capable of carrying nuclear war heads across the Middle East and to major cities in China.[26]

Egypt

Like China, Egypt sees itself within the broader context of its powerful ancient civilization. The most populous Arab state, Egypt has historically been the dominant power in the Arab world. Egypt's foreign policy is influenced by its self-perception as the unchallenged leader of the Arabs. It is also shaped by widespread poverty, overpopulation, high rates of unemployment, and the Arab-Israeli conflict. Geography has profoundly affected Egypt's relations with other countries. It lacks a large amount of arable land. About 96 percent of the population lives on 5 percent of its land. With a population that has grown by about 380 percent since 1900 and cultivated land that has expanded by only about 25 percent in the same period, Egypt is forced to look to other countries for employment opportunities for its citizens.[27] Egypt's serious economic problems also play a role in its relations with the United States, which is the primary source of Egypt's foreign assistance.

Egypt attempted to promote cultural and economic cooperation among Arabs by forming the **Arab League** in 1945. The influx of large numbers of Jews into Palestine, largely to escape the horrors of the Holocaust in Germany and elsewhere in Europe, prompted Egypt to coordinate Arab efforts to prevent the establishment of a Jewish state in Palestine. The creation of Israel in 1948 led to the first war between the Arabs and the Israelis. As leader of the Arab League, Egypt was influential in determining the Arab response to Israel. In fact, given Egypt's military power and its geographic proximity to Israel, the other Arab countries depended on Egypt's support to carry out their own policies against Israel. Israel's seizure of Egyptian and Syrian territory during the **Six Day War** in 1967 strengthened Arab opposition to Israel. When Israeli forces took Gaza and the West Bank from the Palestinians, the city of Jerusalem and other holy places of great significance to Jews, Muslims, and Christians came under Jewish control. Arab nationalism increased after the Six Day War, and countries such as Saudi Arabia, Iraq, Kuwait, Syria, and Jordan saw Egypt as an indispensable ally in their struggle against Israel. The Six Day War also brought the Middle East into the broader rivalry between the United States and the Soviet Union. Egypt grew closer to the Soviet Union. Israel gained increased support from the United States.[28] The Arab attack on Israel in 1973 led to a closer alliance between Egypt and the other Arab countries. The Arabs imposed an oil embargo against the United States and other supporters of Israel, which quadrupled the price of petroleum.

Egypt's leader, **Anwar Sadat,** believed that the cost of war with Israel was too high, despite the support Egypt received from the Arab world. In 1977, Sadat took the

Arab League

An organization that was created to promote cultural and economic cooperation.

Six Day War

Israel seized Arab territories in 1967.

Anwar Sadat

Egyptian leader who made peace with Israel.

Knesset

The Israeli parliament.

Camp David Accords

An agreement between Egypt and Israel that ended their hostilities and granted the return of seized Egyptian land.

risky step of visiting Israel and addressing the **Knesset,** the Israeli parliament. With the strong support of President Jimmy Carter, Sadat and Menachem Begin, Israel's prime minister, met at Camp David in Maryland to negotiate an end to the conflict between their two countries. Egypt and Israel signed the **Camp David Accords** in 1978, which ended hostilities between them and provided for the return of Egyptian land seized by Israel. But peace between Egypt and Israel did not end the Palestinian-Israeli conflict and the broader Arab-Israeli dispute. Egypt's actions led to its temporary expulsion from the Arab League, which moved its headquarters from Cairo, Egypt, to Tunis, Tunisia. The withdrawal of Arab financial support was offset by a large amount of foreign aid that Egypt received from the United States for making peace with Israel.

Progress in negotiations between the Palestinians and the Israelis culminated in the Palestine Liberation Organization's recognition of Israel in 1993. This development helped strengthen Egypt's position in the Arab world. Egypt had continued to work for a negotiated settlement of the Arab-Israeli conflict even after it got its territory back from Israel. The main development that helped restore Egypt's position as leader of the Arab world was Iraq's occupation of Kuwait and the Gulf War. Egypt committed troops to defend Saudi Arabia and the Gulf States from Iraq and to end Iraq's occupation of Kuwait. Conflict in the Gulf had a devastating economic impact on Egypt. Hundreds of thousands of Egyptians lost their jobs in Iraq and Kuwait. However, Egypt's support of Saudi Arabia as well as its willingness to protect Libya from what many Arabs saw as unfair treatment by Western countries enhanced Egypt's position. The Egyptian workforce in Saudi Arabia, the Gulf, and Libya increased dramatically.[29] Like other developing countries, Egypt regards economic development as a main objective of its foreign policy. By returning to the Arab world, making peace with Israel, supporting Arab causes, and working with the United States, Egypt has moved toward achieving that goal.

Mexico

History and geography have shaped Mexico's foreign relations. Mexico's relative weakness and the United States' strength have created a lopsided and unequal relationship between them. As discussed in Chapter 13, Mexico's geographical proximity to the United States brought it into conflict as well as cooperation with its northern neighbor. The United States used its superior strength not only to prevent Mexico from posing a security threat but also to take a large part of Mexico's territory. The power of the United States is a constant reminder to Mexico of its own weakness. Although Mexico is forced to pay attention to the United States, Mexico is often ignored by the United States on many issues. Nonetheless, the geographical proximity of the two countries has contributed to the development of an interdependent relationship between them. On the other hand, the unequal relationship between the two countries has heightened Mexican nationalism and influenced Mexico to adopt foreign policies that are sometimes in conflict with U.S. foreign policies, partly to demonstrate its independence and sense of identity.[30] For example, Mexico strongly opposed America's decision to invade Iraq in 2003. President George Bush's visit to Mexico in 2007 generated widespread protests.

Mexico's desire to play a greater role in world politics has often complicated U.S. policy in Latin America. For example, despite disagreements with Cuba's leader, Fidel Castro, Mexico has not supported the United States' attempts to isolate Cuba. Instead, Mexico agreed not to ostracize Cuba in exchange for Cuba's nonintervention in Mexican affairs. Major steps toward Mexico's more assertive foreign policy were taken by President Luis Echeverria (1970–1976). Mexico strongly supported the developing countries in their effort to create a New International Economic Order (NIEO). To project its power beyond the region, Mexico decided to build closer relations with the other Latin American countries and emphasize its commitment to a policy of nonalignment in international affairs. One of the major differences between the United States and Mexico arose concerning the conflict in Central America in the 1980s. The United States stressed the need for military force to counter Soviet-Cuban activities in the region, whereas Mexico focused on a negotiated settlement. Under Mexico's leadership, Panama, Colombia, and Venezuela formed the **Contadora Group** in January 1983 to find a peaceful solution to the conflicts in Nicaragua, El Salvador, and Honduras. Mexico was concerned about the growing militarization of Central America and U.S. policies that it believed would eventually threaten Mexico itself. Despite its reservations, the United States supported the Contadora peace process.[31]

As a developing society, Mexico has concentrated on economic development in its relations with other countries, especially United States. By signing NAFTA in 1993, under the leadership of Carlos Salinas de Gortari, Mexico consolidated its economic relationship with the United States. Most of Mexico's exports go to the United States. In fact, Mexico is one of the United States' leading trading partners. But this dependence on the United States has influenced Mexico to find ways to diversify its commercial and political partnerships. One of the most important foreign policy initiatives taken by President Ernesto Zedillo was his decision to pursue a free-trade agreement with the European Union to reduce Mexico's economic dependence on America. Despite Mexico's geographic proximity to the United States, many Mexican leaders perceive European economic and social policies as being similar to their own.

Mexico's relations with the United States, as discussed in Chapter 13, have concentrated on immigration issues. The influx of Mexicans into the United States brought the two countries closer together economically and culturally. Just as important as immigration issues is the problem of drug trafficking. Drug smugglers take advantage of Mexico's proximity to the United States, the world's largest market for illegal drugs. Drug trafficking has created serious tensions in U.S.-Mexican relations. Many American politicians blame Mexico for America's drug problems. The **war on drugs,** launched by President Ronald Reagan in the early 1980s, aims at reducing the importation of drugs in an effort to solve the drug problem. The United States concentrates on diminishing supplies as the solution,

Contadora Group

A group formed in 1983 to find a peaceful solution to the conflicts in Nicaragua, El Salvador, and Honduras.

war on drugs

Launched by President Ronald Reagan to keep illegal drugs out of the United States.

FIGURE 14.3 Latin America

N IN THE EWS

Carter's Visit to Cuba

Former president Jimmy Carter made a historic visit to Cuba in May 2002. He is the first U.S. president to

visit the island since Fidel Castro came to power in 1959. He addressed the issue of human rights in Cuba and called for the end of the U.S. embargo against Cuba.

Source: David Gonzalez, "Cuban Dissidents Put Hope in a Petition and Jimmy Carter," *The New York Times,* 14 May 2002, A3.

but Mexico emphasizes reducing the demand for illegal drugs in the United States as the best way to eliminate drug trafficking. In 2006, Mexico proposed legalizing the use of small quantities of certain drugs. However, this idea was abandoned, partly due to U.S. opposition. Although Mexico cooperates with the United States to solve the drug problem, it is concerned about the implications of America's war on drugs for Mexico's sovereignty.[32] Mexico experienced a growing drug problem and escalating violence connected to drugs in 2007.

Cuba

The dispute over the fate of a little Cuban boy, Elian Gonzalez, in early 2000 encapsulated broader issues in Cuban foreign policy in general, and with the United States in particular. Cuban Americans in Miami have influenced U.S. policy toward Cuba since Fidel Castro seized power in 1959. The dispute about whether Elian should stay in the United States with his Cuban American relatives in Miami or be reunited with his father, half-brother, stepmother, and other relatives and friends in Cuba was more about U.S.-Cuban relations than about Elian. Cuba's adoption of communism and its close alliance with the Soviet Union created strong anti-Castro feelings in the United States. American foreign policy toward Cuba aimed at ending communism in that country. Cuba's decision to send more than 25,000 troops to Angola to support the Popular Movement for the Liberation of Angola against groups that were backed by the United States hardened American opposition to Cuba. Working closely with the Soviet Union, America's enemy during the Cold War, Cuba became militarily involved in Ethiopia, Central America, and the Caribbean, areas in which the United States had significant interests and military involvement.

From the beginning, in 1962, the United States imposed sanctions against Cuba to induce political and economic change. Many European countries and Canada, close allies of the United States, believed that isolating Cuba was counterproductive. They established diplomatic relations with Cuba and refused to participate in economic sanctions against it. In response, the United States passed the **Helms-Burton law,** which provides for American sanctions against any foreign companies deemed to be using property that U.S. citizens claim was confiscated from them by the Cuban

Helms-Burton law
A law that called for American sanctions against foreign companies deemed to be using property U.S. citizens claimed was confiscated by Cuba.

government. Cuba's foreign policies during the Cold War concentrated on counter-ing American efforts to isolate Cuba diplomatically, especially in Latin America. Cuba also wanted to play a leadership role in the developing world. This was accom-plished by supporting the Nonaligned Movement, calls for the establishment of a New International Economic Order, educational and technical assistance to Caribbean countries such as Grenada and Jamaica, and military support for libera-tion groups in southern Africa and Central America. Cuba's foreign policy objectives changed with the end of the Cold War. Its major foreign policy goals include attract-ing foreign investment to the island, building international support against American sanctions, and implementing economic reforms that would allow it to play a greater role in the regional and global economy. Similar to China, Cuba is attempting to join the world economy even while it maintains its communist system of government. The strong anti-Americanism of President Hugo Chavez of Venezuela, the election of Evo Morales as Bolivia's president in 2006, and a general turn toward the left in Latin America enhanced Castro's role and facilitated the achievement of Cuba's for-eign policy objectives in the region.[33]

Summary and Review

As globalization increases, the fate of rich countries is increasingly linked to that of poor countries, to varying degrees. Although much of the discussion of foreign pol-icy and international relations is focused on developed countries, especially the United States and members of the European Union, foreign relations are also extremely important to many developing countries. The poverty of developing countries heightens their vulnerability to events beyond their borders, events over which they have relatively little control. Foreign policy making is essentially deci-sion making by countries about their national interests. It involves setting priorities and deciding how to accomplish them. In a general sense, foreign policy deals with efforts on the part of one country to influence the behavior and attitudes of other countries, nongovernmental organizations, transnational actors, and international institutions. The foreign policies of developing countries are expressions of what governments, groups, and individuals determine to be national interests. The for-eign policies of developing countries are influenced by many factors, including (1) the country's geographical location, (2) the level of economic development of the country, (3) the nature of the country's political system and the quality of its leader-ship, (4) the military capabilities of the country, (5) the nature of international public opinion and the priorities of major countries and nonstate actors, and (6) cultural ties with other countries. Despite many similarities among poor countries and their efforts to work together, each region has at least one major country that attempts to influence developments in the area. Because America is a global power with global interests, major developing countries often find that their pursuit of their foreign policy objectives in their regions collides with the interests of the United States.

Key Terms

international
relations   303
Peace of Westphalia
303
national interests   303
Nonaligned
Movement   307
New International
Economic Order
(NIEO)   312
Group of 77   312
Treaty of Rome (1957)
312
economies of
scale   313

regional economic
development
banks   313
Seven Sisters   314
Organization of
Petroleum
Exporting Countries
(OPEC)   314
Southern Cone
Common Market
or the South
American Free
Trade Area
(Mercosur)   315

Association of South
East Asian Nations
(ASEAN)   315
Organization of
American States
(OAS)   315
Opium War   317
ping-pong diplomacy
319
Shanghai Joint
Communiqué   319
Taiwan Relations
Act   319
South Asian
Association for

Regional
Cooperation
(SAARC)   321
Kashmir   321
Instrument of
Accession   322
Arab League   323
Six Day War   323
Camp David Accords
(1978)   324
Contadora Group
325
Helms-Burton
law   327

Discussion Questions

1. As globalizing trends and bureaucratic governmental failure in the developing world render
the nation-state to an ever shrinking role in
human affairs, what actors or alignments have
emerged to fill the void left by decreasing state
power?
2. How do regional organizations fit into the
emergence of globalization? Are they beneficial or harmful to globalization? Explain.
3. Explain some ways that the developed world
ultimately determines the economic disposi-
tion of the developing world.
4. How has the traditional concept of "national
interest" been redefined under the emerging
world order of globalization?

5. How does a country's political system shape its
foreign policy?
6. Is military capability as important for a country today as it was during the Cold War? Why
or why not?
7. What impact has the Six Day War had on
Arab-Israeli relations?
8. What are the reasons underlying India and
Pakistan's dispute over Kashmir? Are the two
sides' aims irreconcilable, or can they mutual-
ly benefit from a peaceful resolution? Explain.
9. Do sanctions ever achieve peaceful political
aims, or are they just another form of coercion
that prolongs conflict and poverty?

Suggested Readings

Bajpai, K. Shankar. "Untangling India and Pakistan."
Foreign Affairs 82, no. 3 (May/June 2003): 112–27.

Cordesman, Anthony H. *The Iraq War*. Westport, CT:
Praeger, 2003.

Evans, H. David, and David Greenaway, eds. *Developing
Countries and the International Economy: Issues in
Trade, Adjustment, and Debt*. Portland, OR: F. Cass,
1991.

Feher, Michel. *Powerless by Design: The Age of the International Community*. Durham, NC: Duke University Press, 2000.

Fukuyama, Francis, ed. *Nation-Building: Beyond Afghanistan and Iraq*. Baltimore, MD: The Johns Hopkins University Press, 2006.

Hakim, Peter. "Is Washington Losing Latin America?" *Foreign Affairs* 85, no. 1 (January/February 2006): 39–53.

Jervis, Robert. *American Foreign Policy in a New Era*. New York: Routledge, 2006.

Korany, Bahgat, with contributors. *How Foreign Policy Decisions Are Made in the Third World: A Comparative Analysis*. Boulder, CO: Westview Press, 1986.

Lopez, George A., and David Cortright. "Containing Iraqi Sanctions Worked." *Foreign Affairs* 83, no. 4 (July/August 2004): 90–103.

Shifter, Michael. "Breakdown in the Andes." *Foreign Affairs* 83, no. 5 (September/October 2004): 126–38.

Swaine, Michael D. "Trouble in Taiwan." *Foreign Affairs* 83, no. 2 (March/April 2004): 39–49.

Zartman, I. William, and Victor A. Kremenyuk, eds. *Cooperative Security: Reducing Third World Wars*. Syracuse, NY: Syracuse University Press, 1995.

Zweig David and Bi Jianhai, "China's Global Hunt for Energy," *Foreign Affairs* 84, no. 5 (September/October 2005): 25–38.

Addresses and Websites

Council on Foreign Relations

The Harold Pratt House
58 East 68th Street
New York, NY 10021
Tel: (212) 434–9400
Fax: (212) 434–9800
http://www.cfr.org/p/

The Council on Foreign Relations, established in 1921, is a research center, publisher, and organization of foreign relations and foreign policy. The group's main goal is to educate Americans on the world and American foreign policy. The Council hopes to strengthen people's knowledge of global affairs while helping create stronger leaders for tomorrow. This website offers various information about global issues and issues in all regions of the world. It provides a wide variety of links on topics such as human rights, peacekeeping, culture and religion, and globalization. The website also offers a media center that houses information on numerous international issues.

Organization of African Unity

Headquarters
P.O. Box 3243
Addis Ababa, Ethiopia
Tel: 11 (251) (1) 51 7700
Fax: 11 (251) (1) 51 2622
http://www.oau-oua.org/

This is the website of the Organization for African Unity (OAU). The OAU, which was formed in 1963, was created to promote Pan-African solidarity and unity. The organization looks to increasing human rights; ridding the region of colonialism and its legacies; and promoting economic, health, and general welfare. The website offers detailed information about the OAU, including a look at the various arms and different treaties and documents of the organization.

Organization of American States

Headquarters
17th St. & Constitution Ave., NW
Washington, DC 20006
Tel: (202) 458–3000
http://www.oas.org

This is the official website of the Organization of American States (OAS). The organization was founded in 1948 to promote unity amongst nations in North and South America. The OAS currently has thirty-four member-states, which work in cooperation for solidarity, security, and regional affairs. This website offers in-depth details regarding the organization and provides information about the current issues before the OAS, as well as contact information for its member-states.

http://www.un.org/

This website takes you to the Internet home of the United Nations, the international governing structure in which many nations participate. The United Nations offers statistics and other useful information about various issues in countries. There are also numerous U.N. councils and programs, and information regarding them can be located on the site. This link is also an excellent source of information on international law and international affairs.

Notes

1. Richard J. Payne, *The Third World and South Africa* (Westport, CT: Greenwood Press, 1992), 3.
2. Donald Nuechterlein, *America Overcommitted: U.S. National Interests in the 1980s* (Lexington: University of Kentucky Press, 1985), 10; and Richard J. Payne, *The Nonsuperpowers and South Africa* (Bloomington: Indiana University Press, 1990), 3.
3. Charles W. Kegley and Eugene R. Wittkoff, *World Politics* (New York: St. Martin's Press, 1997), 45.
4. Richard J. Payne, *The Clash with Distant Cultures: Values, Interests, and Force in American Foreign Policy* (Albany: State University of New York Press, 1995), XVI.
5. John Schmeltzer, "Asia's Travail Trips Up Travel," *Chicago Tribune*, 11 January 1998, sect. 5, 1.
6. Douglas Jehl, "As Oil Prices Explode, What's Next? Voters?" *The New York Times*, 19 March 2000, sect. 4, 1.
7. Adam Zagorin, "Why Libya Wants In," *Time*, 27 March 2000, 66.
8. Richard J. Payne, *Opportunities and Dangers of Soviet-Cuban Expansion* (Albany: State University of New York Press, 1988), 29.
9. Richard J. Payne, *The West European Allies, The Third World, and U.S. Foreign Policy* (New York: Praeger, 1991), 122.
10. James Lee Ray, *Global Politics* (Boston: Houghton Mifflin Company, 1998), 380.
11. Paula Hoy, *Players and Issues in International Aid* (West Hartford, CT: Kumarian Press, 1998), 63; and Peter Isard et al., eds. *The Macromanagement of Foreign Aid* (Washington, D.C.: International Monetary Fund, 2006).
12. Shireen Hunter, *OPEC and the Third World* (Bloomington: Indiana University Press, 1984).
13. Matt Moffett and Craig Torres, "Brazil and Argentina, Long Rivals, Move Closer," *The Wall Street Journal*, 12 November 1998, A25; and Larry Rohter, "Latin America and Europe to Talk Trade," *The New York Times*, 26 June 1999, B2.
14. Peter Eng, "Transforming ASEAN," *The Washington Quarterly* 22, no. 1 (Winter 1999): 64; Ruth Taplin, "Japan's Foreign Policy Towards Southeast Asia," in Richard L. Grant, ed., *The Process of Japanese Foreign Policy* (London: The Royal Institute for International Affairs, 1997), 99; and Jane Perlez, "Southeast Asian Nations Meet to Tighten Economic Bonds," *The New York Times*, 6 October 2003, A4.
15. Payne, *The Third World and South Africa*, 25.
16. Richard J. Payne and Cassandra R. Veney, "China's Post-Cold War African Policy," *Asian Survey* 38, no. 9 (September 1998): 868.
17. Erik Eckholm, "Vote Is Likely to Raise Tension With China," *The New York Times*, 19 March 2000, A1.
18. Ian James Storey, "Creeping Assertiveness: China, the Philippines, and the South China Sea Dispute," *Contemporary Southeast Asia* 21, no. 1 (April 1999): 96.
19. Robert S. Ross, "Beijing as a Conservative Power," *Foreign Affairs* 76, no. 2 (March–April 1997): 39.
20. Hassan Fatah, "Chinese Leader Increases Trade with Saudi Arabia," *The New York Times*, 23 April 2006, A12; David Zweig and Bi Jianhai, "China's Global Search for Energy," *Foreign Affairs* 84, no. 5 (September/October 2005), 25; and Peter Hakim, "Is Washington Losing Latin America?" *Foreign Affairs* 85, no. 1 (January/February 2006), 45.
21. Payne, *The Third World and South Africa*, 67.
22. Payne, *The Third World and South Africa*, 66.
23. Barry Bearak, "Kashmir a Crushed Jewel Caught in a Vise of Hatred," *The New York Times*, 12 August 1999, A1.
24. Victoria Schofield, *Kashmir in the Crossfire* (London: I. B. Tauris, 1996), 3; and Brooke Unger, "The Economist Survey of India and Pakistan," *The Economist*, 22 May 1999, 9–11.
25. Jaswant Singh, "Against Nuclear Apartheid," *Foreign Affairs* 77, no. 5 (September/October 1998): 41; and Dennis Kux, *India-Pakistan Negotiations* (Washington, D.C.: U.S. Institute of Peace, 2006).
26. Nattali Bendavid, "Clinton Ends India Visit With High-tech Talk," *Chicago Tribune*, 26 March 2000, Sect. 1, 4; and "India: Tested Missile Can Hit China," *The New York Times*, 13 April 2007, A7.
27. Gregory L. Aftandilian, *Egypt's Bid for Arab Leadership* (New York: Council on Foreign Relations, 1993), 46.
28. Payne, *The West European Allies*, 79.
29. Aftandilian, *Egypt's Bid*, 54.
30. Roderic Camp, *Politics in Mexico* (New York: Oxford University Press, 1996), 195.
31. Payne, *Opportunities and Dangers*, 108.
32. Peter H. Smith, "Drug Trafficking in Mexico," in Barry Bosworth, et al., eds., *Coming Together? Mexico-United States Relations* (Washington, D.C.: Brookings Institution Press, 1997), 141.
33. Javier Corrales, "Hugo Boss," *Foreign Policy* 152 (January/February 2006), 32–33; and Juan Forero, "U.S. Aid Can't Win Bolivia's Love as New Suitors Emerge," *The New York Times*, 14 May 2006, A4.

Abacha, Sani   General and military ruler of Nigeria from 1993 to 1998. He ruled the nation with an iron fist, and during his reign the country was full of corruption and mismanagement. Political opponents were imprisoned, exiled, or killed; the constitution was discarded; and violations of civil and human rights became commonplace. He died in 1998 of a heart attack.

abed   Term used in the Sudan that is synonymous with the term *slave*.

absolute monarchy   A monarchy where the monarch has absolute power.

Abubakar, Abdulsalam   A general, commander of the country's armed forces, and defense minister, Abubakar became the leader of Nigeria after Abacha's death. He began a process to return the country to civilian rule, allowed exiles to return to the country, and released many political prisoners.

access   The ability to reach the government, politicians, and governmental structures and subsequently have influence on them.

African National Congress (ANC)   Brought about an end to apartheid in South Africa.

African Union   Replaced the Organization of African Unity in 2002.

Agrarian Reform Act of Egypt   Limited land ownership and redistributed Egyptian land among the peasants.

Airbus   The European consortium that had greater economic success than Seattle's Boeing because of its sales of passenger jets to Libya.

Algerian National Liberation Front (FLN)   Created in Algeria in 1954 with the stated objectives of achieving independence from the French and establishing a democratic and socialist state.

Allende, Salvador   The leader of the Popular Unity Coalition, who won the election for the Chilean presidency in 1970. He pursued a socialist policy designed to redistribute the wealth of the nation. Salvador Allende died in a military coup d'état, led by Augusto Pinochet on September 11, 1973.

Al Qaeda   The Islamist terrorist group headed by Osama bin Laden that claimed responsibility for attacking the Pentagon and the World Trade Towers on September 11, 2001. Al Qaeda has claimed credit for various other attacks in Spain, Saudi Arabia, and Iraq.

al-Wahhab, Abd   An eighteenth-century religious scholar who made an alliance with Muhammad ibn Saud for mutual protection. This union began the formation of the modern Saudi Arabian state.

American Colonization Society   Organization in the United States designed to "return" enslaved Americans to Africa. The first group of freed American slaves landed in Liberia.

Americo-Liberians   American settlers of Liberia who were former slaves and who practiced discrimination against the native Liberian Africans.

Amnesty International   One of the best-known human rights groups. Founded in London in 1961 by a group of writers and lawyers, it publicizes human rights abuses in different countries and encourages its members around the world to participate in letter-writing campaigns to seek the release of prisoners of conscience.

animists   People who worship animals, stones, plants, and other objects.

apartheid   A system of legal racial separation and inequality in South Africa, implemented in 1948 and overthrown in 1991.

Aquino, Benigno   A journalist and husband of Corazon, Benigno was imprisoned by Marcos in 1972 and later assassinated.

Aquino, Corazon   The leader of the Philippines from 1986 to 1992.

Arab League   Formed in 1945 by the initiative of Egypt, this organization attempts to promote cultural and economic cooperation among Arabs.

Aristide, Jean-Bertrand   Became leader of Haiti in 1990, following the Duvalier regime. A liberation theologist and Catholic priest, Aristide tackled the drug problem, stopped police brutality, ended the practice of bribery in government, reduced the bureaucracy by 20 percent, raised the minimum wage, and ended police extortion. Under his leadership the nation saw its most democratic period, although he was ousted from power by the military in 1991 and not returned as leader until 1995. He was deposed again in 2004.

Ariyamagga   The Noble Path of Buddhism, which is the path to Nirvana.

Artha   Refers to power and substance through material possessions or high social status for Hindus.

Arusha Declaration   A declaration that called for greater self-reliance and egalitarianism, issued in 1967 by the leader of Tanzania, Julius K. Nyerere.

Ashanti   The dominant group of people in what came to make up Ghana after independence.

Association of South East Asian Nations (ASEAN)   Founded in 1967 by Thailand, Indonesia, the Philippines, Malaysia, and Singapore, with the main focus of promoting economic, social, and cultural progress through international cooperation.

Aswan High Dam   Built in Egypt to expand the amount of land for agriculture by providing relatively inexpensive water for irrigation.

Ataturk, Mustafa Kemal   The founder of the modern Turkish state in 1923 who became a strong advocate for women.

Ayatollah Khomeini   The religious leader of Iran after the Revolution of 1979. The Ayatollah became the most powerful religious leader of the Iranian state.

Aylwin, Patricio   Became civilian elected leader of Chile in 1990.

baht   Thailand's currency.

Bakongo   Angolan ethnic group that dominates the northwest.

balance of payments   A nation's record of economic transactions, especially imports and exports with other countries.

Bangladesh   A country of South Asia between India and Burma on the Bay of Bengal, established in 1971 out of what was formerly an eastern province of Pakistan.

Bani-Sadr, Abulhassan   French-educated economist and first president elected in Iran after the fall of the Shah in 1979.

Bassa   A Liberian ethnic group that makes up 14 percent of the population.

Bay of Pigs   An event that took place on April 17, 1961, whereby a force of 1,300 Cuban exiles, armed and trained by the CIA, attempted an invasion of Cuba from the southern coast of the island.

Beijing Conference   A U.N.-sponsored conference that outlined the major concerns that women have and emphasized respect for the rights of women. It stressed the following: (1) the right of women to decide all matters related to their sexuality and childbearing, (2) an end to the genital mutilation of girls and violence against women because their dowries are too small, (3) the right of women to have access to credit, and (4) the equal treatment of males and females.

beliefs   A set of thoughts and values that encompass the social, political, and religious aspects of life.

Bhutto, Benazir   The prime minister of Pakistan from 1988 until she was ousted from power in 1996.

Bhutto, Zulfiqar Ali   The father of Benazir Bhutto who belonged to one of the most important landowning families in Pakistan. He became Pakistan's leader in 1971.

bonds of nationalism   A set of nationalistic attributes (which include common territory, language, culture, and enemie); it allows people in a nation to feel united with one another.

Bracero Program   A set of agreements between the United States and Mexico that facilitated the migration of Mexican workers, on a temporary basis, to work primarily in agriculture in the United States.

Brahmin   Members of India's highest caste, traditionally those of the priesthood.

brain drain   The migration of highly educated and trained people from poor countries to rich countries.

Brazil's Labor Code   Legislation that outlaws child labor in that country. However, although this is law, many children are employed to pick oranges and work in citrus-processing industries.

bride price   A tradition in Africa where a man has to pay his bride's family for her hand in marriage.

Buddha   An Indian mystic and founder of Buddhism.

Buddhism   A religion founded on the teachings of Buddha.

Buddhist's Double Liberation   Freeing one's mind of its limitations and liberating the community in a nonviolent way from unjust socioeconomic conditions.

bureaucracy   The administrative arm of governments that holds information and expertise regarding carrying out policy and decisions.

bureaucratic corruption   The illegal use of an official position or title for private gain.

Camp David Accords   An agreement signed by Egypt and Israel in 1978 that ended hostilities between them and provided for the return of Egyptian land seized by Israel.

capitulation system   A system imposed on Egyptians by the British, whereby foreign subjects could not be prosecuted under Egyptian laws.

Caritas   The Roman Catholic humanitarian agency of East Timor.

carrying capacity   Refers to the maximum number of humans and animals a given area can support without creating irreversible destruction of the environment and, ultimately, of humans and animals themselves.

caste system   A social arrangement in India comprised of four hereditary classes, including the Brahmans (priests), Ksatriyas (warriors), Vaisyas (farmers and merchants), and Shudras (laborers). The Harijans (untouchables) exist outside of the system and are considered below all castes.

Castro, Fidel   The leader of Cuba under a communist regime.

Catholic Church   A nonstate actor that influenced transitions to democracy throughout the world. The Catholic Church has consistently sought to exert influence throughout the world on a variety of issues, whether they be religious, political, social, or economic.

centralized government   A system of government in which all decisions are made at the center of power.

Chamorro, Pedro Joaquin   A journalist from a wealthy landowning family that had been active in Nicaraguan politics. He married Violeta.

Chamorro, Violeta   The leader of Nicaragua elected after the Sandinista regime in 1990. Chamorro came from a wealthy landowning family and was seen as a figure who brought Nicaragua closer to the United States and brought the country into the capitalist world system.

Chiapas   Southern state in Mexico where entire Indian communities do not have electricity or running water. The area has been left in the preindustrial age.

Chinese Communist Party (CCP)   The main governmental force in China that controls the policy process in all aspects of the government.

Christianity   A religion founded on the teachings of Jesus.

Cicero   (106–45 B.C.E.) A Roman philosopher and lawyer who believed in universal natural rights. He articulated the view that governments as well as citizens anywhere in the world must obey the authority of the higher law of nature.

Ciller, Tansu   The first woman to become the prime minister of Turkey in 1993.

civil wars   Violent conflicts carried out within the borders of a country by warring factions. Civil wars are considered a major contributor to economic disparities.

classical economic model   Emphasizes competition among producers, the growth of production, the efficient allocation of resources, and relatively little governmental involvement in the market.

Cold War   The struggle between the communist Soviet Union and the capitalist United States. The Cold War was defined through nuclear deterrence and proxy conflicts fought by the United States against countries that were Soviet allies and by the Soviet Union against countries and forces that were U.S. allies. The end of this ideological conflict contributed to democratization throughout former Soviet territories.

colonialism   The practice of states controlling areas outside of their territories.

colonization   The subjugation and domination of one country by a more powerful country. Colonization is considered a major cause of inequality between rich and poor countries.

community development   See *grassroots development*.

competitive exclusion   A major cause of migration, it occurs when more land is taken by large agro-export companies. This increases land prices and decreases the land available to small subsistence farmers who are forced to migrate.

Congress Party   The leading party in India after British rule ended that promoted a secular form of governance.

constitutional monarchy   A monarchy whose monarch's powers are allocated in a constitution.

Contadora Group   Under Mexico's leadership, this group—Panama, Colombia, and Venezuela—formed in 1983 to find a peaceful solution to the conflict in Nicaragua, El Salvador, and Honduras.

coup d'état   Military takeover of government.

cultural colonialism   A process in which one culture replaces another culture by indirect forces, such as those of finance and popularity.

cultural ties   Common values, family ties, and historical experiences that shape foreign policy. Countries that share common values and beliefs tend to develop close relationships.

culture   A set of traditions, beliefs, and behaviors that a people express and hold.

Dalai Lama   Tibet's spiritual leader who was forced to flee the nation because of deliberate Chinese efforts to destroy Tibetan culture and religion.

decentralized government   A system of government in which power is divided between a national government and smaller provincial or state governments.

deforestation   The loss of valuable forests due to economic development and the need for forest resources.

democracy   Any system where the majority rules.

dependency theory   The belief that industrialized countries benefit from the present capitalist economic system at the expense of the poor countries, a relationship established by colonialism.

deregulation   An argument that too much regulation is not healthy for society; people believing in deregulation want less regulation and less government in the citizens' lives.

devaluation of currencies   The process in which a country's form of money loses its value. When this occurs, it often takes a larger amount of a country's currency to buy the same amounts of products.

development   Significant and measurable economic growth and the emergence of social, economic, and political institutions.

development theories   Try to explain how countries achieve specific economic and political changes that are based on assumptions or things we take for granted.

dharma   For a Hindu, in a strict sense, this is a religious and moral law that sets the standard for a worthier and more deeply satisfying life.

dictatorship   A form of republic where power is vested in a single person who is not a monarch.

direct rule   A system of governance associated with colonial rule that subjects the colonized nation to the government, rules, and structures of the colonizing entity.

displaced person   Someone who has been forced to leave his or her home because of violence, conflict, persecution, or natural disaster but has not crossed an international border.

Doe, Samuel K.   Successor to Tolbert as leader of Liberia, he was tortured and murdered by members of the Gio group in 1990.

dowry   A price paid by a bride to her prospective husband.

Duvalier, Francois   Nicknamed "Papa Doc," he began a dictatorial reign of oppression in Haiti in 1957.

Duvalier, Jean-Claude   Nicknamed "Baby Doc," he maintained the repressive regime of his father until 1986, under which tens of thousands of Haitians were murdered.

East Timorese   A predominantly Catholic group that comprised 25 percent of the Indonesian population and resisted occupation by Muslim Indonesia.

Economic Community of West African States (ECOWAS)   Composed of Nigeria and fifteen other West African countries, ECOWAS is primarily concerned with regional economic integration, although it created a military force, known as Ecomog, to restore order in Liberia and Sierra Leone.

economic development   One of many factors necessary in the democratization process. The greater economic prosperity, exposure to other cultures, higher rates of literacy and education, increased urbanization, and access to both local and international mass media, a nation has, the more receptive it is to democracy.

economic inequality   A significant cost of uneven development, it discourages investment on a wider scale and encourages the poor and their supporters to pressure governments to allocate resources to benefit those left behind by unequal economic growth.

economies of scale   Deals with the relationship between output and costs.

embargo   A set of punitive sanctions imposed on goods and services by one country or the international community against another country.

equity and human development   An aspect of development that recognizes that economic growth is essential to achieve greater equality in society.

ethnic Chinese   A significant minority in Southeast Asia, they are the main targets of ethnic conflicts in Indonesia. They make up 5 percent of Indonesia's population and account for two-thirds of the nation's private urban economy.

ethnic group   Composed of individuals who generally share a sense of common identity based on a common set of historical experiences, national sentiments, religious beliefs, geographic location, a common language and culture, and, in countries such as the United States, arbitrary racial categories.

ethnic pluralism   The presence of many different groups within a specific geographical boundary.

Evian Agreement (1962)   An agreement concluded with the Algerian FLN by France, which gave Algeria its independence.

extradition   The process of making a person go back to a country where they have been charged with a crime so that they can stand trial.

famine   A situation in which food supplies are suddenly reduced, which causes a large number of deaths.

federal structure   A system of government in which power is divided between a national government and smaller provincial or state governments.

federalism   The sharing of power between the central government and the states or provinces.

female genital mutilation   A practice that involves the removal of the clitoris in its less severe form and all of the external female genitals in its most severe form.

feminization of employment   Women are making significant gains in all areas of employment and are thus leaving the home in increasing numbers to work in the industries of the new global economy.

forced migration   A method of evicting those who are hostile to the government or who disagree with fundamental or revolutionary social and political changes adopted by a new government.

foreign policy instruments   Includes a combination of military power, diplomacy, and economic might. Rich countries have more resources to use in order to accomplish their foreign policies. Many developing countries often rely on military force and diplomacy to achieve their objectives.

formalism   Reminds us of the widespread discrepancy between form and reality, which can take the shape of false reporting or by electing to disregard personnel regulations.

Four Noble Truths   Main concepts in Buddhism including the beliefs: life is suffering, suffering is caused by ignorance, sorrow ends when one is enlightened, and enlightenment is achieved by a course of disciplined and moral conduct.

Free Officers   Comprising Gamal Abdel Nasser, Anwar Sadat, and ten other young army officers, this group ousted King Farouk from power in hopes of ridding Egypt of corruption and creating a more just society.

free-market capitalism   An economic system where the market operates with as little government interference as possible.

Fulani   Making up 11 percent of Nigeria's population, this ethnic group resides in the Northern region of the nation.

Gandhi, Indira   Prime minister who ruled India from 1966 to 1977 and from 1980 to 1984.

Gandhi, Mahatma (Mohandas K.)   A charismatic leader who fought for India's independence from Britain by using his methods of nonviolence.

Gandhi, Rajiv   Became prime minister of India after the assassination of his mother, Indira Gandhi. He was killed in 1991 by a group of Tamil separatists.

Ganges River   A river in India that stretches for 1,500 miles from the Himalayan Mountains to the Bay of Bengal. Because of its life source, almost half of India's 1 billion citizens live along the Ganges.

Gastarbeiter rotation system   A governmental agreement between Germany and unions in which foreign workers or guest workers would stay in Germany for one to three years and would then return to their home countries.

General Act of Berlin (1885)   An act created during the Berlin Conference whereby the European states of Britain, France, Belgium, Portugal, Germany, and Italy officially carved up African territories and spheres of influence among themselves.

geographic location   A factor that affects a nation's international relations with other states. The proximity of one country to another (their geographic location) often helps determine interstate relationships.

Gio   An ethnic group in Liberia that comprises 9 percent of the population.

global companies   Companies that are transnational in orientation; they are said to undermine traditional values by promoting homogenization of consumer tastes and other cultural values.

global interdependence   A phenomenon whereby peoples around the world are becoming dependent on one another in areas of health, economy, environment, culture, and communications.

global warming   A theory that has gained much acceptance and attention in recent years; it is caused by emissions of carbon dioxide into the atmosphere.

globalism   A term that describes an ideology that encourages the establishment of a global market economy.

globalization   The integration of markets, politics, values, and environmental concerns across borders. Globalization is a process in which governments in the poorer countries are being pushed to open up their markets to the world market. It involves technologically driven integration of markets, politics, and environmental concerns across borders.

Gold Coast Constitution (1946)   This constitution created a new legislative council that included elected members. Although the council was only advisory to the British governor, it still was a bold move that gave Ghana a level of political participation not found anywhere else in colonial Africa.

good governance Characterized by the existence of responsible, responsive, and accountable government.

government A mechanism that people employ to organize their affairs and to protect them from internal or external threats.

Grameen Bank An informal lending program that is targeted at rural women. The Grameen Bank started in Bangladesh, but is now an international service.

grassroots development An approach to development where self-reliance and the empowerment of local communities and groups is emphasized.

Green Revolution A massive change in agricultural output that enabled farmers to produce more crops on the same amount of land by using hybrid seeds, chemical fertilizers, pesticides, herbicides, irrigation, and modern farm machinery.

gross domestic product (GDP) The total market value of all goods and services produced by resources supplied by residents and businesses of a particular country, regardless of where the residents and businesses are located, which is considered by gross national product.

gross national product (GNP) The total market value of all goods and services produced by a country.

Group of 77 The economic alliance formed by leaders of Africa, Asia, and Latin America, which included 77 nations in 1974.

growth The development of natural resources and the construction of an infrastructure to effectively utilize those resources.

Guardian Council Iranian religious council set up to ensure that Iranian law complies with the teachings of Islam.

Gutierrez, Gustavo A Peruvian priest who was one of the first advocates of liberation theology, which attempted to explain the relationship between the Christian faith and justice in the world.

Habibie, B. J. Indonesian president who allowed the East Timorese to vote on the issue of independence for East Timor.

Habyarimana, Juvenal Hutu president of Rwanda who died in 1994 when his plane was shot down.

Hajirans The name Gandhi gave to the untouchables; he called them the children of God.

Han The largest ethnic identity in China, comprising 93 percent of the population and controlling the nation's government.

Hausa A Muslim ethnic group of Nigeria that makes up 21 percent of the population and has historically controlled the nation.

Hegira (622 A.D.) The flight of Mohammed from Mecca to Medina to escape danger.

heterogeneous state A state in which people possess diverse cultures.

Hijab Islamic garment that women are required to wear, particularly in Iran, which covers their bodies completely.

Hinduism A set of beliefs, religion, and culture native to India.

historical experiences Factors that aid in the democratic process of a nation. Democratization depends on a particular nation's history and its exposure to different forms of governance in the past.

homogeneous state A state in which people share a similar culture.

honor killing The slaughter of women deemed to be unchaste by male relatives.

horizontal diversity Many different cultures, practices, and customs within a continent or nation.

humanitarian intervention The use of military force against a country that engages in gross violations of human rights.

Huntington, Samuel P. A leading scholar who, along with Janowitz, investigated military intervention in the governments of the developing countries.

Hussein, Saddam Leader of Iraq who led the nation into war with Iran in 1980 and invaded Kuwait in 1990. He was deposed by the United States in 2003.

Hutu Ethnic group in Rwanda that makes up 85 percent of the population. Also an ethnic group in Burundi, Hutus killed huge numbers of members from the Tutsi group.

Ibo Making up 18 percent of the population, the Ibo is an ethnic group located in the southeastern part of Nigeria that resides in the region rich with oil.

identity A conception of the self; a selection of physical, psychological, emotional, or social attributes of particular individuals.

ideology A system of values, beliefs, and ideas that influence economic, social, and political activities.

immigrant Someone who goes to a foreign country as a permanent resident.

import substitution   The strategy of developing domestic industries for domestic consumption in poor nations in order to diminish their reliance on rich countries.

indirect democracy   See *representative democracy*.

indirect rule   A system of governance, associated with colonial control, that allows a nation to maintain its institutions, religion, language, culture, and economic and educational systems.

Indonesia   The largest Islamic country in the world, it transitioned toward democracy after the fall of the Suharto regime in the 1990s.

Indonesia's Transmigration Program   A government-sponsored program that seeks to relocate millions of people and convert 2.5 million acres of rain forest to rice paddies.

Indo-Sri Lankan Agreement to Establish Peace and Normality in Sri Lanka   Signed on July 27, 1987, it called for the introduction of Indian troops into Sri Lanka to enforce a negotiated end to the violence.

influences of developing nations' foreign policy   The foreign policy of developing nations depends on things such as the country's geographical location, the level of economic development of the country, the nature of the country's political system and the quality of its leadership, the military capabilities of the country, the nature of international public opinion, the priorities of major countries and nonstate actors, and ties with other countries.

infrastructure   Roads, railways, ports, and telecommunications or other public works within a nation.

Institutional Revolutionary Party (PRI)   Historical single political party of Mexico that dominated the bureaucracy and federal government until it was defeated in 2000.

interest group   Also known as *pressure group*, it is composed of individuals who share common concerns, but who do not aspire for political positions of power.

internal self-selection   The tendency of individuals to decide not to apply for loans.

International Labor Organization   Part of the United Nations based in Geneva, Switzerland, that deals with labor-oriented issues. This organization adopted an agreement in June 1999 to abolish the worst forms of child labor.

International Monetary Fund (IMF)   Established in 1944 to prevent countries from defaulting on their loans and to make financing available.

international or regional environment   The surrounding societies that facilitate or impede the development of democratic values in other nations.

Islam   A religion marked by the belief in one God and that Mohammed is God's messenger.

Janowitz, Morris   A leading scholar who, along with Huntington, investigated military intervention in the governments of the developing countries.

Jesus   Founder of Christianity and regarded as the son of God, messiah, and Christ.

Jinnah, Ali   Leader of the Muslim League that incited the separation of Muslims from India to form the nation of Pakistan.

judicial systems   An essential element in maintaining democratic freedoms, including political participation that determines the meaning of laws and holds political leaders accountable.

junta   A small group of military officers who run the affairs of a country.

Kabila, Laurent   Leader whose forces launched a successful war in the Congo that overthrew Mobutu Sese Seko in 1997.

Kai-shek, Chiang   Leader of China's Nationalist Party; he was ousted from China and subsequently created Taiwan in 1949.

Kaleen   A label used by carpet manufacturers to demonstrate their compliance with laws banning child labor.

kama   The desire for pleasure, especially through love, which is an acceptable goal in life for a Hindu.

Karma   The Hindu belief that what happens to one in this life is determined by one's good or evil deeds in a previous life.

Kashmir   A disputed region northwest of India and northeast of Pakistan.

Kimbundu   The main ethnic group in the north-central region of Angola.

Knesset   Israeli parliament.

Koran   See *Quran*.

Kpelle   Liberian ethnic group that comprises 20 percent of the nation's population.

Krahn   A Liberian ethnic group that comprises 5 percent of the nation's population.

Ksatriya   Member of a Hindu upper caste that traditionally works in the government or military.

Kumaratunga, Chandrika Bandaranaike   Became Sri Lanka's president in 1994. She promised an end to the violence in the nation and initiated talks with the Tamil Tigers, which resulted in a truce, but later resulted in violence when Tamil demands were not met. She unilaterally offered a peace agreement to the Tamils following the violence, which ultimately failed.

Kuomintang   See *Nationalist Party*.

Kurdish Workers Party (PKK)   Kurdish independence movement in Turkey that uses guerilla activities and other means of violence to achieve independence.

Kurds   Non-Arab Muslims who are the largest ethnic minority in the Middle East. For the last 500 years or more, the Kurdish population has been spread across Turkey, Iraq, Iran, Syria, and parts of the former Soviet Union.

La Prensa   The Nicaraguan newspaper run by Pedro Joaquin Chamorro, who supported the Sandinistas.

labor recruiters   Sometimes called smugglers, these people smuggle laborers from poorer nations into nations such as the United States, Canada, and Western Europe. The recruiters charge substantial sums of money to transport migrants to labor markets and to secure employment for them.

Latin America   Geographic area that includes South America, the countries of the Caribbean Sea and the Atlantic "West Indies," Central America, and Mexico.

legitimacy   The power to govern based on the consent of the majority of those who are governed.

lesser developed countries   See *underdeveloped countries*.

level of economic development   Influences a country's selection of foreign policy goals and how it tries to accomplish them. Richer countries often have numerous interests and vast amounts of resources to pursue these interests. Poor countries, on the other hand, are usually more dependent and subservient in their relations with rich countries.

liberation theology   A political/religious movement that combines the religious notion of salvation and political theory, usually of Marxist origins, as a method for liberating the people from injustices. This movement has been particularly popular among Latin American clergy of the Roman Catholic Church.

limited monarchy   A monarchy where the monarch's powers are limited to ceremonial functions.

Locke, John   A proponent of democracy and the social contract.

Lok Sabha   One of two houses in the Indian Parliament, also referred to as the House of Representatives.

Lost Decade   In Latin America, this was the period in the 1980s that forced many to abandon cultural values that kept women at home when the region faced serious economic decline.

Madres de la Plaza de Mayo   Argentine mothers who marched daily in Argentina, drawing attention to the "disappeared," their relatives who had been killed by the government.

Majlis   The Iranian parliament, set up as part of the Constitutional Compromise after the 1979 Iranian revolution.

maleness of politics   The tendency for politics to be regarded as an activity for men. Under this theory it is believed that politics is closely connected to the traditional fatherly connotation of patriarchy, which excludes women from power, and to fraternalism.

managed transitions   A method of gradually obtaining democracy overseen by an entity of people, usually the military, instead of making a quick democratic change.

Mano   An ethnic group that makes up 7 percent of Liberia's population.

maquiladora   Export factories along the U.S.-Mexican borders that enable Mexican citizens to work within their communities. Single women without children who have completed secondary school are the preferred workers. The maquiladora program was initiated by the Mexican government to encourage U.S. industries to locate on the Mexican-American border.

Marcos, Ferdinand   The leader who imposed martial law in the Philippines in 1972.

marianismo   A Latin American cult of Virgin Mary in which the family is seen as being held together spiritually and emotionally through the mother's steadfast devotion.

McWorld   A term coined by Benjamin Barber to describe a process by which American popular culture and consumerism threatens to overtake the globe.

megalopolises   Large cities in Asia, Africa, and Latin America where people come largely because of the economic, social, and political benefits they offer.

Mercosur   See *South American Free Trade Area*.

Mesopotamia   An area between the Tigris and the Euphrates rivers, sometimes referred to as the cradle of civilization; area is present-day Iraq.

mestizos   A people in Latin America descended from Iberian and Native American ancestry.

Mexican-American War   A war between Mexico and the United States from 1846 to 1848 during which the

United States conquered land from Mexico including present-day Texas, California, Arizona, New Mexico, Utah, Nevada, and Colorado.

middle class   A group of people who fall within a middle income range. Many political scientists believe a large middle class is essential to the acquisition and maintenance of democratic values.

Middle East   An ambiguous concept referring to the countries of the eastern Mediterranean and parts of North Africa.

migrant   A person who moves from one country or area to another country or location.

migration   An integral part of human behavior that involves the movement of people from one place to another.

migration of dreams   Also known as the export of dreams, this is a process that follows the dissemination of information technologies whereby the wealthy and advanced countries pass to the poor and underdeveloped countries pictures, sounds, and other forms of messages of luxury and well-being and results in relative deprivation.

military leadership   The phenomenon of intervention by military leaders in politics and their attempts to control governmental institutions.

modernization   In developing a nation, new values, access to Western ways of life, and often less tolerance for traditional cultures often result. Modernization tends to homogenize cultures, destroy the boundaries that are essential to ethnic solidarity and a sense of identity, and create new identities and rearrange the boundaries.

modernization theory   Also known as developmentalism. This theory proposes that all countries go through stages of development, from traditional through transitional to modern. These stages were also identified as (1) underdevelopment, (2) takeoff, and (3) modernity.

Mohammad (570?–632 A.D.)   An Arab who lived in Mecca, which is present-day Saudi Arabia; he declared that he was given the ultimate form of revelation (Islam) to fellow humans. Messenger of Islam.

Moksha   Liberation or salvation is the ultimate goal of a Hindu.

monarchy   A form of government distinguished by having a monarch, who receives her or his title through divine right or inheritance from a family member. A monarch may be called a king, queen, prince, emir, sultan, emperor, tzar, shah, or pharaoh.

Monrovia   Capital of Liberia, named after James Monroe in 1822, where former American slaves settled upon their return to Africa.

mosques   Religious places of Muslim worship.

Mujahedeen   Islamic holy warriors, supported by the United States, who fought against the Soviet army during its occupation of Afghanistan. The CIA trained Islamic freedom fighters to resist the Soviets, although many of the leaders of the Taliban eventually emerged from the Islamic freedom fighters.

multinational corporations (MNCs)   Companies that operate in more than one country and that depend on interdependence for the operation of their enterprise.

murahaleen   Militiamen on horseback, supported by the Sudanese government, who not only killed civilians but also burned their crops and stole their cattle and other animals.

Muslim League   Muslim party in India that aided in the formation of Pakistan.

Nasser, Gamal Abdel   Became leader of Egypt after Free Officers ousted King Farouk; he was very popular among the Egyptian people. Under his rule, he attempted to nationalize the Suez Canal Company and constructed the Aswan High Dam, among many other things. The charismatic leader died in 1970 of a heart attack.

nation   Refers to a group of people who identify with each other as a political community because of common territorial, cultural, and other similar bonds.

National Action Party (PAN)   The Mexican political party that defeated the PRI in the 2000 elections.

national interests   A set of goals that are essential or beneficial to a country's survival, its economic prosperity, the psychological well-being of its population, and its status and prestige in the region and in the larger international community.

nationalism   A state of mind in which loyalty is given to the nation to which an individual belongs.

Nationalist Party (or Kuomingtang)   Led by Chiang Kai-shek, the party was driven from mainland China after it lost the war with the Chinese Communists; it ruled Taiwan in 1949.

natural disasters   Include drought, earthquakes, volcanic eruptions, hurricanes, tornadoes, and tsunamis. They destroy important economic sectors.

naturalistic theories   Theories in sociology and geography that stress cultural and environmental influences on economic development.

Nehru, Jawahar Lal India's prime minister after independence and head of the Indian National Congress Party, the country's dominant political party.

neoclassical economic theory See *free-market capitalism.*

neocolonialism A new form of indirect colonialism.

neopatriarchy Patriarchal practices that remain underneath that façade of modernity.

New International Economic Order (NIEO) An international platform for nations of the South to challenge the comparative strength of Northern countries to exploit weaker countries. Believing that colonialism and neocolonialism were responsible for the existence of an unfair economic system in which developing nations were disadvantaged, leaders of Africa, Asia, and Latin America formed the Group of 77 (initially composed of seventy-seven countries) to seek ways of warding off the negative effects of developed countries on the South.

New World Information and Communication Order (1980) A resolution passed in a Belgrade conference by the United Nations that advocated respect for each people's cultural identity.

Nike's Memorandum of Understanding Calls on all factories that produce Nike products to comply with the following: (1) government regulation of business; (2) safety and health regulations; (3) local laws providing health insurance, life insurance, and worker's compensation; (4) laws forbidding the use of forced labor; (5) environmental regulations; (6) laws promoting equal employment opportunities; and (7) efforts by external groups to certify that factories are complying with Nike's rules.

Nikkeijin Latin American peoples of Japanese ancestry who are allowed unrestricted employment opportunities in Japan.

Nirvana The ultimate state of liberation from rebirth, the Fullness of Being that no human words can describe.

Noble Eightfold Path Explains ethical norms of Buddhism including Right View, Right Understanding, and Right Thought.

Nonaligned Movement Formed under the leadership of Yugoslavia, India, Egypt, Ghana, and other developing countries, this movement was created to express neutrality in the Cold War.

nongovernmental organizations (NGOs) Groups that are not part of a government, which often have agendas of improving human rights and democratic practices globally.

nonindustrialized countries See *underdeveloped countries.*

North American Free Trade Agreement (NAFTA) An agreement adopted in 1994 that lowers trade barriers among Mexico, the United States, and Canada.

North Korea A communist country, its government's policies have produced and reinforced poverty.

No Sweat A label that is used to verify that clothing, shoes, toys, and other products were not made in sweatshops or by children.

Nyerere, Julius K. Leader of Tanzania who allowed only one party, the Tanzanian African National Union (TANU), to function. He believed that a single-party democracy was not only possible, but that it would allow various groups to compete and enable the people to have a voice in government.

Obasanjo, Olusegun Civilian elected leader of Nigeria who came to power on May 29, 1999.

Ocalan, Abdullah Leader of the Kurdish PKK who was captured in Kenya by Turkish agents in early 1999.

oligarchy A type of republic ruled by a small group.

one child policy A policy in China under which a couple can have only one child except in the following cases: if the first child has a defect; in the case of a remarriage in which one partner does not have a child; if couples are involved in jobs such as mining; or if both partners come from families with one child.

Operation Wetback An operation in which hundreds of thousands of Mexicans were rounded up and deported in response to economic competition and fears about communists entering the United States through Mexico.

Opium War A war fought between Britain and China from 1839 to 1842 over opium and the British occupation of Hong Kong.

oral divorce Allows a husband to divorce his wife simply by telling her that he is divorcing her.

Organization of African Unity (OAU) Established in 1963, this organization committed itself to (1) promoting the unity and solidarity of the newly independent African countries, (2) coordinating the efforts of member-states to improve the standard of living for Africans, (3) defending the independence and territorial integrity of African states, and (4) ending colonial rule and white minority rule in Africa.

Organization of American States (OAS) Composed of the Latin American countries, the Caribbean, the United States, and Canada, the OAS was established in

1948 and attempts to promote the solidarity among the member countries; strengthen their collaboration and defend their independence and territorial integrity; promote the economic, social, and cultural development of member-states; and work toward regional economic integration.

Organization of Petroleum Exporting Countries (OPEC) Formed by major oil-producing nations in response to the control of the world oil market by seven major oil companies.

outcasts See *untouchables.*

overpopulation A major cause of migration that stems from overcrowding, loss of economic opportunities, and unemployment.

Ovimbundu Angolan ethnic group dominant in the south-central region.

Pakistan A country in South Asia on the Arabian Sea that was established in 1947.

Pakistan People's Party (PPP) This political party, under Benazir Bhutto, ran on a platform that promised to eliminate barriers to women's political participation. Bhutto and the PPP wanted to (1) sign the U.N. Convention on the Elimination of All Forms of Discrimination Against Women, (2) improve working conditions and job opportunities for women, (3) introduce maternity leave, (4) repeal laws that discriminated against women, and (5) promote female literacy.

Palestine Liberation Organization (PLO) A Palestinian organization created out of Palestinians' desire to control their political and governmental structures. It was created to promote the self-determination of the Palestinian people on their land.

panchayat Village council seats of India's parliament.

parliamentary democracy A form of democracy in which there is no clear division between the executive and legislative branches of government and where the leader is a prime minister as opposed to a president.

patriarchy A traditional system in which authority is closely related to family and kinship groups and in which the head of the family and group is a male.

patronage The use of political office to hire supporters, which often provokes corruption and proves harmful to the government.

patron–client system A system in which a patron (a person or group) with political ties or power provides a service to a client, who will repay the patron with political support or other means.

Peace of Westphalia The treaty that concluded the Thirty Years' War in 1648.

Pereira de Queiroz, Carlota A physician in Sao Paulo who became the first president of Brazil in 1933.

personal identity Entails a sense of individual autonomy, which gives a person a sense of place within a community or the larger society because of that person's own distinctive or unique characteristics.

peso Currency of the Philippines.

physical terrain A factor that determines countries' international relations. Physical terrain includes the type of land a nation has, such as mountainous, rocky, sandy, or full of forests.

Pinochet, Augusto Carried out a coup that killed Chilean leader Allende, which allowed him to rule Chile under a dictatorship. Pinochet waged a campaign of terror that included raids, executions, disappearances, imprisonment, and torture of his opponents and reversed numerous policies created by Allende. In 1998, he was arrested in the United Kingdom for the involvement of the murders of Spanish citizens in Chile.

plutocracy Rule of the wealthy.

political culture Traditions, beliefs, behaviors, and attitudes related to politics and government.

political development The growth of modern and effective political institutions and practices.

political participation Conventional forms of political participation include voting, supporting particular candidates for political office, running for a position in government, writing letters to the editor of a newspaper about a particular issue, joining an interest group or an organization that tries to influence government policies or decisions, and protesting. Unconventional forms of participation include mass demonstrations, civil disobedience, and sometimes even acts of violence.

political party A coalition of interests whose goal is to gain control of the government by winning elections.

politics The means by which a people organize their affairs.

power-sharing arrangements Essentially, these arrangements divide political power among the different ethnic groups.

preconditions for democracy A combination of factors that provide a fertile environment and foundation for the growth and stability of democratic societies.

presidential democracy A type of democracy in which there is a clear separation of powers and a system of checks and balances.

Pudong A major industrial development zone not far from Shanghai in China.

pull factors   Motivating factors for people to leave their homes for another country. Those include employment opportunities, higher wages, political and social stability, a healthy environment, educational and cultural opportunities, and family reunification.

Purdah   A practice that requires women to wear veils, restricts their mobility and social interaction, and limits access to employment.

push factors   Motivating factors for people to leave their homes that include human rights violations, political oppression, forced resettlement programs, violence and political instability, overpopulation, unemployment, poverty, natural and environmental disasters, and the lack of educational and cultural opportunities.

Qaddafi, Muammar   The leader of Libya when the Pan Am Flight 103 over Lockerbie, Scotland, was bombed. He was accused with being involved with terrorist attacks against the United States and its allies, which led to sanctions on Libya.

Quesada, Vicente Fox   A member of the PAN party who was elected as Mexico's president in 2000. He promised to improve the economy, reform taxes, overhaul the justice system, and give states more power.

Queiroz, Carlota de   The first woman in Brazil elected to Parliament in 1933. She was a physician from Sao Paulo and a member of a traditional and wealthy family.

Quran   The holy book for muslims.

Rajya Sabha   One of the two houses in the Indian Parliament, which is known as the Council of States.

Refah (Welfare) Party   An Islamic political party in Turkey that was banned by the court in early 1998. Many Turks viewed this party as a threat to Turkish society and secular values.

refugees   Migrants who live outside of their country but are unable or unwilling to return because of persecution or a well-founded fear of persecution.

regional economic development banks   Modeled after the World Bank, each region has a bank that aids in providing capital to governments to stimulate economic development, promoting regional economic integration, and providing policy and technical assistance.

relative deprivation   The gap between what a person gets and what that person thinks he or she should get.

remittances   Migrants throughout the world often send money to their families. In some cases, poor countries make arrangements with rich countries to recruit migrants for temporary work, and part of the migrant's wages are sent directly to the government.

representative democracy   A form of governance where citizens elect representatives to vote for them and to safeguard and further their interests.

republic   A form of government that is ruled by a group of people or one person who claim(s) to represent the people.

Restavec system   A Haitian system whereby impoverished parents who cannot afford to raise their children allow them to stay with wealthier families.

Right Concentration/Meditation   The final step in the Buddhist Path that requires a clear and composed mental condition to help in achieving wisdom and avoiding evil. Meditation is considered a form of mental training for an ethical life of the Buddhist.

Right Conduct/Right Action   The fourth step in the Buddhist Path that suggests avoidance of bodily harm to oneself or to others. Right Action means a life full of love, compassion, and abstention from wrongful gratification of one's senses, especially in terms of sexual misbehavior.

Right Effort   The sixth step in the Buddhist Path that expresses that individuals need to be determined to prevent evil within themselves and to choose the moral alternative. Effort is the most important factor for the victory of morality over temptations within every individual.

Right Mindfulness   The seventh step in the Buddhist Path that guides one's mental, verbal, and bodily behavior toward a moral direction.

Right Occupation/Livelihood   The fifth step in the Buddhist Path that suggests a morally acceptable means of livelihood. Occupations that are materially rewarding but morally wrong must be avoided because it is unacceptable in Buddhism to engage in any occupation that could result in harming others.

Right Speech   The third step in the Buddhist Path that involves avoiding false speech, slanderous speech, harsh speech, and frivolous talk.

Right Thought   This Buddhist Path bridges thought and action. It preaches the importance of having thoughts that are free from lustful relations or greed, free from hatred, and free from violent intentions. Thoughts, it is believed, lead to actions.

Right View/Right Understanding   One of the Buddhist's norms that involves an understanding of the power of the individual.

roles   Expectations regarding the skills, rights, and duties of individuals.

Rugmark   A label used by carpet manufacturers to show compliance with child labor laws.

rule of law   The belief that no person is above the law and that all individuals are treated equally under the law.

rupiah   Indonesian currency.

Sadat, Anwar   Successor to Nasser as the leader of Egypt. He reached a peace agreement with Israel, signing the Camp David Accords in 1978.

Sadr, Bani   Iran's first elected president after the Iranian Revolution and the fall of the Shah in 1979. Sadr was eventually forced out of Iran during its transition into an Islamist state.

Sahara Desert   An area that divides Africa into two areas known as North Africa and sub-Saharan Africa.

sale of females   The trafficking of young girls and women, which is rooted in both traditional and economic consideration.

Samsara   The cycle of birth, suffering, death, and rebirth in Buddhist scripts. Hinduism also defines it as the cycle of rebirth.

San Andres Accords   An agreement between the Zapatistas and the Mexican government that granted land and legal rights to the indigenous population.

San Suu Kyi, Aung   A female who won an election in Burma but was denied leadership by the military that retained power.

Sandinistas   The opposition to Somoza regime that adopted socialist policies and failed to bring democracy to Nicaragua.

Satyagraha   A Hindu term that literally means holding fast to truth. Practically, it is a philosophy of nonviolent civil disobedience.

Saud, Muhammad ibn   The leader of a nomadic group who made an alliance with Abd al-Wahhab for mutual protection in the eighteenth century. This alliance led to the formation of the modern Saudi Arabian state.

Seko Sese, Mobutu   The leader of the Congo and close ally with the Angolan group UNITA; he was overthrown in 1997 by a force headed by Kabila.

Selassie, Haile   The leader of Ethiopia who attempted to annex Eritrea in order for Ethiopia to have access to the Red Sea and to avoid being landlocked.

self-selection   Refers to the tendency of individuals to decide not to apply for certain goods and services that may improve their well-being.

self-sufficiency   The ability of a country to produce most or all of what its people consume.

Seven Sisters   The name given to the seven large oil companies that controlled most of the world's petroleum until the mid-1950s.

shaheed   A martyr. Some Muslims believe that it is the highest aspiration to die a shaheed.

Shang Dynasty   Chinese era when written records appeared.

sharaf   A threat to the family's honor caused by an unchaste female family member.

shari'a   Laws based on the Quran and the totality of God's teachings for every Muslim to follow.

Shining Path   A Peruvian rebel movement that was formed by university professors and students who subscribed to the philosophy of Mao Zedong (Mao Tse-tung), the first leader of China's Communist Party. The Shining Path attempts to violently transform society in order to decrease human misery.

Shudra   Hindu caste includes all non-Aryans or those who are not of Indo-European origin, including blacks, Semites, slaves, servants, and even some prisoners of war.

Sikhs' Golden Temple   Regarded as most sacred to Sikhs, it became the center of controversy when Sikh rebels used it as a refuge from Indian security forces.

Sinhalese   Ethnic group of Sri Lanka that comprises 74 percent of its population. This group, dominating the South, is Buddhist and speaks Sinhalese.

Six Day War   A war in 1967 that occurred among Syria, Egypt, Jordan, and Israel.

Sixteen Decisions   The social contract of the Grameen Bank.

social contract   A fundamental principle of democracy, one that is closely related to the ideas articulated by John Locke and others.

socialization   The process that shapes how we see ourselves and those around us, including values that we learn from parents, teachers, religious authorities, our friends, and the media.

social construct   Societies create and use subjective standards to determine who will have a higher or lower status. These standards are subject to change as societies change.

Somoza   The family that ruled Nicaragua under a horrible regime. The Sandinistas were this family's political opposition.

South   See *underdeveloped countries.*

South Asian Association for Regional Cooperation (SAARC)   Formed in 1985 and composed of India,

Pakistan, Sri Lanka, Bangladesh, Bhutan, Nepal, and the Maldives, this organization focuses on trade, development, and stability in order to overcome regional challenges of poverty, underdevelopment, low production levels, and overpopulation.

South American Free Trade Area (Mercosur) Formed by the Treaty of Asuncion in 1991 to reduce trade barriers among its members. Mercosur is composed of Argentina, Brazil, Uruguay, Chile, Bolivia, and Paraguay. It is South America's regional economic bloc, created to strengthen trade throughout the continent, and it is the third largest trading bloc in the world.

sovereignty An authority whose actions are independent of the legal control of another.

Spark Plan A plan implemented by the Chinese government in 1985 to modernize rural industries through technological innovations.

Sri Lanka Freedom Party (SLFP) A Sri Lankan political party that stressed Sinhalese separation and made Buddhism the national religion.

state An internationally recognized, politically organized, populated, geographical area that possesses a government and sovereignty.

state capitalism A system where the state operates to ensure economic competition to secure growth.

status Refers to a person's position in the social, economic, and political hierarchy.

study of international relations The study of the interaction of countries or states. These interactions or relationships are characterized by cooperation as well as conflict.

study of politics The study of government and power allocation and use in society.

subsistence living Independent living where people produce a sufficient amount of food for their survival as an independent family unit.

Sudan People's Liberation Army (SPLA) A political group that has been fighting the Sudanese government since 1983 to achieve secular democracy.

Suez Canal A significant trade route that connects the Mediterranean Sea to the Red Sea.

sustainable development A theory that holds that growth is not inconsistent with using resources in such a way that future generations will have access to them and continue to experience both an adequate standard of living and equity. This theory recognizes the limits of natural resources and the need to redefine development to reflect this reality.

sweatshop Dreary working conditions including the harshness of supervisors, difficult and hazardous jobs, frequent and serious accidents, long hours and low pay, few employee benefits and rights, and generally toxic, polluted, and unsanitary working environments.

symbols of nationalism A set of national representations that includes a common flag, anthem, popular slogans and legends, and historical sites.

Tainos The Native people of Haiti, subjugated, enslaved, and dispossessed by Spanish settlers.

Taliban Islamic movement in Afghanistan that controlled the government until it was ousted by an international force led by the United States after the events of September 11, 2001.

Tamils Divided into two groups, the Indian Tamils and the Ceylon Tamils, this ethnic group makes up 18 percent of Sri Lanka's population. This group, dominating the north, is made up of Hindus who speak primarily Tamil and English.

Tanzanian African National Union (TANU) The one party in Tanzania allowed under the one party democratic system of Julius K. Nyerere.

Ten Fundamental Human Needs Identified by the Sarvodaya Movement in Sri Lanka Includes a clean and beautiful environment, an adequate supply of clean water, minimal supplies of clothing, an adequate supply of food, a modest home, basic health care, basic communication facilities, a minimal supply of energy, holistic education, and spiritual and cultural needs.

theory Predicts how humans behave or how things work in the real world under specific circumstances.

Third World See *underdeveloped countries*.

Third World Socialism An economic doctrine that calls for less private enterprise and a greater role for government in determining economic priorities and in running industries. The most important features of Third World socialism include (1) industrialization through import substitution, (2) protectionism, (3) fixed exchange rates, (4) the development of state-owned companies, and (5) government control of agricultural prices.

Three Gorges Dam Built in China along the Yangtze River to ease flooding and increase electrical power, it is the world's largest dam.

Tolbert, William An Americo-Liberian president of Liberia who was overthrown and murdered by a group of soldiers of the Krahn group in 1980.

totalitarian system A system in which all powers are concentrated at the center of government.

trade The exchange of goods and services among individuals, organizations, nations, and states.

trade barriers Barriers that prevent the free exchange of goods and services and are therefore seen by some as an impediment to economic development. Types of trade barriers include restrictions on imports, quotas, high taxes on imports, and the implementation of price and wage controls.

Trans-Amazon Highway Built in Brazil with funding from the World Bank, the government encouraged millions of landless peasants to move to the Amazon and clear the land for cultivation.

transcontinental migration The movement of persons from one continent to another.

Treaty of Rome in 1957 Established the European Economic Community as an economic alliance. This union also strengthened the political ties of these member-states.

tribalism Usually regarded as an outdated term that has been used by some Westerners to refer to small groups of indigenous people in Africa, Asia, and Latin America.

Tripitaka Meaning "three baskets," the book of Buddhist writings where the Four Noble Truths are explained.

Tudeh Party The communist party of Iran, which played an important part in opposing the government of the Shah Muhammad Reza.

Tutsi Small cattle-herding ethnic group in Rwanda that comprises 14 percent of the population and helped the Germans control the nation upon colonization. This group, also a part of Burundi, exploited and killed members of the Hutu ethnic group.

Uighur Separatists Muslim ethnic minority in China who reside primarily in Xinjiang.

ulema Learned religious men who interpret Islamic teachings.

ul-Haq, General Zia The person who overthrew Zulfiqar Ali Bhutto and subsequently became leader of Pakistan in 1977.

underdeveloped countries A concept that refers to the peoples and countries outside of Europe and North America with few exceptions. Other characteristics of underdevelopment include high mortality rates, high birthrates, low levels of sanitation, high levels of poverty, and large gaps between rich and poor.

unitary system A system of government in which power is centralized.

United National Party (UNP) Political party of Sri Lanka that advocated unity between the Tamils and the Sinhalese.

United Nations High Commissioner for Refugees (UNHCR) Established in 1950 by the United Nations to assist people who have crossed international boundaries because of uncontrollable circumstances at home.

untouchables Hindu outcasts, considered the dregs of society whose mere touch pollutes a caste. Such individuals have no hope of rising in the social scale; they are often stigmatized by Hindu society and left to live in misery of poverty and starvation.

urbanization As countries develop their economies, they become more industrialized and cities and urban areas grow.

Vaisya Hindus working in commercial and agricultural sectors; this constitutes an upper caste.

Veddah Native peoples of Sri Lanka.

veiling Varying from the covering of the face to the entire female body, veiling is a religious/cultural practice that symbolizes gender segregation, the unequal relationship between men and women, and the complex nature of status in some countries.

vertical diversity Occurs when many individuals hold a myriad of beliefs within a continent, region, or nation.

Wahhabi tradition Religious tradition that serves as the basis of Saudi law and social behavior. It was first institutionalized by the Saudi king, Ibn Saud, who worked with Abd al-Wahhab.

wars of national liberation A series of conflicts between colonized and colonizer in which the colonized attempt to gain independence.

war on drugs An American-led campaign launched in the 1980s by President Ronald Reagan to keep illegal drugs out of the United States. The war on drugs was continued under the Bush I, Clinton, and Bush II administrations.

won South Korea's currency.

World Bank A U.N. agency that deals with monetary aid transfers to developing nations usually via a loan program varying from nation to nation.

World Health Organization (WHO) A part of the United Nations that attempts to improve the health of people around the world.

world systems theory Developed by Immanuel Wallerstein, it stresses the role of European capitalism in creating economic groups of countries based upon power inequalities.

World Trade Organization (WTO) An economic grouping of states that seeks to eliminate trade barriers, increase trade competition, set rules for governments to observe in relation to international trade, and stimulate competition within the developing world itself.

Yoruba Ethnic group of Nigeria comprising 21 percent of the population who live in the western part of the nation.

Yunis, Muhammad The founder of the Grameen Bank, which is a lending institution for poor women. He created this institution because he believed that other banks and lenders excluded the poor population.

Zapatista National Liberation Front (Zapatistas) Launched an attack on the Mexican government on January 1, 1994. This group called for the Mexican government to withdraw from NAFTA, ensure the fair treatment for Mexico's indigenous groups, and promote economic development of Chiapas.

Zedong, Mao The leader of the Chinese Communist Party and leader of China in the middle of the twentieth century.

BIBLIOGRAPHY

Acemoglu, Daron, and James A. Robinson, *Economic Origins of Dictatorship and Democracy*. New York: Cambridge University Press, 2006.

Anker, Richard. *Gender and Jobs: Sex Segregation of Occupations in the World*. Geneva: International Labor Office, 1998.

Barber, Benjamin R. *Jihad vs. McWorld*. New York: Ballantine Books, 1996.

Barraclough, Solon L., and Krishna B. Ghimire. *Forests and Livelihoods*. New York: St. Martin's Press, 1995.

Bauman, Zygmunt. *Globalization: The Human Consequences*. New York: Columbia University Press, 1998.

Baydas, Mayada M., Richard L. Meyer, and Nelson Aguilera-Alfred. "Discrimination Against Women in Formal Credit Markets." *World Development* 22, no. 7 (July 1994): 1073–82.

Bhalla, A. S. *Globalization, Growth, and Marginalization*. New York: St. Martin's Press, 1998.

Bird, Graham. *IMF Lending to Developing Countries*. London: Routledge, 1995.

Birdsall, Nancy. "Life Is Unfair: Inequality in the World." *Foreign Policy* 111 (Summer 1998): 76–93.

Bowring, Bill. "The Kurds in Turkey." In Kirsten E. Schulze et al., eds., *Nationalism, Minorities, and Diasporas*. London: I. B. Tauris, 1996.

Bratton, Michael, and Nicolas van de Walle. *Democratic Experiments in Africa*. New York: Cambridge University Press, 1997.

Brecher, Jeremy, and Tim Costello. *Global Village or Global Pillage? Economic Reconstruction from the Bottom Up*, 2nd ed. Cambridge, MA: South End Press, 1998.

Brinkley, Douglas. "Bringing the Green Revolution to Africa." *World Policy Journal* 13, no. 1 (Spring 1996): 53–62.

Brown, Seyom. *Human Rights in World Politics*. New York: Addison Wesley Longman, 2000.

Bryan, Lowell, and Diana Farrell. *Market Unbound: Unleashing Global Capitalism*. New York: John Wiley & Sons, 1996.

Burtless, Gary, Robert Z. Lawrence, Robert E. Litan, and Robert J. Shapiro. *Globaphobia: Confronting Fears about Open Trade*. Washington, D.C.: The Brookings Institution, 1998.

Chase-Dunn, Christopher. *Global Formation: Structures of the World Economy*. Lanham, MD: Rowman & Littlefield, 1998.

Chowdhury, Najma, and Barbara J. Nelson, eds. *Women and Politics Worldwide*. New Haven, CT: Yale University Press, 1994.

Clark, Ian. *Globalization and International Relations Theory*. New York: Oxford University Press, 1999.

Cohn, Theodore H. *Global Political Economy: Theory and Practice*. New York: Longman, 2000.

Coleman, Isobel. "Women, Islam, and the New Iraq," *Foreign Affairs* 85, no. 1 (January/February 2006): 24–38.

Counts, Alex. *Give Us Credit*. New York: Random House, 1996.

Cox, Harvey. "The Market as God." *The Atlantic Monthly* 283, no. 3 (1999): 18–23.

Cravey, Altha J. *Women and Work in Mexico's Maquiladoras*. Lanham, MD: Rowman and Littlefield, 1998.

Destexhe, Alain. *Rwanda and Genocide in the Twentieth Century*. New York: New York University Press, 1995.

Diamond, Larry, et al., ed. "Introduction: Comparing Experiences with Democracy." In *Politics in Developing Countries*. Boulder, CO: Lynne Rienner, 1990.

Dominquez, Jorge I. *Democratic Politics in Latin America and the Caribbean*. Baltimore: The Johns Hopkins University Press, 1998.

Eller, Jack D. *From Culture to Ethnicity to Conflict*. Ann Arbor: The University of Michigan Press, 1999.

Eng, Peter. "Transforming ASEAN." *The Washington Quarterly* 22, no. 1 (Winter 1999): 49–65.

Esman, Milton J. *Ethnic Politics*. Ithaca, NY: Cornell University Press, 1994.

Excurra, Exequiel, and Maria Mazari-Hiriart. "Are Mega Cities Viable?" *Environment* (January–February 1996): 6–26.

Farsoun, Samih K., and Christina E. Zacharia. *Palestine and the Palestinians*. Boulder, CO: Westview Press, 1997.

Fernando, Nilan. "Sri Lanka in 1997: Inching Toward a Durable Peace." *Asian Survey* 38, no. 2 (February 1998): 142–45.

Fieldhouse, D. K. *Colonialism 1870–1945*. New York: St. Martin's Press, 1981.

Fieleke, Norman S. "Is Global Competition Making the Poor Even Poorer?" *New England Economic Review* (November–December 1994): 3–15.

Fukuyama, Francis, ed. *Nation-Building: Beyond Afghanistan and Iraq*. Baltimore: The Johns Hopkins University Press, 2006.

Goldin, Ian, and Kenneth Reinert. *Globalization for Development*. London: Palgrave Macmillan, 2006.

Goldman, Merle. *From Comrade to Citizen: The Struggle for Political Rights in China*. Cambridge, MA: Harvard University Press, 2006.

Greenberg, Karen, ed. *The Torture Debate in America*. New York: Cambridge University Press, 2006.

Greider, William. *One World, Ready or Not*. New York: Simon & Schuster, 1997.

Gurr, Ted Robert. *Minorities at Risk: A Global View of Ethnopolitical Conflicts*. Washington, D.C.: U.S. Institute of Peace Press, 1993.

Hakim, Peter. "Is Latin America Doomed to Failure." *Foreign Policy* 117 (Winter 1999–2000): 104–19.

Hamilton, Kimberly A., and Kate Holder. "International Migration and Foreign Policy." *The Washington Quarterly* (Spring 1991): 195–209.

Held, David. *Democracy and the Global Order*. Stanford, CA: Stanford University Press, 1995.

Henderson, Hazel. *Beyond Globalization: Shaping a Sustainable Global Economy*. West Hartford, CT: Kumarian Press, 1999.

Holton, Robert J. *Globalization and the Nation-State*. New York: St. Martin's Press, 1998.

Hoy, Paula. *Players and Issues in International Aid*. West Hartford, CT: Kumarian Press, 1998.

Hurrell, Andrew, and Ngaire Woods, eds. *Inequality, Globalization, and World Politics*. Oxford, UK: Oxford University Press, 1999.

Ignatieff, Michael. *The Warrior's Honor: Ethnic War and the Modern Conscience*. New York: Metropolitan Books, 1997.

Jameson, Fredric, and Masao Miyoshi, eds. *The Cultures of Globalization*. Durham, NC: Duke University Press, 1998.

Jaquette, Jane S. "Women in Power: From Tokenism to Critical Mass." *Foreign Policy*, no. 108 (Fall 1997): 23–37.

Jervis, Robert. *American Foreign Policy in a New Era*. New York: Routledge, 2006.

Kandiyoti, Deniz. "End of Empire: Islam, Nationalism, and Women in Turkey." In Deniz Kandiyoti, ed. *Women, Islam, and the State*. Philadelphia: Temple University Press, 1991.

Kapstein, Ethan B. *Sharing the Wealth: Workers and the World Economy*. New York: W. W. Norton, 1999.

Kempe, Ronald Hope. *Development in the Third World*. London: M. E. Sharpe, 1996.

Kim, Kwan S. "Income Distribution and Poverty: An Interregional Comparison." *World Development* 25, no. 11 (1997): 1909–24.

Krauze, Enrique. "Furthering Democracy in Mexico," *Foreign Affairs* 85, no. 1 (January/February 2006): 54–64.

Küng, Hans. *A Global Ethic for Global Politics and Economics*. New York: Oxford University Press, 1998.

Lindberg, Staffan. *Democracy and Elections in Africa*. Baltimore: The Johns Hopkins University Press, 2006.

Linz, Juan J., and Alfred Stepan. *Problems of Democratic Transitions and Consolidation*. Baltimore: The Johns Hopkins University Press, 1996.

Lockwood, Bert B. *Woman's Rights*. Baltimore: The Johns Hopkins University Press, 2006.

Mayer, Ann Elizabeth. *Islam and Human Rights*. Boulder, CO: Westview Press, 1999.

McDonald, Brian. *The World Trading System*. New York: St. Martin's Press, 1998.

Mehmet, Ozay, et al. *Towards a Fair Global Labor Market*. London: Routledge, 1999.

Mernissi, Fatima. *Beyond the Veil: Male-Female Dynamics in Modern Muslim Society*. Bloomington: Indiana University Press, 1987.

Nassar, Jamal R. *Globalization and Terrorism: The Migration of Dreams and Nightmares*. Lanham, MD: Rowman & Littlefield, 2005.

Nyrop, Richard F. *Rwanda: A Country Study*. Washington, D.C.: U.S. Government Printing Office, 1985.

Ohmae, Kenichi. *The End of the Nation-State*. New York: The Free Press, 1995.

Payne, Richard J. *The Clash with Distant Cultures: Values, Interests, and Force in American Foreign Policy*. Albany: State University of New York Press, 1995.

Pridham, Geoffrey, et al., eds. *Building Democracy*. London: Leicester University Press, 1997.

Rapley, John. *Understanding Development.* Boulder, CO: Lynne Rienner, 1996.

Rodrik, Dani. *Has Globalization Gone Too Far?* Washington, D.C.: Institute for International Economics, 1997.

Rosenau, James. *Along the Domestic-Foreign Border: Exploring Governance in a Turbulent World.* Cambridge, UK: Cambridge University Press, 1997.

Rostow, Walt N. *The Stages of Growth.* New York: Cambridge University Press, 1960.

Rothchild, Donald. *Managing Ethnic Conflict in Africa.* Washington, D.C.: Brookings Institution Press, 1997.

Sachs, Jeffrey D. *The End of Poverty.* New York: Penguin, 2006.

Sadowski, Yahya. "Ethnic Conflict." *Foreign Policy* 111 (Summer 1998): 12–23.

Sassen, Saskia. *The Global City: New York, London, Tokyo.* Princeton, NJ: Princeton University Press, 1991.

Schiff, Maurice, and Caglar Ozden, eds. *International Migration, Remittances, and the Brain Drain.* London: Palgrave Macmillan, 2005.

Scholfield, Victoria. *Kashmir in the Crossfire.* London: I. B. Tauris, 1996.

Scott, Alan, ed. *The Limits of Globalization: Cases and Arguments.* London: Routledge, 1997.

Sen, Amartya. *Development as Freedom.* New York: Knopf, 1999.

Shaeffer, Robert K. *Power to the People: Democratization Around the World.* Boulder, CO: Westview Press, 1997.

Singer, Marshall R. "Sri Lanka's Ethnic Conflict." *Asian Survey* 36, no. 11 (November 1996), 1146–55.

Singh, Jaswant. "Against Nuclear Apartheid." *Foreign Affairs* 77, no. 5 (September/October 1998): 41–52.

Smith, David, Dorothy J. Solinger, and Steven C. Topic, eds. *States and Sovereignty in the Global Economy.* London: Routledge, 1999.

Smith, Peter H. "Drug Trafficking in Mexico." In Barry Bosworth et al., eds. *Coming Together? Mexico-United States Relations.* Washington, D.C.: Brookings Institution Press, 1997.

Sorensen, Georg. *Democracy and Democratization.* Boulder, CO: Westview Press, 1998.

Spar, Debora L. "The Spotlight and the Bottom Line." *Foreign Affairs* 77, no. 2 (March/April 1999): 7–12.

Stillwagon, Eileen. *AIDS and the Ecology of Poverty.* New York: Oxford University Press, 2005.

Thomas, Caroline, and Peter Wilkin, eds. *Globalization and the South.* New York: St. Martin's Press, 1997.

Tomlinson, John. *Globalization and Culture.* Chicago: University of Chicago Press, 1999.

U.N. Development Program. *Human Development Report 2004.* New York: Oxford University Press, 2004.

Wallach, Lori, and Michelle Sforza. *The WTO: Five Years of Reasons to Resist Corporate Globalization.* New York: Seven Stories Press, 1999.

Wang, Gabe T., and Xiaobo Hu. "Small Town Development and Rural Urbanization in China." *Journal of Contemporary Asia* 29, no. 1 (1999): 76–94.

Weiner, Myron. *The Global Migration Crisis.* New York: HarperCollins, 1995.

Weiss, Anita. "The Slow Yet Steady Path to Women's Empowerment in Pakistan." In Yvonne Yazbeck Haddad and John L. Esposito, eds. *Islam, Gender, and Social Change.* New York: Oxford University Press, 1998.

Wiarda, Howard J. *Non-Western Theories of Development.* Fort Worth, TX: Harcourt Brace and Company, 1999.

World Bank. *India: Achievements and Challenges in Reducing Poverty.* Washington, D.C.: World Bank, 1997.

World Bank. *World Development Report 2005.* New York: Oxford University Press, 2004.

World Bank, *World Development Report 2006.* New York: Oxford University Press, 2005.

The World Resources Institute. *World Resources 1996–1997.* New York: Oxford University Press, 1996.

INDEX

Abacha, Sani, 205, 221
Abed, 261
Abiola, Moshood, 205
Absolute monarchy, 6
Abu Ghraib prison (Iraq), 188
Abubaker, Abdulsalam, 205
Afghanistan
  females in, 167, 170
  foreign relations and, 308–309
  illegal drugs and, 257
  Taliban in, 167, 170
  U.S. troops in, 52
Africa. *See also specific countries*
  agriculture in, 174
  cultural diversity in, 41
  deforestation in, 156
  democratic transitions in,
    204–206
  economic development in, 121
  ethnic conflict in, 256–263, 286
  European colonialism in, 12–13,
    72, 78, 204
  HIV/AIDS in, 126–127
  income in, 86
  language use in, 11–12, 72
  literacy rates in, 126
  overview of, 11–12
  population growth in, 122, 123
  poverty in, 11, 87, 88
  regional inequalities in, 93–94
  religion in, 11
  resistance movement in, 12–13
  role of females in, 165, 166,
    169, 176
African National Congress (ANC),
  204, 242
African socialism, 117
Agrarian Reform Act (Egypt), 219
Agriculture
  deforestation and, 156, 157
  economic development and, 152
  effects of natural disasters on, 120

Green Revolution and, 102, 120,
  153, 284
pollution and, 153
slash-and-burn, 156
technological advances in, 102,
  113, 126
women in, 173–175
AIDS. *See* HIV/AIDS
Air pollution, 154–155. *See also*
  Environmental issues
Al Qaeda, 308
Al Yaqubi, 77
Algeria, 76–77
Allende, Salvador, 202, 209, 222
Amnesty International, 211, 222
Angola, 89, 257
Animists, 100, 261
Apartheid, 96, 176, 204–205, 321
Arab-Israeli conflict, 220, 306
Arab League, 323
Arabs, 19, 42
Arawaks, 226
Argentina
  background of, 16
  disappearances on, 176
  economic problems in, 283
Aristide, Jean-Bertrand, 62
Ariyamagga, 56
Ariyaratne, A. T., 58
Arusha Declaration, 117
Ashanti, 77–78
Asia. *See also specific countries*
  democratic transitions in,
    206–208
  development of governments
    in, 15
  economic crisis in, 122
  economic development in, 119
  ethnic conflicts in, 263–272
  HIV/AIDS in, 126
  natural disasters in, 120
  overview of, 13–15

population growth in, 122
poverty in, 87, 88
prostitution in, 169
religion in, 13, 15
role of females in, 169
urbanization in, 149–150
Assimilation polity, 292
Association of Southeast Asian
  Nations (ASEAN), 315, 320
Aswan High Dam, 158, 220
Ataturk, Mustafa Kemal,
  178–179, 194
Autonomy, operational, 239–240
Axis of Evil, 52
Aylwin, Patricio, 223

Baby formula, 91
Bachelet, Michelle, 178
Balance of payments, 130
Bangladesh
  background of, 14
  child labor in, 142, 143, 145
  consumption in, 124
  Grameen Bank in, 117–118
  microloans in, 175
  political participation in, 177, 178
  solar energy in, 155
  untreated sewage in, 152
Bani-Sadr, Abulhassan, 51
Barber, Benjamin, 36
Batista, Fulgencio, 228
Bay of Pigs, 229
Beatrix, Queen of the
  Netherlands, 165
Beaudoin, Cindy Marie, 27
Beijing Conference, 182
Belgium, Rwanda and, 261, 262
Beliefs, 197
Ben Bella, Ahmed, 76
Berlin Conference of 1884–1885, 12
Berlin Wall, 293
Bermuda, 197